CW00517870

# CHALLENGE

## Books produced by Al J. Venter

*The Terror Fighters;* Purnell; (1969)
*Underwater Africa;* Purnell; (1971)
*Report on Portugal's War in Guiné-Bissau;* California Institute of Technology, Pasadena; (1973)
*Underwater Seychelles;* Verhoef; Victoria–Seychelles; (1973)
*Portugal's Guerrilla War;* Malherbe; (1973)
*Under the Indian Ocean;* Harraps, London; (1973)
*Africa at War;* Devin Adair, Conn. USA; (1974)
*The Zambezi Salient;* Devin Adair, Conn. USA; (1974)
*Coloured: A Profile of Two Million South Africans:* Human and Rousseau; (1974)
*Africa Today;* Macmillan; (1975)
*The Black Leaders of Southern Africa;* Siesta; (1976)
*Vorster's Africa;* Keartlands (1977)
*Handbook for Divers;* Ashanti; (1987)
*Underwater Mauritius;* Ashanti (1989)
*South Africa's Second Underwater Handbook;* Ashanti (1989)

## Novels

*Soldier of Fortune;* W H Allen, London; (1980)

# Southern Africa within the African Revolutionary context

## An Overview

### Edited by
# AL J. VENTER

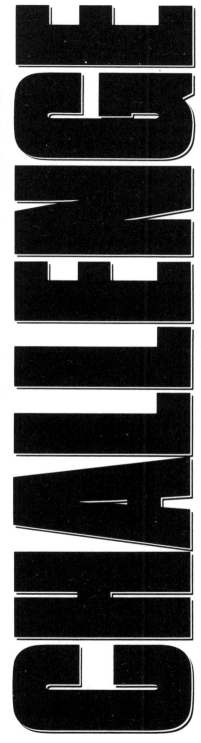

## ASHANTI
## PUBLISHING LIMITED
### GIBRALTAR
A DIVISION OF ASHANTI INTERNATIONAL FILMS

Designed by: Axel Adelbert and Dieter Mandlmeier
Typesetting: Pointset
Photo reproduction: Photo-Prints
Cover colour separations: Hirt & Carter
Printing: Printpak Books
Published by: Ashanti Publishing (Pty) Limited,
             a division of
             Ashanti International Films
ISBN number: 0 620 12190 4     © 1989

*DEDICATION*

*For Johan, Albert, Luke and Leigh
in the hope that South Africa
will be a better place to live in
for the new generation*

# ACKNOWLEDGEMENTS

Many people had a hand in the production of this large work which, we all hope, will ultimately prove to be of some historical value when the next generation looks back on South African society.

One person, more than any other who played an important part in bringing this project to fruition was Madelon, my wife. I would often still find her at her desk at five or six in the morning.

She carried a heavy load in the final stages, not least that of begging or bullying contributors into finishing their proof-reading. That the book was published at all has largely been due to her efforts.

Axel Adelbert originally designed a dummy of *Challenge* for a book fair overseas. He completed this task, producing the final product in printed form in a fortnight. The cover is his. Dieter Mandlmeier and Roy Smith of Pointset were responsible for putting the book together in the end, and they, too, pulled out all stops.

Tom McGhee spent months poring over other people's writings, subbing, often rewriting, always cursing the trend towards modern journalese. A linguist and a purist, he deplores the hand-me-down clichés that form the bulk of modern day writing.

Photographs came from many sources. Some, such as several taken during the Portuguese epoch in Mozambique by Juhan Kuus and John Rubython, were acquired twenty years ago for some of my earlier books. My old *rafiki* Mohamed Amin of Nairobi provided me with others, as did Derek Large and Mike McCann.

Obviously, the book is not without its faults. As with most commentaries on Africa, it will infuriate some and please others. But if in the end we have succeeded in contributing to some understanding of what is happening on this extraordinary continent, then it will have been worth it. Any errors or deletions – whether intentional or otherwise – are the editor's responsibility entirely.

I wish only that I had twice the time and twice the space to include everything that I had originally intended. But it is not given to mortal man to do all he would wish to do.

# CONTENTS

# FOREWORD

This book is about South Africa, a pariah nation that has been appearing as the Demon King on television nightly all over the world and was not expected to survive the 1980s with its present form of government intact.

It is about a nation under great and increasing pressure: social, political, economic and military. During that time South Africa has had to endure a United Nations arms embargo; financial limitations on the international capital markets; trade and oil boycotts in the Middle East; a transport embargo instituted almost thirty years ago that forces South African airliners to fly round the "bulge" of Africa to reach Europe; selective mandatory economic sanctions imposed by the United States, Japan, Australia and New Zealand; a trade boycott by most of Africa, much of Asia and the entire communist bloc; and a strenuous attempt by many black African states to bring South Africa to its knees.

On top of all this the country has experienced the severest drought in living memory and, more recently, appalling floods which by early 1988 had cost billions of dollars, a smouldering war on the northern borders of Namibia and substantial active anti-Soviet support inside Angola for the Unita rebel movement which has cost the country dear in lives and equipment. South Africa should, in theory, be on the verge of collapse.

When historians one day look back at this complex and tormented scene, some of them will certainly conclude that during recent years there were probably times when the present South African government could have – or should have – fallen. The situation has not been eased by the increase of an extremely vocal right wing opposition that appears to be doing its best to emulate some of the excesses of Nazi Germany.

Yet there are few who would maintain with confidence that South Africa is unlikely to be in existence for some time to come. That change must come, and fast, no one will dispute; not even the National Government, now in power for over forty years. What these changes may be are hidden in the future; they are impossible to foresee.

There are also few South Africans who would wish to see the country plunged into the same kind of civil war that ruined Rhodesia and culminated in the installation of a Marxist government in Harare. Many would maintain that if that happens, it will be the fault of the South Africans themselves; and most outsiders would agree.

The effect on some South Africans has been to view the situation with alarm and to vote with their feet. The result is sizeable pockets of Springboks of all colours in places as diverse as Perth and Pennsylvania. The sad thing is that most of these expatriates belonged to the best-qualified professional classes to be found in any country. That is South Africa's loss; and it is a serious one.

At the same time, while some have gone, most have stayed. It is not generally appreciated abroad that in a nation as diverse as South Africa there are more than four million white people who call it home. That alone makes South Africa different from the rest of the extremely varied and volatile continent of Africa.

Unlike Rhodesia or the Portuguese colonies of Angola and Mozambique, or colonial Kenya and Nigeria before them, South Africa has a large community of European origin who effectively control a multi-coloured society of thirty-five million souls and who are in a position to decide for themselves what their future will be. Most of these people are tough, intractable and resolute to stay and defend the norms and standards of a civilised country. Their destinies will not be decided in London or Lisbon, or Washington, or Moscow.

For the first time in the modern era, a white African nation – rightly or wrongly – is able to set its own course wherever it may lead towards its ultimate destiny.

Whether these people vote for P.W. Botha's National Government or not (and it might surprise many people abroad that many South Africans do not) most are well aware of what unmitigated black rule has done to the rest of the continent. Their view may be slanted and jaundiced, but it is the education of their children, efficient medical services, an essentially free press, (the virulently anti-government Archbishop Desmond Tutu is quoted in the South African press just about every day calling for anything from sanctions to the downfall of the government), sincere social programmes, welfare, pension, sound business principles (capitalist as opposed to socialist economics) and a democratic right to the vote as well as a lifestyle that has taken centuries to evolve that are at stake.

The average South African will show you, by example, that all the above would disappear overnight if the principles of "one man–one vote" were applied. On a continent that since 1960 has had far more coups d'état and revolutions than the rest of the world put together, it would be a case of one man–one vote: *once*. In all of black and Arab Africa's 51 countries only one country, Botswana, could be described as a true democracy. The rest are either monolithic one–party states or military dictatorships, some of them the most brutal on earth.

Political and military questions apart, to anyone visiting the country, South Africa – on the surface in any event – appears to be flourishing like no other country in Africa. When you arrive in Johannesburg by road or air you find a great modern metropolis unequalled in Africa; no roadblocks on the road from the airport, no potholed highways, no cattle trucks for railway passengers; but plenty of libraries, restaurants, museums, hotels, game parks and cinemas which all races can now use and, above all, an economy that bustles.

In all its natural disasters of the past few years, South Africa has not been offered a penny of foreign aid. Alone in Africa, the South African government received no American, European, Japanese or Warsaw Pact handouts. Yet in spite of all its difficulties – and an outward flow of foreign exchange and capital – it still somehow manages to balance its budget each year and show a healthy trade surplus. To the gratification of a good number of financial institutions abroad, it has so far also managed to repay some of its foreign loans at a rate unmatched by any other African or South American nation, many of whose debts have had to be effectively written off.

South Africa works: while there is still plenty of urban unrest in some parts, the trains and aircraft run on time, the transport system is well maintained, most children of all races go to school, the old get their pensions on the nail, the civil service, police and defence force have never missed a month's pay, as in so many other African states; and, while there is disquiet about some of the events happening all round here, most South Africans see a hope for the future in a country long ago given up as a lost cause by prophets of doom.

I have thought of compiling a book of this kind for at least ten years now. Having covered most African conflicts, especially those nearest to the borders of South Africa: Mozambique, Angola and Rhodesia in particular, it has concerned me greatly that some of the events being enacted in and around her borders now are essentially a repetition of similar episodes in such places as Luanda,

Lourenço Marques and Salisbury hardly more than a decade ago. I have said as much in several of the books that I produced during that period.

On a purely political level, I warned readers in 1974 of the political destiny of the people of mixed origins in South Africa in *Coloured: A Profile of Two Million South Africans.* I said then that if white South Africans could not come to terms with that group, with whom they share a common history, language and culture, they will never be able to deal with what Stuart Cloete called "the slowly awakening African Giant".

I was not wrong. Two million coloureds soon became three million; and some of the worse excesses in the race riots of the mid–80s occurred among or on the fringes of the coloured community in the Cape. I know; I was living in Cape Town at the time.

I offered another word of caution: "The rumbling political discontent of (so many) million black souls who share their shores and their aspirations is, in reality, only an extension of what is called the coloured problem, magnified in essence, finality and interpretation of the law."

I recorded what was being done to the coloured people then, culpably, tragically and without apology. In compiling this present volume of sometimes controversial views and observations, I have none to make now, either to the Right or to the Left of South African or foreign politics. Conditions are certainly not helped by the unceasing military struggle on the borders of southern Africa.

I, for one, would like to see South Africa survive; so, I am sure, would many others, although the forces arrayed against the country are powerful and intent on its destruction.

These wars have expanded and intensified in the past two or three years, in Angola and Mozambique especially.

Dr Jonas Savimbi has achieved some outstanding successes, though at the price of raising the stakes alarmingly *and* at the cost of loss of domination by the SAAF of the local airspace. Russian MiG–23 fighters and Sukhoi fighter-bombers flown by Cubans and East Germans are technically superior to the rapidly-ageing squadrons of French Mirages and British Buccaneers used by the SAAF.

Because all these problems are not likely to disappear overnight, the time might be ripe for an attempt to put the southern African problem into perspective. For that reason I have called together as illustrious a group of authorities on southern Africa as has ever been published to shed some light on that problem.

They are a diverse lot: journalists, academics, a medical doctor, politicians, soldiers, historians – even specialists in the world of Deighton and Le Carré. Some entertain leftist ideals; others are true-blue Tory. There are a few whose politics would be hard to define.

All have contributed essays of great value. Obviously there are some omissions. The choice, however, was mine, and if I have erred in not including a representative of the fascist AWB or Joe Slovo of the ANC (and perhaps a few dozen very dissimilar people in between) then that responsibility is mine too.

Tom McGhee, for instance, that erudite old hack and, for many years, an outspoken commentator on southern African politics and events, went back to Nigeria after an absence of over twenty years specially to reorientate himself to write the prologue. He lived and taught there for twelve years of his long life before coming to South Africa in the early Sixties.

In the past, people would listen when McGhee talked. Now they will read attentively, for he knows Africa.

So also with David Isby, a military analyst and tactician of note who has been published by *Jane's*. Isby has examined Soviet intentions closely, in Afghanistan, Central America, Europe and now, southern Africa.

Paul Johnson, the eminent author, journalist and historian and former editor of *The New Statesman,* was kind enough to allow us all a peep into his crystal ball. He did so originally at the behest of the Anglo American mining group. His comments are measured and sobering.

Professor Willie Breytenbach of Stellenbosch University deserves special mention, because it was during our early discussions about a book of this kind that the idea first took shape. He was lecturing in London, New York and Pretoria on the subject of "South Africa within the Context of Revolutionary Africa"; and I asked him to provide me with what turned out to be the foundation stone of this publication. He examines in detail a number of African uprisings and revolts from Algeria on and how they compare with similar problems at the other end of Africa.

Several journalists have contributed. My friend and colleague from the days when I wrote for the Argus Africa News Service, Gerry L'Ange (he was then in the United States), has written a chapter on the neighbouring states which he has appropriately titled "Countries in the Cross-fire". He underlines the fact that South Africa is now involved in a limited war. Yet he sees hope, though believing that any recourse to military adventure is ultimately futile. Like me, he has a son who is likely to find himself in the firing line in the not too distant future. My eldest son, Johan, was badly wounded in Angola during his national service (strangely enough, within a mile or two from where I was blown up, 300 kilometres inside Angola) so I have, as it were, a personal interest.

Willem Steenkamp is a writer with whom I have worked for two decades – and he is still going strong. Militarist and raconteur of note, Willem has done two chapters, drawing on his own experiences of many months of cross-border duty inside Angola.

Fred Bridgland and his book on Savimbi: *Jonas Savimbi - A Key to Africa* (Coronet Books, London, 1986) hardly needs introduction. When writing his chapter he met the former head of the Cuban Air Force in Angola, General Rafael del Pino Diaz, who went over to the United States in 1987. That was the first interview that he had given to a British journalist and some of what he was told is recounted in these pages.

Like Simon Barber, a columnist in Washington whose acerbic wit and no-nonsense logic make his columns a delight, Holger Jensen, formerly of *Newsweek,* is based in the United States. Jensen is a much-wounded veteran of Vietnam.

He was with the American media detachment in South East Asia, and he saw the machinations of the American press at first hand. His views of some of his fellow-journalists are unflattering. As the Israelis found out (belatedly), the ego-expanding media can be one of the most ruthlessly destructive organs of modern society and his lessons are illuminating.

South Africa has produced some excellent journalists; some are to be found on every newspaper worthy of note in the capitals of the world. In South Africa they have a peculiar set of problems of their own, skilfully and daringly dodging government restrictions to keep the liberal flame alight. It is that flame that Mr Eugene Terre Blanche has sworn to extinguish.

A former South African spy, Craig Williamson, now a member of the South African President's Council, was asked to write a chapter on the African National Congress. There was a time when he travelled the world (including Moscow) as an ANC plenipotentiary. He has seen that society from the inside and knows very well what Messrs Tambo and Slovo plan for the country that some of their cadres (as well as Azapo) one day hope to rename Azania. I have always regarded "Azania" as an unfortunate choice of name since the literary Azania was hilariously spoofed in Evelyn Waugh's fanciful country so called. In our amazing century that most extravagant satire is in danger of being capped by unadorned fact.

There are the academics; Dr Richard Wood, formerly of the University of Rhodesia; Professor Mike Hough, director of the Institute of Strategic Studies at the University of Pretoria and Professor Deon Fourie, a specialist in Political Studies at the University of South Africa; all have added breadth and depth with their contributions.

Dr Christopher Coker, a lecturer at the London School of Economics, was asked to provide a chapter on the South African–Russian conundrum. His views are an exercise in far-reaching logic, since they foresee a time when incessant American aggression may force Pretoria to come to some kind of strategic arrangement with the Russians.

One of the most controversial contributors to this volume is Major-General Ron Reid-Daly, formerly of the Transkei Defence Force. He has had more experience in counter-insurgency warfare than almost anyone I know, having fought with the British Special Air Services in the Malayan emergency before returning to Rhodesia. There he was instrumental in setting up and commanding one of the best clandestine pseudo-operations yet seen in any modern conflict, the Selous Scouts.

Reid-Daly's views on some aspects of the Rhodesian war, including the fact that the high command was riddled with British intelligence "moles" throws fresh light on some of the more confusing aspects of that débâcle.

Douglas McClure is no stranger to South African politics. Following stints at the universities of Michigan and Edinburgh, he lectured at Cape Town and Witwatersrand universities for a while. Today he sits in the Press Gallery in Parliament.

My own contributions are two-fold; on what I have termed the South African–Algerian connection and on why Portugal lost its wars in Africa; there is something instructive in both subjects.

If we are going to survive we need to examine carefully what happened in Africa in the past and the effect it has on the present. If we do not the consequences are irrevocable.


Al J. Venter
Rivonia, January 1989.

# AFRICA: LOOKING BACK
## by Tom McGhee

Forty years ago, when I was on home leave from Nigeria, I was lunching at the Edinburgh University Club with a number of eminent sociologists. Somebody asked me how things were going in my part of the world; for it was the time of the Great Liberation. I said something to the effect that, although "Africanisation" had already begun, the inevitable rot had not yet had time to set in.

This set the table in a roar of Homeric laughter, and I immediately became an object of great interest. Here was a specimen of the imperialist blimp, *pur sang!* A person who actually believed in things like the White Man's Burden and all the other Kiplingesque baloney.

Well, in fact I didn't. Then as now I thought neither so highly of white (or pinko-grey) skin nor so lowly of black skin as was customary in (say) South Africa or Rhodesia or the American Deep South. I was well aware both of their potential and their actual; the former being that of the general run of the human species in every way, the latter being, in the modern cant, distinctly "disadvantaged". *Tout comprendre, c'est tout pardonner;* and it is necessary both to understand and to forgive Africa. It is indeed all that is said of it: bankrupt, given over to self-serving politicians and crazy ex-sergeants and one-party presidents-for-life; incapable of serious cooperation between states; full of grandiose slogans and paranoid whining; holding out their tin cups to all the "affluent" nations, yet knowing full well the pockets that most of the "aid" disappears into. Incapable of ensuring an honest civil service or police force. Incapable of pulling themselves up by their own bootstraps; if they have any bootstraps after a generation of independence.

If I refrain from turning round to Lord Ritchie-Calder and the other sociological pundits to say "I told you so" it is not out of humility but rather out of a sense of decency. The sociologists at least meant well, they were on the side of the angels; they even got some of their premises right; though my own were based upon firsthand experience while theirs were not.

The most remarkable thing about "our" presence and dominance in Africa was its brevity, excluding the obvious case of South Africa, which is *sui generis.* Effectively Africa was ruled by whites for no longer than the biblical allotted span of a man's lifetime. The Romans ruled the island of Britain for four hundred years, without managing to occupy either northern Scotland or Ireland; and when they left ("scuttled") they left it much as they had found it. But in sixty years or less the Europeans changed Africa far more radically than ever Rome changed any part of its empire. After Rome, northern Europe relapsed into what we choose to call the Dark Age; though we are none too luminous ourselves in this Junk Age. By the middle of this century there could be no relapse, no regression, no return to a simpler age for Africa. We the whites had made quite sure of that.

The history of Africa more than that of any continent has a kind of predestinate inevitability. It is possible to imagine different histories for both the Americas. It is easy to imagine a hundred different histories for Europe, north and south: suppose the Tudors had never happened; a Norman line continued, with no Stuarts and no Reformation; no Thirty Years War; no Prussianism; no disintegration of Austria; no Russian Revolution – no French Revolution, for that matter; no

Napoleon. No Hitler. No Stalin. Europe cries out for such suppositions, such an infinite series of alternative histories.

But the history of Africa could not have been otherwise. It was like a stacked pack of cards or cogged dice.

During the European Middle Ages Africa showed itself perfectly capable of organising large and complex political structures, based on the simplest of technologies; structures large enough and stable enough to be called empires, and congenial and benign enough to deserve the name of civilisation, though without literacy. But it has taken our own astonishing Age (in which *everything* is carried to the point of gigantic absurdity) to demonstrate with its vast junk "media" in a vast global village that "literacy" can be a curse rather than a blessing.

The persistent notion of inherent white superiority is based upon a failure to grasp the unique and unprecedented nature of what happened in Britain in particular and northern Europe in general during the last century. The Industrial Revolution may have been a "progress" in many ways; it was certainly a regress in many others; but from whatever point of view it is regarded it changed all the natural balances of the world. It was a lopsided thing, that perverted and distorted human values, gave the northern nations new and overweening "priorities" and Manifest Destinies. The British and the French and the Belgians and the Germans of the nineteenth century sincerely believed that they had something like a divine mission to go forth and govern the benighted blacks and browns and yellows, to set them to labour on their behalf, and to keep them hewers of wood and drawers of water for the rest of foreseeable history.

But of course history is never foreseeable; and the new and neurotic national rivalries and ambitions created a political situation even more dangerously stressed and unstable than the dynastic Europe of the seventeenth century. When Africa was penetrated and seized (raped or seduced, according to circumstances) nobody, anywhere, could have foreseen the Kaiser war or the Hitler war, which first exhausted and then destroyed Europe. It is pointless to say that if Europe had managed to avoid these apocalyptic destructions all would have continued as before and the white man would have gone on governing and "developing" Africa for as long as the Romans occupied Britain. The Europe that erupted, first in the French Revolution and the Napoleonic wars and then went on to still more and more scientific bloodshed on an increasing scale was desperately sick, with a deadly fever in its blood. Europe and America may have attained an astounding level of technology, but their wisdom and moral sense have declined in inverse proportion.

As it happened, in the nineteenth century Africa was mostly at a material stage of development roughly equivalent to that of thirteenth century Europe; which is not such a bad level in view of the climate, the diseases, the poverty of tropical soils. In Africa there are many rivers but few running streams or steady breezes to turn a simple mill. All societies were based on subsistence tillage, on little plots hacked and burnt out of the forest. Considering the afflictions that they had to survive, the yellow fever, yaws, leprosy, sleeping sickness, malaria, bilharzia, filariasis, dysentery, malnutrition and an appalling range of parasites internal and external, the marvel is that any human beings without the benefits of modern science and medicine could not only survive but thrive in such conditions. No other continent has such a large proportion of deserts, and such parched areas surrounding them, like the Sahel and the Sudan. The economic expansion that took place in Europe was firmly based on agrarian efficiency.

The great Industrial Revolution was preceded by the great Agricultural Revolution; and British agriculture is now one of the most efficient in the world with only three per cent of the population employed in it. When Whitehall tried to introduce large-scale modern methods, like the Tanganyikan Groundnuts Scheme and the Gambian Egg Scheme, and the French made similar attempts in their territories, the results were invariably fiascos; Africa easily defeated the tractors and the deep ploughs. In any case, the seasonal cycle permits only a few weeks of cultivation during the year; for the rest the expensive imported machinery lies idle and rusting. Africa must still be scratched laboriously with the hoe.

Despite all these disadvantages, Africans still managed to feed themselves – just. They had no means of storing food for any length of time, so that they were very vulnerable to drought and famine, with no pharaonic barns against the lean years. They lived in a very delicate balance with nature; but they well understood the necessity of the balance, and preserved it as well as they could.

If Africa could have "developed", or evolved, in free cooperation with the Europeans over the centuries its history might have been better and brighter. But it is a singularly impenetrable continent, with a long surf-beaten coast unbroken by natural harbours and insulated from the north by the Sahara. It was not until 1830 that my kinsmen the Lander brothers sailed down it in a canoe that anybody even knew where the great Niger ran. Like Mungo Park and Barth and Caillé they footslogged over Africa without benefit of Landrovers or fridges or quinine or yellow fever inoculations. They experienced the dangers and discomforts of Africa; yet they were for the most part well received by inhabitants decent and friendly and helpful.

Even so, by then the long-suffering natives had good cause to view strangers with suspicion; for the white men in tropical Africa were mostly interested in African bodies as slaves rather than as souls to be saved or minds to be edified. It is impossible to compute the numbers of Africans shipped across the Atlantic in the west and to the Arab world in the east. At that time slaves and ivory and a little gold were all that could be profitably got from Africa. Perhaps twenty million were sent to the Americas by the busy and murderous middle passage. According to Livingstone, about fifty thousand passed through Zanzibar every year, and for every one that reached the markets something like seven must have died from the rigours of the march or rough castration. This haemorrhage was not confined to the coast; it reached deep into Africa, with the cooperation of local kings and chiefs. The Arabs armed the more warlike tribes with muskets and encouraged them to raid the helpless villagers in deep bush. For at least three centuries Africa suffered this terrible wasting disease with all its disruptions. The slave trade made local wars profitable.

Thus by the late nineteenth century Africa was very weak and Britain was very strong. Given the vast disparity between "advanced" Britain and "backward" Africa it was historically inevitable that the one should use the other as a source of primary materials – and labour – for its own expanding metropolitan industry and worldwide commerce. It began modestly enough with the palm-oil trade. The standard of living of the British population had risen sufficiently to create a great demand for soap. At the point of contact of black and white there cannot at that time have been any very obvious superiority of white to black. The agents who collected the nuts and oil on behalf of Lever Brothers, the "palm-oil ruffians", were a deeply degraded species who lived mainly on trade gin on their hulks anchored in the Guinea river mouths. But thanks to the efforts of a few men of daemonic energy and dedication, the interior was soon opened up to development; which meant that African agriculture now had to accommodate cash crops for export to the metropolis; and the beginning of a cash economy was forced upon them. Of course such idealistic imperialists as Goldie and Lugard were men of the highest honour and integrity, and the statesmen over their heads were reluctant acquirers of unpromising tropical regions that portended more trouble than they were worth. But by then there were large and rich and powerful businessmen itching to get at all sorts of things that the tropics were fruitful of; and their attitude to Africa was rather like that of the Squire to poor little Angeline. They knew what they wanted, and they made sure that they got it.

This was the introduction – the "enlightened self-interest" of European commercial demands – of Africa to the modern world: that of humble suppliers of raw materials to the industrialised north. In theory it was in many ways commendable: Africa had to begin to join the rest of the world somewhere, and it is really quite difficult to see how else they could have begun; it was an inevitable phase.

But as with so many phases that should have been transitory and brief, Africa got stuck in that one. After nearly a century of such "development", it is still essentially a supplier of raw materials, with all that that implies in the way of subjection to the caprices of world prices, which scarcely affect the manufacturers but can be disastrous to the primary producer, who by now had to adapt themselves to the new cash nexus in place of the old subsistence and barter. That is, much of the African production is not suited to its own needs but to those of the North. Africa buys dear and sells cheap. One of the most pernicious results is, increasingly, that countries that used to be self-sufficient in food now import food at great cost. Not merely necessary staples, but luxuries like bread and European beer, for which all Africa has acquired an unfortunate taste.

But as a result of the European skewing of priorities, Africa is now producing coffee and groundnuts and cotton and rubber and cocoa and sugar where it should be growing more and more yams and maize and millet and guinea-corn. Even rice (another crop for which they have acquired a taste) is an over-expensive luxury that they cannot really afford.

So far I have presented the main case against the exploitation of Africa by the whites. But of course there is a brighter picture to present too. Britain did put down the slave trade (although a form of slavery still continued in the form of forced labour), and if large tracts were a kind of tropical Arcadia where nobody did any more work than was necessary to satisfy the basic needs, took no thought for the morrow, yet nevertheless there were certain horrors that cried out for abolition or alleviation, devils that needed exorcism. There still are.

The first heroic generation of white Residents and District Commissioners and District Officers had the difficult and often dangerous task of getting rid of the worst manifestations of superstition, human sacrifice and torture and cannibalism, the impaling of little girls on sharpened bamboo shoots to ensure the success of crops, the savage punishments for small crimes. These abominations were not myths or the creations of over-heated white imaginations; they were real, they were happening then and there; they are still fresh within living memory. It is necessary still to bear in mind the scenes that met the eyes of the expedition to Benin in 1898 – ninety years ago: " ... live women slaves gagged and pegged on their backs to the ground, the abdominal wall cut in the form of a cross and the gut hanging out ... to die in the sun ... sacrificed human beings lying in the path and bush ... the stench was awful. Dead and mutilated bodies everywhere – by God! may I never see such sights again."

The expedition dynamited the juju trees, rather like the English St Boniface hacking down the sacred oaks of the pagan Germans.

Benin was particularly sensational; religious atrocities tend to be so. But even ordinary judicial punishments under the Muslim Fulani rulers in the north were of barbarous severity. Petty thieves had their hands either chopped off altogether or their palms deeply slashed and bound into fists with rawhide strips until they healed as useless lumps. Mary Kingsley records the punishments for domestic slaves in Bonny: "ear-cutting in its various stages from clipping to total dismemberment; crucifixion round a large cask; chilli peppers pounded and stuffed up the nostrils and forced into the eyes and ears (as a Victorian gentlewoman she omits to mention the other obvious orifices); fastening the victim to a post driven into the beach at low water and leaving him there to be drowned or eaten by the sharks and crocodiles piecemeal."

In *Religion and Art in Ashanti* R.S. Rattray describes the punishment for any man guilty of adultery with one of the king's innumerable wives. In all its long-drawn-out elaborateness and fertile ingenuity of torments it is not suitable for quotation. Suffice it to say that it was both varied and thorough.

What used to be the Eastern Region of Nigeria (later the shortlived Republic of Biafra, so great an object of the sympathy of liberal-minded journalists) was – and for all I know still is – especially abundant in horrors. The Ibos and Ibibios and Ijaws were not organised in large kingdoms or tribes like the Yorubas or the Hausas, and human sacrifice and cannibalism were rampant in their dense forests. The Aro-Chuku Long Juju was a cult of widespread terror, whose priests admirably combined slavery and sacrifice with highly profitable extortion and even a prostitution network; an African Cosa Nostra.

So addicted were these peoples of the Delta to "long pig" that the British administration made it illegal to sell any meat without a piece of the skin still attached. The tradition persisted even into my own day. Once when I was "on tour" with a Hausa servant I told him to go and buy a basket of charcoal. He refused point-blank to go on his own: "I fear 'um too much."

I have no means of knowing whether the Ibo "horse title" clubs still continue. They were still vigorous in my day. Elspeth Huxley describes their activities in *Four Guineas:* "That's how almost every horse in northern Nigeria meets its end …Beaten to death by the progressive Ibo in one of their revolting ceremonies …Old horses fetch large prices from Ibos who 'take a title' …joining a society which has a large initiation fee. Once in, each member is assured of a regular income from his share of the initiation fees of subsequent entrants. The initiation ceremony involved the sacrifice of a horse …Generally the horse is roped and thrown and dragged into the juju house, where its throat is partially cut so that blood may drip on to the altar. Then it is dragged outside, its tail cut off, and it may be beaten to death with clubs, or the participants may break its legs and drag it on to a fire. Sometimes, while still living, it is hung up by a rope to a tree. At least five or six hundred horses, and probably more, are dealt with in this way every year."

In the present "climate of opinion" it is considered bad form to mention such matters aloud; I suppose that even to think of them would be regarded as hidden racism. But they still happened; and the record is incomplete if it fails to include them.

My own personal encounter with Africa took place in the post-war period up to the general independence. On the whole I enjoyed my service under the

Colonial Office. Of course we cursed the climate, the perversity of the natives, the hardships we suffered in the cause of bringing light to dark places. But really it was a pretty good life for a young and fit man. One had a pleasant house, with a sufficiency of servants: a cook, a steward, a gardener, a small-boy (who could be of any size and age; it was a function, not a description). On a bush station one was a member of a small white élite, living on the Government Reservation Area, or GRA, far from the native areas with all their stinks and squalor. We had most of the elementary necessities for comfort: mosquito nets, kerosene lamps and refrigerator, and a filter for boiled water. We were well peppered and salted with vaccinations and inoculations and anti-malaria pills; it was considered disgraceful, a sign of culpable negligence, to get malaria. We could ride and shoot. And above all we had the Club.

It is impossible to overstress the importance of the Club all over the British Raj. It was the heart of our little white community, from which all natives were strictly barred. That, after all, was the essential point. Our day was sufficiently taken up by blacks; in the evening it was necessary to get away from them, relax the imperial countenance and let our hair down in our own exclusive company. In the early days there were few white women, except missionaries, who did not count; since they were all teetotal fundamentalists who looked upon the Club as a haunt of debauchery.

Certainly we did drink a lot, our excuse being that we sweated it out as soon as we absorbed it. We were convivial to a high degree. If we found ourselves in a new station with no regular club we formed a Scotch Club; that is, in the evening each of us sent his servants with an armchair and a table and a sufficiency of bottles, porous cooling jars and what not, and a large bonfire would be lit in the middle. As an institution it was very relaxed; conversation could be animated, or one could sit in meditative silence, just as one pleased.

Many held that the rot set in when wives were allowed to join their husbands in Africa. Whereas before men lived the lives of jolly bachelors, making surreptitious arrangements adapted to the local scene, when white women appeared in any number they complicated life. Things tended to get a bit steamy; and it wasn't the women who "got into trouble" but the men. Many undesired and undesirable postings were made in consequence of indiscretions.

The lord of the community was the Resident, who represented the King *in partibus infidelibus.* If you were summoned to the Residency, if only to answer a simple question or receive a brief instruction, you went home first to change into long trousers, a long-sleeved white shirt and a tie before presuming to enter the presence. I myself liked a degree of formality and a firm quasi-military framework. One knew exactly where one was, one accepted a hierarchy and respected the tradition. We regarded ourselves as the heirs of Lugard, and we retained something of the old West Coast vocabulary. Food was invariably the pidgin "chop". We never went to bourgeois shops; we "went to canteens" or "to factories"; and indeed the old trading firms like John Holt's and Leventis and Paterson Zochonis still had something of the primitive character of the early warehouses of the coast and the rivers. When we went "on tour" (any journey) we did not take luggage, but our *loads,* as if we had a gang of porters.

Every government officer was expected to become reasonably proficient in the local language; and of course for the Administration, the "Politicals", complete fluency was a *sine qua non.* By my time what I think of as the Heroic Generation was over, but not forgotten.

They were giants, titans, in the early days, the first thirty years of this century.

Think of what a D.O. was required to do, all on his own. He would probably cover several thousand miles a year on horseback; about three-quarters of his time would be spent in hard, rough travel, accompanied by a servant, an interpreter, a messenger or two, perhaps half a dozen native *dogarai* armed with Snider or Martini-Henry rifles. There would be no other white man within hundreds of miles perhaps, to give advice and support. In his early days he would be ignorant of Hausa or Yoruba or Ibo, and he was expected to master all the local languages as quickly as possible; not a smattering, not a mere "working knowledge", but real conversance with the finer *nuances* of meaning. The sooner he was able to do without interpreters the better, for they were mostly rascals, and mistranslated to suit themselves. Every word he uttered, every action he made, was studied closely, to observe how much he could be taken in by intrigues and wiles. How far could rackets and extortions be carried out under his nose? From the Emir at the top, buying and selling slaves, to his horse-boys at the bottom, stealing the ponies' corn, everybody was in league against the D.O. It was a grand game, and they were all experts at it. A Resident assisted by two juniors had to administer a province over 25 000 square miles, with perhaps a million or more inhabitants. If any trouble broke out, there would be perhaps a company of native troops and perhaps fifty native police.

These were the men who by sheer force of character and cool courage and resolution put a stop to the kind of abominations that I have hinted at. In northern Nigeria they had perforce (by Lugard's principle of Indirect Rule – which had its drawbacks) to base their administration upon a much decayed and corrupt Muslim code of law, which was certainly attuned to the customs and needs of the people; but they civilised and softened it. Instead of being crammed into pitch-dark dungeons with their legs plastered immovably into the thick clay walls, prisoners were kept in new and decent gaols where they were well fed and clad, often in far better conditions than in their village hovels. They were put to useful work wearing a government uniform that they were quite proud of. A gang of working prisoners expected ordinary bystanders to salute the king's uniform and their official status as they passed.

All this was done in the absence of juggling speculators with one foot in Africa and the other in the London Stock Exchange; the kind of get-rich-quick chancer or randlord who brought such contempt and odium on South Africa in the early days of gold and diamonds. There were no money-manipulators or market-riggers in West Africa, with their gimcrack "raids" going off at half-cock. There was no vulgar flag-wagging, no cant about the White Man's Burden. The conquests or penetrations were made with the minimum of bloodshed; and whoever made a fortune out of them, it was not the empire-builders themselves.

There is some genuine gold among the vulgar brass of Kipling, though. He could at times sum up the spirit of true idealism and dedication that animated the imperialists of West Africa as distinct from the self-serving expansionists of the South:

> *Keep ye the Law, be swift in all obedience,*
> *Clear the land of evil, drive the road and bridge the ford.*
> *Make ye sure to each his own, that he reap where he hath sown.*
> *By the peace among our peoples let men know we serve the Lord.*

The lines express a more than Roman sense of *virtus,* justice, order, decency, discipline; the *Pax Britannica* that did for a brief time make Britain the effective policeman of the world in a way that no other nation or superpower has managed to accomplish since. No one had better cause to appreciate the description:

> *Your new-caught sullen peoples,*
> *Half-devil and half-child*

than the officers who came into direct contact with them, like Frank Hives in Iboland. He was a simple man, in the noblest sense, and his springs of action had not been choked up by "racism" in reverse. After rescuing a native policeman from a very unpleasant death he says: "The rescued man ... was soon chattering to his comrades ... His troubles had been more mental than physical, and a native soon gets over that kind of thing, being nearer to childhood than a white man." Heresy, nay blasphemy, nowadays.

Like most people who got to know tropical Africa intimately (including Joyce Cary) he was quite convinced that there was "something in" witchcraft. At any rate many very common-sensical people have recorded some very odd experiences in that line. My own opinion is that there is infinitely more than meets the eye in all human life, that it is the Europeans and North Americans with their materialistic and superficially scientific habits of thought who have lost the sense of the numinous, while the Africans have, or had, retained it to a large extent; decreasingly, no doubt, as they also acquire positivist assumptions. As the Moslems say, even our clothes reek of atheism. After living for years in Nigeria, where men wear loose robes both comfortable and becoming, I found it depressing to come to South Africa, where the blacks wear proletarian Western clothes.

When I first went to West Africa I began to learn Hausa from an old phrase-book. The officer on tour could instruct a servant thus: "Here is sixpence. Go to the village and buy two chickens." By my day the price of chickens had gone up to one-and-sixpence each in the town market; which was no doubt as much as the scraggy local fowls were worth. The large British pennies - solid bronze - had a hole in the middle so that they could be strung like beads. In Kano market the people of the desert would take only silver Maria Theresa dollars. The expatriates called the local currency monkey-money; but you could nevertheless buy a bottle of imported Heineken's for three shillings and a new car for five hundred pounds.

On my last visit to Nigeria in the summer of 1988, I never saw a coin, or a note less than fifty kobos; nominally the old ten shillings. I don't know what the conscientious Muslim gives to the crippled beggar. A penny used to be sufficient to earn Koranic merit.

All Africa, with its half-baked, half-raw economy is desperate for foreign currency, especially pounds and dollars. Yet it recently took me a whole morning, going from one bank to another, to cash a hundred-dollar traveller's cheque. Barclays (in its local protective coloration as the Union Bank) refused even to consider it. I wondered, not for the first time, what banks were for. But I was a fool to go to banks in the first place. All I needed to do was to ask the first prosperous-looking Hausa or Yoruba I met. If I had gone to a Lebanese shop I could have got much more than the official rate.

Currencies are only one of many signs of the lunatic economics of Africa. They used to have a certain stability as long as they were linked to Bank of England sterling; but now they have mostly fallen into "independent" anarchy, except in the old French colonies, where the Paris-controlled CFA franc remains fairly steady. The French retained a far more effective post-imperial presence than the British; and indeed they have got a firm foothold in Nigeria now. For example, you can get any car you like in Nigeria so long as it's a Peugeot. They set up an assembly plant in Lagos a few years ago, and now they dominate the market to the exclusion of all others. In Zimbabwe, by contrast, every second car is a clapped-out Renault 4L that would not be allowed on the roads of Europe.

The Raj in its heyday always thought in terms of railways; and indeed it was by that means that it "opened up" new territories to trade everywhere. But Africa never took to them very enthusiastically, for some reason. In fact, Sierra Leone had no sooner become independent than they pulled up all the existing railway lines and sold the steel to China; an easy (but in the long run expensive) way of making a quick buck; for they have made their own interior almost inaccessible as a result. And of course in the present "economic climate" of Africa there can be no hope of ever replacing them.

If you want to go from Lagos to Kano you can forget about the trains; you either fly or hire a car. And in fact the car is cheaper, faster and far more convenient than either the train or the aircraft. I will not say safer. The African driver is a maniac behind the wheel, and the hundreds of rusting wrecks by the roadside speak for themselves. In my day the natives went everywhere by mammy-waggon, with their pious or philosophical legends: God Sees All; Sea Never Empty; Sea Never Full; What Say They? Let Them Say and so on. They too were far from safe, and when they crashed, as they often did, the driver took to the bush without delay to avoid being killed by the survivors; which was normal practice.

In a doleful commentary on the state of Africa a few years ago *Time* magazine noted that all the "infrastructures" left by the imperial powers had fallen into decay: the roads, railways, hospitals, waterworks and drains had fallen more and more into disrepair or were engulfed by bush. For example, of the sixty thousand miles of good road left by the Belgians in the old Congo only about five thousand miles were still usable in 1984. Yet of all the countries that I have seen recently Nigeria is exceptional in that the roads are actually better than when I knew them thirty years ago. This was a direct result of the oil bonanza, which went to the collective head of the country; but it has made Nigeria easier to get about in.

But I would never attempt to drive there myself. The only thing to do nowadays is to entrust your life to God and a local driver and sit back in Muslim resignation.

All these tarred roads and all these Peugeots are measures of how far tropical Africa has come in the way of Progress. In my day the highest aspirations of an ordinary man was a Vono bed, a Raleigh bicycle and a wireless set. Now he can aspire to bigger material blessings. But intelligent blacks are well aware of the precariousness and hollowness of all this ostensible progress. A Nigerian film-maker (there are such people now) says: "We build palaces but can't run them, we import cars we can't repair, we are attracted by all that glitters. We are slaves to another culture." And it is true. The Africans, like everybody else in the modern world, are fascinated with all the chromium trumpery.

When all these countries acquired their "independence" they immediately set about creating something that took precedence over every other need: a national airline, with their very own emblem on it. For the most part these were technological white elephants, with glass-and-steel airport buildings built in the expectation of traffic that never came, and now crumbling, with lifts and escalators that don't work; high-rise buildings with no water in the taps and lavatories; cement factories built by the Russians with a capacity of fifty thousand tons a year but finding it difficult to turn out five tons. The Canadians built a "semi-automated" bakery costing two-and-a-half million dollars in Dar es Salaam; but since the wheat has to be imported, and Tanganyika ("Tanzania") has no means of buying it, the absurd thing stands idle. But why a bakery in Africa? Why "semi-automated" where there is so much unemployment?

As Count Oxenstierna said three centuries ago: "Dost thou not know, my son, with how little wisdom the world is governed?"

Of course such enormous projects, however useless and wasteful, bring substantial material benefits to those in a position to award or further contracts; so the foreign firms are happy, and the local ministers and nabobs are happier still to acquire more and more such white elephants. Corruption from top to bottom is as serious a haemorrhage everywhere in Africa now as slavery was up to a century ago; and very much more difficult to abolish. Some of the new third or fourth generation leaders, like Jerry Rawlings in the Gold Coast, have tried the brisk policy of shooting ministers and officials who had dipped their fingers too deep in the till, *pour encourager les autres;* but they would depopulate their countries on a Pol Pot scale if they were to deal thus with everybody who took advantage of his position to direct public funds to his own pocket. In all African societies it is taken perfectly for granted that a man of importance should become rich, without much concerning themselves about how. One might go so far as to say that Africans have no civic conscience in a *Gesellschaft* society. In their old *Gemeinschaft* communities they were cocooned within a network of kinship and tribal obligations; and the "extended family" can be very extensive indeed. The richer an African becomes, the more the number of poor relations and hangers-on of all sorts he feels morally compelled to support, widows of cousins, bright remote nephews who ought to get an education and so on. These are the things that he accepts as inescapable duties; and the public funds are capacious; nobody will miss the perks that he considers his due; and public money is faceless and nameless. The *dash* has always been a deep-rooted institution. It would be blatant and intolerable discourtesy to any man of rank or influence *not* to offer him a dash, especially if you need a favour from him. The old white explorers knew that very well, and their baggage consisted mainly of rolls of cloth and other stuff for presents to the chiefs and headmen wherever they passed.

There is no tradition of an honest public service such as developed in Britain and Europe – though not until fairly recently, as it happens. Eighteenth century England (and still more eighteenth century America) took bribes with enthusiasm.

As for the lower ranks of the public service, most of them are too poor to be honest. But that should be regarded as a positive thing rather than a disadvantage; for it is often only by judicious bribery that anything worth doing can get done at all in Africa. Certainly there is no shame or shyness about taking a dash; nor need any be felt by the white man who offers one. It is the custom of the country.

I say this in a spirit of realism rather than cynicism. If corruption is an evil (as it is) it is one that will have to be lived with in Africa for a long time to come. In my day a black nurse in a hospital expected a dash every time she brought a bedpan or changed a dressing. In Lagos, if a child is in desperate need of a blood transfusion to save its life, a substantial dash will have to be placed in the proper hands before that transfusion will be given.

When the government schools were Africanised and black headmasters were appointed, it became necessary for parents to pay a substantial dash to get a pupil accepted. There is no more universal or deep-rooted institution.

When the expatriates left it was generally assumed that nationalist pressures would ensure the ultimate displacement of English by the main local languages.

In fact English is if anything more necessary now as the official language than ever. This, however, is a sign of the development of a genuine national (i.e. Nigerian as such) feeling, rather than the old Hausa and Yoruba and Ibo regional or tribal rivalries. It is a hopeful development, for it means that Nigeria has digested the bitter hatreds that broke out in anti-Ibo pogroms in the North and finally in the "Biafran" war. I could never have foreseen in 1988 that there could be so little ill-feeling. As it is, there are more Ibos and Yorubas than ever in Hausaland, and they appear to be accepted without the least hostility. Nigeria seems at last to be shaking down in amity. Now this is one of the most important signs that I noticed, and I hope that I have not misread it. Tribal factionalism has been another of the many curses of Africa, made particularly serious and acute in the post-imperial age. The time has been when a Hausa or a Yoruba would infinitely rather have had a white man as a superior than an Ibo, and the converse *mutatis mutandis.* I was present at some school ceremony at which the guest of honour was Sir Ahmadu Bello, Sardauna of Sokoto and Premier of the Northern Region. The head boy made such an excellent speech with such aplomb that the Sardauna summoned him, with the obvious intention of furthering his career. But when he learnt that the boy was not a Muslim Hausa, but a Christian Igbirra, his face fell; and he took no further interest in him.

A few years later the Sardauna's own career was abruptly terminated by Ibo officers in a night of long knives.

Television is well-established and very popular, and mostly in English. A good deal of American junk is imported (dirt-cheap, one hopes) – they love bogus all-in wrestling matches; but I greatly admired the local productions, and wish that South Africa would buy some of them. They displayed a talent and freshness and what I can only call sheer charm more than anything on the box produced by the South African Broadcasting Corporation in the white south. The newsreaders, mostly Yoruba ladies with a perfect command of Cheltenham English, are a delight to listen to, as well as to look at.

Nor is English confined to an affluent or educated class. In my experience everybody, at least in the towns, could use it to some degree. Hausas talking to one another throw in phrases of English all the time.

Before I went back recently I had assumed that I could retrace my steps by way of such of the old clubs as still existed. I had assumed the continued existence in each place of the sort of white community that I had belonged to thirty years ago. That was an error. Of the few white faces that I encountered in Nigeria most were French. The clubs still stood, but the light of their life had gone out. It was eerie, disquieting, to go into buildings that I had known as lively centres of white society and find them dim, decayed and deserted. In Kano Club the pool was empty and there were only a handful of Hausas drinking beer – that in itself a significant change; for in my day they would never have done so in public. It was difficult to recognise some of the other clubs. In Zaria Club I found what I take to be the perfect symbol of the change: a snooker-table that I used to play on stripped of its cloth and cushions and pockets, a big slab of slate covered with the dust of years, a neglected gravestone strangely set up on eight legs.

All this merely signified the disappearance of an alien body of strangers, and I had no right to regret that particular change. But one change I did regret was the disappearance of old Kano itself. When I was there it was still much as Clapperton and Lander had known it, a medieval walled city a thousand years old. I had told my driver to take me through the *Kofar Nasarawa*, the Conquerors'

Gate, that I had known so well. Not only was there no *Kofar Nasarawa:* there was no longer a wall. Even the old market, which had once been so full of bustle and colour, where you could see the cattle slaughtered and hacked up in the open, had shrunk to a depressed area of sad tin shacks. Even the vultures that used to be so numerous in Kano had disappeared.

The Africans have never treasured buildings as such. What to history–conscious white men was an ancient city that deserved the same sort of respect as the Tower of London was to its inhabitants only a visible manifestation of the old African way of life that they were ashamed of rather than sentimental about. Sentimentality is a northern indulgence. They were no doubt prouder of the new high–rise bank offices and "international" hotels, the future that they were headed for, than the romantic alleys and *kasuwas* of the old town that they saw as belonging to the past and to poverty. And I wish now that I had never gone back there.

Imitation being the sincerest form of flattery, when Africans were second- and third–class citizens in their own countries they imitated the white masters in some things. Unfortunately, by a sure instinct of perversity they imitated them in all the wrong things and none of the right things. A white man gave orders from behind a desk and never toiled with his hands. Thus an educated, or half- or quarter–educated African desires to give orders to obsequious inferiors, and scorns to work with his hands. He wishes to acquire white man's authority without the white man's efficiency, honesty and civic integrity. Even the most senior white officers lived modestly, even austerely. But when an African makes it to the top of the heap he feels no inclination even to feign modesty and simplicity. The "Emperor" Bokassa's Napoleonic fantasies ruined his country. His neighbour Mobutu builds himself palaces of sybaritic grandeur, combining candy–floss Versailles and Schönbrunns with Disneyland and Coney Island. As I write the Prime Minister of South Africa is being entertained in these surroundings. Mr Botha is a Calvinist and a bourgeois to the core, very much in the line of Paul Kruger; who lived all his days in a plain house in Pretoria, sitting on his *stoep* smoking his pipe and drinking his coffee.

Whatever they may think or say about the iniquities of the Boers, perhaps Paul Kruger offers Africa a better model to imitate that Nero or Heliogabalus.

The new expensive flashy "international" hotels offer a cool refuge from the equatorial heat; but they cut you off from the equatorial life. Thirty years ago, when we travelled we put up at government rest-houses. Some of the newer ones, designated Catering Rest-Houses or CRH's, usually managed by a white memsahib, provided meals. The older ones, which I much preferred, were simple thatched rondavels, and your own servant cooked your chop; delightful; and it cost next to nothing. But now Africa is becoming sophisticated before it has become civilised.

When in the Sixties Africa cast off the imperial shackles it seemed reasonable to adopt some form of socialism; which most of them did. In most cases the mixture of one-party spendthrift administrations and the endemic African corruptions led to swift bankruptcy. The more left-inclined they were, the worse the mess they got into. It is only apparently paradoxical that after "independence" the former colonies and protectorates became more dependent than ever on the industrialised countries of the north. They had pressed for independence too soon, and it had been granted them too soon for their own good. Disaster could have been avoided if they had had the good fortune to be governed firmly and sensibly in accordance with reality. Some, such as Kenya and the Ivory

Coast and Malawi had that good fortune. They still recognised their dependence on the support of the imperial metropolis. They were practical in economics, and they were not in a frantic hurry to Africanise everything. There are now more Frenchmen – and Frenchwomen – in the Ivory Coast than there were under French rule, and there are still fifty thousand whites in Kenya. But those countries that had the misfortune to combine socialism with an irremovable president, such as Tanzania and Zambia, are in serious economic straits. The Zambian kwacha is worthless. By buying them for foreign currencies on the black market, you can fill the petrol tank of a car for less than two pounds, because petrol is subsidised. Since the coppermines are now managed by native Zambians, and expatriates are limited to "essential personnel", production is barely half of what it could and should be. The shops in Lusaka are empty. When a consignment of cooking oil arrives the army has to be called in to keep order. Only two hundred buses out of twelve thousand are still working; the rest are off the road for lack of spare parts. Rubbish is left to accumulate in the streets; there are no trucks to take it away. Bribery is necessary for every elementary transaction. Kaunda has taken elaborate measures to defend himself against popular anger, with electric fences, television cameras, dogs, alarm systems, and even a mined corridor between two aprons of barbed wire; all constantly patrolled. He never divulges his intentions, and travels from his State House prison by helicopter. Wherever he appears in Lusaka, whole blocks are cordoned off and ordinary traffic is diverted. When he meets other African leaders he commandeers aircraft of the national airline, leaving stranded passengers to shift for themselves for days on end. As in old Stalinist Moscow, expatriates with foreign currency can buy all sorts of luxuries in the Free Shop: vodka, chocolates, tinned ham, smoked salmon.

As if Africa had not enough troubles already, now it has the new horror of Aids. A group of Scandinavian doctors in Lusaka took random samples of blood from five hundred senior managers in commerce, the upper ranks of the armed forces and the civil service and bank officials and found that twelve per cent were infected. The figure for Zambia as a whole is over twenty per cent. Two sons of Kaunda himself have died of it.

Presumably the figures for all the rest of Central Africa are comparable.

What struck me most about the places I knew was the obvious and explosive growth. What I remembered as modest villages had grown into large towns, towns that had already been large had swollen and spread into huge sprawling conurbations, with no visible sign of planning or direction. Towns in French West Africa have shape and order and dignity; they were planned *as* towns, not simply left to spread amorphously like mildew. There is no more appalling example of bad planning, or lack of planning, than Lagos, which has grown from a population of a million in the Fifties (and already a horribly overcrowded slum then) to over five million now; a place to be avoided altogether, or got out of as soon as possible. Yet with wise and firm control it could have been as decent and pleasant a town as (say) Abidjan, or even Luanda or Lourenço Marques. As it is, it is a hideous human sump altogether beyond redemption.

And that is how most towns in former British West Africa have grown: stinking conglomerations of rusty tin and open drains, full of unemployment and crime and prostitution. This is a post–colonial problem, created by colonial conditions of trade and industry. No African towns under African conditions ever grew into such monstrous vivaria. The gap between the standard of living of the "developed" and the "under-developed" countries is widening rapidly. To look at Lagos is to despair for the future of all Africa.

But, as Churchill said, "Never, never, never despair." Africa is in a most uncomfortable state of transition from the thirteenth, or even the eighth century, to the twentieth, in the process of getting caught up in the gigantic machine that the rest of us have come to take for granted as our human habitat. I myself feel about it rather like the hero of Scott–King's *Modern Europe:*

*Headmaster:* "Parents are not interested in producing the 'complete man' any more. They want to qualify their boys for jobs in the modern world."

*Scott–King:* "I think it would be very wicked indeed to fit a boy for the modern world."

*Headmaster:* "It's a very short–sighted view, Scott–King."

*Scott–King:* "There, headmaster, with all respect, I differ from you profoundly. I think it is the most long–sighted view it is possible to take."

We began the process of fitting Africa for the modern world without consulting it as to its desires in the matter. Naturally the Englishmen with the fire in their bellies who began the process could not have foreseen where their own world was going. They belonged to the nineteenth century, which was a kind of apogee that we may well look back on with envy. Nothing could have seemed more stable than that world. There had been no serious wars except in the Crimea; although the ugly business in South Africa was a portent of what was to come. But British industry and trade dominated the world, and there was a prospect of almost infinite expansion. Painting the map red had become almost an unconscious habit. And was not that good for the world? The English (and with them all other western Europeans) had no doubts about their own fitness or their right and duty to direct the lesser breeds without the law. It was a time when it was (perhaps for the first and last time) possible for intelligent men to *believe* in the Future as the Middle Ages had believed in the justice and mercy of God; when it was possible to utter words like Progress without embarrassment. If some prophet had stood up and loudly informed them that their Progress was to Hell in a handcart they would not have stoned him; they would have laughed.

With at least the wisdom of hindsight, if no other, we are beginning dimly to suspect that perhaps Europe (and now the white America derived from it) is not so superior after all; that there was something unnatural about the circumstances that led it to think so; and that now we had better begin to concentrate on the novel notion that we are all in the same boat: that the boat is rocking wildly, and is none too seaworthy; and that we had better start sharing out the food and water and oilskins equitably, and give up the notion of eating one another.

There are now about forty countries south of the Sahara. Not one of them can be regarded as inherently stable. Not one is homogeneous within itself, not one is a "natural" ethnic entity, not one is within "natural" boundaries. Africa is a white man's artefact, a thing made, not an organic thing. Their communications, their roads and railways, make no joint sense. Lagos and Porto Novo are fifty miles apart; but to telephone from one to the other the call has to go by London and Paris. As they are, these new states are the wrong size and the wrong shape: too big to be all of a piece, but too small to be economically viable. The demagogues who inherited these fragments of empire were perfectly happy with the situation; it gave them a sphere of operations that they jealously guarded like dogs with juicy bones. The "leaders" ("Take me to your leader") of these new countries are the last men to contemplate any kind of rational rearrangement of peoples and frontiers; and anyway, even if they did, it would certainly lead only to the kind of bloodshed that took place when Pakistan split off from India. It seems that Africa is stuck with these fundamental illogicalities for ever and a day.

Strangely enough it is Europe itself that now begins to set an example and shows how Africa may yet solve its worst basic problems in a positive evolutionary manner. It took the two disastrous wars of our disastrous century to induce the western half of Europe to start making common cause, jammed as they are between the upper and nether millstones of the ineptly lumbering "superpowers". It may be that their post-independence disasters and the European model will likewise induce the Africans to combine into natural regional communities. At present their currencies are valueless outside their borders, except for the French CFA. If you ask a bank teller in Nairobi or Accra to change (say) Nigerian nairas, he will at best smile. It is absurd that a Kenyan shilling should be worth twenty-five to the pound while the Tanzanian shilling next door is (officially) worth only a hundred to the pound and the Ugandan shilling (officially) about three thousand. Yes, of course: Idi Amin, Milton Obote, the meddling governessy socialist Nyerere acting Jehovah. But these anomalies and instabilities are inherent as things are. Africa has no defence in its present state against crazy sergeants and thimble-rigging politicians.

Until it has, there is little hope for it.

One of the craziest anomalies is the present polecat situation of South Africa. However unsatisfactory the internal politics of South Africa may be, its (official) isolation from the rest of Africa is an excellent example of its modern substitute for human sacrifice: cutting off its joint nose to spite its joint face. There never was a clearer case of perverse failure to take advantage of beneficial cooperation, regardless of meddling selfrighteous Congresses and futile obstructive OAU and UN talking-shops.

Africa is pretty sick, and none the better for the innumerable quacks and mountebanks with their political and economic and moral pills. As the most successful states, such as the Ivory Coast and Kenya and Malawi, have shown, Africa needs more than anything a sufficient quantity of benevolent and sensible paternalism. Let democracy come when or if they can afford it; at present they can't. And the rest of the world, particularly the former imperial powers, ought to have the moral courage to *do* something, not just wring their hands; or worse still, wash them. Nothing proclaimed the moral decline of Britain more than when they allowed Idi Amin first to throw out the Indians and then proceed to debauch what Churchill called "the pearl of Africa". The British put the appalling buffoon there in the first place; it was their moral duty to get rid of him by whatever means lay to hand; and I refuse to believe that there were none. I agree with Laurence Sterne: They order such matters better in France. When their equivalent of Idi Amin, the bizarre cannibal Emperor Bokassa, went off his trolley, they hustled him off the scene with the minimum of fuss, and when trouble threatens in any of their African interests a quiet and modest little police action restores order and settles the hash. The former British territories would have greatly benefited by a similar display of gumption at the right moments.

I am no enthusiast for biological engineering; but I wish they could "clone" Margaret Thatcher.

Let me end with a brief exchange between a French soldier and a British soldier when both nations were manoeuvring for position in West Africa ninety years ago:

"You have insulted our flag," said the Frenchman. "The history of Borgu shows how England has overridden all treaties."

"The history of Borgu," replied the Englishman, "has surely yet to be written."

Typical white arrogance, an African would say. But in a real sense General Willcocks was right; and the significant history of Africa still remains to be written.

# GLOSSARY

AFV – armoured fighting vehicle
Aids – Acquired Immune Deficiency Syndrome
ALN – National Liberation Army (Algeria)
ANC – African National Congress
AP – The Associated Press
Armscor – Armaments Corporation of South Africa Limited
Azapo – Azanian People's Organisation
AZASO – Azanian Students Organisation
*baraka:* Special grace or good fortune accorded from on high
*barbouze:* ("false beard") underground government agent (Algeria)
*bidonville:* shanty town
*bled:* French army name for the outback
BBC – British Broadcasting Corporation
BCM – Black Consciousness Movement
BPS – Black Priests' Solidarity Movement
BSAP – British South Africa Police
CAAA – Comprehensive Anti-Apartheid Act
*caid:* Arab local governor
Canu – Caprivian African National Union
CFA Franc – Monetary unit in circulation among former French colonial community
　　in Africa; linked to French Franc. One French Franc equals 20 CFA Francs
CIA – Central Intelligence Agency (United States)
CIO – Central Intelligence Organisation (Zimbabwe)
Cocom – Coordinating Committee
*colon:* European settler
COMOPS – Combined Operations (Zimbabwe)
COSAS – Congress of South African Students
Cosatu – Congress of South African Trade Unions
CP – Conservative Party (South Africa)
CPSA – Communist Party of South Africa
CPSU – Communist Party of the Soviet Union
CPUSA – USA Communist Party
CRUA – Revolutionary Committee of Unity and Action (Algeria)
CW – Chemical Weapons
CSIR – Council for Scientific and Industrial Research (South Africa)
CUF – *Companhia Uniao Fabril* (Portugal)
DFA – Department of Foreign Affairs (South Africa)
DGS – *Direção-Geral de Segurança* (successor to PIDE – Portugal)
*djebel:* mountain
D.O. – District Officer
DOW – Defence Ordinance Workshop
EPG – Eminent Persons Group
FAC – fast attack craft

FALA – MPLA airforce (Angola)
FAPLA – Popular Forces for the Liberation of Angola (MPLA military wing)
*fellagha:* Arab guerrilla (Algeria)
*fellah:* Arab peasant
FIDA – *Feria Internacional del Aire:* International Air Show (Chile)
FLN – National Liberation Front (Algeria)
FNLA – National Front for the Liberation of Angola
FLING – National Front for the liberation of Guinea (Portuguese)
FPLM – Popular Forces for the liberation of Mozambique (Frelimo Army)
FPLN – Popular Front for National Liberation
Frelimo – Mozambique Liberation Front
GAO – General Accounting Officer
GDP – Gross Domestic Product
*glasnost* – "openness"; Gorbachev expression relating to new Soviet era
GNP – Gross National Product
GRA – Government Reservation Area
*Hadj:* title given to Muslims who have made the pilgrimage to Mecca
*harki:* Algerian soldier fighting for France
HIV – Human Immunodeficiency Virus
ICU – Industrial and Commercial Workers' Union
IDASA – Institute for a Democratic Alternate for South Africa
IDR – *International Defense Review* (Geneva)
IFV – Infantry fighting vehicle
ILO – International Labour Organisation
IMEMO – Institute for World Economy and International Relations
ISL – International Socialist League
JDW – *Jane's Defence Weekly*
*jihad:* holy war
JMC – Joint Monitoring Commission
JMPLA – Youth of the MPLA and the Pioneer Organisation for Angolan Children
JOC – Joint Operations Command
*katiba:* FLN company
LC – landing craft
LEW – Lyttleton Engineering Works
MAG – *mitrailleur á gaz* (gas-fired machine-gun); much used by southern African
    security forces
*Maghreb:* (land of the setting sun) Tunisia, Algeria and Morocco
MCW – Military Combat Work
MGL – multiple grenade-launcher
MK – *Umkhonto we Sizwe* (Armed wing of ANC)
MTLD – An early generation Algerian liberation movement
MNR – Mozambique National Resistance Movement (see Renamo)
MP – Member of Parliament
MPLA – Popular Movement for the Liberation of Angola
MPV – mine-protected vehicle
MRL – multiple rocket-launcher
MWASA – Media Worker's Association of South Africa

NACTU – National Council of Trade Unions
NATO – North Atlantic Treaty Organisation
NCO – Non-commissioned officer
NDP – National Democratic Party
NSE – National state of emergency
NUM – National Union of Mineworkers
OAU – Organisation of African Unity
OCC – Operations Coordinating Committee
OMA – Angolan Women's Organisation
OPC– Ovambo People's Congress
PAC – Pan Africanist Congress
PAF – Portuguese Air Force
PAIGC – African Party for the Independence of Guinea and Cape Verde
PATU – Police Anti-Terrorist Unit (Paramilitary Support Unit)
*perestroika* – "restructuring"; Gorbachev expression
PF – Patriotic Front
PFP – Progressive Federal Party
PIDE – Portuguese secret police active in metropolis and overseas provinces
    (succeeded by DGS)
*pied noir:* ("black foot") European settler in Algeria
Plan – People's Liberation Army of Namibia (military wing of Swapo)
PLO – Palestinian Liberation Organisation
PMP – Pretoria Metal Pressings
RAR – Rhodesian African Rifles
Renamo – see MNR, Mozambique Resistance Movement (anti-Frelimo)
RLI – Rhodesian Light Infantry
RSA – Republic of South Africa
SAAF – South African Air Force
SAANC – South African African National Congress
SABC – South African Broadcasting Corporation
SACC – South African Council of Churches
SACP – South African Communist Party
SACP-ANC – The ANC linked to the SA Communist Party; successor to the CPSA
    which went underground in the early Sixties
SACTU – South African Congress of Trade Unions
SADCC – Southern African Development Coordination Conference
SADF – South African Defence Force
SAN – South African Navy
SARH – semi-active radar homing
SAS – Special Air Services (Rhodesia and United Kingdom)
SASOL-NATREF – South African Coal, Oil and Gas Corporation-National Refinery
SATAC – South African Teachers' Action Committee
SDECE – French Secret Service
Swapo – South West African People's Organisation
SWATF – South West Africa Territory Force
UDF – United Democratic Front
UDI – Unilateral Declaration of Independence

UDMA – Algerian United Democratic Manifesto
UN – United Nations
UNESCO – United Nations Educational Scientific and Cultural Organisation
Unita – National Union for the Total Independence of Angola
UNTA – National Union of Angola Workers
UPI – United Press International
UPNA – Popular Union for North Angola
USA – United States of America
USSR – Union of Soviet Socialist Republics
*Wilaya:* one of the six FLN commands in Algeria
Zanla – Zimbabwe African National Liberation Army
ZANU – Zimbabwe African National Union
ZAPU – Zimbabwe African Peoples Union
Zipra – Zimbabwe Peoples Revolutionary Army
ZPRA – Zimbabwe Peoples Revolutionary Army

# THE STRATEGIC SIGNIFICANCE OF SOUTHERN AFRICA IN THE 1990s

## by David Isby

Is there any strategic consequence or value to southern Africa, in either the short or the long term? Or will the internal situation in South Africa so overshadow all the other aspects of the strategic picture as to render them, if not irrelevant, at least outside the first rank of international concern? If it does not, a much broader range of factors and decisions must be considered.

Since 1978 South Africa has had a strong, well considered national strategy that has achieved a number of successes. But ten years is a long lifespan for any policy, and in the late 1980s South Africa has been trying to evolve a new strategy, to be put into effect both externally and internally. The agreements on Angola and Namibia are likely to be its first vital test.

The most critical factor in assessing the geopolitical future of South Africa is the capability of its security forces. The superiority of these forces to all threats, external and internal, made South African strategy workable in the 1980s and offers Pretoria the same hope for the 1990s, even if new strategic approaches emphasise its economic, political and diplomatic power more than its military power.

South Africa's response to the internal dimension of its security problem has been consistent with its response to external threats. The development of nuclear and chemical weapons of mass destruction by South Africa presents the military with a final option, although its use is difficult to envisage in the 1990s. The strategic significance in southern Africa comes also from its natural resources and the Cape sea route. This is also a matter of Russian interest. Despite changes in policy, the Russians remain key actors in conflicts throughout southern Africa, which gives them a broader international significance, as does the Cuban presence in Angola. Elsewhere, there is a second "wind of change" in southern Africa: leaders and economics are both evolving. Whether this will change the strategic future is uncertain, like the impact of Aids and other "wild cards", factors that cannot be reasonably assessed, but will shape the future of southern Africa in the 1990s.

### Inside the Laager: the Internal Strategic Dimension

Paradoxically, the strategic significance of southern Africa in the 1990s will probably be most strongly affected by the element with the least international input. The crucial question, internally, is likely to remain that of state power in South Africa: whether it is unitary and whether those who have it shall be black or white. How it is resolved – and resolution in the 1990s is by no means likely – will have a great effect on the outside world. Politics remains the art of the possible, but it is uncertain what is possible in South Africa; and President P.W. Botha and Oliver Tambo would have widely divergent views. A variety of models and examples has been offered for the possible future of South Africa; the French Algerian, Zimbabwean and the Israeli (especially after the Palestinian uprising began in 1987) experiences are all frequently likened to the situation in South Africa, but all present fundamental differences. If the revolution of the internal situation in the 1990s turns out to be through either repression or revolution, the deciding factors will be military. Otherwise diplomacy and political and economic factors will be crucial.

The prospect of non-military action providing a solution to the future of South Africa seems remote. At present there are no regular negotiations to deal with this fundamental question of power. However, it must be remembered that the talks in 1988 that ultimately led to the end of the wars in Angola, Afghanistan, Iran and Iraq once seemed hardly less incapable of providing a solution.

The South African government wishes to use its gains in the Angola and Namibia negotiations as a springboard for a parallel internal initiative. The difference is that no one on the other side will talk. Even the black leader most closely associated with a negotiated settlement, the Zulu chief Mangosuthu Buthelezi, has made the release from prison of Nelson Mandela, the former leader of the ANC, a pre-condition for talks. But the real criterion for potential internal negotiations is whether Pretoria is willing to hand over more than a cosmetic amount of power. If it is not, neither Buthelezi nor the ANC nor any other opponent of government has anything to gain from negotiating.

Buthelezi has explicitly recognised another crucial question that makes short-term solutions initiated by the black population unworkable: the military power of South Africa. As he says: "P.W. Botha is the most powerful man in Africa... It is madness to declare an armed struggle that you cannot win."

While Buthelezi has emphasised the ineffectiveness of attempts at a revolutionary solution, the corresponding weakness of a negotiated solution was also demonstrated by the efforts of the Commonwealth Eminent Persons Group in 1986. Pretoria supported their efforts, but did not share the Western view that negotiation is the opposite of the use of other forms of state power (raids into Zambia, Botswana and Zimbabwe were carried out while the mission was in progress) and so black agreement did not emerge. The final negotiating terms produced by the Eminent Persons Group were rejected by Pretoria, as they were essentially framed in terms of resigning white rule. The refusal to release Nelson Mandela, the banning of 17 opposition groups in February 1988, who might otherwise have sat at the table opposite President Botha's men, and the biggest political trial in a generation, used to convict much of the UDF leadership of treason in November 1988, suggests that the South African commitment to negotiations is limited to those who would confirm its grasp of state power.

Other South African approaches have likewise had limited success. The local elections in October 1988 did not attract wide support as a first step towards democracy, either internally among the black population (although the 30 per cent turnout in contested seats in the face of intimidation shows that this lack of support was by no means unanimous) or among most Western governments, because it seemed unlikely that many more steps would be taken. All South African internal moves certainly have an external element, like those of its African opposition. While the West, especially the USA, has had, with Russian cooperation, some success in contributing to the agreements on Angola and Namibia and, indirectly, the improved relations between South Africa and Mozambique, they have not succeeded in applying this policy to the internal situation. The international element in South Africa itself depends on to what extent the economic partners of Pretoria can affect its behaviour and to what extent the external supporters of the opposition – African, Russian and Western – can alter it.

With revolution unlikely to defeat the South African security forces in the 1990s, and negotiation now seeming, by common consent, an unlikely short-term possibility, Pretoria may then unilaterally look to concession or repression or a judicious mixture of both as a practicable internal policy. Certainly there are deep divisions within white South Africa on this fundamental matter. The increased strength of the Conservative Party (CP) in recent years is an expression of distrust of a negotiated settlement by a large part of the white population. Parliament becomes less and less relevant as time passes; the government retains its powers assumed during 1984–86 and makes decrees in place of normal law-making. There are fears that the next ten years may see a change to an authoritarian régime, without even a pretence at democracy.

The divisions in white South Africa are not only political. The security services themselves are by no means monolithic in their views of how to deal with the challenges of unrest in the townships, let alone the broader questions. The police tend to see unrest as a police problem, calling for rigorous and effective enforcement, while the army tends to see the situation more as a budding insurgency that demands effective counter-insurgency tactics, including the "winning of hearts and minds", to be successful. Even in the wars in Angola and Namibia, much easier militarily than the situation inside South Africa, the Defence Force was unable to use its undoubted strength to impose its own solution. The utility of military force inside South Africa will probably remain limited throughout the 1990s.

South African strategy is at present linked to economic strength, and its successor in the 1990s is likely to be even more so. Without it, South Africa will be unable to control either the other states of southern Africa or its own townships without the use of armed force. The Botha government's target of 5 – 6 per cent real growth in the early 1980s (now slipped to 3 – 3,5 per cent) necessitated "one economy", economic and social decentralisation and liberalisation that precluded the separate economies of the old-style apartheid still clung to by the right wing opposition. To achieve growth, blacks had to be brought into the economy as skilled and semi-skilled labour. This required the legalising of black trade unions, recognising the permanency of black residence in urban areas, repealing the pass laws, expanding educational opportunities, relaxing group area restrictions, and finally accepting the political strength that economic power would give to blacks, although that strength would still have to contend with the ultimate crux of the colour of state power.

Concessionary aspects of South African policies that emerge in the 1990s are likely to be centred on making the fruits of the economy more readily available to blacks, carrying on the 1980s moves in that direction: new housing in the townships, a 33 per cent increase in spending on black education since 1986 — but all this must take place within the context of the total economy, shaken by the weakness of the gold price (40 per cent of South African exports) challenged by sanctions and disinvestment. Reform is difficult under such circumstances, and the government will run the risk of alienating those whose support it most needs without gaining the loyalty of those who oppose it. The harder line advocated by Pretoria from 1986 is linked not only to the rise of political opposition on the right but also to the reduced effectiveness of their economic leverage.

The "homelands" that were to be the pillars of the old apartheid failed to win either international legitimacy or domestic viability, although they have certainly not been abandoned by Pretoria. The absence of emphasis on failed institutions has also been seen in the emergence of the Joint Management Committees, which can bypass existing government structures, and provides more evidence that the system in South Africa remains resilient and adaptable. Another adaptation was the 1984 constitution. Its tricameral parliament was a recognition that political power was to begin to flow towards the economic strength of the coloureds and Indians. But Pretoria will reject all adaptations that do not mesh with the general national strategy, such as the proposed formation of KwaNatal from a union of Natal with the KwaZulu "homeland", despite its widespread support in the West.

The strategy of Pretoria in the 1980s, even as it is likely to be brought up to date for the 1990s, is unlikely to satisfy black expectations, either those of the labour movement, troubled by a precarious economy, or those of the "comrades" in the townships. But all the choices are not Pretoria's. President Botha's promise in August 1985 that "I will restore order to South Africa and no one in the world will stop me" has been negated by the facts: in 1980 there were 19 terrorist incidents and 234 in 1987, with further increases probable in 1988. More disturbing, 446 African National Congress (ANC) terrorists and guerrillas were captured in 1987 (200 fewer than in 1986) although the bag from the Pan Africanist Congress (PAC) increased from 38 to 85. Instead of sporadic attacks against symbolic priority targets, white civilians are now being targeted. More extensive violence, including isolated industrial sabotage, is probable although this factor is unlikely to be major since only the most desperate individual destroys the means of earning a living.

While the violence has moved beyond the boundaries of the townships, it is far from rampant and has certainly never approached that of the Algerian insurrection. There are no South African equivalents of the mobs of *pieds noirs* lynching Arabs after every bomb explosion in Algiers. As a result of effective policing, the violence remains peripheral to South African life, much as it has been in Israel in the past few years. Fissures and rivalries within the groups committed to revolutionary violence and a willingness by Pretoria to use strong measures at the cost of internal division and external condemnation, are likely to keep this so into the 1990s. Nor, despite the resentments created by apartheid, has hostility between black and white ever been as bitter as that in Algeria or, conceivably, those that may be emerging from the polarisation of Israel. The economic realities of South Africa have forced a certain degree of mutual interdependence. Whether that can ever be the grounds for mutual understanding remains uncertain. The possible political futures for South Africa range from repression to revolution. Either of the extremes is likely to result in a carnage that would sicken Tamerlaine. But in Africa few such apocalyptic solutions of its many problems have come to pass.

The resilience and capability of white South Africa and its means of dealing with internal and external challenges are strategically decisive. Economic weakness has certainly become evident. But, considering its size and its integration into the world economy, South Africa is certainly no Zimbabwe, where the cost of the war eventually destroyed the economy and the resilience of the whites. There is no guarantee that that would ever happen in South Africa. Again, while the whites in Rhodesia could always leave for South Africa, white South Africans have nowhere else to go to. Desperation rarely generates moderation. Demographic change – that great locomotive of discontent in the Israeli-occupied areas – is a long-range challenge. In 1988, blacks outnumber whites by nearly five to one, and may increase to fourteen to one by the year 2050.

In the 1990s, the human rights problem inside South Africa is likely to shape the development of policy in the West. Congress now realises that the USA electorate is less ready to support even pro–Western repressive régimes for geopolitical reasons than it was fifteen or twenty years ago. This knowledge will certainly help to determine whatever policy the Bush administration formulates as its successor to Reagan's "constructive engagement" in southern Africa. But American interest in the internal struggle will take the form of supporting peaceful change, even though the instruments of such a policy, such as the Anti-Apartheid Act, may not be of Bush's choosing.

As 1988 ends, the resilience of Pretoria still appears strong. External actions such as the Angolan and Namibian negotiations and President Botha's diplomatic overtures to African states (in a two-month period he was received by the presidents of Mozambique, Malawi, Zaïre and Ivory Coast) may have given a lead towards similar solutions to domestic problems. It is certainly not unreasonable to consider whether the ANC could be brought to deal with Pretoria as Angola and Mozambique have been, combined with an effort to divert, split, buy off or co-opt ANC leadership, or at least to try to exploit the differences between the various elements of the opposition. Will short-term success lead to a lasting settlement or a passing advantage for Pretoria? This question will determine whether the potentials of South Africa, geopolitical, natural and human, will be wasted or not.

### Nuclear and Chemical Weapons in Southern Africa

Even if there is no single source of clear evidence in the open literature, South Africa must be presumed to have a substantial stockpile of nuclear weapons. South Africa has never signed the nuclear non-proliferation treaty. The Foreign Minister Pik Botha's announcement, in the summer of 1988, that South Africa had the ability to produce nuclear weapons "should we want to" has been the most explicit statement on the nuclear question, although he would not confirm the existence of a stockpile, which is estimated to consist of something like nine to 23 devices at that time. What may have been a nuclear explosion near Marion Island in the South Atlantic on 22 September 1979 also seems to confirm this capability. The Valindaba uranium enrichment plant is probably capable of producing weapons-grade material. South African strike aircraft certainly provide an effective means of delivery, and with aerial repelling, which the South African Air Force (SAAF) is also capable of, could effectively strike anywhere in Africa south of the Sahara.

South African chemical weapons, the existence of which is also not confirmed, may have deterred Cuba and the MPLA (Popular Movement for the Liberation of Angola) from expanding the use of chemical weapons in Angola (as, no doubt, their capability of chemical warfare deterred South Africa). South Africa has delivery systems for chemical weapons also, and its large fleet of crop-dusting aircraft could be used to deliver chemical toxins.

Such atrocious weapons are unlikely to be used in the 1990s. The chief utility of the nuclear weapons would be to deter any serious threat to South Africa from outside. But such threats, for example, a large offensive by an African coalition or a naval blockade or expedition by the United Nations, are remote. The threat of chemical weapons is most effective as a domestic ultimate weapon; armed revolution might provoke widespread use of nerve toxins.

### Resource War and the Cape Route

The resources of South Africa and its geographical position determined its original strategic importance, but it has been overshadowed and perhaps made less relevant in Western calculations by internal and regional situations. These changes have also affected South African defence priorities. The South African Navy is now a coastal rather than a blue-water force. The old ASW Shackleton patrol aircraft and Wasp helicopters were not replaced as their working lives ended. The Buccaneer attack aircraft of the SAAF have largely relinquished the function of a maritime strike force for which they were originally procured.

Despite this shift in emphasis, certain geopolitical realities remain. The Cape route is still the highway by which a great deal of the raw materials for Europe and the Western hemisphere is carried. In 1981, 537 megatonnes out of a total of 738 megatonnes of crude oil imported by the European members of NATO came to them round the Cape. The "supertankers" that carry most of the oil consumed by the world cannot pass through the Suez Canal, and the ever-turbulent situation in the Middle East means that the danger of Suez being shut down, as in 1967-73, can never be dismissed.

Many of the resources that the West needs from southern Africa are simply not available elsewhere outside the Soviet Union. The Russian refusal to rely on southern Africa is shown by the fact that only 2,5 per cent of the vessels using the Cape route are Russian or Warsaw Pact. South Africa dominates world supplies of many essential minerals, especially chromium, manganese, vanadium and platinum, and is likely to do so throughout the 1990s, in the absence of large-scale investment to develop other sources. Gold and diamond production gives South Africa resource value. The importance of South African resources remains a shield against a total trade embargo. The West cannot build a jet engine without South African raw material, and must consider this fact in relation to any potential future government.

## The Soviet Dimension

Russian interest in the future of southern Africa has survived the changes in Gorbachev's foreign policy. Continuity in its policies towards southern Africa is still firm. Despite pressure for an agreement in Angola, even one that would eventually require the Cubans to withdraw, there has been no abandonment of the MPLA, as the degree of Cuban reinforcements and deliveries of arms in 1988 reveal. Russian relations with the ANC and Swapo continue, and while the old commitment to supporting national liberation movements and external communist parties may receive less emphasis under Gorbachev, it has certainly not been abandoned. The Russians realise that such groups, like the general situation in southern Africa, are still excellent tools for influence on or penetration of African resources and the Cape route to the economies of the West, and of the fact that this is one area where economic warfare could be waged in peacetime.

But Soviet Union policy on southern Africa in the 1990s will have to come to grips with a wide range of problems. Arms sales were long the most effective single tool of Russian foreign influence; but, outside Angola, they have been of only limited usefulness in the southern African Frontline States. The use of proxy forces has not expanded beyond the Cubans in Angola, and the Cuban willingness to negotiate its presence may indicate that in the 1990s Havana wishes to shift its attention, although these troops earn foreign currency and allow Cuba to keep up elements of its normal forces that might otherwise have to be demobilised. One considerable change in Russian policy towards southern Africa is in its dealings with South Africa. While not abandoning previous policies, Moscow has shown itself open to a more practical and less ideological set of options in southern Africa. There have also been some moves towards Pretoria: diplomatic activity, journalistic exchanges, increased trade, and the long-standing cooperation on the sale of gold on the world market. Any great change in Russian policy is highly unlikely; but if the West becomes more actively hostile to South Africa and gives more effective support to the Frontline States and South African opposition groups, which are likely to receive less Russian largesse under Gorbachev, Pretoria may conceivably re-align itself to being pro-Russian in its attitude rather than pro-Western.

### Namibia, Angola, Mozambique: The Strategic Test

South African strategy was evolving as P.W. Botha attained power in 1978. Reacting to increased unrest in the townships and the unfriendly régimes in Angola and Mozambique, this strategy aimed at a more refined and less repressive solution to internal problems and tried to "fight forward", to engage hostile forces as far away as possible. South African strategic goals in 1978 included: stopping potential advance of Cuban-backed troops across the border, blocking support for Swapo or the ANC from bordering countries, (reinforced by the six-mile security zones established along South Africa's borders from 1978), and finally, combining South African military and economic power to ensure that the Frontline countries of southern Africa did not act against Pretoria. The main tenor of the 1978 strategy had not been abandoned by 1988, but it had evolved, characterised by the diplomatic offensive, dealings with Mozambique, and negotiations on ending the wars in Angola and Namibia.

The apparent military threat to South Africa will not disappear, since even if the Cubans leave Angola, Swapo or ANC armed forces would be seen as an external armed danger to South Africa. Against these dangers, the South African Defence Force (SADF) has made deep strikes against Swapo and ANC bases and taken part in the wars against the MPLA and, up to 1984, Frelimo. Aggressive South African pre-emptive or retaliatory forward strikes have included proxy, covert or special operations against the Frontline States. South African commandos struck into Mozambique in 1981, Lesotho in 1982, and Botswana in 1985. Air raids have been widespread. But the Frontline States are likely to be unwilling or unable to remove the ANC or similar groups from their territory entirely. Other military actions have developed from South African strategy as well; there has been fighting along the western border of Zambia with South African forces outflanking Swapo bases in Angola. These actions are designed to create and maintain buffer zones forward of the borders, and are considered more effective than relying on barrier defences that need to be strongly manned, especially in spring, when rain and low cloud make air reconnaissance difficult.

South African understanding of the limitations of military strength is not new; it was seen in their unwillingness to continue to prop up the government of Rhodesia in 1979. It was seen in Mozambique when the South Africans were willing to give up their support of Renamo after the signing of the Nkomati Accord in 1984. The South Africans signed the Luanda Accord for a ceasefire with the MPLA about the same time, although it did not last. By 1988, the signing of economic agreements with Mozambique (including debt servicing and agreements on the security of the Cahora Bassa dam), the withdrawal of South African forces from Angola and agreements for a settlement in Namibia show that the South Africans are willing to make this a part of their "forward strategy".

There are now few "low-threat" battlefields left in the world, and what conventional military force can accomplish in a Third World conflict is limited. In Angola, billions of dollars' worth of Russian equipment enabled the garrison at Cuito Cuanavale to hang on in the summer of 1987; but only just. While the South Africans have an impressive record of victory in both land and air, they are vulnerable to attrition of spirit, weapons and money. This has led to increasing problems with numbers of South Africans evading or avoiding military service. It is generally well understood that while South Africa has only a limited number of ageing high–performance aircraft, the Cubans and the MPLA régime appear to have inexhaustible replacements of MiG–23 *Floggers* with all–aspect missiles. Faced with a well–equipped opponent, modern war is an expensive business for economically troubled South Africa.

When the last South African troops left Angola on 30 August 1988, it was unlikely to change the situation in Angola seriously. Unita was certainly helped by South African units, but that was not the most important cause of their success. Communist air–power is unlikely to be able to carry out an effective air offensive against Savimbi. If the Cubans ever withdraw from Angola, the MPLA will certainly have to make a deal with Unita. By 1988 there were already reports of diplomatic contacts between the two Angolan groups, in Zambia, the Ivory Coast and elsewhere. But the essential upshot of negotiation, who shall control state power and whether it is unitary, may not be such an absolute barrier as it now appears to be in the internal state of South Africa. The MPLA will be militarily vulnerable once the Cubans leave, and there are grounds for unity between former comrades–in–arms during the war against the Portuguese.

Attempts to negotiate an end to the war in Namibia are not an abrogation of South African strategy. The South Africans realise that Western attitudes are unlikely to become more favourable in the 1990s, and any attempt to resolve the Namibian problem would certainly improve their international standing. Saving the cost (estimated at R1 000 million a year in the early 1980s) of the commitment as well as shortening the defensive perimeter of the heartland were also obvious factors. The debit side is the possible loss of resources and a geopolitical buffer. While the ability to "meet the enemy in Ovamboland rather than along the Orange" had long justified South African commitment to Namibia, Pretoria may now believe that it can achieve the same results through the other components of their strategy, and turn the Namibian terrain into a barrier against their enemies rather than keep it a logistics headache for the SADF.

If the promise of agreements with Mozambique, Angola and Namibia is fulfilled, at least part of the American "constructive engagement" policy will be vindicated; but such a coincidence of interests between Washington and Pretoria is unlikely to be enduring. Once the conflict on the South African border becomes more diplomatic, political and economic and less overtly military, the ability of Washington to influence developments, which is already limited, may well decrease still further.

## The Second "Wind of Change" in Southern Africa
Macmillan's famous expression is often quoted to the detriment of Pretoria, but change in southern Africa is not limited to inside South Africa. In the 1990s, a generation since independence for most of Africa, there will be many significant changes that South African strategy will try to shape. The driving force of much of the changes seen in Africa will come from changes in leadership, although even in Africa, where institutions tend to be weaker and personal influences stronger than elsewhere, the future is unlikely to be shaped by only a few key actors. The most important task of these new leaders will be to come to grips with broad and deep economic problems. While hopes for economic development remain, the economic situation in most of Africa south of the Sahara remains

disastrous. Regional GDP, both absolute and per caput, continued to sink through the late 1980s, with debt mounting despite the concessions made at the economic meeting in Toronto in 1988. Most governments in southern Africa are trying to get their economies in order. Despite the difficulties of Zambia, there is now more willingness to accept the unpleasant medicine usually prescribed by the World Bank or the IMF. Few now follow the lead of the former president of Tanzania, Julius Nyerere, the "founder of African socialism". Nyerere's successor, Ali Mwenyi, has now turned away from the old policies by devaluing the currency and attempting to reduce bloated public services, The result was a 4 per cent increase in GDP in 1986/7 and rising exports. In the 1990s, it is probable that conventional theories of economic development will be more evident in African decision-making. Even Benin and the Congo, in the north, are turning away from doctrinaire socialism and seeking economic help from the West.

The succession of the Minister of Foreign Affairs, Joaquim Chissano, to the presidency of Mozambique, after the death of Samora Machel in an aeroplane crash in October 1986, has been an example of the predominance of practical common sense over ideology in southern Africa. It has resulted in strong support of Chissano by Washington and London, despite vociferous opposition by some on the US right who continue to support the Renamo resistance movement, and uncertainties about whether the shift of Mozambique from pro-Russian policies is fundamental or simply a tactical move made in desperation. The encouragement of more Chissanos may be one area where Washington, London, Pretoria and the Frontline States might possibly agree.

South African financial difficulties will probably grow worse in the 1990s; nearly US$12 billion worth of debts will fall due in 1990/1, four times the figure for 1988/9. Sanctions and outflow of foreign capital have also hurt. Servicing debts and sustaining the economic growth and strength that South African strategy depends on will become more and more difficult. But the continued weakness of most other southern African states ensures the relative power of South Africa. Those states that have been willing to deal with South Africa have had, on the whole, much better economic success than their neighbours. Botswana is the great success of sub-Saharan Africa. Malawi has performed respectably. Mauritius has no need of help from the IMF and is amortising some debts ahead of schedule.

## Other Winds, Other Changes
Many factors that will influence the strategic importance of southern Africa cannot be predicted. The phenomenon of Aids is one. It is already inflicting terrible damage throughout the "Aids belt" of Zaïre, Rwanda, Burundi, Uganda, Kenya and Zambia. It will have a great impact, even if the belt itself does not grow. The cost of the disease is already evident in the economies of these countries.

It may yet have a political effect, over-stretching the capabilities of poor countries with few resources. There is, however, already much evidence that the belt is spreading. Lusaka is worse than Kampala according to one experienced observer of southern Africa. The leadership classes of these countries are suffering severe casualties. Already by the end of 1988 20 per cent of ANC insurgents captured on South African soil were found to have contracted the disease and it has made inroads into the upper echelons of the organisation.

Countries that depend on the military for their government or their stability are now finding that a high proportion of their officers are infected. Consequently, the use of foreign troops in southern Africa will be more difficult in the 1990s. The Cuban garrison in the oil-rich Cabinda enclave of Angola, in the Aids belt, is believed to have suffered many casualties. But Aids is by no means the only element in the future of southern Africa that it was impossible to foresee. A wide variety of external forces, including elections in the West or possible shortages of resources or another energy crisis could also cause great changes in southern Africa in the 1990s. The heavy economic reliance of South Africa on gold protects it against potential damage if commodity prices fall. Any further economic set-backs in the West would certainly spread to southern Africa if they were prolonged.

Neither brutal repression nor revolutionary change in South Africa is inevitable or even probable in the long term. Neither is desirable in the West.

While the South African security forces still remain invincible (and backed up in the last resort by nuclear weapons and nerve toxins), Angola and Namibia have certainly been lessons on the limitations of military power even when skilfully used. Between the two poles of revolution and repression there is a whole range of futures. South Africa, which has shown itself adaptable and resilient in the past, will no doubt continue so throughout the 1990s.

The potential is there for South Africa to use those qualities, embodied in the evolving national strategy, to aim at a long-term future for all southern Africa.

# THE SOUTH AFRICAN-ALGERIAN CONNECTION
## Why Algeria?
*by Al J. Venter*

Some people in South Africa and elsewhere tend to equate conditions in revolutionary Algeria before independence, when France was still in control in North Africa, with the situation as it is developing in South Africa.

Both states have undergone social and political unrest. There is some similarity in the nature of the struggle: violence, radical politics, nationalist sentiment; on the one hand the majority of Arabs, on the other increasing numbers of more and more politically-orientated blacks; and of course, the eternal African gulf between the haves and the have-nots.

Some say that there are fundamental similarities between the uprisings that have taken place in both countries, and the consequent response by government; brutal and repressive, leaving hundreds of thousands of Arabs dead in Algeria and hundreds of blacks in southern Africa.

History records how the security forces in both countries reacted. In the case of South Africa they are likely to continue to act as they are doing for the foreseeable future. But it would be as misleading to compare the battle of Algiers of the Fifties with the present revolt of the townships as it would be to draw a parallel between Northern Ireland and Vietnam.

Bloodshed, violence, revolution, liberal protest, the abhorrence of brutality and increasing bitterness are all there. But the most important element is the degree of commitment. That rests solely with the level of dedication to the cause by the factions. As we have seen in Iran, Lebanon, Iraq and Algeria, and even in the *Intifada* uprising in Israel, the Arabs show a superabundance of commitment, and they believe that their cause has the blessing of God. Theirs is a glorious death, into the embrace of Allah, they believe.

At the opposite ends of a vast continent with little physical, social, political or cultural resemblance to one another, Algeria and South Africa are as dissimilar as, say, Nicaragua and Greece. Algeria belongs distinctly to the Third World, with socialism as the base of all its political and social ideals. South Africa, by contrast, aspires to capitalist First World status. In some respects it has attained that status.

Yet it is fashionable to compare the two countries for several reasons. Many writers, journalists, politicians, academics and others equate the seven-year French colonial war in Algeria with what is now happening in South Africa. A throng of "guerrilla war specialists", most of whom have never seen or heard action have passed loud judgment. Moreover, they command a large following, not least among the revolutionaries themselves.

As the late Captain Sir Basil Liddell Hart observed, the problems of guerrilla warfare are of very long standing. Yet he wrote, "they are manifestly far from understood". And regional conflicts were far simpler in his day than they are now.

The comparison between Algeria then with South Africa now runs something like this:

If France, a larger, a vastly more preponderant and experienced military power was not able to contain the revolutionary conflagration of what began as a mere handful of Arab and Berber dissidents revolting with only very limited Russian backing, how on Earth can the small white South African population of barely five million ever hold up the march of the same revolutionary process among their thirty million blacks? Given its due, the argument has merit.

But the conditions are vastly different. In fact, all that the Algerian war and the disturbances in the townships of South Africa in recent years have in common is conflict of staggering divisiveness.

There are other anomalies. While General de Gaulle early recognised that it would be impossible for France to keep Algeria French for ever against the vociferous wishes of the great majority of its inhabitants, the South African leadership and most of the people who elected them firmly hold on to their own identity. Many regard their survival as a divine right, and it is they, not the Africans, who resemble the Arabs in piously invoking the help of God in their refusal to share their powers and privileges.

Again, the South Africa of the Eighties is not as Algeria was thirty years ago, or even the South Africa of the time of the Soweto riots a few years ago; for even the government, with all its faults, its reluctance to reform overnight, its intransigence, has come to accept that change is necessary for survival. There is no choice.

As cautious and dilatory as this change appears to critics abroad, some real change has in fact taken place, and more may be expected. Otherwise, the country would already have undergone a real revolution. But change, such as it is, is gradual; too slow for some, and suicidal in the eyes of others – nevertheless change is the only possible solution.

While de Gaulle insisted that there was no solution to the problems of Algeria other than total independence, one only needs to spend a little time north of the Limpopo to accept that in reality, *Uhuru* or simple majority rule in southern Africa would ultimately mean the destruction of most civilised standards as they are understood by most moderate people in the West. Look at the record.

There is in all Africa only one stable multi–party democracy on the continent: Botswana. It is not altogether surprising that it is also Botswana that has borne the brunt of some of the most intense South African military actions across the border.

For the rest, nearly all fifty African countries were created as multi–partied democracies about thirty years ago, generously backed and blessed by European powers. See what that has led to. In that time there have been nearly a hundred changes of government in Africa, many of them violent. At any one time there are half a dozen regional or international conflicts. Lagos, Kinshasa (Léopoldville as it was then), Kampala, Bamako, Lusaka, Dar es Salaam, Khartoum, Addis Ababa, Mogadishu, Bangui, Freetown, Banjul, Niamey, Brazzaville – these do not exhaust the examples – bear little resemblance to the towns that they were when they were still administered from Europe. Lagos is a cesspit, detested by diplomatic personnel of both West and East who have the misfortune to be posted there. Freetown is a slum. Many of the whites have gone. Most had to.

The two outstanding exceptions are Abidjan and Nairobi; but then they both still have a fair number of whites in industry or government or other positions of authority, and they depend on European influences, whether trade or tourism, for their obvious prosperity.

I have not so far mentioned either Luanda or Maputo, the old Lourenço Marques.

Few South Africans do *not* know what happened there when the Portuguese unceremoniously withdrew. The results are there for all the world to see. It is a pity that the *colons* in Algeria had no such benefit of hindsight.

But we must accept that whatever other views or prejudices the bell–wethers of South Africa may have, they certainly do not wish to see their country racked by the revolutionary warfare that destroyed Angola and Mozambique, their nearest and most frightening examples of what happens when black independence runs wild. Nor do they wish to see imposed on their people the harebrained socialism that has brought about economic ruin that can now be seen all too plainly in Tanzania, Zambia, Nigeria, Ghana, Madagascar, Mali and Algeria; all, incidentally, very vocal about the need for immediate black rule in South Africa.

At the same time there is a constant high level of urban and regional conflict in southern Africa that cannot be ignored.

The South Africans, like the French in Algeria, believe that it can be stopped or contained. There will be some bloodshed. Limpet mines and car bombs will never be a tolerable alternative, but history has shown that people quickly learn to live with such dangers and get on with their lives. Others emigrate. Violence serves only to harden attitudes and the determination of both whites and blacks.

How different from Algeria, but then it must be seen from the point of view of the settlers. It was, after all, a colony of France, whatever else the Elysée Palace incumbent chose to call it. South Africa, by contrast, is tied to no apron-strings, European or otherwise.

Walter Laqueur, the internationally acclaimed military historian and strategist, once observed that the situation in Algeria might have been different if France had still been the "mastodon" that it had formerly been. By the time de Gaulle began to prepare for the independence of Algeria, France had already killed 200 000 Arabs, and the French were certainly capable of continuing the war. "But where would it lead?" asked Laqueur.

"The army, seeing no further than the next *djebel,* did not want to be deprived of its victory. It had only one remedy; to break the bone of the *fellaghas.* But this would merely lead to a new war in five or ten years, and by that time the Arabs would be even weightier in numbers."

More important still, and fundamental to any comparison between conditions in Algeria then and South Africa now, Algeria was actually part of metropolitan France. The distance between Algiers and Marseilles was not much greater than from Johannesburg to Durban. We know now that when the crunch eventually came, most of the million–odd Frenchmen in Algeria simply cut their ties and went back to France. The Algerian economy nearly collapsed as a result, and ever since Algerians have been queuing in tens of thousands to leave the country for which they fought so bitterly. Thirty years later the right wing French extremist Le Pen highlighted the presence of so many Algerians in France during the French general elections in 1988. His answer was to kick all the Algerians in France back to North Africa.

The South Africans, by contrast, have no such escape route. The forefathers of many South Africans, including my own, arrived in the country more than three centuries ago. If they lost their country they would have nowhere else to go. *South Africa is their motherland.* Their destiny is in their hands. And that, essentially, is why the comparison fails; the conclusion is derived from false premises.

Whatever the outcome of the present conflict in southern Africa may be – and it has so far been pretty mild, considering that France lost about 2 000 soldiers a year in Algeria during the seven-year struggle there and South Africa has lost fewer than 1 000 lives in over twenty years in South West Africa – the South Africans will in the end be the masters of their own fate. Of that, few people south of the Limpopo, black or white, are in any doubt.

Conflict in South West Africa and occasionally in Angola has demonstrated one of the most obvious differences between the two countries, then and now.

During the past ten years there has grown much more military association between white and black soldiers, not less. This trend is increasing, to the point where, despite intimidation in the townships, most of the fighting in northern South West Africa towards the end of 1988 is done by black troops under white officers. The reverse was true in Algeria, where local Arab recruits played only a subordinate part in the conflict, and often defected *en masse* to the enemy. Once independence had been achieved, Algeria entered its second, internecine stage of violence when these "collaborators" were slaughtered in their thousands in spite of assurances to the contrary at the final Evian agreement which brought peace to North Africa.

The Algerian war was complicated still further by religious differences.

To most of the Muslim rebels – who were regarded as little short of fanatics by the French – they were waging a *jihad* against an infidel power and thus had the blessing of Allah for their cause. Unlike the southern African situation which, with lapses, has been tempered by trying to win hearts and minds on both sides of the fence (the ANC claims it is geared to garnering support from the more affluent, liberal white community), Algeria's conflict often deteriorated into vindictive retribution that spawned bloodshed of horrific proportions. At times senseless torture was the norm rather than the exception; the FLN took few prisoners; those that they caught were brutally murdered. The French were equally uncompromising. And if anyone believes the same of South Africa, I challenge him to put the proposition to a group of troopies on home leave that they have brutally tortured anyone while on military operations on the border and see what reaction this evokes. No serving officer would dare issue such a command; it would be in the newspapers within weeks.

In the broader view of things, South Africa also has one additional factor which did not feature in Algeria; the Bantustans.

Flawed, ultimately doomed to failure because of mismanagement and corruption and very much a stop-gap measure conceived by National Party politicians with one eye on the back door and the other on survival, the Bantustan programme has provided the country with something of a safety valve. Whatever else might be its faults, the programme did give blacks the opportunity to do their own thing; though very much within the ambit of Pretoria's all-embracing influence.

And what it has achieved, is a form of secondary government (and don't underestimate the security connotations, for they are far more brutal and all-embracing in places like the Ciskei, Transkei or Bophuthatswana than they are outside the national states – you only have to hear stories from people who were incarcerated there) which takes some of the load off the central authority. That much Algeria never had.

On a more basic level there are minor differences like sport; minor in the overall shape of things to come but major in the minds of the man in the street. The French in Algeria rarely included the Arab community in national sporting activities, such as they were. A token Arab player would make the local (white) Algerian team and though I speak under correction, Arab football teams were

**Above:** South African soldiers prepare for the demolition of a Russian PT-76 amphibious tank while a SAAF helicopter hovers over the Kunene. This photograph was taken during *Operation Protea* near Xongongo

**Right:** Swapo prisoners brought in by a patrol along the cutline. These men are usually interrogated before being interned.

**Above:** Lagos, Nigeria, is one of the most densely populated towns in Africa. For most of us who lived there, it was both fascinating and frightening.

**Right:** Gate of the Emir's palace in Ilorin in northern Nigeria.

**Below:** An old Hausa man selling wooden hoes in the Kano market.

**Above:** The Clock Square in Dar es Salaam near Liberation Row, where most of the insurgent movements were based in the Sixties.

**Left:** In the francophone African territories many of the colonial administrators and explorers are still commemorated. In the Portuguese-speaking countries such monuments have mostly been destroyed.

**Below:** The Republic of Guinea, which was used as a platform against Portuguese Guinea, has numerous monuments countering imperialism and "martyrs of colonialism".

LA REPUBLIQUE DE GUINEE A TOUS LES MARTYRS DU COLONIALISME

**Above:** Black Star Square, Accra, built in 1957, was the focal point of many insurgent movements which were then proliferating in Africa.

**Below:** The National Assembly in Dahomey, now the People's Republic of Benin, was established on the departure of the French authorities. A few years later, the army took over, and the building has been boarded up ever since.

**Above:** There are many other problems that beset Africa, including poachers. Kenya, once in the vanguard of conservation in Africa, now faces the prospect of losing much of its game, including most of its elephants, by the end of the century.

**Below:** Britain left Kenya with a sound constitution and effective government. This was confirmed by President Jomo Kenyatta, seen here opening Parliament in Nairobi. Since then, one-party rule has become the norm in Kenya and most other African countries.

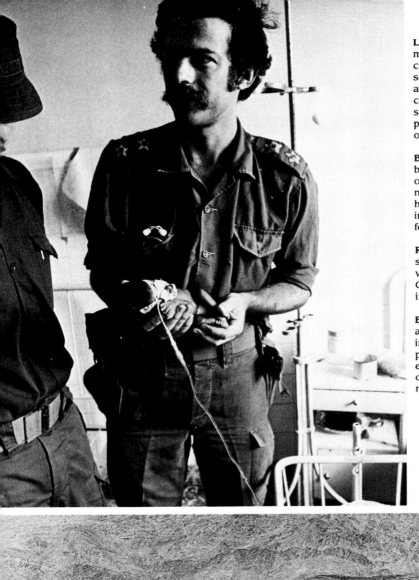

**Left:** A South African medical officer at the civil hospital at Ongiva in southern Angola. All attention was concentrated on trying to save the life of a premature infant born to one of the local women.

**Below:** A forward SAAF base in the arid wastes of south-west Angola near Kaokoveld. In this harsh terrain several important battles were fought against Swapo.

**Right:** Helicopter-borne strike force making its way over the treetops of Ovamboland to a strike in south Angola.

**Below right:** Impala aircraft of the SAAF flying in formation. These planes have provided effective back-up in the operational area when necessary.

**Above:** Civilians in South West Africa represent a wide range of humanity. They include educated Ovambo and Herero businessmen, while these Himba tribesmen are nearer to the Stone Age.

**Left:** South African forces at an operations centre in the Angolan bush in a cross-border strike.

**Right:** A South African soldier in Angola.

**Left:** Progress has come to parts of Africa, but many old traditions remain.

**Above:** Life in the interior of Algeria is much as it has been for a thousand years. With the coming of the French, the ancient traditions were only briefly interrupted.

**Right:** By the time the French army became embroiled in Algeria, it had been at war since the late Thirties: first in Europe and then Indo-China. French units are still active in Chad.

**Below:** Much of the land put aside for use by the Arab peasants was hardly cultivable.

**Above:** Rhodesian soldiers lift a mine from a road north of Salisbury.

**Below:** The magnificent Birchenough Bridge in south-eastern Rhodesia became a focal point for insurgent bands, but it was never damaged.

**Above:** French *paras* kick in the door of a house near Kolwezi during the attack by the Foreign Legion in southern Zaïre in 1978.

**Right:** Members of the élite French paratroopers waiting to go into action in Chad during the war with Libya. France gave effective help to Chad after Colonel Gaddafi had invaded it. France is likely to have a powerful influence in Africa for the foreseeable future.

**Above:** The French army tradition in Chad is still very much as it was in Algeria twenty years ago.

**Left:** France has a long and fine tradition of military service in Africa. The French still maintain over a thousand military personnel in the Central African Republic as part of its Early Reaction Force.

**Below left:** French troops mix easily with the local people in the streets of Ndjamèna (formerly Fort Lamy).

**Below and below right:** Life in the desert was difficult. For the French army in pursuit of the FLN it was even worse.

**Above:** Children were often deployed by the FLN for military purposes during the war. Now they are used by the Polisario Front in the Western Sahara. The same ploy has been attempted in South Africa.

**Right:** Many of the old towns of the Maghreb still look as they did in the late Forties. Little has changed since then, although tourists are now more evident than soldiers.

**Above:** A captured Russian armoured personnel carrier being brought back to South African lines after a long-range attack in Angola.

**Right:** General Jannie Geldenhuys was Military Attaché in Luanda during the early stages of the Angolan war. He gained a good understanding of developing conflicts in the region. Many of the principles observed then have been applied in the South African campaigns in South West Africa and neighbouring territories.

**Below:** Handouts such as these were often dropped by South African forces in pursuit of Swapo insurgents across the border.

MPLA e FAPLAS

AS FORÇAS ARMADAS SUL AFRICANAS
NAO LUTAM CONTRA VOCES.
A SWAPO E UMA DOENÇA E POR CAUSA DELA
VOCES PODEM SER ATINGIDOS.
SE QUISEREM SOBREVIVER DEIXEM DE AJUDAR
E PROTEGER A SWAPO.

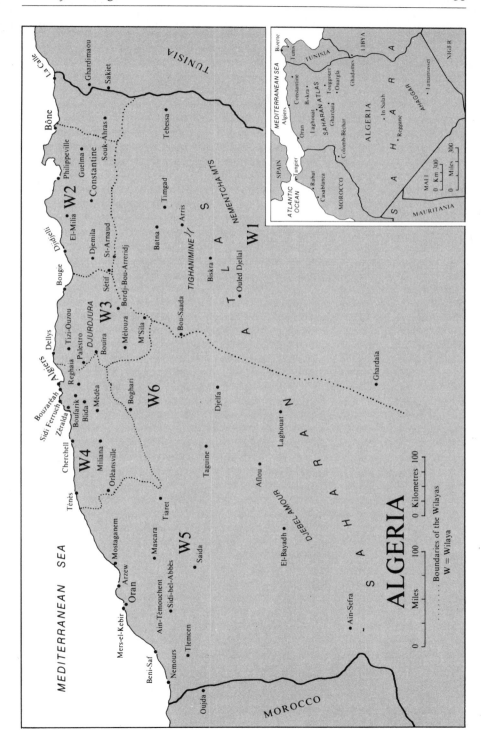

Boundaries of the Wilayas
W = Wilaya

ALGERIA

rarely pitted on a national basis against French teams. Arabs were generally regarded as physically inferior to the average French macho.

How different in South Africa, where sport has been used, effectively, as a lever to break down racial barriers.

Full integration has yet to take place; but if one considers the football, cycling, boxing, athletic and other competitions on SABC television any Saturday afternoon of the week, one might be forgiven for thinking that sport in South Africa is almost as multiracial as it is in, say, Zimbabwe. Not quite, but not far from it, and increasingly so.

The lack of social contact between the *pieds noirs* and the Arabs in North Africa was almost total. It manifested itself constantly. One of the most obvious examples was the absence of intermarriage between Europeans and Algerians. Such unions took place at the rate of less than a hundred a year. Sexual encounters between Europeans and Algerians were limited to the furtive meetings of homosexuals and the commercial transactions of prostitutes. How different in southern Africa, with its diverse mixture of people of mixed blood already totalling almost three million, or ten per cent of the population.

To understand properly what happened in Algeria a generation ago it is necessary to look back in history at the development of the country early last century. Dr L. Hahn is Executive Director, Association of Third World Affairs, Washington D.C. His view is instructive.

Dr Hahn points out that the French entered Algeria in 1830 with a punitive military expedition against the Dey of Algiers, the recognised ruler of a state which for years had maintained diplomatic and commercial relations with several European countries. After the surrender of the Dey, they waged a relentless pacification campaign lasting 17 years against the indigenous Arabs and Berbers, who were fighting to retain the land that they had inhabited for centuries and their Islamic way of life. The conquered territories were subsequently divided into three French *départements*, which juridically constituted an integral part of France.

No other colonial power ever interfered, and Algeria remained French until it became independent.

As Dr Hahn says, the original Dutch settlers at the Cape also arrived at the behest of their mother country, but not as conquerors. They did not defeat or unseat an established ruler, they did not proceed to establish their rule over long-settled natives who, however diverse, shared strong religious and cultural bonds, and they and the natives never became part of The Netherlands.

If we compare the "Europeans" of South Africa with those of Algeria, we find that it is the historical role of the English that somewhat resembles that of the French. But for the Afrikaners, striking out alone and becoming themselves the victims of British colonialism and conquest, there is no parallel in Algeria, says Dr Hahn.

French settlers in Algeria, who began to arrive during the pacification, were soon joined by others from Spain and Italy, who subsequently received French citizenship. This melting process was roughly similar to what occurred among Dutch, German and French settlers in South Africa.

However, despite disagreement with Paris over how much autonomy they should have, the *colons* in Algeria never seriously desired to be anything other than citizens of France. The Afrikaners, by contrast, forged a new nationalism with a new language in a country that they alone occupied or conquered and built into jealously independent republics. They never asked for or got any help from outside, military or otherwise, and they now have no one else to turn to.

Again, the role of some English South Africans may in a way be compared to that of the Algerian *colons,* except that their position as a minority within a dual ruling minority is unique.

As in the case of South Africa, Algeria was bedevilled by the question of what to do with the natives who greatly outnumbered the settlers. Paris, believing in the French *mission civilisatrice,* initiated several efforts and took limited steps over the years to assimilate its Algerian Moslem subjects as full French citizens. First the handful who were willing to abandon their personal status under Islamic law, then special categories of educated Moslems; and finally, in 1947, all Algerian Moslems nominally became full Frenchmen. Early metropolitan French policies, in other words, resembled British policies that entailed a qualified franchise for Africans.

The *colons,* however, always stubbornly resisted all attempts to grant the Arabs anything like complete equality.

Not merely did they wish to monopolise their special privileges; they considered the Moslems inferior; not because of their colour (which was little different from their own) but because of their vulgar contempt for Arab culture and religion. It was a contempt not shared by superior French such as Lyautey, who loved and protected the Moslem way of life.

After the creation of the *Conseil Supérieur* of Algeria in 1894, however, the *colons* accepted direct minority representation of Moslems in Algerian government bodies, something that few whites in South Africa ever knew before the institution of the tricameral parliament.

In 1947, Paris gave them a bicameral Algerian Assembly, to which they elected sixty delegates and to which the Moslem population, over eight times larger, elected another sixty. The dissatisfaction of the *colons* with the "equal" arrangement led to rigged elections and other devices to suppress Arab aspirations; while Moslem dissatisfaction with the obvious inequality led ultimately to revolution.

Most politically-minded Algerian Arabs, who became active after the first world war, at first aspired only to full assimilation as Frenchmen. As a result of repeated rejections, however, they became increasingly attracted to the idea that since they could not become real Frenchmen, they must instead regain their Algerian-Moslem heritage in a separate Algeria.

After the disappointments of 1947, the *Mouvement pour le Triomphe des Libertés Démocratiques (MTLD)* advocated a sovereign Algeria with an Algerian Constituent Assembly elected by universal suffrage without distinction of any kind. A more moderate proposal, advocated by the *Union Démocratique du Manifeste Algérien (UDMA)* called for an autonomous Algeria federated with France and dual citizenship for Frenchmen and Algerians in both France and Algeria.

When Paris made it brutally clear that it would never consider letting Algeria be anything other than part of France, young militants in the MTLD, who subsequently formed the *Front de Libération Nationale (FLN)* began planning guerrilla actions in Algeria.

The FLN theoretically welcomed non-Moslems who shared its aspirations, much as the ANC welcomes non-blacks, although it focussed on the Arab-Moslem heritage of Algeria and its solidarity with others in the Arab world, like the early *Pan Africanist Congress (PAC).*

The FLN turned to violence because there was absolutely no hope of attaining its goal of independence through peaceful negotiations. Likewise, in 1960 the

ANC turned to violence because it appeared impossible to negotiate the end of apartheid through peaceful means. However, whereas the FLN won immediate success, the ANC was crushed inside South Africa, so that the task of flying its flag and furthering the revolution became the responsibility of its external bodies.

Throughout the period of French occupation of North Africa, Arab opposition to rule from Paris was never far from the surface. Many of P.C. Wren's stories about the French Foreign Legion, which kept generations of schoolboys in the English-speaking world enthralled – myself included – were based on actual exploits by the Legion in the Algerian Sahara. Uprisings were brief and bloody; and they were equally brutally suppressed.

By the end of the second world war, the position of France in North Africa had been weakened, and the serious insurrection now known as the Sétif bloodbath broke out in 1945. Nationalist forces alleged that 20 000 Arabs were killed by the French. Official reports give the number of about 1 500 rebels shot by security forces; Walter Laqueur believes that the real figure is probably between 5 000 and 8 000. That was a dangerous conflagration, and it would undoubtedly have drawn the attention of the United Nations if it had been in existence at that time.

Simone de Beauvoir recalls that the French public heard very little about what happened at Sétif. The communist publication *L'Humanité* acknowledged only a hundred or so casualties, while de Gaulle in his memoirs dismisses the whole bloody episode in one terse sentence: "Beginning of insurrection, occurring in the Constaninois and synchronised with the Syrian riots in the month of May, was snuffed out by Governor–General Chataigneau."

Any form of military action must clearly have been sanctioned by de Gaulle's government. It must have been equally aware of the bloodbath; after all, many thousands of people were killed. As one observer said:

"On both scores it is to be noted that the communist ministers shared responsibility without a murmur." But then the French have always taken a solipsistic view of events beyond their borders; they prohibited the sale of arms to Israel, but made a great profit by selling weapons to both sides during the war between Iran and Iraq. They stopped selling arms to South Africa, but still sold them to Angola, dominated as it was by the Russians and Cubans.

There was also the episode of the *Rainbow Warrior* in New Zealand, the less said about which, the better. French morality has always been somewhat selective. Pierre Lellouche, deputy director of the Institut Français des Relations in Paris, writing in *Newsweek*, 31 October 1988, said that while some French moralists were very outspoken about what was happening in Israel, "it took a full week before the French government and French intellectuals finally decided to take a stand on the Algerian carnage earlier that month; and even then criticism was very subdued."

The media, he said, were also cowardly. "The French press took great relish during the early months of the *Intifada* on the West Bank in printing the latest toll of Palestinian casualties, day after day. It failed to react as strongly when Algerians were killing other Algerians – most of them teenagers and children – by the hundred…"

Why? He says the answer lies in the fact that France "still suffers from a guilt complex over the loss of its former African colony and also because the French left is more prone to beat on right wing dictators than on its 'progressive' colleagues".

The truth is that the present Algerian FLN government, one-party and authoritarian, "having carefully eliminated every potential source of opposition has now turned its guns on its youth because it has been unable to provide food, decent shelter or jobs for them". But more of that later.

Going back to 1945, the events at Sétif made an indelible mark on the minds of the Arab people of Algeria. Although they were in fact responsible for the uprising, which left 103 French dead and many more injured, and women brutally raped, including one old lady of 84, they considered that the French "over-kill" was out of all proportion to the events that caused it.

The Algerian poet Kateb Yacine wrote: "It was at Sétif that my sense of humanity was affronted for the first time by the most atrocious sights. I was 16 years old. The shock that I felt at the pitiless butchery, which caused the death of thousands of Muslims, I have never forgotten. From that moment on my nationalism took definite form."

French writers have often described the unfavourable geophysical nature of North Africa. As John Talbot in *The War without a Name* (Faber and Faber, London, 1981) puts it:

"Until the close of the nineteenth century … a scarcity of settlers had given French rule a look of impermanence. In an age of imperial expansion this had been the cause of much worry and regret. Algeria was no El Dorado; in the early years of the French occupation, Algeria was not even an inviting land. Settlers risked being shot by Algerians, bullied by the army, swindled by land speculators, ruined by drought, killed off by disease. Such a prospect limited settlement to 'immigrants of crisis' – victims of hard times, political repression and war. Of those who made the trip against their will, such as the political exiles of the Second Empire, few stayed."

The settlers who did remain tried one crop after another – sugar, cotton, tobacco, tea, mulberries; and all failed. Wheat did quite well, but not well enough to enable growers to compete in the world markets. Fortunes were struck in Algeria only when misfortune hit France.

Even wine was not successful. When the vine disease Phylloxera destroyed the French vineyards in the 1870s, Algerian farmers found a niche for themselves by taking advantage of the disaster in Europe. They grew vines to the exclusion of other crops. When Planchon found a remedy for the disease by grafting French vines on to American rootstocks a decade later, the French industry recovered.

Shipping wine from Algeria to France was a case of coals to Newcastle; and the north African viticulture stagnated.

Even then, most towns were still the domain of the French *colons*, with the Arabs living largely in the countryside. By the early 1950s, about 80 per cent of the Arabs were rural.

Gradually, as the Arab population grew, they began to seep into Algiers, Constantine, Oran and Bône, all of which were essentially French towns. By the middle Fifties Arabs were in the majority though many of them squatted in a plethora of shantytowns that surrounded every commercial centre. As with Crossroads in Cape Town, these were filthy and unhealthy slums where the unemployed or unemployable lived, *bidonvilles* of cardboard and rusty iron, eyesores to the settlers and breeding grounds of revolution.

As Walter Laqueur puts it: "According to the conventional liberal wisdom of the day, the Algerian problem was basically one of poverty, and consequently the solution had to be primarily socio-economic in character."

It was not to be, for several reasons. Politically France was in turmoil. That and the French military defeat in Indo–China resulted in instability both at home and in the African colonies. Algeria was an agricultural country, and although oil had been discovered, production still amounted to only eight million tons in 1960. There was simply not enough money even to attempt to right the balance.

Moreover, nine-tenths of the Algerian economy was in the hands of French interests and 100 000 French settlers cultivated nearly two-and-a-half million hectares, most of it good arable land that they had cleared themselves. On the other hand six million Algerian Arabs tilled little more than four million hectares.

After nearly a century of imperial rule, no event had the signal effect on the mind of the average educated Algerian Arab as the second world war, especially the humiliating defeat of France by Nazi Germany in 1940.

The Islamic psyche has always been particularly sensitive to prestige; *baraka* is the special blessing of Allah on people who have acquired grace. France had suddenly run out of *baraka*. The almighty French were fallible, after all.

Much the same thing happened at the other end of the continent after the fall of the Portuguese African colonies in the mid–Seventies. Suddenly a European power had been overthrown by black nationalists. If it could happen in Angola and Mozambique, then surely the same could happen in Rhodesia and South Africa.

The Rhodesian war intensified greatly after that. The Soweto uprising took place in 1976; little more than two years after the coup d'état in Lisbon in 1974. These events were obviously linked, and they made their imprint on the minds of young people, black and white.

It is also significant that the Algerian war only got properly under way after the ignominious defeat of a French force by the Viet Minh at Dien Bien Phu, an apparently invulnerable strongpoint in the heart of North Vietnam, fortified almost like Verdun. It fell on the eve of the ninth anniversary of VE day, 7 May 1954, at a cost of 13 000 dead among the defenders.

A colonial resistance army had inflicted a terrible psychological defeat on a regular Western army. In the *souks* of Algiers and Oran nationalists took careful note of the event and swore that if the Vietnamese could do that in Asia, they could follow suit in North Africa. Naturally the average French *colon* rejected the idea. Many Frenchmen consoled themselves with the thought that even after the defeat in South East Asia, at least Algeria had remained calm. After all, there had been nine years of tranquillity there after the Sétif *évenements*.

The Algerian revolt began in 1954, and by 1957 the Arab controlling body, the *Front de Libération Nationale* (FLN), thought that victory was at hand. The war went on for five more years.

There is confusion in the minds of some historians who have written on the Algerian war about the early days of the war. Cairo was the main base of most North African revolutionaries, including those from Tunisia and Morocco, and it was from there that many of the early instructions went out to the small groups of nationalists in the principal Algerian towns. The move into the interior came only later.

Officially the coordinating body was known as the *Comité Révolutionnaire d'Unité et d'Action,* or CRUA. Before that there had been others such as the *Parti Progressiste Algérien,* and, after the second world war, the MTLD, led by Messali Hadj, from which CRUA had taken over. For a while the MTLD specialised in crimes such as the occasional bank robbery to raise funds for the movement and sporadic acts of terror; but nothing serious. The head of the *Organisation Spéciale* responsible for such tasks was a man whose name became familiar to many of us living in Europe during the early Sixties: Ahmed Ben Bella. He had served with distinction in the French army during World War 2.

The nine leaders of the CRUA were a diverse lot. Apart from Ben Bella there was Mohamed Boudiaf; Belkacem Krim, a former French Army corporal who had organised a Kabyle *maquis* of his own before 1954, a brigand chief operating in the mountainous region of the Kabylia; Larbi Ben M'hidi; Mohamed Khider, who was older than the rest, had been a member of the French *parlement;* and others, such as Mostefa Ben Boulaid and Robah Bétat. Some were affiliated to the MTLD; others were communists. Quite a few had military experience with the French army. Laqueur says that for all their fervent nationalism, most of the FLN leaders were culturally uprooted men: "Scarcely one of them had a command of literary Arabic."

Thus, with the outbreak of the rebellion, the CRUA was transformed into the FLN with the *Armée de Libération Nationale* (ALN) becoming its military wing in much the same way as *Umkhonto we Sizwe* is the military arm of the ANC.

Unlike similar revolutions in countries as diverse as Vietnam, China, Cuba or Angola, no single outstanding character with unassailable authority emerged from the ranks of the FLN or ALN. Some of the founder members were killed during the war; others, including Ben Bella and Khider, were captured by the French and held until the Evian agreements were concluded.

Since we are all aware that revolutions tend to take on the colour of their predecessors, it was not surprising that several of the leaders who survived the war were ousted by the new generation of Young Turks who inherited Algeria after independence. Ben Bella was overthrown by his army commander, Houari Boumedienne, in a coup d'état less than three years after independence.

Belkacem Krim, ironically, accused the new leaders of Algeria of ideological and economic excesses. He went into exile soon after Boumedienne came to power. In 1969 he declared passionately, after having founded his own expatriate opposition group, that "seven years of independence were worse than seven years of war". Krim was murdered in an hotel room in Frankfurt. His enemy Boumedienne almost certainly ordered his assassination.

Krim was strangled; the same fate that he had determined for his former associate Ramdane Abane, who was murdered in 1957.

The entire situation was well summed up by Alistair Horne in the preface to what is certainly the best book on recent events in Algeria: *A Savage War of Peace - Algeria 1954-1962* (Macmillan, London, 1977): "... the lesson of the sad, repeated failure of moderates, or a 'third force' to compete against opposing extremes is one of constant relevance to the contemporary scene; whether it be Northern Ireland, southern Africa or Latin America. As in 1793 or 1917, in modern revolutions it is the Montagne that triumphs over the Gironde."

Those few military writers who have attempted to chronicle this conflict, such as Alistair Horne, John Talbot, Ferhat Abbas *(Guerre et Révolution d'Algérie),* Charles Henri Favrod *(Le FLN et L'Algérie)* or Germaine Tillion, all declare that one of the difficulties faced by commentators on the war in Algeria was that so few records were kept by FLN commanders.

As Horne says, with the FLN constantly on the move "few men in the field had either the time or circumstances to keep coherent journals". Quite a few were illiterate. Many of the records that would normally have found their way into the archives of the new state were either destroyed or "removed" in the last desperate days of the OAS.

History may have repeated itself in Rhodesia but in a different manner. There, once the victory of Mugabe at the polls had become a *fait accompli,* every government department in Salisbury had several months before the black takeover to set about burning or shredding documents that might have implicated persons who had taken part in the war. Loads of documents stowed in the belly of South African Air Force C-130 transporters were taken from Salisbury to Pretoria. No doubt France did the same when the end was near in Algeria.

Consequently, while much has been recorded and published on the French war effort, most of what has come from FLN sources is either hearsay or has been embellished for later generations. Thus there are a dozen different versions of what happened on the first night of attack. Some reports contradict others. There is even a wide difference in the number of participants that first night; 300 or 400 according to some sources, several thousand according to others. Rhetoric proliferated abundantly.

**The War**
There was a certain logic in the choice by the FLN of November 1, 1954, for the launching of their "jihad" against the French in Algeria.

It was the eve of the Christian festival of All Saints' Day, and most of the devout *pieds noirs,* it was assumed by the FLN leaders, would be off their guard. At least the vigilance of the police would be relaxed. The settlers themselves assumed (just as the Israelis did just before the Yom Kippur War in 1973) the Muslims would surely respect the sanctity of a religious holiday.

They did not. The country had already been divided up by the FLN into six *Wilayas* or autonomous military zones, and there were attacks in each of them. Some were the work of a small group of armed men; in other areas, such as Biskra a group of rebels attacked the police station half an hour before the predetermined hour of 3am.

The attack on the barracks at Batna went off roughly as planned, but not before its occupants were aroused by alarm bells and flashing lights. Two of the guards, 21-year old *Chasseurs,* were mowed down because peace-time regimental orders required that their rifles should be unloaded and their ammunition sewn up in their pouches. They were the first military personnel to be killed in the war.

The first officer was killed by machine-gun fire as he emerged from his quarters in the small garrison at Khenchela. He was a Spahi, Lieutenant Gerard Darneau. Other attacks took place at the Ichmoul lead mine where the guerrillas intended to seize a quantity of explosives but failed; It was the same at the tiny *gendarmerie* post of T'kout and in the Tighanimine Gorge a few hours later. The local bus travelling between Kiskra and Arris was ambushed and a loyal *caid* or government functionary was shot. Two young French teachers were wounded in the attack.

There were five targets in Algiers: the radio station, a fuel depot, the telephone exchange, the gasworks and a warehouse belonging to a prominent French politician. All five attacks were frustrated, largely because the attackers were ill-trained and badly equipped. Similarly in Oran, none of the groups fulfilled their objectives. One of the attacks being launched prematurely, the authorities were on their guard, and by morning eight insurgents had been killed, six of them with weapons in their possession.

Elsewhere in Algeria the attacks took on a similar pattern, some of them successful, many others not, largely because of a lack of modern weapons. A few of the attackers were armed with knives. Ben Bella later said that the FLN began the rebellion with between 350 and 400 firearms, "and virtually nothing heavier than a machine-gun".

Most of the bombs exploded on All Saints' Day were primitive devices made locally by inexpert artisans. Only months later did military supplies begin to arrive in Algeria from Morocco and Tunisia. Alistair Horne says that not a weapon at that time or for several years to come was provided by the communist bloc; nor was more than a modest quantity of guns acquired elsewhere abroad with the slender funds of the FLN. Thus, from the very beginning the theft of French arms from depots or their recovery on the battlefield became a prime military objective. A French doctor reported later that most of the wounds he treated in the early days had been inflicted by hunting rifles and shotguns.

How different in South Africa towards the end of the Eighties, where there are estimated to be thousands of illegal firearms in the hands of black people. By the end of 1988 so much Russian equipment was entering the country that bomb attacks on "hard" and "soft" targets in the Transvaal and Natal were virtually an everyday event.

The French had been warned as early as six months before the attacks on All Saints' Day that an offensive by the CRUA was being prepared. The office of the Governor-General even received a warning from an informer that this was about to take place, but it was apparently filed away in some pigeon-hole and retrieved only after the attacks had taken place.

The French reacted, of course. The Commander-in-Chief in Algeria, General C. de Cherrière, had about 55 000 soldiers at his disposal, though few were ready for action, since most of the best French counter-insurgency forces were either still in French Indo-China or on the high seas on their way home. According to Jacques Chevallier who wrote *Nous les Algériens* (1958), Cherrière reckoned that he had fewer than 4 000 usable combat troops in the entire country when the revolt began. There was only one helicopter in Algeria at the time and eight second world war Junkers bombers. There were 60 000 Algerian troops in the French Army, many of them serving "at home ". These were branded collaborators and became a prime target of the insurgents throughout the war; their families sometimes suffering a worse fate than the men themselves.

Reinforcements soon arrived, however. By the end of that year the French Prime Minister, Mendes-France, had sent 20 000 more troops and twenty companies of riot police.

It took little more than three weeks for an extensive counter- insurgency operation with artillery and air support to get underway. Terrorist attacks on Europeans stopped as suddenly as they had begun.

Many suspects were rounded up, various Arab organisations were proscribed, offices were raided and documents confiscated. Large numbers of innocent people fell into the bag. Curiously, the Algerian revolt raised little public interest in Europe, comparable, say, to Israel's *Intifada* of late 1987 and 1988 or the black rebellion in South Africa which started in 1984/5.

Alistair Horne observes: "On the ground, the physical reaction or over-reaction - was predictable. It was predictable, not specifically because of the *pied noir* mentality, but because this is the way an administration caught with its pants down habitually reacts under such circumstances; whether it were the British in Palestine, Cyprus or Northern Ireland, the Portuguese in Mozambique or the French in Indo-China.

"First comes the mass indiscriminate round-up of suspects, most of them innocent but converted into ardent militants by the fact of their imprisonment; then the setting of faces against liberal reforms designed to tackle the root of the trouble; followed finally, when too late, by a new progressive policy of liberalisation."

Irony has a thousand faces. Is it not strange that Pretoria has reacted in exactly the same way, both in South Africa and in Namibia?

In spite of the accumulation of forces, the war began quite slowly. At first, the rebels were astonished at the fury of the French response, although much of this stemmed from the indignation of the *pieds noirs* over the fact that the Arabs should reject a colonial system that was so obviously of benefit to all. Few French settlers were aware of the hardships suffered by the *fellah* indigenous population; widespread unemployment, and often less than rudimentary education and medical facilities for most Arabs, or of the irreconcilable political differences between the French and the Arabs. To most French people in Algeria, it was fine to have Algerian Arabs working as menials on the farms or in the factories at wages none of them would consider on the mainland, or as domestic servants, but any notion of integration on any other basis was not to be considered.

Some settlers demanded the immediate execution of all captured members of the FLN. In the *Dépêche Quotidienne,* a local senator demanded that "the evil be pursued where it be found and the ringleaders rooted out ..." He also insisted that security measures should be increased and called on his metropolitan associates to create the political atmosphere to launch "the proper solution" to the rebellion.

Obviously, the response of Paris paid dividends. Between November 2, 1954, the day after the revolt began, and early February the following year, not a single *pied noir* was killed by insurgents. Terrorist attacks against the Algerian population continued unabated, however. It was the typical Third World pattern of coercion by violence to make it very clear to the Algerian people that to be associated in any way with French authority meant an unpleasant death. The population was being terrorised into supporting the revolution in much the same way as black dissidents in South Africa used the "necklace" to bring the populace in line with revolutionary activities.

Public opinion in France, meanwhile, was totally behind the settlers. Even the socialist François Mitterrand, then Minister of the Interior, was firmly behind them. "Algeria", he said, in a catchword that was to be repeated endlessly, "is France".

In January 1955, Mendes–France appointed a veteran of de Gaulle's Free French campaign and one of his most trusted lieutenants, Jacques Soustelle, Governor-General of Algeria. It was not a popular choice. Soustelle was regarded with great suspicion by the settlers, and ten years later he was probably the most outspoken and obstinate advocate of keeping Algeria French; he became such a diehard *Algérie française* man that when the war was over he would have been arrested if he had set foot in France again.

One of the principal reasons why Soustelle was regarded with suspicion in Algiers was that he immediately proposed that France should give political rights to the Algerian majority, but only on condition that it did not jeopardise or compromise the political rights of the French settlers. The "Soustelle Plan" provided for increased Algerian representation in local politics, including extending the vote to women, providing schooling in Arabic (a fundamental demand from the outset) and, ultimately, integrating Algerians and French settlers in a political entity composed of nearly fifty million metropolitan French.

In theory the system should have worked, because the changes were profound and far-reaching in principle. But Soustelle had apparently never heard that majorities never share power; which was an axiom as applicable to Algeria then as it had been to Sparta twenty-four centuries ago and to South Africa now. Thus, what was hoped to be a single entity stretching from Dunkirk on the North Sea to the borders of Equatorial Africa thousands of miles to the south was never to be.

The guerrilla war began hesitantly in 1955. Apart from sporadic acts of violence most of the country was peaceful. As John Talbot says in *The War without a Name - France in Algeria 1954-1962*: "For at least a year after All Saints' Day, three of the district chiefs (of the six *Wilayas* or command structures) had almost no followers or weapons at their command. Violence was confined almost entirely to the three *Wilayas* of eastern Algeria, from the outskirts of Algiers to the Tunisian frontier. The western *Wilayas* from Algiers to Morocco were for months nearly as peaceful as Paris on a Sunday morning. For most of the war the Sahara saw more oil prospectors than guerrillas."

By the end of 1955, as a result of concerted undercover work and the deployment of mainland forces and a strengthening of security throughout the country, most of the original members of the FLN had either been killed or gaoled.

But the war gathered momentum. Repression was first replaced by some measure of Soustelle's reform, but it was generally agreed that it made little impression on either the settlers or the Algerians. Although the FLN had few successes, its mere existence was enough to force Paris to deploy huge numbers of men. The French Air Force was expanded and prepared to start its programme of bombing and strafing selected targets. But that was to come later. And when it did, leaflets were usually dropped in advance to give the local people warning of the attack in time for them to seek shelter.

The air force dropped thousands of warnings on *fellah* settlements in the interior. One read as follows:

### APPEAL TO THE MUSLIM POPULATION
Agitators, among them foreigners, have provoked bloody trouble in our country and have installed themselves notably in your region. They are living off your own resources ...

*Soon a terrifying calamity, fire from the sky will crash down on the heads of the rebels.* After which *la paix Française* will reign once more.

With the arrival of the vaunted 25th Airborne Division, the first French paras led by the legendary Colonel Ducournau, who had recently returned from Indo-China, set up headquarters in Arris in the Nementcha mountains near the Tunisian border.

Following the same principles that he had applied in South East Asia, Ducournau decided immediately to apply Mao's maxim of "merging with the people like fish with the water" and pursuing the rebels in their own strongholds. It was not easy. The *paras* had some successes but many failures.

In retrospect, what disconcerted the FLN command was that after the first attacks, most *pieds noirs* resumed their way of life as if nothing had happened. There was no mass exodus back to France and in France itself the war was relegated to the inside pages of the press.

Precautions had to be taken, of course. After the first acts of terrorism in Philippeville and Bône in the east and the increase in military aid from Tunisia and, indirectly, Egypt to the FLN, no one travelled anywhere without an escort. Six months after the All Saints' Day attacks, actions averaged about 200 a month.

That included road ambushes, isolated attacks on farmers and their property, cutting down telephone poles, shooting members of the local militia on leave and occasional skirmishes with the army.

By a year later these figures had greatly increased. According to official reports they rose to 900 in October 1955, to 1 000 in December and to more than 2 500 in March 1956. Much of this activity was due to the opening of the second front. By the beginning of 1957, almost thirty months after the outbreak of hostilities, FLN guerrilla fighters were active in five of the six *Wilayas,* the forces in the west having linked up with their compatriots in the east on the high plateau between Saida and Tiaret. At that stage Soustelle estimated that there were between 15 000 and 20 000 members of the FLN, although these figures included sympathisers and "night-time guerrillas" who would carry on with their normal jobs during the day. The FLN command claimed double that number of loyalists; war always results in hyperbole. But even 4 000 guerrillas raised from a community of almost ten million could hardly be regarded as a nation in arms.

Gun-running increased enormously. As the FLN hierarchy made headway in Algeria, so its influence spread beyond the borders. More money was contributed by friendly Arab states and more weapons made available for the fighters. At the same time the revolutionaries, even during the most favourable times, never had enough modern weapons for every man. Settlers and soldiers were being beaten or knifed to death right to the end of the struggle.

Gradually the war turned from "hard" targets such as police barracks and patrols to "soft" civilian objectives and the socalled "Muslim friends of France". These might include *caids* or village constables or even lower functionaries such as postmasters and tax collectors.

A fundamentalist influence also acted strongly on the rebel forces. Muslims were forbidden to smoke or drink. Penalties were severe; first offenders had their noses or ears cut off; for a second offence FLN cadres would inflict what the army called "the Kabyle smile" - slitting of the throat.

The FLN also turned to economic sabotage; maiming and killing of cattle, rooting up of vines and poisoning of wine vats. Dogs were often found with their throats cut. In May four French civilians caught unarmed on their farms had their throats cut.

In August 1955, there were the massacres at Philippeville. A group of rebels convinced several hundred peasants that the hour of their deliverance was at hand. Armed with axes, knives, sickles and other implements, the mob set upon settlers and Algerians alike.

At the small pyritis extracting town of El Halia, Algerian miners slaughtered European overseers and their families. Some were hacked to death; others were disembowelled; still more had their throats cut while their arms were pinned behind their backs. It was a gruesome report that arrived on the desk of the French Governor-General in Algiers. Altogether about 150 people were killed, about half of them settlers.

The French army and the Foreign Legion arrived on the scene while the massacre was still going on. In reprisal they killed over 1 000 Algerians, including women and children, and took many more prisoners, some of whom later died in custody, although this was strenuously denied by the authorities. The worst fears of the French settlers were being realised.

In Paris, meanwhile, arguments developed between the two factions; the one opposed to greater violence and those who were all for using maximum force to put down the rebellion. The French government maintained that France was facing a revolt of French citizens. They were rebelling against their own government. It was stated that in Algeria the army was not fighting a war but conducting what was called "operations for the maintenance of order".

There were a few parallels with what was then happening in Malaya. The British, like the French, never referred to "communist terrorism" in South East Asia as a war, but rather as an "emergency". This fiction was adopted because to place the country on a war footing would have enormously increased Lloyds' insurance premiums and would have had many other undesirable results. The same motives operated in Algeria also. After all, it was argued, for Algerians to rebel against their own government was to put them *hors la loi*.

In April 1955, accordingly, the government, with parliamentary assent, declared a state of emergency in Algeria, which, although curtailing civil liberties, stopped short of actual war.

In South Africa thirty years later, when faced with the beginnings of a general uprising among the black population, the government of President P.W. Botha, drawing upon both the Algerian and Malayan experiences (and of course what had happened more recently in the Portuguese colonies and the former Rhodesia) acted selectively. Areas were declared to be in a state of emergency and strictures were applied or lifted as circumstances permitted. The country as a whole was never placed under *de facto* military rule (although the military were involved) or the extent of the revolution acknowledged either in private or public. Areas were dealt with piecemeal and, in retrospect, probably a good deal more effectively than any of the previous examples. At the same time, no one in South Africa as the 1980s draw to a close believes that insurrection in South Africa is over, or that it will be for some time yet to come.

But the *évenements* in Algeria resemble those in South Africa in one respect. Conscript soldiers were used to help to put down the insurrection. In France nearly 10 000 reservists were recalled to active service, and there were plans to delay the release of about 100 000 conscripts.

After the Philippeville massacres 60 000 reservists were recalled, and a week later another 120 000 conscripts due for discharge were told that they would be kept under arms. And so it went on, until by 1960 half a million French troops had been concentrated in a country several times the size of France, which was then passing through the most difficult period of its post-war history.

What made the situation in Algeria different from August 1914, when most men of military age gladly rallied to the colours was that fighting in Algeria, in the minds of most, was certainly not defending *la patrie*. The enemy was not battering at the gates of Paris. This was essentially a *colonial* war; an expression which gained ready currency then, and a few years later when small brush fire wars began to break out in various parts of Africa: Kenya, Angola, the Congo, Portuguese Guinea and elsewhere.

The reservists vented their resentment on the government; some by refusing to obey the conscription orders, others by public demonstrations of protest in Paris, Marseilles, Nantes, Calais, Lyons and elsewhere. In 1955 several hundred air force reservists called up, shouted anti-government slogans and pulled the emergency brake handles on their coaches to keep their trains from leaving the Gare de Lyon.

There was also disarray when huge numbers of call-ups arrived at their appointed barracks to find no catering arrangements for them; in the winter of 1955 the men were herded into bleak barrack-rooms without heating or adequate blankets or food. Conditions in Algeria itself were not much better.

The extent to which the war had grown is shown by statistics issued at the time by the French Ministry of Defence. During 1955 the number of French troops in Algeria increased from about 80 000 to nearly 200 000. A year later, in the autumn of 1956, a third of the entire French armed forces were on active service in Algeria.

This was no longer a limited, holding operation to suppress a few disaffected "rebel groups running wild on the fringe of the Sahara". The FLN had grown to its full strength.

Students of military history have found a number of similarities between the Algerian war and what is now happening in Israel.

While political conditions are different, it is the day–to–day association between Jew and Arab and between French settler and native Algerian that requires examination. In both situations the Arabs have been viewed with suspicion and hostility with few exceptions. In Tel Aviv and Jerusalem until recently as in Algiers and Oran then, there was no social contact of any significance between the two sides.

Arabs were all right to do the housework or to labour in factories, but after hours, as in South Africa still, each went his own way. A West Bank or Gaza Arab at a Jewish social gathering is a rare phenomenon. Having spent many months during the past ten years as a military correspondent in both Israel and in Lebanon during the invasion of that sad country after 1982, I found that the tension between the two sides was severe. In some cases hostility to Arab civilians was manifest on the part of Israeli soldiers. Hatred would not be too strong a word; some Jews whom I met were hardly sane on the subject.

David Grossman, an Israeli Jew, did make the effort to try to get to know his fellow countryman of a different creed. For him it was a distressing event. He records his experiences in a book *The Yellow Wind* (Cape: London, 1988). He writes:

"It requires an investment of energy on my part, since I have also trained myself to look at Arabs with that same blurred vision which makes it easier for me (only for me?) to deal with their chiding, accusing, threatening presence, and during this month of encounters with them I must do exactly the opposite, enter the vortex of my greatest fear and repulsion, direct my gaze at the invisible Arabs, face this forgotten reality."

Almost all Grossman's Arab interlocutors express a settled hatred for occupying forces, for Israel and for the Jews. Yet it is a fascinated hatred, with elements of attraction in it. One Arab said: "We need to learn from you and take from you what you can give us." And another: "Israel is, in a way, a positive challenge for the Arabs. It has momentum. It is the resuscitation of something that was almost dead."

It was the same in Algeria. After the war, that Arab state, though embracing Muslim tenets, still maintained strong French traditions; in the civil service, in government (even though it quickly became a one–party state) and in the Algerian Defence Force. They hated the French. They also admired aspects of French culture.

*The Yellow Wind* is pervaded by a sense of impending disaster. An old Arab, Abu Harb, tells the author:

"about the yellow wind that will soon come, maybe even in his lifetime: the wind will come from the gates of Hell (from the gates of Paradise comes only a pleasant, cool wind) – *rih asfar*, it is called by the local Arabs, a hot and terrible east wind which comes once in a few generations, sets the world afire, and people seek shelter from its heat in the caves and caverns, but even there it finds those it seeks, those who have performed cruel and unjust deeds, and there, in the cracks in the boulders, it exterminates them, one by one."

As contrast, Yehoshafat Harkabi is a former Head of Military Intelligence in Israel and is now Professor of International Relations at the Hebrew University: a typically Israeli rolechange. As a writer, Harkabi is perhaps best known for his analysis of the Palestinian National Covenant, an analysis which has become a kind of handbook for Israeli hawks, by reason of its demonstration that the document, which is the foundation Charter of the PLO, is incompatible with the existence of the State of Israel. Yet Harkabi now argues that Israel should ignore that Covenant and its implications and enter into negotiations with the PLO, leading to the establishment of a Palestinian State in the West Bank and Gaza.

Harkabi has reached this position because he has come to feel that continued occupation of the territories is incompatible with the survival of Israel. He writes as a committed Zionist and he believes that the "annexationists" are betraying the Zionism to which they profess extreme devotion: "it is indeed my intention that Israel remain a Jewish state, for this is the purpose of Zionism. Thus annexation of the territories is contrary to Zionism."

While some writers tend to over-generalise and while there are people in Israel actively working towards some form of *rapprochement* between Jew and Arab, these sentiments are not shared by the masses on either side of the divide. In fact, any tourist can gauge the measure of animosity by hiring an Arab guide in a short tour of the Old City (as my wife and I did in September 1988).

Exactly the same situation prevailed in Algeria. The French there made no secret of their disdain for anything Arabic, to the extent of excluding them not only from private and public places such as clubs, hotels, games and so on, but also from access to adequate education or business. Likewise, in Israel now as with Algeria of old, the number of Arab sportsmen willing or able to appear in the national colours could be counted on two hands.

In the Fifties, war followed the outbreak of revolt in Algeria, and thirty years later *Intifada* (uprising) broke out in Israel. The common denominator was or is Arab nationalism.

In both countries hasty soul-searching was followed by some concessions, including an attempt at political concessions. Again in both cases it was too little, too late. And while the scale of hostilities is not comparable, the fundamental irreconcilability of the adversaries in the two states is uncomfortably similar, although the average Israeli would protest that the comparison has no relevance whatever. But it has. As *Time* magazine said in April 1988:

"For 21 years, Israel's leaders have been telling the people that they were 'practically at peace'. Why rush to negotiate some traumatising political compromise? Now the Israeli government says the State cannot negotiate as long as there is trouble in the territories.

"Paradoxically, Israel's moral territory has contracted as its physical space has expanded. Israelis must consider the dangers of the authoritarian temptation. Israel cannot be a 'light unto the nations' if it must exhaust itself daily by beating Arabs into submission." The Israeli-Arab writer Attalah Mansour described the Israelis' predicament with an Oriental image: "Instead of stepping on the snake that threatened them, they swallowed it. Now they have to live with it, or die from it."

Albert Camus in his day, reviewing the Algerian conundrum, said something almost exactly the same ...

Harkabi again:

"Our choice, he says, "is not between good and bad. That is easy. Our choice is between bad and worse. Israel cannot defend itself if half its population is the enemy. The Arabs understand that if there is no settlement, then there will be hell, for them and for us."

That is the real danger, Harkabi believes: "If an individual claims that he can live only provided that he sits on the shoulders of another individual, and further that he has the right to drive his fingernails into the other's body (that is, in this instance by establishing settlements), people will begin to question whether it might be better if such an individual did not exist."

Paradoxically, one of the commonest sentiments voiced in Algeria at the time of the troubles was that most *pieds noirs* wished the Arabs did not exist; or that the army would make them, eventually, cease to exist. All nine million of them.

Various arguments were used, both for and against, by many French writers of the time.

Albert Camus, at the vanguard of the French left, insisted that Paris must acquiesce in the demands of the FLN. He wrote: "In this admirable country in which a spring without equal covers it with flowers and its light, men are suffering hunger and demanding justice." He made several visits to Algeria and was met with vehement hostility by most of the *pieds noirs* with whom he came into contact. On several occasions he was threatened with death.

Camus repeatedly cited the official Maspétiol Report of 1955, which revealed that nearly a million Algerian Arabs, or almost ten per cent of the population, were wholly or partly unemployed. Another two million were seriously under-employed. He made much of the fact that the agricultural worker in rural areas worked only two months a year at the most. Predictably, the French reacted by accusing Camus of selective criticism; asserting that the Arabs were naturally lazy and did not wish to work. Is it not strange that Israeli and South African officials have, more recently, accused the communications media of similar bias? But in Algeria the situation was far more serious.

Critics of Camus could not explain away the fact that the Arabs had fared badly during the recent famine, when he found in Kabuylai families where only two out of ten children had survived. He had seen children in Tizi-Ouzou fighting with dogs for the contents of a garbage can and though these examples are extreme, they were as relevant then to the causes of the war as they would be now.

Meanwhile, conflict intensified. The government of the time, under Guy Mollet, acknowledged that by the end of 1956 France had committed more than 400 000 men to North Africa. As George Armstrong Kelly stated in *Lost Soldiers: The French Army and Empire in Crisis, 1947-1962* (Cambridge, Mass. 1965), there were "perhaps as many as twenty soldiers for every FLN guerrilla in the bush".

Less than ten per cent of this force did fighting. The main task of the majority was to protect the persons and property of settlers and Algerians, to keep the main roads and rail links safe and open and to protect strategic installations from FLN sabotage. The task of the rest, perhaps between 30 000 and 40 000 men, was to hunt down the cadres of the FLN. The term "search and destroy", long familiar to those who have followed the wars in El Salvador, Vietnam, Rhodesia, Namibia and Angola originated with the French in Indo-China. It became typical of the classic guerrilla struggle in Algeria.

By early 1957, one out of every three Europeans in Algeria wore a French uniform. The next time that Africa was so heavily under arms was in the Rhodesian war, which lasted for seven years and ended in 1970. As in Algeria, Rhodesian insurgents in 1965 would certainly have been willing to settle for a good deal less than Robert Mugabe got at the end of the conflict. So, also, the FLN, no doubt, would have been willing to settle in 1956 for less than they were finally granted in 1962.

By early 1956 crucial problems of political and military policy and strategy sharply divided the Algerian Arab leadership both in the country and abroad, to the extent that internecine assassinations within the hierarchy had begun on a grand scale. Fortunately for the rebels, Paris was to know none of this until afterwards; which does not say much for the effectiveness of SDECE, the French secret service.

There are certain similarities between the bombing campaigns carried out by the FLN in the large towns such as Algiers in 1956 and early 1957 and the wave of bomb attacks that occurred in South Africa in 1987/8. The FLN command, aware of the publicity value of bomb attacks, argued that "one bomb in the centre of Algiers is far more newsworthy than countless skirmishes in the countryside with the army". They were correct, of course.

Bombs thirty years ago were a rarity, and they certainly made news. Explosive devices perfectly confirmed Lenin's dictum: "The purpose of terrorism is to terrify."

But that is where the analogy with South Africa ends. Bombs have become so commonplace in South Africa and in many European centres notably in Northern Ireland, that unless they are particularly horrible, they hardly rate as front-page news. Recent history has also shown that the bombing of unarmed civilians is counter-productive. Any support from enlightened "liberals" vanishes as quickly as the puff of smoke that it generates, especially if friends and family are struck.

When bombs began exploding at the rate of about one a day in September and October 1988, South African politics underwent a perceptible change. The main liberal opposition, the Progressive Federal Party (PFP) had taken a somewhat conciliatory line on security operations and the border war, which gave the National Party grounds to accuse them of being "soft on security". Such accusations had often been made in the past, but now they hurt. The only result was a rash of PFP posters all over Johannesburg declaring "Security Yes: Apartheid No".

There is no doubt that such sentiments are a direct result of the bombs; which is not surprising when women and children are being blown to pieces in a dozen different towns in the Transvaal and South West Africa. At public meetings, few subjects elicit as many questions from the public about how the PFP feels about bombs and what it proposes to do. The direct effect is that the carefully nurtured image of the banned and exiled African National Congress as a potentially enlightened and accommodating organisation in post-apartheid South Africa has been almost irremediably damaged.

For a while, in 1987, and early in 1988 there had been real and positive moves towards closer contacts with the ANC. Bombings have all but put an end to those except on the fringe of radical South African politics. How could it be otherwise when it is ANC bombs that were killing and maiming wives, children and friends?

In Algiers the bombs had indeed the required effect; and also a reaction that was not entirely expected.

**The Battle of Algiers**

The square mile of the Casbah in Algiers has often been the subject of films and books. It charmed tourists and filmgoers alike long before the war, and independence brought its quota of socialism and xenophobia. With its narrow, twisting streets, great walls and mysterious passageways, even now it is not unlike casbahs of Rabat, Casablanca and Meknes in Morocco or of Tunis. The enigmatic Casbah has always been a place of intrigue and secret drama; the setting of the romantic but fictitious *Pépé le Moko*.

It was not surprising, therefore, that the FLN should choose the Casbah in Algiers, with its 100 000 Arab inhabitants, as the place to carry the war from the *bled* to the towns. It was regarded by the FLN as an autonomous zone with three branches; intelligence, military and financial. For most of 1956 conflict had been limited to the countryside; the urban or third phase of guerrilla war had begun.

Who fired the first shot in the Casbah is a subject of regular debate. The FLN maintains that it was the French *paras;* and it may well have been, though even Alistair Horne says that it is an over-convenient assumption.

The Algiers network was run for the FLN by Saadi Yacef, the son of a Casbah baker who was said to have worked for the French as a double agent. Yacef was competent and dedicated. Within a year he had about 1 500 operators reporting to his various commanders, many of them westernised Arab boys and girls who had grown up and been educated with the sons and daughters of French *pieds noirs* and who might have passed as French.

Many of the girls, such as Zohra Drif and Samia Lakhdari, both law students in their early twenties, were attractive and often dressed stylishly in Western garb. Drif was a stunner; she turned many heads, French and Arab. She was also passionately opposed to French rule. She called Hitler's invasion of France in 1940 God's revenge on the Frenchmen for what they had done to the Muslim people of North Africa.

This devotee of André Malraux, with his pre-war ideal of a terrorist as the archetypal "solitary, heroic individual" had all the characteristics of a potential killer. She preferred to use bombs. She was a member of an élite squad of about fifty revolutionaries created specially for that purpose, nearly all of them young.

The FLN Algiers Autonomous Zone began making bombs early in 1956. The authorities were aware of it and did what they could to stop it, but with little success. They were fully occupied trying to trace groups of Yacef's assassination squads roaming the streets killing civilians. After the execution of two inveterate terrorists, one of them a cripple, on 19 June 1956, the order came from the FLN Central Command to "take the war to the people". Between 21 and 24 June Yacef's squads shot 49 civilians in the streets of Algiers.

Then, on August 10, an immense explosion ripped through the Casbah, killing about seventy Arabs. At first the authorities gave out that a bomb-making factory had blown up; later a *pied noir* counter-terrorist cell hinted at responsibility, but that also has never been thoroughly investigated. However, it had the effect of giving a new dimension to the war.

A month later Yacef called before him the women Drif and Lakhdari and a more recent member of the group, Djamila Bouhired. He gave them the task of placing three one-kilogram bombs in the heart of French Algiers; at a popular milk bar on the corner of Place Bugeaud; another at the cafeteria in the elegant Rue Michelet, much frequented by members of the smart set, and the third in the terminus of Air France near the centre of the town. Because of a faulty timer the third bomb failed to go off.

The carnage inflicted by the other two bombs was appalling; there were three deaths and about fifty injured, including children. Most of the victims were young people who had nothing to do with the war or its ultimate course. Naturally, the settlers reacted violently; and if one looks at South Africa now, when bombs are a routine event, then one must admit that the white-ruled state at the opposite end of this troubled continent has reacted very differently to similar provocations.

The Algerian bombs were not complex Russian SPM limpet mines such as are often found in South African townships. The metal casings were often roughly welded pipes or machine parts put together in tiny factories in the Casbah. Yacef's bomb-maker was a chemistry student, Taleb Abderrahmane, operating in a secret laboratory, but the products so simply fashioned were effective enough.

So the Algerian conflict spread and intensified from August to December 1956. According to Philippe Tripier, in his notable *Autoposie de la Guerre d'Algérie,* "bombings, shootings, stabbings, and destruction of property soared from about four incidents at the beginning of January 1956 to fifty in July, almost a hundred in September and to roughly four each day in December". Yacef's agents were active everywhere; in cloakrooms, municipal offices, buses, cinemas, restaurants, sports pavilions; and that apart from direct attacks on French government establishments.

The authorities in France became increasingly disconcerted by these events in their nearest colony. The press had become more vociferous, and some sections of society were shocked at the disclosure that some French nationals, though only a few at that stage, had gone over to the FLN. There were several intellectuals, mainly associated with Algiers University, including Professor André Mandouze, Professor of Literature, who gathered together a core of FLN sympathisers. There was also a prominent *pied noir* surgeon, Pierre Chaulet, who, with his wife, carried out numerous operations on wounded members of the FLN, often under very difficult conditions. Both were later discovered and had to flee to Tunisia. They returned only after Algerian independence to settle permanently in the country, although it is said that they soon fell foul of the new order.

Local settlers would have been even more disconcerted if they had known that one of the members of Saadi Yacef's bomb-laying teams was a French girl student at Algiers University, Danielle Mine. She was discovered much later, when it was too late to do anything about her.

In Algeria at that time it was clear to everyone that the country had become untenable. A new face and a new approach were needed to fight the worst urban terrorism that Europe had seen since the end of the second world war. But revolutions were breaking out all over the world. Castro had just landed in Cuba from the ship whose name was later to decorate the masthead of the national newspaper, *Granma.*

Amid some of the worst atrocities in Algiers, General Raoul Salan arrived. He was a man who was to be associated with the tragedy of Algeria until the very end, and afterwards, from exile in Brazil.

Salan was the most decorated French soldier. He had served in various campaigns and had been awarded the British CBE and the American DSO, as well as a long row of French medals. In 1954 it was the sombre visage of Salan that had presided over the defeat of the French in Indo-China.

The press in Algiers quickly christened him the Proconsul, although those who knew him better called him *le Mandarin.* He was probably the most competent French soldier yet to have entered the war. He was also ambitious, but he avoided official ceremonies. His job was to fight, and he made no secret of the fact that he preferred visiting units in the field to receptions.

He needed to know about the war he was fighting from the men doing the work. Salan had always worked that way; and even if his fellow officers were suspicious of his professed vagueness about political ideas and accused him of being a socialist, a freemason and an opium-smoker (all of which charges he rejected with disdain), he quickly stepped into the shoes of the departing Commander-in-Chief in Algeria, General Lorillot.

It was a formidable job. Within sight and sound of his office, people were being killed. In retaliation the *pieds noirs* were sometimes more brutal than the FLN. They asked no quarter and gave none. Algiers had become an almost lawless battleground. The country was now encumbered with a military apparatus of almost half a million men, and although the FLN was being rooted out of some of its lairs by the army, they were still getting results. This was terrorism in its purest form.

Some of the attacks were mindless. After the 74-year-old Amédée Froger, President of the Federation of Mayors of Algeria had been assassinated, the FLN placed a bomb in the cemetery that would have caused further damage if his cortège had arrived in time. The *colons* ran wild. Furious *pieds noirs* hauled innocent Arabs out of their cars or assaulted them in the streets. They left three dead and fifty injured.

Looking back on recent history, we can see that that was exactly the reaction that the FLN wished to provoke. They wanted mobs to go on the rampage; to loot, to kill and inflame passions to such a degree that Arab and French Algerians would never talk to one another again, far less administer the country together at some future time. They wished to make Algeria ungovernable; to force the French to concede that it was a lost cause. Of course they succeeded in the end; and that is why the Algerian revolt is always held up by radicals to prove what sheer brutality can achieve. They have been doing so also in the southern tip of Africa.

In South Africa, with the riots of the middle Eighties, exactly the same system was applied. Political suspects and informers were *necklaced.* Others were brought before tribunals where teenagers were often in charge and in the majority. Many innocent people were sentenced to death.

In three years, tens of thousands of vehicles were destroyed, thousands of classrooms burnt. Parts of South Africa came near to anarchy. Looking at the problem in retrospect, we see some parallels with what happened in Algeria; but the problem was never so severe, for most of the violence was by black upon black. Most white areas never heard a shot. Factionalism and tribalism has been part of the salvation of South Africa so far.

But not in Israel where Algeria is also held up as an example of what could happen if matters get out of hand. The Palestinian command structure in the Middle East, with strikes, shop-shutting edicts, stonings and killings (although on a far smaller scale than in Algeria, largely because of the efficiency of the Israeli security system) has tried to apply the same measures as those employed by the FLN thirty years ago. The only reason why a general military uprising in Israel has been avoided is that its borders are secure. The only people who carry weapons in Israel, apart from small units of the Druze, Circassian or Bedouin minorities, are Jews.

Israel is now probably the most difficult country in the world to smuggle anything into or out of. Checks at Ben Gurion Airport are extremely efficient; as they are on the luggage of anyone who gets on a plane, and at the few Israeli frontiers that can still be crossed by road, such as the Allenby Bridge into Jordan or the Good Fence at Metullah. Vehicles coming into the country at the Allenby Bridge are sometimes stripped. Every part of a car, engine, body, tyres, seats or fuel tanks, is inspected and sealed. It sometimes takes a truck two days to get through the checkpoint, and if a seal is found to be broken it can take another two days for the entire process to be repeated. It is surprising that any bombs go off in Israel at all. Not so in Algeria, with thousands of kilometres of insecure frontiers. The border with Morocco alone is over 1 000km long.

Obviously, Governor-General Lacoste had to do something. Algiers was as much a symbol to the country as Paris was to France or Pretoria to South Africa.

On 7 January 1957, Lacoste decided that a more rigorous approach was necessary. He summoned General Salan and the recently arrived commander of the élite 10th Para Division, General Jacques Massu. He told them that the 1 500 police in Algiers had proved themselves incapable of handling the situation and that after two years of limited hostilities, the situation had deteriorated almost to a level of anarchy. The strike force of 5 000 men would step in and stop the riot. The *paras* had the job of restoring order in a hilly seaside town, then roughly the size of Cape Town. It appeared an impossible prospect.

The FLN had called for an eight-day national strike. Massu reacted by forcibly opening Algerian shops, as the Israelis do in Arab strikes in the West Bank towns of Nablus and Afula now. The French army, though, achieved success, largely because after eight days many shopkeepers feared for their wares if their shops were left open and untended. A strike of one or two days might have achieved better results.

To keep a stable and permanent presence in the Casbah was totally different from patrolling the streets of the rest of Algiers. But with so many stories of FLN atrocities against the French and so many of their fellow countrymen who had fallen victim to terror, the *paras* went to work with a will. In North Africa indiscriminate assassination was followed by systematic torture and brutal and thorough techniques of interrogation. Neither was troubled by humanitarian scruples. They went to the very limits of means that security forces of a civilised country could use.

The *paras* employed a subtle system of control from the beginning. The Casbah had been divided into sectors by the FLN. It was likewise segmented by the army in its own fashion. Each area, each block, each tenement building came under the command of an officer or an NCO, and it was he who made direct contact with the inhabitants.

Once the system was devised and every French soldier was aware of his duty, the senior occupant of a block of flats was ordered to report to army headquarters. Usually this person had achieved a position of authority because of political associations. Some were outspokenly pro-FLN; others were more discreet.

Having been taken to HQ, this "man of confidence" was told that from then on he would be held responsible for any activity that might take place in the building or block. If any acts of terrorism were linked to it he would die; and one of his children, or his wife, would die first.

All the way up the line the system was put into effect. French undercover agents had a free hand in bringing in suspects. Proof of association with the FLN was not necessarily a *sine qua non;* anyone who was even vaguely suspected of anti-government activity in the past fell into the net. Many suspects died while being interrogated.

The measures were draconian. Ultimately they caused so much revulsion that the European (especially French) and American press and TV exposed the brutalities and injustices and helped to bring the war to an end. The iniquitous system was no less repressive and repulsive than that imposed by the occupying Germans twenty years earlier. Since memories die hard, the French establishment came under fire for sanctioning such atrocities. Yet it was no worse than what the FLN were doing, and it is to the discredit of the liberal press that they ignored the one and sensationalised the other. South Africans and Israelis are familiar with the same propensity.

But, as the Nazis had shown, violence is often effective. While the *paras* tended to contrast the disgusting business of fighting terror with terror in the towns with what some of them called "the purity of fighting in the *bled*", there was no doubt that the two tasks were incompatible. Some of the more horrible episodes were then and later written by men who had actually taken part in the military security programme. It also resulted in more French civilians, both in France and Algeria, going over sympathetically to the FLN. There were even some soldiers, men of conscience, who deserted to the other side, although they were only a small minority; and if their *bona fides* were not entirely satisfactory, they were put to death, often in cruel fashion, after being accused of spying. To be shot outright in the Algerian *bled* rather than tortured to death was more than could be hoped for.

The undoing of some of these idealists was what was called the "flic test".

A man was either wholly for the FLN or he was against. Everything was painted emphatically in black and white. There were no greys. Therefore, if a man who had no obvious reason to do so wished to be associated with the movement, he was required to display his hatred for the system by killing somebody who belonged to the governing machinery; usually policemen. Young idealists on the run from the French army were hardly likely to exchange one form of savagery for another, and most refused to do any more killing. They had seen enough. Consequently they were regarded as infiltrators, and few were admitted to the ranks of the FLN.

The FLN was of course aware that the French (like the South Africans) often made use of bogus deserters to infiltrate their organisations. It had been a regular practice in South East Asia, but it did not meet with much success in Algeria.

Meanwhile, in Algiers the *paras* were having some notable successes. They would act on the flimsiest evidence. A man found with money in his pocket would be accused of carrying or collecting funds for the FLN. Under *persuasion* he would eventually disclose to whom he paid the money. The next man would be tortured until he named names, and so on up the line. It was a simple but effective system, and it brought results. Torture was the army's answer to terrorism.

And the soldiers worked quickly. Any piece of information was acted upon immediately, sometimes even before a man's family knew he had been picked up. Surprise was vital to the success of the operation, and it achieved the kind of results that the police within the strictures of the laws of the Fourth Republic had never been capable of.

The army was also methodical. It was answerable to no one, and it devised its systems carefully; areas were cordoned off with barbed wire and regular searches were made. The fact that the Casbah was compact and difficult to control also worked against the FLN; it was a small tactical area that could be worked through, slowly and thoroughly. Gradually the insurgents lost their edge; and it was only a question of time before they lost the battle for Algiers.

By such methods the *paras* gained the mastery of the Algiers Autonomous Zone. They recovered weapons, deprived the FLN of its funds, arrested leaders, stopped recruitment of more insurgents and nearly stopped the bombings, shootings, and stabbings. By mid-April, less than four months after General Massu had faced the Governor-General in his office, he was able to remove every regiment but one from Algiers.

But it was not over yet. With the army out of the way, Saadi Yacef cranked the system up again and started a new wave of bombings and killings. But the new order was short-lived; the Tenth Division was brought back to Algiers, and by mid-September the two principal coordinators of the rebellion, Yacef and his lieutenant Ali la Pointe, were captured and killed. If the means justify the ends, then France had certainly achieved a remarkable success. By October acts of terrorism amounted to only one a month.

Foreign reporters in the country noted at the time a curious anomaly. On the one hand the *paras* were performing miracles in re-establishing the old order and were lauded as the saviours of Algiers. On the other, there was much friction, especially in rural areas, between the *colons* and the army. Soldiers who were doing most of the work guarding the livestock, buildings, possessions and persons of the farmers against terrorism were regarded by the settlers as no better than a necessary nuisance. They manifestly despised those conscripts who chose to work with Arab communities in a bid to alleviate problems.

There was little fraternisation except where it was necessary. Although there were exceptions, the civilians rarely went out of their way to make those responsible for their safety comfortable. They regarded the half-million metropolitan troops almost as an army of occupation.

The soldiers, for their part, regarded the *pieds noirs* as selfish ingrates. The troops were often accused of doing too little to stop the spread of revolt. Sometimes the soldiers intervened to stop French farmers killing suspected Arabs, and of course that provoked yet more animosity.

An appalling massacre of two dozen young French conscripts at a village 80km south-east of Algiers on 4 May 1956 brought the reality of the Algerian war home to Frenchmen. Until then the conflict had been relegated to the inside pages of most newspapers. After only two weeks in the country, a small patrol of young conscripts, most of them from Paris, were ambushed at point-blank range by one of the insurgent leaders known locally as Ali Khodja, a deserter from the army.

The youngsters were no match for the tough FLN regulars. Within minutes most of them were dead. A handful remained alive and while they were being beaten and bound, some of the bodies were barbarously mutilated. Some were disembowelled; others had their testicles cut off and stones stuffed into ventral cavities. Only one man survived the experience; he was later rescued by a *para* strike force in a fight in which the only other French soldier taken alive by the band was killed.

The event was big news, not only in France but also in the rest of Europe and the United States. In France, at last, Algeria had become headlines. This was the worst single loss of the war so far. Nearly all the boys who died were hardly out of their teens. The army, for once candid in its communiqué, admitted that they had been brutally massacred.

About the same time the first reports of torture by the French army in Algeria began to creep into news reports, usually as a result of some young conscript baring his soul while on home leave. No one would speak publicly about such atrocities, and reports were usually discreetly phrased for fear of prosecution. But as the hints and whispers became more widespread, the public began to take notice. It horrified some; it delighted others, who believed that the excesses of the FLN should be returned tenfold.

In clandestinely published tracts, reservists told what they had seen in Algeria of the use by the army of the sun, water, beatings, deprivation of food and water and even more horrifying examples such as electric wires attached to genitals, soda bottles forced into the vagina and anus of victims, nails pulled out with pliers and the local version of the rack; bodies contorted by ropes and weights and bones snapping under pressure. In many cases torture and resultant death were regarded as little more than cold-blooded acts of reprisal. If nothing more, the French army proved itself very efficient at extracting information under severe duress.

The government reacted, of course. Newspapers of liberal tendency were scrutinised. Any mention of torture was forbidden. *The Economist* of 27 July 1957 reported that in some cases "squeezing the press" meant that "for some editors police visits were as routine as visits from the postman".

But although there was solid evidence of the barbarism, including a book by a regular army officer whose early enthusiasm turned to revulsion, most French dailies, except for those like *L'Humanité*, the communist newspaper (which was seized 28 times during the course of the war), kept clear of such controversial subjects.

Those publications that were regarded as being guilty of *injuring the morale of the army* or had published articles that might be construed as a "provocation to disobedience" usually had their editions confiscated before they reached the streets. All publications would be required to provide the authorities with copies of the next day's edition, either the evening before or early on the day when it would appear. These were then circulated among the various ministries responsible for public conduct, defence or security, as well as the prefecture of police. Decisions to prohibit a particular edition were usually made at a fairly low level of command, with the result that rather innocuous pieces would often incur the wrath of the authorities and prevent an otherwise responsible piece of reporting from reaching the public.

But there was no means of preventing foreign papers from covering such reports. Suddenly the Algerian war had become good copy, although much was made of French excesses largely because correspondents were allowed to cover the war from Algiers and, because of FLN xenophobia, very rarely from the side of the rebels. They heard the French side - pro and contra; rarely that of the FLN, who were no less uncompromising and barbarous.

About that time there also began the first discreet, even furtive, attempts to negotiate an end to the conflict directly with the FLN. By March 1956, Guy Mollet had already sent his first "peace mission" to Cairo, led by the Foreign Minister, Christian Pineau, who made a direct approach to President Nasser to put out what was termed at the time "feelers for conversations" with the rebel movement. Much as South Africa has been having "talks about talks", which led to the 1988 series of meetings on Angola, so the French and representatives of the Egyptian government and the FLN dilly-dallied about trying to find common ground to bring about an end to it all.

A series of altogether five such meetings took place in 1956 in Cairo, Rome,

Belgrade and even the FLN headquarters in Tunis (shades of the South African meetings with the ANC?) Naturally, all were hidden under a cloak of secrecy, for it would never have been acceptable to the French public to discover at that early stage that while their boys were dying for "a just cause" in Algeria, their government was actually breaking bread with terrorists.

Alistair Horne in his book *A Savage War of Peace* maintains that Ben Bella considered, even so early, that "peace was within reach". Mollet, in an interview with Horne later, thought otherwise. He said: "Even if Ben Bella had not been sequestrated, I doubt whether things would have turned out very differently, because the FLN never accepted our basic theses that there should be, first of all, a ceasefire." As Horne concludes: "No one will ever know."

The war dragged on. In spite of losses, the French position in Algeria was far stronger than it had been a short while previously in South East Asia. Moreover, Algeria was not a distant colony but in theory an integral part of Metropolitan France. Algeria had no jungles or forests where the rebels could hide and the French Air Force could easily spot rebel concentrations. Most important of all, most Frenchmen at the beginning of hostilities were all for the war; it was only later, as more and more attention by the mass-communications media was focused on the conflict that the public was gradually worn down by an incipient form of war weariness that also characterised the American embroilment in Vietnam. Algeria had become the first of the "media" wars and France paid a heavy price as a result.

For the French there were serious problems. It was not that the members of the FLN were a monolithic party like the communists in Vietnam; there was much internal strife between the various rebel cadres. But they had the advantage of safe borders to cross when the going became really hard; sanctuary in the neighbouring countries of Tunisia, Libya, Egypt and Morocco. Walter Laqueur, in his book *Guerrilla*, considers that the FLN would have been defeated but for external support. He would probably say the same of Swapo in relation to Angola if he were ever to make a study of the conflict in southern Africa.

But whereas the South Africans have taken the war to the enemy, the French dared not do so. As Laqueur says:

"However much the generals might rave, they were powerless to pursue the enemy. Even a minor air attack against an FLN base on the Tunisian side of the border (Sakiet Sidi Yusuf) provoked a major international scandal; a massive attack was altogether unthinkable, since the French government felt it could not commit such an affront to world opinion."

Since then, the United States (in Vietnam), the Israelis (throughout the Middle East and the Maghreb), and South Africa (in Angola, Mozambique, Zambia and Zimbabwe) have emphasised the right of any nation under attack from beyond its own borders to retaliate. Although the "right of hot pursuit", as it is usually called is not codified in any statute book, its frequent and effective application over the past thirty years or so has practically established its validity in most seats of power; in the West, at least.

More serious, in the Algerian war effort was the inherent weakness of the French government to get to grips with some of its problems. The country was passing through its most difficult period since the end of the second world war; there was no real leadership until de Gaulle arrived on the scene; no stable day-to-day government; with the result that the succession of crises in Paris inevitably affected the situation in Algeria.

Keeping several hundred thousand French soldiers on active duty in North

Africa was also costing France a billion dollars a year. It is no wonder, therefore, that the conflict gradually lost support at home. When de Gaulle made his first conciliatory remark that perhaps force was not the ultimate answer to the problem of Algeria, the vast sigh of relief throughout France was almost audible.

It was close. While the French army had at first underestimated the extent of the rebellion, they very quickly brought in the men and systematic measures to deal with the menace. The FLN rebels lost the initiative. They were further hampered by the fairly secure Morice Line along the Tunisian border, which made infiltration from outside difficult; and by the *régroupement* of villages (along the lines of the Portuguese *Aldeamentos* system, which came later) and which effectively "denied water to the guerrilla 'fish'".

Walter Laqueur says that by 1961 the number of *fellaghas* inside Algeria was down to about 5 000 men, scattered in small groups.

The situation was not much better for the French, although they always put on a brave front, especially when the press was about. According to Laqueur: "If FLN morale was low, among the French it was at breaking point." They could not keep huge garrisons indefinitely in all the main towns and huge mobile reserves besides. There were 20 000 insurgents concentrated in Tunis, beyond the reach of the French, and the European population of Algeria was up in arms against the *défaitistes* in Paris.

By now the military commanders in Algeria were paying less and less attention to orders from Paris. In short, France was on the verge of civil war when General de Gaulle took over, and the danger did not pass for several years.

The FLN succeeded in obtaining diplomatic recognition from about twenty countries, including Russia and China. They had set up a government in exile, with the result that when the time came to meet the French face to face at Evian, they could do so with confidence and the effective backing of their own masses.

The end came seven years after the beginning of the struggle, and half a million Frenchmen in uniform were sent home. Tens of thousands of people had been killed. More than a million people were uprooted, and Algeria became a dictatorship where the rule of law was at least as severe as it had been at the height of the war. Socialism was adopted and, now towards the end of the Eighties, it is interesting to look at the results of nationhood in Algeria compared with what might have been if the country had accepted the French offer to make Algeria a real, not merely theoretical, part of France. If the rebels had accepted, Algeria would now certainly be in the European Common Market; and what a different situation that would have created for 1992.

A report was published by Reuters in October 1988 after the riots in Algiers which left 500 students dead. It set forth the position of Algeria 26 years after the county had won its independence from France. It said:

"The typical Algerian youth is poor and angry and is behind the worst violence in the country since independence from France in 1962.

"He is working class, most likely unemployed, and lives in the teeming slums on the edge of central Algiers, where on average nine people share two rooms.

"In the central Casbah district, the old Turkish–built quarter, families of 15 are often crammed into the crumbling old dwellings.

"... Rubbish stands high in the streets; the stench is often overwhelming. Shabby buildings are crumbling and the local municipality cannot afford the necessary large-scale renovations.

"In 1966, Algeria's population was around 12 million. Today it stands at almost

25 million. Two-thirds are under 25 – and they want jobs." More important, Algeria's external debt was in excess of twenty billion dollars at the end of 1988.

*The Economist* was even gloomier:

"Take the economic stagnation of an East European country, mix it with an oil-producer's shrunken earnings and an African rate of population growth, stir in hunger: you have Algeria."

There are still 6 000 Frenchmen living in Algeria and almost a million Algerians in France.

One might well now ask: what was it really all about?

**BIBLIOGRAPHY**

Abbas, Ferhat, *Guerre et Révolution d'Algérie,* Paris, 1962.

Abbas, Ferhat, *La Nuit coloniale,* 1962.

Alleg, Henri, *The Question,* London, 1958.

Ambler, John Steward, *Soldiers Against the State; The French Army in Politics,* New York, 1968.

Andrews, William G., *French Politics and Algeria,* New York, 1962.

Aron, Raymond, *La Tragédie algérienne,* Paris, 1957.

Beauvoir, Simone de, *La Force des choses,* 1963.

Behr, Edward, *The Algerian Problem,* London, 1961.

Bell, J. Bowyer, *The Myth of the Guerrilla,* New York, 1971.

Bell, J. Bowyer, *Transnational Terrorism,* Washington, D.C., 1975.

Bourdieu, Pierre, *The Algerians,* Translated by Alan C.M. Ross, Boston, 1962.

Brace, Richard and Joan, *Ordeal in Algeria,* New York, 1960.

Bromberger, Merry and Serge; Elgey, Georgette; and Chauvel, Jean–François, *Barricades et colonels, 24 janvier 1960,* 1960.

Camus, Albert, *Noces,* Paris, 1938.

Camus, Albert, *The Outsider,* London, 1946.

Camus, Albert, *The Plague,* London, 1948.

Camus, Albert, *The Myth of Sisyphus,* New York, 1954.

Camus, Albert, *Actuelles III Chroniques algériennes 1939-1958,* Paris, 1958.

Camus, Albert, *Resistance, Rebellion and Death,* London, 1961.

Clark, Michael K., *Algeria in Turmoil; A History of the Rebellion,* New York, 1959.

Crozier, Brian, *The Rebels,* London, 1960.

Crozier, Brian, *The Morning After,* London, 1963.

Devillers, Philippe, and Lacouture, Jean. *End of a War; Indochina 1954,* New York, 1969.

Gaulle, Charles de, *Mémoirs d'espoir: (i)Le Renouveau, 1958-1962,* Paris, 1970.

Gaulle, Charles de, *Discours et messages (avec Le Renouveau),* Paris, 1970.

Gendarme, René. *L'Economie de l'Algérie,* 1959.

Giroud, Françoise, *I Give You My Word,* Boston, 1974.

Good, Dorothy, "Notes on the Demography of Algeria," *Population Index,* 28 (January 1961):3–31.

Gordon, David C., *North Africa's French Legacy, 1954-1962* (Cambridge, Mass., 1962)

Gordon, David C., *The Passing of French Algeria,* London, 1966.

Gordon, David C., *Women of Algeria, an Essay on Change,* (Cambridge, Mass., 1968)

Greer, Herb, *A Scattering of Dust*, London, 1962.

Grossman, David, *The Yellow Wind*; Cape, London 1988.

Harbi, Mohamed, *Aux Origines du FLN: la scission PPA-MTLD*, 1975.

Heilbrunn, Otto, *Warfare in the Enemy's Rear*, London, 1963.

Henissart, Paul, *Wolves in the City; The Death of French Algeria*, New York, 1971.

Horne, Alistair, *A Savage War of Peace; Algeria, 1954-1962*, Macmillan, London, 1977.

Hutchinson, Martha Crenshaw, *Revolutionary Terrorism; The FLN in Algeria*, Stanford, 1978.

Joesten, Joachim, *The Red Hand*, London, 1962.

Johnson, Chalmers, *Autopsy on People's War*, Berkeley and Los Angeles, 1973.

Kelly, George Armstrong, *Lost Soldiers; The French Army and Empire in Crisis, 1947-1962*, Cambridge, Mass., 1965.

Kraft, Joseph, *The Struggle for Algeria*, New York, 1961.

Laqueur, Walter, *Guerrilla*, Weidenfeld and Nicolson, London, 1977.

Lartéguy, Jean, *The Centurions*, London, 1961.

Massu, Jacques, *La Vrai Bataille d'Alger*, Paris, 1971.

Massu, Jacques, *Le Torrent et la digue*, Paris, 1972.

Mauriac, Francois, *Bloc-Notes, 1952-1957*, 1958.

Mitterrand, François, *Présence française et abandon*, Paris, 1957.

Moss, Robert, *Urban Guerrillas*, London, 1972.

Motley, Mary, *Home to Numidia*, London, 1964.

O'Ballance, Edgar, *The Algerian Insurrection, 1954-1962*, London, 1967.

Ortiz, Joseph, *Mes Combats*, 1964.

Paret, Peter, *French Revolutionary Warfare from Indochina to Algeria; The Analysis of a Political and Military Doctrine*, New York, 1964.

Pickles, Dorothy, *Algeria and France*, London, 1963.

Quandt, William B., *Revolution and Political Leadership: Algeria, 1954-1968*, Cambridge, Mass., 1969.

Roy, Jules, *The War in Algeria*, New York, 1961.

Salan, Raoul, *Mémoires: Fin d'un Empire: Algérie française*, Paris, 1972; *Algérie, de Gaulle et moi*, Paris, 1974.

Soustelle, Jacques, *Aimée et Souffrante Algérie*, Paris, 1956

Soustelle, Jacques, *L'Espérance trahi, 1958-1961*, Paris, 1962.

Soustelle, Jacques, *La Page n'est pas tournée*, Paris, 1965.

Talbott, John, *The War Without a Name: France in Algeria 1954-1962*, Faber and Faber, London; 1981.

Talbott, John, "The Myth and Reality of the Paratrooper in the Algerian War." *Armed Forces and Society* 3 (Fall 1976): 69-86.

Talbott, John, "French Public Opinion and the Algerian War: A Research Note." *French Historical Studies* 9 (Fall 1975): 354-61.

Thayer, George, *The War Business*, New York, 1969.

Tillion, Germaine, *L'Algérie en 1957*, Paris, 1957.

Tillion, Germaine, *Les Ennemis complémentaires*, Paris, 1960.

Trinquier, Roger, *Guerre, subversion, révolution*, Paris, 1968.

Trinquier, Roger, *Modern Warfare*. Translated by Daniel Lee. New York, 1964.

Wall, Irwin, "The French Communists and the Algerian War." *Journal of Contemporary History* 12 (1977): 521-43.

Werth, Alexander, *The Strange History of Pierre Mendès-France and the Great Conflict over French North Africa*, London, 1957.

# SOUTH AFRICA WITHIN THE
# AFRICAN REVOLUTIONARY CONTEXT

*by Willie Breytenbach*

## 1. Continental Overview

Africa is a continent locked in conflict. History shows that no part of it is immune to violence. The context of its violence, however, has changed over the years. For example, the ideological contents, insurgency doctrines and other new phenomena such as external implication in African revolutions have grown since the second world war.

The oldest of the new revolutions in Africa is the Algerian rebellion of the Fifties and early Sixties. That uprising was launched on 1 November, All Saints' Day, in 1954, three weeks after the secret formation of the Liberation Army on October 10. That was an exceptionally short period of time. In most other cases uprisings occurred only after long periods of mobilisation and the organisation of resistance.

Since then Africa has not been without revolutionary conflict for a single day. As long as contending ideologies, popular grievances, social and economic problems and political crises exist, the longer civil strife will continue. That is particularly true of southern Africa.

The obvious revolutionary battlegrounds in southern Africa are Namibia and South Africa. However, the rest of the continent cannot be excluded from our survey. What has happened in countries such as Uganda under Museveni and in Ethiopia since the overthrow of Haile Selassie in 1974 is instructive. Chad and the Western Sahara seem to have endemic rebellions, with civil wars in the Sudan and Angola. These events all prove that armed insurrections, whether rebellions or civil war, can take place and even succeed in situations unrelated to nationalist or anti-colonial revolutions.

Uganda did not undergo a revolution. It was an internal insurrection that developed into a civil war along the lines of guerrilla warfare. In the end, central government forces collapsed and power was seized by Museveni and his men. It cannot therefore be regarded as a coup d'état either, for Museveni was an "outsider" (though not a foreigner) who did not occupy a position of authority in either the civil service or the armed forces of Uganda.

Ethiopia, on the other hand, was subjected to a coup d'état by the armed forces. But as we shall explain later, it was a coup that turned into a revolution without a guerrilla war being fought.

Guerrilla warfare has become the hallmark of all other revolutions in Africa. Ironically, though, the Eritreans have, since the Marxist takeover in Ethiopia, conducted a full-scale rebellion against the new régime, and adopted a guerrilla strategy in doing so.

But as in all the other revolutions in Africa, with the exception of Algeria, the USSR became an important external supporter of the revolutionary cause there; in the case of Ethiopia, not on the side of the Eritreans (who are Muslims), but on the side of the Ethiopians who, paradoxically, are nominally Christian Copts, now "converted" to atheism.

Soviet intervention became a dominant feature of all the anti-colonial revolutions in Guiné-Bissau, Angola, Mozambique and Rhodesia. The Russians are also committed to supporting what they call the national liberation movements in South West Africa/Namibia and South Africa. From a Russian and also from a revolutionary nationalist point of view, there is not much difference between the revolutionary anti-colonial struggles in the rest of Africa and the South African Communist Party-cum-African National Congress armed struggle in South Africa. In an SACP document dated 1962 entitled "The Road to South African Freedom", according to decisions taken by the ANC at the time of the Morogoro Conference in 1961, the South African situation was regarded as "a colony of a special type". Hence the SACP and the ANC justify both their theories and tactics as fundamentally the same as those appropriate to national liberation movements elsewhere on the continent.

In all these cases, the Russians, first under Khrushchev and later under Brezhnev, were quick to exploit grievances where a violent potential existed, as will be explained later.

Violence is always related to a cause, and it can almost always be traced to grievances, problems and crises in the societies concerned. In that sense the Russians do not create revolutions; they support them.

Some violence in Africa erupted spontaneously, for example the many "incidents" during colonial times such as the early rebellions, post-pacification revolts and so on. In most of these cases the colonial powers easily suppressed the disturbances or else eradicated the grievances through some "reform" or other. Invariably such revolts were weak, mainly because of their spontaneity. Other explanations are their lack of forward-looking ideology and lack of organisational capacity, including a strategy of resistance. There was no theory of violence.

But revolutionary violence has seldom if ever been spontaneous or unplanned; it forms part of a deliberate strategy for change and is usually employed long before fighting begins.

Revolutionary violence without political organisation is unthinkable.

Revolutionary organisation implies concentrating on such things as mobilising support, defining ideologies, creating revolutionary ("alternative") infrastructures, securing external bases and then, as part of comprehensive strategies, decisions on the appropriateness of armed techniques. Quite often military wings take responsibility for such matters. Even the Mau Mau, which was not an insurgency, only an insurrection, had a military wing, the Land and Freedom Army (LFA).

Ironically, violence is more important to the insurrectionist than to the insurgent, although ultimately no insurgency can sustain itself without planned violence. It is therefore a calculated act. Frantz Fanon, the well-known writer on the Algerian revolution, has some valuable comments. He himself had very little to do with the revolution in Algeria. He was more influenced by the events and their aftermath in Algeria, which had a profound impact on his writings. He therefore had some influence on the Algerian leaders. Writing by hindsight, he put great emphasis on violence and on the revolution as a primary peasant insurrection rather than one guided and dominated by the trade unions and the towns. In fact, his insistence on violence was so devoid of theory that one cannot escape the suspicion that his advocacy of violence was probably motivated more by revenge than by a thorough understanding of revolutionary processes.

Revolutionary violence on the continent, often styled "revolutionary terror", should not be confused with so-called "non-revolutionary political violence" of the kind perpetrated by the Basques in Spain, the Baader-Meinhof gang in Germany, or by the Red Brigade in Italy. These organisations are politically angry and are merely intent on making "political statements" through their actions and, unlike the revolutionary organisations in China, Latin America and Africa, are never really interested in seizing power. Some, like the Red Brigades, are interested in radical reconstruction of their societies but are not interested in political takeovers. As such they are not, and do not even aspire to be, guerrilla fighters. Guerrillas fight for political victory, not necessarily military defeat of the target state; and in pursuit of that they employ "revolutionary terror" as a means to that end.

More often than not it is preceded by "subversive" political organisation. However, some South American revolutionary ideologues such as Guevara and Debray (the advocates of "instant action") deviated from this pattern. The death of Guevara (and others such as Marighella) at the hands of security forces, the alienation of their revolutionary *focos* from the sprawling urban proletariats and the poor in the South American cities and *favelhas*, and the failures of similar strategies in a number of South American countries such as Bolivia, Brazil, Argentine and Uruguay, discredited this strategy so much that its legacy was completely lost on African revolutionaries, the "sudden eruptions" in Algeria (1954) and Angola (1961) notwithstanding.

On closer inspection, however, we find that only Algeria showed signs of "instant action" in 1954. The revolts elsewhere, including the Angolan rebellion, were well planned ever since the *União das Populações do Norte de Angola* (UPNA) and the *Movimento Popular de Libertação de Angola* (MPLA) were created in 1953 and 1957 respectively. Still, it took UPNA a full seven years before the revolt in northern Angola was launched in 1961.

Neither the *Front de Libération Nationale* (FLN) — and its military wing the *Armée de Libération Nationale* (ALN), nor the Angolan or any other African resistance movement exactly fitted the model of the Guevarian strategy. Unlike South America, external support patterns always predominated in revolutionary Africa. Organisational structures and ethnic differences were also simply too different for South America to provide useful lessons for revolutionaries in Africa.

In fact, Guevara himself declared that revolutions (presumably of his kind) were "impossible" in Africa. He came to this conclusion after the fiasco of the Congolese rebellion during the Sixties. As will be seen later, Guevara's assessment of the prospects for revolution in Africa was wrong. What had happened with especially the *Partido do Africano de Independencia da Guiné e Cabo Verde* (PAIGC) in Guiné-Bissau, and to a lesser extent with the *Frente de Libertação de Moçambique* (Frelimo) in Mozambique, the Zimbabwe African National Union (ZANU-Patriotic Front - PF) in Zimbabwe, proved that Guevara was far too pessimistic about revolutionary prospects in Africa. Even Angola with all its internal rivalries does not disprove the revolutionary theory. The revolutionary outcome in Angola is instructive, considering the consequences of too many cross-cutting revolutionary alliances, widely different ethnic support patterns, contending ideologies and competing external supporters.

The outcome of revolutions in Africa, especially the anti-colonial revolutions, also showed that early failures can be overcome. Here the failure of the urban uprising by the MPLA in Luanda in 1961, the failure of the rural insurrection in north-western Angola by the *Frente Nacional de Libertação de Angola* (FNLA) also in 1961, the failure of the ZAPU and ZANU infiltrations in Rhodesia in 1965/6, and Amilcar Cabral's acknowledgement in 1969 that the PAIGC had to switch from a proletarian strategy (in the towns) to a peasant strategy (in the Balanta tribal areas in the country) in Guiné-Bissau, are all cases in point.

But switching tactics does not mean striking a winning formula. Although the PAIGC and ZANU (PF) improved their performances, military victory still eluded them. The FNLA is still nowhere near victory, while ZAPU has virtually been swallowed up by ZANU (PF); and the MPLA still fights for survival in a bitter post-colonial civil war. It is still not certain whether the recent peace accords will bring that to an end.

These examples and others to be discussed later show very clearly how dynamic and flexible revolutionary strategies can be. Most revolutionaries benefit from their own experiences and that of others. Their intellectual leadership can put them in positions to learn something that is often lost in peasant insurrections.

One of the greatest lessons that revolutionaries in Africa have learnt is that, although they were easily beaten militarily, fighting was less important than effective political organisation. The old principle that subversion comes before combat is always the best formula for ultimate success despite failure to achieve military victory.

It is a case of the survival of will-power. All African revolutionary organisations have *long* histories. As we shall see later, they have average lifetimes of no less than 23 years, the greater portion taken up by protracted combat preceded by shorter phases of organisation. Only the FLN in Algeria had no significant preparatory phase. The ALN was 21 days old, and the FLN was formed the same day that violence was unleashed. However, its predecessor, the *Comité Révolutionaire d'Unité et d'Action*, CRUA, saw the fate that had befallen the French in Indo-China and believed that an uprising could be successful. From 1953 onwards they carefully planned the rising and the formation of the FLN. Consequently the Algerian insurgency, which was then seen as a mere "insurrectional incident", achieved almost complete surprise.

Yet the Algerian model is not typical of what was still to come in Africa. Apart from the suddenness of the Algerian rebellion, it also differs from the other insurrections and insurgencies in one fundamental respect: the absence of Russian support.

In the rest of the continent anti-colonial rebellions were planned for well after the organisations had been founded. The rebellions in question were both nationalist and Marxist-inspired. This is an irony that Marx himself (though not Lenin) would have frowned upon; for Marx disapproved of nationalism as false consciousness.

Yet despite the ironies the pattern is clear: revolutions cannot take place without ideologies. Ideologies do not "create" revolutions; but they do reinforce the conditions in which they are predicated.

Meanwhile a revolution of a different kind, not anti-colonial, but "anti" nonetheless, occurred in Ethiopia. There the military rebelled against the feudalism of Haile Selassie. It was first thought to be another of many African uprisings followed by one of the many coups d'état. However, the consequences rather than the causes of this coup showed that what had happened in Ethiopia was a far-reaching Marxist revolution. To be sure, the ideology was Marxist, but the style and methods were unmistakenly Stalinist, including at least two purges. A strange thing happened: Praetorians acted for the first time in Africa and perhaps in the world in the name of the proletariat. Marxists came to power without even a party to support them. The party was established only ten years later, when the Workers' Party of Ethiopia was formed in 1984.

Certainly that was a rare phenomenon. Surely a case of Pliny's dictum: *Ex Africa semper aliquid novi.*

## 2. From Reluctant Rebellions to Insurrectional Strategies for Change

The African "warrior tradition" is often cited as one explanation of its modern wars. It is an interesting proposition; but on closer inspection it fails to convince.

The warrior tradition was characterised, according to Ali Mazrui, by its premise of "indigenous fighting symbols". Examples are the Ashanti and Zulu wars of the previous century. These were conventional wars by primitive means. They were the heroic battles of the indigenous armies of pre-colonial African communities against the imperialist intruders from Western Europe who were actuated by the mercantile and expansionist instincts of a Europe reshaped by the British Industrial Revolution and the new nationalisms on the Continent. The quest was for Empire. The spoils were Africa, its land and its resources.

Many indigenous peoples fought valiantly: but sheer power and technology prevailed. But it was not long after that that the first rebellions against the presence and the economic policies of the colonial powers erupted.

Most eruptions took the form of peasant insurrections led by tribal chiefs. All foreign powers felt their wrath. The British, the French, the Portuguese and the Germans were all committed to crushing all resistance, whether "early rebellion" or "post-pacification revolt" as Donald Crummey of the University of Illinois in Urbana-Champaign distinguishes them.

The Germans with Teutonic precision crushed the Maji-Maji rebellion in Tanganyika in 1905 and the Herero and Nama revolts in German South West Africa in 1904-1907. The Portuguese fought the Bailundu War in south-eastern Angola in 1902-1903. During the same period the British faced a series of revolts beginning with the Bambatha rebellion in Natal in 1906, the Chilembwe risings in Nyasaland in 1915 and the working-class protests of Harry Thuku in Kenya in 1921.

Conventional wisdom has it that these rebellions were "provoked", not organised as they would have been if they had been insurgencies. For example, Bill Freund refers to the Herero and Nama uprisings as "revolts of despair". The same is true of Bambatha.

According to Shula Marks, colonial provocation led to the "reluctant rebellions" of Bambatha and his Amazondi tribesmen in the district of Greytown in Natal in 1906. Bill Freund shares the same opinion about the "desperate responses" of Samuel Maherero and Hendrik Witbooi in South West Africa in 1904-1906. Whether provoked or not, these rebellions were entirely different from the early resistances to conquest, premised as they were on "indigenous fighting symbols". Basil Davidson calls that "primary resistance".

These newer forms of resistance were to be associated with "unindigenous" elements and they laid the foundations for the later patterns yet to come, Davidson's "secondary resistance", which included Crummey's "early rebellions" and "post-pacification revolts".

The new patterns of, say, the early twentieth century were characterised by new forms of leadership; for example the rebelling of "minor chiefs" (not kings or paramount chiefs) like Bambatha, the forming of alliances, such as between Maherero and Witbooi, and new leaderships arising from the ranks of detribalised Africans no longer linked to tribal hierarchies, such as John Chilembwe and Harry Thuku, both of whom were commoners and not formal traditional leaders. They arose from new economic pressures, for example, resistance of colonised poll tax payers in Natal during the Bambatha rebellion, the uprising of plantation-workers and wage-earners in Nyasaland in the Chilembwe incident, and the discontent of postoffice and other workers and wage-earners in Kenya in the

Thuku protests in Nairobi.

Not surprisingly, church influences became evident too, as in the case of Bambatha (the Ethiopian church) and Chilembwe (the American Baptists); and the emergence of new social bases of popular protest and class consciousness.

This signalled the end of "indigenous fighting symbols" and the "primary resistance" era. Violence was never to be the same again.

The new patterns introduced by Chilembwe and Thuku have a clear ideological basis. In its rudimentary form it sprang from an awareness of discrimination and exploitation. In South Africa, Clemens Kadalie's ICU fitted this pattern. One of the new political vehicles was socialism, which was to become an important ideological source of legitimation for the increasingly radical anti-colonial struggles after 1945.

The other important incentive for the struggle, indeed the most important one, turned out to be nationalism, especially the associated notions of national self-determination and statehood. But that was still largely absent from the worlds of Chilembwe, Thuku and Kadalie.

The familiar language of liberation also gained momentum only after the war. Even the Mau Mau, not yet concerned about the Kenyan *state,* flirted with "liberation", as witness its *Land and Freedom Army.*

These emergent ideologies and new goals went hand-in-hand with the rise of voluntary political movements and congresses, and the imminent radicalisation of political parties arising from the melting-pot of anti-colonial forces; grievance plus -ism equals action.

After World War 2, nationalist fervour and socialist rhetoric were matched by the "made-in-America" phenomenon of Pan-Africanism. Its founding fathers were black Afro-Americans such as Sylvester Williams, Marcus Garvey and William du Bois. With Pan-Africanism came the era of mass parties, the increasing importance of ideology and a flowering of the "secondary" resistance tendencies such as rebellions, revolts and revolutions.

It was also the era when strategies for change were hotly debated in such places as Manchester (the last Pan-Africanist Congress on foreign soil took place there in 1945), Accra (the seat of Kwame Nkrumah in the Gold Coast: the man destined to become the leader of the first independent black state in Africa in 1957), Nairobi (the centre of the Mau Mau uprising in the Fifties), and in Algiers and its environs, where Algerian Arabs and Berbers and Kabyles had already, since 1954, engaged the French and the white *colons* or *pieds noirs* in savage fighting for the control of Algeria.

In Algeria the FLN *fellaghas* had already decided that the reform debate was over and the fighting was on. It was brutal. The moderation of Ferhat Abbas and his middle-class associates was gone. In their place came the younger revolutionaries of Ben Bella and his cadres. Andrew Wheatcroft describes it as a "very dirty war" and a "catalogue of atrocities". According to the Algerian psychiatrist and revolutionary, Frantz Fanon, born in Martinique and trained in France, violence was the *only* way to defeat colonialism. Strangely enough, Fanon was not a communist. Although he paid lipservice to Marxism, he rejected it. He praised the peasants, not the proletariat.

It is also surprising that with the exception of Kenya and Algeria the anti-colonial struggles of the Forties, Fifties and Sixties were remarkably peaceful. Nationalism in Africa was never really aggressive, despite being "radical".

There are various explanations for that, the first being that mass nationalist movements and parties were quite successful in their attempts to mobilise the masses peacefully; the fact that many nationalist leaders were sincere Christians who had an aversion in principle against violence; the fact that nationalistic leadership was predominantly bourgeois in origin, imbued with the moderate values of their professions such as teaching, the civil service, or as officially recognised chiefs. As such they were the class least likely to resort to mob behaviour and organised violence; and finally, the fact that up to and including the Mau Mau uprising and the Algerian rebellion, the Russians were nowhere in sight. By the time that they took an interest in the decolonisation struggles, organised violence had already become part of the pattern. So to explain the outbreak of armed fighting in Africa only as a result of the "sheer stubbornness of white settlers", as Mazrui does, is to overlook the fact that armed struggles developed in post-colonial Africa as well, for example in Zaïre, the Sudan, Nigeria, Chad, Eritrea, the Western Sahara and so on.

Moreover it was *not* the anti-colonial struggles that first whetted the Russian appetite for African conflict. Ironically, it was the civil war in the Congo, now Zaïre, that precipitated their intervention in Africa. Also, the Russians became implicated in Ghana and Mali, which had fairly peaceful transfers of power.

The Kenyan and Algerian crises, for all their anti-colonial fervour, owed nothing to communist interference. Stalin was at that time too preoccupied with Europe and the Americans. He also had a strong aversion to Third World nationalists, whom he regarded as "firmly entrenched in the bourgeois camp of imperialism". The Kenyan and Algerian revolts were thus the last of their kind.

In the next era, which began with planned insurrections in Angola, Guiné-Bissau, Mozambique, Rhodesia, South West Africa, the Russians were deeply implicated. Yet it is still questionable whether they had a hand in the *Umkhonto we Sizwe* (the armed wing of the ANC) sabotage and bombings that began in December 1961 in South Africa. Whatever the verdict, the weapons used were obtained directly or indirectly from communist sources.

The pattern that emerged showed that things would never be the same again. Certainly not a case of Fanonian violence. It would be subversion first, then violence, and finally combat.

## 3. Revolutionary Violence: Subversion and Organisation Before Combat

Revolutionary violence, sabotage and politically-inspired destruction of life and property, came to Africa during the sixties. It was violence of a special kind, violence that neither erupted spontaneously nor marked a new era in the decolonisation process, which was normally not violent. Instead, revolutionary violence was calculated to effect radical changes in society. The Mau-Mau violence of the fifties falls short of the definition of "revolutionary", simply because it lacked most of the characteristics such as modern ideology of revolutionary organisations in contemporary times.

Effective subversion and organisation also became indispensable. Thomas H. Greene of the University of Southern California dismisses spontaneity as an element in this process. He says that there is no real substitute for revolutionary organisation in the attainment of revolutionary objectives.

Radically-inspired violence was seldom spontaneous and hardly ever a necessary ingredient of decolonisation. It was planned and preceded by political organisation that included tactics of violence as part of wider strategies for the seizure of power and radical transformation of the economic, social and political relations within given systems.

Roy C. Macridis of Brandeis University defines a revolution as acts of organised violence calculated to bring about comprehensive radical changes: "It uses force to destroy and replace those in power." As will become clearer later on, "organised violence" in the revolutionary era after the second world war is necessarily of the *protracted* kind (for example, the Maoist revolution in China lasted for 22 years, from 1927 after Mao Tse-tung proclaimed a "soviet republic" in Kiangsi Province until the communist forces finally triumphed over the nationalist opponents in 1949); and "radical changes in the economic, social and political relations" imply a strong commitment to *ideology* (for example, Karl Marx referred to ideology as "the theory that becomes a material force when it grips the masses". In fact, the function of ideology is so pervasive that it becomes almost the sole *raison d'être* of the explanation, legitimation and direction of "the cause").

In addition to Macridis's definition and its elaboration offered above, two other factors must be emphasised: one, *organising for support and mass mobilisation*; and two, *the securing of external support.*

Although all revolutionaries emphasise violence (the so-called "armed struggle", "people's war" etc.), violence in itself is not the sole objective in the revolutionary struggle. Nor is it the only means employed in the struggle. Unlike terrorists such as the Italian Red Brigade, revolutionaries in Asia, Africa and Latin America use violence as one means in the struggle. Besides tactical considerations, there are also strategic considerations, especially in the notion of violence as "the weapon of the weak". This implies that violence may decrease as strength in other tactical and strategic areas increases. Even a non-radical theorist such as Max Weber saw a correlation between "protest" and "charismatic leadership".

These other tactical and strategic fields may be discussed according to the four elements mentioned above: the protracted nature of revolutions, which allows for time-scales and revolutionary phases; the roles of ideology; the organising of support and the organisational imperatives of mass mobilisation and the securing of external support.

None of the revolutions in Africa was ephemeral. With the possible exception of the Ethiopian revolution, all the other actions ("praxis") were preceded by political phases during which ideological and organisational factors predominated. From a counter-insurgency point of view, this was the "subversive" phase, the "protest" phase.

In Africa the "violence-free" ideology-formulation and organisational phases lasted five years on average. That is the time-scale between the founding dates of the organisations concerned and the first acts of violence.

These dates could be deceptive, as in the case of the South African ANC. It is well-known when violence first occurred (1961), but it is still uncertain when it actually abandoned non-violence.

The ANC was established in 1912, and the "first violence" was only committed in December 1961 after a period of almost fifty years. What is important, however, is to remember that ANC violence in December 1961 resulted from the formation of *Umkhonto we Sizwe* (MK) in June 1961. In this case, therefore, the time-scale was only six months. Where to begin counting is therefore a problem, given the complexities of the history of the ANC of first trying to redress "native" grievances, then the Lembedist black radical influences on the youth wing of the ANC, the banning of the South African Communist Party and its subsequent attempts to infiltrate the ANC, then the resistance to pass laws, the split by the PAC, the Defiance Campaign, and ultimately the formation of MK and Poqo as the military wings of the ANC and PAC.

The first violence of the MK was confined to sabotage and the bombing of government properties. Damage to life and limb was slight. The ANC had not intended it to be otherwise. But that policy changed radically over the years. Many lives have since been lost; and that dates from the time when a strategy of armed struggle was adopted after the Soweto uprisings of 1976. Hints were given at the time of the Morogoro Conference in 1969. But it never came to fruition. An armed strategy was finally adopted in 1979, but not put into effect until March 1985.

Still, it is difficult to know how to begin counting dates in the case of the ANC: should it be December 1961? Or should it be August 1979, when a strategy of armed struggle was adopted? Or when that strategy was actually carried out in March 1985?

It is easier to decide on the length of the preparatory phases of similar organisations in the rest of Africa. The following less ambiguous pattern of an average of five years emerges: Nought number of years in the case of the Algerian FLN-ALN (1954) on the short side of the range, and eight years for PAC in South Africa (1952-1960) and Swapo in South West Africa (1957-1965), on the long side.

Those falling in between are Unita in Angola, two years, from 1964 to 1966; Frelimo in Mozambique, two years, from 1962 to 1964; ZAPU in Rhodesia, three years, from 1963 to 1966; the MPLA in Angola, four years, from 1957 to 1961; the FNLA in Angola, seven years, from 1954 to 1961, and finally, PAIGC in Guiné-Bissau, seven years, from 1956 to 1963.

During these non-violent phases crucial "organisation" took place. That is what is known by counter-insurgents as the "subversive" phase, when "undermining" and "infiltration" take place.

The second factor of ideology is central to the shaping of the nature of subversion organisation and the kind of fighting techniques employed.

Ideology and circumstances such as counter-insurgency responses set the limits within which leaders and followers, the modes of resistance, and external supporters all interact in this comprehensive scheme.

It is a case of ideology playing an invisible yet highly creative part, which ultimately defines the limits of the struggle and serves the purpose of "gripping the masses". The limited and weak ideological base of the Mau Mau in Kenya is often cited as one of the reasons for its easy suppression by the British; it hardly "gripped" the non-Kikuyu "masses" in that country. Ideology *is* important.

Revolutions are normally premised on three types of ideologies: "republican" (the French and the American revolutions), "nationalistic" (the anti-colonial rebellions in Africa and elsewhere), and "Marxist-Leninist" (in the USSR, Cuba and Ethiopia).

These ideological strains are not mutually exclusive, however. They reinforce one another. The first and the last combined in the Russian and Ethiopian revolutions. The first and the second combined in the American revolution; and the second and the third combined in most revolutions in Africa. The only exception is Algeria, where no communist influence was discernible.

In fact, African revolutions have never been dominated by a single ideology. They have always been a mixture determined by historical experience, ideological preference, ethnic grievances and class conflicts.

Even the Algerian revolution, although not Marxist-inspired, was equally influenced by Nasser's insistence on Arab self-reliance (read "socialism" and unity), and by the religious cohesion offered by a homogeneous Muslim faith, ethnic differences between Arabs, Berbers and Kabyles notwithstanding. Together they were the under–classes, subservient to the *colons*.

The Algerian revolution was the only rebellion on the African continent where religious ideologies formed a basis of social antagonism. The French *colons* were predominantly Catholic, the indigenous masses Muslim.

The third factor is organisation and mobilisation. As Claude Welch once wrote: "The guerrilla fighter recognises his initial weakness... and seeks to overcome this through building a strong political foundation." As we have seen earlier, this building process usually lasted for an average of five years in Africa before violence ensued; and it is during this phase that the revolution is "organised". It therefore follows that revolutions are not spontaneous by nature. However, they have causes in the historical experience of the resistors, either as the oppressed, the exploited, or the dominated and whatever. But experience alone is not enough. What is needed is an ideology that embodies a vision; as Macridis puts it: "an ideology that promises so much to the many." But without popular participation all notions will come to nothing. "The many" must be mobilised or they will become dispensable in the struggle.

No revolutionary organisation can survive let alone succeed without people: leaders and followers. Lenin was one of the first revolutionaries to grasp that "leadership", the intellectual element in a revolution, is vital to its performance. Mao Tse–tung agreed. He and Lenin emphasised the role of intellectuals in directing the struggle. According to them the proletariat are capable neither of intellectualising the ideology nor of mobilising themselves.

African revolutionary leaders are no exception. Perhaps the only deviations from this pattern are Swapo, founded by Ovambo migrant workers in Cape Town in 1957, and the Ethiopian Dergue, founded in 1974 by soldiers and joined by workers who pursued Marxist visions in the dislike of feudalism.

All other revolutionary organisations in Africa were founded and were and are led by intellectuals. Agostinho Neto, the first leader of the MPLA in Angola, was a medical doctor and a renowned "protest" poet; Jonas Savimbi, the leader of Unita in Angola, is a Swiss–trained political scientist; Amilcar Cabral, the founder of the PAIGC in Guiné–Bissau, was an agricultural engineer in Lisbon; Eduardo Mondlane, the founder of Frelimo in Mozambique, was a South African educated anthropologist trained in America and Portugal; and Robert Mugabe, who led ZANU (PF) to political victory in Zimbabwe, has six diplomas and degrees obtained in South Africa and the United Kingdom. Generally speaking, ANC leaders belong to the same "learned" category.

The profile of the typical revolutionary leader in Africa is by no means that of a proletarian worker, let alone an illiterate peasant.

Ironically, African "revolutionaries on the left" are in more ways than they would care to admit typical of the bourgeoisie that they profess to despise. Writing about the Algerian revolution Frantz Fanon castigated his fellow revolutionaries for precisely that. After independence, he said, the bourgeoisie reasserted themselves, and the peasant basis of the original revolutionary movement disintegrated. The post–revolutionary régime in Algeria at no time since independence approached the Fanonist ideal except in so far as virtually all the French and Jews have left, mostly to France and Israel.

This tendency defies Marxian theory, which asserts the notion of class struggles and the historical inevitability of the "dictatorship of the proletariat" as a precursor to the establishment of a classless and stateless society. Algeria is still not classless, and judging by its performance in the Western Sahara, certainly not stateless either. Ironically, Algeria is again experiencing uprisings threatening "the state".

The African pattern of revolutionary leadership nevertheless conforms with the other notions of Lenin and Mao, both (incidentally?) communists. But whether they are communists or not, it is sheer common sense that the complexities of revolution-making should require "top-down" (read intellectual vs. peasant and worker) organisation to succeed. That is exactly what happened in the PAIGC, MPLA, ZANU-PF and Frelimo.

Although Frantz Fanon was an intellectual and an influential revolutionary writer, he failed as a visionary. Perhaps he was too obsessed with revenge against the *colons* to be able to challenge *colonialism* comprehensively. His remark that "colonialism only loosens its hold when the knife is at its throat" reveals it all. He will therefore be remembered for his advocacy of violence; nothing more, except that he denounced the bourgeoisie as "parasitic" and "unreliable", and that he preferred the (rural) peasants and the (urban) lumpenproletariat, a class of poverty-stricken squatters and shanty-town crooks as "the best" revolutionaries. In doing so he discarded the working class. That earned him the wrath of Marxists.

That brings us to the appropriateness or otherwise of class analysis in revolutionary theory and in explaining support and mobilisation patterns.

Marxian historians and many social scientists emphasise the importance of class analysis. The general consensus seems to suggest that guerrilla wars in Africa were "peasant" wars, implying, as Bill Freund does, that leaders, fighters and supporters are all peasants. As we have seen, nothing could be further from the truth as far as leadership is concerned.

Insight into this problem was offered by none other than Amilcar Cabral. He insisted on the usefulness of the "rootless young" in the revolutionary struggle and also admitted that ethnic factors were more important than class divisions in the recruitment of PAIGC guerrillas.

Whether rootless or not, youngsters and peasants formed the backbone of the fighting cadres of the MPLA, Frelimo, ZANU (PF), Swapo and the PAIGC. The urban poor, and Fanon's "lumpen" helped the Mau-Mau in Kenya (especially those uprooted from their highland tribal lands by the settlers) and the FLN-ALN in the Muslim casbahs of Algeria.

The ANC in South Africa is quite a different case. To be sure, it is very different by African standards, but not so different according to Marxist perspectives. It developed from a nationalist organisation through various forms of protest into a non-racial body, weak in nationalism but strong in socialism.

Here the combatants appear to be mainly the "rootless young", the fruits of the Soweto uprisings in 1976. Inside South Africa, however, the support base includes student activists and working class intellectuals such as trade unionists. It also includes other youth and protest bodies among the extra-parliamentary civic associations at the community level.

This has become the basis upon which the ANC has tried to build "alternative structures", especially in the black townships. It almost succeeded during the height of the emergency in 1984-1986, when its policy of making townships "ungovernable" and then replacing them with "people's committees" and other "alternative" structures became popular.

This was the recipe for communist, or rather bolshevist, successes in Russia in 1917. Trotsky emphasised the notion of "dual power", whereas Lenin had already demonstrated how effectively the bolsheviks gained power once the take-over was imminent. This was engineered through the preliminary setting-up of *soviets* or peoples' committees in all the large towns. As such the *soviets* operated as "counter-governments" before October 1917. This facilitated the take-over after 8 November, when the *soviets* finally took control. Up to that point, very little bloodshed had occurred (and only in two places, Petrograd and Moscow). However, after the take-over many lives were lost, first in the civil war (1918–1921) and then during Stalin's reign of terror.

In South Africa the state has succeeded in crushing this attempt at "counter-government", "dual power", "alternative structure" initiative.

The chance of "counter-government" succeeding has remained slim, the main reason being that it was never likely that "liberated zones" could be established to provide the territorial foundations of either *soviet* cells in the towns or guerrilla bases, as happened in China in Mao's revolution.

The chances of the establishment of liberated areas of guerrilla-controlled zones in South Africa are remote, if not entirely impossible.

The South African pattern and that of the rest of the continent suggest that Fanon's emphasis on the lumpenproletariat and the urban poor is somewhat exaggerated. It may have been useful in Algeria and in Kenya where the landless Kikuyu formed the backbone of the Mau Mau revolt, but there are strict limitations to the revolutionary potential of lumpen and urban poor. These limitations are well summarised by Sandbrook. He explains that the urban poor normally have "diffuse" family relationships with certain members in rural areas and others in the urban "establishment". This network makes them vulnerable and even unwilling to choose sides in the event of conflict. He also says that the urban poor are not really interested in alternative social and economic dispensations, because they are actually striving towards greater modernity; that they are too poorly organised for trade unionism; and that they have no strong tradition of ideological leadership. In South Africa they are too preoccupied with survival in the face of economic hardship on the one hand and with intimidation in the townships on the other.

Even the rural peasants in their own right present numerous obstacles to "peasant wars" in Africa. After analysing their potential, Welch concludes that peasants are too divided and too conservative, and have expectations too low to promote revolution. They cannot make guerrilla war a practical proposition. In the South African sense, guerrilla wars are even less likely. Unsuitable terrain, long distances, commando action, lack of support by farm-workers and so on make that remote, if not unthinkable.

If class analysis is dubious or inappropriate in explaining the rural support that guerrilla armies commanded, what then is a more appropriate explanation?

First, the importance of the "rootless young" should not be underestimated. They hardly represent a "class", however. The question of class cannot be rigidly cast in "either-or" terms, but should rather be understood as an alliance in forces, for example intellectuals combining with workers and peasants and in various permutations.

Secondly, the other force, apposite in rural areas among the "peasants", is the highly divisive ethnic factor. It has been demonstrated that Amilcar Cabral tried, almost in vain, to mobilise "class" support in the urban areas of Bissau from 1956, when PAIGC was formed, up to 1969: that is for thirteen years; but without much success. His support remained rural; therefore he switched his policy to mobilising the support of the tribal Balantas in the southern marsh-lands of Guiné-Bissau. That provided a solid rural basis of support from which he could effectively use his guerrilla forces against the Portuguese. By 1974 the war was almost won.

Portuguese Guinea was no exception. The ethnic factor, although divisive on a national scale as witness the unwillingness of the Fula to join the PAIGC became the force without which no revolutionary organisation could survive. Algeria, Angola, Mozambique and Zimbabwe offer similar lessons.

In Algeria this necessary cohesion was provided by the Berbers and Kabyles of the Aurés mountain areas east of Algiers. In Angola, Mozambique and Rhodesia the revolutionary movements actually split, ostensibly for ideological reasons, but also for reasons that any anthropologist can understand.

In Angola the split between the three main organisations, the FNLA, MPLA and Unita, followed ethnic lines with the Bakongo, Mbundu and Ovimbundu-Chokwe as their support bases in the rural regions. This problem still plagues Angolan unity. The civil war is being fought along these lines.

In Mozambique a similar pattern emerged with Frelimo enjoying the rural support of the Makonde and Nyanja, but not of the Makua, who, like the Fula, remained pro-Portuguese. In Rhodesia it was ZAPU that commanded the support of the Ndebele, while ZANU PF had the support of the Shona. But because the Shona do not constitute a single ethnic entity, tribally-based rivalries soon broke out. The Ndau supported Ndabaningi Sithole; the Manyika supported both Muzorewa and Herbert Chitepo, the ZANU war leader; the Karanga ironically supported both the Rhodesia army and the ZANU forces; and the Zezuru supported their own man, Robert Mugabe. That is still the situation today.

In South Africa it was common knowledge that the PAC (of the Sixties) had a predominantly Sotho support base as against the Xhosa-based support of the ANC. But this has now changed. Although most blacks in the ANC top structures still appear to be predominantly Xhosa, non-blacks are asserting themselves to an increasing degree. That may explain the ideological shift from blackness towards all-inclusive non-racialism and also the shift from nationalism to socialism. The aversion of the ANC to "group rights" may also be understood in this light.

It is interesting to note that some ethnic groups not only oppose one another within the revolutionary movements but that some have even decided in the past to side with colonial forces. As we have seen the Fula, the Makua, and to a lesser extent the Yao in Mozambique and the Karanga in Rhodesia did so.

In Guiné-Bissau, the Fula are Muslims, and the Portuguese often chartered flights to Mecca to fly their religious elders to the Arabian peninsula on the Hadj.

The lessons to be learnt from these examples are that African revolutions are often complex affairs not easily explained by conventional theories of revolution. The endemic nature of "factionalism", as Professor Henriksen calls this phenomenon, applies to Africa also. Ethnicity, not class, is the main force behind factionalism.

In addition to internal strife among revolutionary movements in Africa, as in Zimbabwe and even more in Angola, counter-insurgency techniques have had profound influences on the shaping of revolutionary strategies. That happened in the Portuguese colonies with their *aldeamentos* policies and in Rhodesia, where blacks were coopted into ruling government structures.

Revolutionary responses to counter-insurgency action are often played down by theorists, or even ignored as forces that have an effective impact upon the shaping of revolutionary doctrines and mobilisation strategies. A good example is the ANC in South Africa. After the first violence of the early Sixties, the treason trials and rigorous police action of the time, they were almost totally destroyed as a force. Then followed the Morogoro Conference in 1969, at which certain policies, "reactive" and "non-reactive", were formed in response to state action in South Africa. But it failed to make any real progress. Then came the labour strikes of 1973 and the Soweto riots of 1976, after which many "Soweto kids" fled into exile and joined the ANC. Then came the era when trade unionism, black local government and new constitutional reforms were being planned and executed in South Africa. As is well-known, blacks were excluded from the tricameral parliament. The result was the formation of the United Democratic Front (UDF) as a "protest movement" against these unacceptable reforms. Rightly or wrongly, the ANC claims fatherhood of the UDF.

Meanwhile an ANC delegation toured Third World Marxist states in 1978 to analyse the revolutions that had occurred there. By August 1979, the National Executive Committee of the ANC adopted a policy reminiscent of the Giap strategy of the Viet Minh and Viet Cong in Indo-China. The struggle then entered a new phase, partly dictated by state counter-insurgency measures and partly by a study of revolutionary experience elsewhere.

That brings us to the last factor singled out for special attention under the broad heading of subversion and organisation; which is the nature and degree of external support.

External support is one of the most underrated factors in the sustaining of protracted struggles and in the shaping of sanctuary and supply strategies. These in turn create external dependence patterns, quite often fatal to revolutionary and post-revolutionary aspirations, especially in the sense of being masters of their own destinies.

It is a serious problem; for not a single revolutionary movement in Africa has ever acted without external support. It began with the FLN–ALN in Algeria being dependent on Tunisian and Egyptian support. Tunisia offered sanctuary and supply routes, while Egypt supplied political and military help. Yet that was not a serious dependency problem, as these relations remained within Muslim and Arab worlds.

In the case of Guiné–Bissau, however, the function was performed by Senegal, marxist Guinea–Conakry and the Soviet Union, which supplied the weapons.

The same pattern existed in Southern Africa. Zambia and Tanzania acted as continental allies. The People's Republic of China and the USSR supplied the weapons. Black neighbouring states offered help with training camps, transit facilities and logistical support. Obviously the revolutionary movements would have found it very hard to sustain their efforts without such support. And since the decolonisation of Angola and Mozambique in 1974/5 took place, these two territories became useful springboards for infiltration into South West Africa and Rhodesia.

It is interesting that Zimbabwe has not been performing the same function in the case of South Africa, as many expected after the Lancaster House constitution was adopted in 1979 and put into operation in 1980. Zimbabwe is a reluctant liberator.

As we have seen, the USSR never became associated with either the Mau Mau in Kenya or the FLN in Algeria. Their first association with "national liberation" movements was their support of the MPLA in Angola and the PAIGC in Portuguese Guinea during the early sixties, despite earlier alliances between the SACP and the ANC.

Philip Nel, a sovietologist at Stellenbosch, explains that anti-colonial movements became linked with the Russian conception of promoting the "socialist world system" through the association of movements of "national liberation" with the fight against "capitalist imperialism". The SACP sees South Africa as a colony of a special type.

Lenin was the first to write about this association; but it was only after Professor Ivan Potekhin became the first Director of the (Soviet) Africa Institute in 1959 that it was translated into practical policy in Africa. Potekhin's grasp came too late for Russian association with the Mau Mau and the Algerian rebellions, but soon enough for intervention in the anti-colonial struggles in southern Africa.

It is now general knowledge that the Congo crises of the early sixties expedited Russian intercession in Africa. The USSR was then under the leadership of Khrushchev. Their implication became reality in 1961. After some blustering, the Russians under Brezhnev adopted a much more subtle policy during the Seventies, which included support for "vanguard" parties such as the MPLA, Frelimo, PAIGC, ZAPU, the Dergue, Swapo and the ANC. A greater degree of selectivity was implied since some were favoured and others excluded. That was the fate of the FNLA, Unita, ZANU (PF) and the PAC.

In Angola this selectivity was exercised at the expense of the FNLA (supported by the American CIA) and Unita (once supported by the People's Republic of China). In Rhodesia it was at the expense of Mugabe's ZANU (PF); and in the case of South Africa, at the expense of the PAC. The last two were to a varying degree supported by the People's Republic of China; but their support has diminished since the death of Mao Tse-tung in 1977.

The Chinese have always had an ideological preference for rural guerrilla wars, because of their own history. Mozambique, Angola, Guiné and Namibia became testing-grounds for that policy.

In Africa the Chinese competed with the Russians for the allegiance of Frelimo, PAIGC and Swapo. Ironically, ZANU (PF) was firmly in Chinese hands. Robert Mugabe, not surprisingly, once remarked that he was a Marxist-Leninist of Maoist persuasion. That annoyed the Russians. It was only after independence that they strengthened their relations with Zimbabwe. For the rest, the Russians were left unhindered.

Of the two great communist powers, the Russians were by far the more successful. They have the support of the Cubans and the East Germans. With the exception of ZANU (PF) in Zimbabwe, all the other Russian-supported "vanguard" parties came to power in Africa. An example is the Preliminary Military Administrative Council (PMAC) or Dergue in Amharic which transformed itself into a fully-fledged marxist party, the Workers' Party of Ethiopia in 1984, after seizing power in 1974. Meanwhile it established close ties with Moscow. Frelimo and the MPLA came to power in June and November 1976. Both had close ties with Moscow before then. Frelimo had also flirted with the Chinese. Even after independence Mozambique never formed very close ties with the Russians.

In Angola the Russians were fighting on different fronts: against the South African and American-backed Unita movement on the one hand, and against the South African and South West Africa Territory Forces fighting the Swapo guerrillas in Angola on the other. The obstinate resistance of Unita and strong South African fighting ability have sucked the Cubans deeper and deeper into the Angolan conflict. The Cubans failed to capture the Unita headquarters at Jamba. They also failed to capture South African positions at Mavinga in the offensive of late 1987. Moreover, the SADF won at Lomba and captured thousands of tonnes of enemy equipment at Cuito Cuanavale in early 1988. The result was that the dependence of both Swapo and the MPLA on the Russians has become still greater. Ironically, this also implied that these Soviet allies were left to the mercy of their masters when Mr Gorbachev started to co-operate with the Americans in the pursuit of peace in south western Africa in 1988.

Dependence on the USSR by Swapo and the MPLA is not the only example of its increase. It has also increased for ZANU (PF), the ANC and the Dergue in Ethiopia, especially since 1977, when the Russians intervened militarily in support of the struggle of the Dergue against the secessionist movements of Tigre and Eritrea and the irredentist and also secessionist movement in Ogaden.

The only examples of reduced dependence are the PAIGC and Frelimo: Moscow has not provided the Mozambicans with the same quality or quantity of counter-insurgency support in their fight against the National Resistance Movement of Mozambique (Renamo).

The lessons to be learnt from these examples of excessive external dependence are that revolutionary successes are no longer dependent solely on the "will-power" of the contestants but more and more on the strength of the external adversaries. That inevitably turns guerrilla wars into "conventional" wars.

No peasant warrior or rural guerrilla fighter, let alone an urban combatant, can endure that kind of violence. The price of insurrection simply becomes too high to pay. However, nationalists will always justify the cost as never too high for freedom. But what is now happening in Angola and in Mozambique, to a lesser extent, provides ample proof of how captive the dependent liberators in Africa have become.

## 4. Revolutionary Wars: Contests of Will rather than Trials of Strength

All African revolutions, with the exception of the Ethiopian insurrection and coup d'état in 1974, have been characterised by protracted guerrilla activities taking place simultaneously.

The average length of revolutionary guerrilla wars in Africa is, as we have seen, eighteen years. Ethiopia is not the only exception in which a revolution without a guerrilla war has taken place. South Africa is another.

The absence of guerrilla war, urban or rural, in South Africa is not due to want of trying on the part of the ANC–SACP alliance. As we have seen, the ANC had decided in August 1979 to wage an armed fight through its military wing, *Umkhonto we Sizwe* and through a "people's war" in South Africa itself. March 1985 was the launching date for that phase.

What the ANC had in mind was a guerrilla war, not a conventional war. It was supposed to be a continuation of the sabotage and bombing campaigns begun in 1961. Now, however, the revolutionary doctrines were fundamentally revised. The violence of the new phase was characterised by the "necklacing" of collaborators, some assassinations, and the detonation of limpet mines and car bombs in urban areas, especially limpet mines in civilian public places and car bombs intended to destroy the personnel and symbols of government authority, such as the car bombs in front of the SAAF HQ in Pretoria and the High Court in Johannesburg.

This phase began in 1984, and it was crushed within two years. A change of tactics was then considered in 1987. The ANC themselves denounced "necklacing" because of public indignation against this atrocity. Their other tactics, school boycotts and making black municipalities ungovernable, ran into difficulties too. Alternative structures, based on the Russian *soviets* of 1917, never materialised. Their main strength still lies in trade unionism. But even there the miners' strike incited by the NUM and Cosatu failed in part, because of pressures on the mineworkers themselves from their home countries (Malawi, Mozambique, Lesotho etc.) in need of miners' regular remittances. For the rest, protest in the townships has run out of steam.

That is largely because of the effectiveness of counter-insurgency measures by the state under the two sets of emergency regulations first proclaimed in 1985. The first apparent success of the "alternative structure" policy ground to a halt with the detention of large numbers of UDF leaders in South Africa; just as Mau Mau resistance became leaderless in Kenya after 1954.

The laying of mines on rural roads in the Transvaal has also been stopped largely by the blocking of infiltration routes through Mozambique, Swaziland and Botswana. A new method now appears to be "conventional" hit-and-run mortar attacks across the Limpopo. But even this tendency receded in 1988.

This might have heralded a new era of guerrilla warfare in South Africa; but so far the attempts have fizzled out. South Africa is not dealing with a fully-fledged guerrilla war, only with isolated incidents of violence more akin to terrorism than to warfare, and on a much lower scale, than, for instance, Northern Ireland.

The Algerian revolution was not a good example of fully-fledged guerrilla warfare either. The conflict there was too brutal, too atrocious. Yet to refer to the Berber and Kabyle *fellaghas* as "terrorists" and not as guerrilla fighters is not correct either. Their revolutionary strategies, including the geographical division of Algeria into operational zones, communication and recruitment policies and command structures, are all typical characteristics of guerrilla warfare, not of mere terrorism.

In one other important respect the Algerian and Ethiopian patterns differed from those in the rest of the continent, including South Africa; the absence of a protracted organisational phase before the outbreak of hostilities. Here the similarities between Algeria and Ethiopia end as far as organisational time-scales are concerned. In Ethiopia, the revolutionaries seized power immediately and quite effortlessly. But in Algeria it took a long and bitter struggle.

That set the example to those revolutionaries yet to come in Africa. Revolutions are more often than not trials of will rather than of strength. That is quite evident in the historical longevity of African revolutions: eighteen years for the average guerrilla war as opposed to five years for the political organisation phase. Fighting has always been a more laborious business than organisation. For example, the shortest period of fighting was that of the FLN-ALN rebellion in Algeria, which lasted only(!) eight years.

All the rest are ten years or longer. For example: Frelimo ten years, from 1964 to 1974; PAIGC eleven years, from 1963 to 1974; ZANU (PF) fourteen years, from 1966 to 1980; FNLA fourteen years, from 1961 to 1975 (and for them the struggle is not over yet); MPLA fourteen years, from 1961 to 1975 for them civil war replaced the revolution; ZAPU fifteen years, from 1965 to 1980 (for them the struggle has turned sour with Mugabe's intention to create a one-party state under ZANU (PF) rule): Unita twenty-two years, from 1966 to the present – first the anti-colonial revolution, then an internal civil war. Still unfinished business: Swapo, twenty-three years, from 1965 to the present, and prospects not improving; and finally, the PAC and the ANC from 1960 and 1961 to the present. For the PAC the prospects are dismal; and for the ANC the end is not in sight either.

Thus, despite the extraordinarily long life of revolutionary organisations in Africa, matched only by Mao's revolution in China (twenty-two years) and Giap's revolution of twenty-nine years, beginning in Indo-China in 1946 and ending in 1975 in Vietnam (contrasted with the rather short life of revolutionary movements in Latin America), the outcome in Africa is not guaranteed to go either the successful Chinese way, or with the exception of Cuba and Nicaragua, the unsuccessful South American way.

Counter-insurgency success or revolutionary defeat is therefore not without historical precedent. Most Latin-American and all colonial insurrections up to and including the Mau–Mau rebellion were defeated militarily. It is probable, however, that white morale was badly shaken by these events.

FNLA and Swapo may also be regarded as "defeated", although Swapo still continues to fight. The externalisation of their struggle with the support of Russians, Cubans, Angolans, and South Africans has converted this war from a contest of will to a trial of external strength. Unita and ZAPU have not tasted political success either but for different reasons.

The most successful of anti-colonial revolutionary organisations in Africa were probably the PAIGC, Frelimo and to a lesser extent ZANU (PF). Yet none of them, with the exception of PAIGC, achieved notable military successes.

As with the FLN in Algeria, "revolutionary success" means *political* rather than military success. In his book on counter-insurgency in Rhodesia, J. K. Cilliers emphasises the necessity of *political* legitimacy and the inherent limitations of violence in the ultimate outcome of counter-insurgency warfare.

Ironically, the only military and political success ever achieved by any rebels on the African continent was not the result of a revolution; it was the result of Museveni's civil war and seizure of power in Uganda in January 1986.

Many coups d'état in Africa are not included in our assessment because coups are takeovers, through unconstitutional means, by people who already occupy positions of power and authority in the military or civil government of the régime overthrown and therefore not guerrilla fighters who resisted the system from outside, as Museveni did.

The pattern of revolutionary wars in Africa therefore suggests that *successful* revolutionary organisation need not win decisive military victories to seize power. Revolutions in Africa differ from coups d'état, civil wars and conventional wars in which *military* victories are necessary.

There is yet another difference, however. Revolutions cannot "erupt" spontaneously; all revolutions are carefully planned and organised. "Surprise" is seldom an element in revolutions, whereas coups are characterised by the element of surprise.

With the advantage of hindsight we may say that guerrilla wars in Africa began with an increase in physical acts, such as violent assaults on life, limb and property and intimidation of the masses and the creation of fear among non-resisters.

Frelimo launched its campaign on 25 September 1964 by attacking an administrative station at Chai and murdering a Dutch missionary, Father Daniels, in the Cabo Delgado District of northern Mozambique. The consequence was *fear*. But it was not really a great surprise; it happened two years after the founding of Frelimo. Similarly Swapo began its first attacks on shops and farms in 1965 and 1966 in Ovambo and northern Namibia almost eight years after its formation. ZANU (PF) began its armed campaign in December 1972 (after abortive attempts in 1966) when it attacked farmhouses and trading stores nine years after its formation, and with the same consequences: not unexpected, but *fearsome* nevertheless.

The purpose of such violence is to frighten, to instil fear. As the title of the novel by Alistair MacLean reminds us, *Fear is the Key*.

With the exception of attempts at urban insurgency in Algeria (1957) and

South Africa (since the late Seventies), the other revolutionary situations in Africa were characterised mainly by an absence of urban warfare. The Algerian *fellaghas* thought they commanded adequate support in the *casbahs*; which was undoubtedly true. But from a tactical point of view street fighting in Algiers never worked effectively. The French simply outgunned them. The French thus demonstrated that a well-trained military force could contain urban violence. The FLN-ALN then retreated to the mountains south-east of Algiers, where they were much more successful in guerrilla warfare. Hence Fanon's obsession with "peasant insurrections".

Writing on the efficacy of urban terrorism, Walter Laqueur reminds us in a recent magazine article that it is easy to think of guerrilla movements that defeated the forces opposing them but "…it is difficult to remember more than a few cases in which terrorism had any lasting effect". It hardly causes disunity among the ranks of the rulers, without which "collapse" is unthinkable.

Africa, with its propensity for rural guerrilla wars, has become anathema to urban insurgencies. That was so until a resurgence of violence hit the South African towns from 1984 onwards. But by 1987 resistance was crushed. We shall say more about that later.

It is as well to remember J. J. McCuen's view expressed in his book *The Art of Counter-Revolutionary Warfare* of the error of trying to understand revolutions as distinct sequences or phases. For example, although the typical sequence is organisation – terror – guerrilla war; and conventional war, revolutionary conventional wars overlap guerrilla wars, and guerrilla wars again overlap terrorism and organisation. The only phase that stands alone is that of political organisation as we have described earlier.

However, since no African revolutions ever really entered a conventional phase – Nkomo's ZAPU tried it but failed – the "highest" stage of revolution in Africa has remained that of guerrilla warfare according to the McCuen model. This phase slots into that eighteen-year period we referred to earlier.

A guerrilla war need not result in military victory. It must be well led, well supported – both internally and externally – well organised and well justified ideologically to be able to sustain the necessary will-power. The ALN demonstrated that in Algeria, where they were well and truly beaten by the French in open combat. In guerrilla fighting, however, they always had inexhaustible resources of staying-power.

The Mau Mau uprising during the early fifties in Kenya was instructive for the lessons that they taught about guerrilla warfare in Africa. First, the Mau Mau was a Kikuyu-dominated peasant insurrection with a modicum of (Kikuyu) squatter support; too narrow an alliance to challenge the authorities seriously. Secondly, it capitalised almost exclusively on ethnic loyalties. That was too parochial an ideology to "grip the masses" of the entire nation. Thirdly, it was too poorly organised to succeed in mobilising revolutionary fervour. Fourthly, there were no intellectuals in its leadership. Fifthly, it was too spontaneous, concentrating almost entirely on grievances of landlessness without envisaging anything beyond that. And finally, they were "trained" only in terror tactics, not in guerrilla warfare. Moreover, they had no external supporters to teach them.

What then is an appropriate guerrilla strategy?

There are three kinds of guerrilla strategies. The first is the essentially Chinese variety of rural guerrilla warfare, derived mainly from the writings and experiences of Mao Tse-tung and Vo Nguyen Giap.

Mao emphasised the importance of rural bases: ("People are to the army what water is to fish"), from where the revolution progresses through the propaganda phase to the phase of (rural) mobile warfare entailing small fighting units (based on "liberated zones"), and finally to the conventional phase, when the large towns are encircled and the state collapses. Giap's strategy is essentially the same, except that rural bases should be run by "people's committees" as a kind of an "alternative structure". Vo Nguyen Giap put less emphasis on the encirclement of the towns.

The Maoist and Giapist strategies are timeless: very little urgency; and premised on the notion of "protracted people's wars". History has taught that these long wars are very difficult to win. In contrast to South America, where many revolutionaries believed in "instant action", African revolutionaries have the patience to endure and to persist.

The PAIGC in Guiné-Bissau came nearest to perfecting a Maoist strategy in Africa. Like Mao, Amilcar Cabral succeeded in establishing rural bases from the inception of PAIGC in 1956 until the war broke out in 1963. Cabral then began to concentrate on the urban areas in Guiné-Bissau. But the tactical switch was too early. The urban areas with their enfeebled urban classes could not withstand Portuguese counter-insurgency measures. Admitting his tactical error, Cabral reverted to the rural areas in 1969. From his bases in the south, and consolidating his support among the Balantas, he swiftly moved into a typically Maoist policy of mobile rural guerrilla warfare. By 1974, when the Caetano regime collapsed in Portugal, "liberated areas" already existed in Guiné-Bissau. The towns were encircled.

Frelimo, ZANU (PF) and Unita experimented with the Maoist model but to little avail. They all had rural bases, mobile units and, to a lesser extent ZANU (PF), had established liberated zones. However, none of them fought conventionally, and none of them offered any real threat to the towns. Places such as Beira, Lourenço Marques, Salisbury, Umtali, Sa de Bandeira and Lobito were always more or less safe. So has Windhoek always been.

Swapo in Namibia comes nearest to an application of typically Giapian strategy. Like Giap, Nujoma does not entertain the notion of encirclement. Not that Swapo has the ability to do so. Paradoxically Swapo was founded by urban migrant workers, but they never had a chance in the towns and are almost completely destroyed as a guerrilla force in Namibia. Their "last stand" is southern Angola, where they are mere spectators at the battles between the Angolans, Cubans and Russians on the one side and the Unita forces and South Africans on the other. Peace initiatives may, however, alter this.

The second kind of guerrilla strategy is the Latin American variety of rural guerrilla warfare. In contrast to the Chinese "people's wars", the South Americans, like Che Guevara and Regis Debray, were known for their impatience and insistence on "instant action". They did not believe in the creation of a revolutionary climate before beginning guerrilla activities. According to them, revolutions could be instigated instantly, the only real requirement being trained focal groups, or *focos* in Spanish.

In the end, Guevara was killed in Bolivia in 1967 and the French intellectual Debray was discredited because his brand of revolution failed so abysmally in South America. One explanation for the failure was that the rural guerrillas or *focos* operated in isolation from urban workers. There was a lesson in that; in so doing the guerrillas dissociated themselves from the urban workers in the factories and shanty-towns. They also underestimated the ruthlessness of South American military dictatorships in dealing swiftly with rural *focos* and with the handful of their urban comrades. In the end they were easily destroyed.

Conclusive weaknesses in their make-up were the lack of organisational strength on the one hand and the lack of any real external support on the other.

Given these factors (and lessons), the destruction of these insurrectional groups was inevitable. It was only a matter of time before a new type of guerrilla strategy developed.

The third kind of guerrilla strategy is entirely new and differs fundamentally from the first two in that it emphasises the concept of *urban* guerrilla warfare – almost a contradiction in terms. Like the second model, it originated in Latin America (where a rural-urban strategy had failed), where this new *urban* strategy came to be associated with the theories of the Brazilian communist Carlos Marighella. (Are there any communists who are peasants?)

Robin Corbett writes about him: "(He) saw insurgency in urban areas as the key to the promotion of revolution. The urban guerrilla should use methods such as murder, sabotage, bombing and kidnapping to ridicule and discredit the authorities, forcing them to adopt repressive measures that would alienate the population, create a socio-political crisis that would lead to the collapse of the government, thus opening the way for a seizure of power by the revolutionaries..."

Marighella's testing ground for his theory was Uruguay and his vanguards the Tupamaros (1963-1973). They were guided by his *Minimanual of the Urban Guerrilla* (written earlier, but published in 1974). The ideal model was Cuba, ironically not Castro, because Castro believed that "the city is a cemetry of revolutionaries and resources".

The essence of Marighella's theory (he was killed in 1969) was to force governments to adopt repressive measures, in other words to instigate antigovernment backlashes. The Tupamaros were intent on doing that in Montevideo, the capital of the then democratic state of Uruguay. Unlike the situations in Cuba and Bolivia, where revolutionary experience existed, the Tupamaros ignored the peasants and concentrated on recruiting well-educated *petite bourgeoisie*. This made sense up to a point, because the upper classes in Uruguay were very rich and notoriously corrupt. But fighting them and their government was not good enough. In the end the Tupamaros failed because they were unable to win the mass support of wide-ranging alliances of sympathisers. Instead the Tupamaros resorted to increased violence after 1972. That turned out to be counter-productive, and also because the then government ceased to operate on "democratic" lines and resorted to equally dirty tricks. Hugh Purcell in his *Revolutionary War: Guerrilla Warfare and Terrorism in our Time*, reminds us of this appalling irony: "By their (i.e. the Tupamaros') revolutionary action they contributed to the collapse of a democratic government which was prepared to be conciliatory and the pushing into power of a dictatorial government which was not."

Democracy has now returned, not through reforms, but after dissent was suppressed — another irony in the complex process of state and nation-building in the twentieth century.

By 1973 the Tupamaros were defeated, and their mentor, Carlos Marighella, who had earlier begun an urban terrorist campaign in his native Brazil, had been killed four years before in a battle with the police in São Paulo. But his legacy was not lost. The South African rebellion of 1984 to 1986 shows remarkable resemblances, the different outcomes notwithstanding.

Africa north of the Limpopo River never witnessed any experimentation with South American methods of guerrilla warfare, whether rural (e.g. Guevara) or urban (e.g. Marighella).

There are, however, remarkable similarities between the central thesis of Marighellian "provocation" tactics and some of the events in South Africa since 1984. That was when the "armed struggle" became so intense that it "provoked"(?) a state of emergency. Also, this latest phase actually began on 21 March 1985, the 25th anniversary of the Sharpeville shootings, when police opened fire and killed twenty people in Uitenhage. By the end of March, arsonists had burnt six schools in the area and black local authorities were on the way to becoming ungovernable. "Armed struggle"? "mass mobilisation"? "provocation"?

Be that as it may, Guevara's dictum that revolutions don't work in Africa has been proved wrong over and over again. The *political* success of the FLN, PAIGC, Frelimo, and to a lesser extent ZANU (PF), are cases in point.

The irony is that none of them, with the exception of the PAIGC in Guiné-Bissau, ever really won military success. The lesson is that revolutions can be won not on the battle ground but after protracted political *and* guerrilla fighting.

It is therefore not necessary for revolutionaries to proceed to the final stage of revolutionary warfare; conventional war. For oriental revolutionaries such as Mao and Giap, military success was important, but military victory itself was never contemplated by most Latin American and African revolutionaries. As we have seen, some African rebellions turned out to be successful revolutions. How?

In Africa revolutionaries are notoriously weak in conventional warfare. Modern warfare should not be confused with Mao's semi-modern "mobile" wars, in which the only requirement is that guerrilla units in the countryside should be as mobile as possible, on foot, not necessarily motorised.

Those insurgent forces that experimented with conventional weapons and fighting methods, such as ZAPU in Rhodesia and Swapo in Namibia, were outfought time and again by the security forces. Swapo has in fact retreated into southern Angola. But as we saw, that theatre of war is no longer guerrilla terrain. It has become the killing-fields of external adversaries who are locked in trials of strength, not in contests of will. Here revolutionary doctrines no longer apply. Diplomatic initiatives have introduced a new dynamic ... at least for the time being.

## 5. Revolutionary "Lessons" for South Africa

South Africa does not fall within the anti-colonial categories of either "primary" or "secondary" resistance, but within the more subtle permutations of the latter: the "take-over" rather than "resistance" categories. The lessons are therefore to be derived from the former. Hence the relevance of Algeria, Guiné-Bissau, Angola, Mozambique, Zimbabwe and Ethiopia. SACP theory places South Africa in this category.

At this point ANC theory differs. It sees South Africa as an independent state with an internal problem, economic and racial. But the complexity of the situation is compounded by the fact that South Africa cannot be equated with any other independent state that has had "similar" problems, such as Ethiopia. The greatest differences between South Africa and Ethiopia are, first, the feudal characteristics of Ethiopia as opposed to the modern industrial nature of South Africa; secondly, that Ethiopia had only a small educated élite and, paradoxically, it was from that class that the challenges to Haile Selassie's régime came. In South Africa, educated élites are found on either side of the revolutionary divide, which produces cross-cutting alliances in both blocs, something that was absent in Ethiopia; thirdly, revolutionary leadership in Ethiopia had some access to government before the takeover in 1974 - witness the fact that the takeover was a coup by army officers, unlike the situation in South Africa where "access to the régime" by the ANC, the SACP and the UDF is very low. In fact, it is so low that black politicians who benefited in some way or another from their "régime access" are regarded as traitors ("collaborators") and victimised for that reason; and finally in Ethiopia no protracted guerrilla war was fought that was preceded by long organisational and violent phases. There the revolution in fact "erupted", unlike the situation in South Africa where the history of revolutionary resistance goes back a long time, including the setting up of external support bases, which was not the case in Ethiopia.

Thus on closer inspection the situation in South Africa resembles, in an ironical way, not the Ethiopian experience but rather the historical experiences of anti-colonial African rebellions, despite the avowal by the ANC that South Africa is not "colonial". (The Russians apparently still maintain the theory that South Africa represents colonialism of "a special kind").

The crucial difference is that all African anti-colonial rebellions were *nationalist* resistances in the first place. In South Africa perhaps *only* the ANC, of those members of the revolutionary alliance, can legitimately claim that title. The rest is problematical: the SACP is hardly nationalist; it is explicitly Marxist-Leninist; whereas the UDF represents a motley collection of "protest" bodies, weak in organisation and divided in ideology, except in their commitment to the Freedom Charter, which is not very explicit either. Its professed "non-racialism" is anathema to nationalist ideologies and, judged by African experience, a feeble force. If nationalism, therefore, as revolutionary experiences elsewhere have taught, is the most effective force in forging cross-alliances, then the most legitimate claims to such symbols of nationalism must go to the forces opposing the ANC–SACP–UDF alliance.

But this ideological weakness of the revolutionary forces in South Africa is counter-balanced somewhat by another ideological phenomenon: the relative weakness of the state and its governmental apparatus in legitimacy. The notion of legitimacy must not be confused with legality or with power. It is "moral authority", which in practical reality means two things: firm government and support by the majority of the people. The first requirement is satisfied by the South African government. Even its strongest critics would admit that. But it falls short of the second. Whether its legitimacy falls shorter than that of the ANC–SACP–UDF alliance is open to debate. Be that as it may, it is one area where the South African government is seriously challenged by its revolutionary adversaries.

An obvious way out of this dilemma would be to get the *nationalists* on both sides of the revolutionary divides together, to agree on the nature of the contending ideologies, and then to *negotiate* a solution as an alternative to the revolutionary conflicts among the parties concerned. The problem with that proposition however, is *what* to negotiate about and *whether* it is feasible to negotiate about contending self-determinations. The commitment to "non-racialism" on the part of many serious contenders for power in South Africa, makes this option a non-starter, anyhow.

Ironically, some African revolutions ended at the conference table, notably Lancaster House in the case of Zimbabwe. But that was *not* negotiation. It was a way of concluding the procedures for the transfer of power. "Negotiation" obviously came too late. But negotiations can also be premature. Some commentators in South Africa have said recently that negotiating will not succeed in South Africa as long as the common belief exists that neither party has utilised all its power bases: the ANC–SACP–UDF alliance its putative legitimacy, and the South African government its existing force – militarily speaking – and other resources such as its industrial power base. The extra-parliamentary forces are essentially an alliance of disparate forces, whereas the ruling élites are more than that. Although somewhat pessimistic about the future, they remain cohesive and united in their resolve to survive.

Therein lie the crucial differences between South Africa and the rest of the continent where revolutions have taken place: in no case did revolutionaries succeed in seizing power from a government as well established on a military and industrial base as strong as that of South Africa. But there are yet other differences:

* Unlike Algeria, the Portuguese colonies and Rhodesia, whites in South Africa are not settlers or colonists, nor is the system colonialist. The revolutionary struggle in South Africa is therefore not anti-imperialist; at most it is anti-establishment. And the "establishment" in South Africa includes both whites and blacks. The labelling of some of them as "collaborators" reinforces this notion.

* The most effective anti-colonial ideology in Africa has always been nationalism. As we have argued, the ANC–SACP–UDF alliance may prove to be a mobilising strength, its weakness lies in its "non-nationalist" appeal. Ironically, PAC and Azapo have a more valid claim to the future than the alliance on those grounds.

* The ideological divisions between socialism and capitalism, between socialism and nationalism, between nationalism and non-racialism make black politics in South Africa, unlike the situations in Algeria, the Portuguese territories and Rhodesia, divisive.

* Despite all its democratic deficiencies, the tradition of liberalism is far more firmly rooted in South Africa than in any of the countries where revolutions have taken place in Africa. That may have paradoxical or unintended consequences. On the one hand, the tradition of liberalism allows of a freer press, freer associations, freer industrial conciliation systems and a much freer judiciary than in any of the quasi-totalitarian systems of Ethiopia and the Portuguese territories. But it offers effective opportunities for the regulation and reduction of conflict in both the state and private spheres. On the other hand, too strong a challenge by the revolutionaries may cause the withering away of such state-sponsored or state-permitted liberties as still exist since the introduction of the two states of emergency. What actually happened in Uruguay and other Latin American countries should serve as salutary reminders of the likelihood of such a situation. Revolutions in all Latin American countries, with the exception of Cuba and Nicaragua, were all defeated by state forces, not because they adopted liberal philosophies making them decently "legitimate", but totalitarian.

* Although deficient in legitimacy, the South African state remains remarkably efficient (though not necessarily cost-effective!) in most of its functions. Many efficient state structures are not altogether lacking in legitimacy or moral authority. Those capable of regulating conflict, such as the industrial conciliation system and judiciary, spring to mind.

* Despite all the (legitimate) rhetoric about the odiousness of apartheid, South Africa has made significant progress in the building of state and national structures to accommodate regional and ethnic variations

effectively. Continued patterns of domination and discrimination make it difficult for these structures to be fully appreciated as legitimate by those who see them as relics of the past.

* Finally, unlike the situations in Algeria, the Portuguese colonies, Rhodesia and Namibia, a full–scale (rural) guerrilla war, if only for logistical reasons, cannot be envisaged in South Africa. The SACP has no capability of war-making, and the UDF has no intention of using the tactics of guerrilla or conventional warfare. The danger of civil war, as opposed to revolutionary subversion, is therefore remote. The South African government has not, by a long chalk, lost control of the country. A very significant yardstick of the ability of the government to sustain itself through periods of crises is the question of retaining the confidence of civil servants. It fails to do so only when it fails hopelessly, especially economically. But that is decidedly not the case in South Africa. It is even more important for revolutionary success to win the loyalty of the armed forces. That was clearly illustrated in Portugal and Ethiopia, where the armed forces rebelled. Even in Algeria large numbers of Muslim soldiers in the French army deserted to the ALN. In South Africa, such situations belong to the realms of wishful fancy. The same applies to the loyalty of black volunteer soldiers in the SADF. That factor alone, however, significant as it is, will not remove the other factors favourable to revolutionary tendencies that have become historical forces in their own right.

These historical elements are not the only similarity between South Africa and the rest of revolutionary Africa. Others are:

* Organisations committed to revolutionary doctrines exist in both. A spontaneous and therefore weak revolt that could easily be suppressed is therefore out of the question. The duration of the struggle so far makes it unlikely that those who believe in "the struggle" or "people's war" will now call it off, unless they are ordered to do so by external supporters.

* The demonstration effect of what can be achieved *politically*, despite military defeat of the insurgents, serves as a reminder of the revolutionary experiences of Africa and what "lessons" they offer.

* Like revolutionary Africa, South Africa also has a distribution problem, i.e. the fair allocation of scarce resources such as power and wealth. These inequalities at the receiving end cause frustration among the have-nots which is easily translated into feelings of deprivation which, together with class antagonisms, provide ready-made causes for radicalism and revolt.

* Because of the clearly polarised "we" and "they" syndromes in South Africa, revolutionaries have very little "régime access" within the system; in fact, none at all. Thus, unlike Ethiopia, where revolutionaries were part of Haile Selassie's system before they overthrew him, and unlike the Rhodesian situation, where opportunities for discussion were created from time to time (such as the "Tiger", "Fearless" and "White Train" confabulations) very little of these opportunities exist in South Africa. Apart from its polarising effect on the body politic, it actually invites foreign intervention on the side of the anti–establishment forces. The enfeebled military position of the ANC and MK deepens their dependence on external allies such as the USSR, and perhaps also on the Americans under a post-Reagan government; would the interests of South Africa in the long run not be better served by talking to the Russians too? Have they not a more consistent foreign policy record than the US Congress, which makes

vigorous efforts to seize foreign policy from the White House and the administration? To thwart such American initiatives, South Africans would be well advised to produce a vision, resulting from negotiations, that went much farther than the promise of a return to the pre-revolutionary status quo ante. Not even a post-Reagan administration or an inconsistent Congress can ignore that. The challenge therefore, is to present an ideology that "grips the masses" to such an extent that it offers enough to all; an offer they can't refuse!

* Time is crucial; but in South Africa the moment for reconciliation has neither passed nor yet arrived. Like ideology, time can be created. But then it must be fully utilized. In this equation the military has only a minor, even though important, auxiliary part to play. The main role is that of the politicians, who must deal with the causes, not the consequences, of rebellion. Otherwise, the anti-insurgent war will sap so much energy that society will simply collapse under the stresses of a siege. Even the enfeebled LFA of the Mau Mau frightened settlers to the point where they at last came to terms with African aspirations. There is a lesson there.

Yet the experience of Algeria, Guiné, Angola, Mozambique and Zimbabwe vividly illustrated the limitations of violence, despite its attractiveness as a counter-insurgency technique. African counter-insurgency wars have yet to demonstrate that violence can swing the pendulum towards lasting peace and prosperity. It merely excruciates the inevitable. For the guerrilla fighter military victory is irrelevant. Setbacks are not defeats. It depends on the will to win. But in South Africa there is no guerrilla war yet. Solutions can therefore still be found without turning South Africa into another wasteland. That lesson should also be heeded by would-be guerrillas.

South Africa is not only the fatherland of the SADF and the anti-insurgent security establishment, it is also a place of *their* own. With Gorbachev apparently in a conciliatory vein, the options for peace have increased, not decreased. And with peace initiatives in south-western Africa on the upsurge, who knows what is in store for South Africa next?

## SOURCES QUOTED

Cabral, Amilcar. 1969. *Revolution in Guiné*. London, Monthly Review Press.

Cabral, Amilcar. 1973. *Return to the Source: Selected Speeches*. New York, Monthly Review Press.

Cilliers, J. K. 1985. *Counter-insurgency in Rhodesia*. Cape Town, David Philip.

Corbett, Robin. 1986. *Guerrilla Warfare: From 1939 to the Present Day*. London, Orbis.

Crummey, Donald (Ed). 1986 *Banditry, Rebellion and Social Protest in Africa*. London, Currey.

Davidson, Basil. 1978. *Africa in Modern History.* Harmondsworth, Penguin.

Fanon, Frantz. 1969. *Black Skins, White Masks: The Experiences of a Black Man in a White World.* New York, Grove Press.

Fanon, Frantz. 1968. *The Wretched of the Earth.* New York, Grove Press.

Freund, Bill. 1984. *The Making of Contemporary Africa.* London, Macmillan.

Greene, Thomas. 1984. *Comparative Revolutionary Movements.* 2nd ed. Englewood Cliffs, Prentice Hall.

Henriksen, Thomas H. 1978. "Lessons from Portugal's Counter-insurgency Operations in Africa", *Journal of the Royal United Services Institute for Defence Studies.* London, June 1978.

Laqueur, Walter (Ed.). 1974. *The Terrorism Reader: A Historical Anthology.* London, Wildwood.

Laqueur, Walter. 1987. "Reflections on Terrorism", *Dialogue,* Vol. 3, 1987.

Macridis, Roy C. 1986. *Contemporary Political Ideologies.* 3rd ed. Boston, Little Brown.

Marks, Shula. 1970. *Reluctant Rebellion.* London, Oxford.

Marighella, Carlos. 1974. "Minimanual of the Urban Guerrilla", in J. Kohl and J. Litt. Eds. *Urban Guerrilla Warfare in Latin America.* MIT Press.

Mazrui, Ali. A. 1986. *The Africans: A Triple Heritage.* London, BBC Publications.

McCuen, J. J. 1966. *The Art of Counter-Revolutionary Warfare.* London, Faber Faber.

Nel, Philip. 1987. *Die USSR en Suidelike Afrika: Aspekte van Beleid.* Stellenbosch, Instituut vir Sowjet-Studie.

Purcell, Hugh. 1980. *Revolutionary War: Guerrilla Warfare and Terrorism in Our Time.* London, Hamish Hamilton.

Sandbrook, R. 1977. "The political potential of African urban workers", *Canadian Journal of African Studies,* Vol. XI 3, 1977.

Welch, Claude. 1977. "Obstacles to Peasant War' in Africa", African Studies Review, Vol. XX (3), 1977.

Wheatcroft, Andrew. 1983. *The World Atlas of Revolutions.* London, Hamish Hamilton.

## OTHER SOURCES CONSULTED

Brinton, Crane. 1939. *The Anatomy of Revolution.* Englewood Cliffs, Prentice Hall.

Chaliand, Gerard. 1969. *Armed Struggle in Africa.* London.

Dostal, Elizabeth. 1986. *Revolutionary Strategy in South Africa.* Stellenbosch, Institute for Futures Research.

Grundy, Kenneth. 1971. *Guerrilla Struggle in Africa: An Analysis and Preview.* New York, Grossman.

Gurr, Ted. R. 1970. *Why Men Rebel.* Princeton, University Press.

Kotze, D.A. 1979 *Rewolusie in Swart Afrika,* Referaat tydens konferensie van die Afrika-Instituut, Pretoria, 1979.

Lodge, Tom. 1983. *Black Politics in South Africa since 1945.* Johannesburg, Ravan.

Maylam, Paul. 1986. *A History of the African People of South Africa.* Cape Town, David Philip.

Russel, D. E. H. 1974. *Rebellion, Revolution and Armed Force.* New York, Academic Press.

Thomashausen, André. 1983. "Experiences and parallels of political change in pre-revolutionary Portugal and South Africa", *South Africa International Quarterly*, April 1983, Johannesburg. S.A. Foundation.

Venter, Al J. 1973. *Portugal's War in Guiné-Bissau.* California Institute of Technology, Pasadena.

Venter, Al J. 1974 *The Zambezi Salient.* The Devin-Adair Company, Old Greenwich, Conn.

Woodward, Calvin. 1983. *Understanding Revolution in South Africa.* Kenwyn, Juta.

# THE VIEW FROM WASHINGTON - US POLICY TOWARDS SOUTH AFRICA

*by Simon Barber*

Many years ago, when (to paraphrase Joan Robinson) Africa was exchanging the misery of being exploited by capitalists for the misery of not being exploited, a British correspondent visited the capital of a fledgling state to observe what the winds of change had left in their wake. His first stop was the still impressive colonial pile that now housed the liberal administration. Inside, there was an air of profound and officious purpose. Morning–coated functionaries toiled importantly at the desks of their former oppressors. Each desk bore an array of telephones (proportionate to the user's rank) into which the official bellowed imperiously. Minions scurried about, efficiently filling the trays marked "in" and emptying those marked "out". In short, a scene of commendable bureaucratic industry. Independence had changed nothing except the faces of the men behind the desks. There was, however, one small discrepancy. The telephone had yet to be connected, and the papers, flowing so smoothly between the trays, were blank. Our correspondent ventured a deferential enquiry. He was told: "But is this not exactly how you people ran things?"

1. In a curious way, it *is* how the United States is running things, particularly (though by no means exclusively) with regard to South and southern Africa. Unprecedented quantities of energy are being devoted to the apparent end of overthrowing apartheid. Yet the means are almost totally unconnected to that end. In 1988, shareholder activists introduced a hundred resolutions at annual general meetings demanding that companies should restrict or sever their ties with South Africa. Dozens of states, cities and universities have sold their stock in companies tainted by South Africa. Some cities, including Los Angeles, San Francisco and New York, have refused to grant contracts to such companies. In one case, Miami, the refusal resulted in the temporary closure of the main sewage plant for want of a part that only a proscribed company could supply. Such behaviour has given rise to an industry that employs hundreds, if not thousands, to administer regulations, hunt down offenders, invent new expedients and proselytise the cause. In Washington, Congress has embarked on a similar pursuit. Scores of resolutions have been introduced to condemn Pretoria for whatever happens to be its current enormity. Highly–convoluted legislation to impose sanctions, coerce allies into following suit, and force out US companies, is weaving its way through the system as this is written, providing work for yet greater armies of administrators, legislative aides, lobbyists, lawyers, and activists, both professional and part–time. And what relation does all this bear to its alleged purpose? In reality, virtually none. Yet no one seems to care in the least.

The explanation is that what is happening here is happening in a sort of discrete universe, a political fourth dimension. In that dimension, the facts as they exist in the other three are of little consequence. It does not matter, for example, that driving out foreign companies will have the perverse effect of making the South African economy more, not less, autonomous, and in the particular case of oil companies it will succeed merely in endowing the government with such precious assets as oil refineries. It does not matter that restricting foreign investment and trade will strip black South Africans of the very tools... economic muscle and accelerated access to knowledge and skills... that are the necessary means of their genuine liberation. It does not matter that officially designating South Africa a "terrorist state", as some are pressing for, may sever whatever bonds still tie Pretoria to norms of Western decency and encourage it to become still more "terrorist". Congressman Howard Wolpe, Chairman of the Africa subcommittee of the House Foreign Affairs Committee is a conspicuous denizen of this strange, illogical universe. One of his favourite incantations is that America must be "consistent": if it applied sanctions to Poland, why not then to South Africa? To that end he demands that South Africa should be totally quarantined, even to the extent of cutting off aid to black South Africans on the grounds that such aid serves only to guild the apartheid cage. And yet, the Solidarity movement in Poland, the repression of which by the state Wolpe draws as a parallel, has expressly recognised that outside support designed to make the oppressed self-sufficient is essential to eroding the totalitarian power of the state.

On the surface, at least, there is a primitive quality in such obduracy. In their efforts to fight apartheid (for that at least is what they pretend to be doing) American policymakers and legislators resemble nothing so much as the Ashanti tribesmen of what is now Ghana. Faced with an irresistible British force, the Ashanti observed that the invaders strung copper wires between regularly placed poles. Believing that to be the cause of the invaders' superiority, they thought they could achieve the same result by stringing vines between trees. That it did not avert defeat they attributed not to the inherent weakness of their totems against breechloading rifles and modern logistics, but to the improper stringing of the vines. Their solution was more totems. So it is, though in an infinitely more complicated way, with late twentieth century Washington.

2. The Ashanti logically emulated. The American politicians and policymakers simulate; which is a more cynical process. The Ashanti had no reason to know better. Their American successors have: their make-believe, designed at one level to make their constituents believe they are taking their responsibilities seriously, is calculated.

Consider the following examples, both hot issues in the 1988 elections: drugs and trade. Each year, Americans spend more than the entire GNPs of many "developing" countries on intrinsically worthless weeds, powders and other chemical substances. The profits are so enormous that the illicit trade has helped to turn many inner cities into battle zones as gangs and dealers fight to maintain their share of the market with automatic weapons. Apart from the damage that the drugs wreak on their users, whole communities are being terrorised. This would be bad enough; but the communities endangered are generally the most depressed to begin with. The drug trade may enrich a handful of dealers, but it also has the effect of driving out whatever other economic activity there is. The tax base shrinks, schools (already demoralised by drugs) deteriorate, generations of poor people are doomed to stay that way. Meanwhile, American politicians do not even begin to have an answer. So, of course, they simulate one. The problem, they conclude, is not gargantuan domestic demand (consumers are "victims") but the foreigners who grow the coca leaves, the marijuana and the poppies to satisfy that demand. Foreign governments must therefore be made to stop the growers. If the governments do not cooperate, then sanctions will be applied. As one congressman yelled recently in the general direction of Peru,

Bolivia and Paraguay: "You want to talk about trade? You want to talk about bilateral loans. The hell with you... first we talk about drugs." The Senate even voted to cut off aid to Mexico. Yet at the same time it has refused to consider placing export controls on ether and acetone, necessary ingredients in the production of cocaine.

In the fourth dimension of politics, economic vitality is bad, especially for the out party. In mid-1988, the American economy had enjoyed five years of sustained growth. Early in the year unemployment reached its lowest point since the early Seventies. Millions of new jobs have been created. Investment, employment, industrial production and productivity have been increasing at rates two to three times faster than those of their main trading partners, budget deficit notwithstanding. It has thus become necessary for the out élites, primarily the Democratic Party, to simulate a crisis. One of the themes they have hit upon is that foreigners, made rich by their chronic trade surpluses with the US ("unfair competition"), are now exploiting the cheap dollar to buy up American land, corporations, even banks, and thereby threatening the very sovereignty of America. This quite deliberately misses the point that the foreign "invasion" is not only keeping the American economy boisterously afloat but is enabling the country to retool for a new industrial era with a minimum of dislocation... just as foreign capital and trade deficits helped to build America in the first place. Capital moves where it will be most amply rewarded and efficiently used, and unless the political Ashanti attempt to scare it off (forcing foreign investors to register and disclose their investment is one small pernicious example of how they might try), the trillion-dollar US economy will remain one of the most attractive destinations. Once arrived, who owns the capital does not much matter. Angry car workers may derive satisfaction from sledgehammering Honda motor cars (Ashanti-ism at its most sublime), but the fact is that Honda is becoming an American company and will eventually build more cars here than back home. That the owners live in Tokyo is almost immaterial; their plant and their assets are in Ohio, creating new wealth and business opportunity in depressed midwestern communities as much as in Japan. To find fault with that requires an alternative logic.

I have given these examples to illustrate how, on matters of central importance, American politicians have become divorced from the empirical world of cause and effect, creating in its place a discrete universe complete with its own language, axioms and internal logic. I have done this in part to reassure South African readers that the treatment they receive from Washington is not uniquely quixotic, but part of a broader pattern. More importantly, it seems to be the only way to begin to make sense of the twilight zone that is US policy towards South and southern Africa. But before venturing into that zone, let's take a cold look at what the region really means to America.

3. For all the prodigious quantities of ink expended in the attempt to elucidate America for South Africans and vice versa, one fundamental point has largely been overlooked. It is this: if tomorrow, the African National Congress were to seize the *Tuynhuys* and turn out to be every bit as vicious as South African propaganda has predicted, it will not have the slightest impact on the continued pursuit of happiness in the United States. South Africa is simply not part of the global web of economic and political relationships upon which American security and prosperity depend. As a result it may be sacrificed on whatever demagogic altar the American Congress and administration may at any given moment find expedient. The old arguments about sea lanes, strategic minerals

and the threat of Russian imperialism have ceased to apply, overridden by technology, economic reality and the growing pathologies of Soviet socialism. If Gorbachev or his successors want Africa, they can have it. The game of nations is no longer about real estate; and besides, in most of southern Africa there are no nations, only cartographic fictions. The subcontinent is returning to the middle ages. There is very little chance, and in Washington no pressing concern, that the slide can be reversed within any significant political timespan. Africa south of the Sahara does not matter here. It is so far at the bottom of all serious priority lists that it is the one part of the earth in which the Reverend Jesse Jackson can be given free rein. It, like Jackson, is out of the loop.

Satellites and nuclear navies have made assets like Simonstown and Silvermine superfluous. Intercontinental missiles and more "conventional" forms of mass destruction have made a protracted war like the last one so unlikely that the contingencies of such a conflict have ceased to be a factor in daily policy planning. That is one reason why successive administrations have paid little more than lip service to a broad minerals policy. There is no urgent need. Besides, mere commonsense asserts that whatever government controls the Reef and Richards Bay will continue to mine and market South African minerals. But even if South Africa were suddenly to disappear into the sea, the disruptions would still be bearable. The US Bureau of Mines has calculated the cost of a total five-year embargo on South African chromium, manganese, titanium, vanadium and platinum-group metals, plus Zaïrean cobalt shipped through South Africa, and it is not excessive: US$9.25 billion, rather less than the B-1 bomber programme and a drop in the ocean of a trillion-dollar economy. Such a price would not be without reward, incidentally, as entrepreneurs rushed in to fill the void with alternative sources, materials and technologies.

Assume, for the sake of argument, that East-West rivalry is not undergoing the substantial transformation that now appears to be occurring, and that, contrary to Gorbachev's assertions, the Kremlin remains ready to take the risks and foot the not inconsiderable bills of Brezhnev's ambition to seize the "treasure house". Even then, I would argue, the United States would not be prepared to challenge it. The global commitments of America are already under heavy siege from a petulant, neo-isolationist Congress, to the point where even the scale of its membership of NATO is being seriously questioned. And thanks to the power of incumbency and what can only be described as the widespread gerrymandering of congressional districts by the Democratic Party, which holds an overwhelming majority in the House of Representatives, the siege will not foreseeably be lifted. To put it in another way: if Washington can barely bring itself to confront the creation of a second Cuba in Nicaragua, it is inconceivable that it would actively oppose the Angolanisation of, say, Zaïre, much less of South Africa.

Every indication, however, is that this is no longer part of Moscow's gameplan. Russian spokesmen have repeatedly insisted that they now see Africa as a prospect no better for cloning into their own brand of socialism than it is for becoming a series of humane Jeffersonian democracies. The effort and expense are too great, the existing failures too devastating an advertisement of the failures of Marxist ideology, the prize too trifling. Whatever geopolitical advantage might accrue to the Kremlin from turning the continent into its zone of influence is offset by the indifference of America. Power is not very useful if it does not grab enough of your adversary's attention to force concessions. In any event, Gorbachev has clearly decided that concessions are much more efficiently achieved by lowering the Russian profile in Africa, and the Third World generally, not raising it. The long-term survival of the Soviet nomenclature demands that the nomenclaturists shall fulfil the material promises of the revolution at home rather than expand the reach of the Russian ruling class abroad. If retrenching backward dependants can earn the Soviet Union access to desperately needed Western technology and flows of capital, then let the retrenchment begin where it matters least and where there is least chance of the West leaping in to claim victory: Africa.

By its actions, if not yet by its rhetoric, the United States is making it clear that it sees no significant role for the southern part of the continent for at least a generation. Once the superpower dimension is removed (and it is the only aspect of the continent capable of keeping American policymakers interested in any consistent way) the place can be left to rot. A little aid may be dispensed now and then as a genuflection to economic development. But the recipients will essentially have been written off. The true tendency was expressed, if in somewhat more high-minded terms, by the then Assistant Secretary of Defence for International Affairs, Noel Koch, in 1985. "We must not, in a fit of philanthropic fervour, seek to do more good for Africa than she can bear; we must not, in a rash miscalculation of the Soviet threat to US interests in Africa, over-react to that apparent threat, or doubt the capacity of Africans at length to deal with it themselves… In the end, the Western democracies will prevail there by the force of our values, by helping where help is needed and asked for, and by otherwise stepping back and letting Africa find her own destiny.

Which she will surely do, whatever policy we here may set, and however we may construe our interests there." In other words, the continent is not worth the trouble, leave it alone.

4. Leaving it alone, through default, neglect or conscious abandonment, is how I believe US policy towards sub-Saharan Africa will resolve itself over the next decade or so. But I am speaking here in real terms. In the Ashanti terms of American policy-making, the picture will appear rather different. To the credulous observer who cannot tell the difference between reality and the twilight zone, it may well look as though Washington is obsessed with the continent, especially the southern bit. The truth, however, is that even now as Congress cranks up for another round of South African sanctions, the subject is anything but South Africa. Because they do not intrinsically matter, South Africa and its neighbours are a pawn in a quite different game. Welcome back to the fourth dimension.

As far as the vast majority of this country is concerned, South Africa, like much of the rest of the world, is an abstraction. A good analogy might be the shadows dancing on the wall of Plato's cave. Few Americans, and fewer still of their politicians, have any concrete notion of what is going on down there in the cave. All they see, and dimly see at that, are silhouettes which they interpret like daydreamers inventing faces in a cloudy sky. In essence, they see the South Africa that they want to see, the South Africa that best serves their agendas and fulfils their prejudices nearer home. Most black Americans, not unnaturally, see a reflection of their own historical sufferings and are justifiably angered. Less justifiably, many of their leaders take the interpretation several steps farther in an attempt to turn the anger to political advantage. They are joined by the left generally: from the soft, unconscious historicists who believe that in any situation like the one they see as existing in South Africa, revolution is inevitable and therefore must not be hindered if America is not going to "get on the wrong side of history"; to the harder, more statist, variants who see South Africa as an epic conflict between "the people" (i.e. themselves) and capital whose existence in hands other than their own bars them from the power that they regard as justly theirs. For most, South Africa is the means to a quite separate end.

To that end, they have created the myth that it is in large measure the Reagan administration, especially since it is largely white and Republican, that is to blame for the horror that the shadows represent. Since the administration quite obviously is not responsible for the creation of apartheid, it must be made responsible for its persistence. This has necessitated the creation of a second myth: that the government could, if it so pleased, end apartheid within a political timespan of (say) two or four, or at the outside, eight years, and then only if it chose to adopt the one policy that no responsible government, in rather fuller possession of the facts, would readily adopt. Which pinions the administration beautifully. Reason asserts that it cannot concede to the myth, but the myth, based as it is on an invincible abstraction, is so powerful that the administration will be damned as racist until it does.

It is for that reason that the opponents of the administration will not tolerate discussion of any approach to South Africa other than sanctions: sanctions are the one measure that the administration will not take, thus proving, under the rigorous terms of the dialectical mythology, that it is succouring apartheid. South Africa, the real place, facing the real nightmare, is of no consequence here. What matters is the apportionment of political power in America. In that struggle, the only question is whether to apply sanctions. They are the subject and they alone. Indeed, I would go so far as to say that if the administration did accede to sanctions (as, indeed, in limited form it did in 1985), its opponents would immediately impose another set of demands that it either could not or would not meet. In fact, that is already happening. The sanctions enacted in 1986 were promptly deemed insufficient, and Congress is now being asked to pile on more. The next step, which I shall describe in more detail later, is to demand that South Africa should be declared a "terrorist state" and placed in the official company of Libya and North Korea.

After simmering gently for a generation, sanctions against South Africa first became a high-priority item on the agenda in November 1984, when a coalition led by Randall Robinson, director of TransAfrica, then a little-known lobbying organisation focusing on matters of black foreign policy, held the first of a series of daily demonstrations outside the South African embassy in Washington. You can argue that the deteriorating situation in South Africa itself, especially as replayed on American news broadcasts every evening, was the cause. That is certainly how it looked. But in that case, why was there not a similar outpouring in 1976, at the time of the Soweto uprising? Why did not Jimmy Carter, then a presidential candidate claiming to be a passionate defender of human rights, espouse sanctions of the severity now fashionable and chastise the Ford administration for failing to take a firmer stand? Why, after his election, did the Democrat-controlled Congress not leap into the fray? Why were there no daily demonstrations outside the embassy then? Surely the crushing of the Soweto riots was just as inflammatory as what happened eight years later? The answer is simple enough. In Carter, black leaders and their progressive allies saw a candidate and then a president receptive to their broader interests. It was enough that he agreed to support a mandatory arms embargo in the US, modestly tightening up a policy that was already in existence. He did not have to be pinioned. In 1984, the circumstances were quite different. Reagan, the ideological enemy whose simple belief in a colour-blind society challenged the very foundations of the power of the established black leadership, was re-elected in a landslide and with scarcely a black vote. A new weapon was needed. And since the American electorate appeared more than happy with the way Reagan was handling their affairs domestically, something else had to be found for which his administration would be blamed and to which it would be impotent to reply. South Africa was the peg. Sanctions were the issue.

It was a stroke of genius. A whole new brand of motherhood had been invented. Even a few conservative Republicans, recognising a cheap and easy way to atone for their oppositon to the other mainstays of the civil-rights agenda ... school busing, for example, welfare expenditure and racial hiring quotas ... rallied to the banner. By September 1985, Reagan was obliged to sign an executive order banning Krugerrands and restricting loans and sales of computers to South Africa. Of course, it was not enough. As I have argued, nothing could have been enough. Enough is not the point. So, in 1986, came the Comprehensive Anti-Apartheid Act, comprising the broadest sanctions that any large industrial nation had ever imposed on South Africa. It, too, was insufficient, but that was the intention. Indeed, a historian may one day look back and say that if the CAAA had a purpose outside the Washington fourth dimension, it was to produce a set of responses in South Africa perverse enough to keep the ideological weapon primed and cocked.

5. By mid-1988, the Democrat-controlled Congress was performing a liturgy whose purpose was to give birth to the Anti-Apartheid Act Amendments of 1988. Note that the CAAA had now become simply the Anti-Apartheid Act. The new legislation was designed to restore the "comprehensive" by means of a "total" trade embargo that exempted strategic minerals representing between 70 and 80 per cent of US exports from South Africa, and also permitted American farmers to continue selling grain and other foodstuffs to the "apartheid régime" (as it is called in the standard incantation). After approving the bill, the House Foreign Affairs Committee issued, as per standard practice, a report setting out the official interpretation of what it meant. You may find it strange that a congressional committee should only decide what its actions mean after it has acted; but remember, we are dealing with another non-Newtonian dimension here. The report itself was stranger still. For example, it stated that in the event of a nuclear accident (say, one of the reactors at Koeberg designed by Westinghouse begins spewing contaminated steam into the Western Cape) the US would be barred from providing technical help even for "humanitarian and public safety" reasons. The grounds for this draconian prohibition were that to allow otherwise would be "inconsistent with comprehensive sanctions", even sanctions so "comprehensive" that they left most trade untouched. Elsewhere in the report, it was stated that one of the prime purposes of the legislation was to "act as a depressant on South African business confidence and its own willingness to invest". Another purpose expressly stated was to require departing American companies to transfer their assets and operations to the ownership or beneficial control of black employees or their unions. Exactly how beneficial such control could be in the economic climate that the bill purported to create was a question, like the contradiction between suffering and a loving God, that only the priestly classes might answer.

It is as a priestly class that Congressman Wolpe and his brethren in sanctions, who include Congressman Ron Dellums and Senator Edward Kennedy, may best be understood. Their thinking is utterly unrelated to the material world. The connection between the methods that they preach (with the encouragement, it must be said of more orthodox priests such as Archbishop Desmond Tutu and the Reverend Allan Boesak) and the outcome that they profess to seek can only be achieved by a leap of faith and the suppression of concrete evidence. To put it another way, no one outside the political fourth dimension has yet been able to establish through what conceivable mechanism the Anti–Apartheid Amendments Act can be translated into a genuinely democratic South Africa. Indeed, in the purely ceremonial hearing that Wolpe foisted on the legislation, only one serious analytical attempt was made; though serious may not be quite the word, in view of what the analyst, one Roger Riddell of the London–based Overseas Development Institute, finally came up with. "Will sanctions have a positive... effect in achieving the political objectives sought?" he asked after half an hour of explaining the economic vulnerability of South Africa. In his view, yes. Why? "There has been no conclusive evidence over the past few years that the alternative strategy of constructive engagement or dialogue with Pretoria has led to change in the intended direction. Indeed, there is evidence to suggest quite the opposite. For instance, as President Reagan observed in his... statement to Congress (on the first anniversary of the CAAA), "I regret I am unable to report significant progress leading to the end of apartheid and the establishment of a non–racial democracy in South Africa". In other words, gentlemen, the Reagan adminstration has been stringing too weak a strain of vine between your trees. The logical solution to your problem is not to doubt the effectuality of vine-stringing, but to try a more magically potent species.

Now you might think that with the benefit of a modern education (though Kennedy had to take some short-cuts at Harvard, for which he was expelled, and Wolpe only managed to get a teaching job at the less ivy-clad University of Western Michigan), the sanctioneers would be able to approach the question a little more rationally than the Ashanti or those bureaucrats bawling down silent telephones. And you would be right. They are fully aware that objectionable truths may occasionally stray into their hieratic envelope. Such truths they take pains to suppress, much as the Inquisition sought to suppress doctrines that threatened its own secular power. Wolpe's hearings were full of dangerous contagions, none more so than James Ncgoya, President of the South Africa Bus and Taxi Association. "We and thousands like us are trying our best every day to build a future for ourselves and our children and our nations," pleaded this visitor from flesh-and-blood, three–dimensional Soweto. "We ask for understanding and assistance ... we have struggled more than you can know. We have gone too far to turn back. Do not take from our hands the tools of liberation we have forged at such a price." Wolpe ensured that like a tree falling in the midst of an uninhabited forest Ncgoya made no sound. His testimony, like all that critical of the bill (including a letter from the Botswanan ambassador) was headed straight for the memory hole.

Kennedy's defence against unpleasant intrusion has been more active. In October 1987, with his *soi-disant* Republican sidekick, Senator Lowell Weicker, the senior senator from Massachusetts asked the General Accounting Office, a government research agency, to prepare a study examining, among other things, "the status of US disinvestment and how it has been implemented and US dependence on South African strategic minerals". The GAO sent a team to South Africa as part of its research. The team interviewed a broad array of those whose liberation Kennedy purports to desire. Many said they had grave reservations about the senator's approach. Unfortunately, as the director of the project, Steven

Sternlieb, later admitted to me, "black opinion was not part of the brief". Kennedy had intended from the start to submit the GAO report in support of new sanctions and had deliberately drafted the terms of reference to ensure that no heretic could be heard. His office also said that it had no objection if the GAO refrained from answering the strategic minerals question until the end of 1988, by which time Congress would have dealt with the legislation and would be in no further need of advice.

Even so, there are moments when even the most zealous defender of his faith must begin to choke on his own contradictions. For a long time it has been one of the most cherished versicles of the sanctioneers' litany that their policies if fully put into effect, would bring apartheid to its knees almost instantaneously. The shamans of the Commonwealth Eminent Persons Group opined in 1985 that their prescription "offered the last opportunity to avert what could be the worst bloodbath since the second world war". Three years later, the House Foreign Affairs Committee offered precisely the same view, citing Their Eminences in support. This is a fairly extended last chance, not unakin to the last chance that President Reagan has consistently been brandishing at General Manuel Noriega of Panama. Indeed, the clock appears to have stuck at thirty seconds or so before midnight, to the point where one wonders whether the priesthood in question does not quietly yearn for a bloodbath to authenticate its orthodoxy. In the mean time, it has decided to emend its theology. Sanctions, even of the most stringent kind, were now a "medium-to-long term" proposition, concluded the Foreign Affairs Committee in its report. Their success would be "at the margin". Consider the logic: this is the last chance to avoid *götterdämmerung*, so we must resort to a *marginal expedient.*

6. On June 12, 1988, Democratic Party functionaries wrapped up work on the draft of the election platform that would be debated at the nominating convention in Atlanta in July, and upon which the nominee, Michael Dukakis, the Governor of Massachusetts, would be obliged to run in the general election. The party had lost the two previous presidential elections by landslide margins mainly because on each occasion its candidate had appeared to have been pulled left by the noisy activists who tend to dominate conventions and the platform. The theory was that the platform should be seen to unify the party. The recent practice, however, has been to use it to console its more radical elements whose candidate has been defeated in the primaries. As in 1984, the defeated candidate on this occasion was the Reverend Jesse Jackson, whose political vision appealed exclusively to electoral minorities, one racial and the other, somewhat overlapping, comprising those whom the economic resurgence of the past five years had left behind. Platforms, on the whole, are meaningless documents, torn up no sooner than a candidate is elected and confronted with the realities of actual government. They rarely do a candidate much good (that he must do for himself) but they can do him harm if they provide ammunition for his opponent. Dukakis's negotiators therefore had to ensure that Jackson's less electable propositions (slashing defence, raising taxes and devoting the proceeds to great new layers of welfare bureaucracy) did not make their way too obviously into the document. For that they had to pay a price.

Two months earlier, the State Department issued a report on the plight of Mozambican refugees. Prepared by a refugee expert with impeccable neo-conservative associations, the report painted the Mozambican National Resistance as an African incarnation of the Cambodian Khmer Rouge. The purposes, besides documenting an authentic horror, were several: to silence conservative demands that Renamo should be officially accorded "freedom fighter" status under the Reagan Doctrine, to prod Pretoria into reaffirming its commitment to the Nkomati Accord, to demonstrate solidarity with Mozambique at a time when negotiations with Angola were reaching a critical phase, and to persuade Congress to drop its quixotic restrictions on aid, military and economic, to the government in Maputo. Logically, Jackson could have had no complaint with any of these goals and should have had nothing but praise for the State Department when he paid a visit shortly after publication of the report. But this is politics, not logic.

Jackson regards southern Africa, indeed the entire continent south of the Sahara, as his sphere, an area in which he is the moral leader of America or, to put it more bluntly, from which he derives the right to blackmail anybody if it suits his purpose. He toured the continent in 1986 with a vast heavyweight–champion-style entourage, and luxuriated in the flattering audiences he was granted by Nyerere, Kaunda and other presidents. South Africa, however, was the great prize, the issue in the headlines, and there he was stymied. Other black leaders with competing credentials, principally Coretta Scott King, the widow of the civil-rights martyr, were making the play, as were the Congressional Black Caucus and Randall Robinson of TransAfrica, the acknowledged driving forces behind the 1986 Comprehensive Anti–Apartheid Act. It even looked as though Mrs King, never a fan of Jackson since he lied about her husband dying in his arms, might be winning a mediator's role when she and President P.W. Botha agreed to meet at the time of Archbishop Desmond Tutu's enthronement. Although the meeting never came off – Mrs King was dissuaded by Tutu and others – Jackson was deeply resentful. It even irked him, as he made clear to the then South African Ambassador to the USA, Herbert Beukes, that Pretoria had given Mrs King a more liberal visa for her trip than it was prepared to grant him. In 1988, as the Black Caucus and their allies cranked up for a new sanctions bill, the preacher was once again left in a me-too position. He may have been the most successful black presidential candidate in history, but he was not being allowed to dominate the prime black foreign-policy question. Then the Mozambique report appeared.

Jackson seized upon the findings, with their implication that South Africa was ultimately to blame for the attempts at genocide by the MNR, to demand that South Africa should be declared a "terrorist state". In his own mind, he thought he was considerably raising the sanctions ante, putting himself in his rightful place at the front of the debate. Ironically, he was in fact achieving rather the opposite, although few noticed it at the time. If a president formally declared a nation "terrorist", the maximum sanctions he may then impose are scarcely more restrictive than those already existing against South Africa under the Comprehensive Anti–Apartheid Act and earlier expedients such as the arms embargo. This, as far as is known, was not Jackson's intention. To judge from his advisers, he apparently believed that the designation would immediately bring down upon South Africa the total quarantine in force on North Korea and Cuba, two other members of the terrorist list.

But there was an added twist: to declare South Africa "terrorist" would mean expanding the *de facto* definition that generally applied only to those countries implicated in acts that endanger American lives or property. That narrow definition enabled Dr Crocker, no friend of sanctions, to deliver a personal warning to Ambassador Piet Koornhof after the murder of Dulcie September in Paris that if South Africa was implicated in a similar incident in the US, it would be placed on the list. There is a reason why the definition is narrow. Expand it, in the manner that Jackson wanted, and it logically begins to cover Israel, which conducts regular cross-border raids in Lebanon, uses surrogate forces, and in 1988 assassinated the PLO leader Abu Jahid in Tunis; tactics strikingly similar to those employed by South Africa.

Studying his demands, the Dukakis camp quickly concluded that South Africa was the issue to concede, the price to pay, the Israeli problem notwithstanding. They offered a compromise, agreeing to insert language in the platform supporting comprehensive sanctions "similar" to those imposed on the terrorist states of Libya, North Korea and Iran. Even though in reality that would have been stronger, Jackson wouldn't have it. The plank had to be his, and his alone, a demonstration that he, no one else, spoke for the party on South Africa. For their part the Dukakis negotiators did not press it. They knew that whatever the platform said about South Africa, however wild the formulation, it was the one question that the Republican candidate, Vice President George Bush, would never raise against them in the campaign. In the dialectics of contemporary American politics, righteousness lies with him who demands the toughest sanctions. For Bush to criticise it would lay him open to a charge of racism.

The following week Jackson himself all but admitted what was going on here. "The focus on ... South Africa," he said, "ratifies my leadership." Precisely. Jackson and his own power were the issue, not South Africa. South Africa was a means, not the end. But observe more closely the manner in which South Africa was used. By calling for it to be designated a "terrorist state", Jackson was making a demand that Dukakis, if elected, would be unable to meet because of the Israeli implication. The candidate had already evaded the simple sanctions trap by saying, repeatedly but insincerely, that he favoured them. So Jackson had to raise the bidding. Now it is unlikely that Dukakis, as president, will be as pertinaciously hounded on sanctions as the Reagan administration was ... for the same reason that Carter was not confronted on the same issue. So what Jackson has done instead is lay the groundwork for a shakedown. If Dukakis takes office in 1989, he will very probably try to forget the South African plank. Jackson will be able to demand a price for letting him forget it.

Lest such cynicism should seem implausible, consider that during the Senate debate on the Comprehensive Anti-Apartheid Act in 1986, Senator Paul Simon, who later became chairman of the Africa subcommittee of the Senate Foreign Relations Committee, offered an amendment to ban South African fluorspar. As it happens, the United States imports precious little of that commodity from South Africa, but that was not Simon's immediate concern. His own state, Illinois, has the only fluorspar mine in the USA and its business was not thriving. Simon proposed the measure so that he could lie to the employees of the mine that he was protecting their jobs. He even uttered the lie on the Senate floor, proclaiming the virtues of saving American jobs in the fight against apartheid. Forty-seven senators voted with him. Or consider a bill to ban South African diamonds proposed by Congressman Mervyn Dymally, in 1988 the chairman of the Congressional Black Caucus. Given the way the world diamond market operates, such a measure would be almost impossible to put into effect without smashing the De Beers Central Selling Organisation, which would in turn cause great hardship for other African diamond producers such as Botswana, and to cutters and polishers in India, Israel and Antwerp. Nonetheless, it was Dymally's express intent to break De Beers, something that even he knew probably could not be done. What was behind this? It turns out that Dymally is a close personal friend of President Mobutu of Zaïre, who has long chafed against the CSO. This friendship is a strange one, given the strong antipathy of the Black Caucus to Mobutu; but it is also a source of patronage for its chairman: with the right contacts, there are plenty of business opportunities in Zaïre. Dymally wanted his friend to think he was being done a favour. Finally, there is the case of Congressman Mickey Leland's bill to bar South African mining houses from investing in the US. Leland introduced the legislation as a favour to a law firm in this district that was representing Newmont Mining in its fight against a hostile takeover bid by Consolidated Gold Fields. Having inspired the measure, the law firm then publicly praised the "author" in an article published in the *Journal of Commerce*. The piece was entitled "Fighting Apartheid Sensibly". Cravenly, rather.

7. Now of course there is a very concrete connection between what is going on in Congress or the Democratic Party and the real world beyond. For as the report by the Foreign Affairs Committee that we discussed earlier states, "The preponderance of those whom blacks have indicated they regard as representative political and economic leaders are currently calling for comprehensive international economic sanctions including disinvestment." There follows a list: Cosatu, NACTU, the UDF, Azapo, the ANC, the PAC, the South African Council of Churches, Archbishop Tutu and the Reverend Boesak. How then can it be argued that the sanctions "debate" is fraudulent? However domestic the underlying motivations, however irrational and unconnected to the realities of apartheid, surely the fact that the people on whose nominal behalf the legislation is to be passed say they want it gives it a certain legitimacy.

Yes, I must confess it would, but only on two assumptions. First that the organisations and individuals cited fully represented the views of their constituents, which even flagrantly biased surveys like that prepared by Mark Orkin in 1987 suggest may not be the case. And second, that Wolpe, or Kennedy, or the Congressional Black Caucus, had stopped for one moment to think about what those they cite in their support are really saying and why they are saying it. The answer is that these people are demanding sanctions because none of their supposed sympathisers has ever offered them an alternative of greater promise. That, in turn, is in large measure because sanctions are too convenient a weapon in the alien politics of Washington to be discarded in favour of something that might work. God forbid that there might be a set of alternatives of which the ideological enemy could readily approve or which might demonstrate the folly of the present course. That would make nonsense of the entire purpose. In a sense, the sanctioneers are guilty of a deliberate con to further their own domestic purposes.

What, from the safety of their separate reality, the sanctioneers have thus achieved is to make suicide the only reasonable option. One is reminded of the phrase *auto da fe*. As used by the Inquisitors, it literally meant "act of faith", a phrase highly applicable to the argument for imposing sanctions in the face of all contradictory evidence. In the minds of the victims of the Inquisition it came to mean something else. Immolation. The modern Inquisitors have given black South Africans no choice but to accept "an act of faith". It is in this light that the decision by Cosatu in July 1987 to call for the erosion of the very economy that sustains it as a union becomes understandable.

To use a grammatical metaphor, the members of Cosatu, like all black South Africans, exist in the passive voice, and have been condemned to do so for many generations. With few exceptions, they are people *to* whom and *for* whom things, some good, most frightful, are done. Their historical experience has been one of being at the receiving end of whatever someone else determined should come down the pipe. Whether it be the abominable social engineering of apartheid or the largesse of a Western multinational, black South Africans have virtually no say in what is fed into that pipe. Their free will is as restricted as that of Homeric characters whose lives were governed by the theocratic machinery of Olympus. Deadly serious though the game is, they are not so much players as playthings. The Olympians of white South Africa and the outside world know that this cannot go on; yet they do nothing to change the fundamental nature of the relation. The fundamental question is: what should "we" do about "them". Variants include: how do "we" control "them"? How do "we" satisfy "their" aspirations? How do "we" empower "them"? In general the answers boil down to some form of cooptation: how do "we" fit "them" into "our" society in a manner that does not radically change "our" lives but improves "theirs" to the extent that "they" will live contentedly with "us", or "we" and "they" can at least live side by side with the minimum of friction.

Cooptation takes various forms, some insidious and coercive, others more genuinely concerned and generous. At one extreme, there is the totalitarian kindness of the Joint Management Committees and their related control mechanisms. Under this method, docility is expected in return for certain material rewards; release from detention, for example, or a desperately needed standpipe. At the other end of the scale, the emphasis is on development, uplift, dialogue and affirmative action. In moral and practical terms, this is infinitely preferable, but the fact remains "we" are still in control of the process and "they" are "beneficiaries"; recipients, not actors. "They" are "victims" whom ... we have a moral duty and politico–economic imperative to devictimise. Further, however noble the efforts of the Urban Foundation or the late Sullivan Signatories Association, it is ultimately "we" who decide what good works need to be done, and "we" who disburse the necessary funds. "They", poor creatures, are merely fodder for projects designed to assimilate them into "our" world.

This is not to disparage such projects, much less to side with those of the sanctioneers who regard them as attempts to gild the apartheid cage. The point is not that trying to redress the consequences of apartheid and indifference is wrong or futile. What must be understood, however, is that by its very nature the effort has contradictory implications: chiefly that even as it seeks to elevate the beneficiary, it impresses on him just how little of his own destiny he controls. His range of options is extremely limited: to be trained, housed, employed, advanced in a way that "we" pretty much dictate, or accept poverty, violence and hopelessness. In such a context, the simple making of a significant decision and of thus becoming, however fleetingly, a free agent assumes an importance, imparts a dignity, that "we" who are lucky enough to enjoy democracy (of a sort) and choices cannot easily appreciate.

Calling for the world to impose sanctions and pull out its investments is just such a decision. Like participating in a protest march knowing that the authorities will respond with arrests and worse, it is a liberating act of free will in a profoundly unfree situation. The consequences are not, at the moment of the act, of paramount importance. What matters, what liberates, is the act itself. Now some who advocate sanctions in South Africa may well have ulterior ideological motives and may believe that resulting economic stagnation and human suffering will help to sow the seeds of revolution. But most, I believe, advocate sanctions simply because it is an authentic act of protest in itself. By a gross irony, the South African state, in denying any real choice to the mass of its population, has left it no option but cry out for self-destruction.

The American sanctioneers have compounded this irony, making it grosser still. They have seized upon black South Africans' desire to be masters of their own destinies and then exploited it for their own purposes, Jackson and the Congressional Black Caucus to humiliate an ideological opponent and expand their own power, Wolpe to build himself a platform, which as one of the least respected members of the House, he could not otherwise have done; and the list could go on. In a sense they have become exploiters, every bit as evil as Pretoria. They have not devised plans or policies that would genuinely contribute to the expansion of choice or freedom, and they have not done so because it does not suit their own agendas. They would sooner lie, suppress and distort, and fight their own petty battles in the fourth dimension, than do anything that might be of benefit in the real world. In a sense *they* are the colonial exploiters of the post–colonial era.

Worse: they have so thoroughly occupied the field with their pernicious dialectics that it has become impossible for those who advocate more fruitful measures even to be heard. If you propose to help to build black institutions, or any way help black South Africans to challenge apartheid in any manner that makes them real actors, in charge of their own fates, rather than cannon- or prison- or unemployment-fodder, you are at best "on the wrong side of history", but more likely a simple "racist". This has left those few with a genuine concern for the future of South Africa not only demoralised but compelled to fight a losing battle of utterly irrelevant terms. For the outside world, the future of South Africa should not be a sterile argument about whether to impose sanctions, as though that were the only problem. But that is exactly what it has become, and no one dare try to change it. Whatever havoc is ultimately wrought upon South Africa is not worth bucking the tide in the US. Indeed, it has got to the point where Vice President George Bush, the Republican Presidential nominee in 1988, could be urged quite seriously by his chief political adviser, Lee Atwater, to support sanctions as the cheapest way to win a few black votes.

8. In mid–1988 there are faint signs of promise in southern Africa, rather smaller than a man's hand to be sure, and starting from an extremely low baseline. Given its wealth and ideals, America ought theoretically to be well placed to promote them; but, as I hope has become clear, seems determined rather to stunt their growth. Dr Chester Crocker, President Reagan's Assistant Secretary of State for Africa, has given it his best shot with a policy he called (but perhaps should not have) "constructive engagement". Yet even he all but foretold his own failure nearly two years before taking office in 1981. "There is simply no solid domestic base," he wrote in the June 1979 edition of the *International Affairs Bulletin*, "for a durable and moderate policy." He was exactly right; how exactly he has spent the last seven years learning.

Among the hints of promise I would identify the following: The thorough-going commitment of Pretoria to what has been called the "political fallacy", the idea that the only kind of power that matters is political and it must be had before all else, has led it into a rigorous assault on its political opponents. The latter, themselves in thrall to the same fallacy, are being forced to recognise its shortcomings and are beginning to unite along alternative avenues, using the tools inherent in their numerical preponderance and their economic power of veto. Under extreme duress, they are beginning to understand the futility of confronting the state at its strongest points ... its security apparatus ... and the wisdom of boring into its comparatively defenceless underbelly to devour it from within. Ironically, they are learning to adapt themselves to their own ends and the very different circumstances, the methods of organisation, unity and infiltration, that brought Afrikaner Nationalism to power in 1948. It is a policy upon which virtually all can agree, from the Marxist academic Neville Alexander to such traditional liberals as Chief Gatsha Buthelezi, from Oliver Tambo to the most execrated township mayor. And although the state may try to bar such an avenue, those who seek it are the very life-blood of South Africa. Throttle that, and the country itself will die. In another irony, the strategy looks superficially like what the state itself is trying to achieve, far more gradually, through economic cooptation. As a result, the state may be lulled into believing that it is ensuring its survival, when in fact it is ensuring its own destruction.

A second area of promise lies in what has been happening inside the American and other foreign multinationals. They too have been subjected to a learning process. Domestic pressure in the US, the disinvestment campaign, shareholder divestment programmes, and, perhaps most importantly, the discriminatory purchasing laws adopted by many city and local governments, have shuttled down the American presence to a core of those companies that are most determined to stay. Over the past five years, as the pressures have increased, many companies (though by no means all) have realised that staying put cannot depend on winning an unwinnable public relations battle in the US ... an attempt upon which millions of dollars have been fruitlessly squandered ... but on becoming indispensable to their employees' aspirations. This development, in yet another irony, has been fostered by the Reverend Leon Sullivan's abandonment of his Principles and rating system in 1987. The Sullivan Code was in its way as much a crutch as a progressive force, directing companies' energies to the pharisaic scoring of points rather than towards discovering and then helping to provide what it was that their employees really wanted. Just as government repression is channelling resistance into paths that it cannot easily control, so many of the surviving corporations are beginning, more than ever, to sympathise and cooperate with the aspirations of their employees. Rather than treating them as cooptable objects of self-serving kindness, they are beginning to treat them as legitimate actors. They are no longer saying: see what wonderful things we are doing for you but asking: What can we do to make ourselves useful? Let me stress, that this is far from universal. But it is happening.

A third component of hope deals with a far broader matter, and it has repercussions not only for South Africa but for the entire region. The lessening of tension between the superpowers, whatever underlies it, is compelling all parties to reconsider their positions. South Africa can no longer pretend that it is a bulwark against communism, because, wrongly or, I am inclined to believe, rightly, the Soviet Union is no longer seen in the West as an imperial aggressor seeking to turn Africa into its private preserve. By the same token, those in the region, the ANC, for example, the MPLA in Luanda or Mozambique's Frelimo, can no longer count on Moscow as a guarantor of their refusal to compromise with political and economic realities. Much as America did after Vietnam, the Soviet élite is turning inwards and reassessing the myths that have long sustained its power. It is coming to realise that, for the time being at least, the preservation of its rule depends less on making its people believe that they are under constant danger of annihilation, 1984-style, than in satisfying their material needs in the manner of Brave New World. Such a shift has compelled the nomenclatura to take a cold look at its Third World protégés for what they are: a huge wasting asset whose chronic failures and frequent resort to barbarity are worse than a drain on the maternal exchequer; they challenge the very legitimacy of the theory upon which the continued rule of the nomenclatura depends. This has profound implications, not only in Angola which by mid–1988 headed the queue of regional conflicts awaiting resolution, but for the future of South Africa itself. For the first time, Russian commentators have been able to say that the South African crisis is infinitely more complicated than a Manichaean struggle between good blacks, supported by the East, and bad whites, maintained by racist capital; that revolutionary violence of the kind that brought their own party to power is not desirable; that negotiation, perhaps even with guaranteed minority rights, may be the only solution if South Africa is not to be turned into yet another gross advertisement for the failures of socialism. Accordingly, all with a stake in the future of South Africa, from the ANC to the Nationalist government, who have looked to the Soviet Union to validate or nurture their programmes, have no choice now but to think again.

Each of these three glints of hope boiled down to one essential idea. However difficult it may be to detect from what seems on the surface to be the ineluctable march of South Africa into the heart of darkness, and however fitfully it may be taking place, a great relearning is in train. Under almost unbearable harassment, black South Africa is learning how to challenge the state in truly effective ways. American and other capital is discovering that pious condescension and public relations are no substitute for genuine cooperation in change. All sides are learning that the historicistic theories of Marxist revolution can no longer be used as a defence against or prescription for the future. And yet (and this is the greatest irony of all) America will probably have no part in bringing these lessons to fruition. Indeed, on its present course, it is doing everything in its power to smother whatever hope there is.

For most American politicians, this is not a conscious attempt, nor am I talking about some grand, lurid American design. Instead I am talking about the devastating way in which the great amorphous mass of American policy-making, with its warring interests, some selfish, some blind, some indolent, some defiantly ignorant, all thoroughly insular, is resolving itself. This country, as long as it uses South Africa to fight its own ideological squabbles, is systematically making itself incapable of the kind of coherence, consistency and commitment that would enable it to contribute anything but obstruction to a situation so complex and distant. All three of these rays of hope American politicians are now, in one way or another, seeking to extinguish. Now that American companies at last begin to discover a genuine role for themselves, Congress wants to throw them out. Black South Africans begin to coalesce round the one kind of revolution that Pretoria cannot stop, and Congress decides to strip them of their most important weapons. The Soviet Union begins to shift from confrontation while American politicians maintain their own self-contradictory agendas, seeking to protract the war in Angola and to encourage one in South Africa, neither of which the Soviet Union sees as in its own interest.

Crocker talked of "engagement", but like the bureaucrats I mentioned at the beginning, this country will never be engaged until it notices that its telephones have yet to be connected. And that won't happen until it takes a genuine interest in who might be at the other end of the line.

# THE FUTURE OF SOUTH AFRICA
## by Paul Johnson

What will be the future of South Africa? Has it a future in its present form? If not, what will the new form be? And when will the change take place? Everyone in South Africa asks these questions, and many in the world beyond too. They are very difficult to answer; much more difficult than most of those who hold strong opinions on South Africa suppose. I think the best way to begin answering them is by putting forward this preliminary proposition: What happens in South Africa will depend to a large degree on what happens in the rest of the African continent. Why so? *Because South Africa is in many respects a typical African country.*

Now this may seem a paradoxical and provocative statement. So let us examine it. First, let us look at the ways in which South Africa is a typical African country, and then at the ways in which it differs from the rest.

There are six important ways in which it is typical. The first is perhaps the most critical. Like every other state in Africa, without exception, it is undergoing a rapid population increase. Africa is the last of the continents to experience what is commonly called the population explosion.

Now very rapid increases in population are not just demographic events. They have important political and often geopolitical consequences. The first population explosion occurred in nineteenth century Europe, which accounts for the phenomenon of European mass-migration and colonialism. It then spread to Asia and South America, both of which, like Europe after 1918, are emerging from the phase of fast growth and the revolutionary turmoils which accompanied it.

In Central America the "explosion" is at its height, and that is one prime reason for the intense political instability and fear we find there.

In Africa it is just beginning, but the curve of population growth is rising rapidly and it is already producing Malthusian counter-effects in the form of over-cultivation, droughts, famines and wars. So far, South Africa has avoided the worst of these but it is feeling intense population pressures, like every other African country.

Demographic growth exacerbates what is the most striking single characteristic of the African continent: its lack of racial, cultural and linguistic unity. No other continent is so fragmented, especially south and south-east of the Sahara. Before colonialism intervened, Africa was beginning to evolve larger units by a process of tribal imperialism.

The effect of the colonial period, which lasted roughly a century, was to accelerate the process, and to transform many thousands of tribal societies into about fifty superficially modern states which are now independent. Scarcely one of them is homogenous. Even small states like Rwanda are split by deep, radical fissures. In the first quarter-century of independence, these divisions have produced appalling civil wars in Chad, the Sudan, Zaïre, Uganda, Nigeria, Ethiopia and elsewhere. Sometimes, as in Angola and Mozambique, these civil wars have a strong ideological element. But in every case the tribal or racial element is there too, and it is usually predominant.

This brings us to the second respect in which South Africa is typical. It is a large and populous African country and its racial problems, like those of Nigeria, Zaïre and the Sudan, for instance, are particularly complex.

There are at present at least five major civil wars taking place in Africa. So far South Africa has managed to avoid a similar disaster, and this is a considerable achievement. But, as in other African states, there are forces pushing towards civil war, and many influential people, inside and outside, who actually want one. The assumption outside the African continent is that any civil war in South Africa would necessarily be between whites and blacks, but of course the reality is much more complicated.

The largest racial group in South Africa is the Zulu – more a national than simply a racial group, since it is divided in turn into about 200 tribes, each subdivided into clans. The next largest group is the whites but these, too, are composed of diverse ethnic and cultural groups – Dutch, English, French and German, for instance, and have two distinct languages, Afrikaans and English. There are important sub-groups too: Portuguese, Greeks, Jews, Italians and the so-called Rhodesian whites. Third in size are the Xhosa followed by the coloureds, the North Sotho, the South Sotho and the Tswana.

In addition to these seven major groups, there are seven minor racial groups, ranging from the Shangaan and the Asians to the Venda. The Venda are the smallest of the main groups but even they have twenty-seven distinct tribes. Indeed, all fourteen of the racial divisions of South Africa contain internal subdivisions. Thus the Asian population is split between Hindus, Moslems, Christians and Buddhists. Among the various groups of blacks the linguistic divisions are particularly important, with four major and twenty-three minor languages spoken.

The third way in which South Africa is typical is that population pressure on the land is driving people into the towns and especially into the big cities. In Cairo, Africa now has its first megalopolis but all over the continent cities like Lagos, Dakar, the Johannesburg conurbation, Kinshasa, Khartoum, Nairobi and Harare are expanding at impressive speed. Most of the new arrivals live in shantytowns, unless deliberate and forceful measures are taken to settle them elsewhere. In these immigrant cities, also characterised by very high and rising birthrates, the statistics of serious crime, especially murder and rape, are appalling.

These burgeoning and ultraviolent giant city complexes pose fearful problems to the authorities in all African countries, and here again South Africa is typical. Governments have found that, unless they respond ruthlessly, the shantytowns and immigrant suburbs quickly become no-go areas for the police and are ruled and partitioned by rival gangs, with the danger of the entire city becoming ungovernable.

So governments respond with what has become the curse of the continent – social engineering. People are treated not as individual human beings but as atomised units and shovelled around like concrete or gravel.

South Africa has moved to end the pass laws and movement control, having been the first to impose them – and this is very welcome – but unfortunately the use of identification papers has spread all over Africa and when movement is restricted the bulldozer is never far behind. Most African governments use them to demolish unauthorised settlements. Vast numbers of wretched people are made homeless without warning by governments terrified of being overwhelmed by lawless multitudes.

In the black African countries immediately south of the Sahara, for instance, the authorities fight desperately to repel nomadic desert dwellers driven south by poverty or drought. When the police fail, punitive columns of troops are sent in.

South Africa has the most efficient, though by no means the largest, internal repressive force on the continent. It is so much admired and imitated by other African governments, who buy or copy South African police hardware when they can. All these security forces are ruthless and liable to act with unpredictable violence. But, unlike the South African police, many are ill-paid and undisciplined and therefore far more brutal. The human cost of social control and social engineering in black Africa goes largely unreported. South Africa, by contrast, has a large, varied and in many ways excellent press. Hence, despite all the legal restrictions on reporting, we know pretty well what goes on there.

African social engineering is perhaps inevitable, given the lack of homogeneity, conducted on a racial-cultural basis. Here again South Africa is typical. All African states tend to be racist. Almost without exception, and with varying degrees of animosity, they discriminate against racial/religious groups: Jews, or whites, or Asians, or non-Moslems, or minority tribes or even majority tribes. There is no such thing as a genuine multiracial society in the whole of Africa. There seems to be no African country where tribal or racial origins, skin colour or religious affiliation are not of prime importance in whether people are accorded or denied elementary rights.

African countries vary in the extent to which their practice of discrimination is formalised or entrenched in law codes and official philosophies. Many have political theories of a sort, cooked up in the political science or sociology departments of local universities. Thus Tanzania has Ujaama, Ghana Consciencism, Senegal Negritude, and Zambia "Zambian Humanism"; Zaïre has a national philosophy named after its military dictator, Mobutoism. Apartheid, whose modern, sophisticated form was put together in the social psychology department of Stellenbosch University, is a typical example of this distinctive African brand of political theory which has developed over the last half-century. Paradoxical though it may seem, apartheid is not a concept which divides the Republic from the rest of Africa. It is, on the contrary, the local expression of the African ideological personality. No continent has ever suffered more at the hands of its politically-minded intellectuals, and here again South Africa is typical.

Those then are the six main ways in which South Africa is very much part of the continent. But there are also five important ways in which it is quite untypical. The first is in wealth and in infrastructure.

South Africa in some ways is a Third World country, like all other African states; but, alone among them, it also has some characteristics of a First World country. Its wealth is both created and intrinsic. It has by far the richest and most varied range of natural resources of any African country. Its settlements, both white and black, were originally poor, entirely agricultural, largely pastoral. But since the discovery of diamonds in quantity in the 1860s, and still more since the discovery of the Rand in the 1880s, it has emerged as the richest depository of minerals in the world, exceeded in quantity only by Soviet Russia.

It exports about eighty-five per cent of what it mines or refines. It is the world's largest supplier in nine key commodities and second largest in two more; in addition it is among the world's top ten suppliers in such basic commodities as copper, tin, nickel and coal. In many essential and scarce metals it has between fifty and ninety per cent of the West's known reserves and over a wide range of important commodities Africa and the Soviet Union between them control virtually all the world's supply and reserves.

The second way in which South Africa differs is that its mineral wealth has become the basis of a modern economy – the only modern economy in the whole of Africa. South of the Sahara, South Africa has under ten per cent of the population. But it has nearly seventy-five per cent of the total Gross National Product. The core of this modern economy is mining, and after the Soviet Union it has the largest mining industry in the world, employing 700 000 people, as opposed to 470 000 in the United States, the next largest. In many important aspects the South African mining industry is the most efficient and technically advanced on earth.

The strength of the mining industry accounts for the third way in which South Africa differs. With very few exceptions – the Ivory Coast, the Cameroons, Kenya, Malawi and Botswana are five which spring to mind – most black states have experienced falls in real income per capita since independence. In some cases the falls have been severe and states have virtually passed out of the international economic system. In South Africa, by contrast, the real incomes of blacks have risen substantially in the last quarter-century. In the decade 1975–85, for instance, black wages in the mining industry more than doubled in real terms, and this improvement has continued despite the severe recession which began in 1984 and from which South Africa is only now emerging.

This improvement in the fortunes of South African blacks is not confined to purely financial matters. Though the education available to blacks there is poor compared to what the whites get, it is good compared to what is available almost anywhere else on the continent. The number of blacks completing secondary education now approximates the white total. So, perhaps surprisingly, does the number of black women with professional qualifications – well over 100 000. There are probably more black women professionals in the Republic than in the whole of the rest of black Africa put together.

Moreover, it is important to remember that this modest but rising prosperity is not confined to blacks born in South Africa. About half of South Africa's black miners come from abroad, chiefly from Malawi, Mozambique, Lesotho, Swaziland and Botswana, and most of their wages are remitted home; so about ten million people, in half a dozen countries, are directly or indirectly financially dependent on South Africa's mining industry.

Their governments are likewise dependent, in varying degrees, on those hard-currency earnings, and pressure from other African governments was one factor which brought to an end the recent mining strike. The point can be summarised quite simply: continuing South African prosperity is essential to the economic well-being of all southern Africa, and in the battle for higher black living standards throughout this subcontinent it is one of the few positive factors.

The fourth way in which South Africa differs from the rest of the continent is that it is in many respects a free country. This difference is very little appreciated in the outside world, but it is of transcendent importance. South Africa is essentially a British creation, and as such was endowed with most of the political and individual liberties Britain evolved over centuries and transmitted to her overseas possessions; not least it enjoys the rule of law, more precious in some ways than the right to vote.

The libertarian endowment has been eroded since South Africa became independent and especially since 1948; but the erosion has gone much less far than in other former British territories in Africa – or in other African ex-colonies given western-style constitutions. South Africa still possesses an independent judiciary, what is in many essentials a free press, and a multi-party parliamentary system, albeit elected on a racially-restricted franchise. No other African state still enjoys this combination of benefits.

With its natural resources, its modern economy, its ability to raise its living standards and its residual freedoms, these four ways in which South Africa differs from other states on the continent are greatly to its advantage. But those four pluses are balanced by a serious minus. The fifth way in which South Africa differs is that it alone, in the whole of Africa, is the object of overwhelming interest in the outside world, an interest which often takes the form of active hostility.

I know of no historical precedent for such widespread and persistent international obsession with the internal affairs of an independent country. The curious thing is that it comes at a time when the outside world has little interest in the African continent as a whole. From the 1860s onwards, for an entire century, outside interest in Africa grew steadily. The continent became part of the European world-system: its wars were Africa's wars, its booms and slumps Africa's, it transmitted its institutions, religion, technology, sports, virtues, vices.

For most of the 1960s, as Africa became independent this interest remained, but with the rise of military régimes, the collapse of economies and the ravages of chronic frontier disputes and civil wars, the world turned its back on Africa – except for the Republic, on which world attention has been increasingly concentrated. It is as though the world, unwilling or unable to do anything to assist the new black states to survive their post-independence mistakes, has selected South Africa to be the moral scapegoat, to carry the burden of the sins of all. Hence the world's focus on South Africa, to the exclusion of the rest of the continent, is itself distorted, since it is not really interested in any aspect of South African life which is not directly related to the race problem.

That those who form international opinion should wrench South Africa out of its continental context, and then in turn wrench its racial difficulties out of their national context, obviously does not make for understanding or wisdom. And indeed the policies pursued towards South Africa by those, at the United Nations, in the United States Congress and elsewhere, who are pleased to call themselves agents and spokesmen of the world's conscience, have been exceedingly foolish and have often achieved the opposite of the ends desired.

Let us look at what has happened since the UN first mounted embargoes, boycotts and sanctions against South Africa. It is a recurrent lesson of history that economic sanctions are usually ineffective against a strong, modern economy. Often they merely enforce improvements, in quite unexpected ways.

South Africa was traditionally a colonial-style economy which exported commodities and imported manufactures. The sanctions imposed over the last quarter-century have simply accelerated its progress towards economic self-sufficiency.

The arms embargo, now more than two decades old, merely led to the creation of an indigenous arms industry. South Africa exploited the technology of its mining industry to become a world leader in the manufacture of conventional explosives, rivalling the hitherto unchallenged supremacy in this field of the United States and Sweden. It also specialises in mine-resistant armoured vehicles, in which it seems to have outstripped all its competitors. From an importer of arms it has become an exporter, selling its products all over the world, but especially to other governments whose needs are similar. Hence the UN, which once instructed its members to stop selling arms to South Africa, is now driven to begging them not to buy arms from her.

Again, the oil embargo had the predictable result that South Africa, in order to make itself more than eighty-five per cent self-sufficient in energy, has created a synthetic fuel industry, whose chief component, Sasol, the semi–public organisation which turns coal into petroleum products, is now the world leader in this technology.

This involved modernising and expanding the coal industry, and as an unforeseen but very important by-product of the embargo, South Africa has created the lowest–cost coal–export trade in the world. It has captured a large slice of the Japanese market and even contrived to export coal at a profit to the United States, something which would have been inconceivable when the embargo was first imposed. These exports are vulnerable to protectionism posing as sanctions, but there is no doubt about their competitive edge.

The latest attempt to exert pressure on South Africa, the disinvestment campaign mounted in the United States and copied to some extent in Britain, appears to have similar results. One of South Africa's weaknesses was that both its mining industry and still more its financial institutions were to a great extent controlled from abroad. The process whereby South Africans have acquired a dominant stake in their own mines has been proceeding for many years, and disinvestment has merely accelerated it.

But in the financial sector the recent changes have been much more important, as British and American institutions have handed over ownership and control to local affiliates or management consortiums, often at bargain–basement prices. South Africa is thus in the process of acquiring what no other African state possesses, and at nominal cost – its own locally–owned array of modern financial institutions. In the end, the result may well be the opposite of what those who demanded disinvestment wished to see, for South Africa is emerging from the process with its economic sovereignty and its power to defy its foreign critics greatly enhanced.

Of course disinvestment was designed to starve the South African economy, and especially its mining industry, of funds. It is hard to see how this purpose was advanced by ensuring that South Africa acquired its own money–raising institutions. The truth of course is that so long as investment in South Africa, especially in mining, remains highly profitable, capital will find its way there.

Now this brings me to one of the main points I want to make. Capital, in searching for a place to rest and fructify, is not interested in United Nations resolutions. It is so with all these impersonal economic forces. The gold price, that primary factor in South Africa's economic health, rises or falls according to principles of motion which are all its own. It is not motivated by political, ideological or humanitarian reasons. So too with capital as a whole. It is deaf to speeches, heedless of "isms", impervious to demonstrations; not least, it is colour–blind. It does not make ethnic or ethical judgments, merely financial ones. It is a rationalising force, the great destroyer of unreason, prejudice, illogicality and ancient follies. For capitalism is not really an "ism" at all: it is merely what happens at certain stages in the development of a free market, unless you do something very forceful and positive to stop it.

Hence, it is the great dissolvent of castes and classes, sweeping away in its impersonal search for profits the artificial inequalities mankind creates among itself, whether based on heredity, occupation, caste or colour. It destroyed the feudal system. Left to itself, it must destroy apartheid.

What is apartheid? It is not, as many people seem to think, the extreme right wing end of the political–economic spectrum. Quite the contrary. It is more accurately described as ethnic socialism, a regressive and primitive system which necessarily involves state interference in every aspect of economic activity, a huge state sector, an ever-growing state encroachment on the national income and a mass of restrictive laws which inhibit the operations of a free market.

Capitalism is incompatible with apartheid for broadly the same reasons it is incompatible with feudalism – it cannot co-exist with a social and political system based on inherited racial caste, which forbids freedom of movement and a free market in labour, and which subordinates all business decisions to the needs of an irrational world-view.

Hence capitalism will tend to destroy apartheid, unless positively prevented from doing so. Indeed we can go further. Being colour-blind, it has an inherent tendency to advance the interests of blacks.

If we look at the aspirations of the blacks in South Africa, not as imagined in theory and from the outside, but as they actually exist, we find that black priorities centre on five practical objects. These are, in probable order of importance: better education for their children; rights of citizenship; the right to own property; freedom of movement and residence; and – a natural consequence of the last three demands – freedom from excessive police supervision. To this I think I would add a sixth aspiration, especially among blacks with good educational and technical qualifications – the right to a job on the basis of merit alone.

Now it is a significant fact, in all these different demands, that the blacks have the vigorous support of virtually the whole of the business community. Nor is this surprising, for such rights are not merely compatible with the capitalist system, they are directly conducive to its successful performance. The needs of capitalism and the hopes of the blacks complement each other. That is why they have a common interest in dismantling apartheid.

Now we know that man does not live by bread alone. But it helps. South Africa's blacks are no different from anyone else. They want better homes. They want cars and appliances. They want better schools and health-care. Probably, most of all, they want a better future for their children. All these, if left to itself, capitalism can eventually supply, as it has supplied them in Europe and North America, as it is now supplying to countless millions in East Asia.

Of course such aspirations cannot be divorced from the political context; but the historical reasons show that where capitalism advances, the vote is never far behind. In Britain, the first wave of the Industrial Revolution was followed, in due course, by the first Reform Bill, extending the franchise and parliamentary representation. In the United States, industrialisation and democracy advanced hand-in-hand. In the long run, the kind of mass prosperity generated by free-market capitalism is incompatible with the denial of political rights.

If we take Europe today west of the Iron Curtain, we find the market system everywhere triumphant, living standards higher than ever before, and – for the first time in history – every single European state is a parliamentary democracy under the rule of law. Are these things connected? Of course they are – for economic freedom and political freedom are indivisible.

Now you may say: But that is Europe, South Africa is different. Of course the differences are enormous. But in the long perspective of history, they are nothing compared to the similarities.

We have seen over the past quarter-century half a dozen states on the Asian rim of the Pacific, with cultural traditions very different from Europe's, create astonishingly successful free market economies, which have brought unprecedented prosperity to their peoples. The number of such states is growing in Asia, as the progress of the pioneers is noted and their example spreads.

Why, given time and patience, should Africa prove any different? It is at this point that I return to my initial contention, that what happens in South Africa cannot be separated from what happens in the rest of the continent. Africa as a whole is a former colonised area struggling hard to find its own forms of political self-expression and make its own way to economic prosperity.

South Africa began to be independent before the first world war, so that it was a generation or more ahead of the rest. But it faced essentially the same problem: how to replace control from Europe?

In answering this question, all the newly independent states have made mistakes. In some cases, Uganda, Tanzania, Ghana, for example, the mistakes have been very serious, near-fatal indeed. But though the mistakes have varied in degree, they have tended to follow a common pattern, what I am tempted to call the political fallacy – the assumption that all economic and social problems are susceptible to political solution, provided it is pursued ruthlessly enough.

The fallacy was stated most clearly in 1963 by Kwame Nkrumah. Africa's aims, he declared, including its unity, constituted "above all a political kingdom, which can be gained only by political means. The local and economic development in Africa will come only within the political kingdom, not the other way round." Well, he was wrong, wasn't he?

Other leaders – Nyerere, Sékou Touré, Mengistu, to mention only three fairly typical ones, made the same kind of mistake, and their countries paid for it. South Africa, too, fell into the political fallacy, which here took the form of apartheid.

All these errors, stressing as they did the supremacy and invincibility of the political, ideological solution, involving, as all did, a great deal of social engineering, of pushing around ordinary men and women, were different forms of state socialism. They have all failed economically; and all, in varying degrees, have led to internal violence.

South Africa has so far escaped the coups and uprisings, the civil wars, which have been the consequence of the political fallacy in so many black African states. But it, too, has paid for the error of apartheid in internal tension, in an immense and repressive security apparatus and in sporadic political violence.

Now it seems that after a quarter-century of putting its trust in the political kingdom, the African continent as a whole is beginning to learn better. It is beginning to grasp that social and economic problems are not susceptible to drastic, simple-minded and abstract political solutions. Throughout the advanced countries of the world, socialism and its monstrous progeny, the all-embracing, all-powerful state, is in retreat. Even in Moscow and Peking it is beginning to shrink. Africa is not immune to this worldwide trend. Slowly, painfully, almost reluctantly, African political leaders are beginning to grasp that the state cannot do all – indeed can do scarcely anything well, except perhaps kill – and that social and economic arrangements are best left to the wit and wisdom of private men and women.

Where the state gives up and retreats, capitalism cheerfully steps in to fill the vacuum. The process is beginning in many parts of Africa. It will take a very long time to bear fruit, for incalculable damage has been done to economic infrastructures which were, even to begin with, inadequate and fragile. However, Africa is at last turning in the right direction.

Now here is the opportunity for South Africa, as the leading economy in Africa – the only modern economy in Africa – to play its part. Can it learn the lessons of its own version of the political fallacy, and dismantle apartheid with all deliberate speed? Can it create by its exertions, and demonstrate by its example, the

**Top:** Aerial view of Lourenço Marques immediately before independence. In those days it was a bustling, thriving town despite the war in the north.

**Left:** Many of an older generation will remember the pavement cafés in Lourenço Marques. Now the faces are mostly black and the fare limited.

**Below:** Maputo is now destitute. Food queues are controlled by soldiers.

**Left:** President Mobutu Sese Seko has played a pivotal role in Angolan/Zairean relations.
**Above:** The face of a South African soldier at war in south Angola.

**Left:** One of the Portuguese mercenaries who later fought for the FNLA in Huambo.
**Above:** Unita troops clamber over a Soviet-built helicopter shot down by an American Stinger missile in the central Mexico region of eastern Angola.
**Below:** Angola's rebel leader, Dr Jonas Savimbi of Unita, briefs the foreign media at his headquarters in the south-east bush at Jamba.

**Left:** The pride of Portugal's fighting forces on parade in the streets of Luanda during the colonial period.
**Above:** Maputo, once known as Lourenço Marques, offers a sad reflection on the image of African Uhuru.
**Below:** Many of the soldiers that fought for the Rhodesian RLI were not yet out of their teens.

**Above left:** A Swapo mine blew off a front wheel of this *Koevoet* Casspir during a pursuit near the Angolan border.

**Left:** South African forces prepare to emplane at the former Portuguese garrison town of Cuamato in southern Angola. The photograph was taken after an attack on the Swapo base in which two South African *parabats* were killed.

**Above:** Caprivi has seen the benefits of the aggressive South African military policy of hitting at the enemy whenever Swapo makes a strike from Zambia. There has been no war in the Caprivi area for nearly seven years.

**Above right:** The South African fleet of three *Daphne* class submarines is tiny by great-power standards, but the squadron has proved a sufficient deterrent to any action by a united African force.

**Right:** Dr Mangosuthu Buthelezi, head of the KwaZulu authority, will undoubtedly play a more forceful role in the future of black and white southern Africa. Many think that he should have been included in the South African cabinet long ago.

An early photograph of Dr Jonas Savimbi with members of his Unita army in eastern Angola. In those days this rebel group was still armed with second-hand PpSh submachine-guns.

**Left:** President Robert Mugabe of Zimbabwe holds the key to future developments in much of southern Africa.
**Above:** Fireforce operations in the Rhodesian midlands. An Alouette "K" Car with cannon mounted hovers over a contact in the midlands.
**Below:** Soldiers of the rebel FNLA movement prepare their weapons for combat shortly after the MPLA takeover of government in Luanda.

**Above:** The Chinese in Africa have played an unusually constructive part, despite the criticism that has been levelled at their activities. But for the TanZam Railway linking Dar es Salaam with Zambia, built by the Chinese, the region would be in an even worse economic state.

**Below:** The man who first attacked the whites in Africa was Julius Nyerere, President of Tanzania. He is seen here with the mad buffoon, Idi Amin Dada of Uganda.

**Above:** President Kenneth Kaunda of Zambia continues to push for full sanctions against South Africa, even though his own country is on the verge of economic collapse.

**Top:** The Soviet Union has flooded Africa with huge numbers of missiles, aircraft, armoured vehicles and military equipment of all kinds. The SAM-8 anti-aircraft missile (codenamed *Gecko*) is one of the most effective Russian weapons in Africa. It has been used against the SAAF.

**Above:** The part played by Cuban military forces in Africa is significant. This parade of Russian military equipment supplied to the Cubans was displayed on a Lenin Day parade recently.

**Right:** Cairo Road, Lusaka, is as well known to members of the African National Congress as it is to recent visitors from South Africa attempting to build bridges between black and white Africa.

**Above:** The dividing line between Angola and South West Africa is the majestic Kunene river, which forms the border between the two countries for some distance.

**Below:** Joachim Chissano succeeded to the presidency on the death of Samora Machel. This historic photograph was taken on 18 September 1974 at a press conference at the Portuguese Governor's palace in Lourenço Marques, where the group of Frelimo representatives had just arrived from Tanzania.

functioning free market economy which alone can provide the dynamism to carry Africa onto the plateau of the affluent society? Can it, emerging from its isolation as the continent scapegoat, take up the role which nature and its own skills surely allotted it – the economic leadership of Africa?

I think the answer to these questions, which are still very much open, will depend in great degree on the young people of all races who are growing up in South Africa today. We look to the old for wisdom, but only the young can supply the idealistic passion which is so incorrigibly a characteristic of tender years.

After the ideological follies of the past quarter-century, there is a spirit of cynicism and moral defeatism in Africa which needs correction. The market system, left to itself, will undoubtedly do the spadework. But, as I say, it is blind, impersonal, materialistic, non-human. It cannot, of itself, supply the necessary corrective of idealism. It needs a moral dimension, and only people can supply that.

Africa needs economic example. But she needs moral leadership too, the kind of moral leadership which recognises how essential economic success is to achieving anything else, which sets about getting it in a businesslike way, but which knows that materialism is not enough.

When I look at the prospects for South Africa over the next twenty years, I am inclined to be optimistic. Twice in my lifetime, once in the early 1960s and again in 1985/6, doomsday predictions for South Africa, foreseeing a crescendo of violence culminating in a destructive change of régime, have been invalidated by actual events.

I no longer have the smallest belief in a catastrophic solution for South Africa. Too many people, of all races, have too much to lose; and too much to gain from the rational alternatives.

However, reason, and the gifts of reason, are the rewards of the open-minded. And, by a curious paradox, South Africa – supposedly obscurantist, inward- and backward-looking South Africa – the South Africa of the *laager* – has in recent years, quite suddenly, become extraordinarily open-minded about its future.

How to face the future has become the leading topic of discussion, more so perhaps than in any other country in the world at present. In this respect, the hostile actions of the outside world have not been an unmixed evil; they have forced, or at least encouraged, South Africans to think deeply and systematically about what they ought to do. As Dr Johnson might have said, the knowledge that one is to be disinvested in a fortnight concentrates the mind wonderfully.

South Africa is beginning to concentrate its mind; and this process must, in my judgment, propel it along the path where the underlying forces of capitalism are already taking it – towards a society based not on class or caste or race, but on merit. So the next twenty years will see radical reform and power-sharing, though whether, in its initial phases, it will be reform from above or reform by negotiation, I am not able to say: a bit of both I suspect.

What I am sure of is that, to be successful, and to lay the foundations of a durable future in the twenty-first century, this process of reform will require not only economic sense and political daring, but also, and perhaps most important of all, moral wisdom.

I would like to end on a heretical note. I wish there were in South Africa today a little more of the spirit of Cecil Rhodes. He is not a fashionable figure today. Indeed, he figures largely in the Left's demonology of Africa. Yet, Rhodes was a genius; and the kind of genius Africa needed then, and needs today.

He was a great business creator, the architect of enormous companies and institutions, most of which survive and flourish to this day. Yet he never made the mistake of seeing money or business or profit as anything other than the means to an end – and that end was human improvement. All his life he had a passion for education, for he saw knowledge as the key to all else.

When, aged 18, he went to the Kimberley diggings, he took with him as the principal part of his luggage an immense Greek dictionary. As a rising entrepreneur, he insisted on keeping terms at Oxford University. And both during his life, and after his death, in his will, he gave most of his fortune to education.

Rhodes was not just a great improver: he was a visionary, ahead of his time. In inventing the mining finance house he was projecting the capitalism of the 1880s forward into the twentieth century. If he were working today, a hundred years later, he would be projecting the 1980s forward into the twenty–first century. He would not be talking in terms of the paternalism which made sense in the 1880s. He would be talking in terms of the partnership which makes sense today – but with exactly the same blend of realism and idealism which marked his whole approach to the development of Africa.

That blend, that combination of practical sense and moral sensitivity, is something the young should study and seek to acquire. For each is ineffectual without the other.

In the long run, the future of South Africa – the future of the continent as a whole – rests in the hands of its own people, of all races, religions and cultures. The outside world can be, at best, of only marginal assistance or hindrance. It cannot do much either way, by showering Africa with aid, or bombarding it with embargoes and sanctions. The international community must realise that Africa has really no alternative but to go it alone as a continent, and work out its own salvation.

Whether it goes it alone in harmony or companionship, or in discord and violence, will depend in great part on the quality and intelligence of the leadership which South Africa, as its most powerful unit, has a duty to provide.

# ANGOLA AND THE WEST

## by Fred Bridgland

*Examination question:* "A liberal is a person whose interests aren't at stake at the moment."
*(Will Player, the San Diego Tribune).*
*Discuss.*

I am a Western liberal democrat, a member of a broad class at the centre of the political spectrum that likes to think of itself as the guardian of decent and humane values in a world in which greed, rapacity and oppression prevail.

I cannot imagine ever being anything other than a member of that class (to be precise, in my case, as a social democrat), but it has been salutary to find, as a result of nearly 13 years of journalism in the Angolan conflict, that liberals can be as cruel as those of ostensibly tougher political persuasions. In relation to Angola, most liberals have been persistently unwilling to accept the intellectual and moral challenges presented by that conflict.

To some extent the liberal failure to defend liberal democratic values in Angola has been understandable. (I include moderate socialists and moderate conservatives, social democrats and true liberals in my term "liberal democrat"). So closed to the outside world was totalitarian Portugal up to 1974 that few people in the democracies understood the dynamics of the country or the importance of its overseas territories. When the imperial pack of cards collapsed as a result of the Portuguese people's demand for more social and economic justice at home, the questions in East Timor, Guiné–Bissau, Mozambique and Angola seemed fairly simple: rule passed from the white minority colonial régime to governments of the black majorities.

Superficial analyses of the post-colonial situation seemed to be confirmed by the fact that East Timor, Guiné–Bissau and Mozambique each had only one effective anti-colonial movement, Fretilin, the PAIGC and Frelimo, and each appeared to be characterised by a high degree of internal unity. The old imperial-cum-fascist order retreated to allow the emergence of a new, bright and shiny future of freedom, peace and goodwill.

Angola, the jewel in the Portuguese crown, was different. Twice the size of France, it had the potential to be one of the most prosperous countries on Earth. It was blessed with fertile soils, great mineral wealth (oil, diamonds, iron ore), immense and diverse forests, abundant bilharzia-free water supplies, a benign climate and rich marine resources.

However, it also had several liberation movements that had fought the Portuguese (and one another) and each had strong claims to at least a share in the spoils of post-independence government. In trying to unravel the mysteries of Angola many people fell at the first hurdle of mastering the acronyms of these competing movements. The main contenders, among others with real legitimacy, were the MPLA (Popular Movement for the Liberation of Angola), the FNLA (National Front for the Liberation of Angola) and Unita (National Union for the Total Independence of Angola).

But who were these movements? How were they to be understood in the Angolan, wider African and international strategic contexts? The international news agencies made confusion more confounded by pinning glib labels on them that acted as a bar to understanding. There was the "Soviet-backed, Marxist" MPLA; the "American- and Chinese-backed" FNLA; and the "Maoist-orientated" Unita, which the *Washington Post* described as "the most dangerously Marxist" of all.[1]

With so much confusion about the various Angolan liberation movements, bewilderment increased in the period between 25 April 1974, when the Portuguese Armed Forces Movement carried out a coup d'état and overthrew the Lisbon dictatorship of Dr Marcello Caetano, and 11 November 1975, the date set for multi-party independence elections in Angola, which were aborted when foreign powers became embroiled there.

Western public opinion on Angola, such as it is, knows that a civil war between the three Angolan movements began with the establishment of the MPLA in power in Luanda after independence.

Opinion is divided about which outside powers first fanned the flames of the internal conflict. On the one hand there is a school that argues that the Americans and South Africans came first and the Russians and Cubans followed only in response to previous interference by Washington and Pretoria. On the other, there is a school that argues the direct opposite.

It is necessary to understand which foreign powers intervened in Angola and to what extent before one can reach a conclusion about present-day Angola. It is also necessary to appreciate how each of the movements might have fared in the promised but aborted independence elections.

The former Tanzanian President Julius Nyerere played an important part in persuading many Western liberal democrats of goodwill that the "Americans and South Africans first" option was the truth. In the mid-Seventies Nyerere was seen by many as the guru of African independence, the philosopher of African democracy and socialism. His influence was very great and his views were not subject to the critical scepticism that they are now.

When President Nyerere spoke many people were apt to believe him unquestioningly. In April 1976, in a BBC interview, he said: "The internal struggle (in Angola) had a lot to do with the Americans. The Americans were there well before November 11, 1975. The Cubans were not there. The original external intervention there was American and South African."[2]

In fact, the place at the centre of the first known foreign intervention in Angola was Nyerere's own capital, Dar es Salaam. Nyerere, who for many years had given support and external training bases to the MPLA, had become deeply disillusioned with the movement. Beset by internal feuds and schisms, the MPLA had been defunct as an effective fighting force against the Portuguese since 1972. Even Moscow, for long the powerful friend and backer of the MPLA, had withdrawn its support.[3] According to Portuguese intelligence, the MPLA had only a few dozen guerrilla fighters inside Angola at the time of the 1974 coup in Lisbon:[4] in the months after the coup the MPLA continued to waste all its energies on internal squabbling, torture and murder. Only in September 1974 did one of three contesting factions, that led by Dr Agostinho Neto, emerge as the best organised and therefore able to command widest external recognition as the "true" MPLA.

But although Neto became established in the eyes of the world as the leader of the MPLA, the legacy of division continued to plague his movement. The president of Zambia, Kenneth Kaunda, became disenchanted with the MPLA even before Nyerere. From the early 1970s Zambia had given the movement camps near Lusaka, the capital of Zambia, and also in the west of the country, near the eastern Angola border. But Kaunda too had witnessed the petering out of the fight by the MPLA against the Portuguese and the bitter and bloody struggle between its factions in Zambian bases.

Zambian intelligence officers told Kaunda that between 12 and 15 supporters of Daniel Chipenda's Eastern Revolt faction of the MPLA had been killed by Neto's followers in August 1974 in one of the remote western Zambia camps. Killings by the MPLA were not new, but the manner of these particular horrors badly upset Kaunda. Five-sided wooden frames had been fitted to the heads of the victims and tightened very slowly until their skulls cracked. Kaunda vowed that Agostinho Neto would never again set foot on Zambian soil; a rift opened up between the leader of the MPLA and the president of Zambia that would be pivotal in the subsequent course of events in Angola.[5]

Soon after the coup d'état in Portugal, Nyerere, knowing the disarray of the MPLA (which enabled the Portuguese to switch troops from Angola to Mozambique), asked Peking to help the FNLA. His intention was to maintain the war effort and spur the new leaders in Lisbon towards ending the colonial status of Angola.[6]

In June 1974, two months before Portugal announced that it intended to give independence to Angola, Chinese arms and military trainers began to arrive in Zaïre, where the FNLA had its bases. By August 1974, when the struggle for leadership of the MPLA was at its height and the movement was militarily impotent, Peking had sent the FNLA 450 tons of weapons and 120 instructors.[7]

John Stockwell, a former officer of the CIA who led its Angola Task Force, alleges that in July 1974 the CIA, noting Tanzanian and Chinese help to the FNLA, began trying to gain influence by giving money to its leader, Holden Roberto.[8]

With independence promised, with the Chinese building up the FNLA, and with the US getting into the act, even if only with small cash hand-outs, it would have been asking a lot of the Soviet Union to stay out of the struggle for Angola. In August 1974 the Communist Party of the Soviet Union announced that it considered the triumphant Neto faction of the MPLA to be the true spokesman of the Angolan people. From that date, precisely at the moment when the struggle against the Portuguese was over and preparations were beginning for the creation of an independent Angola, Moscow resumed the supply of arms to its former client, the MPLA.

Russian aid did not consist of surreptitious hand-outs of pocket money of the kind given by the CIA to the FNLA. The Soviets far outdid the help secured by Nyerere from China for the FNLA. The generally accepted estimate is that the Soviet Union gave the MPLA US$6 million worth of arms in the last four months of 1974. Most were shipped into Congo–Brazzaville, from where they were ferried into remote parts of northern Angola by small boats and light aircraft.[9]

Neto, having emerged as leader of the MPLA, moved swiftly to re-establish the movement in the race for the independence prize. Having regained Soviet backing, he returned to Angola for the first time in nearly thirty years and signed a peace agreement with the Portuguese on 21 October 1974. Neto opened an MPLA office in early November in Luanda, the party's main centre of support. The FNLA also moved into the capital. Neto had a close ally in the new Portuguese Governor-General, Admiral Rosa Coutinho, appointed to Luanda by the Armed Forces Movement after the *coup d'état* in Lisbon. Coutinho, known as the Red Admiral because of his close ties with the Portuguese Communist Party, turned a blind eye to the deliveries of Russian weapons to Neto.[10]

Ominously, more than a hundred people were killed in fights in November 1974 between supporters of the FNLA and the MPLA in Luanda, a portent of later mass killings. But despite these conflicts most people were either hopeful for the future or were hedging their bets, as was one African at a rally who wore a cloak bearing the names of all of the three main liberation movements.[11]

Meanwhile Admiral Rosa Coutinho had met the leader of Unita, Dr Jonas Savimbi, and publicly approved an important political and diplomatic initiative by Savimbi to reach agreement on Angolan independence between Lisbon and the liberation movements.[12] Savimbi began a tour of black Africa in November 1974 to get backing from heads of state for the formation of a united front (though not a unified party) between Unita, the MPLA, and the FNLA. On 18 December Neto, Savimbi and Rosa Coutinho met in the small town of Luso, in eastern Angola. The leaders of Unita and the MPLA embraced and signed an agreement binding them to a common front in negotiations with the Portuguese to form a transitional government. They also agreed on the necessity of including the FNLA in the front.[13]

As 1974 came to an end, Savimbi announced that the Portuguese had agreed to hold talks in Portugal from 10 January 1975 with the MPLA and Unita to decide a timetable for independence. James MacManus, the Africa correspondent of the *Guardian*, wrote: "Unita, long ignored and attacked by the other movements, has emerged as the binding force in the new nationalist union. Dr Savimbi in particular is striving to dampen the tribal and personal animosities that divided the liberation movements so deeply during their 13 year war with the Portuguese."[14]

Savimbi arranged a meeting in Mombasa, under the auspices of Jomo Kenyatta, President of Kenya, to reach a common position between the MPLA, FNLA and Unita before negotiations with the Portuguese. By the end of the talks in Mombasa, from 3 to 5 January 1975, Neto, Roberto and Savimbi had signed a trilateral accord in which they recognised each other as independent parties with equal rights and responsibilities. They also agreed that they were not ready to take over Angola immediately and that a period of transition in cooperation with Portugal was necessary before independence.[15]

The nationalist leaders, thus newly unified, then moved on from Kenya to the Penina Golf Hotel at Alvor, on the southern Algarve coast of Portugal, to discuss the timetable for self-determination. By 15 January 1975 the Portuguese, whose official delegation included Admiral Rosa Coutinho, the MPLA, FNLA and Unita, had hammered out and signed an agreement that set 11 November 1975 as the date for independence.

Elections to a Constituent Assembly would be held in October, and until the day of independence power would be vested in a Portuguese High Commissioner, replacing the traditional colonial Governor–General, and a transitional government, in which the FNLA, MPLA and Unita each would have three ministerial posts. Each would hold the premiership in rotation. The Portuguese would hold three ministries and the office of High Commissioner.

The Alvor Accord also called for the formation of a joint Angolan Defence Force consisting of 8 000 combatants each from Unita, MPLA and FNLA. They would be combined at first with a 24 000–strong Portuguese force, and Portuguese troops over that number would be removed from Angola by 30 April 1975. The

Portuguese troops allocated to the Angolan Defence Force would also eventually be sent home. Their withdrawal would begin on 1 October 1975, six weeks before independence, and be completed by 29 February 1976, eleven weeks after political power had passed entirely into Angolan hands.

Angolans were ecstatic when the transitional government was set up in Luanda on 31 January 1975 under Admiral Rosa Coutinho's successor, General Antonio Silva Cardoso, in the new post of High Commissioner. Superficially, the path to independence and unity in a multi-party democracy looked clear and smooth. Intensive campaigns for the pre-independence elections began.

But, despite all the high hopes, a combination of Russian ruthlessness and Western complacency ensured that independent Angola would be born in blood and tumult.

In December 1974, as Neto and Savimbi embraced in Luso after signing their agreement, a large contingent of MPLA officers was flown to the Soviet Union for military training. Delivery of the US$6 million worth of Soviet arms committed to the MPLA in the last part of 1974 continued even as the Alvor Accord was

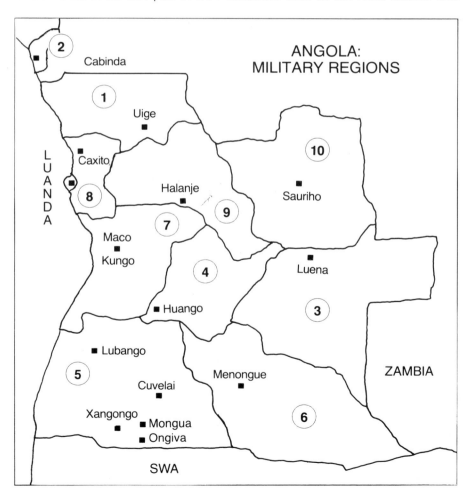

being negotiated and signed.[16]

The inauguration of the transitional government in Luanda was the high point of Portuguese and Western efforts to steer Angola towards independence with some degree of democracy. From then on it was like a hopelessly uneven and mismatched game of poker in which one side (the Soviet Union) was strong, committed and purposeful and the other (the West) was weak, vacillating and faint-hearted. The Soviet Union acted as though it had been dealt a handful of aces and proceeded to play each of them at the right moment. The West behaved as though it had a dud hand; such initiatives as it did take were so pusillanimous or unimaginative as to allow the Soviet Union to respond with force and decision.

After Alvor the United States made two fundamental errors. First, it made no immediate formal protest about the build-up of Russian arms in Angola, and did not do so for another eight months until October 1975. Secondly, its only response to the Russian moves was to give US$300 000 for political organisation to the FNLA, the weakest, most tribal and most corrupt of the three movements. At that stage Unita received no American support because it was an unknown quantity that had fought the whole war against the Portuguese from bases inside Angola: its leaders therefore had not appeared on the international cocktail circuit in the same way as activists of the MPLA and the FNLA.

Through its diplomatic missions in Luanda and Kinshasa, the capital of Zaïre, where Holden Roberto had his headquarters, the Russians soon learned of the new American cash hand-out to the FNLA.[17] As far as Moscow was concerned, this legitimised its own earlier and more substantial commitment. After the Alvor Accord the flow of Russian arms to the MPLA continued and steadily increased. By April 1975 planes were flying Russian arms direct to Angola, and then they began to arrive on board Greek, Yugoslav and Russian ships.

At some time in late 1974 or early 1975 Cuba also began to be deeply embroiled in the provision of support by the Eastern bloc to the MPLA in close cooperation with Admiral Rosa Coutinho. The precise date on which Fidel Castro made a firm commitment to the MPLA is not known. But it was at least eight or nine months earlier than the date of 5 November 1975 given by Gabriel Garcia Marques in his official account of the Cuban intervention in Angola.[18] This assertion was quite simply false, and it was appropriate that a winner of the most important prize for fiction, the Nobel, should perpetuate such an immensely damaging untruth. It was of serious historical consequence because the Marques "facts" have been repeated so often as to have become indisputable truths in the minds of many Western liberals. The Marques account suggested, for example, that the Cubans arrived in Angola only in response to an intrusion into the country by South African forces in October 1975, and that has determined the thinking of many in the West ever since. For example, the American journalist Jonathan Power, writing in the *International Herald Tribune* as late as 4 December 1985, could without fear of contradiction coolly state:

"The Cubans never set foot in Angola until the South Africans invaded Angola during its civil war."

Evidence that the Marques – Power version of Angolan history is mendacious has long been available, but new and ever more authentic accounts of the early Cuban commitment are now coming to light. Two of the most important in 1987 came from Admiral Rosa Coutinho, who described on Canadian television how he worked with the Cubans to undermine the electoral process in Angola, and General Rafael del Pino Diaz, the chief of the Cuban Air Force and one of the planners of Cuban military strategy in Angola for 12 years. In May 1987 General del Pino flew out of Havana in a private plane to Florida to become the highest defector ever to flee his country.

I met General del Pino in Washington and he described to me how, in January 1975, he had been instructed by Fidel Castro to begin preparations for the participation of the Air Force in the internal struggle in Angola.

"I was asked by the General Staff at the end of January to visit Africa to look at airfields," said General del Pino. "I said that Africa was a big place and I would need more precise guidance. Then they said it was southern Africa, and in due course they told me it was Angola.

"Castro assumed that the Alvor Accord was going to be honoured by no one, and he wanted to get ahead of the field; he knew the Chinese and North Koreans were giving aid to the FNLA. The arrangement was that the Soviet Union would send the weapons to Angola and Cuba would send the personnel.

"By March 1975 I was ready to send two officers to Angola to make plans for our (i.e. that of the Cuban Air Force) involvement.

"At the end of that month Lieutenant Colonel Angel Botello Avila (chief of logistics in the Cuban Air Force) and Colonel Jaime Archer Silva (a senior pilot) arrived in Luanda in civilian clothes and stayed in a house provided by the MPLA. In May they flew to Henrique de Carvalho, where they were given the air base by Portuguese military officers, who I suppose were loyal to Rosa Coutinho".

Henrique de Carvalho, renamed Saurimo since independence, is about 800 kilometres inland from Luanda. The instructions given Lieutenant-Colonel Botello and Colonel Archer were to develop the base as the main point of entry into Angola for Cuban weapons and military personnel. It was remote, and Western intelligence would therefore take longer to find out what was happening than if the operation were conducted nearer Luanda. Botello and Archer asked Cuba for 13 more officers specialising in electrical engineering, communications, power generators and fuel. Soon, when Cuba realised there was no concerted Western reaction to its activities in Angola, General del Pino switched his expeditionary air force to Luanda and Cabinda, an Angolan enclave to the north, through which it was easier to organise the airlift of weapons from the trans-shipment point of Brazzaville. "We had concluded that it was better to be a bit more open and less complicated," said the General.

Admiral Rosa Coutinho's role in bringing in Russian arms and later Cuban troops to help to undermine the electoral process in Angola had long been suspected. But he admitted nothing himself until interviewed for *Angola,* a Canadian television documentary shown for the first time on 27 September 1987 on Public Broadcasting Service TV in the United States.

Rosa Coutinho said that although he had helped to set up the Alvor talks and taken part in them, as one of his last tasks as Governor-General of Angola, he was all the time working to ensure that the MPLA came to power without the promised elections being held.

"I think that I fixed the decolonisation process in an irreversible way," Rosa Coutinho told the Canadians. "I knew very well that elections could not be held on the territory during the time that elapsed because Angola was still in a kind of turmoil. If elections were held, it would be a fantasy.

"I stated at the time that the only solution was to recognise the MPLA as the only force capable of directing Angola, and that Portugal should make a separate agreement with the MPLA to transfer the power on 11 November."

Even as the Alvor Accord was being signed, the Portuguese military, under Rosa Coutinho's direction, was allowing Cuban soldiers (as well as Russian) to slip into Angola in support of the MPLA. Juan Benemelis, head of the Africa Department of the Cuban Foreign Ministry from 1965 to 1975, said the first Cubans arrived in early January 1975: "At the moment (of the signing) of the Alvor Accord there were already Cubans about a hundred kilometres south of Luanda in a base in a fort called Massangano. Now the key person in that operation was Rosa Coutinho."

Benemelis, who defected to the United States in 1980 and has written a book titled *Castro - Subversion and Terrorism in Africa,* said that more Cuban military instructors arrived in March 1975 in the Angolan provinces of Cabinda, Benguela and Lobito from depots already established in Guiné-Bissau and Congo-Brazzaville.

As the Angolan crisis deepened Rosa Coutinho, now back home in Portugal, sought increased Cuban intervention to ensure a victory by the MPLA. Benemelis said: "In June 1975 there was a meeting in Havana. General Carlos Fabiao, Colonel Valera Gomes and Rosa Coutinho (all Portuguese military officers) went to Havana and they had a meeting with Senen Casas Requerion, Chief of Staff of the Cuban Army; Julio Casas Requerio, Army logistics chief; Vecino Algret, later one of the Cuban generals in Angola; and Rear Admiral Emigdio Baez of the Cuban Navy... It was a meeting headed by Rosa Coutinho with the high Cuban military in order to develop the military help that the Soviets and the Cubans were providing in a way that would facilitate on the 11 November 1975 the power to the MPLA."[19]

The High Commissioner, Antonio Silva Cardoso, recognised what those sections of the Portuguese forces loyal to Rosa Coutinho were trying to do in Angola. Silva Cardoso attempted to stop the flow of Russian weapons to the MPLA to avoid civil war and permit the elections to go ahead. In April 1975 he ordered Portuguese forces to impound a Bristol Britannia aircraft that arrived at Luso carrying 32 tonnes of arms, manifested as medicines, for the MPLA.[20] In the same month the Yugoslav cargo-vessel *Postoyna,* carrying weapons for the MPLA, was turned away from Luanda by General Silva Cardoso. The *Postoyna* sailed north to the port of Pointe Noire in Congo-Brazzaville, where she unloaded, and the weapons were ferried to Angola in smaller boats.[21]

In May 1975 Silva Cardoso told Jonas Savimbi that he wanted to attack the MPLA base at Massangano and clear the Cuban soldiers from the fort. Savimbi said: "He (Silva Cardoso) told us that he wanted to bomb that fort, so we said 'OK, go and do it.'

"But there were pro-Russians in the Military Council (of the Portuguese Armed Forces in Angola). They warned Silva Cardoso that if he did it they would tell Lisbon and he would be dismissed. Next day we found him very demoralised. He couldn't do anything, even though he wanted to. Portugal was divided, and its will and that of its soldiers in Angola had virtually collapsed."[22]

(In September 1975 Silva Cardoso retired in despair to Portugal, exhausted by his efforts to prevent chaos and to create conditions in which elections would be possible. He was replaced by Commodore Leonel Cardoso).

As Cuban personnel were infiltrated into the country to help the MPLA and the flow of Russian arms increased, the FNLA used part of its cash from the CIA to buy a daily newspaper, *A Provincia de Angola,* and a television station in Luanda. Then in early 1975 Holden Roberto began to move more of his troops from training bases in Zaïre into areas of northern Angola that the FNLA had occupied during the previous September. On 23 March 1975 FNLA soldiers attacked MPLA posts in Luanda, and three days later they attacked an MPLA training camp at Caxito, to the north-east of Luanda, and killed more than fifty recruits.

The aggression was not one-sided. Daniel Chipenda, leader of the Eastern Revolt faction of the MPLA, set up offices in Luanda, still claiming to be the real MPLA. On 13 February 1975 they were attacked by Agostinho Neto's followers, and 15 Chipenda loyalists were killed. Chipenda fled from Luanda and joined the FNLA, taking with him perhaps 3 000 soldiers.[23] Regular orgies of bloody reprisals between the FNLA and MPLA from now on made Luanda a city of terror. By June 1975 about 5 000 people had been killed in the fighting and many others were wounded and left homeless.[24]

Savimbi managed to keep Unita out of the fighting, but he could see that the conflict between the FNLA and the MPLA was intensifying into full-scale civil war. He responded with a two-fold strategy: to get all sides together again at a reconciliation conference outside Angola, and to appeal to the Western democracies to intervene to save Angola's own fledgling democracy.

The credentials of Unita for peacemaking were recognised by the international press corps which had gathered in Luanda to await independence and now found itself reporting the slaughter. Jane Bergerol, the Angola specialist on the *Financial Times*, wrote: "Dr Savimbi is increasingly seen as the mediator who can bring together the three movements... His original claim to fame as the single leader to have spent the war entirely inside Angola has been overtaken by his immediate popularity on the hustings. He also impressed African leaders as a man of compromise leading a party of peace."[25]

A correspondent for the *Gemini News Agency*, Barry Baxter, describing the uneasy peace in the Luanda *musseques* (shanty towns) after another round of fighting, wrote: "In the townships armed men from FNLA and MPLA parade nightly before their headquarters and their flags fly proudly above the remains of their strong-points. Attempts are being made to control the numbers of armed men in the *musseques*.

"Each movement is allowed to occupy 15 buildings with no more than 15 armed men (per building). The rest of the MPLA and FNLA troops must stay in barracks... The first attempts at promoting a truly national army are being made. When I went on patrol with a mixed group I saw that troops from the FNLA or the MPLA are never mixed on one patrol, although Unita soldiers are mixed with troops from the other two. The Portuguese captain in charge told me: 'If we go to investigate trouble in an MPLA area, we can send in MPLA and Unita men. If in an area which supports FNLA, we can send in only FNLA and Unita. We cannot send MPLA into FNLA country.'"[26]

With the diplomatic support of President Kaunda of Zambia, Savimbi was able to arrange Nakuru, in the Great Rift Valley, as the site of the reconciliation meeting. It took place from 16 June 1975 under the chairmanship of Jomo Kenyatta. Savimbi, on his first visit to Luanda in April and May 1975 from his headquarters in the central Angolan town of Nova Lisboa (renamed Huambo after independence), had been dismayed to discover that the transitional government decreed by the Alvor Accord had made little progress towards preparing for the pre-independence elections. A provisional constitution which, according to the Accord had to be ready by 31 March, had not been drawn up. The registration of voters was far behind schedule.

In one of his speeches in Luanda, Savimbi said there was no hope of real independence for Angola unless it was brought in by elections. "We need one flag, one anthem, one army," he said. "How can the Portuguese give us independence with three flags, three anthems and three armies? The liberation movements inside the government are still operating as independent groups.

"We shall all have to make concessions so that we can make independence possible and society viable." Noting the extent to which China was helping the FNLA at Nyerere's bidding and the arming of the MPLA by the Soviet Union, Savimbi warned against making Angola an arena for confrontation between the superpowers, and he recalled one of Jomo Kenyatta's old sayings: "When two elephants fight, it is the grass that gets trampled."[27]

While in Luanda, Savimbi got a taste of the gruesome reality of the conflict between the MPLA and the FNLA. On the night of 28 April 1975 severe fighting broke out between the two movements and continued for three days, leaving more than 700 people dead and more than a thousand wounded. The fighting spread to towns in eastern and northern Angola. The MPLA recruited a mercenary force of 3 500 Katangese gendarmes who had fought on behalf of the anti-Soviet Congolese leader Moise Tshombe in his attempt at secession in the Sixties. Ironically, only a few months earlier the Katangese had been fighting as mercenaries with the Portuguese against Unita and the MPLA. The recruitment of the Katangese, who still had ambitions in Zaïre (as the Congo had been renamed), incensed the Zaïrean patron of the FNLA, President Mobutu Sese Seko, and by mid-May 1975 1 200 Zaïrean soldiers had moved across the border into Angola with French Panhard armoured cars to fight alongside the FNLA. As Angola descended into apparently unstoppable civil war, tens of thousands of Portuguese civilians began to leave the country; Africans left the *musseques* in Luanda for their home villages and foreign consulates began to send home their wives and children.[28]

The truth is that Savimbi, in spite of his efforts to organise the Nakuru meeting, had scant hope of its success. On 4 June just twelve days before the Nakuru talks began, the MPLA had for the first time turned its guns on Unita followers. MPLA troops in Luanda killed a large group of young recruits who were Unita's contribution to the joint Angolan Defence Force. Estimates of the number of dead, in what became known in Unita folklore as the Pica–Pau massacre, varied between fifty, according to some independent accounts, and 260, according to Savimbi. Bodies were mutilated by the MPLA in acts of "pure barbarism", said a communiqué of the Portuguese Armed Forces, whose soldiers helped to collect the corpses from the Unita "peace offices" in the suburb of Pica–Pau.[29]

There was speculation that black radicals loyal to Nito Alves, one of the fiercest of the MPLA leaders, had carried out the attack independently in an attempt to force Savimbi to choose between the other two movements. Lucio Lara, the veteran MPLA ideologist, and President Marien Ngouabi of Congo–Brazzaville had together asked the Prime Minister of Senegal, Abdou Diouf, a sympathiser with Unita, to persuade Savimbi to join the MPLA, arguing that his movement had no future if it tried to act alone.[30]

Savimbi declined the invitation because he believed the MPLA was seeking the help of Unita to eliminate what it saw as the greater immediate danger, the FNLA. "After that they would get rid of us," Savimbi argued. "Everybody was struggling for power. The FNLA also was scheming to use Unita to destroy MPLA, and after that get rid of Unita because Unita was not strong militarily... (After Pica–Pau) many of our members advocated that we should join the FNLA and crush the MPLA once and for all. But in the leadership we knew that the FNLA, despite its numbers, was a hollow movement. Politically they were weak and badly organised. We said we could not form an alliance with them because they were going to lose."[31]

As well as resisting a partisan alliance with either of the other two movements, Savimbi refused to be intimidated into reaction by the Pica–Pau massacre, despite the call for reprisals: "Some of our people accused us of being cowards for refusing to confront the MPLA, but after the massacre even those who argued that the MPLA had something to offer us said it was no longer possible to think of forming a front with them."[32]

Before they went to Nakuru, Savimbi and his senior associates agreed among themselves that the chaos in Angola meant that they could not expect to take immediate power after an election. So they changed their approach: "We said it was absolutely obvious that any election organised in Angola would be won by Unita, but this presented a problem for the FNLA and the MPLA. So we said, let us work out a compromise. Let us say that for five years, from 1975, we all agree on a coalition government so that all the animosities can cool down – then only after five years let us organise elections so that we know who will rule the country with the support of the people."[33]

After five days of talks at Nakuru the Angolan leaders signed a new agreement renouncing force and reaffirming support for the Alvor Accord, the transitional government and the creation of a unified army. But there was no support for Savimbi's proposal that there should be a five-year coalition before the holding of the first election: "No one wanted to admit that they had no majority, so they had to say they wanted elections. Neither the FNLA nor the MPLA could compete with us at the ballot box."

The Nakuru Agreement said: "The holding of elections in Angola is the most adequate form of guaranteeing a peaceful transference of power at the moment of independence." A new timetable was drawn up for preparing the elections – Clause 7 of the 7 000–word agreement reaffirmed October as the date for the elections and called for the Constituent Assembly to meet at the beginning of the following month before Independence Day on 11 November.

The agreement was signed under the benevolent paternal gaze of President Kenyatta. There was much smiling and embracing before international cameramen, although at that very moment Rosa Coutinho was in Havana coordinating increased Cuban military support for the MPLA. In the first few weeks after Nakuru the transitional government drew up a draft constitution and the first 120–man company of the integrated Angolan Defence Force was formed. Clauses 1 and 3 of the Nakuru Agreement called for an end to bloodshed between Angolans, but on 9 July 1975 the heaviest fighting yet between the FNLA and the MPLA broke out and, after three weeks of killing, the MPLA drove the FNLA out of Luanda.

When the new fighting began, Savimbi decided to withdraw his people from the capital, believing that the logic of the continuing MPLA military build-up was that its arms would again be turned heavily on Unita now that the FNLA was out of the way. As they pulled out of the capital in a column of 180 trucks, several hundred members of Unita were killed on 12 July in an ambush at a bridge across the Cuanza River at Dondo, 200 kilometres south of Luanda.[34]

With the expulsion of the FNLA from Luanda and the withdrawal of Unita, the transitional government collapsed, never to be revived. Holding power in the capital, the MPLA declared itself the legitimate heir to political power in Angola. Savimbi's followers called on him to declare war on the MPLA. "But

I told them to be cool, because I was still consulting with my friends among the African heads of state. We were still waiting for arms that we had been promised from China and Rumania. It was no good committing ourselves to a war with the MPLA unless we were strong enough to fight them and keep them out of our areas. But after Dondo the people were all the time crying for war."[35]

Savimbi's attempt to persuade the Western democracies to use their power and influence to ensure an electoral transfer to independence had begun as early as November 1974: "I went to see every embassy of the Western countries in Lusaka. I told them the danger is this one, the danger is this one, the danger is this one... Everybody said, 'We understand you, we are with you' ... but they did not act until the MPLA got us."[36]

Kenneth Kaunda attempted to rescue his friend Savimbi. On 19 and 20 April 1975 he paid a state visit to Washington and was received by President Ford. While public attention was drawn by Kaunda's speech at the White House criticising American policy in South Africa, Namibia and Rhodesia, privately he was warning Ford and his Secretary of State Henry Kissinger of Soviet intentions in Angola and urging them to react effectively and give help to Unita and the FNLA.[37]

Preoccupied with the imminent collapse of the government of South Vietnam (Saigon fell to the North Vietnamese on 30 April 1975 as America began a complete military withdrawal), the Ford administration shilly-shallied. It saw no need for an urgent diplomatic effort to save the fleeting chance that an election rather than a war would determine who governed Angola. It made no move to work through the Organisation of African Unity and the United Nations, or bilaterally with the Soviet Union, to solve the Angolan problem. And, with the Vietnam débâcle afflicting American confidence and *amour-propre,* it was inconceivable that the people could be asked to plunge into another war in a far-off country.

The misfortune for Savimbi was that the overwhelming weight of opinion was that Unita would win more votes in an election than the other parties, if only because the Ovimbundu tribe that formed the core of his support was by far the largest in Angola. As early as 7 December 1974, the *Observer* correspondent in Luanda had written: "Portuguese officials here concede that the MPLA, once thought to be by far the most important of the liberation movements, is not so well supported as they thought."[38]

Western diplomats, for the most part, predicted that Unita would win 35 to 45 per cent of the Angolan vote, the MPLA 25 to 35 per cent, and the FNLA 15 to 25 per cent.

But the ultimate legitimation for Unita came from the OAU, which sent a ten-man fact-finding commission to Angola from 10 to 20 October 1975, the month when the elections to a Constituent Assembly had been intended to be held. Presenting its report in early November, before Independence Day, the commission declared that public support for Unita was greater than for either the MPLA or FNLA. The OAU team again called for a ceasefire, the termination of deliveries of foreign arms, the cessation of external interference and the establishment of a government of national unity. The MPLA, growing in political confidence and by now sure of uninhibited and unashamed military support from the Soviet Union, rejected these proposals and also a proposal to create an OAU peacekeeping force.[39]

On 4 August 1975 Unita entered the war after MPLA troops in the central

Angolan town of Silva Porto fired on Savimbi's personal aircraft. Despite troubles elsewhere in the country, MPLA and Unita soldiers had continued to co-exist uneasily in Silva Porto. But after that incident Unita drove the MPLA out of town and succumbed to a devil's bargain worked out between Gerald Ford and Kaunda to enable Savimbi's movement to survive.

Not only did the West fail to respond openly and effectively in support of the agreed democratic process in Angola, but when it made its inevitable covert moves they were misdirected, inadequate and of a nature that was sure to tarnish the image of the non–MPLA Angolan movements in the eyes of many abroad.

The Western programme to combat the Russians and Cubans had three elements:

* A covert, but limited, supply of arms from the Central Intelligence Agency to the FNLA and Unita.
* The recruitment of Western European mercenary troops to fight against the FNLA.
* Encouraging the South African Defence Force to enter the Angolan war in support of the FNLA and Unita.

The whole enterprise was a disaster from beginning to end.

After Kaunda's visit to Washington in April 1975, President Ford approved and signed in July the expenditure for the covert supply by the CIA of arms worth US$31.7 million to the FNLA and Unita. The sum was the maximum permitted to the President under American law before he had to seek Congressional approval for more funds. After the fall of Saigon and because many Congressmen had been elected on platforms calling for a US withdrawal from Vietnam, such support for a war on yet another continent was unlikely to be forthcoming.

But even the covert funding was intended mainly to support the weak and incompetent client of Washington, Holden Roberto, rather than Jonas Savimbi, the man most likely to have been the choice of the Angolan electors. By the time the CIA funds ran out, Roberto's FNLA had received the lion's share of it and Savimbi's Unita only about US$10 million.

The American subsidy for the FNLA and Unita was puny compared with the weapons worth about US$110 million supplied by the Soviet Union between November 1974 and November 1975 to the MPLA, about twice the amount sent by Moscow during all the previous 14 years, when the MPLA was fighting the Portuguese. By February 1976 the value of the weapons sent by the Soviet Union to its MPLA clients and Cuban allies in Angola had reached US$400 million.[40]

Hamstrung by limits on covert funding, the Americans, supported by Kenneth Kaunda, also decided to ask the notorious moral pariah, the white-ruled Republic of South Africa, to intervene in Angola. Pretoria was further encouraged by a series of nods and winks by West European democracies, who stood on the sidelines wringing their hands as events unwound in Angola but were not prepared themselves to act decisively.

President Ford gave Henry Kissinger the task of signalling to Pretoria that its intervention in the Angolan war would not be frowned upon. As his emissaries he chose Daniel Patrick Moynihan, the American Ambassador to the United Nations, and Mr William Bowdler, the American Ambassador to South Africa. Moynihan gave the message to Pik Botha, the South African Ambassador to the UN, later to become foreign minister: Bowdler's message was delivered to John Vorster.[41] The Defence Minister, P.W. Botha, later to succeed Vorster as

Prime Minister before becoming President, said he personally had watched US planes deliver arms in 1975 to anti-MPLA forces in Angola: they were unloaded by American personnel in the presence of South African troops, who had been asked to help distribute them.[42]

Barry Goldwater, the right wing Republican Senator from Arizona, was blunt about the green light that his country was giving to the South Africans. He said: "There is no question but that the CIA told the South Africans to move into Angola and that we would help with military equipment."[43]

John Vorster went to his grave without ever having directly identified the United States as the country that had encouraged South African intervention in the Angolan war. But an interview that Vorster gave to the *Newsweek* journalist Arnaud de Borchgrave in May 1976 went like this:

> *De Borchgrave:* "Would it be accurate to say that the US solicited South Africa's help to turn the tide against the Russians and Cubans in Angola last fall?"
>
> *Vorster:* "I do not want to comment on that. The US Government can speak for itself. I am sure you will appreciate that I cannot violate the confidentiality of government-to-government communications. But if you are making the statement, I won't deny it."
>
> *De Borchgrave:* "Would it also be accurate to say that you received a green light from Kissinger for a military operation in Angola and that at least six moderate black African presidents had given you their blessing for the same operation?"
>
> *Vorster:* "If you say that of your own accord, I will not call you a liar."[44]

Henry Kamm of the *New York Times* reported a South African "high official", probably Vorster, as telling him that South Africa had gone into Angola on the understanding that the US would provide sufficient arms to make possible an effective resistance to a takeover by the MPLA.

Kamm reported from South Africa: "A high official said in an interview that the South African hope that the weapons superiority of the Soviet-backed forces could be balanced was based on contacts with American officials. He did not name them as he made this statement, but at another point he expressed special disappointment with Secretary of State Henry Kissinger. 'We had been in touch,' the official said. 'We felt that if we could give them (the Americans) a lapse of time they would find ways and means… We accepted the utterances of Mr Kissinger and others. We felt surely he had the necessary pull to come forward with the goods'."[45]

It was shameful that the West had to use a surrogate at all in its attempts to rescue the democratic process in Angola. But there was something especially cynical about its choice of South Africa, not exactly renowned for its championship of the black franchise and a frequent target of verbal attack from most of the countries now urging it on into Angola.

However, even this Western "help" came far too late to prevent the totalitarian take-over by the MPLA. According to a secret memorandum sent by the late Sean Macbride, the fiercely anti-South African former United Nations Commissioner for Namibia, to UN headquarters in New York, the South African invasion force crossed from Namibia into Angola on 23 October 1975.[46]

The Western-backed South African cavalry entered Angola *14 months* after the Soviet Union had begun its programme of arms deliveries to the MPLA in late August 1974, and *nine months* after Cuba began its preparations to send troops to Angola.

In the month before the South Africans crossed the border, at least a thousand Cuban soldiers were disembarked from troopships in Angola. In an increase of the earlier small Cuban military presence, troops and weapons began to be loaded in Cuba on board ships bound for Angola from 7 September 1975. The first ship may have reached Africa as early as 25 September 1975, but of those that were positively identified the *Vietnam Heroico* was among the first to disembark, at Porto Amboim, south of Luanda, on 4 October 1975. Two other ships, the *Coral Island* and *La Playa de Habana,* disembarked on 5 and 12 October. There were about a thousand Cuban combat troops on board these ships along with armoured cars and military trucks. By Independence Day, on 11 November, between 2 800 and 4 000 Cuban troops were in Angola.[47] That number of men could not have been mobilised and transported to Angola by that date if, as Gabriel Garcia Marques asserts and so many others have repeated, "the Revolutionary Government of Cuba decided to send the first military units to Angola to support the MPLA" only on 5 November 1975.

Colin Legum, the English writer on Africa who has a long record of opposition to the white government in his native South Africa, wrote: "The mobilisation and transport of such large numbers would require at least six weeks from the time the decision was taken.

"The Russian and Cuban contention that their military intervention was the result of South African intervention is clearly a *post facto* rationalisation, since they were seriously involved before March 1975, and they had already put their aid programme into its second phase by the beginning of October – fully three weeks before the South African army had crossed the frontier. One Cuban taken prisoner by FNLA gave details of his unit's arrival from Brazzaville in August 1975, almost two months before the South African army arrival."[48]

And even the Deputy Prime Minister of Cuba, Carlos Rafael Rodriguez, admitted that Cuban soldiers were in Angola with the MPLA before there was any South African intervention. His admission was filled out with details supplied by the late Wilfred Burchett, the Australian communist journalist who wrote sympathetically first of the Chinese communists and the North Vietnamese and subsequently became close to the MPLA. Rodriguez told a group of correspondents in January 1976 that Cuba had sent 230 military advisers to Angola in May 1975 to train MPLA forces at Benguela, Cabinda, Henrique de Carvalho (now renamed Saurimo) and Salazar (renamed Dalatando), near Luanda.[49] According to Burchett: "238 was the precise figure."[50]

I have dwelt at length on the timing of the arrival in Angola of the various foreign armies and weapons because beliefs about who was concerned and at what time have been crucial in shaping the attitudes of Western liberal democrats towards the conflict. The many repetitions of Marques's blatant falsehood about the timing of Fidel Castro's decision to commit his Cuban Gurkhas to the Angolan battlefields has helped to persuade many liberals, some gullible, others willing accomplices, that that really was the truth.

Having refused to face these facts with intellectual rigour and courage, democrats of the centre were given a boost by the intervention of South Africa, the country whose unambiguously black and white internal policies provided the most widely-accepted litmus test for the liberalism of white outsiders. In refusing to listen to the complex and difficult arguments of the non–MPLA blacks in Angola, there was the bonus for European and North American liberals of a *frisson* of moral righteousness. They could, in the words of a black American lawyer, a friend of Unita, say to groups other than the MPLA: "We aren't going to give you any guns, but we'll get angry with you if you take your guns from South Africa. But we don't care if your enemy is using the most sophisticated attack helicopters in the business to kill you."[51]

In southern Africa the relentlessness with which white South Africans cling to minority rule is matched all too often by the blind fanaticism with which too many anti-apartheid campaigners are willing to sacrifice others to see its white rulers overthrown. This has become a kind of racism of its own, often more cruel in effect if not intent than the system whose destruction is sought.

Savimbi, who had sought help from the West to save the electoral process but had instead been given South African military support by the democracies, once told me: "I am absolutely without remorse that I have dealings with South Africa... Every black African state is trading with them, including the MPLA."

He did not expect Western armchair critics to understand the attitude of Unita towards South Africa. "But do they believe that black men like us approve of apartheid? Do they think we want to import it to Angola? It is unthinkable. Against whom would we apply it? Ourselves?

"My critics in the West are hypocritical. They say we should not take aid from South Africa for our struggle. But they will never give us aid themselves. They seem to be asking us to commit suicide, to accept being crushed by Cubans and Russians in our own country. We will not do that. To avoid it, we have to take help from wherever it is on offer."[52]

This was a bitter jest, for the MPLA leader Agostinho Neto had once said of the succour he received from the Soviet Union while his guerrillas fought the Portuguese: "That people fighting for their independence will take aid from wherever they can find it is clear. To win our independence we should even take aid, as they say, from the devil himself."[53]

Fidel Castro calculated well the mess in which the Western democracies would find themselves in Angola, General del Pino told me. The Americans would not wish to intervene directly because of the pain and humiliation of the recent withdrawal from Vietnam. The Western Europeans were generally spineless, dependent militarily on the Americans, and they could be depended upon not to intervene in any serious way. The FNLA, the Americans' favourite card, was a hollow shell that could easily be defeated on the battlefields of northern Angola. The South Africans were a more serious matter, but they would not need to be fought. When their presence became known Western democratic indignation would be so intense as to make fighting unnecessary: the South Africans would simply retreat in the face of the vociferous condemnation.[54]

Castro proved to be right in all these calculations.

In the north at first the FNLA made advances, until by the eve of independence Holden Roberto's forces were only thirty kilometres from Luanda. Roberto, who had never in his life been to the Angolan capital, believed that absolute power lay within his grasp, only a few hours away.

At first light on 10 November 1975 about 1 500 FNLA soldiers began to advance in a single column across the broad and marshy valley of the Bengo River, north of Luanda. They were supported by two regular battalions of the Zaïrean Army and a hundred Portuguese-Angolan soldiers. South African artillery on a ridge north of the river aimed their guns with a range of 17 kilometres across the river, where 800 Cubans were dug in on hilltops round the village of Quifandongo. CIA officers, French and British intelligence agents, South African advisers, and

Roberto together watched the beginning of the thrust into Luanda, whose outskirts, dominated by petrol storage tanks, were just visible in the distance.

As the FNLA advanced across the swamp along a narrow metalled road on top of a dyke, a devastating barrage was laid down by the Cubans and MPLA support troops. Heavy mortar shells rained down on the column and salvos of 122mm rockets, fired from forty-barrelled Stalin Organ launchers, screamed into the midst of the soldiers. The South African artillery was no match for the Cubans' brand-new Russian hardware. Most of Roberto's dozen armoured cars and a half-dozen jeeps armed with anti-tank rockets were knocked out within an hour.

Roberto's men panicked and got bogged down in the swamp. Cubans dashed forward in jeeps to fire RPG-7 rockets and anti-aircraft guns along the dyke among the demoralised Africans. Hundreds of FNLA men and Zaïreans were killed, and five of the Portuguese. The 26-man South African contingent escaped with radio and decoding equipment to a nearby beach, from which they were flown by helicopter to the South African Navy frigate *President Steyn* waiting five kilometres offshore.

This disaster, which became known as "Nshila wa Lufu" (Death Road), broke the FNLA, which never recovered. It retreated in undisciplined panic from one town to the next, as and when the Cubans and MPLA decided on methodical thrusts north towards the border of Zaïre.[55]

The West, which had judged badly in believing the FNLA had either the resolution, discipline or popular support necessary to break through into Luanda, now compounded the error. The contribution of the Western democracies to the Angolan imbroglio plumbed its most contemptible depths. Mercenaries in Britain and the US were recruited with crisp new hundred-dollar bills, by courtesy of the CIA, to beef up and reorganise the FNLA. The quality of the mercenaries was even lower than most of the breed. Most were from the ranks of the young unemployed of the mid-Seventies, and many were the most socially inferior of their generation; poorly educated, from poor homes, intellectual innocents in an African country that had long since lost its own innocence.

Militarily they were a failure, and they became part of a horror story when a former British parachutist, Costas Georgiou, also known as "Colonel" Callan, killed 14 of his fellow mercenaries, stripped their bodies and left them to rot unburied. Callan and 12 other mercenaries were subsequently captured by the Cubans and sent to Luanda to face trial by the MPLA for war crimes. For months the mercenaries became the focus of attention by the news media, so distracting attention from the deeper questions underlying the conflict. They were a propaganda gift to the MPLA. Their trial in June 1976 was a spectacular news event, and, although its legal validity was disputable, the bestiality and futility of the acts committed by the defendants shocked people everywhere and strengthened sympathy for the MPLA. In the immediacy and drama of the trial, the aborted elections and the question of whether the MPLA was a legitimate government got buried.

During the trial the West took a severe drubbing, especially when it became clear that Prime Minister James Callaghan's Labour government had turned a blind eye to the recruitment of mercenaries in Britain and allowed them to pass through London Airport without passports. The Angolan People's Prosecutor, Manuel Rui Monteiro, described the accused as "professional murderers in the pay of imperialism". The verdicts were virtually pre-ordained as the MPLA received publicity of a value that it could never have bought for itself. Four men, including Callan, were sentenced to death and shot by firing squad on 10 July 1976.

The others were sentenced to long prison terms.[56]

The South African invasion force which Sean Macbride identified entering Angola in late October 1975 made spectacular progress in the south. Three separate columns of South African troops in light Panhard armoured cars swept more than 600 kilometres into the country before pausing at Cela, about 300 kilometres south of Luanda. The confidence of the invaders was high, but they lacked bridging equipment for difficult river crossings on the approaches to Luanda and Pretoria refused to provide paratroopers to attack behind the entrenched Cuban positions. From late November onwards, the South Africans began to encounter much stronger organised resistance by the Cubans, who by then were also receiving better equipment than their first contingents from across the Atlantic. Cuban weapons included Russian T-34 and T-54 tanks, PT-76 light amphibious tanks and missile-firing MI-8 helicopters.

But most serious, in the long run, was the exposure of the presence of the South African force in Angola by Reuter's Central Africa correspondent in despatches on 14 and 22 November 1975. The Reuter reports persuaded Nigeria, the most powerful country in black Africa, to end its calls for a Soviet withdrawal from Angola and to switch support from Unita to the MPLA, to which the Lagos government sent US$20 million.[57] John Stockwell, the head of the CIA Task Force in Angola, wrote of the revelation by Reuters: "The propaganda and political war was lost in that stroke. There was nothing the Lusaka (CIA) station could invent that would be as damaging to the other side as our alliance with the hated South Africans was to our cause."[58]

With South Africa exposed, more and more black African states gave the MPLA recognition as the legitimate government of Angola. In Pretoria officials debated whether to prolong the South African intervention in Angola or to withdraw. At the same time a crucial shift of opinion on Angola had begun among liberal congressmen and senators in the United States.

On 5 December 1975 Senator Dick Clark, a Democrat from Iowa, set in motion a process that made the South African withdrawal absolutely inevitable when he recommended to the Senate Foreign Relations Subcommittee that all covert aid to liberation movements in Angola should be stopped. Since September Clark had been convinced that the CIA was cooperating directly and illegally with South Africa, and he was determined that it should end.

Voices were raised against Clark. The US Ambassador to the UN, Patrick Moynihan, warned the General Assembly that it should not settle for the "big lie" that only one country, South Africa, had intervened in Angola: "At just the moment, with the European colonisers of the seventeenth, eighteenth and nineteenth centuries departing, at just that moment, a new European colonising, colonial, imperial nation appears on the continent of Africa – armed, aggressive, involved in the direct assault upon the lands and the people of Africa.

"Which of the great powers has not condemned all intervention in Angola? We know very well which has not. It is the Soviet Union which has not, the European power now engaged in colonial expansion in the continent of Africa. The Soviet government, far from condemning intervention, has acknowledged it, saying it is assisting its friends in Angola and saying that it would continue to do so..."[59]

Kenneth Kaunda, who had assiduously cooperated with the Americans and John Vorster on South African intervention in Angola, made several speeches emphasising that Soviet intervention in Angola had preceded that of America and South Africa. He asserted that Unita and the FNLA had had "every right to request arms from the USA when the MPLA received such arms from the Soviet Union..."

"If the United States is asked by any Angolan party, who am I to say the USA should not respond?... Once Portugal was out of Angola, there was no justification for Soviet support of the MPLA. I feel we must speak plainly on Angola. We must be morally and politically courageous and tell the Soviets: 'You are wrong.' We in Africa must look at Angola in a sober, cool way, not emotionally. And much as we condemn South Africa's presence in Angola, we cheat ourselves if we think by condemning South Africa we are settling things."[60]

Andrew Young, the black American leader destined later to become US Ambassador to the United Nations in Jimmy Carter's administration, visited Lusaka and joined in the condemnation of the Soviet Union. At the opening of a new "Martin Luther King Library", in the presence of Kenneth Kaunda, he praised Kaunda's daring in meeting Vorster and said that King would have done the same thing. Young called on the United States to stop sending grain to the Soviet Union unless Moscow stopped the flow of arms to Angola.

But most voices were raised in favour of the easy way out. Senior statesman Hubert Humphrey reflected the dominant mood in the Senate when he explained (just as Neville Chamberlain in the Thirties had dismissed Czechoslovakia as a small, far-away country of little concern to Britons) why his vote would be cast against further arms for Unita or the FNLA: "The United States had better start taking care of things it knows how to take care of. We know so little of Africa, the 800 and some tribes that make up Africa... I say it is like a different world."

John Tunney was one of the most vulnerable Democratic senators standing for re-election in 1976. In California he faced a tight Democratic primary against the anti-war activist Tom Hayden, who was backed by his wife Jane Fonda and the Fonda fortune. An undistinguished senator who had taken little interest in defence or foreign affairs, Tunney was in urgent need of instant visibility and an improved status as a "dove". Angola came as an answer to his prayers. Senator Alan Cranston and other leaders of the Democratic Party appealed to Senator Clark to let Tunney take the lead on the drive to cut off aid for Angola and Clark reluctantly acquiesced.[61]

On 19 December 1975 the Senate voted in favour of the Clark amendment by 54 to 22, and the supply of American weapons to Angola was severed. Tunney was gleeful about the fate of Unita. "Savimbi has no illusions about how swiftly the end is coming," he said. "The war in Angola beyond guerrilla fighting is almost over."[62]

Tunney lost his seat in the Senate in the 1976 election and was cast into oblivion. But his opportunism helped to condemn tens of thousands of Angolans to death, for the Clark Amendment, which he hoped would save his career, in fact only helped to complicate and prolong the Angolan civil war.

As the vote on the Clark Amendment took place, an emergency meeting of the OAU in Addis Ababa on Angola was being planned for January 1976. South Africa, which had decided to withdraw from Angola after the capture by the Cubans of seven of its young soldiers, agreed to pleas by Kaunda and Savimbi to stay on until after the meeting in Addis Ababa in the hope that a diplomatic settlement of the conflict could still be achieved. South Africa, having been urged to intervene in Angola by the US administration, was dismayed by the decision of the Senate, but felt even more betrayed by the failure of the American government to block a resolution by the Security Council of the UN calling on South Africa to pay war damage reparations to the MPLA.

Both Savimbi and Kaunda pleaded with South Africa not to withdraw. On the last day of 1975 Kaunda summoned Mr Brand Fourie, the head of the South African Foreign Ministry, from Cape Town to Kaunda's ancestral village in eastern Zambia. As the old year went out, Kaunda told Fourie, whom he had come to know well in the course of more than twenty rounds of clandestine talks in the last six months of 1975, that South Africa should either go forward all the way to Luanda, or withdraw from Angola entirely. But, said Kaunda, his recommendation was for South Africa to go forward. Fourie said it was impossible for South Africa to make that kind of commitment because such countries as the US and France, which had secretly backed South Africa, were now "getting off the bandwagon".[63]

In Johannesburg the Defence Minister, P.W. Botha, who was responsible for the Angolan strategy, said: "If the West does not want to contribute its share for the sake of itself and the free world, it cannot expect South Africa to do it... South Africa is not prepared to fight the West's battle against communist penetration on its own."[64]

Before leaving for the crucial fight in Addis Ababa, Savimbi said that the US Congress should not have abdicated its responsibilities: "The history of this century and the next one should not be made around Vietnam. In Vietnam the United States was on the side of the minority. In Angola it is the opposite. The majority of the people are with us and the MPLA wants to impose its will by force on the majority."

"The Senate really snatched defeat from the jaws of victory," said Bruce Porter, a former economic attaché at the US Consulate in Luanda in 1975. "The Senate voted against US involvement thinking that we were, in the words of one, backing the wrong horse. Actually we were backing the right horse. We were backing the group (Unita) that had the majority support of the Angolan people... "[65]

On 12 January, the last day of the meeting in Addis Ababa, Kaunda outlined the Zambian view of the crisis in the country next to his own: "We are not an electoral college. We have not come here to confirm any one political party as the government of Angola... Zambia wants a progressive and non-aligned Angola completely free from external pressures." And in a scarcely veiled allusion to the Soviet Union, he said: "Africa must understand that imperialism is imperialism. It knows neither race nor colour nor ideology. All nations which seek to impose their will on others are imperialists. Africa must not permit those imperialist Trojan horses which come under the guise of furthering the cause of liberation to divide us."[66]

But black Africa, torn between its detestation of white minority rule in the south and its fear of Russian and Cuban intentions on black-ruled territory, did divide: 22–22 to be exact, with two abstentions, on two motions; the first by Leopold Senghor, President of Senegal, calling for an Angolan ceasefire, the withdrawal of foreign troops and the reconciliation of the three movements to form a government of national unity; and the second by the head of the Nigerian army, Brigadier Murtala Muhammed (destined to be assassinated the following month), which called on the OAU to recognise the MPLA as the legitimate government of Angola. Although the meeting failed to produce a vote condemning South Africa, the two abstainers, the host nation Ethiopia and the chairman nation Uganda, soon afterwards recognised the MPLA, and after that there was an avalanche in favour of the Popular Movement. Within six weeks the MPLA had been recognised by 41 of the 46 OAU members, and on 10 February 1976 Agostinho Neto's government became the forty-seventh member of the pan-African group.

On 20 January 1976 South Africa began its total military withdrawal from Angola and completed the operation by the end of March. Savimbi, now left entirely alone to face the advance of the MPLA and the Cubans through central and southern Angola, spoke with more regret than bitterness about Americans such as Tunney, Clark and Humphrey who had opposed help to his movement: "We deplore that they want to defend democracy and freedom for themselves in the United States, but want dictatorship for us... They are working a contradiction... It is too simple reasoning for Senator Humphrey to say that Angola is too far away... They are defending an undemocratic society for us. For Angolans they want the Cubans and their Russian tanks and jets to impose on us a system."

Even Andrew Young, the advocate of sanctions against the Soviet Union when he was in Kaunda's presence, eventually joined the pack. He described the Cubans as a force for stability in Angola and asked: "If we can trade with a pro-Soviet Angola, why not also with a pro-Soviet Zaïre and a pro-Soviet Zambia – indeed, a pro-Soviet Africa?" To which President Mobutu of Zaïre replied: "Is that the position of the Carter administration? If it is, we should be told about it and we shall then be in a better position to arrange for our own surrender on better terms today than tomorrow."[67]

Senator Clark said the US should acknowledge that "the tide of history" was on the side of the MPLA and begin negotiations with the movement with a view to recognising it.

Savimbi, however, said that the MPLA would never win acceptance. Unita had fought for liberty from the Portuguese. "Now we are fighting again for the liberty of our people. We will fight until one day the world consciousness will understand that between justice and injustice there is no choice. The Russians and Cubans are slaughtering our people. The South African presence was just a pretext for the Russians for the invasion of our country using the Cubans. Now that there are no South Africans at any of the fronts, why are the Cubans continuing to advance and kill our black people? Why don't they stop?"

It was at that point that Fidel Castro made his first serious miscalculation. He did not foresee that Africans would have the determination and acquire the ability to resist what they saw as a new colonial domination of their country.

In fact, although the FNLA was now moribund, Jonas Savimbi and his followers began an epic resistance that by 1988 had demoralised the Cuban expeditionary force in Angola so much that it was beginning to threaten the internal cohesion of the Cuban state itself.

From March 1976 Savimbi led his people on a 3 000 kilometre "Long March" into the interior of Angola that lasted seven months. Many died, some from starvation, some from exposure, as they crossed wide rivers and marshes during the freezing nights of the short southern Angolan winter, and others by gunfire as dissident Angolans were hunted down by Cuban and MPLA troops.[68] Now Savimbi was an embarrassment to Western governments. None gave him any chance of survival, and most probably wished him dead so that they could get on with the job of establishing normal relations with the "legitimate" Angolan power, the MPLA. But Savimbi and Unita did survive and ensured that the war, pronounced finished by nearly all commentators after the Cuban victory in February 1976, would continue.

Meanwhile, with Savimbi gone and Angola ceasing to be a question, Henry Kissinger tried to restore American prestige in southern Africa by visiting the continent and outlining a programme for black majority rule in Rhodesia, a definite timetable for Namibian independence and warning South Africa to end its discriminatory policies.[69] Jardo Muecalia, a young Angolan on Savimbi's Long March, remembers tuning in on a small radio to one of Kissinger's speeches on Africa and being appalled by the lack of any mention of Angola: "I realised then that no one outside cared for us, that we had only ourselves to rely upon. Steel entered my soul that day."[70]

Savimbi's advice to his followers was: "If we survive, then things will begin to change around us." For a year, from February 1976 to March 1977, they were entirely on their own. But in March 1977 several thousand Katangese gendarmes and other exiles from Katanga crossed the border from their camps in Angola into the Shaba province of Zaïre (formerly Katanga) and headed towards the important copper-mining town of Kolwezi. The gendarmes, who had supported Moise Tshombe's unsuccessful attempt at secession from Zaïre in the Sixties, had fled to Angola, where they fought first as mercenaries with the Portuguese against the MPLA and Unita, and then with the MPLA against Unita. They had been trained by the Cubans to return home and stir up revolution in Zaïre.

Now Savimbi received a call, by an envoy, to travel through Namibia to see President Mobutu, who wanted to know as much as possible about the Katangese in Angola. At the same time, Savimbi was given an introduction to King Hassan of Morocco, who provided training at Marrakesh for some of the officers while the Chinese gave Unita arms. An accumulation of support began which also included France, South Africa and Saudi Arabia. By 1981 Unita had pushed forward from its bush stronghold in south-east Angola and captured the small administrative centre of Mavinga, 250 kilometres north of the Namibian border. Unita had also shot down, with a SAM-7 missile, an Antonov-26 transport plane carrying MPLA troops and captured the two Russian pilots.

But the cause of Unita remained unpopular among liberal democrats, who preferred to identify with the MPLA. The British liberal *Guardian* newspaper, for example, wrote admiringly of the declared goal of the MPLA to create a fully-fledged Marxist-Leninist "revolutionary democratic dictatorship," failing apparently to recognise the terrifying irony in the MPLA's own self-description.[71]

By February 1988 Unita, after its long siege of the strategic Cuban air base of Cuito Cuanavale in southern Angola, was in a stronger position militarily and diplomatically than ever before. Mikhail Gorbachev was indicating through his envoy, right wing West German politician Franz Josef Strauss, that Moscow was looking for ways of disentangling itself from Angola. General del Pino declared emphatically that the Cuban military top brass and the ordinary people were fed-up with a war to which they saw no end: only Fidel Castro and his brother Raul Castro, the defence minister, continued to see support for the MPLA as an internationalist adventure and ideological imperative. Many young Cuban boys never came home, and some who did had contracted Aids, the new and dread disease that had all Central Africa, including Angola, in its grip.

In late 1985, ten years after Dick Clark stopped all American military aid to Angola, his amendment was repealed in the Senate, and American arms again began to flow to Savimbi under the auspices of the Republican President Ronald Reagan. But still Unita, the movement that the OAU had said would win an electoral contest in Angola, was suspect to Western liberal democrats, who continued to be critical of the support that the movement received from South

Africa. Still Savimbi was unrepentant. "No one can sincerely tell us that it would be better to be massacred by the Cubans rather than accept aid from South Africa," he told a French journalist. "We want to live and we want our independence. To be promised the posthumous title of revolutionaries does not interest us."[72]

Western conservatives exaggerated Savimbi's pro–Western sentiments to suit their own prejudices and preconceptions about southern Africa. But liberals and progressives, still avoiding objective assessment, emphasised the supposedly conservative virtues of the MPLA to support their case for the Luanda government. In one of the most bizarre examples, Anthony Lewis, the *New York Times* columnist, quoted an unusual supporter for his argument that the United States should extend diplomatic recognition to the Marxist government in Angola.

In Luanda, Lewis met T.J. Fahey, an executive of the General Tire and Rubber Company of Akron, Ohio, which had a 10 per cent shareholding in a state-owned Angolan tyre company. Fahey told Lewis: "We are delighted to be here. They pay us meticulously – our fees and the salaries of our people. I'm just an old peddler, but I think it's a tragic mistake that we don't recognise Angola. Here is a country with incredible buying power and a need for every product on Earth. I'm talking about America's commercial self-interest."[73] Fahey's argument was a strange one for Lewis to make so much of, for he was putting the standard case of a capitalist travelling salesman. Fahey would have argued in the same way if he were selling tyres to South Africa, Chile, China or the Central African Republic. Traders of that kind admired Mrs Indira Gandhi for her suspension of democracy in India and Mussolini for making the trains run on time.

If Lewis had heard Fahey expressing the same views in Warsaw or Pretoria, his wrath would have descended upon the "old peddler". It was strange that Lewis did not point out to his readers that all opposition to the MPLA had been outlawed. He also failed to mention that in the six months on either side of his visit at least 43 Angolans had been put to death by the MPLA in the three main towns for their opposition to an autocracy they had not chosen.[74]

And neither Lewis's voice nor that of any other Western liberal democrat was raised when in November 1986 the MPLA President of Angola, Eduardo dos Santos, told his people that democracy was dead in their country and had been confined to a museum.

Scarcely any Western newspapers reported dos Santos's funeral oration for the freedom of Angola.

Referring to the 1975 Alvor Accord, which promised democracy, the President said: "All Angolans know that this document lost its validity long ago. It has become obsolete and should have a place in our museum."

The need for one man–one vote, multi-party elections in Angola is as rarely heard from the lips of Western liberals as is the call for similar elections in South Africa from, for example, the American Right.

It is, of course, much more difficult for liberal democrats to argue the case for liberty in Angola than in South Africa: the chances of being misunderstood, of getting dirt on one's trousers by taking a direct hand in the human problems, are infinitely greater. There are few easy cheers or slaps on the back to be won in calling for freedom in Angola. But democrats of the centre who truly care should not flinch from analysing carefully what happened in Angola simply because they fear that their motives will be misinterpreted and abused. They should get to grips with the real dramas being played out in a country that has suffered more war deaths than any other on the African continent in the last ten years.

Any investigations of the dramatic stories that individual members of Unita have to tell show that at least they have earned the right to be heard.

Western liberals argue, rightly, for free elections in Namibia and the withdrawal of foreign forces, i.e. the South Africans. But they choose to ignore the thorny logical concomitant that their arguments raise; for if nothing less is good enough for the people of Namibia, then why should anything less be good enough for the people of Angola? Why should they not enjoy free elections and the withdrawal of foreign troops, i.e. the Cubans? Or is there something inferior about Angolan blacks that they should have no right to the same privileges as the neighbouring people of Namibia? In the absence of support from a power that is acceptable to the sensibilities of Western liberals, it is the moral duty of those liberals to suggest some other realistic course of action to Savimbi and his followers than mere abject submission to the MPLA, the Cubans and the Russians. Western liberals have no right to recommend as suitable for Africans political systems that they would fight against if they were imposed on themselves.

It is time for Western liberals to change course and make a tough-minded reassessment of what has happened in Angola. So far, their spinelessness has surrendered the high political ground to the Western Right. South Africa refused to consider independence or elections for Namibia while the Cubans remain in Angola and there are no elections there. South Africa increased its military strength many times over because of the Russian and Cuban presence in Angola.

Angola itself has fallen into economic and social chaos because of the stubborn clinging to power by the MPLA, which was kept in office only by the Cubans and Russians. South Africa was reluctant to venture upon any significant internal reform as long as the chaos in Angola persisted. If liberals do not begin to speak up now (and, more important, to think rigorously) they will still be refusing Savimbi and other Africans from Unita access to their drawing-rooms in Hampstead and Greenwich Village when Savimbi and his people are welcome in the halls of Moscow and Havana.

### General Rafael del Pino Diaz

Cuba's acceptance at the end of 1988 of an accord in Geneva which required it to withdraw its entire 54 000-strong military expedition force from Angola is the kind of military manoeuvre that the Grand Old Duke of York would have understood.

(The popular song tells us how the Duke – in the course of one battle during Britain's late eighteenth century war against France – marched his troops "to the top of the hill and he marched them down again.")

Fidel Castro had frequently asserted that his troops, who began to arrive in Angola in early 1975, would never leave until apartheid had been dismantled in South Africa. But pressure from new Russian leader Mikhail Gorbachev and from within the Cuban military top brass forced him to change tack.

Convincing proof of disillusion among the senior Cuban military officers came when the deputy commander of the Cuban Air Force, General Rafael del Pino Diaz, defected to the United States in 1987. In long and intense debriefings, he charted the collapse of Cuban morale in the thirteen-year-old war in the former Portuguese colony.

At a heavily guarded site in Virginia, General del Pino told me that he and many of his fellow officers had expected that Castro would eventually be forced to withdraw from Angola. "The prevailing opinion within the military was that the war was lost," he said. "Angola was a dead-end, the Cuban Vietnam. Only

Fidel and Raul Castro (the vice-president, Fidel's brother) had any faith in victory."

Del Pino, the most senior military officer to have defected from Cuba, was in direct charge of his country's warplane squadrons in Angola until the day of his defection, 29 May 1987.

"The anti-war feeling at home now is more dangerous to Castro than the social impact of bringing back the soldiers, which is also recognised as a huge threat," said del Pino.

More than 400 000 Cuban soldiers have been rotated through Angola in the last 13 years, which means that in a country of only seven million people every family has been affected by the war. Del Pino said more than 10 000 Cubans had been killed, wounded or gone missing in the conflict. "The cause of most intense grief is that the boys die and are buried over there, and that the bodies are never returned to the families," he said.

There was growing concern, too, over the many young men returning infected by Aids, who were being placed in isolation in a special sanatorium called *Los Cocos.*

Del Pino is one of the most flamboyant products of the Cuban Revolution, acknowledged as the hero of resistance to Washington's abortive invasion at the Bay of Pigs in 1961 when, as a young pilot, he shot down two B-26 warplanes.

Reflecting on how the peace process in southern Africa accelerated throughout 1988, del Pino described to me how he could have rewritten the subcontinent's history back in 1976 – *if* he had got his man.

Del Pino was commander of the Cuban Air Force in Angola when in March 1976 he received an order from Castro to kill Jonas Savimbi (leader of the Unita resistance in Angola to Castro's Marxist clients, the ruling MPLA).

For Castro and del Pino, the death of Savimbi at that time would have amounted to little more than tidying up at the end of a gloriously successful operation in which the small Caribbean island state had humiliated the combined might in Angola of the United States, South Africa and Western Europe.

Del Pino flew at the head of a squadron of MiG-21s which on 13 March 1976 launched three attacks on the village of Gago Coutinho, near the Zambian border, where Savimbi and the tattered remains of Unita were holed up. They pounded it with rockets and destroyed a Fokker Friendship plane which was the guerrilla leader's last link with the outside world.

As he returned to base, del Pino assumed Savimbi was either dead or walking fast towards permanent exile.

At this time, del Pino argues that Castro had calculated most of the factors to perfection in Angola.

After the Portuguese colonial power withdrew on 11 November 1975, Castro saw that his forces in the north could easily defeat the corrupt and inefficient FNLA, heavily supported by the CIA. In the south he could rely on international opinion to drive out the South Africans without firing a shot. And so it happened.

"But he made one little mistake, which ultimately proved fatal," said General del Pino. "Castro never thought that Savimbi was going to resist. I remember one of his phrases before we attacked Gago Coutinho. He said: 'Don't worry, we've already won the war.'"

Savimbi, who had campaigned for elections in Angola and had learned guerrilla warfare in Mao Tse-tung's China, survived del Pino's assault. And instead of fleeing toward towards Zambia, he led his people on a 3 000 kilometre Long March into the interior of Angola. Many of his followers died of starvation or were killed by the Cubans and MPLA. They survived for a year without outside help before aid began to trickle in again – from China, France, South Africa, Morocco, Zaïre.

"Castro was drunk by the success in Angola," said del Pino. The Cuban leader envisaged the end of Pretoria's rule in Namibia and the collapse of apartheid in South Africa. Hard though it is to imagine now, army territorial reserve units in South Africa back in 1976 were preparing for Cuban armour to come rolling across the *veldt* and up the green farming valleys of the Drakensberg.

By 1979, however, Cuban euphoria was subsiding. Unita began to bring down helicopters as its guerrillas learned to stand their ground.

Del Pino cited a series of other events marking the shift of fortunes in Angola. Among them were:

* The 1983 siege by Unita and the South African Defence Force of the south-eastern garrison of Cangamba. More than 1 000 MPLA soldiers were wiped out after some 100 Cuban troops were helicoptered to safety at a critical stage of the battle. Del Pino showed me a complete file he brought from Angola, via Havana, of every radio message exchanged by the Cubans during the Cangamba battle.
* The loss of young Cuban pilots with no training in night flying ordered by local commanders to carry out night attacks on Unita guerrilla positions.
* The discovery in 1985 that his own son and a planeload of Cuban troops, on duty in Angola, had become lost and then been captured in Zaïre because of unserviced navigation equipment aboard the aircraft.
* The increasing use of Angola as a punishment posting for Cuban officers who had failed elsewhere. Colonel Tortolo, commander of the small Cuban garrison on Grenada, was reduced to the ranks and sent to Angola after the 1983 US invasion of Grenada.
* Del Pino's deep disagreement with Soviet and MPLA plans for a single-pronged armoured offensive into Unita territory in August 1987. Del Pino lost the argument, helped plan the offensive and then fled into exile before the assault began. The offensive was beaten back by Unita guerrillas and South African planes and artillery. Thousands of MPLA soldiers died and Soviet military equipment worth hundreds of millions of dollars was destroyed or captured.

Del Pino was scheduled to meet Savimbi, the man he once sought to kill, in November 1988 on Unita territory in Angola. But the delicacy of the Angola/Namibia peace negotiations, which resulted in the 22 December 1988 New York Accords, requiring South Africa's withdrawal from Namibia and Cuba's pull-out from Angola, led to an indefinite postponement of the encounter at Washington's insistence.

**FOOTNOTES**

1. David Ottaway, the *Washington Post,* 1972.
2. Nyerere made his remarks in Lusaka in an interview for the BBC World Service. Replying to them on 27 April 1976, US Secretary of State Henry Kissinger said: "I know we did not do anything on a substantial scale in Angola until there was massive Soviet and Cuban intervention."

3. John Marcum, *Lessons of Angola,* Foreign Affairs, Volume 54, No. 3, April 1976, p413.

4. Henry Kamm, reporting from Lusaka for the *New York Times,* 8 June 1974, at the time of a visit there by the then Portuguese Foreign Minister, Mario Soares.

5. Kaunda's reaction to the MPLA killings was described to the author and Reuter's then manager for Africa, Shake Guebelian, in a meeting with Sikota Wina, member of the Central Committee of Zambia's ruling UNIP party, in Lusaka in December 1975. Wina's story was subsequently confirmed to the author by senior Zambian intelligence officers, who said they had shown photos of the MPLA victims to Kaunda.

6. David Martin, *The Observer,* 24 August 1975; Martin Meredith, *The First Dance of Freedom - Black Africa in the Postwar Era* (Hamish Hamilton, London, 1984), p292.

7. John Marcum, *The Angolan Revolution,* Volume 2; *Exile Politics and Guerrilla Warfare (1962-76)* [The MIT Press, Cambridge, Massachusetts, 1978], p246.

8. John Stockwell, *In Search of Enemies: A CIA Story* (Andre Deutsch), p67.

9. British intelligence sources; also John Marcum, *The Angolan Revolution,* Volume 2, pp253 and 432; and Douglas G. Anglin and Timothy M. Shaw, *Zambia's Foreign Policy: Studies in Diplomacy and Dependence* (Westview Press, 1979), p312.

10. John Marcum, *The Angolan Revolution,* Volume 2, p252; Robert Moss, *Sunday Telegraph,* (London), 30 January 1977.

11. *Report from Portuguese Africa* (ed: Michael Chapman), 13 December 1974.

12. *Diario De Noticias* and *O Seculo,* 29 October 1974.

13. *The Times* (of London), 19 and 20 December 1974; *Zambia Daily Mail,* and *Times of Zambia,* 20 December 1974; *Sunday Times* (of London), 22 December 1974; *Trust* Magazine, Lusaka, May 1975.

14. The *Guardian,* 30 December 1974.

15. Colin Legum, *Africa Contemporary Record, Annual Survey and Documents, 1975-76* (Africa Publishing, New York).

16. John Marcum, *The Angolan Revolution,* Volume 2, p253.

17. John Stockwell, *In Search of Enemies: A CIA Story,* p.68.

18. The 8 000–word Marques account appeared originally in *Proceso,* in January 1977. It was also serialised in three issues of the *Washington Post,* 10–12 January 1977, under the title *Cuba in Africa: Seed Che Planted.*

19. Speaking in the documentary programme *Angola* on PBS–TV, 27 September 1987.

20. *Report from Portuguese Africa,* 25 April 1975.

21. David Martin, *The Observer,* 24 August 1975.

22. Savimbi, interview with the author, Jamba, Angola, 25 February 1983.

23. *Report from Portuguese Africa,* 14 and 28 February 1975.

24. Jane Bergerol, *Financial Times,* 14 June 1975.

25. *Financial Times,* 14 June 1975.

26. *Gemini News Agency,* in the *Times of Zambia,* 7 June 1975.

27. *Africa Development,* May 1975.

28. Tony Hodges, "How the MPLA Won in Angola," in *After Angola: The War Over Southern Africa* (editors: Colin Legum and Tony Hodges) (London, Rex Collings, 1976), p50; *Report from Portuguese Africa,* 9 May 1975.

29. *Angola Report* (editor: Michael Chapman), 13 June 1975; and Fola Soremekun, *Angola - The Road to Independence* (University of Ife Press, 1983), p137.

30. John Marcum, *The Angolan Revolution,* Volume 2, p260.
31. Savimbi, interview with the author, Rabat, Morocco, 19–21 January 1980.
32. Savimbi, interview with the author, Rabat, Morocco, 19–21 January 1980.
33. Savimbi, interview with the author, Rabat, Morocco, 19–21 January 1980.
34. Savimbi, interview with the author, Rabat, Morocco, 19–21 January 1980.
35. Savimbi, interview with the author, Rabat, Morocco, 19–21 January 1980.
36. Savimbi, speaking to reporters in Lobito, Angola, on 14 November 1975.
37. Douglas G. Anglin and Timothy M. Shaw, *Zambia's Foreign Policy: Studies in Diplomacy and Dependence* (Westview Press, 1979), p329; Arthur Jay Klinghoffer, *The Angolan War: A Study in Soviet Policy in the Third World* (Westview Press, 1980), p89; *The Times* (of London), 7 January 1976, referred to Kaunda's April 1975 appeal to Ford "to reverse what he considered to be a tide sweeping the MPLA to victory."
38. John Borrell, *The Observer,* 7 December 1974.
39. John Marcum, *The Angolan Revolution,* Volume 2, p262; Arthur Jay Klinghoffer, *The Angolan War: A Study in Soviet Policy in the Third World,* p65.
40. John Stockwell, *In Search of Enemies: A CIA Story,* p232; and Western intelligence officials to author.
41. Bernard Nossiter, the *Washington Post,* 3 February 1976.
42. John Kane-Berman, the *Guardian,* 21 April 1978.
43. Michael Wolfers and Jane Bergerol, *Angola in the Front Line* (Zed Books, London, 1983), p8.
44. *Newsweek,* 17 May 1976.
45. *New York Times,* 7 February 1976.
46. Document coded sdg/smcb of 2 November 1975 from Sean Macbride to UN Secretary General Kurt Waldheim.
47. Arthur Jay Klinghoffer, *The Angola War: A Study in Soviet Policy in the Third World,* p112; Robert Moss, *Sunday Telegraph,* 30 January 1977; John Stockwell, *In Search of Enemies: A CIA Story,* pp170 and 231; Jorge Dominguez, *Cuba: Order and Revolution* (Bellknap Press of Harvard University Press, 1978), pp354–355.
48. "The Role of the Western Powers in Southern Africa," by Colin Legum, in *After Angola: The War Over Southern Africa* (London, Rex Collings, 1976), pp21 and 40.
49. *Granma Weekly Review,* 2 May 1976; Barry A Sklan, *Cuba: Normalisation of Relations,* Issue Brief No. IB75030, Congressional Research Service, Library of Congress (3 March 1976), p23.
50. Wilfred Burchett, *Southern Africa Stands Up* (Urizen Books, New York, 1978), p34.
51. Clarence McKee, a Washington DC attorney, in the PBS-TV programme, *Angola,* 27 September 1987.
52. Interview with author, south–eastern Angola, 25 February 1983.
53. Agostinho Neto, in a broadcast, August 1969, as quoted in Basil Davidson's *In the Eye of the Storm: Angola's People* (Penguin), p290.
54. General Rafael del Pino Diaz, to the author, Washington DC, December 1987.
55. The description of the failed FNLA assault is based on accounts by Robert Moss in the *Sunday Telegraph,* 30 January 1977; by John Stockwell in *In Search of Enemies: A CIA Story;* by Michael Wolfers and Jane Bergerol in *Angola in the Front Line;* and by Dirk and Johanna de Villiers in *PW - A Biography of South African President P.W. Botha* (1985).
56. *Baltimore Sun,* 3 February 1976; *New York Times,* from London, 3 February

1976; John Stockwell, *In Search of Enemies: A CIA Story,* p224; *Amnesty International, Political Imprisonment in the People's Republic of Angola,* p16. (A shocking account of the mercenaries' behaviour and that of the MPLA commander who confronted them in war, Major Victor Correia Fernandes, is given by two British mercenaries who escaped death and capture, Chris Dempster and Dave Tomkins, in their book entitled *Firepower.* Published by Corgi in London in 1978, it makes sickening but salutary reading.)

57. Jean Ziegler, *Les Rebelles - Contre L'Ordre du Monde* (Editions du Seuil, March, 1983), p259; Lagos Radio External Service, 8 November 1975.
58. John Stockwell, *In Search of Enemies: A CIA Story,* p202.
59. Daniel Patrick Moynihan, addressing the UN General Assembly, 8 December 1975.
60. *Zambia Daily Mail,* 7 January 1976.
61. Margaret Calhoun, paper on the Portuguese coup and African decolonisation to graduate course on National Security Studies, Georgetown University, Washington DC, February 1987.
62. *Washington Post,* 7 February 1976.
63. Brand Fourie to author, Johannesburg, August 1985.
64. Reuter's, Johannesburg, 21 December 1975.
65. Speaking in the documentary programme *Angola* on PBS–TV, 27 September 1987.
66. Zambian Information Services Background 1/76, 13 January 1967 – full text of Kaunda speech.
67. Margaret Calhoun, Georgetown University paper, February 1987.
68. For the full story of Unita's Long March see chapter 20 of Fred Bridgland's book *Jonas Savimbi: A Key to Africa* (Coronet, London, March 1986).
69. *New York Times,* 27 April 1976.
70. Jardo Muecalia, interview with the author, January 1988.
71. The *Guardian,* 2 March 1981.
72. *Tribune,* Paris, 11 September 1982.
73. *New York Times,* 23 January 1981.
74. Amnesty International, *Poliltical Imprisonment in the People's Republic of Angola* (London, March 1984).

# WAR IN RHODESIA - CROSS-BORDER OPERATIONS
*by Ron Reid-Daly*

"Tactics based on deception and surprise are the hallmarks of a victorious commander." *Sun-Tzu* 350BC

"Conventional military forces are invariably characterised by their rigid adherence to orthodox tactics. Unorthodox forms of warfare leave them confused and confounded." *Mao Tse-tung* (2000 years later)

"A few using intellect are a match for hordes of heavily armed automatons." *Laurence of Arabia*

"In the struggle for life and death there is, in the end, no legality." *Winston Churchill*

It would be impossible to condense into one chapter in any detail the facets and phases of the Rhodesian war. The purpose of the writer, therefore, is to sketch an outline of the war concentrating upon the strategy and tactics of both sides using the personal experiences of the writer as a baseline.

Predictably, the demise of Rhodesia has given rise to a rash of authors detailing why Rhodesia lost her war. Most borrow heavily from the theories of "counter-insurgency experts" and what not. One such writer's conclusion deserves mentioning: "Ian Smith and his inflexible colleagues had been entirely circumvented in a revolutionary struggle of classic proportions fought on a total frontage." Then, sarcastically: "It could be proudly asserted that Rhodesia had never lost a single battle but had most ignominiously lost the war." This particular writer, a South African army officer, was very careful, obviously with an eye to his army career, to omit any reference to the role of South Africa coupled with customary British perfidy which in the last analysis sealed the fate of Rhodesia. Another writer, Ken Flower, the former head of the Rhodesian Central Intelligence Organisation, who was widely regarded (with justification) as a British "mole" lashes out at all and sundry in his book and makes it clear that if he had been allowed to run the show, things would have turned out decidedly better. His grovelling to Mr Mugabe, whom he describes as "the best of four prime ministers he has served", is nauseating. As it has turned out Flower might as well have told the truth, for his death before his book was published has removed any chance that the questions the book raises can ever be answered.

That said, let it not be thought that the writer considers the Rhodesian security forces to be without blemish – far from it. The essence of a report that an American "think tank" produced after the massacre of a body of US Marines in the Lebanon during 1983 is worth repeating. It was reported that not only did the United States Defence Department reject this report but also made great efforts to have it suppressed. It implied...

"that the guerrilla terrorists have no stauncher and more helpful ally than the mentality of the professional soldier. Professional soldiers' minds are set – by training and discipline – into inflexible moulds. Their actions and reactions in given situations follow the step-by-step instructions laid down in service academies and practised endlessly in manoeuvres and war games. They are therefore, largely predictable.

"The terrorist or any other irregular, on the other hand, has an open mind; he is an improviser and innovator. He relies upon imagination and ingenuity which, for the most part, have been forced to atrophy in the officers and men of professional armies."

The Rhodesian military, and police force for that matter, did not entirely escape this defect, particularly at their higher levels of command. Much of the fault lay in the fact that many of them had no practical experience of insurgency warfare and therefore had to turn to their text books for answers.

When Cecil Rhodes formed his column of pioneers to settle in Rhodesia in 1890, he knew that despite his signed treaty with Lobengula, the king of the warlike Matabele, his settlers would have very little chance of survival unless they were accompanied by a military force capable of giving them adequate protection. Rhodes's expansionist dreams had not found favour with the whole of British public opinion of the time. The British Empire had reached its zenith, and was about to enter into its decline. As one would expect, the main opposition came from the liberals and the churches. These expressed their strongest opposition to what they saw as yet another chapter of immoral conquest and subjugation of the coloured races of the world by the white man. The reality of the situation was that the Matabele, an offshoot of the Zulu, had themselves invaded what was to become Rhodesia. In the process they had begun a reign of terror, for every winter, selected impis would invade Mashonaland and slaughter the Shona who, although numerically stronger, were weak because they had no such military ardour and tradition like the Matabele impi. Shona women and children who survived these attacks were brought back to the King's military base of Bulawayo as slaves, while plunder in the form of Shona cattle swelled the royal herds. All this of course was conveniently overlooked by the liberal opposition to Rhodes; for then, as now, any horror committed by blacks upon blacks was either ignored or palliated.

In contrast to the Shona the Matabele were organised on a military basis on exactly the same lines as the Zulu nation from whom they had sprung; and foremost in the minds of Rhodes and his planners was the fact that in 1879 a Zulu army, armed with cowhide shields, *knobkerries* and spears, had wiped out a British column of 3 000 regular soldiers armed with the most modern weapons of that age.

To give the column the necessary military protection but at the same time to deny propaganda ammunition to the vociferous opposition, Rhodes decided to create a protective police force. Thus the British South Africa Police came into being: a fine professional force whose destiny and that of Rhodesia, were to be so closely linked in the settlement and creation of a country that was later described by visitors as the Jewel of Africa. It would be interesting to ascertain whether any other country in the world had its police force before the country itself came into being!

The term British South Africa Police arose from the fact that until that time no name had been found for the new country. In keeping with British love of established tradition, the British South Africa Police persuaded the government not to change their title when the new country was finally given the name Rhodesia. This always created some confusion in the minds of new migrants and visitors, who understandably thought that it was a South African Police force.

The British South Africa Police, consisting of about 500 men, was organised into five troops of mounted men. Three of these troops were ordered to escort the pioneer column through Matabele territory to Mashonaland, in accordance with the treaty entered into between Lobengula and the British South Africa Company set up by Rhodes with the blessing of the British government. The journey through Matabeleland was uneventful. Because of the cost of maintaining this police force, and the fact that Lobengula showed no sign of breaking his treaty, most of the British South Africa Police were disbanded. These men joined the settlers whom they had escorted in their search for farms and mining claims. The disbanding of these men was to prove a grave mistake in the war and rebellions that soon followed. It cost the settlers dear in human lives and nearly destroyed Rhodesia in embryo.

By July 1893 the Matabele had been defeated, Lobengula was dead, and the white settlers had expanded their holdings into Matabeleland. Respite from war, however, was brief; and in March 1896 a rebellion among the Matabele broke out. To the astonishment of the settlers, the Mashona far from being grateful to the whites for saving them from the annual depredations and butchery of the Matabele, also joined the Matabele in rebellion against the white settlers. After a series of *indabas* (peace talks) with the Matabele, peace was concluded with them in October 1896. Surprisingly, in view of the poor military abilities of the Shona, it took another year to crush the Mashona rebels; but it was accomplished in October 1897. The cost to the white settlers was a tenth of their number killed or wounded, which was considerably more than the revolts that have taken place in Kenya and Algeria in our own time.

The wars of Chimurenga, however, had one great advantage, for they gave the settlers the opportunity to break the military power of the Matabele, which they did, decisively. The suppression of the Chimurenga revolt meant the end of the Matabele as a military threat, and from that moment on the Shona people were spared from the horrible debilitating raids upon their people. They were able, under the paternal guidance of the white settlers, to develop civilised skills and receive an education. The same was true of the Matabele nation. From 1896 to 1967, when the third and last Chimurenga War broke out, Rhodesia enjoyed a period of peace and tranquillity probably unsurpassed in Africa. This was borne out by the fact that the British South Africa Police up until 24 July 1960 had a proud record of not shooting anyone since the rebellion of 1886, a total of 64 years.

During the revolts it became belatedly clear to the settlers that they would need some form of military organisation to neutralise any further insurrections of that kind. It was also clear that if such troubles were to be avoided, the British South Africa Police Force would have to modify its military character to some extent and concentrate upon proper police work. Thus, although the Force retained a distinctly military quality and was regarded as Rhodesia's first line of defence, Territorial Volunteer Units were set up in most of the larger towns, where drill-halls were built to train and administer them until the mid-1930s. All military instruction was a police function until then, when a small number of policemen were detached as the nucleus of a military instructor corps, known as the Southern Rhodesia Staff Corps. Their task was to train and administer the Territorial Army.

It will be seen, then, that the Rhodesian Army was a direct descendant of the British South Africa Police, or BSAP. That was always recognised by the Rhodesian Army in two ways. First, if ever the BSAP paraded with the military, they took pride of place, on the right of the line. Secondly, to show their origin, the Rhodesian Army flag embodied the colours of the BSAP, blue and old gold.

The introduction of a properly instituted army did not receive general approval by the BSAP as a whole. Many policemen, particularly those in the higher ranks, regarded themselves more as cavalrymen than policemen, and bitterly resented the loss of their status as the Rhodesian first line of defence. They could not or would not recognise the obvious fact that a policeman's training, task and attitude is almost diametrically opposed to those of a soldier. It was an attitude that created much unnecessary friction between the police and the army and hindered cooperation between different branches of the security forces, which of course is very necessary in an insurgency war. The BSAP jealously regarded the maintenance of law and order as their preserve and an area where they would not allow the army to intrude. In fact, on the dissolution of the Federation of Rhodesia and Nyasaland the Commissioner of the BSAP recommended to the Southern Rhodesian government that government should enlarge the BSAP Support Unit at the expense of the army.

Matters came to a head on 28 April 1966 when the Rhodesian Special Branch became aware that the small rural town of Sinoia was to be a rendezvous for seven fully armed terrorists who had entered Rhodesia from Zambia with the task of attacking Sinoia, a task that might well be described as military. The Commissioner of Police, however, apart from a request to the air force for helicopter support, chose to ignore the army completely. The police, a mixed bag of Special Branch black and white officers in *mufti,* local farmers who had been signed on as police reservists, and uniformed regular members of the BSAP, were formed up into a triangle inside which the terrorists, according to police information, were supposed to make their rendezvous. Most of this force were armed with first-world-war Lee-Enfield .303 rifles and a few revolvers. And to ensure that the scenario had all the ingredients of a disaster, the police had no radio to communicate with the helicopters that they had requested.

The terrorists duly arrived for their rendezvous by car, but, whether by design or by accident, turned off into the bush well away from the police triangle. This unexpected change to the plan created consternation among the police commanders. To be fair to them, however, it was only much later that it became generally appreciated that the "K-factor" was vital and had to be taken into account in any security forces planning. The air force, however, having the whole operation under surveillance from a helicopter at high altitude, quickly grasped the true situation. A Gilbert and Sullivan situation now developed, for the pilots, having no ground-to-air communication with the police, had to land, instruct the police, and get airborne once more. All surprise was of course lost, and the terrorists, now aware of their danger, took cover in the elephant grass.

Eventually two sweep lines were re-formed facing each other about a kilometre and a half apart. Confusion reigned as the pilots tried to orientate and direct the police sweep lines by hastily arranged hand-signals while desperately trying to avoid colliding with one another. Astonishingly, in spite of the total confusion and the large volume of uncontrolled fire that sprayed the whole area, all seven terrorists were killed. One was killed by helicopter fire and the rest by police on foot, who were directed by the helicopters to their targets hiding in the long grass, thereby hoping to escape detection. Thus the exercise, in spite of being such a comedy of errors was in fact a success. But the police and the precious helicopters were lucky not to have been hit by their own fire.

The Rhodesian Army, incensed at being left out of what they saw, correctly, as their proper function, made strong representations at an Operations Coordinating Committee (OCC) meeting that followed. The result was that a decree to the effect that any area in which there was terrorist activity must have all counter-insurgency measures coordinated and planned by a Joint Operational Centre. The authorisation of such JOCs could only come from the OCC. Yet the astonishing thing was that the Rhodesian Army, some of whom had served in the British Army during the Malayan emergency, had prepared military textbooks that not only laid down counter-insurgency tactics but also the command and control techniques. And while the Rhodesian Army deserved praise for what appeared to be its far-sightedness, it was not really so. One wonders what would have happened if the British War Office had not reversed their decision to send the first Rhodesian SAS volunteer contingent to Korea instead of to Malaya.

The first experience of counter-insurgency that the Rhodesian Army got was in 1951 when Rhodesia, as part of the British Commonwealth, sent a hundred men to serve in Malaya. This force, consisting of volunteers, had actually formed to serve with the Commonwealth Division in Korea. The insurgency war in Malaya was not going at all well at that time, and a new strategy for the security forces had been drawn up. It took three forms: control of the population by the creation of controlled fortified villages in which the rural population was resettled; denial

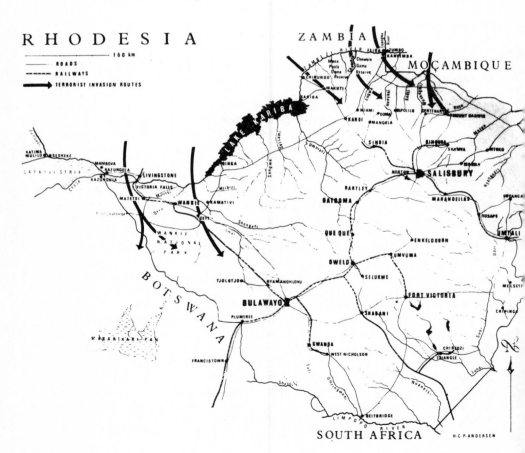

of food and munitions of war to the terrorists; and centralised planning and command of all elements of the security forces and government agencies engaged in the day-to-day prosecution of the war. Part of this strategy was to be the creation of a Special Force Unit, whose task was the destruction of terrorist jungle bases by means of deep penetration patrols. Someone in the British War Office noticed the Rhodesian contingent were destined for Korea and decided that because Rhodesians were more familiar with the bush than the average British soldier, they would be better suited to Malayan conditions.

When the Rhodesians returned from their tour of duty in Malaya they found that while some interest was shown in their operations, there was a decided lack of interest in the inclusion of the counter-insurgency doctrines and techniques into normal training, that they had so painstakingly learned in the Malayan war. Conventional training, as in the second world war, was rigorously retained. Indeed, it was only when the emergency in Kenya began to assume serious proportions and more troops from Rhodesia and Nyasaland had returned from duty in Malaya with experience of counter-insurgency to swell the ranks, that steps were taken to include counter-insurgency as a separate subject in all Rhodesian military training schools.

Again, in true military fashion, instead of carrying out a detailed study of the ideas and tactics of the Malayan campaign, the Rhodesians clung obstinately to Malayan practices whether they met the criteria imposed by Rhodesian terrain, vegetation, population and geographical circumstances or not. It was only when counter-insurgency operations began in earnest that the Rhodesian Army began to realise that, while the general principles were sound, there was a vast difference in their practical application in all areas. The very soldiers who had promoted this new form of warfare (regarded by the old desert soldiers as radicals) now themselves became rigid adherents of the "Malayan Way" and resented any changes from what they themselves had been taught. It was a clear example of an old but very true saying: The army always enters a new war well prepared for its last war.

This perennial habit went even farther than most in the Rhodesian Army. Only two units of the Southern Rhodesian Army actually served in Malaya; the Far East Volunteer Unit, an all-white unit that served as a Squadron in the British Special Services Regiment, and the Rhodesian African Rifles, an all-black regular battalion officered by whites with a sprinkling of white warrant officers in key administrative posts. The Far East Volunteer Unit was all-white, consisting of 90 per cent volunteers from civilian life and 10 per cent regular soldiers. On completion of their tour of duty most of these men returned to their civilian occupations. The Rhodesian African Rifles was in fact the only regular infantry battalion in the Rhodesian Army.

The creation of the Federation of Rhodesia and Nyasaland in 1953 resulted in an immediate increase in the centralised defence force of the three territories. The Federal Defence Force inherited two regular battalions of the King's African Rifles from Nyasaland (now Malawi), one regular battalion of the Northern Rhodesia Regiment and one regular battalion of the Rhodesian African Rifles from Southern Rhodesia. To balance the racial composition of this force more all-white units were formed. These were a battalion of the Rhodesian Light Infantry, a Special Air Services squadron and an armoured-car regiment. The normal supporting corps such as artillery, signals and service units, were built up proportionately. In addition to these regular units there were three active white territorial battalions that could be mobilised within 24 hours, plus at least two more all-white reserve battalions who would need a week to ten days to mobilise. It was by African standards a very formidable, well-trained military force. The cherry on the top however, was the air force. At the breakup of the Federation it had a strength of over one hundred aircraft and comprised Hunter fighters, Canberra Bombers, Vampire fighters, helicopters, Provost trainers and Dakotas for transport and dropping parachute troops.

On 31 December 1963 the Federation of Rhodesia and Nyasaland came to an end. Although it had been economically sound it really had no chance from its inception, because the blacks, apart from their deep suspicions and mistrust of each other, saw it as a crafty plan by the whites to ensure their domination of the numerically superior blacks in the three territories of the Federation. When the parts were divided, Southern Rhodesia came out by far the best from a military point of view. Nyasaland and Northern Rhodesia retained their own old battalions with the addition of a few aircraft. Southern Rhodesia, however, gained the Rhodesian Light Infantry, the Special Air Services squadron and most of the aircraft and personnel of the Rhodesian Air Force. All these units were destined to play important parts in the war which began in earnest in 1967. Southern Rhodesia lost politically, however; for Britain, with unseemly haste, ignored Southern Rhodesia and set Nyasaland and Northern Rhodesia firmly on the road to independence. Poverty-stricken Nyasaland became independent Malawi on 6 July and on 24 October of the same year Northern Rhodesia, nowhere near as well developed as Southern Rhodesia, became Zambia. Southern Rhodesia, by far the most progressive and dynamic of the three territories simply reverted to its condition before federation: something like a dominion, which had actually been its status for over forty years.

Such perfidy and duplicity alienated the whites of Rhodesia against their mother country to a degree that was ill-understood by Harold Wilson's Labour government. They forgot that on every occasion, beginning with the Boer War (which broke out only eight years after the settlement of Rhodesia) the Rhodesians had flocked to offer their services to Britain. During the first world war no fewer than 64 per cent of the total white population of Rhodesia served in the armed forces. In the second world war conscription was brought in *not* to call men up but to prevent the whole male population from joining up and totally disrupting the Rhodesian economy and essential services. It is little known that Rhodesia supplied more troops per head than any other country in the British Empire.

The stage was thus set for the Rhodesians to map out their own future, and they did so by a unilateral declaration of independence on 11 November 1965. With hindsight, it is interesting to speculate what the present situation would have been if the British government of that time had given Southern Rhodesia its independence. If conditions had been built into the instrument that granted Southern Rhodesia its independence making the political progress of the Rhodesian African an unconditional factor, together with financial and economic inducements, a very different situation might well have ensued. Certainly many thousands of lives might have been saved; for it could well have mitigated if not altogether prevented the effects of the war that followed.

The first real action of the war took place in August 1967. A group of eighty well-armed terrorists, members of the Zimbabwe People's Revolutionary Army (Zipra) and members of the South African African National Congress (SAANC), crossed the Zambezi river in the gorges, fifteen kilometres below the Victoria Falls. (The exact point was located after the operation by Sergeant Anthony Grace of 2 Rhodesia Regiment with the help of a captured terrorist). The group were moving southwards, their objective being the confluence of the Tewani and the Nata rivers, where they intended to set up a base camp. This was to be the operational base for both factions of the terrorist group. From there the SAANC terrorists would launch attacks into the Northern Transvaal, while Zipra directed their operations to the Matabele areas of Rhodesia. The terrorists made the elementary mistake of choosing the vast uninhabited Wankie Game Park as a sanctuary from the attentions of the Rhodesian security forces.

Tracks of this group were observed by the Inyantui river near the main Victoria Falls road. This time the BSAP, in accordance with the new instructions from the Operations Coordinating Committee, (OCC), alerted the Rhodesian African Rifles, who had established a headquarters base at Wankie. The RAR was the only Rhodesian battalion that had any real battle experience in counter-insurgency warfare, having served as a battalion during the Malayan emergency from 1954 to 1957. Although 10 years had elapsed, a considerable body of black and white officers, warrant-officers and NCOs were still serving with the regiment. The Commanding Officer and nearly all his company commanders had been through the Malayan campaign.

Accordingly, the Rhodesian African Rifles regarded themselves as the counter-insurgency experts and a cut above the rest of the army. The all-white Rhodesian Light Infantry were a special target for criticism from officers of the RAR. Their view was that the better-paid RLI was an unwarranted luxury because the cost of maintaining it was equal to the cost of two African battalions, and African soldiers of the RAR were better soldiers than the men of the RLI, certainly in counter-insurgency action. Events, however, were to prove otherwise. In view of this wealth of experience, one would have expected the highly-disciplined, well-equipped RAR to make short work of the terrorist group. But they failed to do so, and in fact suffered several nasty reverses.

On Sunday, 13 August 1967 an RAR patrol consisting of eighteen African soldiers and some members of the BSAP led by Captain Peter Hoskins were on the tracks of the terrorist group. At 1.20pm they were ambushed by the terrorists. A very dubious contact with 22 terrorists then ensued for seven and a half hours, during which Captain Hoskins was badly wounded and left to fend for himself. A search party, despatched after dark, recovered him at nine that evening. Next morning another RAR patrol that had been moved up as support during the night went into the battle area. They found that the terrorists had retired during the night, leaving five of their dead behind. The casualties of the security forces were two African soldiers dead, two white officers of the BSAP, one white army officer and two African soldiers wounded.

On 22 August Lt Smith's platoon was ambushed. Lt Smith and his platoon warrant officer were killed. His troops broke and fled, leaving packs, equipment and machine-guns behind, which the terrorists duly collected. The capture of this equipment introduced another nasty element into the operation, which now began to assume the proportions of a military disaster. Worse was still to follow. On 22 August aircraft of the Rhodesian Air Force carried out strikes against suspected terrorist concentrations. At 16h30 two RAR platoons decided to base up together. This was a very unusual procedure, and one can only assume that the two white platoon commanders had decided that a greater concentration of troops would help to encourage the decidedly nervous RAR troops. Even stranger, an air strike was in progress nearby at this time. The terrorists that the air force were seeking were not in the strike zone, however, but near the two RLI platoons, keeping them under observation. A clearing patrol met two of these terrorists, who were dressed in captured Rhodesian Army kit. The terrorists called out a greeting in Sindebele, then at once opened fire on the patrol and wounded the warrant officer who was leading it. The troops at the base camp heard the gunfire but ignored it, thinking it was part of the air strike. They continued basing up until a hail of gunfire ripped through the base camp, followed by hand-grenades. In the words of the platoon commander, Lt Winnall, "there was chaos". Once again the troops, now thoroughly demoralised, retreated in panic, leaving weapons and equipment behind them.

Next morning an RAR platoon cautiously entered the contact area. There they found the bodies of two terrorists and two members of the security forces, one white police officer who had accompanied the patrol and the other a lance-corporal of the RAR. The military situation was not good, for within two days the security forces had lost four men killed to the terrorists' six.

Fortunately it was not all bad news. An RAR platoon commander, Lt Ian Wardle, a Rhodesian born, who was commissioned at Sandhurst, where he acquired his colours for boxing and a very pukka upper-class English accent came to the fore. Wardle was never reluctant to apply a modicum of pugilistic persuasion to his African troops to keep them at the peak of efficiency.

They in turn regarded their leader with the utmost respect. During a patrol his platoon came across the tracks of terrorists. Lt Wardle's observations and instructions to his somewhat apprehensive platoon, delivered in a plummy English accent, deserves repeating: "Gentlemen, as you have undoubtedly observed, we have the tracks of a group of the enemy. The procedure from here is really quite simple. We shall follow those tracks until we come across the enemy, and when that happens we shall kill them. If you don't (tapping his FN rifle) I shall kill you!"

Such was Ian Wardle's determination that his patrol covered 54 miles in 48 hours. True to his character, Ian always led his troops from the front, and during a brief pause he heard a safety-catch being slipped off. The terrorists he was following had ambushed their own tracks, and Lt Wardle's patrol was in the middle. Ian attacked immediately and when the action was over, eight terrorists lay dead and six had been captured. Ian Wardle, whose black soldiers had responded so well to his combination of ruthlessness, fearlessness and professionalism which was so much needed at that time, did much to restore the black soldier's faith in himself.

But one good action was not enough to restore stability to the jittery RAR Command Centre or the morale of the troops. Two actions were hurriedly taken to retrieve the situation. No.2 Commando of the all-white Rhodesian Light Infantry battalion (RLI) was hastily despatched to raise not only the strength of *Operation Nickel* but also the morale of the black soldiers who, it was thought, would take fresh heart on seeing their white comrades fighting alongside them. The second action was the sacking of two company commanders who had served with the RAR in Malaya as platoon commanders.

This was the first real taste of active service by the RLI; and in their first contact, supported by their black comrades of the RAR, they gave an early indication of the great reputation as fighting men that they were to establish as the war progressed. Corporal Emil Taljaard of No.2 Commando 1 RLI tracked down a group of terrorists with his section of eight men. (At that time the RAR were patrolling in platoon strength.) Corporal Taljaard's section caught up with the group and in a contact that lasted barely ten minutes it was all over. Four terrorists lay dead. The RLI suffered no casualties. When *Operation Nickel* ended the terrorists had suffered thirty killed and twenty captured. The rest escaped to Botswana and made their way back to their bases in Zambia. The security forces lost seven killed and thirteen wounded. These casualties from their point of view were extremely high.

This in turn had an unfortunate result: the terrorists were credited with a military skill and aggressiveness that they did not actually possess.

In the post-mortem that followed this operation the reputation for efficiency, professionalism and fighting spirit of Zipra increased to such an extent that it was decided as "lessons learnt" that henceforth the security forces would not patrol in less than platoon strength. Tactics on this principle were worked out, and all units of the Rhodesian Army received printed leaflets informing them of the new tactics and formations to be adopted. RAR officers toured units to lecture on *Operation Nickel*. It was fortunate that elements of the RLI had taken part in this operation, though only at its end. For the RLI, while listening to the RAR officers with great interest did not believe, in the light of their own experience, that the new tactics propounded by the RAR were the right tactics. In the euphoria that followed the victory of the security forces, no one outside the RLI drew the right conclusions from the actions fought by Corporal Taljaard's small section of the RLI, or for that matter, the effect that Lt Wardle's leadership had achieved by forceful positive action. The doctrines and tactics of the "Malayan Way" came under fierce criticism from the young RAR subalterns who had endured their first baptism of fire under its principles. They were not, in fact, entirely correct. There was nothing wrong with the principles adopted from the Malayan campaign; what was wrong was that incorrect tactics had been derived from those principles and their effect on Rhodesian local conditions had not been properly assessed, as we have already mentioned. The Rhodesians thus succumbed to the old army weakness of being trained for the last war. The very soldiers who had tried to persuade the old desert soldiers to incorporate counter-insurgency in the teachings of the Rhodesian military schools, defeated their own object by adhering rigidly to the "Malayan Way", and they deserved to be sacked.

We have dealt with *Operation Nickel* in some detail, within the limitations of one chapter. It should be clearly understood that we have not done so to denigrate the RAR, for all else being equal, they were a fine unit. But things had gone seriously wrong in this, the first serious counter-insurgency engagements that the RAR had fought in a local action. A combination of factors was responsible: aggressive leadership at platoon-commander level was, in the main, conspicuously absent: leadership at company-commander level was hopelessly incompetent and certainly added to the uncertainty and hesitancy displayed by some of the platoon commanders in contact with the enemy. The tactics used belonged to another war in another place, and RAR senior commanders showed no flexibility or initiative by quickly changing their tactics and *modus operandi* when they discovered that the "Malayan Way" was not suited to African bush. The RAR did not lack courage, for later, as the war progressed, a former subaltern of the RAR serving with the Special Air Services Regiment won the Rhodesian equivalent of the VC and two private soldiers who volunteered for the Selous Scouts won a silver and a bronze cross each. This double made these two men the most highly decorated non-commissioned officers in the Rhodesian Army, a record not matched or beaten throughout the war. Other black volunteer RAR soldiers performed astonishing acts of bravery while serving with the Selous Scouts, and made a great contribution to the reputation earned by that regiment.

This operation also showed that the greatest advantage that the security forces possessed, the Air Force, had not been used to maximum effect. Five Alouette 111 helicopters had been acquired by the Rhodesian Army in 1961, followed by three more in August 1963. At least five helicopters, therefore, were available for service during *Operation Nickel*. Five Alouette helicopters could carry twenty fully-equipped men (a significant number in counter-insurgency) to any point swiftly and precisely. Yet there is no record of any swift encirclement of terrorists with helicopters when contact was made during *Operation Nickel*. It is astonishing that, although the Rhodesian security forces possessed helicopters for six years, no battlefield tactics incorporating this most valuable implement had been worked out. Helicopter training for the infantry consisted in emplaning and deplaning drills, the selection of landing zones, and how to direct a helicopter to them. More astonishing still, little of tactical value concerning the use of helicopters emerged at the de-brief of *Operation Nickel*. More attention was given to a more efficient method for ground troops to bring in air strikes, which were much favoured during this operation.

There were two reasons for that. From the formation of the helicopter squadron the air force had made it plain that the helicopter was to be regarded as a *support* weapon. Its sole function was to ferry troops into a contact area and evacuate the wounded and prisoners, the latter for immediate interrogation. Helicopter pilots were forbidden to get involved in a battle. To reinforce this principle even more firmly the Air Vice Marshall of the time, during a stormy Operations Coordinating Committee meeting after the Sinoia débâcle, made it clear that the principle of minimum force would be rigorously adhered to, and he would not allow his aircraft to be used for killing if ground forces could command a situation themselves. He thought that this would save lives and prevent the creation of a host of martyrs!

It was a disappointing debriefing, and at the end of it it was clear that nothing of any real value in new tactics had been learned. The army had overestimated the potential of the enemy and had therefore decided upon ponderous platoon and company tactics, which were altogether unsuitable. The fact that both the air force and the army failed to appreciate the vital tactical role that the air force could play in counter-insurgency was still more serious. Another important aspect that played a vital part in the operation was tracking. But that was hardly mentioned in the debriefing. Perhaps that was because the RAR soldiers were drawn in the main from the rural tribal areas, where tracking was a natural skill that African boys learned in their traditional role as custodians of their fathers' cattle. This again was a serious omission by the Rhodesian Army. Soldiers returning from Malaya in 1953 brought with them an understanding of the importance of trackers in counter-insurgency warfare in the bush. Although pamphlets were produced with instructions for follow-up procedures which of course was based upon the tracker, nothing was done to teach tracking.

It was fortunate for the army that a young SAS subaltern, Lt Brian Robinson, had been sent to Britain on attachment to the British Special Air Services Regiment. It was from these experts that he became aware at first hand of the true functions of a special-force soldier. The techniques of working behind the enemy lines, locating enemy camps and leading conventional troops in to attack them as well as deep-penetration clandestine patrols, were a revelation to him. A devoted disciple of Special Force operations emerged from this experience which, unfortunately for Robinson, was abruptly terminated when Rhodesia declared its independence.

A tour of duty with the SAS in Borneo was cancelled, but the experience of talking to the seasoned veterans of the British SAS revealed one thing that was to transform the conventional attitudes of the Rhodesian Army: which was that if a soldier had to operate in a bush environment he had to become as one with the bush; and the ability to track and anti-track was a vital need.

On his return from Britain, Robinson lost no time in propagating the lessons that he had learnt, and it was at that time that he met a territorial officer, Lt Alan Savoury, a man destined to play a highly controversial part later in the war. Alan Savoury was an ecologist of note with a vast and detailed knowledge of the bush. The two were complementary, one with experience of special forces, the other an expert in bush lore. Selected members of the Rhodesian SAS were moved into remote areas of the bush, and between Robinson and Savoury military tracking techniques came into being.

The principle of four-man tracking, for example, began with Savoury teaching tracking as a single-man operation. Robinson, looking at this from a military point of view realised that the tracker was most vulnerable and would be the first man to move into an ambush if an enemy group realised that they were being followed and set up an ambush on their own tracks. He then devised the four-man principle: one man tracking, one man on either flank of the tracker to give him protection, and the fourth man in the rear with a radio controlling the group. Following behind, euphemistically called a "tactical bound" (that is 100 – 200 metres depending on the thickness of the bush) would be the follow-up troops, often referred to as the "beetle crushers" because of the noise they made. The method here was that the trackers, moving silently, using dog whistles inaudible to an untrained human ear, would by stealth and bush skill track down and locate an enemy camp or ambush. They would reconnoitre the position, report back to the commander of the follow-up troops. (If speed was required it would be done by radio). The follow-up troops, led by the tracker combat team, would move forward and launch a pre-planned attack. The tracker team, because of the paucity of their numbers, would if at all possible remain out of contact, so that they would not suffer casualties themselves and would be ready to be called forward at the end of the contact to resume the follow-up of any survivors.

Colonel Spencer Chapman, a British officer who spent most of the second world war in the Malayan jungle with partisan forces, titled a book that he wrote of his experience *The Jungle is Neutral;* and he was right. The bush, to a human being brought up in an urban environment, seems a frightening place. Such a man has to be taught that the bush is indeed neutral. If you know it, it will help you, but if you don't, it simply watches you. The more knowledge and experience he has the less insecure he will feel. Knowledge of the vegetation, the habits of wild animals, particularly snakes, and the ability to find water in arid areas, makes a man confident in his own ability to survive and even live comfortably in the bush. Alan Savoury and Brian Robinson spent many hours passing on this knowledge to their trackers. They in turn rapidly passed on the information to the rest of the SAS Regiment. The SAS suddenly became the trackers and the bushmen of the army and nearly lost their true role: for when *Operation Cauldron* erupted, tracker teams from the SAS were in great demand.

Interesting developments also took place in the dress of the trackers. Army boots were the first thing to be discarded; they were cumbersome and left distinctive tracks. Canvas hockey-boots were much favoured because they had no heel and made anti-tracking easier. *Veldskoen* and running shoes were also used, without socks. Even worse in the eyes of horrified conventional soldiers were camouflaged shorts and T-shirts. But there was much sense in this dress. Canvas shoes allowed a more silent approach. The absence of socks meant that the trackers' feet were not rubbed raw by a combination of hardened unwashed socks, which often attracted grass seeds and burrs to aggravate chafing of the skin. Bare legs and arms exposed more skin for its natural cooling function, which made the tracker more comfortable in the blazing heat of the Zambezi Valley. Long trousers, apart from the heat they retained, were unsuitable for quiet movement; a man wearing long trousers subconsciously realises that his legs are protected and tends to move *through* vegetation instead of round it, as a man with bare legs would do. Streaks of soot or coloured cream on the arms and legs were sufficient camouflage. A tracker needed silence more than anything else, because his very life depended upon it.

When the news of the SAANC association with the Zipra incursion reached Pretoria there was some fluttering in the dovecotes. Within hours, Pretoria offered Rhodesia a detachment of South African Police and a number of helicopters for use against them. This offer was accepted with alacrity by Prime Minister Ian Smith, who also saw the political advantages. He brushed aside the objections of his military commanders, who were confident that they had complete control of the situation.

Many unkind things have been said about the performance of the South African Police contingents. They had some difficulties to begin with, but in fairness to them many were not of their own making. The SAP, like the BSAP, regarded themselves as the first line of defence against insurgency. Both police forces made the mistake of failing to recognise that there are fundamental distinctions between the policy, nature and culture of a police force and those of an army.

A policeman's policy is essentially to use the minimum force to maintain law and order. To the general public he is a visible custodian and prop of the laws that govern and regulate the life of a nation. His deportment and behaviour must be such that the public will respect him and regard him as a friend and a protector. If the police have applied the correct attitude, goodwill will be tempered with respect, so that familiarity does not breed contempt. He is essentially a *reactor;* his daily duty will consist in *reacting* to the *actions* of criminals and lawbreakers. His career begins on the bottom rung, and he will work his way upwards through a series of examinations and time barriers. The time restrictions are designed to ensure that by the time he is ready to be considered for a commission, he has not only acquired wide and varied experience but, more important still, he is mature. Maturity is most important in a police officer because he will be confronted by innumerable problems that affect the general public and demand an immediate solution. Experience and knowledge give the police officer an ample reservoir to draw upon, enabling him to make the right decision.

By contrast, the military attitude is straightforward; the soldier's task is to defend the integrity of his country with whatever force is needed to effect that. The only deviation from the military style is when they are in support of the police in internal unrest when, like the police, the principle of minimum force is observed. The culture of the army is very different from that of the police. An army officer needs certain academic qualifications and has to pass an Officer Selection Board which will determine whether he has qualities of leadership. If he passes he is required to undergo an officer-cadet course, normally of eighteen months' to two years' duration. If he passes his career is only beginning, and while his opposite number in the police is gaining practical experience by training on the job, the young army officer will begin a series of progressively more difficult courses with built-in time barriers and examinations. His success in these, plus his practical performance, will determine his speed and level of promotion. The army officer is therefore academically better prepared for war, even if he has to resort to war games and exercises to try to reproduce realistic war situations. And if, through no fault of his own, he had been "trained for the last war" he simply has to orientate his training and experience to a new situation.

When the SAP first arrived in Rhodesia the only training that most of them had had was riot training, which is perfectly useless for a bush war. The Rhodesian Army, therefore, had to bleed their units of men that they could not really spare to form training teams and put the SAP through quick rural counter-insurgency courses. One of the great defects inherent in using police in any army role immediately became evident. The need to have a mature officer in the police force caused an immediate difficulty: many officers were found to be simply too old to patrol effectively in the heat of the Zambezi Valley, and some were grossly unfit and overweight. The reasons why the army employed young and fit officers aged from nineteen years upwards now began to make sense to the police; for their most important quality, dynamic energetic leadership, was neutralised. The constables and young warrant officers and NCOs, however, were very good material, and many a young RLI subaltern, short of troopies looked enviously at these men who never seemed to be lacking in numbers. Operationally they did not achieve a great deal, and indeed they suffered many casualties. If young Rhodesian or South African Army officers had been attached to lead them, there is little doubt that they would have given a very good account of themselves. Generally they were used to fill a gap in operational areas not deemed operationally vital to the Rhodesian Army. The South African Security Police, operating alongside the Rhodesian Special Branch, were on home ground, doing a job they understood and were trained for. They encountered no real difficulties and found themselves in a wonderful position where they could report home not only on terrorist activity but also on the Rhodesians themselves. The presence of the SAP in Rhodesia gave Vorster a lever and a whip to use when attempting to compel Ian Smith to accept terms of settlement. By that time they had become an integral part of Rhodesian military strategy, and the possibility of their withdrawal meant that the gaps in the defence system would have to be filled by further call-ups of territorial soldiers, whose morale at that time was beginning to wane.

The Rhodesian Light Infantry, an all-white unit, had taken serious note of all that the RAR had to tell them about *Operation Nickel,* and had followed up with a careful study of their debriefing notes. They were not at all convinced, however, that the RAR tactics, which had been drawn up as a result of lessons learnt from that operation, were correct. Much discussion had taken place, and eventually the Commanding Officer, Colonel Jack Caine, and his second-in-command, Major John Hickman, requested that all commandos should be allowed to experiment with various formations and those adjudged to be best should be adopted by the battalion as standard drill. Rhodesian officers' messes were modelled on the British system, and the practice of talking shop in the mess was severely frowned upon. In this case, however, the custom was ignored, and ferocious arguments and counter-arguments went on into the early hours of the morning. Then there were the frightful experiments in bush or on ranges with live ammunition, grenades and mortars. It was a miracle that the RLI survived these experiments to fight. As it turned out, in typical RLI fashion, every commando was convinced that theirs was the right answer. The CO, knowing that open warfare was at hand, wisely left every commander of commandos to his own devices.

As it happened, the judge of the right tactics for the RLI was near at hand. Unknown to the security forces, a group of 125 terrorists had crossed the Zambezi from Zambia into the Chewore wild life area during the last days of 1967. Throughout January and February 1968, they had begun to establish a series of base camps about twenty kilometres apart across the floor of the uninhabited Zambezi Valley. The plan was to make a permanent infiltration route south of the escarpment, which they would ascend and make contact with the local African tribesmen on the highveld. Unfortunately, believing that the area was uninhabited, they began shooting for the pot while carrying supplies from camp to camp. An observant game ranger noticed a change in the habits of the game, and on investigation he came across strange human spoor where none should have been. He quickly reported this to the security forces, and on Saturday night 13 March 1968 a call was put out in cinemas and on the state and commercial radios ordering all members of the RLI to return to barracks immediately. By 11pm that night the RLI, girded for battle, were setting out from Cranborne Barracks for their baptism of fire in the fierce heat of the Zambezi Valley.

Major Hugh Rowley, who commanded 3 Commando RLI, took over operational command from an RAR major whose company was engaged in border control at Chirundu. The major, dressed for battle in RAR fashion, had everything from a scarf round his neck to a panga and a shooting-stick, which knocked over all the tin tea mugs as he swung it about giving incomprehensible orders to the RLI. He was in a total flap. Major Rowley took his commando into action, and the fruits of the RLI think-tanks immediately became apparent. His first decision was to place two call-signs on the tracks: the first to track down and neutralise the terrorist group, while the other backtracked to find out where they had come from. Game park trackers were allocated to troops, and the follow-up began.

The terrorists were moving in two groups: a reconnaissance group of about sixteen men well ahead of the main group, which had a strength of sixty. The tracks of the terrorists were easy to follow, and to speed up the follow-up the RLI devised a technique known as leap-frogging. It required that the tracker team (comprising four men) should be lifted by helicopter to fly in the general direction of the tracks for a specified distance. The trackers would land and carry out a 180 degree search across the direction of the line of the terrorists' march while the helicopter hovered out of hearing but within radio contact. If the tracks were found again, the trackers would assess how far they were behind the terrorists. If the trackers judged themselves to be two to three hours behind the terrorist group, the helicopters would ferry forward all but one stick (five men) to the follow-up group, and the pursuit would continue. At all times a stick of RLI was left on the original tracks in case the trackers lost their freshly located spoor or, as sometimes happened, the trackers had landed on the spoor of *another* group of terrorists. The other important part of the drill was to ensure that a stick or troop was back-tracking the spoor to find the camp or crossing-point from where they had come.

Subtle judgement was needed to control these operations, for if the tracker team were put down too near to the terrorist group they would alert them, and they might take one or more of the following actions:

1. set up a dog's-leg ambush on their own tracks;

2. split into smaller groups and make for a pre-arranged rendezvous, e.g. a *koppie* or river junction, or one of their own subsidiary camps. Each group would then set off at top speed anti-tracking as they went.

The effects of these tactics on the follow-up troops were:

If the four-man tracker group did not pick up the ambush, the security forces were likely to suffer casualties. If the terrorist group split into small groups and anti-tracked, the follow-up by the security forces would be seriously slowed down, and even if the group were brought into contact it would be an unimportant engagement as the main group would escape. Communications, always vital in any kind of warfare, had also been changed by the RLI think-tank. The Rhodesian Army had been through the whole range of British and Australian Army high frequency long-range (company and battalion level) and VHF short-range radio sets. The radio set desperately needed by the Rhodesian infantry was a light-weight VHF set with a range of ten to 15km on the ground and, most important, capable of communicating with aircraft. It was fortunate that such a set, the A60, had been produced by a South African firm to Rhodesian Army specifications just before *Operation Nickel*. This set, although cumbersome and crude compared with later models produced as the war progressed, was still far ahead of British or American sets and proved a great boon to the Rhodesian Army. But the Zambezi Valley is a vast area, and a radio distance of 12–15km is not of much value when troops or sticks are patrolling 30–50km apart from one another.

To overcome this handicap, a light aircraft was used to circle the operational area and act as an airborne relay station. Troops operating on the ground would pass situation reports (sitreps) and their positions by coded map references (locstats) on the hour every hour to their JOC, so ensuring that their JOC commander was kept up to date. If a contact was made, the relay aircraft imposed radio silence on the entire net so that it was uncluttered and the call-sign engaged in the contact was unhindered. The operation of the net, of course, required slick radio procedures. The snag about this procedure was that it effectively removed an aircraft from the war. The RLI again devised an improvement to this system. High above the Zambezi Valley near the Chewore river there is a large flat-topped eminence, Charoma Kadoma. A complement of soldiers and signallers were placed on this height and a new relay station known as "Cloud Base" came into being. "Cloud Base" using the ordinary A60 had a range of between 80 and 110km, was able to switch call-signs to different frequencies in the event of a contact, so that normal communications were not interrupted. It ran an administrative channel, so that the operation channels were not cluttered with administrative matters and, of course, it ran throughout the night, which was a great comfort to the five-man sticks dotted across the valley. This system, however, developed only after the first few days of the operation, and it became one of the most important means of command and control of all the succeeding operations of the Rhodesian war.

The first contact of *Operation Cauldron,* as it was code-named, was made about 7.30am on 18 March 1968. Lt Bert Sachse with an understrength troop of about twelve men and a SAS tracker combat team had spent the previous day leap-frogging on tracks directed by his company commander Major Hugh Rowley. (A full troop of RLI was 25, unlike a platoon, which has a strength of forty.)

The tracks of these terrorists were found again on the morning of 18 March by the SAS tracker control team. The follow-up began, and after tracking for about two kilometres contact was made with the terrorists. By midday the contact had been concluded and ten terrorists shot dead. Another was found in the contact area next day, bringing the total to eleven. On the security forces' side, one soldier had been killed and two wounded. The Rhodesian Light Infantry had opened its batting average with a vengeance, but much more was to follow.

*Operation Cauldron* lasted for two-and-a-half months and ended on 31 May 1968. During this operation, of the 125 that entered Rhodesia, 69 terrorists were killed and fifty captured. The security forces lost six men killed.

On 16 July another group of terrorist tracks was discovered south of Chirundu, heading south. Once again the RLI deployed, and in a matter of days all but two of the group of 28 were put out of action, the score being twenty terrorists killed and two captured. The RLI suffered one man wounded. The Rhodesian Light Infantry, ably supported by the air force and the trackers from the SAS, had been outstandingly successful. Their ingenuity, initiative and aggressive fighting spirit had instituted a brand-new set of tactics that was unbeatable in African bush conditions. They had also neutralised the reputation for success that the terrorists had acquired after their engagements with the RAR in *Operation Nickel.* The RLI had shown in no uncertain manner that the terrorists were no match for them and would never be a serious military danger to Rhodesia. A sense of euphoria filled not only the Rhodesian military commanders but also their politicians; and in their swelling pride and patriotism the real point escaped them. The terrorist forces had adopted the wrong strategy; they had ignored the people and chosen military action in the bush. Now they had learned a hard lesson, and while the Rhodesian security forces, complacent in the afterglow of their victories and convinced that they now had the right formula, the terrorist leaders immediately set about changing their strategy.

Their conclusion that they could never compete militarily with the Rhodesians and must therefore follow the counsels of Mao Tse-tung was perfectly correct. The target must be the black people of Rhodesia and the war, from this moment on, was to assume a totally different dimension.

It was, in fact, the moment of truth for Rhodesia; but no one recognised it. It was the time to capitalise on the defeat of the terrorists by bringing the African population effectively into the political arena; but for various reasons that never happened, and the die for Rhodesia was irrevocably cast. *Operation Nickel,* and more particularly *Operation Cauldron* were, in the writer's opinion, the most significant operations of the war. The military had recovered from near-disaster in *Operation Nickel,* but brilliant tactics and competence at all levels of the RLI in *Operation Cauldron* blinded the army, the police and the government once again to the fact that, as with the "Malayan Way", the terrorists, having used the wrong strategy, might well correct the error in the next round.

In the lull that preceded it, troops patrolled the uninhabited border areas with renewed vigour and assiduity. Now aware of the need for trained trackers they set up a school for tracking and bushcraft at Kariba.

Every unit sent men on basic and advanced courses, and most regular units added a tracking platoon or troop to their establishment. Simulated follow-ups in counter-insurgency exercises using the new tactics perfected by the RLI were regularly practised. The air force, which had been extensively used in *Operation Cauldron* was very much a part of these exercises, although helicopters were still regarded primarily as a support service. The Rhodesian Special Air Services Regiment was at sixes and sevens among themselves, for suddenly, apart from their tracking and bushcraft skill there seemed to be no place for them in the bush war. Externally, small operations were taking place, most of them in Zambia.

But these operations were restricted to a small number of men and did nothing for the morale of the rest of the SAS. The intelligence for these operations was provided by the Central Intelligence Organisation under its director, Ken Flower. Poor intelligence and a lack of experience in that area resulted in the failure of a number of clandestine operations. In the course of one, three SAS men were killed when an explosive device that they were about to take across the Zambezi to Zambia in a canoe went off prematurely. It was a hard way to learn that these operations demanded first class up-to-the-minute intelligence, careful detailed planning and flexible minds to cope with situations when things went wrong. But learn they did, and the men of the SAS went on to carry out some astonishing external operations that demanded every ounce of professional skill and courage.

I have made no mention of any advance intelligence on terrorist activities and intentions provided to the army before any large-scale terrorist incursion was made. The reason for that is simple: there was none. The Central Intelligence Organisation, whose explicit task was the acquisition of such intelligence, had failed dismally. The acquisition and dissemination of intelligence before the creation of the Federation was the responsibility of the BSAP. On the dissolution of the Federation, which took place on 31 December 1963, the government of Southern Rhodesia, conscious of the vital need for accurate intelligence, set up a Central Intelligence Organisation (CIO). It came under the umbrella of the Prime Minister's Department and it consisted of eleven branches.

The important branches from the military point of view were Branch 1, which was the BSAP Special Branch, primarily responsible for all internal intelligence, and Branch 2, responsible for all external intelligence. Branch 3 was Military Intelligence, which became productive only in the later stages of the war; and then only with radio intercepts.

The man chosen as head of this organisation was an Englishman, Ken Flower. Flower was a former trooper who had risen through the ranks and become an officer in the BSAP. He had no intelligence background, training or experience whatsoever. Obviously he was conscious of that deficiency, for he talked the Rhodesian government into sending him on a three-week visit to various divisions of British Intelligence in England, where it was rumoured that he was immediately recruited by them. Certainly his behaviour during the war, and particularly towards the end of the war, was inexplicable unless the rumour was true. Military officers, particularly those in the Special Forces, were acutely conscious of the fact that, apart from the Sinoia incursion, the security forces had received no advance warning of any crossings. This was shown by the large-scale crossings of terrorists that led to operations *Nickel* and *Cauldron*. In his book *Serving Secretly* Flower makes much of the fact that he had seasoned the terrorist organisations with a sprinkling of informers who kept him abreast of their intentions. If in fact they did, Flower was remarkably slow to pass this intelligence to the military, as is borne out by the fact that from *Operation Nickel* onwards there was not a single occasion in which the CIO gave the military precise advance information of any terrorist incursion into Rhodesia. On page 109 of his book he contradicts himself and admits that the CIO had failed to provide intelligence that might have anticipated *Operation Cauldron*.

There was a distinct Vicar of Bray quality about Mr Flower. His protestations of being totally against UDI and the Rhodesian Front and making his feelings perfectly clear to all ring somewhat hollow. If the sensitivity to possible disloyalty in the commanders of the security forces was such that General Anderson, the commander of the Rhodesian Army, was sacked, how much more likely was it that Flower, in view of his delicate position, should have been sacked first?

During 1967 the Rhodesians began joint operations with the Portuguese Army in the Tete Province of Mozambique. This took the form of providing a squadron of helicopters to enable Portuguese troops to move swiftly into the vast bush areas. The writer accompanied the Rhodesian Air Force as a liaison officer and in the course of duties became the first Rhodesian to lead Portuguese troops in action. It came as a great shock to him when he became aware of the extent to which Frelimo had infiltrated and subverted huge areas of the northern districts. It did not need great genius to see that this situation, bordering on Zambia, was a heaven-sent opportunity for the Rhodesian terrorists, because it provided a protected, well-administered route, using the Frelimo infrastructure, to the borders of Rhodesia. Yet when he returned from these operations and reported to a meeting attended by the Prime Minister, Ian Smith, he was publicly pooh-poohed by Flower, who told the Prime Minister that his information did not tally with Reid-Daly's and that he believed "Lt Reid-Daly was overstating the situation."

The chickens came home to roost. For some months Detective Section Officer Peter Stanton and Winston Hart of the Special Branch had been informing their headquarters that Zanla elements were in Mozambique. All they got for their pains was to be told that they were alarmists, and Winston Hart was forbidden to go into Mozambique. In March 1972 Peter Stanton received intelligence that elements of Zanla were at a Frelimo base near the Rhodesian border. Permission to investigate the area was given by the Portuguese Army and in a subsequent attack launched on this base by the SAS a large number of documents were captured. They included a notebook that gave conclusive proof that the Zanla terrorists were indeed in Mozambique. Special Branch HQ now became greatly concerned at this discovery, but not the CIO, which dismissed it as a trick to deceive the Rhodesian security forces. In the early hours of 21 December 1972 a farmhouse in the Centenary district in the north of Rhodesia was attacked by a group of terrorists. The last battle for Rhodesia had begun, and once again the security forces, in spite of all the accurate signals put out by the Special Branch, were caught napping, because the CIO had failed to produce any external intelligence to corroborate the information that the Special Branch had thrust under their noses.

Elements of the Rhodesian security forces promptly arrived at the Centenary Police Station, and with their customary efficiency deployed immediately with SAS trackers. But apart from one small contact there was nothing; tracks simply dissolved into the tracks of the local inhabitants or, in some cases, were swept away by the locals with branches. The slick tactics evolved during *Operation Cauldron* that had met with such success now proved fruitless, and the morale of the soldiers began to sink rapidly.

The extensive network of Special Branch informers, so painstakingly built up over a number of years, collapsed as the terrorists, now firmly ensconced among the local tribesmen, began their brutal disciplinary killings. Members of the Special Branch, who had performed so well up to now in building up a close rapport with the army, were now looked at askance, even with outright hostility.

The Department of Internal Affairs, whose task was to administer the Tribal Trust Lands, also got a rude shock. Under their very noses for the past few months, Zanla political commissars had been crossing the border and subverting the tribesmen. Significantly, the chiefs and headmen were their first target, the very men that the District Commissioners relied upon to help them in the administration of the Tribal Trust Lands and provide them with a network of information.

The Rhodesian security forces were back to square one. Mao Tse-tung's teachings, so simple yet so effective, had been employed with great success, and they had rocked the Rhodesian security forces. The obvious had totally escaped them; and they could not be excused for their lack of perception. In an attempt to stop the infiltration of Zanla groups, the SAS were withdrawn from the operational area, where they had been engaged on ordinary infantry tasks and tracking duties. Captured terrorists interrogated by Special Branch had given the Rhodesian forces a fairly comprehensive picture of the infiltration routes used by the Zanla terrorists. Brigadier John Hickman planned an operation that required the infiltration of the SAS by parachute. The SAS would act as eyes and ears for the army and wherever possible destroy small groups of the enemy. In an exercise that was to last almost a year the SAS operated well inside Mozambique, and in the later stages they worked in four-man sticks. But despite a considerable effort on the part of the SAS the infiltration of Rhodesia continued. There were too few SAS and too much ground for the operation to succeed.

The well-known flair of the Rhodesians for contriving unorthodox solutions in times of crisis retrieved a serious situation. With hindsight one can only speculate what effect these new tactics, that were about to be used with astounding success might have had on the war if they had been introduced two years earlier.

Experiments with "pseudo-operations" had been taking place behind the scenes for some time. In 1966 a mixture of army and Special Branch under Senior Assistant Inspector Oppenheimer carried out a series of experiments on the "pseudo" concept. No real success was achieved, and it appears that the *modus operandi* included bushcraft, tracking and patrolling in four-man groups dressed as terrorists. The idea was that superior bushcraft would enable these teams to locate terrorist groups and attack them. Unfortunately, the idea was shelved, which was a great pity; for although they were on the wrong track they had an excellent idea that simply needed to be directed into the right channel. By January 1973 the pressure on Special Branch informers was such that Superintendent Tommy Peterson of the Special Branch was given permission to resurrect the idea. An all-African team was put together. Military personnel, both black and white, were added to this complement, with the Special Branch officers Winston Hart and Peter Stanton attached to teach the teams how the terrorists worked.

While nothing much was gained from the point of view of killing (the original concept), a substantial amount of information became available to the security forces. CIO, Special Branch and the army, realising that they had something that might well be an effective substitute for the gap in Special Branch intelligence, took the idea to Ian Smith, who gave it his warm blessing. A new dynamic dimension was added to the war. It would be interesting to a student of counter-insurgency warfare to study how various situations brought about different developments in tactics and procedures as the war progressed.

The SAS performed a great service for the Rhodesian Army by teaching it to be conscious of bush conditions and skills in tracking. The confidence that that bred in the ordinary soldier had a great effect on the disproportionately high casualties that were inflicted upon their enemy with very few casualties to themselves. The RLI had the foresight to place a correct construction upon *Operational Nickel.* They regarded the tactics and formations produced by the

RAR as a result of their experiences as negative, defensive tactics. They discarded them and developed their own. And when their turn came to face their baptism of fire they responded magnificently. Their command, control and leadership at battalion, company and troop level and their imaginative use of air and ground tactics designed to bring the terrorist to battle were superb. The highly professional Rhodesian Light Infantry, ably assisted by the Rhodesian Air Force, had demonstrated conclusively that in the bush they were a formidable fighting machine.

Now, at a critical stage of the war, when intelligence, the vital ingredient in a counter-insurgency war, had all but dried up, a new dimension, pioneered by the Special Branch and the army, was about to make a significant entry into the war. In November 1973, the decision to form a "pseudo" unit, to be known at the Selous Scouts, was made; a decision that was to create a weapon destined to wreak havoc on the terrorists. For at the end of the day, 68 per cent of all terrorist deaths within the operational areas of Rhodesia were directly or indirectly due to Selous Scout "pseudo" operations.

By January 1974 the first sub-unit to have been trained in the "pseudo" principle was deployed. Much thought had been given to their role and method, and it became immediately apparent that for maximum long-term success, "pseudo" teams should be used only to pinpoint terrorist concentrations. Having done that, they were to bring conventional troops to the target by means of talking a helicopter-borne force in by radio or leading them in on foot. By 26 May the same year the correctness of this decision was evident, for 53 terrorists had been killed and nine had been captured. Of this total 45 killed and seven captured had been effected in ten days by the Rhodesian Light Infantry, who were directed to two separate concentrations of terrorists by the Selous Scouts. The morale of the security forces rose rapidly, and once again they felt that they were in control of the situation. The Rhodesian Air Force provided indispensible support and they were to introduce new tactics with devastating effect. It had now become clear to the Air Force that their defensive supportive role of merely carrying troops by helicopter into battle was wrong. The ability of a helicopter to hover, or orbit in a tight circle gave the attacking infantry forces two great advantages over terrorist groups brought to contact. Unless the bush was extremely thick the helicopter provided the infantry commander with his own observation platform directly above the area, and he could be kept in the picture as to the terrorist movements and exact positions. The machine-guns mounted on the helicopter could put down intense fire-power from which a terrorist would find it difficult to escape. The air force went one better and mounted a 20mm cannon on every fifth helicopter. The company commander (normally RLI) flew in the helicopter with the cannon which was known as a K(kill)-Car, and from that position, circling the battle area, he controlled the contact. Later an attack aircraft was added, and also a Dakota transport aircraft which could deliver twenty parachute troops as stops or back-ups. This configuration was known as a Fire Force.

With the Selous Scouts to pinpoint terrorist concentrations this combination was able to destroy more terrorist forces than any other unit in the internal operational areas.

Two other measures designed to remove the African tribesmen from close contact with Zanla forces now began to be put into effect. The Rhodesian security forces, mindful of the lessons of Malaya, persuaded government that two courses must be adopted as a matter of urgency. In consequence a minefield obstacle was laid across the path of the infiltration from the Musengezi to the Mazoe rivers. This was doomed to failure right from the start, because the security forces, astonishingly enough, ignored a fundamental military tenet: an obstacle is not an obstacle unless it is covered by view and fire. The terrorists, therefore, had plenty of time to breach these minefields, which they did, in spite of suffering a considerable number of casualties. The second measure was to move numbers of the rural population into fortified villages, which aroused a considerable amount of resentment against government. While not criticising the removal of the population from the influence of Zanla, I believe that a much more effective block to the infiltrators would have been to concentrate more manpower and effort to increase the efficacy of the minefield. A series of section-posts built along the minefield would have provided the necessary surveillance and firepower to make the minefield an effective barrier. The guard force stationed in the protective villages would have been far better employed on surveillance along the minefield than guarding the villages. The Rhodesians, although in somewhat haphazard fashion, were on the right track. Looking back, it appears obvious that, flushed with their earlier successes, they had still not grasped the seriousness of their situation; or in spite of all their experience in Malaya, they had not grasped the essential elements that had to be incorporated into a comprehensive strategy for the conduct of the war.

General Peter Walls, the Commander of the Army, stated that if some of the lessons and experience of Malaya and Kenya had been applied earlier in the war, the Rhodesians might well have nipped many of their troubles in the bud.

It was immensely frustrating to army officers, particularly those who had served in Malaya, to witness the same fundamental mistakes being repeated and not to be able to do anything about it. The lack of a clear, unambiguous strategy to be employed by all forces and agencies of the security forces proved to be the greatest impediment in the prosecution of the war. Much of the failure was due to the system of command and control, which was essentially control by committee. The idea of the Operations Coordinating Committee with subordinate Joint Operations Committees at the lower levels was a product of the Malayan emergency. In essence it was the correct system for a counter-insurgency situation; but what was overlooked was the fact that in Malaya a Supreme Commander – as the name implied – had total and absolute command. The reason for the creation of such a post was obvious. Rule by committee, unless it is ruthlessly controlled, seldom produces the best answer to a problem. Appeasing conflicting opinions is a pusillanimous dodge often used by the chairman of a committee, with the result that weak, diluted solutions are accepted when bold unpalatable action is needed. A competent Supreme Commander provides stiffening and, if necessary, can override inept decisions.

The British South Africa Police was acknowledged to be a professional, highly competent police force, but none of their senior officers had any experience in counter-insurgency warfare as the army had. They were touchy about their function of maintaining law and order, and they resisted any action by the army that appeared to usurp their responsibilities. The question that bedevils a counter-insurgency war, particularly in its early stages, is: when is the situation to be regarded as outright war? For while the maintenance of law and order is unquestionably a police function, the security of the nation is no less the responsibility of the military. Taken to a logical conclusion therefore, there must come a time when insurgency is as serious a danger to the survival of the nation as invasion by a foreign army. In the case of an invasion the military would immediately assume command. Is it not pertinent, therefore, to ask whether there is not a time in an unconventional war when the integrity of a nation is in serious danger and when the military must assume total responsibility for its defence?

The question of a Supreme Commander was raised by both senior and junior army officers, who realised that the committee system, so alien to the military method of direct command, was largely responsible for the woolly thinking and inertia that clogged the minds of those responsible for coordinating the efforts of the forces. The response from OCC to their request was immediate and direct. There was no question of the appointment of a Supremo either now or in the future, and the idea was to be dismissed. More agitation from military officers followed. The obvious choice, as it appeared to the army, was General Walls. OCC, led by Ken Flower, were obdurate; they would never serve under an army officer. Flower's narrow view, as expressed in his book, was that if the army took over the war could be considered lost. General Walls, as part of the OCC, had to remain silent, which left two policemen and the Chief of the Air Force to vote. Thus, in spite of the clear lesson of General Templar, whose appointment brought sanity and cohesion to the chaos in Malaya, the policemen won the day.

Decision, or rather indecision, by consensus remained characteristic of the war for three more years until, in 1977, a Combined Headquarters was established and General Walls was appointed Supreme Commander. But the sands of time had for the most part run out and left him barely two years to reverse nearly five years of muddle. To weaken his position still further he was denied the rank and absolute power over the control of operations, unlike Gerald Templar, so that his wings were still clipped.

The early stages of the Malayan emergency, like many other rebellions or insurrections, caught the government and its security forces with their trousers down. The British authorities realised that to achieve success they needed a strategic plan. The man chosen to produce such a plan was a soldier who had served with distinction in Burma in the second world war, General Briggs. The Briggs Plan, as it was called, was based upon four main principles:

1. Deny the terrorist access to the civilian population.
2. Deny the terrorist access to food.
3. Destroy the enemy in his rear areas, i.e. his base camps, training camps and his courier lines of communication.
4. Hunt him down with conventional troops on continual patrols in the jungle fringes. ("Hearts and minds" came later with General Templar.)

The army were the prime movers in getting the idea of protected villages put into effect. If the protected village and the minefield barrier had been more effectively carried out the security situation in the *Hurricane* operational area in the early years could have been radically changed. Judicious positioning of the minefield barriers and effective surveillance could have channelled infiltrations into areas cleared of the population where they could have been dealt with using the RLI tactics of *Operation Cauldron* or the Selous Scouts to bring in "fire forces". At that stage of the war very little attention had been given to an important requirement of the Malayan Briggs Plan, which was that the enemy must be defeated in their base areas. There is little point in conducting internal operations, no matter how successful, if an inexhaustible stream of reinforcements can enter the country with impunity.

On 25 April 1974 the Portuguese army mutinied and in a *coup d'état* took over the government. That had the most serious implications for the Rhodesian security forces, for when Mozambique was pushed into independence it extended the borders open to infiltration by 1 100 kilometres. Security forces now had to guard 3 000 kilometres of hostile borders. Many officers of the Rhodesian Army were actually pleased, particularly those who had served in the Portuguese Army. They saw the absence of the irksome restrictions that the Portuguese placed upon Rhodesian forces operating in Mozambique as a wonderful opportunity to "shut the tap off" by using large numbers of troops in Mozambique.

The idea had much merit, for Frelimo, in the conventional sense, was nothing but a rag-tag guerrilla band with no effective means of policing its own country. The Selous Scouts saw an excellent opportunity to infiltrate the Zanla forces, and in accordance with the Briggs Plan, to destroy the enemy in their bases. Their request to reverse the gains by Zanla was turned down.

It is hard to believe that the Rhodesians gave Frelimo a two-year respite to get their house in order. Zanla, seizing this marvellous opportunity with both hands, rapidly organised training camps and infiltration routes from the Muzengezi river in the north to Malvernia in the Gaza Province in the south. On the Zipra front, the SAS began small but effective operations against jumping-off camps in Zambia, while the Selous Scouts carried out a number of successful abductions of numbers of the Zipra hierarchy in Francistown, Botswana. In these operations black Selous Scouts proved conclusively that they had more than the necessary courage and skill to engage in this type of operation. Indeed, they were the only troops who could have carried them off, because a white man would never have been allowed near the target.

By January 1976, Zanla, having put their two years' respite to good use, had established themselves in base camps down the Eastern Border and into the Gaza Province in the south of Rhodesia. Large incursions had taken place down the length of this border, followed, somewhat belatedly, by the establishment of more Joint Operational Centres to deal with them.

The demand for Selous Scouts to pinpoint targets increased accordingly; but fortunately the foresight of General Walls had allowed for a considerable increase in the strength of the Selous Scouts, who were able to meet most of the demands. It was belatedly obvious that the Rhodesians had almost committed national suicide by granting Zanla such generous time to organise themselves. The commanders of the two Special Force units begged to be allowed to "turn the tap off", but the OCC, under pressure from Vorster, vacillated.

Finally in June 1976 the Selous Scouts were given the green light to strike a transit camp in the small town of Mapai in Gaza Province in Mozambique. The strike, using vehicles and Frelimo uniforms was successfully carried out. That was followed by the first important external strike of the war when in August 1976, 72 black and white Selous Scouts wearing Frelimo uniforms and with vehicles painted in Frelimo colours drove into Mozambique and attacked Nyadzonia base. The camp was occupied by 5 000 terrorists, of whom 3 000 were trained and standing by to infiltrate the eastern districts of Rhodesia. The attack was not allowed any air support and relied upon complete surprise. Surprise was achieved, and the Scouts motored back to Rhodesia leaving over a thousand terrorists dead. They themselves had only four slightly wounded.

The raid was a great success and gave a great fillip to the Rhodesian public and security forces. To obtain permission to attack the camp the Selous Scouts circumvented the regular channels and went direct to the Commander of the Army, General Walls. There was great opposition from the director of CIO, Ken Flower, when the plan to attack Nyadzonia was put before the OCC for ratification.

Perhaps it was a simple case of professional jealousy, because the Special Branch unit of the Selous Scouts and the Rhodesian Air Force had pinpointed the exact whereabouts of the camp. For reasons of his own Flower did not want the camp attacked.

The CIO, true to form, despite being responsible for providing such information, had no idea that the camp even existed. It was a state of affairs that was to persist to the very end of the war. Flower in his book states that it was a refugee camp occupied by men, women and children, and he must have known as he wrote that he was telling a gross untruth. Documents, prisoners and photographs were brought back to prove otherwise, although it was hardly necessary in view of the concrete evidence that the Scouts had before the raid.

It was a pity that Edmund Kaguri, the political commissar for Zanla Central Committee, who was captured, died of his wounds before the Scouts got back to Rhodesia. Significantly, in the furore that followed this attack, no photographs of dead women and children were displayed, only photographs of able-bodied young men clad in military uniforms. In any case General Walls and the rest of the OCC would never have agreed to allow such an operation to take place unless they had been ninety per cent certain, at least from the intelligence and air photographs, that it was beyond doubt a terrorist camp.

Apart from Flower there were others who were most unhappy. Perhaps it was symptomatic of the stress that the officers and men of the army were now being subjected to. The SAS, an all-white unit, became particularly bitter about the Selous Scouts, accusing them of encroaching on SAS territory. This was a rather puzzling attitude, since the SAS at that time could hardly put ninety men in the field. Nor had they any black soldiers. It was more important that there were now well over 10 000 terrorists spread over 3 000 kilometres of hostile border, more than enough to occupy the attention of the whole Rhodesian Army.

In any case General Walls commanded the army, and it was his prerogative to say who should do what.

In spite of the success of Nyadzonia many more months were to pass before more strikes on large terrorist camps were carried out, and although the fire forces reaped a terrible harvest, the rate of attrition was not nearly high enough to compensate for the flow of hundreds of trained and semi-trained terrorists crossing into Rhodesia. The absence of a total strategy and the inertia bred by command by committee for five years had brought the country, in spite of the splendid successes of the security forces, to the brink of disaster. The soldiers had preached; the civilians led by CIO had vacillated. It has become standard practice for analysts of the Rhodesian war to castigate the Rhodesian Army for failing to grasp that counter-insurgency warfare is essentially a battle for the people. And they have been totally wrong in this opinion, for it was the army that preached this gospel from the very beginning of the war.

The army can certainly be blamed for tardiness and a lack of flexibility in their tactics, but never for failing to understand the requirements to combat counter-insurgency. It was horses for courses as far as the army was concerned, and at JOC meetings the responsibility for African Tribal Affairs, for example, rested with Internal Affairs, not the army. Similarly, every intelligent person knows that the army is or should be an instrument and extension of the national political aims, and a soldier does not get mixed up with politics. That was the attitude of the army throughout the war.

Politically Ian Smith was under heavy pressure from John Vorster to meet

Henry Kissinger. Earlier, in January 1975, as an inducement to get nationalist leaders to attend a conference at the Victoria Falls, South Africa had withdrawn her policemen from Rhodesia. On 9 August 1976, the day when the Selous Scouts attacked Nyadzonia camp, twenty-six of the forty helicopters on loan to Rhodesia from South Africa were withdrawn, together with fifty pilots and technicians. Inexplicable delays in road and rail traffic suddenly occurred, which resulted in many other shortages. Rhodesia was left with two weeks' fuel to fight the war. Such arm-twisting treatment forced Ian Smith to accept the Kissinger proposals, which were commonly referred to by the Rhodesians as the "Kiss of Death". The bitter saying went round the security forces: "With friends like these who needs enemies?"

It so happened that Vorster's efforts came to nothing for the Geneva talks based on the Kissinger proposals broke down in January 1977. In fairness to the South Africans it must be said that they were in fact the main target of American pressure. The Americans knew that without South African help Rhodesia was finished, and they forced South Africa to apply the pressure. The war, which had actually increased in intensity during the peace talks, raged on with higher rates of killing than ever.

In March 1977 Combined Operations Headquarters was formally instituted, and General Walls was made Supreme Commander. External operations were intensified. The biggest operation of the war was carried out by the SAS and the RLI, supported with every aircraft that could be put into the air. In the early part of 1977 officers of the Special Branch attached to the Selous Scouts and the JOC at Umtali, on the eastern border of Rhodesia, became aware through interrogation of captured terrorists of a camp that had become a substitute training and deployment base for Zanla after the Nyadzonia base was destroyed. Lt-Col. Brian Robinson was now commanding officer of the SAS, which had been expanded into a full regiment. The SAS, strangely enough, had been somewhat put out by the success of the Selous Scouts at Nyadzonia, which they regarded as their pigeon. Chimoio Base presented the SAS with an excellent opportunity to level scores with the Scouts. Brian Robinson summoned his intelligence officer and ordered him to gather every scrap of information that he could on this terrorist complex. The I.O.'s first port of call was the CIO, with which they had a much better *rapport* than the Selous Scouts. There, gathering dust, he found piles of reports on the camp by Special Branch officers in the forward areas. Having identified the position of the camp the I.O. arranged for the air force to photograph it. The results were astonishing. The camp known as Chimoio was estimated to contain between 9 000 and 11 000 persons. A head count of the rifle range alone showed 700. Detailed planning now took place between Group Captain Norman Walsh and Brian Robinson. Altogether twelve representations were made before COMOPS, alive to the danger that the base presented to Rhodesia, agreed to the attack.

On 23 November 1977 a force of 97 SAS and 88 RLI men in a joint force of parachutists and helicopter-borne troops attacked the camp. The attack by the ground troops was preceded by a strong air-strike. It was typical of the aplomb of the Rhodesian soldier to fly eighty kilometres and launch himself at an enemy who numbered 11 000, 4 000 of them trained and armed. The raid was a great success: 2 000 terrorists were killed, to two Rhodesians killed and eight wounded.

Twenty-four hours later the same force struck again, this time at a camp at Tembue. It was situated north of Cahora Bassa, some 225 kilometres from the Rhodesian border. To reach the target, the Rhodesian Air Force, as at Chimoio, had to establish an administrative base deep inside Mozambique to refuel the helicopters. A number of terrorists were killed in the complex, but it was by no means as successful as the attack on Chimoio camp. Immediately after these attacks the Selous Scouts sent a column into Mozambique to blow up five bridges. The purpose of this operation was to block access to the south to the terrorists and channel them into the Rusape area where the topography lent itself to operations by the Scouts. External actions followed thick and fast, but it was the proverbial case of shutting the stable door after the horse had gone.

On the operational side much had happened. The advent of a supreme commander had done much to stabilise the military, who welcomed a strong hand. There were difficulties, however, mostly arising from a combination of personality clashes and a chain of command starting from COMOPS, which effectively kept the army commander from control of his troops. The army believed that, like General Templar in Malaya, the Supreme Commander's prime function should be to coordinate the energies and activities of all the military, police and other bodies engaged in the fight against terrorism. Having formulated a strategic plan, he would issue broad guidelines upon which JOCs would base their own plans. COMOPS, however, took over direct command of units such as the SAS and the Selous Scouts, and eventually the conduct of all operations. While that did not seriously affect the Selous Scouts, because they had always come directly under General Walls, it did create strains in army headquarters, because the staff had to immerse themselves in the work necessary to support the decisions of COMOPS without having taken part in the planning. Bitter feelings were aroused when senior officers were given instructions by junior officers in COMOPS. It may well be that the antics of some senior officers were such that the Supreme Commander no longer trusted their judgment. One, for example, was found drunk after a traffic accident outside the official residence of the Prime Minister. That, of course, is not necessarily a sin, particularly in soldiers; but this particular gentleman compounded his problem by being clad only in his underpants with a highly embarrassed lady in his car.

The early part of 1978 saw a new transitional government with Bishop Muzorewa as its head. Internal and external operations were intensified and the security forces made prodigious efforts to stabilise and reverse the trend of events in an attempt to give the transitional government breathing space to survive and develop strong African support. Zanla refused to join or collaborate with Muzorewa, and the outside world, while pleased that the blacks apparently now ran the country, still hesitated because they knew that as long as Zipra and Zanla boycotted Muzorewa the war would still go on. The army psychological unit made great efforts to sway the African population to support Muzorewa, but the years of neglect to influence the African people took its inevitable effect. It is difficult to convince people unless they can be shown that the insurgents are losing the war; so the psychological unit had an impossible job. Moreover by that time most families in the operational areas had a kinsman or two with the terrorists. The problem had got beyond any solution. There had been a great improvement in intelligence. Special Branch, particularly those of its members attached to the Selous Scouts, had never given up and had served the security forces with exemplary loyalty. The Selous Scouts, because of their close association with the African peasants and the terrorist network, collected better intelligence than the rest of the Rhodesian intelligence put together, both internal and external. Apart from their normal acquisition of intelligence in the course of their duties, they had first call on all captures. And recent arrivals had much to tell, such as routes in and out, contact men, location of training camps, names and so on. Much of this intelligence lay in Selous Scout offices gathering dust. The Special Air Services had no such facilities and because of their external missions they were always on the lookout for intelligence. The two regiments decided to pool their resources: the SAS intelligence section would be responsible for external intelligence and the Selous Scouts for internal intelligence. For a time all went well; but the volume was such that the Directorate of Military Intelligence had to be approached to provide staff to help in the processing of the intelligence. Unknown to the SAS and the Scouts, the Special Branch, the CIO and Military Intelligence were vehemently against the idea, which in retrospect must have seemed a threat. Ken Flower of the CIO protested to General Walls, with the result that the whole notion was shelved. There was one bright spot, however. Military Intelligence acquired an intelligence gold-mine of its own. The Rhodesian Corps of Signals had in the ordinary course of their duties been monitoring the Frelimo radio network. The amount of intelligence that this produced was enormous, and it proved a most valuable means of confirming kill rates after strikes across the border.

Special Branch, for reasons of their own, were extremely wary of Military Intelligence, and such was their concern that they forbade the passing of Selous Scout debriefing reports to them. Although this decision had nothing to do with the commander of the Selous Scouts, he became the target of their hostility, and an attempt, again symptomatic of the times, was made to destroy his credibility and get him removed.

During July 1978 the director of Military Intelligence and his second-in-command, trumped up accusations that AK-47 rifles were being sold to the American Mafia and considerable quantities of poached ivory were being exported illegally to South Africa. How they imagined that the Scouts were able to get away with that when they were living cheek-by-jowl with the Special Branch they did not say, and one can only conclude that they imagined the Special Branch was part of the conspiracy. The Army Commander, although he denied it on oath a few months later, granted permission for a "bug" to be placed on the telephone in the office of the commander of the Selous Scouts. The second-in-command was a rare bird. His first choice of service had been the air force, but he failed the pilot selection board and joined the army. His frustrations and desire to be a pilot were still so strong that he acquired a derelict Harvard trainer aircraft, which he parked in his back garden. Whenever the urge to fly came upon him he would don a leather flying helmet, get into the aircraft and for an hour or so fly blissfully to the clouds. This was the man in charge of counter-intelligence in the Rhodesian military forces, which shows how seriously that service was taken.

To place a "bug" in the telephone of an officer entrusted with the most sensitive of operations can only be regarded as the height of irresponsibility, particularly over something so patently ludicrous and spurious as running Russian weapons to the Mafia. More so when he and his director knew well that the security of the Selous Scouts was entrusted to the Special Branch, to whom he could have made representations. Unfortunately for the trio the "bug" was discovered. The commander of the Selous Scouts was furious and made some caustic comments to the Army Commander, for which he was court-martialled.

Members of the court martial, which was held in camera, were treated to the unedifying spectacle of a general denying on oath any complicity in the sordid affair, while his director and second-in-command of the Directorate of Military Intelligence and his director of Military Police swore on oath that he was involved. The commander of the Selous Scouts was "reprimanded", which is the army's way of saying "We understand why you did it, but you shouldn't have done it. It was naughty and don't do it again".

The affair, of course, was followed with great interest and concern throughout the army and indeed among the general public, to whom the Selous Scouts had become a heroic legend. In the discussions and speculations that followed the court martial, many reasons were put forward for the motives behind this extraordinary affair. The commonest held by the fighting element of the army was that it had been a deliberate attempt by the CIO and military intelligence to remove the commander of the Scouts in preparation for the sellout of Rhodesia.

An interesting fact was uncovered by Inspector Winston Hart of the Selous Scouts Special Branch, when he was investigating the affair after the "bug" had been discovered. Military Intelligence had also been investigating General Walls and were trying to implicate him in the movement of money to South Africa, a fallacious charge that had as much substance as the weapons to the Mafia, because the General, like most soldiers, was as poor as the proverbial church mouse. Perhaps this nasty episode was nothing more than a symptom of the stresses and strains of fourteen years of war. There was no light to be seen at the end of the tunnel – the "chicken run" had been renamed the "owl run" – the owl being a wiser bird than the common fowl.

Morale had taken a steep dive among the soldiers of the territorial forces; not on account of the fighting but the length of time they had to spend on military service – six months of every year. Many of them, unable to maintain their businesses or farms, joined the security forces permanently for the duration of the war. Among the regular units morale remained high, mainly because of the high casualty rate that they were inflicting upon the terrorists both internally and externally.

By the middle of 1978 moves were afoot to form an interim government that would command the support of substantial numbers of the African population. Several black nationalist leaders, some with direct terrorist links, combined with members of the existing government to form a transitional government. It was realised that if that government were to have any standing with the African population they would have to prove that they had a sizeable number of the terrorists behind them. Two nationalist leaders, both churchmen, declared that huge areas of Rhodesia were infested with terrorists who had changed sides because of the African flavour of the Interim government, and were now solidly behind the new government. That caused a rush of blood to the head of those advising the new government, consequently the Special Branch and the Selous Scouts were given the task of training, administering and feeding all the terrorists who came in from the bush in support of Bishop Muzorewa's African National Council or the Reverend Ndabaningi Sithole's ZANU.

It so happened that most of the "boys from the bush" turned out to be vagabonds and loafers recruited in the townships. However, in accordance with orders issued, training began with top priority being given to this policy. The theory was that "auxiliary terrorists", as they were called, would be trained, then given selected areas to control and keep free from the real terrorists. It was thought that this force would have a better *rapport* with the indigenous population and would by subtle propaganda wean it to the side of the new government. It was an interesting idea, but it did not work, mainly because the population saw through it at once. The behaviour of these auxiliaries toward the tribesmen was unsatisfactory, and whatever popularity they had managed to drum up dwindled rapidly.

A similar idea, this time using Frelimo deserters and dissidents, was put into practice externally with great success. A gentleman in the CIO who rejoiced in the name of the Silver Fox made a study of Mozambique with particular reference to the popularity of Frelimo among the rural population. His studies showed that there were large areas where they were extremely unpopular. An old but powerful radio transmitter was commissioned and virulent anti-Frelimo propaganda was pumped out. The response was amazing: hundreds of Frelimo deserted to found the National Resistance Movement, but without success, since it existed in name only. The SAS were given the job of training and advising (and usually found themselves leading them, too) MNR commanders on anti-Frelimo operations in Mozambique. It was a very successful idea with enormous possibilities; the pity was that it came too late in the war to have any serious effect on the outcome of the sellout.

On 21 December 1979, exactly seven years after the terrorist attack on Alterna Farm, which heralded the final seven-year phase in the fight for Rhodesia, Muzorewa, Mugabe and Nkomo signed a ceasefire agreement. A Commonwealth supervisory force began to arrive in Rhodesia to keep the ceasefire and hold the ring for the election that was to follow. Lord Soames was already in Salisbury, and Rhodesians, tight-lipped and mindful of perfidious Albion, watched the Englishman with anger mixed with apprehension as to their future. Their apprehension was justified, for *Operation Con JOB* was about to be launched. Sixteen assembly points had been set up in which, in accordance with the Lancaster House Agreement, all terrorists in Rhodesia were to report with their weapons and remain until "fair and free elections" had been held. The idea was to prevent terrorists from intimidating the voters. The result was exactly as predicted by the Rhodesians. Thousands of youths known as *mujibas* (the eyes and ears of the terrorists) reported to these points with elements of the terrorist forces. Most of the terrorists, however, remained in the Tribal Trust Lands, and set about a systematic campaign of intimidation among the tribesmen.

The morale of the Rhodesian forces, which had sunk low because of the way in which events were turning out, rose sky-high when they were told at a meeting held at the Rhodesian Air Force Base that Mugabe would not be allowed to win the election. It was made clear that there would be no hesitation in using force to ensure this if unforeseen circumstances made victory for Mugabe a possibility. All unit commanders were told to get the message across to their troops as a matter of urgency to sustain morale. A two-phase plan was then drawn up. *Operation Hectic* entailed the permanent removal of key personnel in the terrorist hierarchy, beginning with Robert Mugabe. *Operation Quartz* entailed the destruction of all terrorists concentrated at the assembly points. Some assembly points would be attacked by conventional ground forces, others would be bombed from the air. But although the staff work and planning was excellent, things began to go wrong from the outset. The SAS and the Selous Scouts between them made no fewer than four attempts on Mugabe's life, but inexplicably, on each occasion something went wrong. Once Mugabe had actually got to the steps of an aircraft bound for Bulawayo when he suddenly stopped and returned to Salisbury. Waiting for him at the press conference that he was to address in Bulawayo there was a Selous Scout posing as a member of the press corps. The Scout had already placed a microphone packed with high explosive and fitted with a radio–controlled detonator on the dais.

That was the last straw, and it was obvious to the commanders of the Special Forces regiments that a highly–placed source had access to their plans and was warning Mugabe. Their suspicions focused upon Flower, whom they had always regarded as a traitor. They remembered that it was always Flower who attempted to dissuade the OCC from consenting to attacks on external bases, and that when a Supreme Commander had been appointed to remove the power of the OCC to veto such attacks, suddenly, after several very successful attacks, the army found nothing but a succession of empty terrorist camps. In spite of the failure of Phase 1, rehearsals went ahead for Phase 2, *Operation Quartz*. All troops concerned were in position ready to go into action, on the code–word. On 4 March the soldiers eyes were fixed on their watches, uneasy as the time moved inexorably towards 9am, when the results of the election were to be released. But no code–word came. Reaction among the troops was mixed; some believed that Mugabe had lost the election and there was no need for the operation; others had more than a suspicion that something had gone dreadfully wrong, and they were right. The news came over the radio – the unthinkable had come to pass: Mugabe had won a resounding victory. Even the final Special Branch plan to switch the ballot boxes had been foiled by Flower. British Intelligence had pulled off a masterly con job, ably assisted by traitors. Special Branch officers were summoned by Flower to a special meeting at Combined Operations. The purpose was to tell Special Branch that Mugabe's victory had come as a great surprise, because it had not been considered a possibility. That was an out–right lie.

Because the black Selous Scouts and many Special Branch officers had repeatedly warned their superiors, to quote the Scouts, "that if you whites are stupid enough to allow elections Mugabe will win hands down." The reasons for Mr Mugabe's spectacular win, apart from treachery in high places, were quite clear.

1. First, there was the natural desire of the African people to be masters of their own destiny, though not necessarily with Mugabe as their master.
2. Secondly, in order of importance, there was the great desire on the part of the African people to end the war so that they could get back to normal life. They knew that if Mugabe did not win the election the war would continue, even if at a lower level, because a large section of the population, for example Nkomo's Ndebele and Muzorewa's following would not be involved. African logic therefore was that if Mugabe was voted in the war would stop.
3. Thirdly, although it must be accepted that while Mugabe had a considerable groundswell of support it was by no means as strong as the election appeared to indicate. A vicious campaign of intimidation preceded the election, and even when the voters were lining up to vote Mugabe's thugs were patrolling the queues and making the voters perfectly aware of what they could expect if they failed to vote for Mugabe.

The bones of Rhodesia have already been picked by authors who hoped to be first with their comments. Most of them have simply likened the fight for Rhodesia to similar campaigns elsewhere and have trotted out the same stale reasons, some of which are in fact pertinent. Two stock truisms emerge: that the political aspirations denied to the black people for so long were what triggered off the explosion; or, if it is a military writer that the lessons of Malaya and Kenya were ignored and the war was lost in the Tribal Trust Lands. The writer can only agree with the first; he would point out that it is possible to maintain the status quo if the government of a country with a subject population has the necessary military strength and the determination to hold on to its power. Ignoring hearts and minds for the moment, one need only look at the various empires that flourished and prospered only for as long as the governing power kept its strength, resolution and confidence. The Roman Empire was the classic example. To retain its position the Roman Army was totally ruthless in suppressing any threat to the sovereignty of Rome. There was no United Nations nor were there Leagues of Human Rights or any such humanitarian bodies to deter the army from keeping the integrity of the Empire intact. Rome defeated itself by internal strife and corruption and lost the will to rule.

The German Army during the 1939/45 war occupied most of Europe and had millions of hostile subject peoples under its control. Despite the fact that the Germans were fighting on two fronts and had to contend with resistance groups, the various *maquis* had very little effect upon the German war effort; for, like the Romans, the Germans were totally ruthless in dealing with insurrection.

Obviously the methods used by the Roman and German armies could not be used in Rhodesia. It is not the writer's intention to churn over political questions except to say that the failure to admit the African population in the political life of the country in good time was a cardinal error. However, that was a political matter, not within the scope of the Rhodesian Army; and the writer confines his remarks to the part that the military played in the war. The most glaring mistake was this: until the appointment of a Supreme Commander the Rhodesian Army had no general strategic objective to base its tactics on. Failure to extend the war to the external bases of the enemy in the early stages of the war lost the Tribal Trust Lands to the terrorists. If that had been properly executed, particularly when Frelimo had just taken over from the Portuguese, the need for protected villages would have fallen away. Again, if the MNR idea had been put into effect at that time (and it is conceded that it might have been too early) the Rhodesian Army could have fought most of its war in Mozambique. Petty jealousies between Special Force units exacerbated by certain senior officers in COMOPS, severely limited effective external operations in the surrounding Frontline States. A special forces headquarters should have been formed when the Selous Scouts Regiment was established to ensure the best operational value from them. A sustained tactical plan to channel terrorists into selected killing areas to suit Selous Scouts "pseudo" and fire force operations should have been drawn up. A plan to deny Gaza Province to the terrorists and force them to deploy in the eastern districts, which was excellent for "pseudo" operations was discontinued in favour of more spectacular operations, again because there was no general coherent strategic plan. Perhaps at the end of the day it could be said with truth the astonishing decision to give the terrorists a two–year respite to organise themselves on the northern, eastern and southern borders of Rhodesia actually lost the country, because the security forces were simply unable to contain the flood of terrorists who entered the country in vast numbers from all sides.

The early stages of the war must also be taken into the reckoning. Operations *Nickel* and *Cauldron,* as we have shown, set the Rhodesian Army firmly on the wrong track; for the successes that they won led to tactics entirely unsuited to action against terrorists in the inhabited areas. That should have been foreseen, for if the idea of the Selous Scouts had been introduced earlier, a different situation would have resulted.

On the credit side, there must be few events in history in which a small army has had to contend with such heavy odds plus economic sanctions and world-wide hostility. The sins of omission and commission at higher levels did not deter the Rhodesian security forces from doing their duty with rare skill and dash; and many of their operations must remain models of courage and fighting spirit.

## MORE THOUGHTS ON THE URBAN CONDITION WITHIN THE SOUTH AFRICAN CONTEXT

The insurgent, his *raison d'être,* his aims and the means that he uses to achieve his aims must be thoroughly understood if he is to be defeated. The means that he uses to achieve his political aim are often devious. It should never be forgotten, however, that his civil and military actions are totally subordinate to his political aims. Mao Tse-tung, emphasising the importance of a good public image to engender popular support said: "If guerrilla war is without a political objective, it must fail; likewise, if it maintains a political objective incompatible with the political objectives of the people it will not get their support, and the war will also fail." Total enlistment of the masses is the key to success in a guerrilla war.

## GOVERNMENT FORCES

It follows, then, that if the insurgent is to be defeated, he must be confronted by security forces and a government more determined and skilled than himself in civil and military counter-measures. Unfortunately these two areas are often grossly misunderstood.

The realities and practicalities of an insurgency war often escape the conventional military mind because of a tendency to cloak them in academic semantics and definitions. It has been said that irregular and psychological warfare belongs more properly to the social sciences. The average soldier confronted by an irregular war situation has never studied the social sciences and it is probably just as well, for he would flounder even more deeply into a morass of academic theory that he would not always understand. It is important that the theory and the practical application of civil and military measures in an insurgency war should be clearly and simply defined, and that all concerned in the prosecution of the war understand precisely what their function is.

A Frenchman writing under the pseudonym of Colonel Nemo said: "Regular armies have hardly ever succeeded in gaining the ascendancy over guerrilla operations of any importance. Perhaps that is because of a subconscious desire to hide this importance that the great commanders have minimised the role of guerrilla operations."

## STRATEGY AND TACTICS
### Insurgents

It did not need a military genius to predict the strategy and tactics that insurgents would adopt to attempt to overthrow the government of South Africa.

The insurgent is essentially a propagandist. All means to promote his propaganda are grist to his mill. He is an agitator, who uses violent confrontation as a means of personally enlisting the masses against the government. In that way he binds them to his movement by a literal pact of blood. He endeavours to inflame emotions generated by acts of mob violence to a critical point so that a state of revolution becomes general throughout the country. The geography and grouping of the population of a country will dictate the type of insurgency war to be waged, i.e. whether urban or rural. The choice of the urban mode in South Africa, therefore, will not have surprised anyone.

From a propaganda point of view the urban mode has much more scope to offer than does the rural. A rural insurgency war is usually spread over great distances with poor communications making it difficult for the news media to cover events. By contrast the urban scene is readily available to the media. Insurgents can manipulate mob action at will and force the security forces to react. They are also able to manufacture incidents that the outside news media can use to prodigious effect to propagate the cause of the insurgent. The lack of faith shown by the average American in his "cause" during the Vietnam war can be directly attributed to the fact that the war was brought into his sitting-room every evening. As it happened, such scenes of violence numbed his mind and sapped his morale. The American citizen - like the American Army - lost his will to fight and win. The adverse publicity that the RSA has received abroad as a result of exposure of riots in black townships should be a significant warning to all in authority. As we have seen, any reaction by the security forces to a situation brought about by insurgent action, however justifiable and sensible in the circumstances, can have disastrous repercussions on the image of the country. Security forces under the constant focus of the outside media have a heavy responsibility. Their task is onerous enough in ordinary circumstances, since they have to fight insurgency on one hand yet avoid any action that might discredit the security forces and therefore the country as a whole.

The initiative belongs to the insurgent; it is he who decides when the war will begin and what form it will take. The security forces have to play a waiting game. They have to disperse themselves to cover areas of potential threat. Their task, particularly in the towns, is defensive. They must maintain and restore order; protect property and life. The political nature of the struggle imposes limitations on the actions of the ordinary government forces. The only course open to the security forces by which they can compete with the insurgent, using his own fundamental tactics, is by skilful use of specially trained special forces. But whatever form their tactics take, there is one imperative to which all efforts of the security forces must be subjected: the first stage of an insurgent campaign must not be allowed to develop into its next logical stage.

**Security Forces**
The main object of the counter-insurgency training and practical experience has been in rural operations. What the present situation now demands urgently is a well-conceived urban strategy expressly designed to beat the insurgent or at least to contain him. Failure to achieve that could have very serious consequences. But before any such strategy is put into effect, one prime requisite must be resolved; that is the *status* of the insurgency campaign; that is, is it to be conceived simply as industrial unrest, or is it to be regarded as outright revolutionary warfare? This is extremely important and there can be no pussyfooting or equivocation. The sooner the country is apprised of its situation the better.

History has shown that a blinkered or sheltered approach often has an extremely bad effect on the morale of a population when at last they understand their true situation. We may recall the uproar that ensued when a Rhodesian Police Provincial Commissioner, concluded his farewell speech at a dinner by saying to his Commissioner:

"Sir - for years you have treated us like mushrooms - you have kept us in the dark and fed us on shit."

Whatever faults the Rhodesian displayed he was never afraid to speak up; and this story should serve as a reminder that the mushroom treatment is not the best guarantee of either military or political success. It is important then that the realities are recognised and faced in the earliest stages of a revolutionary war. Failure to do so will result in the insurgent increasing his initiative and his control over the situation, with a consequent rapid expansion of the war. The security forces, by contrast, lacking in positive direction, will feel helpless and become frustrated by their inability to get to grips with the problem.

### Joint Operations Centres

We have spoken of the urgent need to determine the exact nature of a state of unrest as early as possible. There is yet another very important reason for that: the often vexed question of command and control. In the early stages of all insurgency wars this contentious problem inevitably seems to arise. In spite of past lessons, it appears that the wheel has to be invented anew at the beginning of every war with all the resulting frustrations to the fighting troops, while rivalry between services and interference from politicians and heads of civil service departments, nullify work and ability. While the security forces bicker and lose the opportunity to gain the initiative so vital in the early rounds, the insurgent, clear in his aim and free from such in-fighting makes deep inroads into the local population, making good use of the breathing space given him by the security forces.

The British encountered these problems in Malaya in 1948. After some severe military reverses they devised a system of command and control by a series of committees at various levels. They realised, almost too late, that the principal ingredient of success against insurgents is the ability to coordinate the actions of all the civil, police and military forces of government. This principle has now been adopted by most countries with problems of insurgency.

But every system has its own inherent weaknesses and command by committee certainly has its share. What I.L. Janis says of government by committee is also true of command by committee: "Another hazard of modern war is government by committee." Four of the worst military disasters in recent American history (the Bay of Pigs, Pearl Harbour, the Korean War and Vietnam) are directly attributable to the psychological processes that altered group decision-making. These American disasters show very clearly that even the combined intellects and specialised knowledge of highly intelligent men are no proof against decisions so totally unrealistic that they subsequently tax the credulity of even those who made them. Far from diminishing the chances of ineptitude, the group actually accentuates the effects of those very traits that may lead to incompetence in individual commanders. The system of this process, which Janis calls "group think", include:

1. An illusion of invulnerability that becomes shared by most members of the group.
2. Collective attempts to ignore or to rationalise away information that might otherwise lead the group to reconsider shaky but cherished assumptions.
3. An unquestioned belief in the inherent morality of the group, thus enabling members to overlook the ethical consequences of their decisions.
4. Stereotyping the enemy as either too evil for negotiation or too stupid and feeble to be a serious danger.
5. A shared illusion of unanimity in a majority view aggravated by the false assumption that silence means approval.

6. Self-appointed "mind guards" to protect the group from adverse information that might destroy complacency about the effectiveness and morality of their decisions.

The problems inherent in command-by-committee have been dealt with previously. One wonders, in the light of the recent tragedy in Soweto where members of the police force were shot and killed by an army ambush group, whether the time has not come to appoint a South African Supreme Commander.

One of the interesting facts that emerged in the Rhodesian war prior to the appointment of a Supremo was that it quickly became standard practice, by mutual consent, for the senior army representative at the Joint Operational Centres to chair all JOC meetings. This came about because, as the tempo and the pressures of the war increased, the police and other security agencies became aware that Rhodesia was in the throes of a real war. This kind of conflict was not a temporary situation but needed the combined resources of the entire nation to combat it. Also, war is the business of the military. The police play an important ancillary role, but one that is subservient to the military command structure.

**Township Tactics**
A soldier trained for rural insurgency is often at a loss when confronted by urban insurgency for the first time. He should not be however, for he has a number of advantages over the urban insurgent that he had not possessed when fighting the rural insurgent. In a rural situation the aim of the insurgent is to subvert the countryside. By skilful use of small groups spread over as large an area as possible, he endeavours to force the security forces to spread themselves as thinly as possible over as wide an area as possible. Thus he reduces the potency of the security forces and can even weaken them to the extent whereby they become the targets instead of the attackers.

To answer such tactics the security forces often have to take a calculated risk and denude selected areas of troops. The danger here is that these areas will immediately be declared "liberated" areas by the insurgents. Unless the security forces have a first-class intelligence service that enables them to group and strike accurately and at will, they are at a serious disadvantage, and are in fact losing the war.

The urban insurgent, however, has no such advantage. The fact that he operates in the townships means that he is concentrating his forces in a small area. Security forces, therefore, have the advantage and can make good use of concentration of force. Security forces can achieve one thing that is almost impossible in the rural scene: they can dominate the ground.

By dividing the township up into sectors down to section level and actually living in these townships, security forces will command the terrain. Consideration should be given to the following:
1. *Strongpoints.* The construction of strongpoints at strategic positions will enable special forces to impose a strong network over the entire township.
2. *Patrols.* Active patrolling by day and night will make it difficult for insurgents to assemble mobs to stir up riots. These patrols should be by foot and vehicle and carried out continually by day and by night.
3. *Reaction Units.* These should be vehicle-borne, positioned at strategic points ready to react to reports by patrols.
   Each company, for example, should have its own reaction unit.
4. *Surveillance.* All high points should be occupied and used for surveillance.

Fixed-wing aircraft at high altitude in radio contact with troops are also a useful tool for this task.

5. *Helicopters.* A small fire force comprising selected men provides a valuable means of pursuing and capturing ringleaders. Ringleaders and agitators are thus deprived of their normal cover, that of the mob itself.

   Stone-throwing gangs can be similarly dealt with. A good surveillance network can pinpoint houses in which such people have taken refuge. The use of helicopters makes their capture an easy matter.

6. *Special Forces.* Urban insurgency is a tailor-made situation for special force operations. Their ability to provide good up-to-the-minute intelligence makes their deployment imperative.

7. *Intelligence.* If security forces are to be able to make the best use of the advantages that urban insurgency affords them, including the concentration of both forces, it is necessary for all intelligence services to cooperate closely at the various JOC levels.

8. *African Troops.* The maximum use of African troops should be made even if they are split up to accommodate the presence of white troops. The use of black troops does much to reduce the propaganda value of conflict between black and white. Black soldiers understand the sensibilities and values of their people, and above all they have the ability to communicate and tell the people exactly why they are there, and what the government is trying to achieve.

## CIVIL ACTION PROGRAMMES

It has been said that an anti-insurgency campaign must be 80 per cent civil action and 20 per cent military. Nevertheless *all the civil actions in the world will be to no avail if the military actions are not successful.* It is therefore the prime function of the military to prosecute a vigorous and unrelenting campaign against the insurgents. In that way a firm platform is provided so that political and civil reforms and actions can be carried out without interference. Civil actions are the business of the civil authorities, not the army, although they obviously have their part in the planning of operations at JOC level.

## CONCLUSION

These reflections are concerned mainly with the military aspects of an insurgency war. Nevertheless most if not all of these wars must have a "cause" - a promise of better things that will initiate and sustain a struggle, often against apparently insuperable odds. The task of the security forces, while civic and political action takes place, is to neutralise the revolution by nullifying its promise. And that is done by military action that clearly shows the insurgent that he cannot and will not succeed.

# POLITICS OF POWER - THE BORDER WAR
*by Willem Steenkamp*

When South African troops marched out of southern Angola on August 30, 1988, their departure signalled a break in the more or less predictable annual pattern to the counter-insurgency war in South West Africa/Namibia which had developed over about two decades of intermittent fighting, in which nature and various geographic and demographic factors had combined to dictate both the shape of the war and the calendar of the year's activities for both sides.

Whether the pattern has gone forever or will return in the event of the peace process breaking down remains unclear at the time of writing, but this is the way it used to be:

First and always there was the rain. Northern Namibia and neighbouring Angola have two rainy seasons: a short one in the last two months of the year, and a long monsoon that starts in January and goes on till roughly the end of April. The combatants on the border watch for the rain clouds as anxiously as the farmers, because their lives, too, might depend on when the heavens open.

Near the end of the year, a little before the short rainy season was due to hit northern Namibia, the fighters of the People's Liberation Army of Namibia (Plan), military wing of the South West African People's Organisation, would begin to prepare in their Angolan camps for infiltration southwards across the border.

Some would be veterans who had survived previous infiltrations, others would be fresh from training. Still others – particularly from the mid-1980s onwards, when Plan started suffering manpower shortages as a result of falling recruitment, war-weariness and heavy losses – would be Swapo members who had been serving in conventional-warfare units of FAPLA, the Angolan ground forces, and had to be retrained in the arcane skills of infiltration.

Infiltration was a tiresome business because the camps were deep inside southern Angola: bitter experience had taught them that permanent bases within 200km or so of the border were vulnerable to lightning pre-emptive attacks from the south, even when they were under the protection of their allies of FAPLA. But there was no alternative. No matter how much the world protested, the South Africans were never hesitant about bursting onto Angolan soil to break up a planned movement southwards. It was a startlingly successful tactic, and the majority of Plan's dead in the border war were lost on Angolan and not Namibian soil.

If there were no such attacks the infiltration would begin on the eve of the rains. The guerrillas moved south to the "shallow area" just north of the border, dodging various enemies such as the Unita rebels, or possibly the fierce black soldiers of the South African Defence Force and South West Africa Territory Force, who operated almost continually in southern Angola.

If they escaped all these dangers they restocked from hidden caches if necessary, and began to filter in small groups over the "cutline", the actual border, and into western and central Ovamboland. This has always been the favourite infiltration area because more than half of the Ovambo tribal nation lives there, and Swapo is still 90 per cent Ovambo. At this time of the year conditions are at their most favourable. The grass is tall and the bush thick, providing maximum cover; the *oshonas* or level areas become large shallow lakes, and there is plenty of drinking water, while the heavy rain slows down SADF and SWATF follow-ups making it easier to hide one's spoor.

Several months of activity followed. In earlier days Plan fighters often took the initiative; but the tide began to turn in the early 1980s, and from about 1985, thanks to heavy losses and continual harrying by the security force's policemen, soldiers and airmen, Plan began to concentrate mainly on intimidation, mine-laying, political activation, minor sabotage and the occasional "stand-off bombardment".

This last usually consisted of setting up a mortar near some base, or centre, firing a series of bombs at the target and then decamping, leaving the hardware behind, with a security force unit hard on their heels. It was not a particularly effective technique: because the insurgents were never able to "shoot in" the mortar, accuracy was usually doubtful and in most cases little damage was done.

Generally speaking, Plan infiltrators in the later years of the insurgency tended to avoid clashing with security forces, so that most contacts were initiated by the government soldiers; according to a security force spokesman: "We find that ground-level detachments are dodging directives from higher up to be aggressive".

All this activity took place within a day or two's walk of the border: it has been years since Plan fighters have ventured far, if at all, from Ovamboland. In 1983, 1984 and 1985 small teams from their élite "Special Unit" penetrated farther south, to the white farming areas round Tsumeb, but each team suffered almost 100 per cent casualties, and afterwards there was no repetition of what was obviously little more than a suicide mission.

In April the rainy season peters out. By that time, in an average year, the insurgents would usually have lost about 50 per cent of their initial strength, the rest running the gauntlet of police and army border patrols to return to Angola for what Plan called "rehearsals", leaving a small cadre behind to keep the home fires burning.

When the ground had dried out to some extent it would be the turn of the security forces to go on the offensive, with the SADF and SWATF carrying out seek-and-destroy missions to clear a general area or hitting some particular Plan base or bases. Through the years the SADF and SWATF have learnt to operate at any time of the year if necessary, but the dry season was when they preferred to make large-scale incursions into southern Angola. Wheeled vehicles moved more easily over dry roads and across country, the supply process was simpler and flying weather was better for the ground-attack aircraft and helicopters.

On the other hand, as was mentioned earlier, this was not an inflexible rule, and at least two of the known large-scale incursions in the recent past took place in the rainy season. The short lesson was that there was little place to hide in southern Angola, and that no time of the year was really safe.

At the time of writing (November 1988) the war in Namibia had been in progress for so long that many of the infantrymen fighting in it had not yet been born when its first shot was fired in 1966. It had become part of life for South Africans and Namibians, so that it was not uncommon to see father and son both wearing the orange-white-and-blue ribbon of the border campaign medal, awarded for service in the same area 15 or more years apart.

It has always been a much misunderstood war, mainly because most of the observers who passed judgment on it were either handicapped, although not inhibited from commenting, by simple ignorance of the military factors, or whose dislike (overt or covert) of South Africa, one of the main belligerents, resulted in muddled thinking.

The confusion was heightened because critics or observers tried to superimpose the experiences of other countries on the vast stretches of bushland in northern Namibia and southern Angola, rather than apply the accepted principles of a counter-insurgency war to the actual circumstances.

This being the case, it would be fair to say that the border war has been neither "another Vietnam" for any of the main participants, although it might have begun to seem so for the large garrison of Cubans stationed in Angola (numbering something like 50 000 at the time of writing) nor "another Rhodesia".

Protracted and sporadic in nature, it has been, in fact, a classic example of the rural insurgency (or counter-insurgency) struggle as described in the writings of Mao, Giap and General Sir Walter Walker. This includes the semi-conventional attacks into Angola (and, in two cases, Zambia) in the past decade, which should be seen for what they are: logical extensions of the counter-insurgency campaign, rather than uncontrolled military adventures, as they have been represented in some quarters.

Every counter-insurgency war is unique in the sense that its structure and tactics are dictated not by textbooks but by the economic, historical, cultural and demographic factors peculiar to that particular theatre of conflict. So it is with the Namibian campaign, which is why it cannot be compared to Rhodesia, Vietnam or Malaya.

But there are also a few other peculiarities that set it apart from most other counter-insurgency conflicts.

The government concerned, that of South Africa, is neither a colonial régime nor an indigenous one which, like South Vietnam's, relies on the goodwill of a foreign power. It is an African government viewing the Namibian insurgency as a matter of survival rather than an inconvenient hiccup in its foreign policy, and it has been rich enough to fight on by itself to the bitter end.

The matter of wealth is where any intended comparison with Rhodesia falls flat. Rhodesia was basically an undeveloped country because, like so many other southern African nations, its population was small, its economy largely agricultural, its more sophisticated needs being catered for by neighbouring South Africa.

South Africa, on the other hand, is an advanced state, certainly by Third World standards. It has a well-developed economy – based on its strategic mineral riches, industrial infrastructure and huge (albeit mainly covert) trade with Africa – which remains basically sound in spite of long-standing misuse by the politicians, and a large enough manpower reservoir of all races to sustain a long-term small war without ruining its commercial sector.

Another important factor is that its military and industrial planners long ago discovered the secret of waging what has been called a "poor man's war", partly by practising stringent military economies and running a cheap defence force consisting largely of national service conscripts, short-term professional volunteers and well-trained reservists.

As a result, the cost of the war has not been so high as to cause much inconvenience. Recent estimates put it at about US$500 000 a day at the low end of the scale, and at the high end about a million: either figure is modest compared with total annual defence expenditure, which was about US$2 billion in 1987/8.

The only time when the war ever became seriously expensive was during the 1987/8 fighting in Angola, when South Africa made comparatively heavy use of conventional weapons such as tanks and artillery, using up inordinate amounts of fuel and ammunition in the process.

Critics who would love to castigate the South African government for military over-spending suffer embarrassment when the annual defence estimates appear. Total defence expenditure, which includes large sums used for developing and building weapons it cannot import, has actually declined slightly in real terms in recent years: the 1987/8 military estimates came to no more than 4,7 per cent of the gross domestic product, putting South Africa in the same bracket as Britain, Yugoslavia and Malaysia.

Even the pariah status that most of the world has conferred on South Africa has helped Pretoria to conduct the Namibian war in its own way. It cannot be forced by threats of cutting imports of weapons and equipment because the international arms boycott has compelled it to develop an armaments industry which is now so sophisticated that it actually "exports" to a number of other countries. Similarly, diplomatic pressure is difficult to exert because it has been thrown out of virtually every international organisation.

Economic sanctions have not proved the decisive weapon that they seemed because South Africa deals with too many important trading partners in Europe and elsewhere, and has a virtual monopoly of too many vitally important minerals such as platinum, of which it possesses almost the entire world's supply. Three years ago veiled (but unrealised) threats that South Africa might consider imposing its own strategic mineral boycott sent quiet ripples of unease through the industrialised capitals.

Having little need, therefore, to bow to criticism, since an outlaw by definition is beyond the laws of the society that cast him out, South Africa has been able to wage the counter–insurgency war in the right way.

It has not been impatient. SADF planners have never been under any illusion about the chances of achieving a "quick fix", and experienced local observers recall that as long ago as 1976 senior military officers were making it quite clear that there would be no rapid resolution of the border struggle. As a result they did not hesitate to apply all the tried counter–insurgency techniques, such as constant patrolling and "hearts and minds" schemes.

At the same time the South Africans enjoyed, at least up to the end of August 1988, the vital ingredient needed in a war of this type: the ability to take the war to the enemy in the form of "external operations", or extra–territorial pre-emptive attacks.

Critics of the South African presence tend to condemn the known border-crossing operations as "invasions", but this is an over-simplification of a very precise vocabulary of border-war terms.

The nuts and bolts of a counter–insurgency campaign are the follow–up actions after a contact or an attack, when the insurgents are withdrawing or scattering; and the hot pursuit operation, in which a security force unit chases a band of insurgents till they have been killed, captured or lost.

An external operation, on the other hand, is a deliberate and often elaborately planned attack, usually on a much larger scale, carried out beyond the international border and designed to pre-empt a known or suspected action by the insurgents before they can set it in motion. However, like hot pursuit and follow-up, it is just an outgrowth of the border war.

Needless to say, it is not always easy to define precisely the nature of each operation, because depending on the circumstances one may have, or develop, some characteristics of another type. A follow–up often turns into a hot pursuit, which then becomes an external operation scheduled to last several days, and that in turn develops into an incursion, with security forces spending weeks or months on Angolan soil.

On the other hand, the security forces might spend months gathering intelligence and planning a sudden swoop on a particular target in an operation involving up to 2 000 men or so, backed by armoured cars, infantry fighting vehicles, ground-attack aircraft or even field artillery.

Outside observers are prone to the popular misconception that South Africa has launched hundreds of external operations into Angola. In fact that is not so. Since the first one, *Operation Reindeer* in 1978, there have been no more than eight or nine "externals" of substantial size, though of course scores of follow-ups, hot-pursuit actions and minor incursions have taken place. At times small security force units have operated in southern Angola for months on end.

The confusion has been compounded by the Angolan government's habit of camouflaging the actions of its enemies, the Unita rebels, by blaming them on the South Africans, even when they have taken place so far inland that only a madman would have undertaken them.

The Angolans have also habitually exaggerated the scope of such external operations that actually took place. The border war is a low-intensity conflict engaging comparatively few combatants, even when the fighting spills into Angola. Three thousand of all ranks would constitute a large external force; in the most daring one so far only about 300 men took part.

Some external operations have lasted days, others weeks, still others months. All have had the same object: to seek out and destroy or disrupt Plan activities in Namibia. So far not one has failed to do so, and some have had lasting effects on the insurgency.

The essential part of the daily counter-insurgency effort has always been the endless grind of patrolling, with the constant prospect of a follow-up, and the endless waiting; but most of the "kills" so far, and most of the blunting of Swapo's cutting-edge, have taken place not in Namibia itself but north of the border.

There is another important dimension to the border war. When experts write about this war or that they often forget to take into account the people who are actually fighting it.

The first aspect of this matter is that the South African and Namibian soldiers, airmen and marines engaged in operations do not suffer cultural shock of the type experienced by, say, Americans sent to Vietnam or British troops in Malaya, even though they are a motley, polyglot array who speak half a dozen different languages and range in colour from coal-black to pale blond.

For South Africans serving "on the border", as the popular phrase has it, the ethnic and cultural variety found in the operational area was always a familiar one, with a fairly small local communications problem with the population because in Namibia, as in much of South Africa, Afrikaans is the *lingua franca*.

Nor has there ever been a sense of fighting in a foreign country: to all intents and purposes Namibia became a province of South Africa when its German colonial rulers were defeated in 1915, and it is only recently that Namibians have begun to feel a distinct sense of national identity.

In any case, from the early 1980s onwards most of the actual counter-insurgency fighting was progressively taken over by native Namibians of the 30 000 strong South West Africa Territory Force rather than members of the South African Defence Force.

The second aspect is that there has never been a military manpower problem in either South Africa or Namibia.

In Namibia the manpower is raised by recruiting volunteer all-regular tribal battalions from inhabitants of the operational area. No conscription has ever been needed because up to now recruiting drives for these units have always been vastly over-subscribed; the attractions varying from anti-Swapo feeling and tribal factors to the more materialistic lure of good pay and perquisites.

This system is supplemented by conscription for two years in urban and rural areas outside the operational zone, and at the time of writing this does not appear to have encountered any serious difficulties.

In South Africa, on the other hand, the government conscripts only white men, and takes so many each year that it does not always know what to do with them; the vast majority of whites do not seem to be opposed to either conscription or operational service except on a personal level, for example inconvenience and career delays, and some thousands have emigrated to the United States, Australia and elsewhere. Even so there are up to 68 000 conscripts in uniform at any given time.

A small minority of whites object in principle to military and quasi-military service; of these, some have left the country, while others have taken advantage of various non-combatant and civilian service accommodations for conscientious objectors. A very small hard core rejects both options and prefers to go to gaol.

There is also a vast pool of active reservist soldiers of the Citizen and Commando Forces, which consist of volunteers and former national servicemen with an obligation to periodical service. (In South Africa the word "commando" retains its original meaning, that of citizen-soldier. The difference between the two forces is that the Citizen Force is mostly conventional and comprises all arms, whereas the Commando Force consists only of counter-insurgency light infantry).

Black, Asian and "coloured" South Africans of both sexes are encouraged to volunteer for military service, either for two year terms or as regulars of the Permanent Force, and there is no shortage of recruits. (One old-established regiment, the coloured South African Cape Corps, regularly turns away two or three applicants for every one that it accepts).

No doubt this will seem strange to the outside observer, but closer examination explains the phenomenon.

Non-white politics is riddled with internal schisms. It has the full range of persuasions, from extreme left to far right, with some organisations as rigidly racist in structure as their pro-segregationist white equivalents. Just before this was written, for example, conservative and left wing blacks were literally coming to blows in various areas.

Then again, the SADF is remarkably free from segregation of any kind. While basic training is usually segregated, advanced training or specialist training is not; all members receive the same pay of rank, white troops salute non-white officers, and at times, such as in the tough Marine Branch of the South African Navy, both trainees and instructors are inseparably mixed. There are no promotion barriers, and a number of non-white officers have reached the rank of colonel.

These are not token appointments. Black officers and non-commissioned officers often occupy executive posts and enjoy the full privileges of their rank. As in many other armies, military service offers not only employment but also a means of upward social mobility.

At the time of writing, the war in Namibia had reached the self-sustaining phase, with the original causes becoming dimmer because recent events provided the fuel for those to come; this was even more the case because many of the original grievances that sparked the insurgency had disappeared along the way.

At this time old-fashioned apartheid is nearly dead in Namibia. The territory has a semi-autonomous "interim government", drawn from a variety of political parties, which is almost totally black and on a basis of popular support is certainly more legitimate than most African military and civilian dictatorships.

Ironically, too, Namibians of all races are now talking about independence from South Africa, a notion once bandied about only by the insurgents: it is an important change, indicating that the unsought appearance of a conscious national identity is developing where none existed before.

To understand the situation it is necessary to know something about Namibia itself.

Unlike many other African territories, there is no long tradition of nationhood in the sprawling tract of land, of more than 800 000 square kilometres, that was formerly called "South West Africa", is now officially "South West Africa/Namibia" and at some stage in the future will be simply "Namibia". Indeed, up to about a century ago neither its inhabitants nor outside observers regarded it as one territory.

For thousands of years it lay almost unknown to anyone except its inhabitants, protected from the outside world by the barrier of the ferocious Namib desert, which runs along the entire coastline and north into neighbouring Angola. In the eighteenth and nineteenth centuries, as travellers from outside gradually began to venture into its interior, the northern part became known as Damaraland and the south as Great Namaqualand.

The name South West Africa which described the area covered by both territories, was not coined till the mid-nineteenth century. The new name was not the precursor of a sense of national identity; for several decades more, South West Africa remained what it has been, a cockpit of sporadically warring clans and tribes of various races and cultures.

Strangely enough the first people to give South West Africa any coherence of identity were the Germans, who began to colonise it from 1883 onwards and eventually controlled everything between the Orange river in the south and the Kunene river in the north (although the precise northern border was not settled till the 1920s, years after the Germans had relinquished power).

For over thirty years the imperial flag waved over what was then called German South West Africa. Then in 1915 the South Africans invaded on behalf of Britain and defeated the Germans. After World War 1 the League of Nations entrusted South West Africa to South Africa as a Class C mandate, to be governed as a virtual extra province for the benefit of its inhabitants.

Class C mandates were created for territories which, the League of Nations had concluded, were not capable of being turned into viable independent states.

A national consciousness did not begin to take root till the late 1950s, when Africa began to approach the era of independence, and the concept did not really begin to sprout till 1964, when the United Nations unilaterally decided to name the territory Namibia. The South African government continued to call it by its original "national" name till the 1970s, when the term South West Africa/Namibia was coined to indicate its new status.

Namibia as it exists today is bounded in the west by the Atlantic Ocean, in the east by Botswana, in the south by South Africa and in the north by Angola. Most of it is an elevated plateau between 900 and 1 200 metres above sea-level, with mountain ranges running north to south for most of its length.

It has an almost infinite variety of terrain. Its bleak littoral is known as the

Skeleton Coast, and for centuries it has been a notorious killer of men and ships, although redeemed by the diamonds and other minerals found in its deadly sands. The south and east vary from dry bushveld to semi-desert, while north of the central high-grass plains it is typical African savannah country, flat and with abundant bush.

What this fascinating and often savagely beautiful territory lacks most of all is people. It has less than a million inhabitants. In 1970, just after the outbreak of the border war, the population mixture was as follows: 342 000 Ovambos, divided into eight tribes; 90 000 whites, mainly of Afrikaans, English and German ancestry; 49 000 Kavangos; 49 000 Hereros; 44 000 Damara; 33 000 Namaqua (formerly known as Hottentots); 25 000 East Caprivians; 21 000 nomadic Bushmen; 18 000 Batswana and other tribesmen, mainly drifted over from neighbouring Botswana; 16 000 Kaokolanders; and 16 000 Rehoboth Basters, descendants of pioneering half-castes who moved up from the old Cape Colony in the mid-nineteenth century.

There has been a considerable amount of urbanisation, but most of these groups are still closely linked to their traditional regions. The Kaokolanders, Ovambos, Kavangos and Caprivians have their tribal homelands in the far north, immediately south of the border with Angola. The whites, Hereros and coloureds mainly inhabit the central part of the country and the Namaqua the dry south.

It is an indication of the low intensity of the border war that since the 1970 census the population has increased rather than declined, and no part of the territory has been laid waste. It is remarkable, in fact, how little the struggle has affected daily life in Namibia. South of the black tribal areas it has always been barely noticeable, but for the occasional urban bomb blast, and in places regional economies have actually benefited from the conflict; ironically, probably the greatest consequence of the war has been the abolition of most segregation laws.

The beginnings of the border war can be traced back thirty years to 1957, when a group of expatriate Ovambos led by a former railway policeman, Herman Toivo ja Toivo, assembled in Cape Town, 2 000km south of their homeland, and founded a political movement called the Ovambo People's Congress.

The OPC was an organisation typical of its time. The era of *Uhuru* was dawning in Africa, and former rebels were preparing to seize the reins of power all over the continent; and had indeed already done so in Ghana.

It was all a great inspiration to the Ovambos. Largely left alone by both the German conquerors and their successors, the South Africans, the Ovambos were culturally more or less intact, and they were an intelligent and hard-working people. Most important of all, they made up nearly half of the sparse population of South West Africa. A united Ovambo people would obviously be the main political factor in a future South West Africa free from South Africa.

The OPC was a typical "liberation organisation" in yet another way. A number of its founder-members were overtly members of the South African Communist Party, and the OPC, like the African National Congress and other liberation movements, saw no harm in dual membership. Thus was forged a strong link with Moscow which has never been broken, although it would be an over-simplification to describe the OPC in its various later guises as simply a communist organisation.

In 1959 the OPC renamed itself the Ovambo People's Organisation, and in 1960, to broaden its potential appeal, the South West African People's Organisation (Swapo). In spite of that, however, Swapo seems not to have managed to broaden its base of tribal support to anything like a national representation: it certainly enjoys a measure of support among other ethnic groups, with spokesmen and leaders from all races. But 95 per cent of all Swapo insurgents killed or captured in the border war are Ovambos, mainly from the two main tribes, the Kuanyama and Ondonga. Several insurgents who have given themselves up have complained of discrimination.

In one case in 1980 a surrendered insurgent caused amazed laughter among foreign correspondents to whom he was shown when he said in all seriousness that he had given himself up because of the racial discrimination practised against him in Swapo. He explained that as a member of the Damara (a tribe so oppressed before the first whites arrived that it had even lost its language) he had been addressed as *kwangara*, which means roughly "serf", and habitually given menial tasks to carry out.

It is also significant that after more than twenty years of warfare the main operational area is still confined to Ovamboland.

From the beginning the cause of Swapo was total independence from South Africa, with a national government based on one man–one vote. Perhaps it was an over-simplified statement of intent, given the tribal hostility of the pre–colonial era and the fact that the territory had been made a Class C mandate in the first place, but it also powerfully appealed to the emotions.

What made the cause even more attractive was the fact that Ovambos were genuinely handicapped by the apartheid system which had been imported from South Africa, complete with all its major and minor segregation laws, and were deeply frustrated by the migrant labour system, which fettered their freedom of movement.

Twenty years later, Swapo appeared to have abandoned its aspirations to a one man–one vote democratic government; in a spectacularly tactless interview broadcast on South African television in February 1982, the Swapo leader Sam Nujoma dismissed suggestions that there might ultimately be a non–Swapo black majority government in Namibia, saying: "The question of black majority rule is out. We are not fighting even for majority rule. We are fighting to seize power in Namibia, for the benefit of the Namibian people. We are revolutionaries. We are not counter–revolutionaries."

Attempts were later made to discredit this embarrassing outburst by suggesting it had been doctored by South African propagandists, but these attempts never succeeded because the words were so obviously free from any subsequent editing.

Needless to say, Swapo soon came under the attention of the efficient security branch of the police, and by the early 1960s the top leadership had gone into exile abroad, where it has remained ever since. One of the exiles was Nujoma, who fled because of his part in fomenting unrest in Windhoek; most members of the top leadership are his contemporaries, and like him have clung to power.

In 1962 the leadership of Swapo decided to launch an "armed struggle", and formed a military wing called the People's Liberation Army of Namibia (Plan). As a result, Swapo now consists of three distinct parts. The political headquarters is in exile abroad and Plan concentrates on the "armed struggle" from its bases in Angola. At the same time, oddly, the so-called internal wing of Swapo operates openly and legally inside Namibia.

About that time (1964) Swapo acquired an ally in the form of the Caprivian African National Union (Canu), a nationalist movement consisting of tribesmen from the Caprivi Strip.

Recruiting for Plan was slow at first, but eventually 900 recruits were gathered, some by the time-honoured method of offering youths bogus scholarships for overseas study, and given basic training in Tanzania, while those selected for advanced specialised courses were then sent to Algeria, Cuba, Egypt, China, the Soviet Union, North Korea or Red China.

The first phase of the border war may be said to have begun in September 1965, when six trained Plan insurgents infiltrated Ovamboland and began the usual political activation. They also gave elementary military training to about thirty young Ovambos and sent them home to await activation.

By that time word of their activities had reached the ears of the police and surveillance began. No immediate action was taken, and in February 1966 a second small group infiltrated south from Angola, only to come to a speedy inglorious end. Having murdered two Angolan shopkeepers and an Ovambo (apparently believing they had crossed the border into South West Africa) they dispersed, but three members were later arrested in the neighbouring tribal territory of Kavango by police acting on information from local inhabitants.

In July 1966 a third group crossed the border and fired the first shots of the war when they launched a series of attacks on Ovambo tribal chiefs, fired at a white farmer's house in the Grootfontein district just south of Ovamboland, and shot up the South West African border post at Oshikango.

In August the authorities began to strike back. The original group's camp at Ongulumbashe was attacked by helicopter-borne policemen, who killed two insurgents and captured nine more, making further arrests later on the strength of information supplied by the local inhabitants.

In December another group of insurgents entered Ovamboland, and in the next few months was active in both Ovamboland and Caprivi. An intensive activation and recruitment campaign was launched and a number of armed attacks were carried out on tribal headmen and others, culminating in the ambush of a police patrol in March 1967.

Soon afterwards, however, most of the insurgents were rounded up by the police. This was the first of a series of set-backs: in ensuing months a field commander called Tobias Hanyeko was killed in a fight on a barge on the Zambezi river and many other insurgents were shot dead or captured in a series of police actions. By March 1968, 160 insurgents were behind bars, several were dead and the situation had become so quiet that the police counter-insurgency unit withdrew.

The withdrawal proved to be premature. In October 1968 two large groups of insurgents crossed over from Angola and revived the insurgency, but the police reacted immediately. Within a week no fewer than 56 insurgents had been arrested and by the end of the year losses had been so great that the Plan operatives withdrew.

The area remained quiet throughout 1969 and 1970, but in 1971 there was a new infiltration, not only from Angola but also from Zambia, which shares a common border with Caprivi. In May 1971 the first mine incident of the war took place, when a police vehicle was blown up near Katima Mulilo, capital of Caprivi. Various other incidents in the next eighteen months caused a number of deaths among policemen and civilians, since this was before the era of mine-protected vehicles (in the development of which South Africa is now a world leader as a result of the border war).

By 1973 Plan had recovered from its set-backs and launched an intensified campaign of political activation, intimidation and terrorism, especially in Caprivi. There were ambushes of police patrols, and on one occasion a police camp was shot up with recoilless guns. No serious government casualties resulted; in the case of the bombardment the attackers themselves suffered casualties before fleeing across the border to Zambia; but it was obvious that the insurgency had become too great a burden for the sparsely-manned territorial police force, which as late as the mid-1960s had numbered only about 600, enough to maintain order in the entire territory.

As a result it was decided that the South African Defence Force should take over responsibility for counter-insurgency operations in the border operational area, leaving the police to concentrate on their normal duties, although still maintaining their small anti-terrorist unit. So began the second phase of the war.

By the time the SADF moved in, a combination of activation and intimidation had aggravated the situation (from Pretoria's point of view) to such an extent that Plan was able to turn the 1973 elections into a farce in which just 2,7 per cent of the border population wanted, or dared, to vote.

The SADF tackled the situation with an orthodox combination of heavy patrolling and hearts and minds activities (later called "civic action"). Progress was slow at first, although some recovery was seen in 1974.

In 1975, however, there came a significant turn of events in neighbouring Angola, which began to fall apart under the ministrations of the left-leaning government that had temporarily replaced the Portuguese dictator Marcelo Caetano in 1974.

At the time Caetano was ousted the three insurgent organisations operating in Angola, the Popular Movement for the Liberation of Angola (MPLA), the National Front for the Liberation of Angola (FNLA) and the National Union for the Total Independence of Angola (Unita), had all been virtually neutralised. The anti-Caetano coup gave them a new lease of life, especially the overtly Marxist MPLA, which was particularly favoured by the Portuguese government after the coup.

By mid-1975 all public order in Angola was breaking down and ever larger numbers of South African troops were deployed in the border operational area. These developments made it more difficult for Plan to operate, and another election held that year saw a 55 per cent poll in spite of an intensified wave of terrorism, including the assassination of a widely respected senior traditional tribal leader called Elifas, who was also Chief Minister of the Ovambo internal government.

In the last part of the year the Portuguese began preparing to withdraw from Angola with the intention of handing over, without benefit of elections, to a tripartite government which was to consist of joint rule by the MPLA, FNLA and Unita. It was obviously an unworkable arrangement, and well before the agreed date of independence (October 11) open warfare had broken out. By that time the MPLA was openly receiving aid from Russia, Cuba and other countries of the Eastern bloc, and the FNLA and Unita urgently asked South Africa for help.

There was a certain irony in this, because Unita and Swapo had always been closely linked by tribal affiliations and often dual membership; but at the clandestine urging of the American Secretary of State, Dr Henry Kissinger, the Prime Minister of South Africa, John Vorster, acceded to the appeals by sending small numbers of instructors to the two organisations.

Inevitably this help grew (although South African troops never exceeded more than 2 000 during the active stage of the war), and by October 1975 the SADF was operating alongside the two insurgent movements, with four mixed task forces led by South Africans winning a string of victories that took them to just south of the capital, Luanda.

In the short-term, *Operation Savannah,* as the South Africans called the incursion, had both good and bad effects on Plan's campaigns. SADF activities in southern Angola severely restricted its jumping–off operations there. On the other hand, the preoccupation of the South Africans with Angola resulted in a lessening of counter-insurgency activities, which in turn enabled Plan to intensify its campaign in Ovamboland.

In March 1976 the South Africans withdrew from Angola, militarily undefeated but stymied by political developments, which included the abrupt abandonment of the Angolan venture by the Americans. The withdrawal marked the end of the second phase of the border war and the beginning of the third. The seeds of the present situation were sown then, for the situation changed so much that new norms had to be applied.

The most important consequence of the American–South African failure was that for the first time Swapo acquired an asset generally held to be essential for a successful insurgency: a safe border over which it could operate and behind which it could seek sanctuary and general support.

The Portuguese had been pro–South African, and until Caetano fell Swapo had had to operate clandestinely from Angolan soil. Now the insurgents could operate openly, and with the full support of the new MPLA régime in Luanda. It was a much–needed shot in the arm for Swapo, and it would not be an exaggeration to pin–point March 1976 as the point when the border war began in earnest.

On the other hand, there were certain disadvantages for both Swapo and Angola in the new scheme of things. Obtaining the support of the MPLA meant that Swapo had to break its old links with Unita, which was based partly on tribal affiliations (the northern Namibian border is a totally artificial creation dividing one tribal nation, the Ovimbundu). This was an important factor, because Swapo was so heavily dependent on tribal feeling for its recruiting and clandestine activities.

For Angola it meant the beginning of a long agony with few compensations. When South Africa withdrew from Angola the South African generals advised Jonas Savimbi of Unita and Holden Roberto of the FNLA to save themselves from extinction by going back into the bush and fighting the new MPLA government as they had fought the Portuguese, but this time with South African help instead of that of the Eastern bloc.

South Africa kept its promise, and although the FNLA has dwindled into insignificance, Savimbi not only survived but has enmeshed the MPLA in a protracted civil war, which by 1988 had ruined its economy and caused great suffering among the population.

By then he had reached the point where he was no longer obliged to rely on (or obey) South Africa. He was receiving help from the United States and several other countries, and not only controlled a "liberated zone" in south-eastern Angola (the most illustrious status symbol to which any guerrilla leader could aspire) but was active in most other parts of the country. So far the Luanda government has not been able to wipe him out, and at the time of writing Savimbi is in the enviable position, by insurgent standards, of being the only one who can stop the war.

The South African investment in Savimbi proved profitable in its effects on the Namibian border counter-insurgency effort. In exchange for succour and support, Swapo had to cede most of its manpower assets to the MPLA government for employment as guard forces or in the field against Unita. As a result, only about 15 per cent of the total strength of Swapo was actually available or trained for infiltration. According to estimates by various experts this meant that in 1988 the insurgents had perhaps 1 500 trained or partly-trained men available for infiltration into Namibia, and only a few hundred south of the border at the best of times.

In the short-term, however, the benefit of the South African withdrawal was all Swapo's. Backed by the MPLA logistic system, supply from the Soviet Union and elsewhere became much easier; it could set up a network of training camps for its recruits and develop forward staging areas and command headquarters within easy reach of the cutline.

The immediate result was an intensification of the border insurgency. On 25 October 1977 an SADF spokesman, Major-General Wally Black, stated that contacts between security force patrols and Swapo groups were averaging about a hundred a month. There were about 300 insurgents operating in the border area, he said, while about 2 000 were grouped in Angola for deployment in Ovamboland, and another 1 400 in Zambia, aimed at Caprivi.

At that stage the conflict was still largely what Black described as a "corporals' war", because the average security force patrol was composed of a ten-man section led by a junior NCO.

But within two days of Black's announcement it became clear that the days of the "corporals' war" were over. On 27 October a group of about eighty insurgents crossed the cutline and made contact with a much smaller security force patrol. The security force patrol attacked instead of retreating, and with the aid of reinforcements fought a running battle that lasted four days and left 61 Swapo dead for the loss of five security force men killed and another mortally wounded.

The size of the Swapo group was directly linked, South African military analysts believed, to attempts to wreck the latest attempts by the "Western Five" (the US, Britain, France, West Germany and Canada) to reach a negotiated settlement in Namibia. However, they also believed that it might indicate that Swapo intended to increase the pressure and push the struggle out of its activation-and-terrorism stage into the next step in the classic development to semi-conventional warfare.

The new year proved them right. From 3 January 1978, members of Plan in Ovamboland and Caprivi were involved in a series of contacts, laid numerous mines with lethal consequences, kidnapped 119 children and killed several blacks (including a member of the Ovamboland internal cabinet) and two SADF officers. In late April a large group of insurgents, numbering about a hundred, clashed with a patrol.

Almost unnoticed in the commotion was an announcement by the then GOC (General Officer Commanding) South West Africa Command, Major-General Jannie Geldenhuys, that a security force patrol had pursued a Swapo gang over the border into Angola and killed eight of them.

It was not the first of the border war and would not be the last, but the simple hot pursuits and follow-ups were about to be supplemented by full-blown external operations, which were to make so much difference to the border war that it would probably be accurate to say the conflict had reached its fourth phase.

The decision to launch large-scale pre-emptive attacks was taken in December 1977, at a most unlikely place: a holiday cottage at a resort named Oubos on the east coast of South Africa.

The little house was unpretentious; but it belonged to the Prime Minister, John Vorster, and he was joined there by several senior military officers for discussion of the deteriorating situation in Namibia.

The officers put forward their case for launching a pre-emptive attack to dry up the increasing flow of infiltrators at its source. Vorster was reluctant; he was a cautious man, and he had painful memories of how the political failure of *Operation Savannah* had destroyed years of covert effort that he had put into reaching a form of détente with neighbouring states. But eventually he agreed, with the proviso that such operations should be undertaken only after they had been approved of at the highest political level (this rule, as far as is known, is still strictly applied).

Planning soon began on the first external operation. Code-named *Bruilof* (Wedding), it was scheduled for the end of April 1978. Little is known about the objectives and extent of *Bruilof,* but it is believed to have envisaged assaults by ground forces and helicopter-borne paratroopers on six Swapo forward bases in the vicinity of a minor landmark on the Angolan map called Chetequera, about 25km north of the cutline.

Troops had already been assembled for *Bruilof* when it was abruptly cancelled for reasons that have never been revealed, although it was probably because of a breach of security. However, most of the planning was incorporated in a revised scheme, *Operation Reindeer.*

This is not the place to describe each external operation in full, but it is useful to say something about *Reindeer,* because it was the first and the most important operation, not only in the sense that a failure might well have caused Vorster to pull in his horns but also because of its long-lasting effects on Plan. In some ways it was also the riskiest of them all.

*Reindeer* was scheduled for the beginning of May. It was an altogether more ambitious plan than *Bruilof.* The Chetequera network of bases remained a target, but it was no longer the main objective. Instead, *Reindeer* was to be a multiple operation including simultaneous attacks on three widely separated targets.

Target Alpha (or Moscow, as the insurgents called it) was the former copper-mining town of Cassinga, 250km inside Angola, which military intelligence had identified as the main forward operational headquarters of Swapo for southern Angola and a training camp capable of housing up to 1 200 insurgent recruits.

Target Bravo (Vietnam to Swapo and the Angolans) was to be the network of six bases in the vicinity of Chetequera, which contained the forward Swapo headquarters for Western Ovambo and an important supply depot.

Target Charlie, the third part of *Operation Reindeer,* was a series of small bases and suspected bases between 17 and 21km east of Chetequera.

In the case of Cassinga it was an ambitious operation, considering that the South Africans had very limited resources at their disposal.

The plan called for a softening-up aerial attack on Cassinga by SAAF fighters and bombers. That would be followed by an overflight of transport aircraft which would drop about 250 men of the small but efficient South African force of paratroopers under the command of Colonel Jan Breytenbach, then generally regarded as the toughest and most experienced fighting soldier in the Defence Force.

With this small force, backed up by a mobile reserve of 120 men which would be held airborne along the cutline for the duration of the operation, the planners proposed to overrun Cassinga by a swift, violent assault, if possible capturing the local Plan commander, a veteran bush-fighter called Dimo Hamambo. The paratroopers would destroy all munitions, equipment and weapons and try to bring back trained insurgents for interrogation as well as documents and other intelligence material, particularly documents of Russian origin to prove that Swapo was directly linked to the Soviet Union.

The paratroopers were given an extra task of great psychological importance: they were to liberate Sapper Johan van der Mescht, the only South African soldier ever to have been captured by Swapo, who was believed to be held in Cassinga.

Once finished (the paratroopers over-confidently estimated that Cassinga could be overrun in about 45 minutes) the attackers would be evacuated by waves of helicopters which had refuelled at a temporary base or "helicopter administrative area" (HAA) which was to be established at first light on D–Day, 22km from Cassinga.

It was a small force for the task at hand: Breytenbach would have to attack with three nominal rifle companies, each of only two platoons, and two independent rifle platoons. The only support weapons would be four 60mm mortars without base-plates, equally divided between two of the companies, and some captured RPG-7 anti-tank rocket-launchers.

The size of the attack group and its emergency reserve was determined not by purely military considerations but by the lack of enough suitable fixed-wing transports from which to drop them, and of the helicopters, which were the only means of getting them out at the end of the operation.

An attack on Cassinga had, in fact, been excluded from the planning of *Bruilof* because it was too dangerously deep inside Angolan territory for extraction by helicopter.

What made it worse was that, thanks to the arms boycott, the South African Air Force possessed so few of its large helicopter, the Super Frelon, that most of the paratroopers would have to be retrieved by smaller Pumas, some of which were old and short-ranged.

Cassinga itself would be no walk-over. Swapo spokesmen and sympathisers later denied that Cassinga was an armed installation, describing it as a camp for refugees from "South African repression" with only a "camp defence unit" of 300 men, but aerial photographs showed that the town had an extensive network of deep Russian-type zig-zag trenches, bunkers and various other indications of strong defences meant for a much larger force (mercifully for the South Africans' peace of mind, they did not know that it also had some anti-aircraft guns).

Another complication was that a force of tanks and mechanised infantry, manned by FAPLA and some Cubans, were stationed at Techamutete, only 16km to the south. Although the force was small, four or five World War 2 T-34 tanks and about twenty-four old BTR-152 armoured personnel carriers, it presented a threat out of all proportion to its size because the paratroopers' strongest firepower would consist of their small patrol mortars and what RPG-7s they could carry with them.

There was also the possibility of hostile air attack, since MiG-21 fighters had been seen in Angola as long ago as early 1976.

Altogether the margin for error was perilously small, and the chances of walking out if the extraction failed were even smaller; more than ten years later, hindsight makes it clear that the Cassinga drop was the chanciest of all the South African border operations.

But Breytenbach and his paratroopers brimmed over with confidence, and a strong case for going ahead was presented by the Chief of the Army, the ascetic and aggressive Lieutenant-General Constand Viljoen, an artilleryman turned parachutist. He argued that the potential benefits far outweighed the dangers, and in the end he had his way.

By comparison, the attacks on Chetequera and Charlie were straightforward, although the former was apparently also a fairly formidable target. The bases were manned by about 900 to 1 000 insurgents, and were known to be heavily defended with deep trenches and bunkers and a variety of support weapons, which included 82mm recoilless guns, 82mm mortars, RPG-7 rocket-launchers and 14,5mm anti-aircraft guns.

Chetequera itself was to be attacked by an under-strength mechanised battle group known as Juliet, manned by young national servicemen, most of them inexperienced, with a very thin sprinkling of regulars of the Permanent Force. Its commander was Commandant Frank Bestbier, a veteran counter-insurgency fighter who had also had a taste of semi-conventional warfare in *Operation Savannah*.

While Bestbier was attacking Chetequera, two independent units were to attack the southernmost bases. When the fighting was over the assault forces would link up and withdraw south across the border.

The Charlie bases were to be overrun in sequence by members of 32 Battalion, a regiment of expatriate Angolans under Commandant Deon Ferreira, with air and artillery support.

After nerve-racking last-minute delays *Reindeer* was carried out on 4 May. The attack on Cassinga began well with a devastating air attack that caused such heavy damage and casualties that the defensive reactions were temporarily paralysed.

This made up for a bad drop far from the target which resulted in many paratroopers having to ford a river before going into action. The cause remains uncertain to this day: the SAAF says the designated dropping zone was too small, while the paratroopers say they were dropped several seconds too late.

However, the success of the air attack gave the paratroopers enough time to change the direction of their main attack from west-east to south-north. Just after two in the afternoon they had attained most of their objectives, although the commander, Dimo Hamambo, had escaped in time to save himself and the prisoner, van der Mescht, turned out to have been moved elsewhere; and the helicopter extraction began.

The evacuation came near to disaster by the approach of the Techamutete force (a situation made even more serious by the fact that the Chief of the Army, Lieutenant-General Viljoen, had himself flown in to be with the troops at Cassinga and now stood a strong chance of being captured).

The Techamutete force was beaten off by SAAF Mirages and Buccaneers, and by the paratroopers themselves, although two tanks came to within whites-of-the-eyes range of the landing zones. One was knocked out with air-to-ground rockets and the other was neutralised by repeated low-level "buzzing" by a Buccaneer pilot who had run out of ammunition. Eventually the evacuation was completed, and that evening the entire assault force was back at the Eenhana border base, with the exception of one soldier who disappeared so completely that no trace of him has ever been found.

The other casualties amounted to three dead and 11 wounded. It was an astonishingly light rate, considering the hours of heavy fighting; according to the SADF at least 600 inhabitants of Cassinga were killed, most of them uniformed members of Swapo, and another 340 wounded, while 16 members of the

Techamutete column were killed and 63 wounded. Materially, too, the attack had cost little. The parachutes and some equipment had had to be left behind, and two Buccaneer strike fighters had suffered slight damage.

At Chetequera the attack also went off successfully. Battle–Group Juliet's main attack had gone in slightly askew, necessitating an unscheduled return sweep through an untouched portion of the base, but eventually Chetequera was completely overrun at a cost of two deaths and a few wounded. The independent combat teams inflicted some damage on the southern bases without suffering any casualties, and by mid–morning of 5 May the whole force was back over the cutline.

On 6 May five rifle companies of 32 Battalion began their sweep of Target Charlie by chasing some insurgents out of a base at Minguila, and by 8 May they had overrun and destroyed a string of other camps, some defended and others abandoned, unfortunately suffering several casualties from their own artillery fire because of bad communications.

*Operation Reindeer* had been an unqualified success. Plan had lost a total of about 1 000 members killed and 200 captured, while its attempt to infiltrate had been seriously interrupted and large amounts of valuable intelligence material had been captured.

Some observers believe, in fact, that it has never really recovered from this devastating blow, and certainly it suffered heavy losses for a considerable time after *Reindeer* because the only way it could keep up any sort of limited activity was to deploy half–trained recruits, operating in large groups under the leadership of a few experienced men.

It also provided much food for thought. From the South African point of view the most important lesson was obviously that launching external operations was undoubtedly the correct action. Heavy patrolling and civic action could suppress the insurgency, but by the nature of things the initiative would almost always remain in the hands of the insurgents, and it is an old military axiom that one cannot win a war by fighting defensively.

By launching external operations, however, maximum advantage could be taken of the strong points of the SADF: its conventionally trained manpower, its heavy weapons and its control of the air. Swapo would be forced to move its headquarters and jumping–off points inconveniently deep into Angola, and its leadership would live in constant fear of a sudden South African attack. Combined with ordinary pacification operations inside northern Namibia itself, it would be possible to grind down the Swapo war effort from both ends and lessen the advantage of the safe border.

So it has proved. There has never been another airborne external operation, although paratroopers have been in action on numerous occasions; but almost every year has seen at least one formal external operation (and a few informal). Most of the military deaths suffered by Swapo have been in external attacks, not as a result of internal patrolling.

There were no more external operations in 1978, although in August Zambian-based Plan fighters mortared and rocketed the Caprivian capital of Katima Mulilo in revenge for Cassinga. This triggered a counter-bombardment of the Zambian town of Sesheke, and then a retaliatory raid, best described as partly a follow-up and partly hot pursuit. The raid resulted in the destruction of several Plan bases and a serious and permanent decline in the Caprivian insurgency.

In early 1979 two simultaneous external operations took place, one (*Operation Rekstok*) into southern Angola and the other (*Operation Saffraan*) into south–

western Zambia. Neither achieved any great success, although at least two temporarily evacuated permanent bases were destroyed; but one beneficial effect of *Saffraan*, from the South African point of view, was that it inflicted further damage on the local capability and morale of Plan.

This was compounded two years later by a serious split between Swapo and the Caprivi-based Canu, because the members of the latter were mostly being deployed in Ovamboland rather than Caprivi. Many were thrown into Zambian prisons at the request of Swapo, and as a fighting force the movement ceased to exist. Many took advantage of a South African offer of amnesty to return to their homeland. As a result, insurgent activity in Caprivi dwindled to such an extent that the area is now regarded as a kind of rest zone, and its garrison spends most of its time on border-control tasks.

In June 1980 the next external operation took place, when several mechanised battle-groups were launched on a large complex of bases scattered over about 65 square kilometres, code-named "Smokeshell" by the South Africans, in the Chifufua area, about 180km inside southern Angola. The pre-emptive attack, *Operation Sceptic,* was memorable as the first thrust at a new type of Swapo headquarters.

The lesson of Cassinga had been taken to heart: there were no buildings, defensive bunkers or lines of trenches. Instead, Smokeshell was carefully camouflaged, with bunkers built under trees and used only for shelter, and everything that could not be disguised was widely dispersed.

The battle-groups crossed the border near the Eenhana base at dusk on 9 June and travelled northwards all night and half of the next day before hitting Smokeshell with a three-pronged attack immediately after an artillery bombardment. The attack took the defenders completely by surprise, but the lack of orientation marks in the dense and featureless bush, and unexpectedly stiff resistance, particularly by Plan anti-aircraft guns used as ground weapons, caused the attack soon to degenerate into a series of confused skirmishes that did not end till dusk on 10 June.

*Operation Sceptic* had been designed as a sharp attack followed by an early withdrawal, but intelligence on the spot from documents and prisoners indicated other important bases to the west in the vicinity. While mopping-up continued at Smokeshell, part of the force was sent to attack the new targets. In the end *Operation Sceptic* lasted nearly three weeks, leaving about 360 insurgents dead for the loss of 17 South Africans and Namibians, while hundreds of tons of munitions and equipment were destroyed and a great amount taken back for examination.

During the extended second phase of *Sceptic,* the South Africans encountered two new phenomena. For the first time they came up against semi-mechanised Plan elements in the form of two columns (both were hit by air attacks and then destroyed by the ground troops); and during the withdrawal an Angolan column attacked one of the battle-groups instead of staying out of what amounted to a domestic squabble.

The intervention of the Angolans was a significant indication of the way things were to develop. At that stage South African policy was still to avoid contact with the Angolans unless Plan insurgents were inextricably mingled with elements of FAPLA. Since then the policy has changed. South African and Namibian policy is still to avoid collisions with FAPLA unless absolutely necessary, but they will not hesitate to do so if the Angolans are seen to be threatening their operations in any way. For example, SAAF aircraft will carry out pre-emptive strikes on distant Angolan air defences to preserve their superiority over a local combat zone.

*Sceptic* was a salutary experience for the South Africans. It was the first time they had fought real armoured-infantry actions since the latter days of World War 2, and the 17 fatalities were shockingly high for a nation that still adhered to the old Boer tradition of keeping casualties as low as possible.

Nevertheless it had been a success, and had dealt a further severe blow to Swapo operational capability and morale.

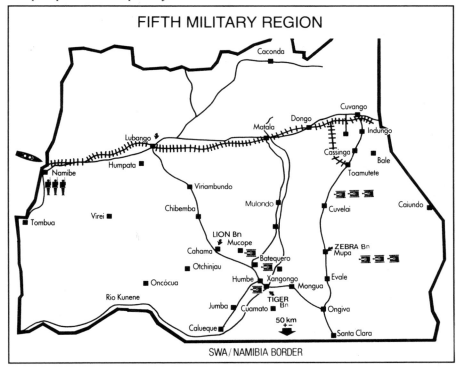

FIFTH MILITARY REGION

SWA/NAMIBIA BORDER

*Sceptic* was followed in August 1981 by *Operation Protea*, the most elaborate external attack so far. By that time the military complexion in southern Angola was changing in response to the external operations, and now a fairly comprehensive network of missile sites and radar installations was in operation. It was the beginning of the end for the halcyon days when the South Africans could operate virtually as they pleased in southern Angola, secure in the knowledge that the enemy could not divine their movements and in any case could not dominate his own airspace even it he wanted to.

*Protea* was preceded by a series of foot operations against Plan bases and logistic routes east of Ongiva (formerly Pereira d'Eca), an important town in southern Angola north of the border crossing-point at Oshikango and the location of one of three regional Plan headquarters for the activities in Ovamboland.

One of these foot operations, code-named *Carnation*, was still in progress when the beginning of *Operation Protea* was heralded by a successful pre-emptive air strike on the radar installations at Cahama to the west. At the same time a large mechanised force moved rapidly up the Kunene river to prevent any interference by the ground forces stationed at Cahama.

A second mechanised force then crossed the border and headed 70km northwards to Xangongo (formerly Vila Rocades), an important military centre which also had several Plan camps in its vicinity. After a brisk fight the South Africans defeated a composite FAPLA–Plan force on the southern fringes of the town and also beat off an attempt by mechanised FAPLA forces to break through to Xangongo from a base at the near-by village of Peu Peu.

Leaving behind mopping-up elements, which destroyed or seized a huge amount of vehicles, equipment and munitions, the South African body headed for Ongiva. After defeating a FAPLA armoured force at Mongua, about 40km east of Xangongo, it reached Ongiva on 26 August. It was offered stiff resistance by a mixed force of FAPLA and Plan armoured infantrymen with artillery support, and did not capture Ongiva till 28 August, killing several Russians in the process and capturing one.

The South Africans destroyed all the munitions and equipment they could not take back, and on 1 September the last of the western covering force was back on Namibian soil.

*Protea*, too, was counted a success. About 1 000 members of Plan and FAPLA had been killed, including senior Plan officers, and a huge amount of booty had been brought back, including tanks, artillery pieces, anti-aircraft guns, ammunition of all kinds and about 200 lorries. South African deaths amounted to ten and losses of equipment were modest.

Like its predecessors, *Protea* provided indications of how things were to be in the future. Not only were Angolan air defences promising to become a serious threat to external raiders, but Plan and FAPLA were fighting side by side in integrated conventional units.

In November 1981 the South Africans launched a second external operation, code-named *Operation Daisy*, which was based at least partly on information gained in *Protea*.

A mechanised force crossed the border and set up tactical headquarters at Ionde, 120km inside Angola, then sent its main body farther north to the area of Bambi and Chetequera (not to be confused with the Chetequera of *Operation Reindeer*), more than 300km from Namibia. On 4 December Chetequera was attacked and captured after being thoroughly bombed and strafed by SAAF aircraft, and after sweeping the area for a fortnight the South Africans withdrew.

*Daisy* would now probably be regarded as daring to the point of foolhardiness. Given the state of shock after *Protea*, it was a feasible enough operation. Yet even then there was an ominous portent of things to come: a number of intrusions by Angolan MiG-21s into the airspace staked out by the South Africans. The MiG-21s did not present any real threat, although one was shot down by a SAAF Mirage flying a combat air patrol.

There were no large external operations during 1982, although two small raids developed into considerably larger cross-border fights.

Swapo had begun opening up an alternative infiltration route that ran from south-western Angola down into desolate and almost desert Kaokoland, then swung eastwards towards Ovamboland, the purpose being to over-extend the security forces and at the same time break in a new corridor into the main operational area that was not so closely watched. South African intelligence got wind of the new route, and in March 1982 a few Puma and Alouette III helicopters and 45 men of 32 Battalion took on a Swapo transit camp in the desolate Marienfluss area just north of the Kaokoland border.

The foot-soldiers were dropped off by the Pumas and proceeded to capture the camp in an action extending over eight hours, with the Alouettes providing close support. Curiously, the battle was directed not by the commander on the ground but by the senior helicopter pilot, a captain whose only experience of infantry work was a year as a conscript in a training battalion before joining the SAAF.

However strange this management of *Operation Super* (as it was retrospectively named) might seem to the orthodox, it was a system that had evolved more or less spontaneously in the course of many small actions, and it worked very well at that level. In the case of *Super* it resulted in more than 200 insurgents killed for a loss of three, and the total disruption of the new infiltration route.

A slightly more elaborate foray was *Operation Mebos* in July and August 1982. It was devised to wipe out a Swapo forward headquarters controlling insurgent activities in eastern Ovamboland, and it became a string of small actions in the hunt for the elusive Plan headquarters that lasted into August. Eventually the headquarters was cornered at Mupa by one of the élite Reconnaissance Regiments (the South African equivalents of the Special Air Services). Most of the command echelon escaped, but the "reccies" went on tracking them down till the operation was stopped and withdrawal begun.

*Mebos* was accounted a success because it completely disrupted the command-and-control machinery of Plan in the region for a considerable period. It also resulted in the deaths of about 345 insurgents and the capture and destruction or evacuation of valuable intelligence material and a large quantity of stores and munitions, including 1 000 mines, deadly weapons much favoured by Plan. This was offset, in South African eyes, by the high death rate of 29 suffered by the SADF, although the figures were inflated by the fact that 15 of those died in a single incident, when a Puma full of troops had crashed on being hit by ground fire, killing all on board.

More than a year passed before the next large-scale external attack. In late 1983, however, South African intelligence began to notice indications that an unusually large infiltration was being prepared for the long rainy season of 1984. This included plans for a penetration of the white farming area south of Ovamboland.

*Operation Askari* officially got under way on 6 December. In many ways it was similar to previous external operations. In others it most certainly was not. For one thing, it was on a larger scale than most of its predecessors. Eventually the South Africans were fielding four mechanised groups of about 500 each and various foot-infantry elements, while on the other side thousands of FAPLA and Plan troops were involved, separately and in combination.

For another, there was a much stronger emphasis on conventional weapons. Both sides used a considerable amount of artillery, and SAAF aircraft shot up the main Plan headquarters near Lubango, 300km north of the border, not only to remind the occupants that they were vulnerable even when sheltering under the air-defence umbrella, but also as a diversion plan to make them think that they might be faced with a ground attack as well.

For the first time, too, FAPLA and Cuban forces not only had T-54 tanks but used them offensively instead of defensively, as in an action on 3 January 1984, when a FAPLA brigade and two Cuban battalions fell on one of the mechanised groups while it was attacking a Plan tactical headquarters and base area just north-east of Cuvelai, 200km from the border. A fierce battle followed in which the Cuban and FAPLA forces lost over 300 killed and 11 tanks knocked out. But for the inept handling by the Cubans and Angolans of their armour, Cuvelai might have been a serious defeat for the invaders.

*Askari* ended on 13 January, although at least part of the forces taking part did not withdraw to Namibia. Now the South Africans could count the cost. Altogether 21 members of the security forces had been killed, most of them during the battle for Cuvelai, and there was much food for thought. For one thing, it was obvious that the "easy" external operation was now rapidly becoming history. Nothing that has happened since then has provided any proof to the contrary.

One of the immediate results of *Askari,* apart from the damage done to the operational capability of Plan, was that the Angolans had been hurt badly enough to talk about peace. On 14 February 1984 South Africans and Angolans met at the Mulungushi Conference Centre at Lusaka in Zambia for intensive talks refereed by the Americans.

The result was the creation of the South African–Angolan Joint Monitoring Commission (JMC), which was to oversee the removal of foreign troops (Cubans, South Africans and Swapo) from most of southern Angola. It was a strange affair, unparalleled in southern African history, and it was tackled with admirable energy by those on the ground; but it did not succeed.

The South Africans could not compel Unita to leave the area (and in fact did not really wish the rebels to leave), although they did persuade them to keep a low profile, while the Angolans made no serious attempt to stop Plan from travelling through and even living in southern Angola.

The JMC was formally disbanded in February 1985, with officials putting a brave face on the matter and asserting that it had achieved its purpose. It had not, but its operations in southern Angola, combined with unremitting pressure exerted in the "shallow area" and Namibia itself, had had an inhibiting influence on Plan activities; so much so that no new external operation took place till *Operation Egret* was launched in September 1985.

*Egret* was negligible compared with *Askari* and some of its other predecessors. South African intelligence had received word that hundreds of members of Plan were congregating in the "Dova Triangle", not far from the border. The purpose of the gathering was to give refresher training to infiltrators and to re-train some semi-conventional troops whom in desperation it had borrowed from FAPLA because of its crippling shortage of manpower. They would then filter into Ovamboland as soon as the short rainy season began at the end of the year. A secondary but important purpose of the assembly was, according to documents found on a dead intelligence officer in the ensuing operation, to give their sagging morale a shot in the arm.

A number of vehicle-mounted "Romeo Mikes" (reaction force teams) from 101 (Ovambo) Battalion, supported by a few helicopters, was sent to the scene with orders to avoid contact with FAPLA forces at almost any cost. A few skirmishes took place in which a number of members of Plan were killed or captured, and the teams then returned to their home base, having effectively scattered the concentration without any losses to themselves except a Casspir light armoured personnel-carrier which had one wheel blown off by a mine but had been repaired on the spot and driven out.

Since *Egret* only one other easily classifiable external operation is known to have taken place up to the time of writing. That was in October 1987, when a mixed force of the SADF and SWATF penetrated some distance into Angola (apparently to Cuvelai, although both the distance covered and the name of the operation are still secret) and wiped out a Swapo camp, killing

150 insurgents for a loss of 12.

I say "easily classifiable" because of the South African movement into southern Angola in 1987 and 1988, which ended in the heaviest fighting on Angolan soil since the civil war broke out in 1975: the difference being that this time the primary target of the South Africans was not Plan, but the Cubans and Angolans.

The train of events that led to the fighting began in July 1987, when the Angolans made a determined effort to capture an important Unita stronghold in the south-eastern province of Cuando-Cubango, the town of Mavinga.

Mavinga is vital to Jonas Savimbi's insurgency because it has an all-weather airfield to which vital munitions and supplies, such as the American Stinger anti-aircraft missiles, are flown from Zaïre and South Africa. Without Mavinga Savimbi's "capital" of Jamba would become untenable and would probably have to be evacuated, resulting not only in a serious psychological defeat but also a grave set-back to the insurgency.

Under the command of a Russian general, Konstantin Shagnovitch, two combined FAPLA, Cuban and Russian armoured columns totalling about 25 000 men and masses of heavy weapons set out, one from the northern railway town of Luena and the other from the forward air base of Cuito Cuanavale, south-west of Mavinga. The columns were intended to grind slowly but remorselessly towards their goal, cross the Lomba river and take Mavinga by late September, when the Angolan President Eduardo dos Santos would be visiting Portugal.

In the event the operation was a total fiasco. Savimbi had appealed to South Africa for help, and the South Africans had responded by launching what they called *Operation Modular*. The long lead time enabled the South Africans to move a large number of their excellent towed G-5 155mm artillery pieces up to the Lomba river area, and a few of the G-6 self-propelled version, heavy and light armour and mechanised and motorised infantry.

Savimbi bloodily repulsed the advance from Luena with his conventional troops, then with the help of the South Africans broke the other thrust and sent it back to Cuito Cuanavale in disorder. He then proceeded to take advantage of the situation by capturing a length of the strategic Benguela railway line west of Luena.

By the end of November the situation had cooled to such an extent that the South Africans began to withdraw some of their troops. In mid-December a copious flow of FAPLA reinforcements to the Cuito Cuanavale area led to the execution of two more combined efforts (known as Operations *Hooper* and *Packer* in the SADF). Between early January and late February 1988 combined Unita and South African forces inflicted several more defeats on the Angolans and Cubans, cleared the area east of Cuito Cuanavale and besieged the base itself.

The South Africans then stayed in place, although steadily reducing the size of their contingent, till they pulled out altogether on 30 August in accordance with a ceasefire negotiated with Angola and Cuba, by which time an estimated two divisions of Cubans had been moved hastily into the south, although they were not located in such a way that they were in direct contact with the South African forces.

The failure of the Lomba river campaign, to give it a name, was a severe blow to the Angolans and their allies. Apart from the sheer humiliation of it, they lost 4 000 or 5 000 dead, including a large proportion of their leaders, and a vast amount of weapons and equipment estimated to have a replacement value of US$1 000 million. Even worse for the Angolans, Savimbi's guerrillas, who operate in about two-thirds of the country, were given a free shot in the arm because Luanda had pulled out counter-insurgency troops from as far away as the northern oil enclave of Cabinda to assemble a large enough attacking force.

The campaign was at no time an external operation of the type pioneered by *Reindeer* in 1978. For one thing, it was not a raid intended to pre-empt Plan operations. Originally it had been intended as a limited operation (fewer than 3 000 South African and Namibian troops, including both "teeth" and "tail") designed to take the pressure off the south-western flank of Unita until the advance from the north had been dealt with.

It is difficult to analyse a campaign that took place so recently, but it may be that the fighting at and after the Lomba river was the model of a new type of external operation.

It was certainly the most advanced form of conventional warfare that southern Africa had seen so far. Rivers were crossed not by wading but by means of bridge-laying trucks; tanks fought tanks, sometimes at point-blank range; towed and self-propelled field artillery engaged targets up to 40km away; the latest Russian Mi-24 helicopters criss-crossed over the battlefield and were shot at with Stinger missiles; Mach 2 fighter aircraft took part on both sides, as did Russian weapon systems which were so new that some of them had never before come into Western hands.

It was altogether a frightening glimpse into the future, especially for old sweats among the South Africans and Namibians who could remember rattling over the border in 1976 in Unimog trucks mineproofed with sandbags and conveyor belts; their heaviest weapons a few old Bren or Vickers guns and some World War 2 bazookas.

It cannot be mere coincidence that 1987 saw a marked interest in conventional armoured warfare emerging in senior South African military circles. Since the early 1970s the SADF had maintained a conventional force of two divisions, but for obvious reasons much of the practical stress had been laid on the counter-insurgency warfare. Then suddenly conventional warfare was in again.

Why? Probably because with most of the fighting in Namibia now being handled by SWATF the SADF has had time to stand back and re-assess its real function, and a clique of bright young SADF colonels has begun preaching a doctrine in which Guderian and Rommel rub shoulders with Patton, Mao Tse-tung and the Israelis.

It is a curious mixture, but one well adapted to local circumstances. As elucidated by Colonel Roland de Vries, commanding officer of the South African Army College, the doctrine calls for high mobility by night as well as by day, maximum violence in execution, flexible thinking and the greatest possible use of deception. It is based on three premises: that there will probably be a hostile air environment; that the enemy will probably be numerically superior; and that the fighting will have to be concluded in only a few weeks, because South Africa, unlike Israel and other countries, has no generous allies to resupply it at short notice.

Who is this new doctrine to be used against? In principle, any enemy that attacks South Africa. In practice, the only immediate contenders would be the Angolans and their allies.

At the time of writing a tense situation prevails along the Angolan border with Namibia. North and south of it there are well-armed conventional forces, and if the peace accords fail and the counter-insurgency war is resumed they could be at one another's throats again.

The conclusion is that while there is a Swapo menace to South African interests there are also strong reasons for physically supporting Savimbi. At the time of writing, more than 80 per cent of the available manpower of Plan is actually deployed full-time with FAPLA in the war against Unita, and if they were not they could be removed from their present conventional role and used for infiltration into Namibia instead. If Unita were to be decisively defeated it would be back to 1978, and the South Africans have said in so many words that they will not allow ten-years' hard work to be wasted.

The composition of the fighting troops in Namibia has greatly changed in more ways than one since the military took over responsibility for operations in 1973.

In the beginning most of the troops were national servicemen from South Africa and Namibia who had been given six months' basic training and then sent on active duties for the rest of their year's compulsory service; a few regulars of the Permanent Force; and a motley array of tribal policemen, trackers and guides.

From 1976 onwards the national servicemen were augmented by reservists called up for three months at a time. Some of these came from the Citizen Force (which is manned by volunteers and former national servicemen with an obligation to periodical service) and the rest from the Commando Force.

From 1980 onwards the mixture began to be diluted as the fledgling South West Africa Territory Force became established. The number of Citizen and Commando Force units called up for border service was reduced to a trickle, and ever fewer South African national servicemen were used there: now at least 70 per cent of the "bayonets" serving on the Namibian border are members of SWATF, not counting the few thousand conventional-force reservists stationed there for a few months at a time in case of a Cuban move south across the line.

Its detractors describe SWATF as a mere "surrogate force", the South African equivalent of the Cubans in Angola; but that is an over-simplification, even though it is true that SWATF still dances to South African tunes.

At the time of writing the SWATF has a strength of about 30 000 and is rapidly assuming more and more responsibility for fighting the border war. It is the result of three needs: political expediency, military realities and perspicacious planning.

In the first place it is a child of politics. For years Namibia dominated the headlines in South Africa and elsewhere, often in a negative form, not to say hostile, to the government.

Every South African casualty was named and publicised, the sums spent on operations there were criticised, dismal warnings were uttered that Namibia would be the South African Vietnam, the government was accused of sending South African boys to their deaths in a country not their own and into a war that could not be won.

It was a verbal bombardment that began to affect even the most loyal supporters of the government.

In the second place it was obvious to military planners that the old expedient of calling up South African battalions of reservists and sending them to the border for three months at a time was not an efficient use of assets.

Acclimatisation, re-training or refresher training, familiarisation with the area, acquiring tracking skills - all cut into efficiency and operating time; it also removed abilities from the economy and it was not difficult for Plan to calculate when battalions were due for replacement and to put the knowledge to good use.

In the third place, it was obvious that Namibia was moving inexorably towards independence. It was also obvious that if Swapo was not handed the reins of government, as happened to the MPLA in Angola and Frelimo in Mozambique, the insurgency would continue.

Even if the insurgency did not, a unilateral South African withdrawal would leave Plan and its allies, the Angolans and Cubans, as the only armed force in a power vacuum.

That being so, it made sense to South African military planners to lay the foundations of what, all going well, would be a non–Swapo defence force for Namibia.

All these considerations, and no doubt others, contributed to the decision to form SWATF on 1 August 1980.

Its future as the Namibian defence force is still as cloudy as the general prospects of Namibia; but in all other respects the decision has been a complete success from the point of view of the South African government.

Because it is mainly Namibians fighting other Namibians, losses are of less concern to South Africa, and some (but certainly not all) of the steam has been taken out of accusations about the South African army of occupation. In South Africa, in fact, Namibia has largely ceased to be a matter of public interest except when South African troops become casualties.

From the military point of view, the stratagem of fighting fire with fire has succeeded excellently. Familiarity with local areas and customs, meshed with efficient support services and good training and leadership, so that at the time of writing Swapo losses had been consistently high for a number of years.

After less than 10 years of its existence SWATF has assumed a character of its own. It is still under ultimate South African command and it has an SADF general at its head, but it has its own uniform, organisation and badges of rank. It is developing its own tradition and its own mythology, imponderable but essential ingredients of a successful military force.

Thanks to SADF administrative backing, the SWATF is "long on teeth and short on tail". At present it is organised as follows:

The General Officer Commanding SWATF is based in the territorial capital, and Namibia is divided into seven "sectors" or military districts. Each border sector also has responsibility for external operations in its equivalent north of the cutline.

The South African Defence Force still controls the three that cover the operational area: Sector 10 (Kaokoland and Ovamboland), Sector 20 (Kavango, Bushmanland and West Caprivi) and Sector 70 (East Caprivi), even though most of the troops are members of SWATF. This is obviously because all external operations are launched from these sectors, usually Sector 10.

SWATF controls the other four: Sector 30 (HQ at Otjiwarongo), Sector 40 (Windhoek), Sector 50 (Gobabis) and Sector 6O (Keetmanshoop).

The Reaction Force consists of two elements:
* A motorised conventional–warfare brigade made up of three motorised infantry battalions and an armoured car regiment. One battalion is made up of full–time national servicemen, but the others are manned by reservist Citizen Force soldiers of all races, called up selectively, then trained at 2 SA Infantry Battalion Group at Walvis Bay, with advanced training at the SWA Military School at Okahandja.
* Six full–time light infantry battalions, manned by volunteers locally recruited

from particular ethnic groups, with a sprinkling of outsiders to provide the necessary special abilities. Each battalion trains its own men and has a particular area in which it works, year in, year out. There is a battalion of Ovambos, two battalions of Bushmen, a battalion of East Caprivians, a Kaokoland battalion and a Kavango battalion.

The Area Force consists of 26 part-time units, manned by a mixture of volunteers and reservists of all races fulfilling a non-continuous obligation. They vary in size and structure according to regional requirements, and they operate in their home areas.

Elements that are not part of either the Reaction Force or the Area Force include one engineer and one signals unit, a parachute battalion and a specialised unit whose men hunt insurgents on horseback or scrambler motorcycles. There is also an "air force" in the form of 112 Squadron, whose civilian light aircraft are flown by their owners.

The border war is a strange mixture of old and new. The horse soldier is back; he can move far and fast, yet silently. Motorcyclists are noisy, but useful for circling ahead *en masse* of insurgent groups making for the border after a contact. Tracking, that most ancient of hunting skills, is an essential ingredient of follow-ups, and is practised by soldiers of all races. The little Bushman soldiers, hardly a generation away from the nomadic hunter-wanderer life, are probably the best at it; but other soldiers, both white and black, can follow an insurgent's almost invisible spoor at a walk, and sometimes at a trot.

But it is the helicopter that dominates the war. South African Air Force pilots fly their old Alouette IIIs, Pumas and Super Frelons with great dash. They have many duties, ranging from evacuating casualties under fire (each "casevac" chopper carries a medical team, and the SADF says that battlefield casualties have a better survival rate than the American wounded in Vietnam) to dodging missiles while giving close support to ground troops.

A few years ago the Chief of the SAAF, a much-decorated former fighter pilot whose service went back to the World War 2, paid the "chopper jockeys" a compliment that they have treasured ever since: in his opinion, they were the rightful heirs of the "Spitfire spirit" of 1939 to 1945.

Three of the SWATF border units deserve special mention. The first two are 201 and 203 Battalions, both manned by Bushmen. Some are former Angolans, others are from west Caprivi. Their reasons for enlisting in the SWATF are complex. As always, there is the prospect of doing a job that is fairly easy and also very well-paid by their standards. For them the battalion, with its distinctive badge, a white-breasted crow, becomes almost like a tribe that looks after them and their families.

Then there is the historical factor. For centuries the Bushmen have been persecuted by blacks, and in the battalion they have a refuge. Their memories of the past are so strong that according to one officer of the black Caprivi battalion, Bushmen are happy to take the point position in a patrol as long as they are within sight of the white officer or NCO, because they firmly believe that the blacks regard them as expendable and will desert them in an encounter with the enemy.

So they flock to the sign of the white-breasted crow, bringing with them both skills and problems. The languages of the Angolan and Caprivian Bushmen are as dissimilar as Swedish and French, so their instructors teach them to speak Afrikaans, not only so that they have a common tongue but also because it is the one language almost every Namibian understands.

The existence of Afrikaans as the common language is an interesting illustration of how different from popular conceptions the situation in the territory is.

It began at the Cape of Good Hope in the late seventeenth century as a simplified form of Dutch, then proceeded to develop on its own lines, acquiring many local words and also a strong infusion of vocabulary and structures from Indonesians sent to the Cape as slaves or political exiles. It matured into a full-fledged language with an extensive literature, and now it is spoken as a home language by millions of South Africans of several races.

The official Swapo line is that it is the tongue of the "Boere", the white oppressors, but the facts tell a different story. The truth is that Afrikaans in an early form was brought to Namibia not by white people but by Hottentot and coloured travellers who began to move into the then uncharted wilderness of Great Namaqualand from the late eighteenth century onwards, some to get beyond the reach of the colonisers and others fleeing retribution for serious crimes.

It is probable that when Namibia at last attains independence the official language will be English, a link with the outside world. But it is probable that Afrikaans will always be the *lingua franca*, and at present there is no substitute for it.

The Bushmen are not auxiliaries but proper soldiers. Their training is a specially devised blend of twentieth century fighting skills with their ancient skills and customs.

One of these, of course, is tracking. Many Bushmen have an almost mystical feeling for their surroundings. Instructors emphasise the military aspects of their tracking abilities and teach them others that they have partly lost. When they are finished, the Bushmen are peerless at following up withdrawing insurgents. They are also renowned for their ability to find cunningly concealed mines; an instinctive understanding of spatial relations, makes them first-rate at using grenade-launchers; and they never get lost, even in the most trackless bush.

The third border unit that deserves mention is 101 (Ovambo) Battalion. As with the Bushmen, the men of 101 Battalion are given training suited to their background. They are mainly used in highly mobile reaction force teams, or "Romeo Mikes", mounted in heavily armed versions of the light Casspir armoured personnel-carrier used by the SWA Police, often operating inside Angola.

Here, too, tribal traditions are preserved as far as possible. Each intake of recruits builds its own traditional beer-hut at the regimental barracks near Oshakati, and they have developed a special drill performed to chants led by a tribal singer.

The following interview with a recent past commanding officer gives a good picture of 101 Battalion, how it developed and what it does:

*How and when did 101 Battalion start?*
In 1974 it was decided to train Ovambo soldiers for the protection of key points. It was not then a military unit. There were only forty men. At the end of *Operation Savannah* (in 1976) it was realised that it was impossible for any other units to operate in Ovambo without Ovambos, so it was decided to start an Ovambo battalion.

About 200 men were recruited and deployed under the operational control of 53 Battalion, and it was a success. The battalion grew; it was named 35 Battalion and later 101 Battalion, and now it numbers more than 2 000.

*What are your tasks?*
First, tracking and destroying the enemy. Second, supporting the other units

operating in SWATF. Third, training Ovambo soldiers. We also have the self-imposed task of training the soldiers' families and keeping in touch with the local population.

*How are you organised?*

We're organised in six operational companies. Two are modular, that is self-contained, companies of about 250 men each. The others are 150 men each. The modular companies are deployed round Etale base (near the Oshikango border gate) and are mainly used for civic action and protection.

The other companies are our reaction force; 40 per cent of all our successes are due to these companies.

There is also a mounted company – horses and motorcycles – at Okatope, and an intelligence company that supplies guides, interpreters and trackers, which is permanently attached to Sector 10 Headquarters. We also have a Civic Action company, and there are various supporting elements, like cooks and clerks.

*Where are your men trained?*

Unlike other units, we train them ourselves: just now we have 300 men under training. We also train them up to section leader, that is, corporal. We already have an Ovambo officer, an Ovambo warrant-officer and many non-commissioned officers.

*How do you educate a soldier's family?*

It's often found that a soldier's family lags behind. We had to rectify this situation, so we took them into the unit as civilian employees and pushed them through. We had one girl trained as a typist, but then she found a better-paying job and left us.

*You say you keep in touch with the local population?*

It's the easiest task because we are the local population.

*What is the Ovambo soldier's motivation?*

I don't believe anybody would be in SWATF without pay, so that's an influence. But I think he has a total understanding of why he is here. Most of my troops were born in this struggle, and they have suffered with their families, and so they're here to perform a task.

*Why is there only one Ovambo lieutenant?*

It takes a long time to train an officer... We only really began training these people in 1975. At first they were used as attached personnel, so there was no rank structure.

*What's your opinion of the quality of the Ovambo soldier?*

My personal opinion, after five years in this unit, is that he is the best fighting soldier in the whole world, and I have facts to prove it... They have a natural "feel" for military matters, and we use their knowledge.

*Is vengeance by Swapo on Ovambo soldiers a problem?*

If only one per cent were aimed at Ovambo soldiers, that would be a lot. There have been cases where the soldier's wife lived among the local population. But there is no indication that an Ovambo soldier's wife is a more vulnerable target than anyone else.

*Do your soldiers live in the camp?*

Between operations a soldier doesn't live in the unit. He lives in his *kraal*, where he relaxes and often picks up information.

*Have any Ovambo soldiers been "turned" by Swapo?*

We have no indications that any have been turned or that large groups have crossed over. In 1982, I remember, one member went over.

*Are there any Swapo members in your ranks?*

No one can say. My soldiers bring the recruits. That's the first stage of selection.

*What language do you use?*

Afrikaans. About 99 per cent of my troops can't speak English. But two-thirds of the unit can't speak Afrikaans either, only Kwanyama. We take those who can speak Afrikaans, and we have white and coloured interpreters. The junior leaders soon learn the language. They teach one another... it's a pretty relaxed process.

*What does a Reaction Force team consist of?*

Thirty to forty men with two officers, four cars (Casspirs) and one armoured logistics vehicle, a Kwêvoël, with supplies and fuel for 14 days.

*Where is Swapo recruiting at present?*

At present Swapo is not recruiting... it kidnaps.

*Are there any indications that more Ovambos are interested in joining 101 Battalion?*

Yes. At the last recruiting drive I needed 250, and at least 2 000 or 3 000 appeared. Yet economic conditions weren't bad.

*What has the psychological effect of the war been on Ovambo youth?*

Ten years ago it was common to hear remarks being passed, and to see black power salutes among young people. Now all the kids salute me. In fact, I get more salutes from them than I do in my unit. But I don't dispute that there is a negative element.

*How many whites are in the unit?*

There are not more that 200 South African and South West African whites in the unit... more than 70 per cent of SWATF border troops are not white.

*How often do you deploy the Reaction Force teams?*

Every day of the year. We look for enemy tracks.

*Do you visit the* kraals *for information?*

We *are* the local population. So the troops treat the people in the *kraal* as I would treat my neighbours. That's one of the causes of our success. We are the nation, we're part of Ovambo.

*What is the level of education among the troops?*

The average is Standard I. They aren't stopped from going further. But when they have grown up there's no further need for school.

*What is needed to end the war?*

If there is independence and Swapo isn't on top the war will go on.

*Do you personally think the war will go on and on?*

No. We're reversing the process here.

There is a sort of unself-conscious schizophrenia about 101 Battalion that one finds only in first-class units. In base its soldiers are very "smart" in the old military sense of the word. In the bush they switch to different norms.

Here, slightly adapted for the sake of clarity, is part of a despatch that I wrote after riding with a "Romeo Mike" team during *Operation Egret* in 1985:

> The Puma helicopter drops into a clearing somewhere south of Dova, where four bush-bashed Casspirs are waiting for us. A TV cameraman, a photographer and I tumble out of the chopper and for a moment think we have fallen among lunatics.
>
> Back at their base near Oshakati, the officers and men of 101 Battalion stalk about in very soldier-like fashion in their form-fitting browns with sewn-in seams, snappy berets and the regimental brown leather belt with its shiny

rhino-head badge, throwing high-ball salutes at every bit of rank in sight. Out here it is another matter.

The preferred form of dress, if there is one, appears to be a black T-shirt bearing a silver eagle with a broken AK-47 in its claws, a pair of baggy issue nutria trousers and comfortable yellow Tsumeb *velskoene*. Headgear includes issue bush-hats, camouflaged peaked caps of uncertain origin, and (I can scarcely believe my eyes) a leather cowboy hat such as one buys in fancy boutiques. Only the weapons are standard issue.

The only sane person, as far as we can see, is the commander of the operation, Major Don Ehlers (the name has been changed at the request of SWATF). He is sitting in his Casspir, sipping from a fire-blackened "fire bucket" (issue canteen cup) and talking in mysterious acronymic tongues with his commanding officer at the tactical headquarters many kilometres away.

Below and around him, however, an unholy racket is going on. The Ovambo soldiers are conversing with one another at the tops of their voices, and the sprinkling of whites with them are not far behind in either loquacity or volume.

But the stores brought in by the Puma, I notice, are being stowed away with speed and efficiency. There may be a lot of jabbering going on, but it is apparent that each man knows his job.

Ehlers, his face under his camouflaged cap as dirty and dusty as those of his men, welcomes us, and within a few minutes the Puma and its escort are flapping away southwards and we are heading north.

I have been on other external operations, but never one like this. The Casspirs travel fast through clump after clump of anonymous bush. Ehlers and his drivers obviously know exactly where they are, although they do not consult any maps as far as I can see.

I notice, too, that everybody is armed to the teeth with a variety of weapons and explosives. The Casspirs all carry single or twin machine-guns, there is a variety of light machine-guns and assault rifles in the hands of the troops, and more munitions are crammed into various crevices in the vehicles.

The talking and banter go on, no matter how bumpy or unpleasant our passage. I begin to notice the interaction between individuals. Two who particularly attract my attention are a white boy named (I think) Piet, who is an attached "tiffie" of the Technical Services Corps, and a black lad of about the same age named Phuma, who was wearing the leather cowboy hat on my arrival.

They are about as different as two youngsters can be. Piet is a blond Afrikaans national serviceman from the Transvaal and Phuma is a Permanent Force member of SWATF. But they have a common tongue, Afrikaans, and service in the "Romeo Mikes" has obviously dissolved the barriers of race and culture.

They share everything, I notice: cigarettes, titbits from their ration packs, a battered service pistol, a filthy pillow, even that incongruous cowboy hat. They wrangle, joke and indulge in constant horse-play.

One incident tells it all. Phuma is a chicken addict and when we stop at a *kraal* he slips off and acquires a suitable fowl, which he cooks at the earliest opportunity.

He is no gourmet chef. He roughly plucks his chicken, rams it into an empty cardboard ration-pack box and drops it on a fire. The plastic round the box goes up with a whoosh and a terrible smell while Phuma proudly looks on.

Then someone shouts: *Opsaal!* (saddle up) and the Casspir engines start. Phuma snatches up his chicken, knocks off the curling bits of charred cardboard and leaps on board as our Casspir draws away, then sets about dismembering the charred bird.

Ehlers drives by and shouts: "Hey, Phuma, give me a bit of chicken!" Phuma throws him a gory drumstick and Ehlers goes on his way, munching.

"Hey," says Piet, nudging Phuma, "Give me a bit of chicken, man. Come on, we're both wearing the uniform."

"Ja," Phuma says, "But *I'm* PF." They and the others scream with laughter.

So it goes. There is no apartheid in 101 Battalion. Yet in the evenings, when the teams have based up, the whites get together for a natter and a ration-pack supper while the blacks congregate in small groups to resurrect some *mahangu* porridge that they have been carrying since the previous evening. Tomorrow they will join forces in their Casspirs again. It is all as natural and amicable as breathing.

Once again I am struck by the way they base up. There is no confusion, no wasted movement. They are veterans and they know what they are doing.

After two days we have our first taste of action. There is the unmistakable dull thump of a mine, and we find one of the Casspirs hunched over with its near front wheel blown off. Its occupants are unhurt but shaken.

But the damage is clean; a helicopter flies in a drive-shaft, Piet and his mates take the necessary markings from the Kwêvoël armoured logistics vehicle that accompanies every "Romeo Mike" team and get to work. Within less than two hours the damaged Casspir is serviceable again.

Then, after hours of grinding through the bush with the trackers loping tirelessly along in front of the Casspirs, several contacts are made.

One breech-bolt after the other clacks home on a cartridge, and suddenly the laughing and skylarking stops and the erstwhile clowns are grim and silent, their eyes glistening.

The action starts, and a number of Plan officers and men are killed or captured. One of the dead is an intelligence officer; among the papers in his leather despatch-case is a no-excuses order to ginger up both the morale and the training of the infiltrators.

Another officer foolishly tries to make his escape on a bicycle instead of lying low. He is knocked head-over-heels by a bullet through the thigh, and Ehlers personally jumps out and captures him.

The insurgent, apparently no more than 19 years old, is grey with pain, and probably fear, if it is true that his commissar has told him he can expect instant torture and death. But Ehlers whistles up an Ovambo medical orderly, who comes running up with his pannier, expertly splints the broken thigh and gives him a pain-killer.

A helicopter is called to take him back to Oshakati, and in the mean time he is laid out under a tree, while nearby an Ovambo soldier rides about on the captured bicycle, dodging shafts of vernacular wit from his mates.

A helicopter is called to take him away for immediate interrogation. While we wait for it to arrive one of the white sergeants engages him in conversation.

"Why are you fighting for Swapo?" the sergeant asks.

"I'm fighting against apartheid," the youngster replies.

"What do you mean by apartheid?" the sergeant asks.

"I can't go into a white bar," the youngster says. "I can't marry a white *meme* if I want to, and I have to carry a pass in a white area."

"You bloody fool," the sergeant says in amazement, "where did you hear that shit? All the pubs in South West have been 'open' for years, and they've changed the law: if you want to marry a white *meme* you can, if you can find one that's willing. And nobody carries passes any more."

After a moment the youngster turns his head away.

"I can't talk any more now," he says. "My leg's hurting too much."

The sergeant walks away, shaking his head. "Where's that bugger been for the last ten years?" he asks me.

In due course the helicopter bears the prisoner away and Ehlers climbs into his Casspir.

"All stations, this is Zero," he says into the microphone. Then, using a colourful expression that I am certain is not found in any manual on voice procedure, he gives the order to proceed with the operation.

A key player in the border war is the SWA Police counter-insurgency unit, which has accounted for more insurgent "kills" in the country than any military unit.

It has never been an ordinary police unit. It was founded in June 1979 as an outgrowth of the security branch of the South African Police. (Namibia did not get its own police force until several years later.)

Named *Operation K* and known as *Ops K,* it was originally composed of ten black and white security policemen and 64 locally recruited "special constables". It was designed for very rapid intelligence gathering and swift exploitation of the knowledge gained, with heavier fire support from an attached sub-unit of the Reconnaissance Regiment: but this proved a cumbersome arrangement, and the unit acquired its own small fire force and then three Hippo mine-protected vehicles to speed up its foot operations where necessary.

It also acquired an enduring nickname of undetermined origins: *Koevoet,* Afrikaans for crowbar. The use of *Koevoet* was discouraged and dropped after a sustained campaign by opposition politicians and newspapers who accused the unit of atrocities, and *Ops K* was dropped when the SWAPol took over the unit: but it lingers on.

*Koevoet* saw action from its inception, and by early 1984 it had killed 1 624 insurgents in more than 700 contacts. Since then its rate of kill has only fallen when there was a shortage of insurgents in the operational area, and its own deaths have been few.

*Koevoet* is now divided into three units, based respectively at Opuwo and Oshakati in Ovamboland and Rundu in Kavango, and each consists of an intelligence and covert operations team and a number of platoon-sized fighting groups, each equipped with four Casspirs, a mine-protected logistics truck and a mine-protected fuel bowser.

The groups are deployed according to the needs of the situation, operating away from bases for up to a week at a time. Operating completely separately from the military and free from restrictions as to battalion or even sector boundaries, they rely heavily on information given to them by the local population and follow up immediately, with trackers following spoor on the run while the rest of the group follows in the vehicles. Once they catch up with the insurgents they lay an ambush or attack on foot or mounted, depending on the circumstances.

White members are regular policemen who have passed the standard SWAPol counter-insurgency course and volunteered for Force K service, black members (the majority) are selected from the auxiliary special constables serving in Ovamboland and trained up to standard.

*Koevoet* is a controversial unit. Its detractors still accuse it of atrocities. Its supporters reply that if its members were as brutal as reports allege they would not be able to operate with such success, because the local population would not help them (*Koevoet* itself says that only if one of its members commits an offence will he be prosecuted).

Considering the *modus operandi* of *Koevoet*, this is a difficult argument to answer. At the same time there is no denying the fact that some members of *Koevoet* have been found guilty of such offenses as murder and assault. The greatest problem in apportioning guilt is the fact that many of the loudest accusers are Swapo sympathisers who could hardly be expected to be unbiased.

There are three permanently stationed SADF units which have played an important part in the border war, especially the external operations: 32 Battalion, 2 South African Infantry Battalion Group, and 61 Mechanised Battalion Group.

32 Battalion is the only unit in the SADF that can be described as a mercenary regiment. It originated during *Operation Savannah* in 1975, when part of the FNLA broke away under one Daniel Chipenda and moved southwards. When the South African withdrawal from Angola began in early 1976, the "Chipenda Faction" faced extermination and was clandestinely evacuated to Namibia. There most of its men, unemployed and bitterly opposed to the Marxist MPLA, volunteered for military service.

The battalion, led mainly by whites (although this is changing) is stationed at a remote camp called Buffalo Base in the operational area. A truly élite force whose emblem is a silver buffalo-head badge worn on a distinctive beret made of camouflage cloth, 32 Battalion consists of at least eight companies who are acknowledged to be the best light infantry in southern Africa.

It is usually deployed in companies or multiples of a few companies, and it operates almost exclusively north of the border, sometimes in mine-resistant vehicles but usually on foot. It has played a leading part in almost every external operation and in hundreds of small actions, some of which take it into the bush for weeks or months at a time.

Needless to say, it is loathed by the Angolans and enjoys a fearsome reputation abroad. It has been widely accused in the *Guardian* and other newspapers of committing ghastly atrocities. The usual reply by its members is that if they were as brutal as the reports allege they would not be able to operate with such success because the local population would not help them.

Time has caught up with the now grizzled survivors of the Chipenda faction who fled south in 1976. But the ethnic character of 32 Battalion remains the same, because although they are cut off from their homeland in northern Angola, their sons are now reaching enlistment age and joining the regiment.

Theoretically, 2 SAI is not stationed in Namibia at all, because its base is in the Walvis Bay area. Walvis Bay is a sore point in Namibian politics. It is the most convenient and in fact the only usable commercial port. It was annexed by the British in the nineteenth century, long before the arrival of the Germans, and it therefore became part of South Africa when it was given its independence in 1910. Eventually, no doubt, Walvis Bay will become a part of independent Namibia, but in the mean time it remains part of South Africa. It is there that 2 SAI, one of nine infantry training battalions of the SADF, is based.

As an all-arms unit 2 SAI was engaged in *Operation Savannah* in 1975/6, and elements of it have taken part in many subsequent operations, because SWATF is essentially a light-infantry force without conventional equipment.

Because of the strong counter-insurgency character of the SWATF "61 Mech" (which is stationed at its own base in the operational area) has been deeply engaged and suffered considerable casualties in the past ten years, particularly in external operations. Like 2 SAI, it is an all-arms unit manned mainly by conscript national servicemen with a few regulars of the Permanent Force.

Unlike the former, however, it has no training function; like 32 Battalion, it is primarily a fighting unit that acquired a formidable reputation and proved an excellent source of regular and non-regular leaders.

With the border insurgency edging towards the quarter-century mark, one might well ask: When will the war end?

It is the sort of question that can have several answers, depending on the persuasions of the replier.

The easiest is that it will end when Namibia becomes independent under a government that includes or is dominated by Swapo. However, things might not be as simple as that.

For example, what if elections before independence bring about a government that is *not* dominated by Swapo?

The question that outweighs every other is how much popular support Swapo would get in an election.

Swapo claims huge support in Namibia, particularly in Ovamboland, but that remains unproved, since it has never taken part in any popular test of strength, and has boycotted and tried to prevent all elections in the past, even when the South African government offered to let them take place under international supervision.

Energetic work by propagandists has planted the idea in many people's minds that an overwhelming victory by Swapo is inevitable, and that might be so. On the other hand, some observers point out that a significant bloc in Ovambo-land, which is bound to be the main electoral battleground because Ovambos make up nearly half the total population of Namibia, is demonstrably hostile to Swapo.

For example, they say, it is significant that the most resolute opponents of Plan are Ovambos serving in 101 Battalion of the SWATF and the counter-insurgency police unit, who could probably muster a large body of votes between them.

The reasoning of this argument is as follows: There are roughly 2 000 trained soldiers and recruits serving in 101 Battalion at any given time, and probably at least double that number who have served their time and retired, while the figures for the police would probably be about half that; and all have good reasons for not voting for Swapo.

The various black border units have provided a great deal of lucrative employment in the tribal areas, with a lot of money being pumped into the local economy; many soldiers and policemen, or their families, now run a variety of small businesses and cottage industries on the side, and many businessmen have scored from supply and other contracts.

The military and civil "capital" of Oshakati, formerly "just a bloody hole in the ground", as a local government official once succinctly put it, now has black-owned supermarkets, garages, pubs, panel-beating shops, curio factories and a variety of other enterprises patronised by both the locals and the large numbers of expatriate soldiers and government officials stationed there or passing through.

Nearly all these businesses are owned by Ovambos, since whites have never been allowed to settle in the tribal areas. It is unbridled capitalism in action, and its practitioners know that Swapo is a decidedly socialist organisation; so an election would tell whether the almighty banknote speaks louder than the ubiquitous AK-47 among the Ovambos, who are well known as the most commercially-minded people in Namibia.

There are other influences at work. Apart from Oshakati there are no big towns and in Ovamboland generally sub-chiefs and *kraal* headmen still exert great influence on their subjects. As a rule these traditional functionaries are anti-Swapo, not only because they are conservative but because the insurgents have been trying for years to break down the ancient tribal structures, and have assassinated many of them. They and their tribal policemen, of whom there are a large number, know perfectly well that under Swapo rule their future might be very precarious.

The same factors apply elsewhere in the operational area; particularly at the Rundu base in Kavango, and Katima Mulilo in Caprivi; if one counts the families (and in typical African fashion the families in the tribal areas tend to be large and strongly loyal to the group) the anti-Swapo elements could muster a very effective electoral bloc in any fair election with a genuinely secret vote.

Threats by Swapo in the past about dealing harshly with "puppets", not to mention group and racial suspicions, some of them going back hundreds of years, will probably also play some part. Given their history of persecution by blacks, the soldiers of the two Bushman battalions and their families are likely to vote solidly against Swapo. The same would probably be true of the Kavango and Caprivian battalions.

Outside the operational area virtually every racial group has at least one ethnic party, although there are also several multiracial parties, ranging from left wing to conservative. Some of the ethnic and non-ethnic parties support Swapo or are at least neutral to it, while others are firmly against it; only a fair election would polarise them.

On the other hand, after over twenty years there is a certain amount of war-weariness, at least in Ovamboland, and according to the security forces Plan propagandists are operating clandestinely in Ovamboland, their theme being that in spite of any conciliatory noises that Sam Nujoma might make, Swapo will keep on fighting if it loses the pre-independence election. Needless to say, the argument that "only I can stop the war" is a powerful one.

But again, much depends on how convincingly Swapo can represent itself as the "strong man", which has always been a factor to be reckoned with in Africa. Old Namibian hands recall that in its heyday, in 1975, as was noted earlier, 55 per cent of the people in the operational area voted in a general election in spite of the best efforts by Plan to dissuade them, and militarily there can be no doubt that the war has not gone well for the insurgents.

The truth is that very few insurgencies have ever succeeded in directly overturning the government that they are fighting. When that government has fallen, it has usually been because its economy collapsed or it lost heart or support, and because it attempted to fight defensively.

Whatever its other faults, the South African government has not succumbed to any of these ailments, and at the time of writing after more than twenty years of "armed struggle" Swapo is no nearer to winning militarily than it was when the first six trained insurgents filtered into Ovamboland in 1965.

It is worth noting some remarks made by Major-General Georg Meiring when he finished his tour as General Officer Commanding SWA Territory Force in December 1986. He said that Plan was on the losing side, because the border war had demolished two fallacies: that time was always on the side of the insurgent, and that a counter-insurgency campaign could not be won.

"We have been fighting for twenty years," he said, "and *they* are deteriorating. They are losing here and at the same time we are winning, two entirely different things.

"The terrorist cannot win because each terrorist is a political commissar (but) his fighting ability is not very good. Yet you must have a fairly good fighting capacity... After twenty years you'd expect that any properly inspired people would have achieved something."

As long ago as early 1988 the security forces confidently asserted that they had Plan on the run and had virtually reversed the progression of the war, so that the insurgents were now back to where they had been five or ten years earlier.

The evidence that they offered was convincing. Caprivi has not had an "incident" for ten years, while by the end of 1987 the small Swapo presence in Kaokoland and Kavango had been reduced to nothing. Even Western and Central Ovamboland, the old recruiting-ground for Swapo, had only a handful of active insurgents; in September 1988 the government planned to abolish the longstanding curfew in Ovamboland, although the proposal was deferred because Swapo reneged on an undertaking to observe an extension of the Angolan ceasefire.

Plan certainly has never managed to extend its activities beyond Ovamboland in any significant way. Its best effort was the short-lived insurgency in Caprivi in the 1970s, by courtesy of the Caprivi African National Union. Attempts to stir up the Kavango tribal homeland have failed, partly because of security force counter-measures and partly because Kavango tribesmen feel little sympathy with Ovambos.

Its "Special Unit" was so totally defeated in the white farming areas in Tsumeb during the early 1980s that in November 1986 General Meiring was confident enough to say that it was possible that the much-vaunted unit had been disbanded altogether. A Swapo spokesman retorted from Luanda that "that is just the speculation of the Boers", but it is a fact that up to the time of writing there has not been another attempt to operate in the Tsumeb area.

Lately there have been a number of bomb outrages in towns inside and outside the operational area, most notably in Oshakati, where 25kg of explosive detonated in a crowded bank in February 1988 killing 18 people, mostly black. One of the wounded was the daughter of the anti-government Bishop of Ovamboland (the Swapo spokesman promptly denied responsibility, saying that the bomb had been detonated by South African agents for propaganda purposes).

The security forces say that the slight rise in bomb outrages inside and outside the operational area results from a change of tactics forced on Plan by the remorseless pressure exerted on it in the past few years. Planting a bomb is cheap in effort, risk and logistics, and is guaranteed good publicity, particularly when the dead are foreigners, such as a United States military attaché who was killed by an explosion at an Oshakati garage in 1985.

A Swapo spokesman more or less confirmed this in November 1986, when he told a reporter that Plan intended to intensify its bombing campaign in the large towns such as Windhoek, Swakopmund, Tsumeb and Walvis Bay.

"We intend to take the war to new areas, to targets in the cities," he said. "We will make the price of their occupation of our country a high one."

Plan has certainly never held or even established a "liberated zone" anywhere; in fact, the only permanent base that it has ever had on Namibian soil was at Ongulumbashe, which was destroyed by the police in August 1966, and it has never been able to inflict serious casualties on its enemies or overrun anything more significant than a small temporary base; while from 1985 to late 1988 its sabotage rarely amounted to anything more than inconvenience to the local population.

There was an increase in "incidents" in September and October 1988, which the Namibian security forces ascribed to the fact that strong Cuban forces had moved into southern Angola from mid-year onwards. The presence of the Cubans had damped down Unita activities in the immediate vicinity, thereby making available for infiltration some of the Plan soldiers permanently serving in FAPLA.

In late October 1988, according to the spokesman, the infiltrators were engaged in a fourfold programme:

* Political activation in the Ovamboland "shallow area" immediately south of the border, the theme of which was the putting into effect of UN Resolution 435 in Namibia and the determination of Swapo to fight on if it did not win the pre-independence election.
* Abduction of schoolchildren, who were taken into Angola for political indoctrination and training in handling weapons and explosives so that they could later be infiltrated back into the operation area. The spokesmen said that they had positive information about this from interrogation of captured insurgents.
* Attempts to persuade members of SWATF and the SWA Police to change sides. If they did not, action would be taken against them during the election.
* Building up caches of weapons and explosives, particularly in the traditional pro-Swapo area of Ombalantu, in preparation for the impending short rainy season.

Between 1 September and 10 October, they said, the local population had made 89 reports of enemy presence to the security forces, and on investigation 39 directly involved Plan. That showed an increase for the same period in previous years (17 in 1987, 23 in 1986). The incidents included two stand-off bombardments, neither of which caused any casualties or damage, seven acts of sabotage of telephone poles and irrigation pipelines; a civilian woman killed in an explosion; eight mine detonations, in one of which a child was killed; 19 encounters with the security forces, all initiated by the latter; two cases of theft and one of murder.

Altogether 72 insurgents were believed to have been involved, of whom twenty had been shot dead and five captured.

The large number of reports mentioned above seemed to indicate that the military were still reaping the benefit of an ill-advised temporary return by Plan to old-style "hard" intimidation about four years before the time of writing. The "hearts and minds" workers energetically exploited the resultant ill-feeling which proved so injurious to the insurgents that they called it off; however, the main benefit to the security forces was an increase of several hundred per cent in the flow of information from the population, which was naturally exploited to the greatest possible extent and proved to be a long-lasting phenomenon.

Spokesmen of the security forces recently told me that they ascribed the increased flow to several different motives: indignation at the heavy-handedness of Plan; the fact that the security forces pay well for information and reward deserters and turncoats with jobs, clothes and money; and the waning influence of Plan.

The local population had abandoned the old play-it-safe method of passing information to the security forces, but only weeks after a sighting of Plan. Instead "the terrorists can't be in the country for more than six days before the information reaches us; and this is in the heart of central Ovamboland."

The most immediate benefit had been information that led to the detection and lifting of three or four mines for every one detonated, as a result of which "we are winning the mine war".

The increased abduction of children indicates that Plan is still suffering from its constant lack of personnel. In 1978 it had about 16 000 trained or half-trained insurgents. By the early 1980s this had been reduced to something like 12 000. Five years later in mid-1988, it admitted to being down to a little over 8 000 (the SADF puts its present strength at 8 700).

The fall in numbers can be attributed to two causes. The first is the appalling casualty figure: the 10 000th insurgent to be killed in the border war was shot as long ago as 1986, and in the past few years Plan has lost the equivalent of a battalion annually – more than 600 were killed or captured in 1986, and 746 in 1987.

The losses were compounded by the increasing shortage of recruits in the 1980s as the tide of military events turned against Plan and harrying by the security forces made it progressively more difficult for the insurgents to abduct large numbers of schoolchildren.

By the mid-1980s this dearth of manpower resulted in infiltrators becoming perceptibly younger and less well trained. Many of them, according to security force spokesmen, were obviously from the so-called "stud camps" that Plan is said to have been running in southern Angola for many years.

The stud camps are an article of faith in the ranks of SWATF. They are supposed to have been established as institutions where the hundreds of small children kidnapped over the years could be raised as fighters, their numbers augmented by babies born to Ovambo girls who had fled north or been abducted over the border by kidnappers.

Do the stud camps exist? The security force asserts that it has convincing evidence that they do. Those hostile to the government deny it. On the other hand, there is independent confirmation that as long ago as 1985 a number of captured Plan fighters, while Ovambos rather than Angolans, displayed such abysmal ignorance of Namibian developments in the past ten years and of local conditions that it was obvious that they had been out of the territory for many years.

Members of Plan like these actually benefit the security forces, because they are such obvious strangers that they carry no weight with the local population.

Security force spokesmen also say that the fact that Plan infiltration groups began operating in much smaller groups in the mid-1980s (the easier to dodge government patrols) did not pass unnoticed by the local people and had an adverse effect.

As a result, according to a spokesman, "the locals will talk with Swapo but not join them, and the flow of intelligence to the security force, particularly concerning the presence of Swapo and mine-laying, has doubled. There are other weaknesses that I could mention, but they are still sensitive at this stage."

However, infiltration never stopped, and deserters were few. Why, then, did they keep coming? Security force spokesmen put it down to four reasons:

* The policy of Plan is not to tell members in base camps of operational losses.
* The fighters are constantly brain-washed by their political commissars,

who tell them ghastly stories about the torture and death that await any prisoner.

* Because their base and training camps are situated far inside Angola, it is difficult for any dissident fighter to escape. Later, when he goes south, he is part of a group.
* Harsh discipline is enforced in the camps, with frequent death sentences passed on murmurers.

No doubt there were other reasons: the bitterness engendered by the war itself; old memories of contemptuous treatment by some whites, still fresh in many a proud and warlike Ovambo who went north at some point; ideological conviction; the continuing international publicity that gave Swapo leaders new faith that in spite of their military reverses they could still emerge the winners. The large-scale movement of Cubans into southern Angola from mid-1988, too, was probably a great booster of morale.

The Cuban move southward and the international peace talks may have saved Swapo from the worst effects of war-weariness at high level, which by 1988 had persuaded many senior members that the time had come to talk instead of continuing with a fruitless war, or run the risk of political events passing them by.

As recently as 1987 spokesmen for the security forces said that there had been unmistakable signs of dissension in the upper ranks of Swapo, some believing that many of the original objectives of the movement had been achieved and that it was now time to negotiate a place in the political structure as Namibia stumbled towards independence; a view which, needless to say, was bitterly opposed by the radicals and time-servers.

There was some confirmation of this in 1986, when more than a hundred members of the upper echelon were arrested on the grounds that they were South African spies. The South African espionage and counter-intelligence services maintained a discreet silence, but they knew the arrests were symptoms of a far more serious crisis afflicting Swapo, and that the "spies" were in fact people who had called for a laying down of arms in favour of entry into the political process.

The security forces were naturally not slow to take advantage of the dissension, and the high command of Swapo eventually became so sensitive about it that "if we catch a suspected detachment leader and then let him go again he's soon arrested by them and neutralised", according to one spokesman.

Much of the immediate future of Namibia is tied up with the reaction of Swapo to events in the next few months after the time of writing.

If Swapo wins the pre-independence election and shows signs of fulfilling its leader Sam Nujoma's prediction in that fateful 1978 TV interview, that "the people" would "do away with" the "traitors" serving in SWATF and the "puppets" of the internal political parties, it could set off a new cycle of violence.

In recent times Swapo has moderated its tone, but outsiders trying to understand the situation in Namibia should bear in mind that the concept of a loyal opposition is strictly Western, clearly contrary to African traditions, and it was abolished as soon as possible after independence by most African countries. The notion still survives in a fairly pure form in only two countries on the continent: Botswana and, ironically, South Africa.

On the other hand, if Swapo loses the election, would the present command be willing to admit that they had lost the military part of the war and that it was time to enter the political arena?

Officially abandoning the "armed struggle" and thereby conceding defeat to "the Boers" would be humiliating, and aggravated by the fact that for years they have been disseminating wildly exaggerated claims to running a "liberated zone" in Namibia and inflicting heavy defeats on the security forces. A re-entry into politics would mean working alongside those very "traitors" and "puppets".

On a more personal level, most of the top leaders of Swapo have spent more than twenty years in self-imposed exile. They have grown old and comfortable in their headquarters abroad, funded by a variety of sympathetic persons, organisations and nations. No doubt they remember what happened to the founding father of Swapo, Herman Toivo ja Toivo. Released by the South Africans a few years ago, after more than twenty years in jail, he has not become the leader of Swapo again, but has been relegated to the status of Grand Old Man. Would the same happen to them once the young Turks, both those in Luanda and those operating in "internal" Swapo, plunged into the political mainstream?

So they might decide to fight on, as their activitation teams are said to be promising the Ovambo people, which would also set off a new cycle of violence.

Yet Swapo must inevitably play an important part in the Namibian political process; even the other political leaders admit that its participation is necessary if there is to be a lasting solution. There is no doubt that Swapo would command a very large following, if only because there are far more Ovambos than anyone else in Namibia.

# WHY PORTUGAL LOST ITS AFRICAN WARS
## By Al J. Venter

*According to the November 1988 issue of* National Geographic
Magazine, *three-quarters of American adults cannot find the Persian
Gulf on a map of the world, in spite of American military activity
there during the Iran-Iraq war; and twelve million of them don't know
that their capital is Washington. Most South Africans, however, are
familiar with recent history in their own backyard, particularly the
wars in Rhodesia and the former Portuguese territories in Africa.*

But ask the average school-leaver in Johannesburg or Cape Town why these
wars were fought, and the answer would probably be something vague about
terrorism. Nothing about insurgency, the Third World or OAU politics, exploitation
of the masses by an imperial power, or colonial rule; just *terrorism*.

Few have any real knowledge of the intensity of these campaigns, which lasted
twenty years. Nor that great numbers of lives were lost; a few thousand whites,
tens of thousands of blacks; or even that South Africa on occasion was drawn
into the periphery of several of them. South African special forces took part
in vital operations in Mozambique, South African officers served in Rhodesia,
and our pilots flew clandestinely into Angola when the Portuguese were still
there, mostly in the south of that country, which is more than five times the
size of the United Kingdom.

For that reason few South Africans can hardly be familiar with the problems
facing a country like Malawi, which was almost totally dependent on the very
limited road and rail links through Portuguese-controlled Mozambique for its
survival. Survive it did, ultimately, but it was close, as Frelimo gradually achieved
a strangle-hold on much of Tete Province; the same Tete Province that was
later to have such a significant and adverse effect on the war in Rhodesia.

In February 1973, I travelled through Tete for three days, and much of what
happened was recorded in *The Zambezi Salient,* published in South Africa and
the United States (Keartlands, Johannesburg and the Devin-Adair Company, Old
Greenwich, Connecticut the following year). My notes of the journey, in convoy,
read like a thriller; there were mines, snipers, chaotic organisation in the Portuguese
forces and a convoy that would have been a write-off if it had happened anywhere
else but in Africa. There were dozens of mines, yet not a single truck was destroyed;
we were sniped at by Frelimo for two days out of the three, and not one of
us was hit. We had only 134 kilometres to cover to reach the sanctuary of
the Malawi border.

The nature of warfare in Africa, in Eritrea or Chad, has greatly changed in
the past ten years. In Mozambique it was almost as if the war was on "hold"
for most of the nine-and-a-half years that it was waged in this East African
territory, which had been colonised by the Portuguese for 500 years.

Whatever else, the trip between Tete and the Malawi border shed some
interesting light on the African conflicts of the Sixties and early Seventies.

We left Tete at dawn on 16 February; a straggling line of cars and trucks
rumbling across the huge bridge over the Zambezi that became as much a
landmark in its area as the skyscrapers of Beira or Lourenço Marques farther
south as the war went on. There were heavy machine-gun emplacements at

various points along the bridge; searchlights cast eerie shadows on the early morning mist on the river. We paid the toll at the far end and moved on. The road was not yet tarred, and in Tete we had seen too many wrecked trucks blasted by mines not to be aware of what lay ahead. Some of the vehicles were bound for Blantyre; others for Zambia and Zaïre. Normally they would have used the Botswana route, but apparently the Rhodesians had been active in the area and had temporarily immobilised the Kazungula Ferry; or that was what we were told. Hence the longer, more circuitous route through Mozambique. In any event the Tete route was preferable to Zambian Army checkpoints often manned by drunk or drugged Zambian soldiers.

On leaving Tete we were told that the journey would last eight hours, but still within sight of the bridge we had to wait four hours for our Portuguese army escorts to arrive; and that in the stifling heat of the valley.

A crowd of officials, all in uniform, arrived to check our vehicles. Any cameras? Binoculars? Tape recorders? Each of us was required to complete forms in triplicate which indemnified the Lisbon government against any loss of life or material that might be suffered along the way.

Of the 35 vehicles assembled in line at the checkpoint, only our Landrover and a small English car on its way to the Zambian Copperbelt were not military or carrying goods. Consequently we were soon approached by a young Portuguese lieutenant, Enrico Chagas, on his way to join his unit at Mussacama. He was born in Mozambique and educated in South Africa, spoke excellent English and while he was with us he gave us an intelligent commentary on the war. It was a fascinating insight into a conflict which, even at that late stage, rarely reached the front page anywhere outside the Portuguese sphere of influence.

According to my diary : "Chagas, born in Africa, was casual about most things, including the possibility of ambush. It seemed incomprehensible to him that he could ever be taken by surprise in the bush country he knew so well. An ambush while travelling in convoy, he said, was 'just so much noise. Mines, yes,' he said, 'but ambushes...'"

We covered 18 kilometres the first day. We passed houses by the side of the road, abandoned, scarred by shells and bullets, their windows and doors torn out of their frames. There was no evidence of any human presence in the region apart from our own; the *kraals* and villages were all burnt or abandoned.

It was a race between the Mozambique Liberation Movement, Frelimo, and the Portuguese government, not only for the hearts and minds of the people but also for their bodies. Tens of thousands of Mozambican civilians were rounded up and corralled in collective villages, or *Aldeamentos*. The rest fled into the bush or into the arms of Frelimo.

Several times we skirted large holes in the road: mines. Strips of crumpled metal were scattered along the verge. On one occasion the wheelless, buckled front suspension of a truck lay in the bush nearby. Twice we stopped while army engineers cleared mines from the road ahead. Chagas said he had lost three members of his unit because of mines in the past three months. He said his men called the Tete Corridor "The road to hell".

Next day we had hardly set out before the engineers detonated a mine *in situ*. It had been badly laid, and the spotters travelling in the first truck had no difficulty in observing a disturbance in the murram near the place where Frelimo had laid the mine, probably the night before in readiness for our early departure. It could not have been more than a few hundred metres from where we had slept.

The second day also brought snipers; sporadic shots rang out across the valley and were answered by bursts of automatic fire from our Portuguese escort. They followed this half-hearted response by lobbing six or eight light mortar bombs in the general direction of where the shots had come from; there was no talk about sending anybody into the bush to answer the threat, or perhaps making a flanking movement. Our escorts were part of the convoy and had no intention of leaving it; the enemy was in the bush and there he remained. That was that!

During the rest of the journey insurgent marksmen fired at us, perhaps three or four shots every hour.

At one point we were stopped for several hours while the army cleared 14 mines, two metal anti-tank TM-46s and a dozen plastic anti-personnel mines. At that point the firing from the bush became intense. Not long afterwards two Portuguese Air Force Alouette helicopter gunships arrived and raked the surrounding bush with heavy machine-guns for ten minutes, setting it on fire and, no doubt, frightening wildlife for miles around. The snipers withdrew for the rest of the day.

During the entire journey of the convoy, only one truck was damaged; not very badly, because it had run over an anti-personnel mine. We waited while wheels were changed, with much banter. We relieved our tense bladders and went on.

At last we reached Mussacama. Just before midnight there were lights ahead, and we found a settlement swathed in mist in the mountains above Capirizauja. The place was guarded by a soldier in an improvised machine-gun turret. My diary reminds me that at least the beer was cold.

All this happened more than 15 years ago; and still the war goes on.

Drivers on the Tete run in 1988 still speak of mines and the occasional sniping attack; only these days there are more ambushes and many more casualties than before. Now the Zimbabwe army, sometimes backed by a Tanzanian detachment, does the guarding and the fighting. Frelimo has replaced the Portuguese. Lourenço Marques has been renamed Maputo and every statue, public square or building associated with Portuguese imperialism has been removed or renamed. Radical graffiti and the *metical* have replaced the old order and people are still getting killed.

The enemy now is Renamo, a movement long linked to South Africa but since abandoned to its own devices. Renamo has acquired or captured enough weapons and ammunition to keep the killing going for years still.

If ever there was an example of what the Americans call the Domino Principle – the overthrow of an established government by political or military action, and the country then being used as a springboard to attack other countries in the vicinity – then the collapse of the Portuguese empire in Africa provides one.

After the coup d'état in Portugal in 1974 and the abrupt withdrawal of Portuguese forces from Guinea, Angola and Mozambique, severe pressure was brought to bear on the Rhodesia of Ian Smith. That war intensified greatly after 1975.

The same happened in South West Africa, where conflict also became more intense, to the extent that some of the heaviest fighting yet seen in Ovamboland took place in 1976 and 1977. It is significant that the worst black riots in South Africa took place in Soweto in June 1976. That was not long after South African forces, which had blitzkrieged their way almost to the gates of Luanda in *Operation Savannah*, were forced to withdraw from Angola after the American Congress had forbidden further dealings with the racist South Africans, despite guarantees

**Above left:** Unita column crossing the Lombo river north of Jamba in eastern Angola. The logistics are primitive but effective.

**Above right:** Dr Jonas Savimbi, leader of the rebel Unita movement in Angola. The future of Angola, whichever direction it takes, will have to include this man, who has been fighting for twenty years.

**Below:** Wreckage of a Cuban MiG jet fighter brought down by an American *Stinger* missile by Unita forces in eastern Angola.

**Above left:** Alouette helicopters, now in their twenty-fifth year of service with the SAAF, provided the main support for many incursions into Angolan territory.

**Left:** Burnt-out Russian truck with anti-aircraft gun mounted. Taken in a South African raid across the border in Angola.

**Above:** During the war many of the best counter-insurgency units attached to the South African Defence Force became increasingly multiracial. The Ovambo battalion was one.

**Right:** SAAF aircraft score hits on an Angolan garrison town occupied by a Swapo battalion in the arid south-west near the Kunene river.

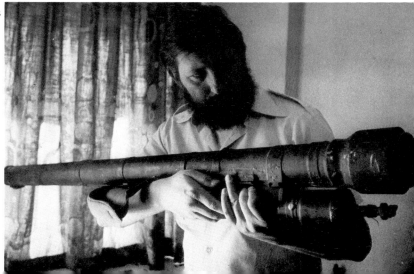

**Below right:** Al Venter with one of the captured SAM-7 anti-aircraft missiles taken in *Operation Protea* in Angola. Swapo did not prove very effective in the use of these Russian guided missiles.

**Above:** A huge arsenal of anti-tank mines taken during *Operation Askari.* This was one of the most decisive blows against Swapo during the war, which has now been waged for more than twenty years.

**Far left:** Bunkers sheltering Swapo insurgents on the battlefield at Cuamato.

**Left:** A Swapo woman fighter captured by South African forces. These women were not very effective in the field and were used mainly to "entertain" male units away from home for long periods.

**Above left:** Grenade assault on a Swapo bunker in southern Angola which yielded a large store of arms. Almost the entire Swapo unit was wiped out.

**Above left:** Members of the élite Selous Scouts before being airlifted by an American helicopter bought from the Israelis. Most of the operations took them into either Mozambique or Zambia.

**Far left:** A column of Selous Scouts on its way to an insurgent base near Chimoio in western Mozambique.

**Left:** A Rhodesian paratrooper attached to one of the special forces units before a jump. To some of these youngsters war still seemed an adventure.

**Above:** Break for a smoke for the column in Mozambique.

**Right:** The man responsible for the destiny of Rhodesia at the most crucial time in its history, Ian Douglas Smith.

**Above:** Rhodesian army column on the main road between Beit Bridge and Fort Victoria. All civilian vehicles travelled under this kind of protection.

**Below:** An historic picture from the early days of the war, when dogs were used in pursuit operations in the Zambezi Valley.

**Right:** The Rhodesian government printed thousands of posters offering rewards for information leading to the capture of insurgents or their weapons. This programme had a good deal of success and obviously caused damage to the ZANU and ZAPU movements.

# REWARDS

You are reminded that large rewards continue to be paid to those persons who give information leading ctly to the death or capture of terrorists and their weapons.

Do not be afraid to report all you know about the whereabouts of terrorists and their weapons because identity will be kept secret and the reward you earn will be paid to you privately. You can choose to be in cash or the money can be put into a Post Office or Building Society savings account in your name.

Look at the amounts shown against the terrorists and their weapons in the photograph below.

KET
CHER
00

SENIOR
TERRORIST LEADER
$ 5000

TERRORIST
$ 1000

TERRORIST
GROUP LEAD
$ 2500

TERRORIST
MACHINE GUN
$ 500

LAND MINES
$ 1000 EACH

PERSON
EAON
$ 300

Other terrorist weapons not shown in the photograph above also qualify for the payment of a reward. e amounts vary according to the type of weapon and the quantity thereof.

## REPORT QUICKLY!

**Above left:** Unita men inspect a PT-76 amphibious tank captured in one of the battles during the Cuito Cuanavale campaign.

**Left:** Captured Russian T54/55 tanks after being abandoned in battle by FAPLA soldiers in eastern Angola.

**Above:** A Unita brigade commander explains the plan before an attack on an MPLA strongpoint.

**Right:** Unita women recruits being drilled in the early days of the civil war. Since then, Savimbi's forces have been driven out of Huambo (Nova Lisboã) but many clandestine attacks have been made on it, the second biggest town in Angola.

**Below right:** Members of a Rhodesian Special Forces unit deep inside Mozambique prepare defences after having taken one of the main bridges on the Umtali-Maputo rail link.

**Above:** Members of a Unita patrol prepare to set plastic explosives on a railway bridge near Huambo. Most of the bridges on the Benguela line have been destroyed, and it will take at least ten years to get the system operational again.

**Below:** Members of Unita inspect an unexploded Russian bomb dropped in eastern Angola.

**Above:** A comrade helps a wounded Unita man after a series of battles round Mavinga in Angola.

**Below:** Unconventional, but effective, transport brings a group of Unita men to a position in eastern Angola.

**Above:** Lieutenant-Colonel Dave Parker, commanding officer of the Rhodesian Light Infantry, confers with the airwing section at Mount Darwin, while a SAAF pilot looks on. Colonel Parker was killed in an accident not long after this photograph was taken.

**Left:** The business end of a light machine-gun manned by a Rhodesian soldier during the war.

**Right:** Three dead Rhodesian insurgents are lined up for villagers to identify. The posters indicate the "crimes" that they were alleged to have been guilty of.

**Above:** A primitive but effective Russian mine-layer captured by South African forces during cross-border operations. These vehicles lay the TM-56 anti-tank mine.

**Below:** Mirage aircraft with long-range tanks being prepared for strikes into Angola at the air force base of Ondangwa, in Ovamboland.

from the Secretary of State, Henry Kissinger. The South Africans cut their losses and withdrew to South West Africa. In Soweto the word went round that "the Boers" had suffered a severe defeat.

The end of Rhodesia came five years later. The urban disturbances and dislocation of the 1984–86 riots need no amplification. All these events are linked; and when South West Africa becomes independent in the not too distant future, more trouble will break out in the South African townships and, perhaps, in the white suburbs this time.

That is a classic example of the Domino Principle. Angola was used as a springboard for hostilities against South West Africa, just as Rhodesia was attacked by an independent Mozambique under the radical Frelimo government of Samora Machel.

Some people question this theory. They argue that if the Domino Principle is valid, then something similar should have happened after the Saigon government had surrendered to the Hanoi tanks in 1975. They point to the Thai government, still as staunchly pro-Western and as intact as ever. And so are the Philippines, although Manila is becoming increasingly embroiled in an incessant communist-backed guerrilla war. Neither of these states near the eye of the Vietnamese storm have been affected by the Domino Principle.

But what of Laos? What of Kampuchea, or Cambodia as some of us still prefer to call it. It was, after all, the insane mass-murderer Pol Pot who renamed it. Both were overthrown. In Cambodia the world witnessed genocide on a scale not seen since the end of the second world war; several million Cambodians were slaughtered by the local equivalents of the Chinese Red Guards run amok. A clique of radicals who wished to destroy all evidence of twentieth-century progress, culture or enlightenment. Unfortunately, they also eradicated much of their own history by burning every book they could lay their hands on. It is a pity that as much attention was not focused on Cambodia then as Israel is getting now with the *Intifada* uprising; or South Africa when its blacks were setting each other on fire with "necklaces" and fire bombs.

Portugal, at least, was spared much of the bias so evident in the Middle East and southern Africa now. Few journalists were allowed into the African territories to report on conditions there. Thus, by comparison, the world outside knew little of what was going on in Angola, Portuguese Guinea or Mozambique at a time when Vietnam was the biggest story of the decade. It is no coincidence, perhaps, that both Vietnam and the conflict in the Portuguese African dominions extended over roughly the same time-span.

The significance of events in Portuguese Africa was also overshadowed by the Watergate scandal, monetary instability everywhere, the rise in the price of oil, accelerating inflation and continued tension in the Middle East. In some cases, the collapse of Portuguese authority in such outposts as Lourenço Marques, Bissau, Luanda and São Tomé hardly merited comment.

In South Africa this lack of interest in a war taking place on its own doorstep was unforgivable.

There was of course some interest. But most people were unaware of the protracted guerrilla campaigns being fought in Tete, Eastern Angola and Zambezi Province; all these regions, incidentally, nearer to Johannesburg than Cape Town.

The first book to appear on the war in Angola, where conflict was at its fiercest, was published in South Africa by a *British* company, Purnell in 1969;[1] eight years after it all began with a series of attacks when insurgents pushed southwards out of the Congo (now Zaïre) into northern Angola between 15 and 17 March

1961. When I visited the country for the second time in 1968, it was said that 17 000 Portuguese whites (the real figure is probably nearer 500) and between 20 000 and 30 000 black Angolans had been killed; most of them in the first three days of the fighting, which was to continue for almost 15 years. And yet most South Africans still regarded Angola as a holiday resort.

One has a sense of *déjà vu* when reading the blurb on the dust jacket. I quote, because what I wrote in 1968 raised a titter among clever South Africans; and South African politicians were no less guilty at the time than South African journalists and academics:

"The guerrilla war in Angola is not an isolated example of insurgency warfare in Africa. Similar wars are being fought in Guinea on the west coast of Africa and Mozambique to the east. The Rhodesians and South Africans, of late, have also experienced the first thrust of a well-trained, well-armed guerrilla force which is using every trick in the book of unconventional warfare to secure an advantage.

"The war in Angola is a harsh campaign. Black guerrillas dictate the way it is fought... They only engage in battle when they are confident that they have a material advantage. It is for this reason that a Portuguese army of almost 60 000 men is tied down to counter a guerrilla threat of barely a sixth of that number.

"But tactics and statistics apart, the Angolan war is also significant historically. It is not generally realised that on its outcome – one way or the other – may depend the future of the whole southern African subcontinent."

In my prologue I added a note to say that the book "is a chronicle of... what may be expected in other southern African countries in the foreseeable future." That was twenty years ago.

The question remains: why, then, did the Portuguese lose their wars in Africa? They had been established on the continent for five centuries. There had been numerous attempts at revolts, especially in Angola, and all had failed. Of all the European colonial powers, the Portuguese had proved the most durable; there was little overt racism in any of the territories, and certainly there was no apartheid. Angola at that time was regarded in Western capitals as the future Brazil of Africa. Even Mozambique, closely linked economically and in some respects emotionally with South Africa, appeared impervious to change. Then came the revolutionary Sixties.

One man was responsible for much of the change to come. His name was Julius Nyerere; Prime Minister of the independent British colony of Tanganyika and later President of the Republic of Tanzania.

Nyerere was one of four African heads of state with strong links with the radical British left, especially the London School of Economics. The others were the *Osagyefo* Kwame Nkrumah of Ghana, Milton Obote of Uganda, and the only African head of state still in power, Kenneth Kaunda of Zambia. It is significant that all four leaders chose the Socialist path; the economies of all four countries are now in ruins.

Ideologies apart, Nyerere embraced every revolutionary who came his way after independence in 1961. Within a year "freedom" movements from Angola, Mozambique, South and South West Africa, Rhodesia, and even a few countries not yet independent, such as Nyasaland and Kenya, had set up offices along Liberation Row in Dar es Salaam. The town had become the hub of the new African revolution.

Even in those days Nyerere was astute enough to realise that as a consequence of such actions, hostile nations to the south might be tempted to infiltrate the government offices or try to "destabilise" the nation. Therefore security in Tanzania was stringent. I went into Dar es Salaam several times during the Sixties and was always aware that my movements were closely watched. It was often nerve-racking. One British journalist with South African connections took a photograph near a bridge on the Rufiji river south of Dar es Salaam. He was seen by one of the local commissars, arrested and brought to trial on charges of espionage for a foreign power. He served the seven years of his sentence under the most abominable conditions in a gaol in Dar es Salaam.

I usually stayed in the Kilimanjaro Hotel, and my baggage was regularly searched. Although the *lingua franca* is Swahili, most people in authority spoke English, which made it doubly difficult for the Portuguese to maintain effective intelligence once Nyerere had opened up the war in northern Mozambique across the Ruvuma river.

Let us give Nyerere his due. Regardless of his public rantings or private conversations with visiting politicians or journalists – and Nyerere was most charming and erudite in conversation – he was an early champion of the principle of Africa for the Africans. He wanted white rule in Africa destroyed, and he constructed his entire political and economic system to that end, first by supporting Frelimo in their war against the Portuguese in Mozambique and then Swapo in South West Africa.

Later this principle was extended to include Rhodesia and Angola, and even now radical South African movements have offices in Dar es Salaam. Much of the war materials used by Swapo in South West Africa were first channelled through Dar es Salaam, at least until Angola won its independence.

Although the distance between Pretoria and Dar es Salaam is greater than between London and Athens, Tanzania still sticks resolutely to the term "Frontline State", even though the Portuguese left Africa 15 years ago. As with so much of Africa, it is rhetoric that makes political points in the end.

In retrospect, the Tanzanian irritant was a trifle compared with other problems that Portugal encountered during its African military campaigns.[2]

There is little doubt that the three wars generated strong anti-colonial hostility in Portugal and elsewhere, especially among the European NATO allies of Portugal. Portugal said much about its historic and civilizing mission in Africa, but that was dismissed as the cynical propaganda of a tottering dictatorship.

As the historian and political commentator Kenneth Maxwell writes:

"Portugal was the last European power in Africa to cling tenaciously to the panoply of formal dominion and this was no accident. For a long time Portugal very successfully disguised the nature of her presence behind a skilful amalgam of historical mythmaking, claims of multiracialism, and good public relations. The reality was something different ... Economic weakness at home made intransigence in Africa inevitable. It was precisely through the exercise of sovereignty that Portugal was able to obtain any advantages at all from its civilizing mission. And these advantages were very considerable: cheap raw materials, large earnings from invisibles, the transfer of export earnings, gold and diamonds, and protected markets for her wines and cotton textiles."

Vietnam meanwhile had provided Europe and America with a huge anti-war lobby which, when circumstances permitted, was conveniently switched to focus attention on what was going on in Africa, not only the Portuguese war effort but also in Rhodesia and, more recently, South Africa.

The Sixties were the great years of Liberty, Equality and Fraternity; and in the eyes of the libertarians Portugal was badly out of step.

The attitude was also adopted by the educated classes in Portugal itself. While popular stereotypes had depicted Portugal as a stagnant backwater for almost three centuries, students, professional people, academics, the military, government officials and politicians in this nation of ten million people became increasingly sensitive to the opprobrium resulting from the reactionary policies of the Prime Minister, Antonio Salazar, who suffered a stroke in 1968. Optimists on both sides of the Atlantic had hoped that under Caetano the country would enter a more liberal phase. It was not to be. Some faces changed, but politics in general did not.

The Brazilian political commentator Marcio Alves wrote:

"To hold on to the Empire was fundamental for Portuguese fascism. Economically, the African territories – and especially rich Angola – were so important to Portuguese capitalism that Caetano took over from Salazar on the condition that they would be defended."

Part of the trouble was that in the Portuguese African possessions no political solution to the problem was either found or even sought. These people had 500 years of fairly successful African rule behind them, and things continued very much as they had in the past. That rule was not only brutal but also repressive and exploitative. Forced labour was still exacted.

The Portuguese secret police, (PIDE) – later replaced by the DGS, *Direção-Geral de Segurança* – was almost a government in itself. Its methods were most brutal, and in some respects could compare with those of the Nazi SS or Sawak in Iran. Matters were exacerbated during later stages of the African conflict by an almost total break in communications in some areas between the security police and the Portuguese defence forces. There were several cases in Tete and Nampula where liberal Portuguese officers informed Frelimo sympathisers of future movements by PIDE in the interior. They knew that such information would be passed on to the revolutionaries and made use of.

As a result of all these factors, there was little development of any real value in either Mozambique or Angola until the last stages of the war. In Portuguese Guinea no real advance was possible because of the forbidding nature of the mostly swamp terrain. There was also little development, economic or otherwise, in Portugal itself, with the result that it was the second poorest country in Europe after Albania.

A great deal of money was spent on the African war effort. At one point, the government in Lisbon voted 45 per cent of the entire budget to the military which is roughly what Israel spends on defence now, but then Lisbon did not have Uncle Sam meeting much of the bill. Yet there are some who maintain that although Portugal was poor when the war ended, and it was not economic policies that caused the collapse of its authority in Africa; it was just as poor when it all began. They say that as a politician Salazar was a disaster. But he had been trained as an economist, and in that he excelled; he treated the coffers of the nation as his own, and in so doing acted like a miser.

David Abshire and Michael Samuels in their book *Portuguese Africa - A Handbook* (Pall Mall Press, London, 1969) say that during the wars, the Portuguese were able to maintain their gold and foreign reserves at a fixed ratio of between 56 and 57 per cent of sight responsibilities. In spite of increased expenditure on defence and the need for external public borrowing, Salazar actually managed to increase Portuguese reserves of gold and foreign exchange during the war years. Herein lies an example for South Africa, labouring under similar pressures.

As a general policy, the Portuguese authorities attempted to stimulate economic activity not by monetary manipulation, but rather to adjust the volume of money to the level of economic activity. Despite three African wars, gold and foreign exchange reserves throughout this period exceeded a year's imports. They were actually larger than the reserves of Western countries of comparable size.

But it was politics that ultimately dealt the death blow to any aspirations that the Portuguese might have had of holding on to their African possessions.

There was little imagination among the ageing leaders to inspire them to improve the political situation either at home or abroad, or to strengthen the military situation. If ever there was an example of political leadership having atrophied while in power, Portugal provides it. Salazar had been in power since 1933. When Caetano succeeded in 1968, the same people who supported Salazar ended up in the Caetano cabinet. There was therefore no change in form or content.

Of course, Africa was prominent in the minds of both Salazar and Caetano; and, curiously, South Africa became the focus of attention on several occasions. Salazar, it was disclosed after he had died, was obsessed with the idea of a Mozambique UDI, much as Rhodesia had declared its independence in 1964. This obsession later became almost a mania; Salazar believed that there were people in Mozambique plotting with the South Africans to overthrow the government in Lourenço Marques.

Matters were not helped by the many South Africans who wished to invest in the Mozambican economy. Although it was permitted at first on a small scale, it was only in 1966 that any considerable foreign investment was allowed into Angola and Mozambique. But by then it was too late. Because of his UDI fears, Salazar permitted little economic development in the Portuguese possessions.

Angola was the one region where the possibilities of independence from Portugal had been mooted for decades. Had the war not arrived, there is little doubt that Angola would have followed Rhodesia into UDI. Douglas Porch, in his book *The Portuguese Armed Forces and the Revolution* (Croom Helm, London, 1977) mentions an air force colonel in Angola who said:

"In 1965, most of us already thought that Angola should become an independent and racially mixed country like Brazil. We saw that we could not win in the colonies. It was impossible to continue. Freedom had to come gradually because the people were not prepared for it. The military would be very useful in preparing the political solution. It was a task which we could not do in two months, but in six or seven years. We had to prepare the government and the local governments. The army had to maintain independence, build up the armed forces and so on."

Compared with other colonial interests in Africa, such as the British, French or Belgian, Portugal was further inhibited by the fact that it had no choice but to continue as before in its African possessions. If a neo-colonial option had been possible, such as was adopted by Britain and France after giving independence to their African colonies - but at the same time maintaining strong economic links with them - no doubt Portugal would also have adopted it.

But Portugal was poor. It is still poor by European standards. It would not have been able to retain any real economic ties with either Angola or Mozambique if it granted them independence earlier. Both countries are now far less dependent on the former metropolis than say, Kenya or Zambia or Sierra Leone - or even Nigeria - are on Britain; or the Ivory Coast, Morocco, Cameroun or Chad are on France.

The real downfall of Portuguese interests in Africa ultimately lay with the armed forces.

There was great dissatisfaction among members of the Portuguese armed forces over service in Africa. A two–year period of service in Africa was usually followed by six months at home and then another two years' service in Africa. That practice had a serious effect on morale in the war zones; there was also bad feeling between regular soldiers and conscripts, particularly within the junior and middle ranks of officers. The MFA or Armed Forces Movement which eventually organised the coup d'état of April 1974 recognised that no political development was taking place either in the defence forces of Portugal or in the African territories. General de Spinola actually said so in his book *Portugal and the Future.* But more of that later.

Significantly, some Portuguese officers (as with some South Africans of similar persuasion) tended to equate their military efforts in Africa with the French in Algeria. Porch draws the analogy by stating that in Portugal, as in France, the circumstances for the military coup were provided by a long and exhausting colonial war. The differences were crucial, however, for French soldiers felt that they were within spitting distance of victory and reacted against what they believed to be governmental betrayal. Portuguese officers were locked in a pointless struggle to maintain a burdensome empire. Portugal's colonial wars sapped the country's strength, made her appear ridiculous in the eyes of the world and ruined the army by flooding it with half–trained conscripts whom the government attempted to promote over the heads of long–serving regulars. The latent resentment which gradually built up to boiling point in the officer corps was a combination of bruised national pride and wounded professional vanity, an explosive mixture of sentiments which the Portuguese military establishment shared with revolutionary soldiers in Egypt and other Third World countries. The Portuguese experience proves that the increasing professionalism of the armed forces can hasten its entry into the political arena rather than discourage it, as American historian Samuel Huntington has argued. Professional discontent creates shop floor militancy and the coup substitutes for the strike.

In retrospect, it is astonishing that Portugal never considered transferring families to the African colonies for these extended periods of anything up to five years. Their principal argument against such a step was the UDI bogey; it was feared that too many metropolitan Portuguese would be sent to the African colonies and then begin to think for themselves.

Occasionally one found a member of a family, usually that of an officer, comfortably off and able to afford such a luxury, in one of the African capitals. While I was covering the war in Portuguese Guinea in 1971, the beautiful new wife of a young *Alfares* shared our table when her husband was in the bush. She had stayed on at the hotel for almost a year and was not dismayed by the prospect of a second year in such a dreadful tropical backwater as Bissau. Unlike Luanda or Lourenço Marques, it was almost totally black and, to her, quite alien.

There were none of the pavement cafés that we knew in Mozambique; no good beaches, no parks. Only the jungle and the war. The hotel, the Grande, was a grim, rambling, stuccoed doss–house that was older than the century. The age of air–conditioning had yet to arrive; only the bar showed any animation; it was raucous by midday.

Then there was the question of money. As any soldier will tell you, he can do without women, but not his beer. The Portuguese army drank *vinho,* and when they could afford it, *aguardente.*

Four or five years in Africa was not eased by the fact that a Portuguese soldier's pay was derisory. A brigadier serving in Africa in 1971 got about US$250 a month. A private got perhaps US$40 and perks were few. Home leave outside the period of service was almost unheard of; and anyway, who could afford a ticket? Even if he travelled steerage on one of the many Portuguese liners serving the African colonies, time was against him, as they stopped everywhere on the outward and homeward runs.

The pay structure was pitiful, almost Third World by comparison. No doubt this factor ultimately played a role in switching the allegiance of the armed forces.

Pay Scales – January 1974 (Exchange rate about R1 = 40$00.)

| | |
|---|---|
| General (4–Stars) and Admiral | 18,900$00 Escudos |
| General and Vice Admiral | 17,200$00 |
| Brigadier and Rear Admiral | 15,500$00 |
| Colonel and Navy Captain | 13,900$00 |
| Lt–Col. and Commander | 12,300$00 |
| Major and Lt–Commander | 11,400$00 |
| Captain and Navy Lieutenant | 10,400$00 |
| Army Lieutenant and Navy Lt.j.g. | 7,300$00 |
| Lieutenants and Guardo–Marinha | 6,000$00 |
| 2nd Lieutenant or Navy Ens | 4,700$00 |
| Sergeant–Major (adjutant) | 5,700$00 |
| First Sergeant | 5,400$00 |
| Second Sergeant | 5,000$00 |
| Sub–Sergeant | 4,700$00 |
| Corporal | 4,700$00 |
| First Corporal | 3,400$00 |
| Second Corporal | 3,300$00 |

By way of comparison, Porch observes that not long after the war started a colonel of an infantry regiment stationed in Portugal earned 10,200 escudos a month. A British Colonel earned fractionally less than double that figure, while a French Colonel earned about 5 or 6 per cent less than his British counterpart.

Physical conditions were also bad. Military camps at such remote corners of the empire as N'Riquinha, Nambuangongo and Cabinda in Angola, and Zumbo, Tete, Zobue and Guro in Mozambique, or any one of the postings in Portuguese Guinea were usually barbarous and unhealthy. In some places the tribesmen lived under better conditions than their "protectors".

Sanitary conditions were often shocking, at least to those accustomed to South African standards.

Malaria was not the danger that it is now, but it took its toll in spite of quinine. Many soldiers went down with hepatitis, mainly because of poor hygiene in the kitchens and latrines. This was, after all, Africa, and flies were always a pest, but no one seemed to care. In some places there were inadequate supplies of fresh water.

During a visit to the military hospital at Tete in February 1973, we found one young soldier alone in a ward with terrible leg and abdominal wounds caused by a mine. The stench in the ward was inconceivable; it hit us in the face like a foul wet rag when we entered the building.

The boy was obviously in terrible pain and distress; even to this inexperienced observer it was obvious that gangrene had set in. I was with a group of South Africans at the time, some of them nurses, and we said so to the Portuguese doctor who accompanied us. He dismissed the suggestion. On pulling back the bedclothes, we could see that part of the boy's upper thigh that had not been wrapped in bandages had turned an evil shade of green.

I resolved then never to get wounded in that war. It would have been a better fate for him to have got a bullet between the eyes than to suffer the inevitable lingering death that he was condemned to. Of course, other Portuguese soldiers could see this dreadful spectacle; and it must have had a very damaging effect on morale.

Portuguese Guinea was the main cause of the decay that set in among the Portuguese armed forces. By 1972 it had become apparent to even the most sanguine supporter of Portuguese rule in Africa that the war in this pestilential jungle and swamp on the west coast of Africa between Guinea and Senegal could not be won.

There were several reasons. The terrain made any proper military operations not only ineffectual but often impossible. The navy was as much involved as the army, and both forces had different ideas about fighting a hidden, well-armed and aggressive enemy.

Moreover, unlike Angola and Mozambique, the country was almost totally undeveloped; there were no industries, hardly any exports. The first question that most conscripts asked on arriving in Portuguese Guinea was: "Why are we here?" The country had none of the towns, industries, diamonds, coffee or hardwoods of Angola; or any of the pleasant amenities of Mozambique. By 1961 the African colonies had actually begun to make a small profit for the metropolis; not Portuguese Guinea.

Furthermore, the country was tiny, only a little bigger than Lesotho, and its borders were therefore constricting. Portuguese garrisons were regularly, sometimes devastatingly, shelled or rocketed from neighbouring territories. And while lack of space and ability to manoeuvre should work against the guerrilla fighter, it also worked against the Portuguese armed forces.

There was yet another insoluble problem. It would have been easy for the Portuguese to withdraw from Guinea; but it would have been impossible without abandoning the other two; the Domino Principle would have taken effect at once.

The most active Portuguese command constantly advocated cross-border raids to prevent attacks by insurgents who found safe havens in neighbouring territories; they were always refused. As a result of being unable to take effective retaliatory action, largely from fear of foreign disapproval, neighbouring states continued to provide support and succour to a variety of insurgent movements in the Congo (later Zaïre), Zambia, Tanzania, Senegal, Guinea (Conakry) and Malawi.

What Portugal feared was further isolation if it were to strike back. Criticism from abroad had begun to hurt.[3]

On a more fundamental level, looking back at a succession of Portuguese African wars that lasted thirteen years, none of the six counter-insurgency principles expounded by the American guru of guerrilla warfare in the West, John McCuen, were followed by the high command. Although there were often subtle variations on these same themes, they are worth examining, especially since South Africa now finds itself in almost the same position as Portugal did twenty years ago.

**1. Self-preservation and extermination of the enemy:** The Portuguese authorities were unable to preserve their own society because the people and the armed forces eventually turned on them. That was a *political* reaction. Nor were they able to protect their *physical* entities because once Goa had been invaded by India, the principle of survival had been eroded. The Goan fissure caused the whole empire to crumble.

The Portuguese army could not annihilate the enemy because they could not hit at them, at source, in their bases. They might have done better if they had followed the example of the Americans (in Vietnam), the Israelis (Middle East and Maghreb) and the South Africans (Angola, Mozambique, Zambia and Zimbabwe) of hot pursuit to dissuade supporting nations from helping insurgent movements. Israel and South Africa have been particularly successful in this method because their policy has been "no holds barred".

**2. Establishment of strategic base areas:** The Portuguese were able to apply this principle in Angola by creating a three-tier "area of regional priority" grid. In so doing, they were able to keep the revolutionary movements out of Portuguese "vital" base areas. These included areas round Luanda, the capital, and the oil-producing regions of Cabinda. They were not so successful in Mozambique and not at all in Guinea.

Although the war in Mozambique was restricted to the north, guerrilla activity was still capable of restricting movement and economic activity in some vital areas; notably in the rich farming regions on the Beira–Umtali axis, along the Zambezi, and the semi–tropical north.

In Portuguese Guinea, the insurgents at the end virtually had the run of the country.

**3. Mobilising the masses:** Portugal was unable to mobilise its own masses, either at home or in Africa, largely because there was no political vision of the future and, even more important, no hope for the ordinary man.

**4. Maintaining external support:** While the Portuguese swam against the anti-colonial tide, they were able to maintain most of their ties with their friends and allies. They stayed in NATO despite strong protests from some nations, particularly the Dutch. They stayed on friendly terms with their oldest ally, Britain; they also used the strategic value of the Azores Islands as a lever against any adverse steps that the Americans might take, and made capital of the long-term strategic value of Angola to the West. Strategic associations with South Africa and Rhodesia, largely the result of necessity rather than of choice, were also of some importance.

But what the Portuguese were able to achieve abroad was largely neutralised by their inability to find an acceptable African solution to their problems, at a time when much of Africa had been granted independence by its former European masters.

**5. Unity of effort:** This principle, if not entirely ignored, was usually applied in a half-hearted manner. The political and military establishment was not effective either in command or in the execution of commands. There were serious differences between senior commanders on the one hand and Governors-General in the "Overseas Provinces" on the other. The problems were still further compounded by the machinations of various ministries at home who had their own ideas about how affairs should be conducted. There were also differences between regional governors about fundamentals and, most important of all, between the various arms of the security forces. This became worse as the army was gradually vitiated by radicals: the *Militianos*.

**6. Channelling:** The Portuguese supreme command was unable to minimise its war effort. They were fighting wars in three different regions, each of which contained seven or eight distinct operational areas; all of this over huge distances.[4]

Nor could they separate the war in Guinea from the others. There was intense rivalry between the arms, with much evidence of "empire-building" by some officers. We have the same situation developing within the South African Defence Force and other security services in this country.

Finally, the structure of the Portuguese armed forces was ill-designed.

The staff corps was an anachronism. Brigadiers were two-a-penny; there were more generals and admirals in the Portuguese army and navy than in any other comparable defence force. Few of them had ever heard a shot fired in anger. Few had exercised active command while they were still captains or majors, in Africa or anywhere else, with the result that they never learnt to understand some of the crucial problems at middle-command level.

Curiously, and in spite of all this, the Portuguese defence establishment had evolved an excellent counter-insurgency doctrine.

This was begun in 1962, soon after the first outbreaks of violence in Angola; it eventually comprised four huge volumes drawing on the experiences of every modern conflict: the Americans and French in Vietnam, Britain in Malaya, Borneo, Cyprus and Aden, France in Algeria, and such obscure conflicts as that of the "Huk" uprising in the Philippines; and many others.

The entire principle was brilliantly applied by the staff corps; but they lacked the attitudes and planning experience of officers who had seen active service.

Thus, while the planning was thorough and technically competent, the execution was inferior. On more than one occasion I heard South African officers who had come into contact with the Portuguese forces discussing the excellent theory, and how some very well constructed operational plans had fallen flat because the work on the ground was so poor.

Yet, by comparison with other African colonial wars, Portugal did not suffer severe casualties during the thirteen-year campaign in Guinea, Angola and Mozambique. Official figures from the book *Africa: A Vitoria Traida*, published in Lisbon by Intervenção soon after the coup, show that from May 1963 to May 1974 Portugal lost altogether 3 265 men killed in action in all three theatres of war. This bears little resemblance to the 2 000 men *a year* that France lost in Algeria over seven years; or less than a thousand South Africans killed in over twenty years of fighting on the Angolan border.

In the Portuguese territories another 3 075 men died from other causes; mostly disease and accidents, mainly on the roads. The number of deaths on the roads is not at all surprising, since the crazy driving of the Portuguese seemed to indicate some kind of death wish. We were far more likely to die in some traffic disaster than from enemy action.

The Portuguese have a name for this special kind of madness. *Loucara* they call it; a fatalism or super optimism that was also reflected in the way they fought their wars. There was none of the regimentation or militarism of the Germanic races, but some Portuguese soldiers were often unusually brave.

These figures are based on those provided by official Portuguese sources:

**TABLE 1**

**Casualties — Portuguese Armed Forces in Africa — Averages**

| Description | During the war in respective Theatres of Operations (a) | | | During the war in the 3 Theatres of Operations | | |
|---|---|---|---|---|---|---|
| | Guinea | Angola | Mozam-bique | Total | Average per day | Average per day per thousand |
| | (1) | (2) | (3) | (4) | (5) (b) | (6) (c) |
| Killed in action | 1 084 | 1 142 | 1 039 | 3 265 | 0,80 | 0,0075 (d) |
| Died from other causes | 791 | 1 529 | 755 | 3 075 | 0,76 | 0,0070 |
| Total dead (1 + 2) | 1 875 | 2 671 | 1 794 | 6 340 | 1,55 | 0,014 |
| Wounded in action | 6 161 | 4 472 | 2 245 | 12 878 | 3,16 | 0,030 (d) |
| Accident casualties | 2 167 | 6 595 | 6 279 | 15 041 | 3,69 | 0,034 |
| Total (4 + 5) | 8 328 | 11 067 | 8 524 | 27 919 | 6,86 | 0,064 |
| Disabled (e) | — | — | — | 3 835 | 0,94 | 0,0088 |

(a) The following figures were listed in Guinea from 1 May 1963; Angola from 1 May 1961; Mozambique from 1 November 1964, and in the three theatres of operations up to 1 May 1974.
(b) In the case of Guinea, 4 016 days were used as a basis for calculation; 4 746 in Angola and 3 647 in Mozambique, giving an average of 4 076.
(c) From 1961 to 1973, the total number of troops in the three theatres of operations reached 1 392 230, which corresponds to an annual average of 107 095. The indices for this annual average and for the average duration of the war were calculated on 4 076 days.
(d) According to the *Field Manual* 101-10-1 (1972) of the United States Army, and based on relevant figures of the second world war in Europe, the indices correspond to a theatre of operations in classical, non-nuclear warfare.

   If these figures are applied to the total number of troops deployed throughout the duration of the war in the Portuguese overseas territories on a daily basis, it would be equal to 61 112 killed in battle, 240 083 wounded in battle and 707 154 casualties through accidents and sickness. The second world war lasted seven years; the Portuguese wars lasted 13 years in all.
(e) The number of medically processed Army cases of combat and service accidents up to 31 July 1974. Figures relating to the navy and the air force were unobtainable.

Porch says that there were also probably about 80 000 civilian casualties and between 100 000 and 150 000 guerrilla casualties in all three colonies together. Certainly the strain on Portuguese manpower was such as to cause the age of conscription to be lowered to 18 in 1967 and the term of conscript service to be extended from two to four years by the addition of two years' compulsory service overseas. However, not all those called up actually served. As opposition to the wars grew in Portugal itself, so avoidance of the call–up increased. It is estimated that 110 000 Portuguese failed to report for military service between 1961 and 1974, either through deliberate avoidance or absence abroad, since over a million Portuguese were emigrant workers by 1974. In the last call–up before the coup of April 1974, less than half appeared.

As the defence establishment grew, the universities were called upon to provide many of the junior officers needed to fight the wars in Africa. Most of these were enlightened people; they had seen the dictatorship in Lisbon at first hand and they knew what it had done and was still doing to Portugal.

Few were under any illusions that they were fighting "a just war" as the Americans like to phrase it. Nor were they welcomed by the regular officers of the army and air force; men who had spent years in uniform struggling up the slow ladder of promotion. And in the Portuguese army it was *very* slow. A man rarely reached the rank of Colonel before he was fifty. These men resented the newly commissioned lieutenants and captains who, as it seemed to them, had usurped their positions. There was much dissension and distrust between the two groups.

Ultimately, it was these liberal officers and their undermining of the Portuguese war effort both at home and abroad that led to the formation of the Armed Forces Movement and the coup d'état of 25 April 1974.

Within a year Portugal was out of Africa.

### Portuguese Guinea

The war in Portuguese Guinea was like none of the other colonial wars in Africa during the Fifties, Sixties and Seventies. It was the only conflict that a European colonial power in recent times actually lost in the field. Yet none of the towns were overrun by insurgents; the Portuguese never fled in disarray or were driven into the sea or forced to abandon strategic positions.

By the time the young officers of the Portuguese Armed Forces Movement had seized power, defeat hung heavily in the air in the streets of Bissau, Cacine and Bafata further into the interior, and the fighting cadres of the *Partido Africano de Independencia da Guinea e Cabo Verde* (PAIGC) knew it.

This conflict also bore little similarity to the British campaign against the Mau Mau in Kenya during the late Fifties; or the seven–year French campaign against the FLN in Algeria. It was also totally different from what was going on in Angola and Mozambique. This was a conflict that increased in intensity as it progressed. It began as a series of sporadic, indecisive skirmishes along the southern frontiers with the Republic of Guinea (Conakry), then the strongest ally of the Soviet Union in West Africa. Conakry, at that time, was to Moscow what the island of Diego Garcia in the Indian Ocean is now to Washington; a strategic listening post, a refuelling stop for aircraft and ships and a vital part of American interests in a sensitive part of the world.

In Portuguese Guinea — a tropical spit of land fringed with islands — the black leaders took the initiative from the start. A small group of disaffected African intellectuals, educated at Coimbra or Lisbon and then granted "most privileged" *assimilado* status, first urged the Portuguese to withdraw from Guinea in the late Fifties.

A year later the same nationalists, some of them now in self-imposed exile, were issuing decrees from Conakry in the Republic of Guinea. Portugal, they said, should get out of "our Guiné–Bissau" immediately. They demanded that Portugal should hand over the reins of nationhood to the African population of about 600 000.

The government would not hear of it. So, when these demands met with no response, the black workers were urged to civil disobedience. The Portuguese reacted vigorously. Only after some dissident Africans had been shot by Portuguese police during a violent strike for higher wages at Pidjiguiti Docks in Bissau on 3 August 1959, a date subsequently commemorated by the guerrillas, did the possibility of armed conflict seriously enter the picture for the nationalists. War broke out three years later in January 1963. It lasted 11 years.

At first a number of fragmentary nationalist organisations were formed by the young firebrands in Bissau and the few who had already sought sanctuary elsewhere. Most of this activity was, of necessity, underground. From 1956 there were several organisations launched. Only two were able to survive.

The first was Amilcar Cabral's PAIGC, which in its day was generally regarded as one of the most potent and successful black guerrilla organisations in Africa. It was also one of the most efficient organisations in its tactics and military successes. Cabral was killed by his own men in Conakry in January 1973 and replaced, first by Dr Vitorio Monteiro, a former bank clerk in Bissau, and then by Aristides Pereira.

The other rebel movement in Guinea was FLING *(Front de Lutte de l'Indépendence Nationale de Guiné)*. FLING was based in Dakar. It comprised at least four combined nationalist movements and was regarded by the Portuguese and the West as somewhat more moderate than the decidedly socialist PAIGC.

Both groups nevertheless, had a common determination that the Portuguese must go, by whatever means. Both also approved of the violence that broke out as a result of what they called Portuguese "intransigence". There was, however, some disagreement on questions of policy, including the leadership, the timing

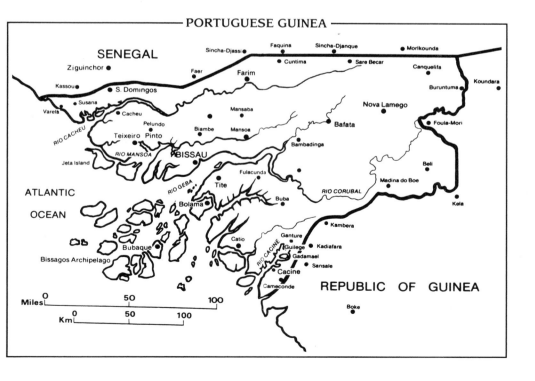

PORTUGUESE GUINEA

of the takeover and the eventual nature of the government which they proposed to set up once the imperialists had been expelled.

FLING indicated that it would not exclude the possibility of some kind of loose economic and cultural alliance or federation with Portugal, similar to that between, for example, the Ivory Coast or Cameroun and France.

PAIGC had their own views on this matter and took the Nyerere line. Africa, as Cabral and his lieutenants asserted, is black, not European. Moreover, the PAIGC was resolved on an essentially socialist type of government along Cuban or Algerian lines, with all aspects of government, including politics, economics and military affairs answerable to the Party and the Party alone. Here Cabral made it clear that he had learnt much from such men as Sékou Touré and Castro.

But despite their differences, the two organisations cooperated as long as they faced the common enemy. Apart from military activity they also launched a joint propaganda campaign, which drew attention to the monopolistic nature of commerce, trade and industry in Guiné-Bissau. Their targets were the great Portuguese cartels, the *Banco Nacional Ultramarino* and Jorge de Mello's *Companhia Uniao Frabril* (CUF).

Both these firms had vast holdings in metropolitan Portugal as well as in the overseas provinces and had an important influence on the course followed by the wars in Africa, mainly through powerful family connections at the highest levels of government in Lisbon.

Until the war began in the early Sixties, CUF ruled the economic roost in Portuguese Africa. All trade passed through the books of the company and no foreign or domestic business was tolerated unless it had first been approved by CUF. It was always conducted through company channels, with appropriate percentage rake-offs. There were many abuses, many of them at the expense of the indigenous population.

The war in Portuguese Guinea was a grim affair. Because of the small size of the country and its uniform terrain of impenetrable swamp and rain forest along the coast, where the tides sweep inland daily for nearly half the length of the country, rising slowly to the savannah plain in the interior, much of what had been learnt of modern unorthodox warfare in Angola, Malaya, Cuba, Algeria and Indo-China was put into effect by the opposing forces. In contrast to Angola and Mozambique there was little organised terror and mass slaughter. In Guinea, from the beginning the struggle was a military one in which both sides used tactical action to make gains. It was a textbook guerrilla war. It was also a testing ground, for many of the methods devised by the guerrillas in Portuguese Guinea with their foreign helpers were later used in the south. Widespread use of the anti-personnel mine was one.

Ideals had also changed radically since the early days. While the campaign was launched by the black nationalists with characteristic spoutings about "imperialism" and "exploitation of the poor by the rich colonials", and the Portuguese retaliating with equal fervour for what they succinctly called "Christ and Country", Portuguese Guinea quickly became a centre of the conflict between East and West.

The military configuration in Portuguese Guinea was one of striking contrasts.

There were the Portuguese, who had material though discreet support from much of Europe, their NATO allies, including the United States, and a variety of Western-orientated nations. On the other side PAIGC was backed by Russia,

China, Cuba, Algeria and most East European states, all channelling aid through Sékou Touré's Marxist republic. As with Angola, Mozambique and more recently Swapo, more help for the guerrillas came from the moderate liberal nations such as Sweden and Canada and various churches and philanthropic organisations in America. Such contributions were mostly fed through "neutral" Dakar.

There were racial aspects in this war from the beginning. At first it had the character of a confrontation of blacks against whites. Over the years, however, the Portuguese had reduced colour to a position of minor importance, mainly because of economic considerations, and relied increasingly on black volunteers.

The only white faces in the ranks of the guerrillas were their Cuban and Russian advisers and the rare Portuguese defector who had joined the ranks of the PAIGC. Occasionally a member of the French Left, a follower of Régis Debray or some other revolutionary would also appear. In the eyes of the Central Committee, said one neutral observer at the time, a white Portuguese would always be a white Portuguese. Nothing else.

Although the intentions of a deserter from the Portuguese army might have

**TABLE 2**

**Desertions from the Portuguese Army in the Three African Theatres (1961 to 1969)**

(Not including personnel who did not report for active service after call-up)

| | GUINEA | | | ANGOLA | | | MOZAMBIQUE | | |
|------|---------------------|------------|------|---------------------|------------|------|---------------------|------------|------|
| Year | Effective Manpower | Desertions | % | Effective Manpower | Desertions | % | Effective Manpower | Desertions | % |
| 1961 | | | | (a) 39 469 | 2 | 0,05 | | | |
| 1962 | | | | (a) 43 956 | 0 | 0 | | | |
| 1963 | (a) 12 960 | 4 | 0,31 | (a) 47 789 | 4 | 0,08 | | | |
| 1964 | 12 491 | 3 | 0,24 | 45 791 | 14 | 0,31 | 19 049 | 4 | 0,21 |
| 1965 | 19 462 | 5 | 0,26 | 61 676 | 20 | 0,32 | 26 139 | 0 | 0 |
| 1966 | 23 239 | 3 | 0,13 | 60 457 | 6 | 0,10 | 33 913 | 3 | 0,09 |
| 1967 | 24 250 | 0 | 0 | 62 013 | 3 | 0,05 | 39 728 | 0 | 0 |
| 1968 | 25 631 | 5 | 5 | 66 138 | 1 | 0,02 | 41 824 | 3 | 0,07 |
| 1969 | 28 446 | 12 | 12 | 64 596 | 8 | 0,12 | 43 604 | 3 | |
| | | 32 | | | 58 | | | 13 | |
| Total | | | | 103 (b) | | | | | |

(a) Estimated numbers.

(b) In Vietnam, according to the *US Statistical Abstract; 1975*, Department of Commerce, Figure 531, p327, the average number of desertions per thousand, between 1967 and 1974, was 23,4 with a maximum of 33,9 in 1971. *(Not including those who fled to other countries prior to call-up to avoid military service in either Portugal or the United States.)* These figures are 180 and 181 times, respectively, in excess of those experienced by Portugal during its overseas wars.

been sincere, the leaders of the PAIGC considered that he was of more value outside the fighting zone, preferably behind the Iron Curtain or under the control of the exiled, communist *Frent Patriotica de Libertação Nacional* (FPLN), with its headquarters in Algiers. A constant preoccupation with security was a trait that the PAIGC seemed to have inherited from the Portuguese.

Curiously, the desertion figures for the Portuguese army in Africa were modest. There were only 103 desertions throughout the thirteen-year period of the war in all three territories. The figures in Table 2 are from official Portuguese sources.

Porch tells us that as the war crept on more and more good officers began to slip away, usually into the metropolis. Their numbers are obviously not included in the above figures. He maintains that some were politically motivated, many more were spurred on by economic considerations. Some officers failed to return from holidays abroad. There was also the incident involving 15 engineering cadets, regarded as the cream of the Military Academy, who walked across the frontier to Spain in 1973 after completing their four-year course.

If the nature and mechanics of this war were interesting, the fortunes of the two opposing factions were even more so. Almost unknown to the rest of the world, apart from a few Africanists who made it their business to keep themselves informed of events, the battle in Portuguese Guinea raged for years without attracting much attention from abroad.

The fortunes of both sides see-sawed with the international standing of Portugal. In the early years things went badly for Lisbon until about the middle Sixties. At that time Portuguese fortunes were at their worst, when Salazar's often ill-conceived control from abroad was firmest. Only when he was replaced by the more liberal Caetano, who promised a more relaxed and open régime, did conditions improve. The ebb and flow was slight, but the advantage always seemed to be with the guerrillas.

Within a year of the first isolated FLING attacks on Susana and Verela on the north-western Senegalese border in late 1962, the Portuguese High Command was admitting that the "terrorists" controlled about 15 per cent of the country.

But the fighting in 1962 was only a foretaste of things to come, and the attacks in the north were regarded as little more than "civilian disturbances". Although war was never formally declared, the real conflict was regarded by both sides as having begun with an attack on Tite, Buba and Fulacunda in January 1963.

Tite was occupied by a battalion of two companies under the command of a major. Buba and Fulacunda were garrisoned by one company each.

Only one Portuguese soldier was wounded at Tite, although the guerrillas managed to destroy the ammunition dump. Next day they ambushed a car travelling between Tite and Fulacunda and killed all its occupants, at the same time they attacked a section of Portuguese soldiers on patrol near a village east of Tite. In this action two Portuguese soldiers were killed. From then on things became serious, both for Portugal and Cabral's band of insurgents.

Two years later Cabral was asserting that the area under his control had risen to 50 per cent. By 1971 PAIGC was able to say that all but the last 20 per cent of the country round the capital was theirs.

Cabral always maintained that the 80 per cent that he said was his, was his to control and use as he thought fit. He told me so when I met him at the meeting of the Organisation for African Unity in Addis Ababa in 1971. There, he told me, he only needed to take Bissau and he would have the entire country in his pocket. The first time he said it was in 1965. He was still saying it when he died.

The Portuguese fought the war in their own way, and it bore little resemblance to what happened in Angola during the Eighties.

The Portuguese certainly preferred the safety of their camps and fortified villages after dark. But as I observed during my visit, there were large areas where movement at night was unrestricted and free from control. I went into them myself, often uneasy, expecting the worst from what I had heard abroad; but I was soon reassured by the nonchalance of my often unarmed Portuguese hosts. It was unlikely they would tempt fate in a moment of bravado, or perhaps to give a visiting correspondent the impression that the war was not so widespread as was generally believed, but at the same time I cannot believe they would have looked for trouble just to make such a point. Certainly, there is no other army that I know of or have been with where the officers and men are not required to carry their weapons at all times when entering a "hot" area. But then the Portuguese tried to be individualists in so many different ways; they were often foolishly unconventional.

There were other places where I did not feel safe even with an escort of eighty men.

The Portuguese had complete air supremacy during daylight and they used it to full advantage. This was to change completely in the following year, when Russian SAM-7s drove the Portuguese Air Force out of the skies in Guinea and gave the insurgents a new and formidable edge. Soviet missiles first appeared in March 1973, three PAF aircraft being lost in two months. By September the PAIGC claimed to have downed 21 Portuguese war planes.

The foreign journalists who visited Portuguese Guinea included an American, Jim Hoagland of the *Washington Post,* and the West German veteran Peter Hannes Lehmann and Gerd Heidemann of *Stern.* They generally agreed with my own opinion that there were few zones actually "held" by the black guerrillas. The guerrilla bands seemed to be applying Mao Tse-tung's theories on unconventional warfare, always on the move, striking unexpectedly here and there, but making few solid gains with the intention of holding an area in the face of counter-attacks. When, in 1971, the rebels announced that their forces had entered the third, or "mobile warfare" stage, which is the equivalent of full confrontation, the statement was contradicted by the facts.

Basil Davidson's observations in 1967 agreed with those of the PAIGC, but then Davidson did not even concede that the Portuguese could fight. It matters little how well they fought; they were at war in three separate zones for 13 years and lost thousands of men on a defence budget in all three conflicts of less than US$450 million a year. They fared badly in Guinea and Mozambique, but the war was won in Angola. The table on the next page speaks for itself.

By the time I arrived in the country in 1971 things had changed for the better from the heady days of 1967, when General Arnaldo Schulz held precarious command over the rapidly falling fortunes of Portugal in this war.

Then a new man took command, General Antonio de Spinola. Like his predecessor, he distinguished himself in Angola. Although Spinola had shocked the established order, he was, like General Bettencourt Rodrigues in eastern Angola, getting results in this hard and still undecided war until the time when the air force lost the initiative.

One of the conditions imposed by Spinola on being offered the command in Guinea was that he should have total control of the country without any

**TABLE 3**

### Killed in combat, per year, in the Three Theatres of Operations

| Description | 1961 | 1962 | 1963 | 1964 | 1965 | 1966 | 1967 | 1968 | 1969 | 1970 | 1971 | 1972 | 1973 |
|---|---|---|---|---|---|---|---|---|---|---|---|---|---|
| GUINEA | | | | | | | | | | | (a) | | |
| Operational deaths | | | 36 | 77 | 81 | 118 | 136 | 109 | 112 | | 263 | | 106 |
| | | | (b) | | | | | | | | (a) | | |
| Deaths per thousand | | | 278 | 6,16 | 4,16 | 5,08 | 5,61 | 4,25 | 3,94 | | 3,33 | | 3,64 |
| ANGOLA | | | | | | | | | | (a) | | | |
| Operational deaths | 134 | 113 | 83 | 101 | 27 | 90 | 88 | 115 | 76 | 123 | | 62 | 41 |
| | (b) | (b) | (b) | | | | | | | (a) | | | |
| Deaths per thousand | 3,39 | 2,62 | 1,74 | 2,21 | 1,41 | 1,49 | 1,42 | 1,74 | 1,18 | 1,08 | | 0,95 | 0,64 |
| MOZAMBIQUE | | | | (c) | | | | | | (a) | | | |
| Operational deaths | | | | 2 | 73 | 108 | 93 | 91 | 126 | 257 | | 131 | 123 |
| | | | | (c) | | | | | | | | | |
| Deaths per thousand | | | | 10 | 2,79 | 3,18 | 2,34 | 2,18 | 2,29 | 2,88 | | 2,72 | 2,27 |
| THE 3 THEATRES | | | | | | | | | | | | | |
| OPERATIONS | | | | | | | | | | (a) | | | |
| Operational deaths | | | | 180 | 241 | 316 | 317 | 315 | 314 | | 836 | | 270 |
| | | | | | | (d) | | | | | (a) | | |
| Deaths per thousand | | | | 2,32 | 2,24 | 2,69 | 2,52 | 2,36 | 2,30 | | 2,08 | | 1,83 |
| Deaths per | | | | | | | | | | (d) | | | |
| thousand/average | | | | | | | | | | 2,23 | | | |

(a) It was only possible to obtain the absolute figure for the period and the average for the corresponding year.

(b) Figures obtained on the basis of the estimated number of troops deployed.

(c) Figures relevant only to the period of November and December 1964.

(d) In Vietnam, for the US Armed Forces, from 1964 to 1972, the annual average was 14,7 per thousand and the maximum reached in 1968 was 23,5 per thousand (from the *Statistical Abstract of US*; US Department of Commerce.)

direct supervision from Lisbon. He also insisted that he should be allowed to choose his own staff. Both demands were granted by the Ministry of War, which is undoubtedly one of the main reasons why the war at least turned in favour of the Portuguese, although only temporarily.

One of the men he chose was a young captain, Otelo Saraiva de Carvalho, and it was he who escorted me while I was in Portuguese Guinea. He was a charming, erudite intellectual in uniform and he became prominent in Lisbon at the time of the coup d'état, as one of the radical hardliners who demanded nothing less than a fullblown communist government for the country. After a series of bomb attacks in the early Eighties he was gaoled for anarchy and little has been heard of him since.

One of the first changes insisted on by General Spinola showed his grasp of guerrilla warfare. Following the example of Sir Gerald Templer in Malaya in 1952, he assumed total responsibility for both civilian and military organisations in the enclave. This proved extremely valuable in his attempts to come to terms with the liberation forces.

He also sliced through bureaucratic red tape and interdepartmental hostility which, until then, had become characteristic of the Portuguese war effort in Guinea, and to a lesser extent in Angola largely because this territory was almost self-governing.

Schulz had been both civil and military governor of the region, but his hands were tied by Lisbon. Many of the plans that he tried to put into operation were thwarted. In retrospect it is clear that the blame was his for tolerating such interference in a rapidly deteriorating situation.

Another result of Spinola's rule was the execution of many long-overdue political and economic reforms. The changes for the better came too late, but in the last analysis, Spinola stole much of the rebels' thunder, for they too promised changes, and were prevented by the war from carrying them out.

The PAIGC took their country into independence with an explicitly socialist programme. Since then the country has lapsed into a sorry state. Bissau was a backwater when I went there in 1971. Now it has shrunk to an urban wasteland where the laws are draconian and readily enforced by the gun.

So much for the independence of the Republic of Guiné-Bissau.

The man running the war during my visit was the ascetic and intellectual career officer, General Antonio de Spinola; the man who was to write the book that eventually altered the course of the political and military fortunes of the Portuguese in Europe and in Africa. General Spinola was a taciturn conservative. He was always seen in public with his monocle and, in spite of the oppressive west African heat, leather gloves. He was certainly of the "old school" and regarded as a father figure by his men; they all stood in awe of him. Few could match his abilities as thinker, tactician, historian and, ultimately, as a visionary.

During my own sojourn in Portuguese Guinea I met him on several occasions, both formally in his office and in the more relaxed environment of the local festival, and occasionally while with Captain Otelo de Carvalho at Military Headquarters in Bissau. The last time I saw him was on the evening of the day we had departed in a clapped-out DC-6 carrying war wounded and troops on their way back to Lisbon. We were loaded to capacity, and it was clear that the aircrew had difficulty in gaining altitude. It took us three hours of preparation to get off the ground. About an hour out of Bissau one of the port engines failed; we turned round, dumped fuel, and minutes later a second engine cut out.

The pilot made straight for Dakar; if we had to land in "enemy" territory, then so be it. Eventually we managed to limp, without stopping, from Dakar to Bathurst (now Banjul) in Gambia and on to Bissau. It was a terrifying experience.

Because it had taken us so long to get off the ground that morning, I asked Captain Otelo Carvalho for authority to be put on the next day's Boeing flight to Lisbon at the expense of the army. I was to meet the Ghanaian Minister of Foreign Affairs in Accra in two days and the delay could have had serious results.

Only one man in the country could give us a decision; so Carvalho and I went to see the General.

I explained the situation through an interpreter (he said he spoke no English, but I heard otherwise from several other senior Portuguese officers) and without a moment's hesitation he agreed, I was to be given a ticket for the scheduled journey.

In my discussion with General Spinola, I found him a man who echoed many of the sentiments expressed by the Lisbon hierarchy.

His role, he said, was a civilising one; he meant to crush the enemy and was well on his way to doing so. At the time, early 1971, Spinola had actually – after the Shulz débâcle – succeeded in reversing the course of the war. There was an air of optimism among the senior functionaries whom I met in Bissau, and that was reflected later in my book.[6] But that was before SAM–7s arrived.

Porch maintains in his book *The Portuguese Armed Forces and the Revolution* that although Spinola's book, *Portugal and the Future* was published in 1974, it was already written by 1971, which means that he was probably working on the manuscript or had just finished it while I was in Bissau. When I met him face to face, he hardly seemed the man who was later to say that war was at the root of the Portuguese problems; or that "the future of Portugal depends on an appropriate solution to the problems raised by the war which, by consuming lives, resources and talent, increasingly compromises the rhythm of development which we must have to catch up with other countries".

I could not have met a more determined or articulate exponent of hardline tactics. He was as uncompromising about the PAIGC as he was when we discussed the difficult terrain in which his men had to fight. I quote from my own interview:

"You ask whether a military victory is possible for the Portuguese in this province? I say to you that we are already achieving victory with our forces in that we are guaranteeing and underwriting the security of the Guinean people." He accused the PAIGC of kidnapping young people to feed their war machine, of a meddlesome Soviet Union trying to implicate others in the struggle, and a conflict that already involved East and West for the domination ... of parts of the south Atlantic and West Africa as a whole.

Spinola could have been a spokesman for the American State Department of the day.

The book was widely read by Portuguese officers. It was immensely popular and bought by the lorryload throughout the country, although it was banned in the overseas provinces. But even there it was smuggled into colonial messes and quietly circulated.

For the MFA, *Portugal and the Future* was a godsend. It provided the revolutionary movement with its political guideline, and there are many people who cite General de Spinola's book as catalyst of the movement. That was contested by Otelo de Carvalho, on the grounds that Spinola was not radical enough. Before the coup the MFA was regarded as "Spinolist" both in doctrine and in leadership.

Needless to say, having been used by the young officers of the MFA to achieve their ends, they ditched Spinola as quickly as they had embraced him as soon as they were in power. Within a year Spinola was forced to flee into exile in Brazil. In Portugal he was regarded as a traitor by many although he was one of the most resourceful and competent leaders that the country has produced this century. He never disguised his contempt for the "hermits in power" in Lisbon.

At the time the young MFA officers had need of a general to lend prestige to their movement. First they had tried General Kaulza de Arriaga, but when it seemed that this staunch rightist, although accepting that change was necessary, was likely to end up using them instead of them using him, they opted instead for Spinola, whose book, of course, was the cherry on the top of all this subterfuge.

One of the interesting sidelights of the book was the attitude of the then Prime Minister, Caetano, who saw the sinister hand of international Marxism everywhere.

General Costa Gomes, one of the brains behind the revolution and the dismantling of the African empire, sent Caetano a copy of the book. In *O Depoimento* (which was later published in Rio de Janeiro after Caetano had himself sought sanctuary in Brazil) he wrote:

"On the 18th, I received a copy of *Portugal and the Future* with the friendly dedication of the author. I could not read it that day, nor the following one, which was taken up by the council of ministers. Only on the 20th after a tiring day did I pick up the book after 11 o'clock at night. I did not stop reading until I reached the last page. And when I closed the book, I had understood that a military coup d'état, which for some months I sensed had been brewing, was now inevitable."

Next day he called Spinola and General Costa Gomes, then Chief of the General Staff of the Portuguese Armed Forces, into his office "for the most serious and disagreeable conversation of my life ... General de Spinola's book contained a critical opening section which could not fail to influence the desire of the armed forces to continue to defend the overseas provinces, and to weigh on public opinion, affecting international affairs and reducing the already narrow margin of manoeuvre open to the government in its foreign policy ... Written by the vice-chief of the general staff and approved by his superior ... it opened a breach between the Prime Minister and the highest chiefs of the armed forces.

"It would be impossible to continue to govern with an insubordinate officer corps and discordant military chiefs."

Today Spinola is back in Lisbon and is once again a highly regarded elder statesman. His honour has been resuscitated and apart from being elevated to the rank of Field Marshall, this retired officer is entitled to a permanent office, with attendant adjutant at Defence Headquarters in Lisbon.

## Angola

Captain Vitor Alves hardly seemed the sort of man to fit into a revolutionary mould.

He was light of frame and sharp of face and intellect, with the bearing of a professional military man. Most of the time I spent with him on our first meeting was at his base at N'Riquinha in the south-eastern corner of Angola near the Zambian border. N'Riquinha – on the Cuando river, which in 1987 became the international focus of attention when Unita and South African forces fought against a combined Cuban and MPLA army for the domination of the region – was as remote a colonial posting as could be found on any continent. Even in Portuguese times it was known as *Terras do Fim Mundo:* Land at the End of the Earth.

Although he was only a captain, Alves had certainly unusual qualities.

He was married to Theresa, the daughter of a Portuguese Admiral, which in itself made him a member of the élite. His own background was upper class. As I spoke to him over a glass of *Constantinho* brandy, I had the impression of a man with a well-furnished intellect who could quote Proust or Sartre as easily as Che Guevara.

I did not know it until later but Guevara occupied a prominent place in the life of Alves; he had read everything that Guevara had written. On 25 April 1974, now a Major, he became a member of the triumvirate, with Otelo de Carvalho and Vasco Lourenço, that was the nucleus of the Coordinating Committee of the Armed Forces Movement, which was responsible for the coup. He had become a revolutionary but he never allowed his radical politics to disrupt our friendship.

Yet Alves the political malcontent was a very different man from Alves the operational officer in the field, or the Alves who came from Angola to South Africa to visit me after I had launched my first book on guerrilla warfare. We were to see each other often in the years before April 1974; I visited him and Theresa on several occasions at their modest apartment on the outskirts of Oeiras, near Lisbon. On one visit I spent a week there while waiting to enter Guinea. Coming back late at night on one or two occasions I was surprised to find Alves deep in conversation with a group of fellow officers. I paid little attention at the time, because I knew he was on a staff course and probably engaged on some project or other. That was early 1971.

I recorded in the book that N'Riquinha was a small trading post established by the colonial authorities in the last century... "It is now a vital link in the chain of Portuguese military command." I also recalled that Alves bore a striking resemblance to the South African heart surgeon Chris Barnard. My report continues:

"The area under his command is the south-east corner of the country, an area of more than 30 000 sq km, or roughly the size of Switzerland. It is his duty to garrison certain villages in the area, maintain them with supplies by road at regular intervals, keep infiltrators who come across the frontier in check, act as guardian and protector to the African refugees who return to Angola and, on average, fight about one action a week against insurgent units in his area.

"Captain Alves had a company of 165 men and five officers under his command.

"Alves himself had trained the men of his company in Portugal, and they had all come out to Africa by sea four months previously.

"They knew their *Capitão* and had a healthy respect for him which was entirely reciprocated. They had frequently been in action during the four months. In this time Captain Alves had lost one man killed and three were injured, one of them seriously. Their tally of insurgents killed, wounded and captured was impressive – well into three figures."

Of his men Alves said: "These are my sons; to each I must be father, judge, disciplinarian and confidant. I must take them all home with me at the end of the two years because I am responsible for them." When there were problems, he wrote to their families, wives or sweethearts.

By 1968 the Captain had been in the army for 11 of his 33 years. Part of his African military career had been served in Mozambique, where he met and married a young student from Rhodesia. While he was serving his country, his wife looked after their children and studied at Lisbon University.

Captain Alves spoke four languages fluently: English, Portuguese, French and German. But his roots in Africa went deep. He liked to think of himself as having adopted the continent as his own; "an adopted son of Africa."

"I have drunk of the waters of Africa. It runs in my veins. I do not think I could live anywhere else for very long," he would say.

He believed that all men, black and white, were equal, and said so. He had never been able to understand the logic of apartheid, but he was too discreet to be overtly critical in the presence of the South Africans with whom he sometimes came into contact, since his area butted on the Caprivi Strip, under South African control. Like the commandos, Captain Alves was a man *sui generis*, but he was no killer.

Writing nearly ten years after the event on the nature of the MFA revolution, Porch makes some interesting comments on Alves as a young officer. The political leanings of a handful of the MFA élite went back long before the war and the guerrilla insurgence, he said.

Like Nasser, Sadat and Gaddafi, some left wing officers (including Alves) had been conspicuous as cadets. Classmates of... Alves at the Military Academy noted that (he) had been politically active even then. One of his associates, a naval lieutenant, had even slept with a copy of Lenin under his pillow. They managed to convert one or two close friends to their revolutionary views, but the mass of the force remained unaffected.

The N'Riquinha posting must have suited Alves's temperament, for in spite of his excellent counter-insurgency track record, much of his time was spent

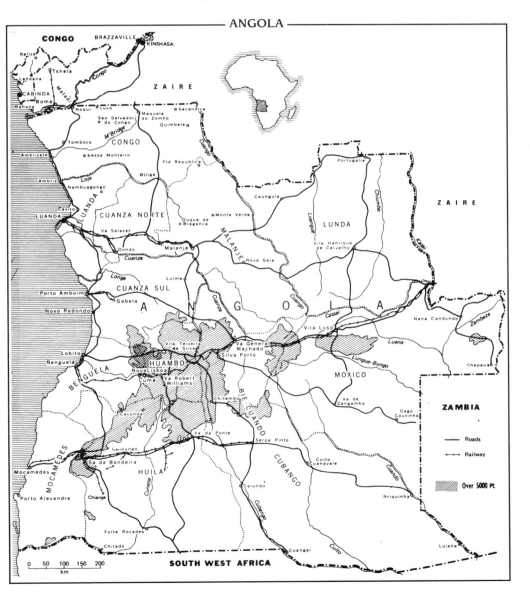

ANGOLA

on the enormous task of rehabilitating civilian refugees who crossed the border. The flow averaged about twenty a day and was steadily growing. Most had arrived at Portuguese camps in the bush and asked to be allowed to live at the "Big Town", as N'Riquinha was already known to the natives. The post had a population of about a thousand. It was the largest concentration of people for 500 kilometres.

Refugees arrived at the camp with nothing – no clothes, no blankets, not even cooking utensils. Many wore only loin-cloths. Without blankets, they suffered during the bitterly cold winter nights. All had to be fed, and the sick had to be separated from the sound.

Each family was allotted a small piece of ground outside the main camp where they could build a hut.

"When you see those poor emaciated people rolling up here, people who have lived in terror for two years and have probably not known whether they would ever see another sunrise, only then do you realise the cost of this war in human terms," Alves said, looking at a lorryload of people who arrived soon after we landed.

"We offer them what we have. We feed them and clothe them. I have some clothes and blankets – all new, good stuff captured from the terrorists. At the present rate we shall soon have enough for everyone. Only yesterday I found a cache of blankets, boots and shirts at a hiding-place south of here."

The group that had arrived was in a pitiable state. They were simple people, some very old, others very young, clutching wide-eyed at their mothers' breasts. All the children were suffering from malnutrition. They were *Camaxis*, river people who lived on the Zambian border. These were the same people who were later to rally round Dr Savimbi after he had launched Unita as a guerrilla movement.

Here and there new arrivals would spot an old friend among those already settled and exchange greetings. For a minute or so they would clap and then shake hands six or eight times. The process would be repeated three or four times in succession, after which everyone would squat down on their haunches and exchange news.

Later that morning the elders of the new group called at the mess to express their thanks.

The camp at N'Riquinha grew its own vegetables. The Captain was also building up a herd of cattle, pigs and goats to supplement their diet, cut off as they were from the rest of the country. Supply columns reached them only once a month.

While with the unit I even managed to persuade the Captain to let me shoot an antelope for the pot. With an antiquated .303 I downed a huge eland at 400 metres in the dry, desert-like terrain. It eventually took 10 men to lift the animal onto a Unimog to get it back to base.

It was the medical problems that worried the Captain most. Many of the new arrivals needed treatment. All suffered from malaria or tick fever. A number of the children had a severe skin disease that attacked the area round the groin and buttocks and made walking painful. It was very contagious, but fortunately the clinic had developed a lotion that seemed to help.

Dr Manuel Carlos Guerra was in charge of the N'Riquinha clinic. He had already spent two years in Africa, conscripted from a prosperous practice in Oporto. He had volunteered to stay on and help, and he had been posted to N'Riquinha, as "punishment", from another camp near Luanda. "They would not give me the research facilities I needed, so I kicked up hell," he said.

He had three serious diseases to cope with at the camp. All affected children severely; trachoma and skin and bone diseases caused by lack of vitamins over a long period. Kwashiorkor was also a great problem among the new arrivals, but it was relatively easy to treat.

In the four months that he had been at N'Riquinha he had saved the sight of five children with advanced trachoma. He was treating dozens of others in the camp for this disease, which is rife throughout all black Africa.

The Captain said that Dr Guerra had only recently returned to N'Riquinha after two weeks in hospital. A parasite had lodged in the doctor's genitals. Deciding that he could not afford the time to be treated in Luanda, he tried to operate on himself; but passed out halfway through surgery. He had to be taken out by air the next day.

Like many Portuguese army camps in the African interior, N'Riquinha had its own school. Young NCOs taught the refugee children the three R's; all in Portuguese. This was considered part of the "preordained" mission of "civilizing Africa" as so many Portuguese politicians phrased it at the time. Although many of the children had never heard the language before they arrived at the centre, they were soon speaking it among themselves as they played between the barrack huts.

More from my notes:

"Water," Alves said, "is a great problem in this country." There was little rain for much of the year, and there were fifteen metres of sand over the bedrock; even more in places.

A large detachment of men spent most of the day at the hand–pump to provide enough water for the garrison and civilians. Captain Alves said that a new electric pump would soon be installed, and it would provide enough water for irrigation. He intended to teach the villagers to grow crops for profit.

"It helps them and it helps me if they make money. They can't live on charity forever," he said.

Alves believed that if he could make the area economically viable (and he thought he could do so in a year), it would also be a defence against insurgents. "The people would then wish to protect their livelihoods against terrorism," he said.

He hoped soon to be able to grant a concession to one of the villagers to set up a store, as a few of the villagers already owned small herds of cattle. Some were collecting skins to barter. He was confident that the economic potential was there.

The garrison at N'Riquinha had a routine all its own. Apart from the water fatigue, there were few duties in the camp. Some of the younger Africans were being taught cooking and carpentry and to help as medical orderlies. One bright young fellow from Barotseland had asked to be taught hairdressing. He was being trained as a barber's assistant. Three others were learning elementary engineering in the vehicle pool.

Monday was the big day at the camp, when the aircraft arrived from Luso with the mail and supplies. It was a day for taking things easy.

The officers carried the tradition a stage further by wearing civilian clothes on Monday. "It's their Sunday," said Alves; "It's the day when one soldier from each platoon has dinner with us and it's our way of keeping in touch with the men."

The Bushmen were an interesting group at N'Riquinha. These little people, who have lived for thousands of years in the Kalahari Desert further south, are now found in a few parts of southern Angola. Since the war began they had been hunted like vermin by the rebel MPLA largely because the insurgents and the Portuguese recognised their ability as trackers. Bushmen were often used in follow-up operations against insurgent groups; they paid a terrible price and continue to pay even to this day. South African forces on cross-border raids into south Angola in the Eighties often rescued Bushman families used as slaves by MPLA functionaries. The Bushmen at the N'Riquinha camp numbered about twenty.

Captain Alves explained that the war in his area was different in many ways from the campaigns being fought near Luso farther north. It was more protracted. The enemy were not seeking Portuguese units; they were more intent on infiltrating through his sector (Sector CC) to the west.

"They come through here from staging areas in Zambia. Usually they are well armed and carry heavy loads of supplies for the terrorists operating in the interior. The position is rather like that of Sector D in the north. This is the hinterland they have to cross to get there and our job is to stop them."

When contact was made with a group of insurgents it was simply a matter of trailing them through the bush and trying to force them to make a stand. Often, if the terrain allowed it, the Portuguese would move ahead and try to set up an ambush.

"The object in this kind of warfare is to draw the enemy to a place where you can attack him," said Alves. He had tried a number of ruses in the four months he had been there, with some success. In his first months at N'Riquinha he had followed a group for forty days, and he was eventually responsible for the destruction or capture of an entire MPLA unit.

"That was my forty days in the desert. It was a gruelling, disheartening experience, but it was stamina and perseverance that paid in the end. We killed 31 and captured 12."

On that operation Captain Alves lost a man. A sergeant was also badly wounded in the leg and belly.

But Captain Vitor Alves at N'Riquinha could not be regarded as typical of the average Portuguese army officer on active service in Africa. He was much more efficient and dedicated than most, but then the war in the East (*Zona* ZIL) was barely two years old by the time I got there and morale among the troops on the ground was still high. The *miliciano* malaise had not yet set in.

Because his posting was remote and the war in his sector not nearly so intense as elsewhere, Alves was no doubt spared many of the frustrations of the Portuguese army and air force fighting in the region north of Luanda. This was the *Dembos,* also known in the local military jargon as "Comsec D". A dreadful region of mountains, impenetrable jungle and tropical rivers and diseases, the operational area began 70 kilometres north of the capital; throughout the thirteen-year campaign it was one of the most strongly-contested areas of the war. Portuguese civilian and military casualties in Angola were the heaviest in the *Dembos.*

Angola was mainly divided into three distinct spheres of operations by its military planners, which defined the extent and intensity of operations allowed in any particular area. Grading was according to a level of strategic priority; for example, the first or number one zone was in the extreme east of the country and the *Dembos* to the north.

Because the land frontiers with Zambia and Zaïre were almost 2 000km long, the Portuguese admitted that it was difficult to control infiltration in the regions. The natural terrain also gave the insurgents a distinct advantage; the jungle in the north and the huge arid wastelands to the east were subjected to "very heavy subversion", and were consequently regarded by the Portuguese as "killing zones".

There was little regard for the indigenous population, and although it would be an exaggeration to say the Portuguese killed anything that moved, there were places where it was true enough.

The most active insurgent movement in the east was the MPLA or *Movimento Popular de Libertação de Angola*, the organisation which by force of arms and Cuban help eventually wrested the country from the two other movements once the Portuguese had pulled out. The MPLA were also active on a more limited scale north of Luanda.

Unita, in contrast, was later limited to positions across the main infiltration routes from Zambia and Zaïre on the Lungwe and Bungue rivers south-west of Luso.

The second zone was defined as the "sporadic limitation" zone. It included much of the central parts of the country, including the rich farming highlands round places like Nova Lisboa and Serpa Pinto. Here fighting was much less intense than in, say, the *Dembos;* but there was guerrilla presence in places, and they were attacked, usually effectively, whenever contact was made. Much of the agricultural wealth of Angola lay in this belt, and the fact that it remained one of the most prosperous parts of the Portuguese empire until the last Portuguese soldiers had been withdrawn indicates the poor success of the insurgents.

Lastly there was the third or "latent war zone" which centred on areas around Luanda, the Diamang diamond fields in the north-east near Henrique de Carvalho and the Cabinda enclave, north of the Congo river with its rich resources of oil.

Luanda, Cabinda and the Diamang fields were areas of great strategic importance. If there was any infiltration in these areas the Portuguese spared no effort to stop it. They were usually successful, since Luanda very rarely saw any real action; a few bombs during the course of the war but never any concerted activity by the rebels. In the case of Cabinda and Diamang (which survived intact throughout these protracted hostilities) it was obvious to all that some sort of "payola" was in operation, because the efforts of the guerrilla bands there were futile. They were near to hostile borders, and a concerted campaign could quickly have crippled both, if there had been any measure of intent.

When the war began in 1961, most of us who were covering the African sphere were aware of the existence of two countries called the Congo: one, the former Belgian possession later renamed Zaïre, and the other a "people's republic", always qualified by its capital, Brazzaville. It was no secret that as active as the Americans were in "old Leo", or Leopoldville (now Kinshasa), so were the Russians in "Brazza".

The unseen hand of intrigue had a strong influence on the fortunes of these various military campaigns, since it was as much a trial of strength between the "super powers" as a rebellious campaign against the imperialist Portuguese.

For some reason the Chinese never seriously entered the fray, although they provided some help to Holden Roberto's *Frente Nacional de Libertação de Angola* (FNLA), which, although later superseded by the MPLA, still continues as a fighting force to this day. Only now the enemy is no longer the Portuguese; it is the Marxist MPLA, which holds on to Luanda as its seat of power.

Like Unita, the FNLA has continued the struggle, though at a much reduced level when compared to Jonas Savimbi's Unita movement which is concentrated in the eastern and central regions of a country larger than Texas, much of it then still untouched by the twentieth century.

The presence of the Chinese in Zaïre was anomalous, since the power most active there was the United States. The CIA headquarters for the region was in Leopoldville. At that point relations between the Americans and the Chinese were so bad that if they had been neighbours they would probably have been at war. The thaw came only later when Nixon took office. The movement that benefited most from this hostility was the FNLA.

Matters were complicated still further a little later when Mobutu took over as president of Zaïre; and even if Washington had wished to ditch the inept, unpredictable and corrupt Holden Roberto they could not have done so, because he was Mobutu's brother-in-law. It was all very complicated.

On my visit to the *Dembos* operational area north of Luanda in 1968, we were taken to the region in an old Portuguese Air Force Nord Atlas transport aircraft. The road was too precarious for such a long ride, we were told. Although we were later to traverse vast distances in convoy and were exposed to our share of snipers and mines, I never ceased to marvel at the way in which these intrepid airmen took their lumbering transports into tiny bush air-strips that would have looked difficult enough for someone flying a Piper Cub.

It was a war of improvisation; and since Portugal was one of the poorest of Western nations, they had to improvise well.

We landed at Santa Eulalia, effectively the "operations room" of Sector D. It lay about half an hour's flying time by Nord Atlas from Luanda. En route we dropped supplies by parachute to a small camp ten minutes' flying time from Luanda. None of us had known that the war had advanced so far south.

From a row of prefabricated wooden bungalows in the middle of the camp, Brigadier Martins Sorrés and his six young staff officers conducted the war in their area.

We found Santa Eulalia surrounded by a double barbed-wire fence two metres high. Arc-lamps with protective wire covers punctuated it every dozen yards or so. Machine-gun turrets at six or seven vantage points round the perimeter stood out against the horizon. With the squat brown buildings in the middle, Santa Eulalia looked like the army camps built round Kuala Lumpur during the Malayan "emergency".

The headquarters and its garrison of 300 was the stock pattern of most army camps in Angola. It was built in 1961, soon after the first wave of attacks swept in from the two neighbouring Congos, barely a year after they had been granted independence.

An elaborate system of bunkers and tunnels, typical of jungle warfare throughout the world, wound past the buildings to the outer defences. If the camp was attacked, my guide explained, it was possible to move in complete safety between the central control position and any other building in the camp, including the hospital. Casualties could be brought back from the most forward positions through the tunnels.

"We find the tunnels a most effective precaution. As in Vietnam, the enemy often creeps up in the darkness and lets off a salvo of mortar bombs before they melt away into the night. Even with the arc-lamps it is difficult to see further than fifty metres beyond the fences," he said. Santa Eulalia had not yet experienced that kind of attack, but other Portuguese positions in Sector D had. The tunnels had helped greatly.

I did not envy the task of the men who built these defences in that stifling tropical heat.

Santa Eulalia was actually two camps in one. A second section had been set aside near the air-strip where air force personnel were billeted. Their area was also fenced off, and the army was responsible for security.

Santa Eulalia had originally been a coffee estate. Sector D even now still produces the best coffee in Angola, and at that time the farm continued to operate as a flourishing commercial venture a few hundred metres away.

In the surrounding area there grew thousands of neat rows of stubby coffee bushes. The plantation created a patchwork pattern against the surrounding evergreen jungle and stretches of open grassland. The jungle had to be kept back constantly with machetes. The owners and workers, black and white alike, were armed and held responsible for their own safety. Every farm was linked by radio with the central military headquarters in the area, which could send help within minutes if a farm was attacked. Much depended on the strength and fire-power of the insurgent force. Farm-owners often dealt with small attacks on their own.

We were told that no troops were stationed on the huge cooperative estates which stretched for miles over the undulating country. The pattern was similar to that of Kenya at the height of the five-year Mau Mau emergency.

Brigadier Martins Sorrés was a tall, slim, unassuming soldier who might well have been mistaken for a bank official. He had been fighting the insurgents from Santa Eulalia for most of the seven years that the war had been in progress at the time of our visit. When the first invasion of Angola took place he had been Governor of the Province of Luanda, and it was his task to organise effective counter-measures to save the country from being overrun by guerrilla bands.

"That there were attacks in 1961 at all is partly our fault," he told me at lunch soon after I arrived. "We had been warned by the Portuguese Embassy in Leopoldville, six or eight months before the first bands pushed across the frontier. Intelligence reports from the embassy indicated that certain elements in the Congo were training a *Freedom Army* which would soon be used to launch an attack on Angola.

"The first reports were dismissed by both the civil and military authorities. By the time the gravity of the problem was realised, Holden Roberto's army had crossed into Angola in their thousands."

The insurgent army had covered the distance between the frontier and the capital within days. The Portuguese were caught completely off their guard. The few Portuguese militia and police in the area (there were only 8 000 men in the security forces in the whole of Angola at the time; 3 000 Portuguese and 5 000 African) were accustomed to years of unopposed rule and were no match for the huge mobs that stormed through hastily erected barricades and defences.

"The rebels had the upper hand from the start. They held on to it until Lisbon was able to send in reinforcements. At times it was touch-and-go whether they would be able to take Luanda or not. At one point they reached the outskirts of the town, and it was only loyal African troops who pushed them back.

"Many of those African troops who saved Luanda are now in command of their own units in this jungle. They were brave men. Portugal does not forget," said the Brigadier.

Meanwhile Roberto's men were laying waste farms and buildings. Everyone in their path was killed - black, white, old or young; even babies were not spared. They were often cut open and stuck on to stakes along the road. Some of the things they did were atrocious. At one logging village in the north eight Portuguese men, women and children were fed lengthwise through the circular saws.

"Those were the scenes that greeted us in the early days. It was enough to make any God-fearing man throw up his hands in horror and ask what had become of humanity," he said.

The explanation for the early success of the rebels was simple, he maintained. Many of them believed that they were protected by the spells of their witch-doctors and that the bullets of the enemy would be turned to water. They thought they were invincible and nothing could stop them. "And it is in fact difficult to stop a man who thinks that," he said.

"When they attacked they came on screaming and firing their weapons. Others followed behind with spears and machetes. They were fearless and ruthless."

It was more than a month before the Portuguese found their feet again. The Brigadier held on with what little he had at his disposal. Everyone who could gave a hand.

Conditions had changed by the time we arrived. Much of the country north of Sector D and stretching towards the coast is jungle swamp. It was known to the Portuguese military authorities and the insurgents as Sector A. Malaria and other tropical illnesses were rife.

"We patrol where we can, but it is impossible to create a no-man's-land as the Americans have done in Vietnam. If you clear the jungle one week, it grows a foot high the next, as it does here," he said.

It was the nearest thing to the Ho Chi Minh trail in Africa – all 200 kilometres of it. Of the 5 000 or 6 000 rebels in Sector D at the time, the staff officer reckoned that 90 per cent had entered the area down this trail from the Congo. It took them six weeks to cover the distance. The others had travelled from the south-east from Zambia or joined the insurgent army in the sector itself.

"They come down the trail with everything they need on their backs – guns, ammunition, explosives, food, medical supplies, propaganda handouts and anything else that they may think necessary to wage war against us. They have already managed to bring 250kg aerial bombs into the sector, carried on a litter between four men." The task must have demanded enormous efforts. The country is extremely difficult. There are few roads and no bridges across the fast-flowing rivers that enter the sea nearby.

The bombs were used by the insurgents as mines. "A large bomb will blow up a large vehicle; so they bring these 250kg monsters down to blow up our Panhards. They've never succeeded yet. They are far too big and bulky, and we spot them every time. God knows what they cost in sweat and blood to get down here."

Most of the men garrisoned at Santa Eulalia were used for tactical and support purposes by other Portuguese units in the vicinity. With about two dozen trucks and helicopters on hand in an emergency, the garrison was highly mobile.

Like Captain Alves in the east, they had the task of protecting the local African population.

The camp at Santa Eulalia had its own clinic, surgical theatre and dental unit. Soldiers needing treatment were flown in by light aircraft or helicopter from other camps. Serious casualties were cleared from Santa Eulalia to the military hospital in Luanda usually on special litters fitted to small, single-engined aircraft. Helicopters landed on a concrete slab behind the clinic, which was used as a tennis court by the officers off duty.

On a return trip from one of the camps in the interior, we had with us a young soldier who had been bitten in the face by some tropical insect. It had affected his sight and hearing, and he was only half-conscious. The doctor was considering moving him to Luanda if he got any worse. "We don't get this kind of case often, but the jungle certainly keeps us busy with some extraordinary ailments," he said.

One man, a former waiter from Coimbra, had been brought in on a stretcher. He had a form of elephantiasis. His body, arms and legs were grossly swollen. His face was grotesque. It seemed as if he had been severely beaten round the eyes. It took an insect the size of a flea to do that to him, the doctor said.

"All we could do was give him the usual drugs and hope for the best. Antibiotics had no effect."

It was aspirin, strangely enough, that cured the soldier, quite by accident. On the second day he complained of a violent headache. "He was already dosed with drugs, so we gave him aspirin. Within a few hours the swelling was down. A week later he was back with his unit. Extraordinary!"

The war in Angola lasted 13 years. It took a heavy toll in men and equipment as it progressed. Gradually, though, from about 1971 onwards, the security forces managed to achieve a momentum that all but thwarted insurgent attempts at subversion by about half a dozen different organisations, all operating from vantage points across the border in Zambia, Zaïre or Congo–Brazzaville.

## TABLE 4

### Casualties of the Portuguese Armed Forces in Africa — killed, wounded and injured to 1 May 1974 (a)

| | Guinea | Angola | Mozam-bique | Total | Percentages of Total | | |
| --- | --- | --- | --- | --- | --- | --- | --- |
| | | | | | Guinea | Angola | Mozambique |
| KILLED IN ACTION | | | | | | | |
| Navy | 42 | 13 | 14 | 69 | | | |
| Army | 981 | 1 088 | 970 | 3 045 | | | |
| Air Force | 55 | 41 | 55 | 151 | | | |
| | 1 084 | 1 142 | 1 039 | 3 265 | 33 | 35 | 32 |
| DEATHS FROM OTHER CAUSES (b) | | | | | | | |
| Navy | 51 | 59 | 15 | 125 | | | |
| Army | 690 | 1 344 | 646 | 2 690 | | | |
| Air Force | 50 | 126 | 94 | 270 | | | |
| | 791 | 1 529 | 755 | 3 075 | 26 | 50 | 24 |
| DEATHS (1 + 2) | 1 875 | 2 671 | 1 794 | 6 340 | 30 | 42 | 28 |
| WOUNDED IN COMBAT | | | | | | | |
| Navy | 376 | 71 | 27 | 474 | | | |
| Army | 5 522 | 4 205 | 2 149 | 11 876 | | | |
| Air Force | 263 | 196 | 69 | 528 | | | |
| | 6 161 | 4 472 | 2 245 | 12 878 | 48 | 35 | 17 |
| INJURED IN ACCIDENTS | | | | | | | |
| Navy | 122 | 194 | 50 | 366 | | | |
| Army | 2 014 | 6 303 | 6 030 | 14 347 | | | |
| Air Force | 31 | 98 | 199 | 328 | | | |
| | 2 167 | 6 595 | 6 279 | 15 041 | 14 | 44 | 42 |

(a) In the case of Portuguese Guinea, calculated from 1 May 1963; Angola from 1 June 1961; and Mozambique from 1 November 1964.

(b) "Other causes" include vehicle accidents, accidents with armaments, other accidents, illness and missing. Fifty per cent of all Portuguese casualties in 1970 were attributed to mines.

Considering that conflict in Angola had begun three and a half years earlier in Angola than in Mozambique and that the Portuguese were caught totally unprepared in Angola, it is noteworthy that the number of battle casualties in all three territories was almost the same for the period under review: 1 142 in Angola, 1 084 in Guinea and 1 039 in Mozambique.

There were nearly 50 per cent more military personnel wounded in action in Guinea than in Angola, which in turn had a higher casualty rate than Mozambique. There were more air force and naval personnel killed in action in both Guinea and Mozambique than in Angola. In distance covered, the air force was more active in Angola than in Guinea.

Most Portuguese living in Angola when the conflict ended say that by 1973/ 4 the war was at its lowest ebb during the entire 13 years of hostilities. Unita, which had always maintained a low profile during the Portuguese era and only really came into its own when it was directly threatened with annihilation after independence, was down to a few hundred active combatants by 1974. There were, of course, thousands of supporters in the towns, but they had little strength in the field.

The FNLA, never an organisation that excelled in combat (even after independence, when the movement was nearly destroyed by a combined Cuban and MPLA force in a series of battles north of Luanda, in which the South Africans also had a hand) was totally bogged down in the *Dembos* by early 1974.

By 1973 Holden Roberto had about 6 000 men in the field between Luanda and the Zaïre border. There were 200 more in the east of the country, but they were of little consequence. Generally, their level of training and preparedness was inferior. Considering their supporters, Tunisia, Morocco, Zaïre, Algeria, Egypt, India, Red China and the United States, it should not have been. Following a pattern which was later adopted by Swapo, their principal successes lay in intimidating unarmed civilians and force-marching bands of kidnapped schoolchildren across the border to training camps in Zaïre.

Idle and undisciplined as the FNLA were, the MPLA, by contrast, faithfully followed the principles of building up good relations with the local people. What FNLA soldiers simply stole, the MPLA asked and paid for.

Agostinho Neto, the MPLA leader and subsequent Angolan Head of State, said that political indoctrination was at least as important as military. The one went hand in glove with the other.

Naturally, it was the MPLA commissar who got results at the expense of the undisciplined and drunken FNLA thug armed with an automatic weapon. Neto and his backers well understood the task of the guerrilla in the field.

It is not generally known that very early in the war Cuba had shown an interest in the many guerrilla insurrections that were then taking place. Che Guevara had been to Brazzaville in the early Sixties. A year or two later he went into northern Angola on operations with a rebel unit.

Raoul, Fidel Castro's brother, also visited the region. Both men must have been impressed with what they saw, or at least with its long-term potential, for soon after the coup d'état in Lisbon and long before the first South Africans had set foot on Angolan soil, Cuban units were being clandestinely infiltrated into northern Angola by way of Brazzaville and Pointe Noire. (See Bridgland; Chapter 7.)

By 1972 the MPLA had 17 "squadrons" in the field in eastern Angola.

In theory, each squadron should have been composed of about 1 300 men, but these figures were often down to only 200 or 300, largely as a consequence of Portuguese attrition. By 1973, even the South Africans acknowledged that the MPLA, which drew most of its support from the Russians, had about 4 000 men deployed in the eastern parts of the country, all well armed but with indifferent morale. There were 300 MPLA soldiers in the *Dembos,* north of Luanda, isolated and poorly armed, operating ineffectively among bands of FNLA guerrillas, who as often as not would attack MPLA soldiers because they were regarded as "communists". That was probably a result of Western influence within the ranks of the FNLA.

The main support for the MPLA, undoubtedly, came from the towns; and here the cadre and cell system made great inroads into an indigenous population that saw little hope in anything that Lisbon might offer. Blacks as well as whites and mulattoes rallied round the MPLA standard; in fact it gave Angola its first real multiracial consensus in the period leading up to the coup.

After the revolution and the entry of Cuba into the fray, most white supporters of the MPLA left the party in disgust. Most of them went back to the metropolis. But, as with South Africa and the ANC in 1988, it was whites who engineered many of the more notable political successes of the revolutionary movement. Some of them also saw action against the Portuguese forces in the field. But they too had no real share in the final sharing of power after 1975.

It is not surprising to find that the political and administrative structure of the MPLA then was not very different from that of the African National Congress now. The only real difference was that the MPLA were able to "export" their apparatus to some of the liberated regions of Angola, while the ANC still remains confined mainly to Lusaka.

There were nine departments within the MPLA. These were concerned with Information and Propaganda, in which they were often streets ahead of the Portuguese, who always regarded journalists with great suspicion; External Affairs; Political Orientation; Logistics, Education and Culture; Finance, Communications, Mass Organisations and Medical Assistance Services.

One of these coordinated the activities of four mass organisations: UNTA (the National Union of Angola Workers); OMA, the Angolan Women's Organisation; JMPLA, the Youth of the MPLA and the Pioneer Organisation for Angolan Children. There was also a Centre for Revolutionary Instruction, which was responsible for the military and political "enlightenment" of everybody from the age of five upwards.[7]

It was all fine in theory, and as long as the MPLA were on the defensive it worked well. Once they had attained power, most of these bodies deteriorated into typical hide-bound East European bureaucracies that became so top-heavy with party functionaries that they eventually calcified.

With that, Angola became virtually ungovernable and the civil war began in earnest. We have seen the results.

Perhaps because of the large settler population in Angola, which rose from about 45 000 in 1940 to about 200 000 in 1960 and almost double that by the time of the coup d'état, and resulted in a more direct "hands on" approach to fighting insurgency (because these people had more to lose than, say, conscripts fighting in Guinea), both the MPLA and the FNLA began to lose ground from 1972 onwards. By April 1974 most Angolans and guerrilla veterans agree that if the revolution had not taken place, Angola would have been "pacified" within a year. The number of *effective* guerrillas in the field was down to a couple of thousand. Most had abandoned the cause, and if the rest had not fled to sanctuary across the border, they had returned to their villages in the interior.

Even Vitor Alves, in an interview with *Expresso* on 20 September 1975, spoke of the poor quality of the guerrilla opposition. Another officer spoke about the poor training of the insurgents. They had suffered many losses; most new recruits thrown into the fray were not prepared for the complex nature that the guerrilla fighting had developed, the aggressive dedication of the settlers' resistance, of new well-trained regiments such as the *Flechas* (Arrows), which established a pattern for élite South African units such as 32 Battalion, which was based on these black commando units.

The *Flechas* were mostly deserters from the guerrilla fighters who had been efficiently organised by the Portuguese into special forces. They knew the country that they were operating in and were familiar with the tactics and the psyche of their old comrades in the bush. Generous bounties for the numbers of insurgents killed provided the necessary motivation to fight.

It was also the *Flechas* who brought a new dimension into the fight often subsequently emulated by the South Africans in infiltrating and disrupting insurgent movements across the border in Zaïre or Zambia. As Porch says, all factors together, "coupled with three tribally-based liberation movements which faced enormous logistical difficulties and spent almost as much time killing each other as fighting the Portuguese, could only have had a dispiriting effect on the *freedom fighters*".

At the end of the Angolan war most of the *Flechas* moved south and under South African patronage were formed into one of the best counter-insurgency units yet to appear in southern Africa. Most of the activities of 32 Battalion, which was led by white officers, were in Angola, often hundreds of kilometres into the isolated interior, striking at Swapo base camps, ambushing supply columns and attacking and laying waste the Swapo support and command infrastructure. To the end, most black members of 32 Battalion were Portuguese-speaking.

The tribalism that hampered the efforts of the liberation movements against the Portuguese in the early Seventies was as disruptive in its effects then as it was later when the various factions jockeyed for power. Even now the MPLA and Jonas Savimbi's Unita movement draw their strength from tribal bodies.

The Mbundu (not to be confused with Savimbi's Ovimbundu) consists of a group of Kimbundu-speaking tribes spread in a broad band from Luanda as far east as Mavinga. These people provided the bulk of the MPLA "intelligentsia" as well as its political and military leaders, and the first president of Angola, Agostinho Neto. The Mbundu are staunchly Catholic as a result of strong historical Portuguese ties, and they are distantly related to the Protestant Bakongo tribe that spans the Angolan-Zaïrean border. These religious differences were further complicated by tribal and then political differences, which to this day make any form of association between the MPLA and the FNLA almost impossible.

In 1973 there were about two million Ovimbundus living in eastern Angola. These were the original inhabitants of the Benguela Highlands; a nation of traders and farmers who were always on fairly good terms with their colonial masters, to such a degree that MPLA commissars sometimes accused their leader, Jonas Savimbi, of collusion with Lisbon in attempts to end the war. There is little doubt that if the Portuguese had been able to reach an accommodation with any of the tribal groups seeking independence, they would have preferred to deal with Savimbi and his Ovimbundus.

The Ovimbundu people are now preponderant in numbers. In 1973 they constituted almost 40 per cent of the population against about 25 per cent for

Neto's Mbundus and 12 per cent for the Bakongos of Holden Roberto's FNLA. The only shortcoming of Savimbi's people is that they are not as warlike as either the Bakongo or the Mbundu (they obviously had less contact with the church), although circumstances in Angola during the past 15 years have considerably changed that characteristic.

There were several other factors that had a bearing on Portuguese military successes in Angola. Perhaps the most important was good leadership by the Angolan command. In my own opinion, one man above all others was decisive in the uncertain fortunes of war in Angola: Brigadier Bettencourt Rodrigues, formerly a Portuguese military attaché in London.

I got to know this man quite well over the years, and I was always impressed by his very un-Portuguese approach to problems. An aristocrat to the core and embodying a proud tradition that had once been the hallmark of a nation of seafarers and explorers, Bettencourt Rodrigues would always go to the heart of the problem from the outset. He never wasted time on idle words.

I first met him because I had been in the Republic of Guinea (Conakry) where the Russians were very active against Portuguese forces in their enclave to the north of the country. He had called me in to his office in London to ask about a Russian transmitting station at Koundara on the Guinea-Senegalese border. It was apparently responsible for much of the PAIGC guerrilla activity in the east of the Portuguese territory. This had been pointed out to me by a group of American Peace Corps workers stationed at Koundara, and I had written about it in one of my articles.

Bettencourt Rodrigues was promoted from the staff corps to command the eastern region of Angola (*Zona* ZIL), and was regarded by most foreign military observers as one of the best senior officers in the Portuguese army. In two years he transformed a moribund campaign to one in which the insurgents were surpassed militarily and tactically. It was a remarkable achievement, and if there had been more of his ilk Portugal might still be a dominant force in Africa.

There were other reasons why Portugal did better in Angola than elsewhere. While the Portuguese were bogged down in swampy Guinea and barely managing to maintain their presence along the Mueda Plateau in Mozambique, Lisbon poured millions of *contos* into improving the transport network in Angola. No doubt the main incentive was the rich profits in mining and agriculture; but at any rate Angola had the benefit of good new roads and railways.

When I travelled through Angola in 1964, it was hardly possible to move in some areas without a four-wheel-drive vehicle, and not at all during the long rainy seasons in the north. Up to early 1974, the authorities had completed almost 10 000 kilometres of tarred roads, several times the length of all-weather roads at the time of the first rebel attacks from the Congo. In the same period the number of primary schools was increased from less than 4 000 to 5 000. There was little unemployment; the nation thrived in spite of the war or perhaps *because* of it. That was also true of South West Africa and before then, of Rhodesia for a time.

Nowhere was this prosperity more evident than in Luanda. John Miller of the *Daily Telegraph* described it as "... a handsome city, which need not fear comparison with any other in tropical Africa." Those of us who came to know it well found it an excellent place to visit. The life of most of the inhabitants, both black and white, the hotels, the businesses, the blocks of flats, the factories, the fine tropical beaches and tourist haunts were more like the Algarve than Africa. Luanda was often referred to as the third biggest Portuguese town, after

Lisbon and Oporto: although there were then almost as many Portuguese expatriates living and working in Paris to evade conscription as in any of them.

How different now. The change hardly bears comment; it is too appalling. Five hundred years of European tradition in Africa has been destroyed and to paraphrase Graham Greene, left to rot like a log on the beach in the sun.

## Mozambique

Some people in southern Africa and elsewhere believe that war can be a nourishing experience, provided of course that the casualties are not too high. There are also some strategists who maintain that that should have been South African policy from the beginning. As soon as it became clear in the Fifties and early Sixties that a military situation was developing, first in the Portuguese territories, then in Rhodesia, and ultimately in Namibia and South Africa itself, it was argued that a restricted conflict and the battle experience gained in it could be valuable later, when the country would really need to protect its people. Now, an entire generation of South Africans have seen service on the border. Most of the operational commanders were first blooded in Angola, and their tenacity and experience is now evident. They include General Jannie Geldenhuys, head of the Defence Force; Chief of the Army, Lt-Gen. "Kat" Liebenberg and Major-General "Witkop" Badenhorst, now Chief of Staff Intelligence. These men — and many others at all levels of command — have long experience of real conflict in the various African theatres of military activity.

But in Mozambique the war was debilitating from the start. The first 250 guerrillas were trained in Algeria (as were also the first 300 MPLA insurgents) and they opened their campaign on 25 September 1964 with their first foray into northern Mozambique. Mueda and Cabo Delgado immediately became contested regions, and remained so for the next 11 years.

Forewarned by the uprisings in Angola and Guinea, Portugal had already built up its strength to about 16 000 men in Mozambique, although at first it had only five aircraft available.

By 1973 the figure had grown to about 70 000, and the air force comprised twelve Fiat G-91s, fifteen Harvard T6s which I found to be ubiquitous in all the war zones, fourteen Alouette and two Puma helicopters, five Nord Atlas transports and seven DC-3 Dakotas. Although some of these planes were hit by ground fire and the occasional SAM-7 missile, the Portuguese air force in Mozambique suffered relatively few losses compared with what was then happening in Guinea.

On one occasion a DC-3 carrying foreign military attachés and members of the senior Portuguese military command was hit by a SAM-7 in one of the engines. The crippled plane nevertheless managed to land safely.

The Portuguese took some time to learn to use their Alouettes effectively. When these helicopters first arrived in Mozambique some unit commanders would try to squeeze five or six men on board, besides the usual two-man crew, although it was designed for a maximum of four passengers. French technicians attached to the Portuguese forces warned them this kind of weight would strip the gearbox if they were not careful; so numbers were later reduced. It was difficult when there were casualties, since the use of helicopters was so limited in this war.

Most of the infiltration by Frelimo took place across the Ruvuma river separating Mozambique from Tanzania; the target was the heartland of the traditionally bellicose Makonde people, who lived on both sides of the river. The Makonde had never been totally pacified in five centuries of colonisation, and they proved to be natural allies of Frelimo, although they were cast aside once independence had been achieved. Later, when Zambia entered the fray, Frelimo groups would come through from Lusaka and cross into the western regions of Mozambique.

## MOZAMBIQUE

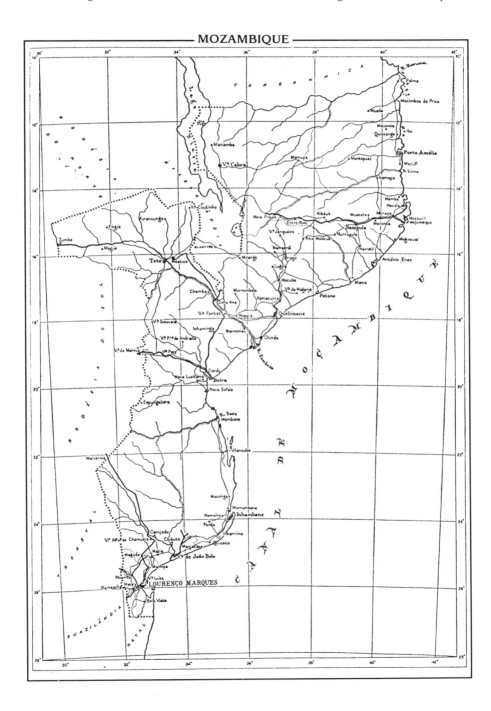

It was then that Tete became the guerrilla cauldron, from which the conflict was ultimately extended to Rhodesia. In 1967, the war progressed farther southward from the Makonde country to Niassa.

Ian Beckett tells of this period: "The size of Frelimo units steadily increased as the movement approached a maximum strength of perhaps 8 000 guerrillas by 1967/8, but these numbers subsequently declined after the internal splits within Frelimo of 1968/9, as represented by the disputes of the Second Party Congress and the assassination of Eduardo Mondlane.

"Frelimo did succeed in closing many sisal plantations along the northern frontier, but had been mostly contained when General Kaulza de Arriaga, who had become Portuguese ground force commander in May 1969, undertook a large-scale offensive, *Operation Gordian Knot,* in the dry season of 1970. Involving some 10 000 troops, the campaigns continued for seven months, in which time Arriaga claimed to have accounted for 651 guerrillas dead and a further 1 840 captured, for the loss of only 132 Portuguese. He also claimed to have destroyed 61 guerrilla bases and 165 camps, while 40 tons of ammunition had been captured in the first two months alone.

"The coordination of heliborne assault after initial artillery and air bombardment, followed by mine clearance and consolidation on foot, undoubtedly severely damaged Frelimo's infrastructure in the north. But, in the manner of such large-scale operations, it did not totally destroy the guerrilla capacity for infiltration, which Arriaga's critics maintained that his predecessors had achieved at much less cost and effort. Further operations were thus required in the north such as operations *Garotte* and *Apio* during 1971."[8]

The problem with *Gordian Knot* and similar operations is that in military jargon, when a counter-revolutionary campaign becomes spectacular (and they were spectacular, since they involved nearly every man in the security forces who could carry a gun, including office staff, cooks and bearers), the writing is already on the wall.

Yet, when the Ruvuma and Tete regions were visited by the South African vice-consul in Luanda (now Brigadier) "Kaas" van der Wals, he did not think the war was going too badly for the Portuguese. He was soon made aware of the fact that, as a result of very heavy insurgent attacks in Tete Province, Rhodesia was suffering because of the inability of the Portuguese upper ranks to cope with the situation.

They tried hard to clear Frelimo out of Tete, but they were unsuccessful. By then *Operation Hurricane* had been launched into the adjacent Mount Darwin area of Rhodesia by the Zimbabwe African National Liberation Army (Zanla), the military wing of Robert Mugabe's Zimbabwe African National Union (ZANU).

Ron Reid-Daly, then an acting captain with the Rhodesian Light Infantry, was the first Rhodesian officer to be attached to Portuguese forces. Other Rhodesian officers, including some Rhodesian SAS specialists, were also seconded from time to time. Some of their comments about the way in which the Portuguese fought their war in Mozambique (and, ultimately, why they eventually lost it) are illuminating.

From Reid-Daly's experience with the British SAS in Malaya, it was clear from the start that the top Portuguese brass in Mozambique had no ready understanding of the nature of guerrilla warfare, and they were certainly far behind anything that the British had experienced in Borneo, Malaya or even Kenya during the Mau Mau rebellion. That was surprising, since many Portuguese commanders had by then seen service in Angola and Guinea.

The counter-insurgency pattern was the same each time. Some intelligence of guerrilla activity would come in and the local garrison commander would spend days getting together a force of several hundred men who would make a huge cross-country sweep, often 500 men strong. They would never act immediately on a tip-off, with the result that when an operation was at last launched, the birds had usually flown.

During bush operations everything in their path would be destroyed; livestock would be slaughtered, crops and villages burnt, the local people rounded up for questioning and anyone acting in a suspicious manner would be arrested and taken back to base. Tribesmen who attempted to escape this treatment were regarded as "fleeing terrorists", and they would be shot and the death recorded as a "terrorist kill".

If they escaped into the bush, well and good; there was no question of sending a force to follow them. By nightfall the unit would be back at base, congratulating themselves on a job well done. Naturally, any one of the local people who had experienced one of these Portuguese "search and destroy" missions was by then firmly a supporter of Frelimo; the business of "hearts and minds" came only much later. In that way many neutral tribesmen soon became Frelimo sympathisers.

The *Aldeamentos* programme of resettling rural communities in organised camps was by then already in full swing in all three African provinces. Large numbers were moved into areas where they would be under Portuguese control, and, in theory, out of reach of the insurgents. The justification for this policy was ostensibly that it denied the guerrillas the ability to wage war because there would be no popular indigenous support and no food, which was supposed to be essential for survival in the bush.

In reality, although a million people, roughly 15 per cent of the population, were resettled in Mozambique, the programme failed utterly. Beckett[9] says that a third of the food grown in the *Aldeamentos* went straight to the guerrillas.

Sometimes the *Aldeamentos* programme was welcomed by the black leaders of the Muslim Yao and the coastal people, who were opposed to Frelimo influence because it was largely tribally based. Most correspondents who visited the war areas up to the 1974 coup tended to disregard the fact that although guerrilla activity was extended to the Niassa region in 1967, the Makonde and the Nyanja were only two of 19 tribes from nine main ethnic groups speaking 17 different languages in Mozambique. For that reason the war was confined to the north. Lourenço Marques, with its tourists and bright lights, might have been in another country.

In the actual fighting, the South Africans and the Rhodesians found the Portuguese clumsy and inept. Their patrols were too large; thirty or forty men at a time when people like Reid-Daly were used to four-man "sticks" and achieving good results with such small numbers.

Most of the failures, the Rhodesians believed, resulted from a lack of regular professional troops and the fact that most of these boys from the metropolis neither understood Africa nor wished to be in Africa in the first place.

Their radio communications were poor, which was probably one reason why they worked in such large numbers; the fear of being overrun by the enemy, as in Vietnam, was a real one in the minds of such unprofessional soldiers.

Again, their radio sets were unwieldy American instruments designed rather for vehicles than the backs of soldiers in the bush, and they probably dated from the Korean war; communication with base was a long and complicated business. At one main base the Portuguese were using large antiquated German sets from the second world war.

During all the operations in which the Rhodesians took part in the Tete panhandle the Portuguese were found to be completely base-bound. They fought much as the Americans had fought in Vietnam.

The upper command was quite happy to let the insurgents control the bush while the Portuguese held on to the towns, communications links and strong-points. Reid–Daly said that in Tete, patrols lasting from four to six weeks should have been normal, supplied by air. The idea was regarded as preposterous by the upper command. At that time, the Portuguese would not consider anything beyond three days, spending every night in camp if at all possible. The Rhodesians always emphasised the need to dominate the bush by night as well as by day, and although the Portuguese officers agreed, they very rarely did anything about it.

The ability of Frelimo to move freely at night was clearly illustrated by the number of mines, both anti-tank and anti-personnel, that they were able to lay. This freedom extended all the way from Ruvuma to Tete. During one morning's clearing operation in the Mueda area, Portuguese sappers cleared 189 mines along ten kilometres of track, about a third of them TM–46s. The rest were APs. There were roughly fifty mines laid in the short three-day journey I completed from Tete to the Malawi border in 1971.

Physically, the Rhodesians regarded the average Portuguese conscript as "a poor physical specimen". They could not march any distance without frequent rests. Most of these young men had come from poor backgrounds, and although they did their first PT the day they joined the army in Portugal, they were barely fit or strong enough to meet the fairly rigorous demands of their officers. There were exceptions, of course. One of their worst faults on the march was that the column was noisy and straggling. They talked loudly instead of maintaining silence, which even Frelimo knew was absolutely necessary in counter-insurgency warfare.

At night, Reid–Daly found, when an ambush had been set up, the Portuguese soldiers would cough and fidget. "It was as if they were warning the enemy to keep clear, so that they would not be compelled to fight. It was an impossible situation."

On the other hand, some of the *Flecha*, parachute and black commando regiments were excellent operators in the bush. Most of them were superior to Frelimo, and most of the kills in Mozambique were attributable to them and to the air force.

While most operational plans were carefully prepared by the brigade staff, Reid–Daly found that they seldom allowed the battalion commander any scope for flexibility or personal initiative. It all had to be done according to the book. There was a marked reluctance to change plans in spite of fresh information and developments as the operation progressed.

A sorry example of this was the failure to capitalise on the discovery, towards the end of 1967, of a huge insurgent camp, about 500 yards across, by one of the helicopters during an operation in the mountains near Cahora Bassa. It was only a day later that an infantry attack was launched, because the Portuguese were not prepared to change the original plan and the sequence of events that they had mapped out.

Reid–Daly was with them at the time. He insisted that they should scrape together another body of men and try a vertical envelopment. That would have been possible, because there were eight Alouettes available. The operation only got off the ground several days later, and it was unsuccessful.

The Portuguese soldiers were very badly equipped, considering the nature of the war. Apart from the standard G–3 rifle of .762 NATO calibre, they had no night illumination flares, no Claymores and none of the elementary means of protection.

They had no idea of how to use smoke grenades to call up helicopters, or how to use small mirrors to attract the attention of aircraft – many little things that most Western forces take for granted. Whereas the Rhodesians maintained excellent liaison between pilots and ground forces, that never existed in Mozambique, and no one ever took steps to improve the situation. They just were not talking to each other. Another device taught by the Rhodesians and eventually taken up in Mozambique was to set up radio relay stations on hills. Rhodesian officers began to take some of the elementary equipment that was lacking, which attracted great interest. Reid–Daly even ran a course showing them how to make a simple Claymore mine from a plough–share.

He and other Rhodesian officers also explained to them the principle of a stop group in a frontal attack. They needed to work hard at it, for the Portuguese choice of positions was usually bad; they did not plan escape routes, and were simply not trained for that kind of warfare which by then had become second nature to Rhodesians and South Africans.

The very idea of taking a prisoner immediately after a skirmish was frowned upon. Although not all Frelimo captives were shot, they would argue that they *ought to have been.* It depended on the attitude of the officer in charge at the time. On more than one occasion Reid–Daly stepped in; it took a long time for the army to understand the need for interrogation and the importance of proper intelligence. PIDE, the secret police, was always calling for prisoners, which sometimes resulted in friction.

The Rhodesians noted that Portuguese military vehicles, the West German Unimog and the French Berliet, and their maintenance, were excellent. Like their uniforms, of which they were issued two per tour of duty, it was all they had and they looked after them. But not their weapons.

Perhaps because the G–3 was virtually proof against stoppage, few Portuguese soldiers bothered to clean their guns, either before or after an operation. They would smile among themselves at Rhodesian officers who took great care of their rifles at all times. One young captain told Reid–Daly that the last place where he had seen a man actually cleaning his rifle every day when not ordered to do so was Goa, after he had been captured by Indian troops.

Morale among Portuguese forces was seriously affected by the lack of facilities for the evacuation of casualties. That was due mainly to the shortage of operational helicopters. Also, while most of the camps had medical officers, most of them were young conscript students who did only the bare minimum. A man injured by a mine would usually have to be moved to an airstrip, where a small plane could be landed. Depending on how remote a base was, that could take a whole day. Many Portuguese died of wounds because of such delays.

The Rhodesian officers found it curious that the Portuguese in Mozambique had never developed reconnaissance patrols. They would seldom reconnoitre a position beforehand, or use aerial photographs for intelligence purposes once a known Frelimo camp had been spotted. Instead, they would deploy special forces in an operation which would often include the necessary primary reconnaissance with the attack; very much a hit–or–miss affair.

Reid–Daly spent some time with one of the *Flecha* units; he became a close friend of Colonel Oscar Cardoza, who was brought from Angola to establish the *Flecha* concept in Mozambique. Unlike so many of his fellows, Cardoza proved to be an excellent soldier and tactician.

While the *Flechas* worked in smaller groups they also lacked scouting ability. They were composed mostly of captured terrorists, turncoats and local recruits and were paid bounties for kills, captures or recovery of weapons. Their training was hard and simple. Discipline was draconian. A petty misdemeanour would be treated as a serious offence.

But they made good soldiers. Their ability to shoot straight with a rifle was unmatched even in the Rhodesian army; they either got one- or two-inch groups at fifty yards or they were thrashed by their officers.

The *Flechas* considered a 40 kilometre patrol between sunrise and sunset as normal, in spite of the difficult mountainous and jungle terrain. Some Rhodesian SAS men who worked with them were amazed at their ability to keep going and were themselves hard-pressed to keep up the pace. They were also militarily correct in their actions; they would cross a river or other obstacle by first sending two sections tactically across, scouting the area and then bringing the rest of the group through. During the entire day they had only one break for a smoke, that respite that most soldiers regard as a natural right.

The Rhodesians achieved some success in Mozambique. They managed to teach some units how to run a proper operations room and to set up an efficient Joint Operations Command. Trackers gradually began to come into their own, and here members of the SAS under Brian Robinson played an important part. Unfortunately, in the long term there were simply too many Portuguese and too few Rhodesians to have any real effect on the war.

The Rhodesians never succeeded in goading the Portuguese into effectively following up tracks after a contact. Under Reid-Daly, they would often refuse flatly to go into the bush unless a large force had been mustered, with helicopter support. The result was that Frelimo units were able to snipe at Portuguese patrols with impunity. They knew that the Portuguese would rarely detach men from a column to go after them.

To the conscript army, capturing a Frelimo camp was the pinnacle of success, even though it had often been abandoned because the rebels had foreknowledge of the attack or could hear them coming. Holding ground was the ultimate achievement, even if they abandoned that ground an hour later.

Reid-Daly recommended on his return to Salisbury that RLI units should be allowed to work with the Portuguese, not so much for political reasons, but rather to demonstrate what ordinary young soldiers were capable of when properly led and trained. He knew that the presence of special forces like the SAS might have been regarded by the Portuguese command as an attempt by the Rhodesians to "show them up", with consequent bad feeling.

In the opinion of most Rhodesian and South African soldiers who came into contact with the Portuguese, the quality most needed was initiative. As it was, it was almost entirely lacking. Occasionally a brilliant officer would be encountered; a man who knew the war, the enemy, the ground on which he was fighting and capable of inspiring his men to better results; but they were rare.

Discipline was also bad; and it has been well said that an army usually reflects its national character.

Thus the Portuguese, while respectful to their officers (except during the last phase of the war after the coup d'état), were sloppy in dress and bearing and slack in military operations. Often a battalion commander would be of the best type imaginable, but he would lack good professional officers to support him. Senior commanders usually had a handful of regular officers supplemented by many more *milicianos,* temporary officers from the universities.

There were other problems. A battalion colonel would often have senior visitors from Nampula, Beira or Lourenço Marques; brigadiers and generals, breathing down his neck in his own operations room, often countermanding instructions that he had just given to his men in the field. Four or five would sit about and veto the next phase; at other times they would change his entire operational plan. Such a scene, witnessed twice by Reid-Daly, was not a rare event; it happened often in all theatres in Mozambique. Certainly it would never have been tolerated in Guinea, or to the same extent in Angola, where the conflict was much more professionally handled. In Mozambique the high command had lost control. As correspondents we were all aware when visiting Mozambique, that Arriaga (the "Pink Panther" as his men called him) was frequently accused of employing too many subordinates who had failed elsewhere. He was recalled in July 1973; but by then the damage had been done.

Mozambique, from the beginning of the campaign in 1963, was never imbued with the kind of determination displayed in Angola or during the early stages in Guinea; the belief that this was a war that could be won. Even to the end, it was never lost; but there was no will to win either.

Because it began late and most intelligent Portuguese knew that Mozambique was their third African war and that Portugal was becoming over-extended, the Mozambique campaign lacked the necessary impetus for any effective or lasting counter-insurgency measures. Everything was done spasmodically; the Portuguese never held on to the initiative gained by operations like *Gordian Knot.*

As Beckett says, the Portuguese had growing problems in Mozambique by 1974, but not serious enough to ensure military defeat. We must therefore look elsewhere for the failure to consolidate the Portuguese position along the Ruvuma and to take advantage of the serious splits that were developing within the Frelimo hierarchy.

Porch speaks of deteriorating morale among regular cadres. This was manifested in the steady desertion rate in Portugal itself.

Nor were matters helped by Salazar, who, like Hitler before him, ignored the advice of his generals. He was warned repeatedly against fighting on more than one front at a time; he had three fronts in three different regions of Africa. To give him his due, there was not much he could do about it.

Again, the antiquated Portuguese war machine had been souped-up by trebling its strength from 60 000 in 1960 to 210 000 twenty years later. Caetano admitted in 1974, when he was in exile in Brazil, that "we had no organisation capable of directing the army in operations." Most of the Portuguese defence was haphazard and piecemeal, which, as Porch says, meant that the army was "ill-equipped to cope with a long war."

Matters were further compounded by the fact that relations between the Portuguese army and the settlers in Africa were bad. In Mozambique particularly, the colonists doubted the ability of the Portuguese army to fight. They questioned their courage, their morale and their integrity. They also hated the increasing reliance of the army on black troops. There were economic factors also. The Portuguese civilians were among the most heavily taxed in Europe. In Lourenço Marques they used to say that when the army arrived, prices went up. There was no love lost between settlers and soldiers.

The crunch came in January 1974, when a group of whites attacked an officers' mess in Beira after the murder of a white civilian. This event accentuated the isolation of the army still further. It resulted in the closing of the army rest centre in Beira.

The official military publication *Revista Militar*[10] gives some indication of the ratio of black and white soldiers towards the end of the war. These figures themselves are illuminating, giving a clear indication of the increasing need for indigenous troops to do their fighting for them. It is significant that in January 1989 the ratio between black–white troops on the Angolan border was even higher. Most of the units deployed in northern Namibia were black.

| Guinea | | Angola | | Mozambique | |
|---|---|---|---|---|---|
| Black | White | Black | White | Black | White |
| 24 800 | 6 200 | 37 800 | 25 000 | 19 800 | 24 200 |

No one can predict what might have happened if the war in Mozambique had continued. Although Frelimo were not successful in taking strong–points, they had extended the war to such a degree that so much attention was devoted to protecting the Cahora Bassa dam that the rest of Tete had became guerrilla country, which the Rhodesian insurgents used to good advantage.

By 1972 Frelimo was beginning to move south and east from Tete. The Vila Pery area was infiltrated that year and the Beira region in 1973. So constant were attacks on the Umtali–Beira rail link (one of the lifelines of Rhodesia) that they eventually stopped running trains at night. Armoured mine detectors known as *zorras* were placed ahead of the engine on this line.

Frelimo was equally active against the local population. In the Tete region alone more than fifty traditional chiefs were murdered in 1971, most of them because they refused to pay cash or tribute to marauding bands. Hundreds more were murdered in other areas. The level of hostilities had also escalated meanwhile. Mozambique, says one report, accounted for twice as many Portuguese casualties in the three months, November 1973–January 1974, than either Guinea or Angola.

Speaking in Lourenço Marques two weeks after the coup d'état in Lisbon, General Costa Gomes, one of the architects of the revolution, said: "Our armed forces have reached the limits of neuro–psychological exhaustion." These were strong words, and they have often been quoted since. Rightly or wrongly, General Costa Gomes echoed the sentiments of the nation. It was time for Portugal to vacate its African possessions.

To quote Beckett in conclusion: "In military terms, neither the Portuguese nor the guerrillas had won or lost; but, as in many other counter–insurgency campaigns, the outcome had been decided elsewhere."

So it was also in Angola and Guinea. In Rhodesia a rebel insurgent government attained power less than seven years later.

## FOOTNOTES

1. *The Terror Fighters,* Al J. Venter, Purnell, Cape Town, 1969.
2. Based on an unpublished thesis on the subject by Brigadier W.S. van der Wals, Pretoria, 1988. A good deal of first-hand information was supplied in a personal interview, 1988.

3. A few attacks were launched, such as the abortive seaborne invasion by exiles of the Republic of Guinea (Conakry) on 22 November 1970. These were rarely competently carried out.
4. With over 150 000 men in Africa by 1970, the Portuguese deployment represented a troop level in proportion to the Portuguese population as a whole, five times greater than that of the United States in Vietnam in the same year.
5. Porch, Douglas; *The Portuguese Armed Forces and the Revolution:* Croom Helm, London and Stanford, 1977.
6. *Portugal's War in Guiné-Bissau,* Al J. Venter; Munger Africana Library, California Institute of Technology, Pasadena, 1973.
7. *MPLA-Angola No.4;* LSM Information Centre, Richmond, Canada, 1973.
8. (Eds.) Beckett, Ian F.W. and Pimlott, John; *Armed Forces and Modern Counter-Insurgency,* Croom Helm, London, 1985.
9. *Ibid.*
10. No.11, November 1974, pp571–2.

## BIBLIOGRAPHY

Abshire, D.M. and Samuels, M.A. (ed.), *Portuguese Africa: A Handbook* (Praeger, London, 1969)

Alberts, D.J. "Armed Struggle in Angola" in B. O'Neill et al, (ed.), *Insurgency in the Modern World* (Westview Press, Boulder, Colorado, 1980), pp235–68

Barnett, D. and Harvey, R. (ed.) *The Revolution in Angola: MPLA Life Histories and Documents* (Bobbs, New York, 1972)

Barnett, D. *With the Guerrillas in Angola* (Liberation Support Movement, Seattle, 1970)

Beckett, F.W. and John Pimlott (ed.) *Armed Forces and Modern Counter-Insurgency;* (Croom Helm, London, 1985)

Bender, G.J. "The Limits of Counter-Insurgency: An African Case", *Comparative Politics* 4/3, 1972, pp331–60

Bender G.J. *Angola under the Portuguese* (Heinemann, London, 1978)

Biggs–Davidson, J. "Portuguese Guinea: A Lesser Vietnam", *NATO's Fifteen Nations* 13/5, Oct.–Nov. 1968, pp21–5

Bruce, N. *Portugal's African Wars* (Conflict Studies, London, Paper No.34, 1973). Later expanded into *Portugal: The Last Empire* (David and Charles, Newton Abbott, 1975)

Cabral, A. *Revolution in Guinea* (Monthly Review Press, New York, 1969)

Calvert, M. "Counter-Insurgency in Mozambique", *Journal of the Royal United Services Institute,* 118/1, 1973, pp81–4

Challiand, G. *Armed Struggle in Africa* (Monthly Review Press, London and New York, 1969)

Cornwall, B. *The Bush Rebels* (André Deutch, London, 1973)

Davidson, B. *The Liberation of Guinea* (Penguin Books Ltd, Harmondsworth, 1969)

Davidson, B. *Walking 300 Miles with Guerrillas through the Bush of Eastern Angola* (Munger Africana Notes No.6, Pasadena, 1971

Davidson, B. *In the Eye of the Storm* (Longman, London, 1972)

Davidson, B. *The People's Cause* (Longman, London, 1981)

Davidson, B. *Slovo, J. and Wilkinson, A.R. (ed.) Southern Africa* (Penguin Books Ltd, Harmondsworth, 1976)

de Arriaga, K. *The Portuguese Answer* (Tom Stacey, London, 1973)

de Spinola, A. *Portugal and the Future* (Johannesburg, 1974)

Ehrmark, A. and Wastberg, P. *Angola and Mozambique: The Case against Portugal* (Pall Mall Press, London, 1963)

Fields, R.M. *The Portuguese Revolution and the Armed Forces Movement* (Praeger, New York, 1975)

Gallagher, T. *Portugal: A Twentieth Century Interpretation* (Manchester Univ. Press, Manchester, 1983)

Gibson, R. *African Liberation Movements* (Oxford Univ. Press, Oxford, 1972)

Henriksen, T.H. *Mozambique: A History* (Rex Collings, London and Cape Town, 1978)

Henriksen, T.H. "Some Notes on the National Liberation Wars in Angola, Mozambique and Guiné-Bissau", *Military Affairs*, 41/1, 1977, pp30–6

Henriksen, T.H. "People's Wars in Angola, Mozambique and Guiné-Bissau", *Journal of Modern African Studies*, 14/3, 1976, pp377–99

Henriksen, T.H. "Portugal in Africa: Comparative Notes on Counter-Insurgency" (Orbis, Summer 1977), pp395–412

Henriksen, T.H. "Lessons from Portugal's Counter-Insurgency Operations in Africa", *Journal of the Royal United Services Institute*, 123/2, 1978, pp31–5.

Henriksen, T.H. "People's Wars in Angola, Mozambique and Guiné-Bissau", *Journal of Modern African Studies*, 14/3, 1976, pp377–99

Humbaraci, A. and Muchnik, N. *Portugal's African Wars* (Macmillan, London, 1974)

Jundanian, B.F. "Resettlement Programmes: Counter-Insurgency in Mozambique", *Comparative Politics*, 6/4, 1974, pp519–40

Marcum, J.A. *The Angolan Revolution* (MIT, Cambridge, Mass., 1969 and 1978; 2 vols)

McCuen J.J. The Art of Counter Revolutionary Warfare (Faber, London, 1966)

McCulloch, J. *In the Twilight of Revolution* (Routledge and Kegan Paul, London, 1983)

Middlemas, K. *Cabora Bassa* (Weidenfeld and Nicholson, London, 1975)

Mondlane, E. *The Struggle for Mozambique* (Penguin Books Ltd, Harmondsworth, 1969)

Morris, M. *Armed Conflict in Southern Africa* (Howard Timmins, Cape Town, 1974)

Munslow, B *Mozambique: The Revolution and Its Origins* (Longman, London, 1983)

Newitt, M. *Portugal in Africa: The Last Hundred Years* (Hurst, London, 1981)

Porch, D. *The Portuguese Armed Forces and the Revolution* (Croom Helm, London and Stanford, 1977)

Sobel, C.A. "Portuguese Revolution", 1974–76 (Facts on File, New York, 1976)

Sunday Times Insight Team, *Insight on Portugal: the Year of the Captains* (André Deutch, London, 1975)

Swift, K. *Mozambique and the Future* (R. Hale, London, 1975)

Venter, Al J. *The Terror Fighters* (Purnell, Cape Town, 1969)

Venter, Al J. *Portugal's War in Guiné-Bissau* (Munger Africana Library, California Institute of Technology; Pasadena, 1973)

Venter, Al J. *Portugal's Guerrilla War* (Malherbe, Cape Town, 1973)

Venter, Al J. *Africa at War* (Devin–Adair, Old Greenwich, Conn., 1974)

Venter, Al J. *The Zambezi Salient: Conflict in Southern Africa* (R. Hale, London, 1975)

Wheeler, D. "African Elements in Portugal's Armies in Africa," *Armed Forces and Society*, 2/2, 1976, pp235–50

Wheeler, D. and Pelissier, R. *Angola* (Praeger, London, 1971)

Wheeler, D.L. "The Portuguese Army in Angola", *Journal of Modern African Studies*, 7/3, 1969, pp425–39

Wilkinson, A.R. *Angola and Mozambique: The Implications of Local Power, Survival*, 16/5, 1974, pp217–27

Wolfers, M. (ed.) *Unity and Struggle* (Heinemann, London, 1980)

# ANC CLANDESTINE OPERATIONS
## by Craig Williamson

Political violence is no stranger to the African continent, where the exploitation of terror and intimidation has virtually become an accepted part of the social norm. The determination of the ANC to come to power and replace the existing government in South Africa has progressed through a series of turbulent and often contradictory phases since the decision to adopt violence. Even the decision itself reflected these peculiarities for it was taken (under SACP[1] pressure) without so much as informing or consulting the ostensible leader, Chief Albert Luthuli, in 1961, with the formation of the MK (*Umkhonto we Sizwe* - Spear of the Nation) the so-called military wing of the movement. In recent years the strategy has been substantially broadened to include an extensive propaganda campaign both outside and inside South Africa, together with the manipulation or creation of many front organisations in the educational, cultural, labour, religious and political-cum-constitutional spheres.

These tactics taken together have created a new level of revolutionary warfare which is a serious and novel development for South Africa. "Revolutionary war" is generally defined as the process whereby politically-inspired and organised communities make an effort to seize control of the decision-making institutions of a nation, by means of unconventional warfare and various forms of terrorism designed to win the social and political support of a wider community or at least their acquiescence. It is commonly agreed that 1976 marked the turning-point in the development of this strategy, when the ANC began its second *Umkhonto* campaign.

Such an operation was a far cry from the original South African Native National Congress founded by the esteemed group of educated African leaders and chiefs who had met in Bloemfontein in 1912. Their purpose was to create an inter-tribal community that would develop into a means of creating a nation from the multifarious black peoples of South Africa. John Dube was chosen as their first president, symbolising the essentially Christian, conservative, reformist and élitist nature of the organisation and its ambitions: the gradual improvement of the lot of the educated and cultured African.

In 1923 the organisation changed its name to the African National Congress, but remained a small group of moderates, which nearly vanished into oblivion during the 1930s. This was mainly the result of conflict between the original moderate nationalists and the newer communist members. Pixley Seme, its leader at the time, a respected lawyer, sought to make the ANC a self-help organisation designed to encourage Africans in the commercial world by means of African Congress Clubs, although such ideals were far beyond the capabilities of the financial resources and organisation of the ANC. Seme was a far-sighted man, despite the shortcomings of his organisation, and he made a sincere attempt to preserve the traditional values and culture of his people at a time when he recognised the inherent instability and disorder created by the industrialisation, commercialisation, urbanisation and the operation of Gresham's Law in the minds of rural men and women.

It is easy to see, with hindsight, the lost opportunities. Seme's dedication and sincerity went unacknowledged by the whites, who themselves were just recovering from the damage of the Boer war, Union in 1910, the first world war and the subsequent economic depression. Successive South African governments found themselves preoccupied by attempts to heal the scars of British imperialism. Reconciling these stresses obsessed the white authorities and the electorate to the exclusion of black concerns and aspirations. When dissatisfaction broke out it was ruthlessly dealt with by Smuts and Hertzog. Efforts to resolve white disputes cut directly into African interests. For example, in 1936 Africans were removed from the common voters' roll in the Cape Province.

Because of the emphasis that the ANC placed on economic questions, there was very little effective opposition to such legislative measures. When Dr Alfred Xuma became president of the organisation in 1940 he did so against this obviously ineffectual background and, not surprisingly, set about trying to make the ANC an effective force. The organisation was redesigned and streamlined, a full-time staff was appointed, subsidised from Dr Xuma's funds. The ANC was given a new constitution, it recognised the equality of women and sought a more representative and broadly-based membership. Through his inspired leadership the finances were put on a sound footing and membership greatly increased. It was during this period that the South African Communist Party (CPSA)[1] increased its infiltration of the ANC despite Xuma's Christian, moderate and reformist policies.

By contrast the CPSA began in 1921 as an organisation dedicated exclusively to the promotion of white interests (it regarded blacks as "pastoral" and therefore irrelevant to the class struggle of modern industrialised society) but was soon forced to realise that a ready-made revolutionary support base existed among the dispossessed African proletariat. By the late 1920s the SACP was paradoxically striving for the creation of a "bourgeois" black independent republic as a first step towards a workers' democratic socialist republic. Josiah Gumede, President of the ANC at the time, earned the disapproval of his fellow-members when he responded positively to such overtures and even accepted an invitation to visit the USSR. In 1930 he was voted out of office and replaced by Seme! The response of the CPSA to this slight set-back was a classic illustration of how a perfectly legitimate organisation can be slowly and secretly infiltrated and turned into a communist front.

Black members of the CPSA such as Gaur Radebe and Edwin Mofutsanyama were henceforth ordered to join the ANC with a view to gradually working their way into positions of influence and power. At first such men were few and apparently insignificant in the general scheme. However, the reforms introduced by Dr Xuma in the 1940s served as a stimulus to younger and less restrained urbanised Africans. They believed that the time had come to take the initiative and go on the offensive, and their opinions were voiced by Anton Lembede, Oliver Tambo, Nelson Mandela and Walter Sisulu. These men formed the basis of the ANC Youth League from 1948 which had a lasting influence on the ANC's future policy and direction. It was responsible, for example, for the formulation of the Defiance Campaign of 1952, elements of which were rejuvenated and used by black activists in later unrest in the black townships. Lembede, a devout Catholic, was convinced that the ANC needed an all-embracing ideological framework within which its members could take active steps to realise their aspirations. The Afrikaner Nationalists both intrigued him and exemplified the quality that had been missing from the ANC.

Lembede therefore embarked upon a programme that he called "Africanism", a form of black consciousness thirty years ahead of its time, which emphasised the importance of pride in one's cultural and historical heritage and a determined and resolute outlook for the future: a sort of Pan Africanism. He treated the CPSA and Marxism with contempt and distrust, and rejected its notions about class and its predominantly Jewish white English-speaking leadership. Unfortunately for the ANC, and perhaps for South Africa, Lembede died still young. His premature death in 1947 provided the opening for which the CPSA had been patiently waiting. His successor, Ashley Peter Mda, who shared his ideological predilections, was himself sickly, and the Marxist faction of the ANC seized the leadership before the moderates could do anything to stop them.

An important event in the take-over of the ANC by the CPSA occurred in 1949, when at the annual conference of the ANC the Youth League ejected Dr Xuma and replaced him with a liberal figurehead, Dr James Moroka. Walter Sisulu was elected Secretary-General, and two communists, Moses Kotane and Dan Tloome, were elected to the Executive Committee (NEC). The appointment of Kotane in particular must have been seen by the CPSA as a notable victory, for he was a graduate of the Lenin School in Moscow, and Secretary-General of the CPSA. As a direct result of the new order, a radical programme of action was formulated, calling for strikes, civil disobedience, boycotts, stay-aways and general lawlessness.

So pervasive was the CPSA, and through it, foreign Marxist disruptive influence in South African politics, that the government was forced to pass the Suppression of Communism Act of 1950. On the one hand it effectively prevented the CPSA from publicly sustaining its campaign of subversion, agitation, propaganda and destabilisation. On the other hand, so wide was the legislation in the broad interpretation of its application, that many individuals, who later bitterly regretted their decisions, were driven into the all too willing arms of the Marxist movements which had been seeking just such an influx of recruits. The CPSA was driven underground and many of its black members subsequently diverted their activity to the ANC, while Indian communists joined the South African Indian Congress, itself enjoying considerable respectability in the Asian community because of its association with Mahatma Gandhi. While it is popular in leftist-liberal circles to condemn the manner in which this legislation was introduced, it should not be forgotten that CPSA involvement with the trade unions had given rise to riots, strikes, demonstrations, sabotage and subversion. The last straw was when the CPSA and the ANC announced their plans for a Freedom Day demonstration all over the country in April 1949. Although the government prohibited these demonstrations, violence broke out and eighteen were killed and many injured. A committee to investigate communism in South Africa had been established by the National Party government when it came to power, and after a thorough study the Suppression of Communism Bill was introduced by the future first State President, C.R. Swart.

By 1951, prominent communists such as J.B. Marks were being elected to positions of influence in the ANC. Marks became president of the Transvaal ANC, a position for which he had been groomed at the Lenin School in Moscow. Another communist, David Bopape, became secretary of the Transvaal Executive Committee. Gradually the ANC Youth League revealed its true colours by its recommendations and the ANC itself discarded the notion of "Africanism" promoted by Lembede as a solution to the problems of South Africa. As the influence of the CPSA grew within the organisation, disaffected Africanists broke away to form a rival body, the Pan Africanist Congress (PAC). Although the splinter faction hoped that they could preserve the original principles of the ANC, as stated in 1912, they adopted a stringent form of racialism similar to that ascribed to Mao Tse-tung. The ANC itself increasingly allied itself with other organisations and came increasingly under communist control. Besides the South African Indian Congress, the South African Congress of Democrats, a communist front for whites, took shape, consisting almost entirely of former white members of the CPSA.

At Kliptown, near Johannesburg, in 1955, these alliances were given formal coherence with the creation of the Congress Alliance at a meeting attended by about 3 000 people, at which the Freedom Charter was adopted. Although written with some eloquence, the document clearly lays the foundations of a future Soviet-style constitution. Two members of the CPSA, Lionel Bernstein and Joe Slovo, played a prominent part in the drafting of the Charter. A flood of communist literature poured from under the banner of the ANC, foreign policies were adopted identical to those of the Soviet Union, and members of the ANC, among them Walter Sisulu and Duma Nokwe, were treated to free trips to the Eastern bloc from funds provided by the South African Congress of Democrats.

In 1952 Moroka was replaced as president of the ANC by Chief Albert Luthuli, a Methodist lay preacher of great courage and dignity who argued strongly for participation by blacks in government without total abrogation of white power. Ironically, action by the government against Luthuli made possible the last communist nail in the coffin of the ANC, for by exiling him under house arrest miles away from the ANC headquarters in Johannesburg, crucial decisions were made by the CPSA clique about which he was neither consulted nor informed. To his eternal credit, Luthuli never advocated violence, although he was a firm proponent of passive resistance.

The Sharpeville shootings in 1960, which resulted in 69 dead and over 180 injured, gave further fuel to the ANC propagandists, despite the fact that the demonstration had been instigated by the PAC and not the ANC. Although the South African Police were to carry the brunt of the blame for the shootings, it is seldom, if ever, mentioned that several days before the events at Sharpeville, nine policemen had been hacked to death by a mob in Cato Manor, near Durban. As a result of the trend of events, the government withdrew the Pass Law legislation for a while. The ANC showed its gratitude for this gesture by calling for a nationwide strike. The government responded with legislation prohibiting the ANC and the PAC. This drove the ANC underground, and so under total communist control. This historical account of the development of and subsequent prohibition of the ANC and the CPSA is a matter of record. What is not, however, are the clandestine attempts to create a socialist South Africa, by international Marxism.

In the years leading up to the banning of the ANC, the CPSA under the tutelage of the Moscow party, planned to gain control of an organ of African nationalist politics in South Africa. Liberal apologists for the ANC and its terrorism still try to explain that the ANC resorted to armed violence only after all other peaceful political platforms had been denied them by an unreasonable white government. The reality is very different. There has been for many years an organised Marxist conspiracy devoted to the establishment of a South African Socialist People's Republic. In 1854 Karl Marx showed his interest in South Africa in an article written for a Cape Town paper, *Die Zuid-Afrikaan*. In 1900 Lenin wrote about South Africa in the first issue of *Iskra*. He also wrote about South Africa in his *Notebooks on Imperialism - Imperialism - the Highest Stage of Capitalism*. Engels wrote about South Africa in his supplement to Marx's third volume of *Das Kapital*. But perhaps the most significant indication of Marxist preoccupation with a socialist revolution in South Africa was shown by Lenin's agent, Mikhail Volberg. Volberg arrived in South Africa in 1913, and stayed there till 1919 under the name of Michel de Velmont. The Tsarist secret police were after him for his role in the abortive Russian revolution of 1905. Because he could no longer remain safely in Europe, Lenin despatched him to South Africa, where he spent six years doing Lenin's work and reporting regularly on the growth of the Marxist movement at the southern tip of Africa. In 1917, after the successful Bolshevik revolution, de Velmont joined Lenin in Moscow.

It is surely no coincidence that soon after Volberg's arrival in South Africa the 1913 miners' strike took place, which was stopped only when the government deported several of the leaders back to Europe from whence they had come. These people had all been associated with the South African Labour Party, which was at that time affiliated to the Second Communist International.

In 1917 the South African International Socialist League, which was a radical breakaway group from the Labour Party, enthusiastically hailed the success of the Bolshevik Revolution in a pamphlet in English, Zulu and Sotho, titled *We are South African Bolsheviks,* and during that same year the ISL shared a platform with the ANC for the first time, when they jointly protested against the Native Administration Bill.

After the success of the Bolsheviks in Russia, Lenin did not rest in his efforts to broaden his Russian success into a worldwide socialist revolution, nor did he forget South Africa. In 1920 he convoked the Third Communist International, better known as the Comintern, at which the ISL was ordered to return to South Africa and to take the leading part in uniting all the socialist splinter groups in South Africa into a single disciplined and centralised communist party. One of the leading lights in the Marxist movement of South Africa at that time, David Jones, who attended this meeting, was ordered to remain behind in Moscow as Lenin's assistant in the Comintern administration. He also acted as its executive member for Africa.

Communist interference in South African politics immediately increased after the formation of the CPSA and its affiliation to the Comintern. In 1922 the leaders of the CPSA were deeply implicated in the miners' strike, ironically enough under the slogan of "Workers of the world, unite and fight for a white South Africa". In *Lenin's Complete Works* mention is made of Lenin's instructions for agents of the Comintern to be sent to the Rand during those years. However, at that stage of the communist movement in South Africa it concentrated its attention mainly on the whites. The party took a very chauvinistic view of the socialist revolution. Racism, paternalism, discrimination and the other political features that later became known as "apartheid" were not their concern. The communists of those days cared only about a socialist revolution in South Africa, and they had decided that only the white working class had revolutionary potential. The black population was regarded as mainly pastoral and therefore outside the proletarian class struggle of the capitalist world, and therefore irrelevant to revolution. Nevertheless, after the disastrous failure of the 1922 miners' strike and other incidents inspired by the party, communist theorists began to seek a new strategy for a revolution in South Africa. From 1924 it began to pay increasing attention to black political organisations, and particularly to the growing black trade union movement. Ironically, it was not Lenin who laid the foundation of the present communist domination of the black political armed struggle in South Africa. It was Stalin who saw revolutionary potential in hijacking the black nationalist movement in South Africa. The formulation of this policy took place at the Comintern meeting of 1928, at which the CPSA was ordered to put into effect the so-called Black Republic policy, whereby a two-stage revolution in

South Africa was adumbrated. The first stage comprised support for the forces of democratic black nationalism to precipitate a black-dominated (i.e. majority) bourgeois democratic unitary state, based on one man–one vote. The second stage of revolution could be the socialist revolution, which would transform the "democratic republic" into a "socialist people's republic".

Marxist–Leninist revolutionary theory requires that to bring about the radical transformation of society, armed force is an essential element. For that reason, once it had been decided to hijack the ANC as a revolutionary vehicle, it became necessary to change its policy from participation in the political process to armed destruction of the existing order. The party therefore began to infiltrate their members into the leadership of the ANC and to seduce existing African nationalist leaders to the socialist cause. Through these leaders, they also shifted ANC policy to become more and more aggressive, which they hoped would provoke the government to ban the organisation, in which event they would, they thought, convince all the leaders of the ANC of the necessity of armed struggle as the only effective political weapon left to them.

While all this was going on within the party and the ANC, Stalin was acting on other levels against South Africa. In May 1927 the Special Branch of the London Metropolitan Police raided the offices of the Russian trade organisation ARCOS. Documents seized in the raid proved that the Russians were running a spying and subversion network from London with its tentacles all over the British Empire. Among the documents seized were lists of contracts and post-boxes for the use of Russian agents in South Africa. The secret war for South Africa had begun.

In 1961 *Umkhonto we Sizwe* was formed under the leadership of Nelson Mandela, who was appointed on the recommendation of Moscow, a decision of which Andrei Gromyko remains proud to this day. Joe Slovo and Ruth First were to play significant roles in the MK from a variety of international European capitals, principally London. As Mzala stated in a recent article in *Sechaba,* when the MK was formed its cadres were unarmed and it lacked personnel who had been trained in revolutionary warfare. Those who were ultimately selected and sent abroad for training returned to South Africa to train the recruits who had joined just before the arrests in Rivonia in 1963. They were key members of the ANC, known to the security forces for their political militancy, although less for their qualities of leadership. Their survival in the new terrorist role had limited chances, and the subsequent arrests smashed all the regional command structures that had been established.

The plan drawn up by the ANC–SACP, *Operation Mayibuye,* was to send abroad a first group of 120 trainees, who on completion of their training would land by ship or air simultaneously in four groups of thirty each, at selected areas, armed and equipped in such a way as to be self-sufficient for at least a month, in the course of which they were to join locally-recruited terrorist bands. That was to coincide with an extensive propaganda campaign both inside and outside South Africa and a general call for an unprecedented mass struggle throughout the country both violent and non-violent.

It was further envisaged that these platoons of thirty men each would split into sections of ten, which would then operate within selected areas and link their terrorist activities with local groups. In the first phase, the choice of these areas would be based on the nature of the terrain, with a view to establishing bases from which attacks could be launched and to which they could retreat. The designers of *Operation Mayibuye* argued as follows:

"... We must not underestimate the fact that there is a terrain in many parts of South Africa, which although not classically impregnable, is suitable for guerrilla-type operations."

Ironically, they cited as examples the actions conducted by the Boer commandos in the plains of the Transvaal against the British.

Their conception of clandestine operations were greatly influenced by the Cuban revolution, in which the general uprising had been triggered by organised and well-prepared terrorist actions during the course of which substantial support had come from the local population, which detested the Batista government. The ANC did not expect such a struggle to end quickly. It had to be protracted, since they could expect virtually unlimited material help from sympathetic governments. In the last analysis the ANC would have to rely on the enemy as its main source of supply. In the 1960s it was decided that terrorist operations would therefore be designed mainly to disarm the enemy.

In 1967, three years after the Rivonia trial, another attempt was made to infiltrate armed units into South Africa. Although it was not so elaborately worked out as *Operation Mayibuye* in the early 1960s, the plan envisaged that a large armed force would pass through Rhodesia and split into smaller units upon arrival in South Africa. The shortcomings of this plan were mainly due to the way in which the operation began. In coordination with the Zimbabwe African People's Union (ZAPU) of Joshua Nkomo, plans were made to dispatch a hundred terrorists to South Africa through Rhodesia. On learning of the plan, the Rhodesian government invited the South African Security Forces into Rhodesia, and military actions at Wankie and Sipolilo cut the operations short. It is doubtful whether these units, even if they had reached South Africa safely, could have managed to survive for long in the absence of an established political infrastructure to receive them and provide their first local recruits.

With the adoption of the Strategy and Tactics Document at the First National Consultative Conference of the ANC in Morogoro in 1969, the first comprehensive guideline for the ANC since *Operation Mayibuye* was drawn up. It envisaged the military strategy as forming part of, and guided by, a broader political strategy to ensure that revolutionary battles were fought on all possible fronts, using not only a terror faction, but also mobilising various sections of the community. Ideologically the document placed the intended South African revolution within the international context "during the epoch of the transition from capitalism to socialism". This radicalised the strategic perspective of the ANC more than any other document or proclamation since 1912, and it recognised that South Africa was, above all, an industrialised capitalist society. Curiously enough, the document still saw the rural areas as the main theatre of terrorist operations, although the ANC was only too well aware that this did not alter the fact that only the "industrial proletariat" should be the vanguard of the revolution.

While the ANC claimed in theory to be planning for a clandestine guerrilla war rather than a general uprising, concentrating on the rural areas where the state was considered to be at its weakest, rather than the towns where the security forces could be readily mustered, the practical application of this policy turned out very differently. In theory the idea was to disperse the security forces from their urban concentrations into the countryside, thereby making the big towns weak links in the security chain. This rather odd reasoning was based on the notion that urban guerrilla warfare would be difficult to initiate, because the black townships were far from the major towns and industrial centres. It was believed that the potential guerrilla army was already surrounded in the ghettos by the security forces. Again, in the 1970s the reality proved to be the contrary. The MK found it very difficult to mobilise and politicise the rural masses, while the more educated, urbanised blacks proved far more susceptible to agitation, propaganda and subversion.

Both the government and the ANC recognised that the support of the population was what the final success of their campaigns would depend on. Indeed, the ANC quoted Lt-Gen. Allan Fraser on that. Writing in 1968, when he was Officer Commanding Joint Combat Forces of the SADF, Fraser had said:

"The objective for both sides in a revolutionary war is the population itself. Military tactics are well and good, but they are really quite useless if the government has lost the confidence of the people among whom it is fighting. And by the time their confidence has been lost, more armed force will cause the population to become more antagonistic."

To its vexation the ANC found itself compelled to watch while new black political forces used existing state structures for a programme of mass mobilisation. Thus towards the end of the 1960s the school children and university students formed the South African Students' Organisation (SASO), followed by a rapid growth of militancy in the black trade union movement, culminating in the mass strikes in Natal in 1973. Thus the ANC realised that a new phase in the struggle had been reached, in which the black political apathy of the previous year was slowly being eroded, and that they could no longer merely conduct the "liberation" of black South Africa as an externally based military operation. In their own analysis of the events of 1976, the ANC found itself admitting that it had been caught off guard. While admitting that its underground machinery was already at work in factories and academic institutions, the ANC pointed out that the level of organisation and internal leadership at that stage had not yet reached the point "where the vanguard movement could masterfully and boldly knit together the various threads of popular initiative and energy into a well organised nation-wide uprising, or probably even arm the people for a general insurrection."

Certainly there can be no doubt that as the events of 1976 unfolded, the underground organisation and structures that existed did their best under the circumstances to capitalise on the unrest by coordinating the various half-organised activities, and where they undoubtedly succeeded was in providing safe routes and other assistance to many of those predominantly teenage schoolchildren who wanted to leave the country to take up ANC pledges of schooling and university abroad. When the schools and universities turned out to be terrorist training camps of a most brutal kind, many of the children desperately tried to return to South Africa. Such "defectors" were either summarily put to death as traitors if they were caught, or were returned to their camps, where they were paraded as examples of "bourgeois deviationism". The few who did make it back to South Africa brought harrowing tales of beatings, starvation, medical neglect and torture. More wisely, many endured the military training and indoctrination, only to hand themselves over to the security forces the moment they had been infiltrated into the country. From these disaffected cadres and other sources, a steady stream of information flowed to the South African authorities, and a composite picture was carefully formed.

As a consequence of the 1976 riots the ANC began a phase of "armed propaganda", designed to make its presence felt throughout South Africa and to make international headlines. Psychologically it was designed to accustom the black population to the idea that the state was not invincible. Attacks on police stations, economic and civilian targets were intended to prove that the ANC was a force to be reckoned with. The fact that innocent black and white civilians were murdered in the process was justified by the assertion that the ANC had been "forced" to adopt violence because of the intransigence of the state. It was an assertion that put the ANC into the same category as any other international terrorist organisation.

If the acts of sabotage themselves were characterised by their sporadic and indiscriminate nature, the cost to the ANC in the manpower attrition rate was great. Private studies in South Africa by independent analysts have shown that ANC sabotage cadres and cells had an average lifespan of not more than six months.

To the ANC, the problem lay not in its adopted strategy or its interpretation. It was considered to be at the tactical level of practice. Trained terrorists were entering the country successfully, supposedly fully equipped to survive, only to rely on the assumption that the "masses" were clear about the need to fight the government, particularly after the Soweto unrest. However, according to ANC sources, on numerous occasions they discovered that the population did not understand who the terrorists were, and even more significantly, that political consciousness and readiness to support the terrorists could not be assessed from headlines about mass turnout at political funerals. When cadres found it impossible to hide "among the very people they had come to fight for", they sought refuge in dug-outs far from the target population.

This was a most unsatisfactory position for the ANC. The outlying terrain was hardly the place for revolutionary warfare, which by their own definition means direct engagement *with* the local population not *for* it. Theory teaches that revolutionary armed struggle develops from the "grass roots of the masses" when the overwhelming majority of the population are presented with no alternative but to fight. The idea was not original; it had been borrowed from that great failed revolutionary, Che Guevara.

Many factors had facilitated the launching of this second *Umkhonto* campaign, both internally and externally. The Portuguese withdrawal from southern Africa in the mid-1970s greatly expanded the territory accessible to the ANC, and made it possible to exploit not only Mozambique but also Swaziland as launching pads. In 1978 a delegation from the ANC under the leadership of Oliver Tambo went on a study tour of Vietnam. They made a detailed study of the methods that had been used against the French and the Americans in Indo-China. They had discussions with political leaders and military commanders, including General Vo Nguyen Giap and General Van Tien Dung. This visit confirmed their belief that the armed struggle had to be based on and grow out of mass political support and that it must involve as wide a range of the people as possible. All terrorist activities had to be guided at every stage, by political mobilisation, organisation and resistance, with the object of progressively weakening the grip of the state on political, economic, social and military power, and by a combination of terror, intimidation, subversion, agitation and propaganda. The other factor that emerged from the Vietnamese visit was the degree of patience required, based on confidence in ultimate victory. The ANC discovered that the North Vietnamese, despite set-backs, betrayals and disappointments, never took short-cuts; they understood that a revolution was a process that required the organisation of people from one stage to another. Their revolutionary "mass bases" had been built by long and patient work and with the experience of organisation and "political education" round the daily life and needs and aspirations of the population. Patient organisation had proved to be the decisive factor.

After the analysis of the Report of the Mission to Vietnam, and basing their assessment on recent experiences in South Africa, the ANC decided that it needed three years of active political mobilisation and organisation, in both town and country before they would be ready for a "people's war". They were satisfied that no amount of mopping-up could uproot a revolutionary force that had become part and parcel of the civil population: no creation of protected villages could prevent attacks on the pro-government local population. A new political machine was trained, and political cadres entered the country not to shoot people or bomb power stations, but to begin a resolute single-minded campaign of political organisation.

As the extent of infiltration of South Africa was gradually increased, the South African security forces, the police, the Defence Force and specialised units found themselves compelled to devote greater attention to the frontiers and even to the neighbouring states beyond the frontiers.

The other crucial lesson derived from Vietnam was the overriding importance of the security forces, in particular the army. If the security forces are still intact in morale and material, if there is no appreciable degree of disaffection within it resulting in its commanders and rank-and-file losing their loyalty to the state, then such an army is capable of frustrating any attempted revolution.

The apparently successful MK attacks of the early 1980s were not, in fact, a result of a general increase in the ability of the organisation. They were rather "armed propaganda" designed to give the impression of a far greater ability than they actually possessed. These spectacular attacks were all conducted by the so-called Special Operations Section of the MK which at that time fell directly under the control of its Chief of Staff, Joe Slovo. The Special Operations Unit was in reality a Communist Party-controlled unit that could draw on the help of other Moscow-controlled parties. The attacks carried out by these units relied to a large degree on the support given by foreigners and white South Africans; for example, at least three holders of British passports living in the UK were responsible for the 1981 122mm missile attack on Voortrekkerhoogte. In the case of the 1980 SASOL-NATREF attack, while the actual placing of the limpet mines was done by black members of the Solomon Mahlangu Squad, the reconnaissance and the establishment of the arms caches were carried out by whites. In the case of the attack on Koeberg, a foreign engineer, who had been infiltrated into one of the contracted construction companies was used to identify a vulnerable feature of the construction and to place the explosives.

The central element in all of these attacks was the participation of highly trained members of the international communist brotherhood and the use of operational bases in the neighbouring states. The response of the South African security forces was decisive. On 31 January 1981 South African forces attacked and destroyed an ANC base in Matola, near Maputo, including the so-called "Terror Nest", HQ of Solomon Mahlangu's squad. In December 1982, South African forces raided Maseru in Lesotho and killed ANC members in "safe houses" throughout the town. Since that time, several attacks by the South African security forces have been made against ANC bases in neighbouring states. During the same period internal security at key points was intensified, and other internal security measures were taken to frustrate hit-and-run attacks from outside the country, all of which meant that not only did the ANC lose its ability to carry out high-level terrorism, but also that the ability of MK was broken, and military support for planned political actions could not be put into effect.

Parallel to their military activities, the ANC hierarchy spent the early 1980s concentrating on "internal political reconstruction". These mechanisms were established to regain control of political organisations active in SA, such as labour, youth, civic and community associations. On 20 and 21 August 1983 a meeting took place near Cape Town of more than 12 000 people who called for the creation of a national organisation, to be called the United Democratic Front. The meeting heard a message of greeting and solidarity from Nelson Mandela and other incarcerated leaders of the ANC, who were given a standing ovation. The three presidents elected were old stalwarts of the ANC: Oscar Mpetha, Archie Gumede and Albertina Sisulu.

Just over a year later, in September 1984, the most sustained outbreak of unrest in black areas in South Africa began. However, while the political will and ability to organise mass unrest existed, the revolutionary forces lacked everything but the most rudimentary military support. In 1985 the South African security forces perfected their National Security Management strategy which, together with the 1986 National State of Emergency, led to the greatest political and military set-back to the ANC since its formation. During the Second National Consultative "Kabwe" Conference of the ANC, in 1985, a heated debate arose during which blame was freely laid by the political and military leaders of the ANC on one another. Joe Slovo, as Chief of Staff of the MK, received severe criticism for his lack of military success against the racist régime. He turned the tables by making the point that military success in a revolutionary struggle depends on the level of political support existing in the community. He said it was wrong to assume that a revolutionary struggle could be won by military action alone. Slovo, like other ANC–SACP leaders, sees the strategy of revolution as a flexible one in which use is made of various tactics, including armed struggle and terrorism. Nevertheless, emphasis is placed on the political struggle, led by a professional revolutionary cadre. The premise is that the masses are weak and uninformed and that their support must be gained through agitation, infiltration and intimidation. Lenin ordained that the armed struggle should be subordinate to the political struggle, and in that, even Slovo had to admit that the ANC had failed.

In a remarkable confession the ANC was forced to conclude that in street battles, behind township barricades and even in stayaway strikes, the MK had been defeated by the security forces. If the outcome of a revolution depends on the sympathy with the revolution in the security forces of the state, apart from any economic and political difficulties, the South African government was far from being overthrown by violence alone.

The ANC has been compelled to accept that history and circumstances demand a uniquely South African solution to ensure the success of a revolution. A recent article in *Sechaba* by Mzala neatly agreed with the findings of the Second National Consultative Conference held in Kabwe at which the Strategy and Tactics Commission decided on a seven-point approach:

1. People's war and insurrection
2. The Bantustans
3. The working class
4. Military combat work
5. Embryos of people's power
6. Coordination of rural and urban guerrilla warfare
7. Action against the enemy's support base

Seeing the situation in the townships as conducive to further action, the National Executive Committee (NEC) of the ANC called for the building up of arms caches in the vicinity of all the large towns so that units could be equipped at short notice for the "emergency insurrectionary conditions". Careful studies of the main urban nerve centres were called for, so that forces could be concentrated at key points during an urban insurrection to select important targets. Mass organisations at the popular level in the Bantustans were to be created so that they could be drawn together with the urban revolutionary base at the proper moment.

The NEC recognised the need for a closer look at the self-governing states, reluctantly acknowledging that they had created a vast bureaucratic apparatus and civil service employing a wide range of black professionals who enjoyed the benefits of public office. It was believed that the security forces of these states opened up new opportunities for disaffection and recruitment, which tied in well with the observation that such homelands greatly expanded the accessibility base for infiltration into South Africa. Situations such as land-hunger, social stratification and the existence of a semi-urban proletariat were considered ripe for exploitation and manipulation for the promotion of the objectives of the ANC. Even more sinister was the programme announced for "collaborators" such as Chief Buthelezi and Lennox Sebe, whose "counter-revolutionary roles" had to be exposed and dealt with.

As for the contribution of the working class, the revival of the South African Congress of Trade Unions (SACTU) and the "popular upsurge" in working-class consciousness among black rather than white workers, indicated a favourable trend that deserved encouragement. The working-class was now seen as the "key force in our revolution" and had to find expression in three fundamental divisions of the struggle: the broad mass-democratic movement, the underground and the MK itself. It was at that time that the groundwork was laid for a future workers-versus-state confrontation epitomised by the resurgence of Cosatu in 1985, representing nearly half-a-million workers throughout the whole national economy. The ANC-SACP stratagem of "internal reconstruction" of the later 1970s succeeded in two areas, the labour front and the "extra-parliamentary" organisation front. The SACP, through its labour front, SACTU, has over the past ten years made deep inroads into the leadership of the emergent black trade union movement in South Africa. Unions and the extra-parliamentary front form an important part of the ANC-SACP revolutionary policy of mass mobilisation.

As for Military Combat Work (MCW), the commission argued that it was high time that the principles of MCW were applied to the question of the armed struggle. The combat forces of the revolution comprises three arms: the urban and rural combat groups, sabotage units and people's defence units based in the factories, townships and rural areas; the "people in arms" – i.e. "the advanced and active elements of the masses" prepared and trained by the vanguard formations; and those elements within the security forces of the ruling structure prepared to defect at the decisive moment. A milestone in that section was the call for a centralised command with one line of communication from top to bottom, from national leadership to regional and district level. The policy was clearly enunciated.

"MCW builds up the revolutionary army of the people, wages all-out war against the enemy, works to disintegrate the enemy armed forces by undermining them from within, and whilst engaging in combat utilises all forms and methods of struggle, involving all the progressive forces of the people, to a stage where power can be seized by a nationwide insurrection. Unless the above is attended to as a matter of strategic necessity, we are afraid we shall continue to remain distanced from the internal situation and therefore unable to properly enter the fray."

By late 1985 the embryos of people's power were said to be taking shape in the form of the so-called Mandela M-Plan, particularly in the Eastern Cape and parts of the Vaal Triangle. This entailed establishing a cell on every street and every block to serve as the foundation for the alternative government. Each cell would be commanded by a steward, with seven cells constituting a zone under a chief steward. Four zones formed a ward. Although in theory each central committee, zone committee, ward committee and street committee, down to cell level was supposed to comprise a political member, a finance member, a propaganda member and an MK member, it seldom happened in reality. In theory, certain members of each committee at each level were also supposed to be members of the subversive organisation, but by no means were all supposed even to know of its existence. In practice it was difficult to find adequate numbers of "reliable" members to fill the available positions. The commission concluded that in the failure of an early seizure of power, the committees would not be able to sustain or finance any of the basic requirements of "alternative" municipal government for any length of time, which would in turn discredit the committees. It goes without saying that the "people" exercising "people's power" in such "alternative" organs of government would all be members of the ANC, and SACP or any other approved front organisation such as the UDF. The origins of the South African "M-Plan" go back to the 1952 ANC Defiance Campaign, but the basic plan has been part of every Marxist revolution since 1917 in Russia.

Analysing the relation between urban and rural warfare, the commission found that the ANC had not and was unlikely to have a reliable support base for advance into the rural areas, which were nowhere near as politically organised as the urban areas, whence most of the MK were drawn. Thus it was decided to make a detailed analysis of who owned the land, what the racial distribution was, how many agricultural workers were migrants or permanent residents, what organisations already existed, and how accessible they were to infiltration and manipulation. It was considered necessary to examine the possibility of agricultural unionisation and the extent of the government's defence infrastructure on the *platteland.*

Finally, it was noted that the government had taken the initiative in adopting the MARNET farm protection system, based on the Rhodesian and Malayan experiences, and had made rudimentary attempts to mobilise the civilian population against the expected offensive by the ANC. They stated with engaging candor that the ANC could no longer allow the activities of the MK to be determined solely by the risk of civilian casualties: "We believe that the time has come when those who stand in solid support of the race tyranny and who are its direct or indirect instruments, must themselves begin to feel the agony of its counter-blows." At the same time, however, the political seduction of the white community was to play an increasingly important part in the legitimisation of the ANC, and in the attainment of that objective the PFP youth organisation was explicitly named, along with the End Conscription Campaign, the UDF and white trade unions, as well as those churches and religious organisations with a record of opposition to the government.

The ANC-SACP attitude towards religious organisations opposed to the government is that their members should infiltrate such organisations which will provide them with a relatively "safe" political home when other organisations are more easily curbed by State action. The members of ANC and SACP within the religious organisations will then also be able to "guide" the organisations into conflict with the State. Physical expression was given to these programmes by ten main categories of terrorism which emerged in the early 1980s and have continued, with certain refinements and changes, down the years to the present. In the mid-1980s a specific campaign of assassinations was launched against perceived "collaborators" of the racist régime among which were numbered black policemen, civil servants, "impimpis" (informers) and "uncooperative" trade unionists.

Limpet mines and explosives of Russian origin were planted in electricity sub-stations and oil refineries; security forces made increasing contacts with terrorists after helpful information had been provided by vigilant members of the public. Administration offices and police stations were attacked because they symbolised the authority of the government. Pamphlet bombs were detonated in urban areas and bombs set off in busy city centres. A few military targets were also attacked, and the diplomatic offices of TBVC (Transvaal, Bophutswana, Venda, Ciskei) states.

While in the main the incidents took place at no particular time, most of the attacks were confined to the townships or the city centres of Johannesburg, Pretoria, Durban, Port Elizabeth and Cape Town. Certain sabotage attacks had spectacular results and were clearly intended to gain widespread international publicity for propaganda purposes.

Local grievances and popular dissatisfaction with the government, insurrection and violent conflicts all helped them in their attempts to make the townships ungovernable and create "liberated zones". There were a number of hand-grenade attacks, petrol or acid bombings and sniper or machine-gun attacks on policemen and town councillors and their buildings.

On 12 June 1986, at a joint sitting of the three Houses of Parliament, the State President declared a national state of emergency. The NSE followed almost as a logical consequence of the rising spiral of unrest that had taken the forms described. During the course of his speech the President pointed out that Oliver Tambo had delivered a policy speech in early January of the same year in which he had declared:[2]

* The ANC would "continue to make South Africa ungovernable"
* the ANC would build its forces "into an ever more formidable united mass army of liberation, an army that must grow in strength continually"
* the goal of the ANC was "the destruction of the 'apartheid régime' and the transfer of power to the people"
* the ANC would heighten "its mass political advance on all fronts" and would intensify its "resolute military offensive"
* the ANC would work for the "political mobilisation and organisation of all the oppressed and exploited – in particular the working class"
* the ANC offensive "must spread to every corner of our country, encompassing cities, towns and the countryside".

During the first five months of 1986 there had been an alarming increase in the nationwide unrest. Between September 1984 and May 1986 the consequences of such activities included:

* 3 477 private houses of blacks either seriously damaged or destroyed
* 1 220 schools badly damaged or destroyed
* over 7 000 buses and 10 000 other vehicles either badly damaged or destroyed

* large–scale intimidation
* consumer and rent boycotts
* disruption of black education and democratically elected municipal government
* the establishment of street committees and "kangaroo" courts
* 573 deaths from black–on–black violence
* 295 victims of the 573 murdered by the "necklace" method.

In May 1986 the South African government learned of plans by radical groups directly or indirectly linked to the ANC, such as the United Democratic Front and Cosatu to hold mass marches into white areas, incite student uprisings throughout the country, encourage strikes and stayaways, and carry out widespread intimidation, sabotage, arson and general destruction. If such plans had come to fruition they would certainly have exacerbated the insurrection and would probably have led to much loss of life, injuries, destruction of property, and a general collapse of national and international confidence.

The President said that the increase of violence perpetrated by persons and organisations was of such a nature and extent that it seriously endangered the safety of the public and the maintenance of law and order. Because the ordinary laws were inadequate to enable the government to ensure public safety and maintain public order a national state of emergency was to be imposed throughout the country, including the self–governing states, to create a situation of relative normality so that every citizen could perform his daily work in peace, business could carry on and the reform programme to which the government was committed, could be continued.

Because of the important part played by the mass–communications media, both at home and abroad, the government also deemed it necessary to limit the extent to which the media could report irresponsibly on a wide range of subjects, particularly insurrectionary incidents and other matters affecting the security of the state. About the same time the so–called "alternative media " began to make their presence felt by consciously or unconsciously promoting the objectives of the instigators of unrest. The ANC had clearly accomplished their mobilisation with considerable success and as Ted Koppel of the ABC *Nightline* expressed it:

"... The media, particularly television, and terrorists need one another... They have what is fundamentally a symbiotic relationship. Without television, international terrorism becomes rather like the philosopher's hypothetical tree falling in the forest – no one hears it fall and therefore it doesn't exist." Despite the imposition of the media regulations, the press continued to criticise the South African authorities both vehemently and openly across a wide range of national affairs.

However, the imposition of the state of emergency caused a marked decline in insurrectionary actions. From May 1986 to May 1987 the number of such actions fell by 79 per cent. By May 1987 the black death rate attributable to insurrection had fallen by 94.9 per cent. The state of emergency also permitted the resumption of schooling and essential administrative work such as refuse removal, water supply, electricity, street maintenance, sewerage, public transport, fire fighting and postal services. Clinics and other medical services were able to resume work in black areas formerly out of bounds to them because of the violence. Social workers returned to the townships, and recreation facilities were no longer called "freedom parks". The efforts by the ANC to establish an "alternative" authority were seen by the population as having been a failure.

Even more important, despite the sanctions campaign orchestrated by the ANC internationally, after the imposition of the state of emergency, business confidence greatly improved, investments returned and economic growth became more promising.

The ANC–SACP revolutionary strategy rests on four legs:
* the armed struggle;
* mass mobilisation – i.e. UDF and Labour;
* ANC–SACP structures, and
* the International Front – i.e. world anti-apartheid, sanctions movements, etc.

The South African government and its security forces have proved over 27 years that they have the answer to at least three of these revolutionary components.

The South African counter-revolutionary strategy stands on three legs:
* the maintenance of law and order by the security forces. This includes the removal from society of revolutionary leaders and their organisations, by means of special powers if necessary;
* good government, in the sense that socio–economic and other frustrations and grievances are effectively dealt with and not exploitable by revolutionaries;
* constitutional and political reform to create a society in which revolutionary demands will produce no response.

It was and is this strategy which has once again undermined and called into question the very basis of the ANC's long term revolutionary effort.

On 8 January 1987 the ANC celebrated its 75th anniversary in Lusaka in the Mulungushi Hall, with fifty foreign journalists, and many diplomatic representatives from the Eastern bloc and Western countries present. While Oliver Tambo addressed the ANC in Lusaka, representatives of the National Executive Committee addressed gatherings at satellite centres all over the world in a slick PR exercise that ensured much international publicity. While the speeches for public consumption displayed great panache and confidence, their bombast was very different from the private misgivings and reservations admitted to trusted confidants.

The failure of the 1986 year of revolution, in which the decisive seizure of power ought to have been achieved, meant that the ANC was compelled to fall back on the attempt to impose international sanctions by the traditional Western allies and trading partners of South Africa. That campaign met with more success than the revolutionary proposition, although the imposition of such measures could be attributed less to the success of the revolutionary zeal of the ANC and SACP than to the changing winds of political expediency blowing through some Western democracies for the benefit of certain interest groups playing domestic politics for their own ends. Moreover, the chain of command, control and intelligence within the MK machine itself was not running as effectively as it might. This was particularly evident in the youthful "comrades" roaming the townships, who seemed to have become a law unto themselves, capable of damaging rather than advancing the tactical operations of the ANC in the country as a whole.

Off the record, the ANC announced that a great intensification of violence against the civil population would take place in the future although ostensibly it would be aimed at the state. Such an objective had its drawbacks, because the other primary desire professed by the ANC was to win over significant numbers of whites to their cause, or at best to neutralise their effectiveness in the fight for the state. Furthermore, to wage such a terror campaign would incur the risk of alienating sympathy and support from Western governments and institutions.

Clearly the state of emergency had considerably retarded the revolutionary impetus of the ANC, if not its potential, and forced it to return to the policy of "armed propaganda". The effect has been to cause a reappraisal of their old political approach, and to compel them to invent a new political policy, encapsulated in the "post-apartheid project". The new approach has not passed through the ranks of the ANC without considerable opposition, which demonstrates the split between those who seek to continue the armed struggle and those who are convinced that the time has come to exploit some of the opportunities presented by the new constitutional disposition, facilitated by the new tricameral system. To suggest that a terrorist organisation is divided into "hawks" and "doves" may seem incongruous. However, if the disastrous effects of the strife between the two factions is any criterion the assassination in Paris of Dulcie September and the attempt in Maputo to assassinate Dr Albie Sachs, who favoured a more flexible approach reveals a profound and bitter disagreement over the future policies. The rash of terror bombings aimed at mainly civilian targets during 1988 was also linked to this strife.

The factions are represented at the top of the structure by men who have given long and loyal service to the organisation. Those who support the flexible approach are led by Thabo Mbeki, a member of the ANC NEC, the SACP and Director of Information and publicity for the ANC. The faction favouring a hardline is led by Chris Hani, a fellow ANC NEC and SACP member who is also Chief of Staff of the MK machine. Thabo Mbeki, a son of the recently released and subsequently restricted Govan Mbeki, has already paid a heavy price for his moderation. Those in the inner circles of the ANC say that Mbeki has destroyed his chances of succeeding Oliver Tambo as leader of the ANC, as had been assumed. Hani, in turn, has made it clear that he too aspires to the Presidency. Hani is a protégé of Joe Slovo.

A clear sign that the ANC–SACP leadership is dissatisfied with the progress made by those in charge of internal political organisation is the open shift in emphasis to the internal labour movement, which has always been a priority of the Communist Party. This is shown by the rapid promotion of the former MK Chief of Staff, Joe Slovo first to the SACP Chairman and then General Secretary, where he will, *inter alia,* play an important part in manipulating the internal labour movement. In response to this change of tack the South African government promulgated legislation to curtail the revolutionary potential of the trade unions to interrupt the process of political reform.

Such moves merely show a change of emphasis. The armed revolutionary struggle has certainly not yet been abandoned, but strengthened in a certain political direction. The arrest of a white terrorist unit in the Transvaal, betrayed from inside the ANC, confirms the role that white SACP members continue to play in the ANC. The huge quantities of armaments captured with them also confirms Hani's warnings that the ANC proposed to intensify the armed struggle, notwithstanding their numerous attempts to improve their "image".

The ANC have also compiled their own constitution for a post-apartheid South Africa. It is the result of two years' hard work, and is potentially the most important document on ANC policy to have emerged for many years. It states its commitment to a mixed economy, a bill of rights, a multi-party government and a unitary state. It will guarantee freedom of religion and of the press, and women's rights and the rights of workers to organise independent trade unions and to strike. It favours a presidential rather than a Westminster system, but it will not have the status of the 32-year-old policy statement, the Freedom Charter. The document is clearly designed as a matter for discussion to legitimise the ANC both at home and abroad. The Freedom Charter itself has often been criticised for being out of date, having emerged from the very different circumstances of the 1950s, and for the vagueness of some of its policies.

This new document is important because it expresses a general trend within the ANC in the past few years to devote time and resources to studies of post-apartheid policies on such questions as health, education and culture. The ANC Department of Education has begun a far-reaching study of post-apartheid education. The analysis begins with a detailed examination of the present situation, such as the number and distribution of educational institutions and the race, language, sex and geographical factors that would have to be dealt with. Yet another element in the "institutionalisation" of the ANC is the appointment of its first ambassador to a pro-western African country, with the accreditation of Tami Sindelo, from the ANC African desk in Lusaka, to the Kenyan government. The appointment is the result of long negotiations between President Daniel arap Moi and the ANC. Diplomatic observers say that the development is a significant step for the organisation towards acquiring greater support from certain African capitals for its claim to be a government in exile. The trend is significant, for the ANC has also been invited to send representatives to Nicaragua, Brazil and Argentina. These postings have not yet been publicly announced, but the ANC is reshuffling its representatives everywhere. Most of its postings are for three years, but some people have been in one place much longer than that. In several socialist countries the chief representatives are given full diplomatic status, while in others they have quasi-diplomatic status.

It is conceivable that a faction of the ANC may yet be persuaded to extend their new policy of "legitimisation" to the ultimate step of taking part in the South African parliamentary system, if their other efforts should continue to fail. In May 1986 the SACP issued a policy directive arguing that the movement must not mechanically dig in its heels against any future possibility of negotiation or compromise. Virtually all revolutionary struggles in the post-war period reached their culmination at the negotiating table, it said. Such was the case in Algeria, Vietnam, Mozambique and Angola. The SACP has said that the movement has to judge what interim compromises are justified to reach the ultimate goal of power. The notion is reinforced by the observations published in an 1986 edition of *Sechaba,* in which it was stated that talks with South African representatives from commerce and industry could create an opportunity for businessmen to cooperate with revolutionary forces. The somewhat facile argument was that businessmen might be prepared to go along with the revolutionary struggle as long as their interests were not threatened.

In short, the future ambitions of the ANC appear to include:
* promoting division among whites;
* exploiting existing divisions in white society to diminish the power base of the government;
* swinging white liberal organisations, politicians and movements on-side to project a moderate and reasonable image and so improve its chances of recognition as a valid alternative government-in-exile;
* showing up the South African government as unreasonable and the cause of internal conflict;

* bringing greater pressure to bear on Western governments for further sanctions against South Africa to overthrow the government, by eroding the means to pay for its defence and reform policies.

1988 sees the ANC revolutionary strategy for South Africa in a crisis. The morale of the organisation is lower than ever before. Their deep depression is partly a reaction to the false euphoria of 1984 and 1985 when, as in 1961 and 1976, "liberation" was considered to be imminent. The resilience, ingenuity and resources of the South African government and its security forces have again proved superior to the military and political strategy of the ANC. That has led to obvious frustration in the MK, and the bombs in public places that kill mostly black civilians are evidence of that. The organisation that could once boast of its ability to sabotage a nuclear power station, of ungovernability in liberated zones and of the imminent collapse of the South African state is now reduced to malicious blows against ordinary innocent people. The turnout in the October municipal elections further eroded the ANC's support base. The ANC–SACP alliance has proved over 27 years to be the most incompetent and least successful Soviet-backed revolutionary organisation in the world. Nowhere else has a revolutionary group supported by the Soviets been so decisively battered time and again and put back to square one.

The passing of the Brezhnev–Andropov–Chernenko era and the dawning of the Gorbachev era, with its remarkably promising *glasnost* and *perestroika* policies, could not have arrived at a more unfortunate time for the ANC. While under no illusions that *glasnost* and *perestroika* mean a retrenchment of global Soviet aspirations, in the short term this new approach to realpolitik in Moscow means that internal economic development in the Soviet Union has now become the highest priority, as opposed to the promotion of international revolutionary socialism.

What does that mean for the ANC–SACP alliance? Men like Joe Slovo in Lusaka and Najibullah in Kabul have undoubtedly been affected. The Kremlin does not waste resources on those who fail to deliver the goods. The ANC is in danger of losing the factor that makes it unique in the revolutionary struggle in South Africa, its military and propaganda support from a great world power, so that it could soon be reduced to the same status as all the other extra-parliamentary groups competing for power in South Africa.

Their alienation from home has denied them the political experience to make a significant mark on the evolving political dispensation in South Africa, which is now proving a serious handicap. The challenge to all South Africans, irrespective of political colour, is the answer to the question: are you for or against violence as a solution to the problems that South Africa will have to contend with in the 21st century? Many members of the ANC have come to the conclusion that violence is not the answer; but once they say so, they will compel the ANC to undergo a painful change. This re-alignment, which must take place in the ANC to bring it back to reality, will not be between those seeking socialism versus black nationalism: it will be for evolution versus revolution. There are in the ANC some moderate communists who regret ever having embarked on the armed struggle and radical nationalists who now seek power through the barrel of a gun. The organisation is suffering from ideological inertia, corruption, financial mismanagement, disillusionment, abuses of human rights (especially sexual) and from a general lack of faith in the old tribal leadership and direction of policy. The strife caused by Xhosa domination refuses to fade away. Many MK cadres spend much of their time smuggling Mandrax and stolen cars.

Those in the ANC who believe that, if Cuba, Angola, Swapo and the Soviet Union can settle their differences in south–western Africa with the South African government through negotiation, then so can the ANC, must assert themselves against those who believe that power sharing is a sell–out and that people's power via the barrel of a gun is the only solution.

The whole of South Africa is awaiting that event with great interest, for until it happens the country will be the poorer.

**FOOTNOTES**

1. The movement was originally known as the Communist Party of South Africa or CPSA. The movement was banned in 1950 and went underground. In 1961, following the declaration of "armed struggle" the movement re–emerged as the South African Communist Party or SACP.
2. This quote by Oliver Tambo was used in Parliament on 12 June 1988 by the State President, P.W. Botha and is therefore privileged.

# THE MEDIA WAR
*by Holger Jensen*

Bad news being good news, South Africa has had a relatively late start as a media "story". As one who had grown up there and always assumed that the attention of the world was riveted on the country's racial problems, I shall never forget my amazement when I first came to the United States in early 1963 to find that many middle-Americans didn't even know where South Africa was. One fellow traveller on a Greyhound bus thought it was a naval base in Mississippi. A black newspaper in Los Angeles offered me a job, sight unseen, because the editor thought anyone from Africa had to be black. He politely but firmly withdrew the offer when I walked into his office ... apartheid in reverse. And, speaking of apartheid, a seemingly intelligent, college-educated friend in California thought it was a Dutch after-dinner drink.

The 1960 Sharpeville riots, while making the rest of the world vaguely aware that all was not well at the bottom of the Dark Continent, hardly made apartheid a household word. It took Soweto, more than ten years later to do that. And even then South Africa did not stay in the headlines for long. There were plenty of other conflicts to divert the world media: Vietnam, genocide in Cambodia, the Yom Kippur war, the Turkish invasion of Cyprus, the Lebanese civil war, a run of hijackings by Palestinian terrorists and, nearer home, the Rhodesian war.

I was a foreign correspondent in all of the above, first with the Associated Press, later with *Newsweek,* and it was Vietnam where I first witnessed the adversarial relationship between a country at war and its own journalists.

Not all, of course. The old hands who had covered World War II, Korea, the communist insurgency in Malaya and other conflicts where print journalists who were censored and otherwise subjected to wartime controls were invariably horrified at the antics of their younger colleagues. But Vietnam did not lend itself to an Ernie Pyle. Even the most patriotic flag-waver could see there was something dreadfully wrong. The South Vietnamese did not want to fight their own battles, they didn't want us there and many American soldiers didn't want to be there either. All this was quite apparent to correspondents who accompanied the GIs into battle, and we reported as much.

Nevertheless, there were some who thought we should win. We may have had serious misgivings about the war, why we were there in the first place, but having made the commitment, rightly or wrongly, the only thing left was to get the job done and withdraw with honour. Others who advocated an immediate pullout ...without victory ...still drew the line between healthy scepticism and outright disloyalty.

But there were some who, either through ignorance, naïveté or misplaced liberal ideals, actually aided and abetted the enemy. We called it "pulling a Jane Fonda", referring to the actress's notorious trip to Hanoi while Americans were dying on the battlefields of South Vietnam. Even she has since admitted that she was used by the communists, who reaped a propaganda bonanza. Her visit certainly helped to whip up anti-war sentiment in the United States, which led to a suspension of American bombing raids on North Vietnam at a time when it was ill-advised to do so.

The Vietnam press corps numbered more than five hundred at any time. The war was a media event, the "big story", and those who wanted to make their bones as war correspondents had to be there. Like the US army regulars who felt they needed a combat tour to further their careers, so too did journalists flock to get their Vietnam tickets punched. There were representatives of all the big papers and television networks, editors from weeklies in Iowa and Kansas, writing "hometowners" about the GIs from their communities, and freelancers hoping to get their first crack at a staff job. There were also the hangers-on: adventurers, war freaks, peaceniks, press groupies, authors soaking up local colour for their books and dopers drawn by the cheap drugs of South East Asia.

Sean Flynn died in Cambodia trying to live up to the screen image of his father. Hunter Thompson, the author who sought literary inspiration in LSD, stumbled through Vietnam in a marijuana-induced haze, blearily comparing helicopters to giant grasshoppers. Michael Herr came on an assignment for *Esquire* magazine that grew into his best-selling book "Dispatches". Nicholas Proffitt of *Newsweek* distinguished himself as a war correspondent and went on to write "Gardens of Stone" and "Embassy House". It is significant that the anchormen of all three prime-time television news shows in the United States are veterans of Vietnam.

Anyone and everyone who showed up in Saigon and could prove some affiliation to the media, however tenuous, was issued a press card by the Military Assistance Command, Vietnam (MACV). The Saigon command made no distinctions between those who worked for the *New York Times* and leftist rags like the *Village Voice* or *Berkeley Barb*. All were given an honorary rank of major in the US Army, with PX privileges, priority on military transportation and unrestricted access to the war. With a few exceptions, accredited correspondents had the right to enter any military installation and witness every military operation in the country.

You could literally "bump" a lower ranking soldier off a Huey gunship and take his place on a heliborne combat assault. You could come and go as you pleased , write or film what you pleased and give the folks back home your perceptions of the war. The men and women who had such formidable powers were not all bad, but they were not all good either; and their perceptions varied greatly.

Some never ventured out of Saigon, accepting the colourful fiction dished out by the US Embassy and military briefing officers at the "Five O'Clock Follies". Others spent weeks in the field, coming back gaunt, withdrawn, with that hollow-eyed look that spells combat fatigue. They despised the "Saigon Warriors", who in turn despised the combat correspondents for failing to get the "big picture". There were some in both groups who lived up to Vice President Spiro Agnew's caustic description of the press as "nattering nabobs of negativism". They spent all their time covering the downside: the lies, the corruption, the cowardice, the massacres of Vietnamese civilians, the "fragging" of officers by mutinous enlisted men and the latters' drug problems. But there were just as many sober, responsible journalists who tried to present a fair and accurate picture of what was going on.

Wars are a nasty business, guerrilla wars are particularly nasty and few stand up to the harsh glare of publicity. But did the press lose the war in Vietnam, as General William Westmoreland alleged in his celebrated lawsuit against CBS Television?

Not exactly. The war was lost by politicians, as most wars are. They refused to sanction an invasion of the North, which would have ended the whole thing quickly and cleanly. They sent reluctant draftees to fight a guerrilla war that should have been fought only by military professionals, then placed impossible constraints on them, in effect making the war unwinnable. American soldiers, at times, couldn't fire unless fired upon; they were not allowed to cross borders in hot pursuit of the enemy and they could not, until it was too late, interdict enemy supply lines in Cambodia and Laos. The longer it dragged on, the more unpopular the war became, the more mistakes were made and the more the US government tried to cover them up.

Body counts were inflated. The lieutenant wanted to please the colonel, who wanted to please the general, who wanted to please the Pentagon, which wanted to please the president. So everyone multiplied by three. Defeats became victories. And everyone from the president down was caught out in the most outrageous lies. CBS was quite correct in exposing the absurdity of General Westmoreland's body counts; those who kept track of such things calculated that we had wiped out the Viet Cong three times over by the time they marched into Saigon.

You don't get a good press by lying to it. And in a nation that prides itself on its First Amendment rights, you certainly can't count on all your journalists being "on-side". Yet US military commanders in Vietnam went to inordinate lengths to cater to the press, in effect inviting them to critique a no-win situation. Non-American journalists, even those from notoriously irresponsible Fleet Street tabloids, simply couldn't understand this "let-it-all-hang-out" philosophy. They saw it as self-flagellation, a curiously American phenomenon that periodically manifests itself in such scandals as Watergate and the Iran-Contra affair.

What made it worse was that Vietnam was the first television war. Americans could tune in to its horrors in living colour on the six o'clock news, just before dinner, and if they didn't catch it on TV they could read about it at breakfast in their morning paper. It didn't take them long to realise that things weren't going as well as their government was telling them. While President Johnson was seeing a "light at the end of the tunnel", the Tet offensive was being played out in American living rooms. While President Nixon was bragging about how successfully the South Vietnamese had taken over the US military role, Americans were treated to the sight of their valiant allies clinging to helicopter skids to escape the fighting in *Operation Lam Son 719*.

The relentless coverage of Vietnam by the media certainly fuelled the American anti-war movement. Students at tidy little colleges like Kent State and Berkeley not only learned that war was hell, they also found out that it was mismanaged. Likewise, coverage of the student demonstrations sapped the morale of the grunts in Vietnam. The power of the press forced one president, Johnson, to abandon his political career. It exposed the hypocrisy of another, Nixon, by showing (with graphic pictures of US helicopters evacuating people from the roof of the US Embassy in Saigon) that our withdrawal from Vietnam was less than honourable. And, by being free and therefore not an effective propaganda tool for the US government, the press often played into the hands of the enemy.

Even those of us who wanted victory found ourselves inadvertently helping Hanoi. *Lam Son 719,* the 1971 invasion of Laos, was the first serious test of Nixon's "Vietnamisation" policy, an effort to block North Vietnamese supplies coming down the Ho Chi Minh Trail network. Using only South Vietnamese ground troops, with US air support, the operation was a fiasco. At first the communists offered very little resistance, cleverly sucking the South Vietnamese thirty miles across the border. Then they clobbered them with everything they had. The United

States lost something like six hundred helicopters in 45 days and the South Vietnamese retreat was a chaotic rout.

Medevacs were mobbed by unwounded soldiers who threw away their weapons and clung to helicopter landing gear in their frantic efforts to flee Laos. When overloaded choppers began to develop hydraulic problems and crash, the US Command ordered its pilots to grease their skids. That did not deter the terrified Vietnamese, who tied themselves on with their pistol belts. American pilots then began scraping them off on trees, returning to their bases in South Vietnam with arms, legs and other grisly remnants still tied to their skids. I took a picture there that won the Associated Press Managing Editors Award for the best news photo that year. A few months later it appeared on the cover of a North Vietnamese propaganda book describing the glorious communist victory.

For the South Vietnamese and their American allies it was a defeat, there was no getting round it. Pictures don't lie. But sometimes they need explaining. I lost another photographic award because the story that accompanied my pictures put them in perspective, and thus robbed them of their shock value. It was your typical "Zippo Raid" ... American Marines torturing Vietnamese peasants and torching their hooches. But I had been with that particular patrol for more than a week. The Marines had been ambushed daily, sometimes twice a day, suffering 50 per cent casualties. When they entered that village and found only old men, women and children they knew it was VC-controlled ... the young men were waiting in ambush outside. And when they dug up communist weapons buried under the floors of the huts, they were understandably enraged. So they burned the village down.

It was one instance where the US policy of allowing correspondents to accompany troops in the field actually paid off. If no journalist had been there and witnessed the events leading up to the raid, word of what had happened would have leaked out eventually and it would have been portrayed as another "atrocity".

That is not to say that there weren't any. Plenty of atrocities were committed by both sides. And it is true that some apologists for the communists seized upon those committed by Americans while blinding themselves to those of the enemy. The My Lai massacre had far more exposure in the American media than the North Vietnamese ambush of a civilian refugee column fleeing Quang Tri in 1972. But then Hanoi wasn't as open with the press as the American side.

Few countries are; certainly not South Africa. If the American attitude to the media errs on the side of tolerance, Pretoria's errs on the side of repression. It can best be described as a "controlled democracy", verging on autocracy. Television, as presented by the South African Broadcasting Corporation, is government-subsidised, and therefore government-controlled and totally ineffectual. The Afrikaans newspapers, though vigorous, are mainly government-supporting with a journalistic tradition based more on obedience than independence of spirit. And the English-language press is a chained dog: it can bark, but it can't bite.

South African newspapers continue to bark, often loudly, at the government through critical editorials. Visitors to South Africa are often misled by their vitriolic content, saying: "But this press looks free". That is music to Pretoria's ears. But the reality is that the press can't bite with investigative reporting that may reveal government corruption or unnecessary restraints on civil liberties. And even the barking has little effect, since most of the voters who elect the government speak and read Afrikaans and are hardly aware of what the English-language papers are saying.

It was not always so. Before the National Party came to power in 1948, South Africa could boast a proud and free press. And in the next thirty years, as the Afrikaner leaders systematically set about muzzling their English-language watchdogs, the press achieved some of its finest hours. Newspapers like the Johannesburg *Star* and the *Rand Daily Mail* fought apartheid tooth and nail with some great investigative journalism. John Vorster was chased out of the premiership into the presidency, and finally overthrown, as a result of exposés written about the "Information Scandal", South Africa's Watergate. With him fell the Information Minister, Connie Mulder, and the Information Secretary, Eschel Rhoodie, both charged with using public funds to establish an ostensibly independent but in fact pro-government newspaper and with buying influence abroad.

It was precisely that kind of journalism that the government wanted to stifle, and it did so with powerful effect. A steady progression of laws eroded the freedom of the South African press. Investigative reports into mistreatment of prisoners led to sweeping prohibitions on writing about prison conditions. Now it is even illegal to take a photograph of the outside of a prison. Reports of police brutality provoked the draconian Police Act, under which the state can call on editors and reporters to prove that any story critical of the police is backed by irrefutable evidence, failing which they face heavy fines and imprisonment up to three years. The Catch 22 is that newspapers are prevented from getting such evidence because the Act forbids photographing a police officer making an arrest or taking a picture of a person in police custody. Other legislation shields the military from press scrutiny and bars reporting on strategic industries, such as oil procurements from abroad, the Sasol coal conversion plants and Armscor's exports to the Third World.

The more the government controlled the media, the greater the contempt it displayed for the press, and the easier it became to enact even more restrictive measures. By the time I returned to South Africa as a correspondent for *Newsweek* in 1979, long before the present state of emergency, more than a hundred laws and regulations were on the books. Their effect showed bleakly in South African newspapers. They had become subdued, a pale shadow of their former selves, practising what amounted to self-censorship. Foreign correspondents, of course, were not fettered by the same restraints – a cause of some chagrin to Pretoria. But they had not yet focused their unrelenting attention on South Africa, and were still regarded as more of an irritant than a thorn in the side of the government.

During the Carter administration, which sent relations between the USA and South Africa plunging into the cellar, and the early years of the Reagan administration, which revived them with Chester Crocker's concept of "constructive engagement", South Africa remained pretty much of a non-story. Though all the most important American publications and TV networks had representatives in Johannesburg, they spent most of their time covering Rhodesia. South Africa was fairly peaceful at the time. President P.W. Botha was taking his first tentative steps toward apartheid reform, revolutionary to Afrikaners but cosmetic to Americans, which hardly made for headlines back home. Rhodesia, on the other hand, had a war going on with all the right elements of a good story: a small, plucky nation defying its British parent; stalwart white farmers holding off the guerrilla hordes; Selous Scouts performing feats of astonishing bravery, and even a few American mercenaries applying the lessons that they had learned in Vietnam.

Unlike South Africa, Rhodesia enjoyed a generally good press abroad. The whites were good guys: friendly, hardy folk who had carved a nation out of the bush. They were quite willing to live in harmony with the black majority ... they just didn't want to see their country go down the tubes. The black guerrillas were bad guys. Atrocities such as the shooting down of a civilian airliner at Kariba, the murders of farm families and missionaries and the slaughter of black civilians in the Tribal Trust Lands had convinced most foreign correspondents that they were not the "freedom fighters" they professed to be. And Robert Mugabe had published a communist manifesto that clearly showed he was more interested in imposing a one-party dictatorship than in parliamentary democracy.

So, while the Rhodesian army was secretive and the Salisbury government not particularly cooperative, the press was sympathetic.

Most correspondents respected military secrets, refrained from writing about sanctions–busting and tried not to be too critical of puppet premier Bishop Abel Muzorewa, even though they knew full well that Ian Smith's boys still ran the show. When the war ended there were few journalists, even bleeding–heart liberals on the *New York Times* and the *Guardian*, who did not feel that the Lancaster House Agreement was a sellout. The "Last White Christmas Party", a nostalgic wake hosted by the foreign press corps shortly before the country became Zimbabwe, saw many beery salutes to Rhodesian gallantry and bitter denunciations of British perfidy. And when Mugabe's North Korean–trained Fifth Brigade began massacring Joshua Nkomo's supporters in Matabeleland, not a few of us dolefully reported: "We told you so."

The great difference between South Africa and Rhodesia, of course, was *apartheid*. Rhodesia had no legislated discrimination, no denial of black voting rights. Despite its racial overtones, it was impossible to depict the Rhodesian war as a conflict between blacks and whites. There were more blacks than whites being killed by their own kind. In that respect ... black–on–black violence ... the South African situation is similar to the Rhodesians. But Pretoria failed to get that point across to the outside world when its townships exploded and South Africa became a "media event".

When the violence erupted in 1984 the Foreign Minister, Roelof "Pik" Botha, who controls the Information Department, favoured full coverage by the media in the hope that it would generate tolerance and sympathy for South Africa's plight. He persuaded President Botha to give it a try. The latter did so against his better judgment. South African leaders are mostly dour, Calvinistic types who feel intensely uncomfortable with the international press, distrust foreign journalists and find it difficult, if not impossible, to explain things in the Afrikaner context to sceptical newsmen with a broader perspective. They come across as bumbling Neanderthals who can't even speak decent English. P.W. was no exception. He felt that he had already been burned by the foreign press. The president, at considerable risk to his own political standing, had embarked on a programme of cautious apartheid reforms which he thought would be hailed as an important advance in the United States. Instead he found them dismissed as inconsequential abroad, while suffering a considerable backlash from his Afrikaner constituents at home.

He had a point. Although the unrest was sparked by a severe economic crisis, it was aggravated to an alarming extent by continuing demands in the United States and other parts of the world for disinvestment, which fuelled the fires and played into the hands of the African National Congress (ANC). In this the press certainly played an important part.

It was never believed at the time that South Africa would be vulnerable to economic sanctions. Rhodesia, before it became Zimbabwe, had proved that a small and weak country could stand up to international boycotts and sanctions as long as it had one economically powerful and sympathetic neighbour, in its case South Africa. Taking heart from this example, South Africans themselves had always believed that sanctions would be more of a nuisance than a danger. But a combination of political and economic factors forced them to revise their thinking.

The country had been weakened by a four-year recession that caused growing black unemployment. The gold price fell disastrously, wiping out foreign exchange reserves. Bishop Desmond Tutu, not really a person of great stature, received the Nobel Peace Prize and suddenly became the darling of American liberals. The media and activist groups, having no Vietnam to cover at the time, latched on to the South African story with enthusiasm, and international banks began to take notice. South Africa had been prepared for sanctions and disinvestment, but all the worst-case scenarios painted by its intelligence organisations envisaged a more gradual process, with the screws being turned in public by United Nations resolutions and individual foreign governments while "constructive engagement" continued under the table. What was not expected was that big American and European banks would suddenly decide, privately and on their own initiative, collectively, to refuse to renew loans to South Africa.

This sent the economy reeling. Blacks, chafing as always under apartheid, also became unemployed and hungry. The stage was set for another violent confrontation, and the ANC, which had already established a foothold in the townships, took advantage. It ordered its cadres to eliminate all blacks who assist the white government in administering the townships – in effect launching a campaign to make parts of South Africa ungovernable. The instructions to terrorise or kill black councillors, civil servants, policemen and other collaborators were carried out with startling ferocity and efficient organisation. Those not beaten to death with *knobkierries* (clubs) or hacked with knives and *pangas* (machetes) were "necklaced", i.e. they had a petrol-soaked tyre placed round their necks and set alight. As a result, many blacks in government jobs at the provincial and municipal levels fled, resigned or simply hid in their offices, refusing to work outside.

The technique was familiar to those who had covered the Vietnam war, where the systematic assassination of village leaders had been used by the Viet Cong to destroy the administration of the Saigon government. Terror succeeds where minor officials go unprotected.

Pik Botha saw it as a golden opportunity to convince the world of the threat that South Africa was facing. Most of the violence was occurring in the black townships. Most of the victims were black. ANC documents captured by the South African security forces proved that its National Council was dominated by communists who were taking their instructions from Moscow. Surely the world would understand. So, for a period of nine months or so, South Africa experienced a brief renaissance of press freedom. Correspondents were allowed to go into the black townships, encouraged to take pictures of the rioting and allowed to accompany the security forces trying to contain it. And for a while the policy worked: the world was shocked by television footage of a necklacing and the murderous antics of the "comrades", gangs of black youths roaming the townships in search of victims.

But the presence of television cameras seemed to goad black radicals to further excesses against their own kind and even greater defiance of the white authorities. Also, as often happens on American TV screens, the networks preferred to show pictures of white police bashing blacks instead of blacks bashing blacks. Foreign correspondents, and many South African journalists, for that matter, found that they could not ignore apartheid, the underlying cause of black discontent. Pretoria began to get a bad press again, and it retaliated, as it always does, by clamping down. The imposition of a state of emergency, with accompanying press restrictions, successfully silenced unfavourable coverage; but it also left the world unaware of how bad things really were. And it made it more difficult for the South African government to justify full use of its military strength in putting down what amounted to the early stages of a classic communist insurgency.

The bloodshed continued, but after mid-1985 it was virtually ignored. In the Eastern Cape Province, where most of the ANC-instigated violence was happening, black townships were made ungovernable. Police and army units patrolled the streets by day but spent most of their time picking up the mutilated corpses of "collaborators" who had been necklaced by kangaroo courts at night. In Soweto and other black townships on the gold-mining Reef, the ANC was broadcasting instructions to its cadres to form revolutionary block committees, another stratagem ominously reminiscent of the Viet Cong, to collect rents and fees that the government could not collect, conscript guerrilla recruits whose loyalty the government could not win and determine the curriculum for schools that the government could not control.

A small war was fought in Alexandra, outside Johannesburg, in which police were fired on with AK-47 rifles and had Russian hand-grenades thrown at them. More significantly, again like the Viet Cong, the ANC guerrillas forced black civilians to help them by digging trenches in the ground as "tank traps" for troop carriers and armoured cars used by the South African security forces. Similar battles were fought in other black townships elsewhere: in Natal Province near Durban, in the Eastern Cape round Port Elizabeth and Cape Town, the seat of Parliament.

By early 1986 more than 1 200 had been killed, most of them blacks, more than five hundred homes belonging to black policemen had been firebombed and the government had to move black members of the security forces and their families into fortified housing complexes to protect them. P.W. Botha, in fact, conceded in a rare interview with the editor of the *Washington Times* that 14 per cent of the black townships were effectively beyond government control. Since they were all urban townships, the percentage of the black population that had fallen under ANC domination was actually much higher. Ironically, however, most South Africans didn't even know what was happening in their own country. While they were nearer to it than the rest of the world, apartheid kept them out of the townships and their own press was muzzled.

The emergency regulations, which are still in effect, prohibit journalists from entering demarcated areas, such as black townships, and report, photograph or televise any unrest, riot or demonstration. The laws are so strict that newsmen who inadvertently stumble across a disturbance must ignore it and leave the scene immediately. Stories about military movements, preparations or actions taken by security forces cannot be published until cleared by censors. Any police officer above the rank of colonel can stop the presses of any newspaper if he deems it necessary. The Minister of Law and Order can ban or suspend publication of any newspaper for reasons of national security.

Two publications were shut down in 1988: the weekly newspaper *South* and the Catholic Church periodical "*New Nation*". Defending this action, the Minister of Home Affairs, Stoffel Botha, told Parliament: "Sectors of the press in our country are more concerned about the concept of press freedom than the existence and effect of publications which promote subversion and revolution. It is stated that actions such as those taken by the government amount to a violation of democratic principles. The contrasting question that I wish to pose is this: Should the government, in the name of democracy, simply allow fear, hatred, intimidation, murder, mutilation and other similar evils to be furthered by certain publications? That is nonsense."

True enough. South Africa is a country at war and no publication should be allowed to further the cause of revolution. Here, in all fairness, it must be pointed out that many of the country's press curbs would not have been imposed had it not been for some very irresponsible reporting by the media. And it is important to note that even with its wartime restrictions, South Africa's press is still more free than that of its black neighbours. Journalists in Zimbabwe, Zambia, Mozambique and Angola are not even allowed to bark. All of them routinely practise self-censorship because it's downright dangerous not to.

As John Simpson, BBC's Diplomatic Editor, commented in *The Listener* on 26 May 1988: " ... it is worth remembering that at least half the countries of the world are likely to refuse access to (British) camera crews, or else to sanction filming only what it wants the world to see. Mujahideen guerrillas took a number of Western journalists with them into Afghanistan, but there was never film of the US and Chinese advisors working at Mujahideen training camps inside Pakistan."

Al Venter, in completing his series *Africa in Focus* for television, sometimes had every shot and angle monitored by state-appointed security officers while working in places like Egypt, Liberia, Burundi, Nigeria and Zambia, and was controlled to a lesser degree in several other African states. In Kenya, filming these days is not possible without a government representative being present. In Tanzania any form of reportage outside the ambit of the government information department is forbidden. One British journalist was gaoled for seven years during the Seventies for taking a picture of a bridge south of Dar es Salaam. He was accused of photographing "a sensitive military target".

Equally bizarre was Al Venter's arrest in Khartoum in the Sudan after a soldier had spotted him taking a picture of his hotel. He was frog-marched across the city to police headquarters and kept in custody for a day. Only when he reported the incident the following day by way of a story to the London *Daily Express,* for whom he was stringing at the time, was any apology forthcoming.

Thus, if one compares South Africa to the black dictatorships around it, then Pretoria's treatment of the press is relatively benign. But if the government wants to portray itself as the last bastion of democracy on a chaotic continent, then it must be judged by Western democratic standards.

Another comparison frequently voiced by South Africans is that of Israel, which too has had to impose stringent press curbs to prevent inflammatory reporting on the Palestinian uprising in the occupied territories. But that hardly helps Pretoria. The West Bank and Gaza Strip are not part of Israel ... they used to belong to the Arabs before the Six Day War of 1967 and still are technically under military occupation ... and there is a big difference between governing one's own country and occupying someone else's. Pretoria would not like to be perceived as an occupation power, since this would imply that the black parts of South Africa actually belong to the ANC.

The only parallel that does apply is an unfortunate one. Both Israel and South

Africa have indulged in overkill. Their emergency regulations lend themselves to abuse by government officials and military censors who are not always qualified to judge the content of the press. Even responsible newsmen are being silenced in the name of "national security" and the innocent are being punished along with the guilty.

The ever-increasing burden of anti-press legislation has become a nightmare for South African editors. They must now delegate normal editing tasks to underlings while they concentrate on the legal problems of publication. The average South African editor, who must bear responsibility for all violations of the emergency regulations, now sits beside a computer monitor with all the laws and enactments, checking the reports and dispatches of the day, deleting phrases and sentences likely to result in penalties against his newspaper. Anthony Heard, a former editor of the *Cape Times*, summed up the situation when he told a foreign correspondent: "I am today more a lawyer than an editor." He wasn't a good enough lawyer, apparently, for he is now out of a job. Those others who are still employed have grown weary of the daily strain of putting out a newspaper under the plethora of intimidatory laws. It shows in their product.

The foreign press, for its part, has simply given up trying. TV networks depend on footage for their news programmes. If film is not forthcoming, the event becomes a non-story. Most American networks have pulled out their correspondents and maintain skeleton staffs of local stringers, who spend their time being denied permission to film anything. The larger newspapers still have staff based in Johannesburg and Cape Town, but they have transferred their experienced old Africa hands to other more productive assignments and replaced them with novices, newcomers to Africa and the news business, who have no regional perspective, no background in war reporting and no knowledge of the country they are covering.

To them apartheid is simply a catchword, good for a headline or two because it always elicits a knee-jerk response from American liberals. They see things in black and white, without the nuances of South Africa's ethnic mosaic. They have no grasp of tribalism, the deep-rooted divisions within the black community that make *Inkatha* as much an enemy to the ANC as the white régime in Pretoria. They are totally mystified as to why President Botha should be concerned about a man like Dr Andries Treurnicht. They cannot differentiate between Afrikaner *verligtes* and *verkramptes* because, in the American context, there is not much difference. So their political assessments are shallow, and their reports on the security situation, having been censored, are regarded with suspicion by their editors. Most stories about South Africa these days wind up on the inside pages of American papers, buried among the truss ads.

Pretoria would appear to prefer it that way. The government blames the foreign press for much of South Africa's problems with the outside world. The US media are seen as a wolf pack that always hunts in unison and runs one way at a time, showing little independence of thought or genuine attempts at analysis, focusing only on what will appeal to a sensation-hungry American audience without delving into the deeper complications of South African problems. Articulate radicals like Bishop Tutu get more coverage than Afrikaners trying to explain their point of view in a second language. Television cameras follow those who make flamboyant statements or burn and riot. Newspapers and news magazines all too often go for cheap kicks.

"The trouble with American correspondents who come here to report the situation is that everyone is trying to win a Pulitzer Prize", complains one South

African official, with some justification. The new crop of American journalists does adopt the bandwagon approach. They all try to leap on it whatever direction it is going in, lest they be left behind and thus be seen as "missing the story". Often the bandwagon is going the wrong way. For example, the story put across to Americans, generally speaking, is that South Africa should be governed by blacks because they are in the majority and have been suppressed by the white minority. Scant attention is given to what sort of black government would emerge, or the concerns of white South Africans who fear that their well-developed and fairly advanced nation may be ruined like Angola and Mozambique.

All these are valid criticisms, particularly when applied to the foreign press corps as it now exists in South Africa. But Pretoria must share the blame for its plight. Its treatment of the press is often as stupid and shortsighted as the treatment of South Africa by the press.

Successive Nationalist governments have always adopted the Chinese Communist approach to the press: i.e. "if you aren't for us, you're against us." Afrikaner leaders have never been able to distinguish between balanced coverage and hostile coverage. They are extremely thin-skinned, excessively defensive about apartheid ... a policy that is essentially indefensible ... and intolerant of criticism. President Botha may see himself as a reformer, but he is no exception to his predecessors when it comes to favouring the stick over the carrot in dealing with the media. And he must bear the responsibility for creating what amounts to a public relations disaster during one of the most critical periods in South African history.

By stifling the South African press, Botha silenced those who were in the best position to give balanced reporting of what was going on in their own country. He forgot, if he ever knew it at all, that new and inexperienced foreign correspondents often use the local press as a guide and reference for their own stories until they themselves become familiar with the situation. An even worse mistake was chasing out or discouraging those foreign correspondents who, if not sympathetic to South Africa, at least understood what it was all about.

Pretoria is well aware that the largest and most influential media organisations in the United States are owned and dominated by liberals. That is one of its most frequent complaints. What it is not aware of, apparently, is that many correspondents who were assigned to cover South Africa for those organisations in the late 1970s and early 1980s were not so liberal. Most were old Africa hands who had witnessed the disastrous consequences of so-called "independence" in the Frontline States. Most were veterans of the Rhodesian war and its bloody aftermath in Zimbabwe, when blacks turned on blacks. They may not have approved of apartheid, but they understood the dilemma of white South Africans and they knew there were no simple solutions. They were, in fact, some of the best friends that South Africa ever had.

The country lost Alan Pizzey of CBS, a Canadian who won his spurs in Rhodesia, moved to Johannesburg and provided the best and most balanced coverage the country had ever received on American TV. His network pulled him out of South Africa and transferred him to the Middle East because he was too good to waste on a story that couldn't be filmed. South Africa lost Alan Cowell of the *New York Times,* an Englishman formerly with Reuters who had lived in Zambia and Rhodesia, knew what he was writing about and was always scrupulously honest in presenting both sides of the story. He was probably the most sympathetic *Times* correspondent that Pretoria would ever get, given that newspaper's notoriously anti-South African stance. He was certainly less biased than Michael

Parks of the *Los Angeles Times,* who set out to win a Pulitzer Prize, and did.

South Africa did not lose Peter Younghusband, who has a wine farm in Paarl and never intends to leave, but it lost his influence on *Newsweek,* another publication with a decidedly liberal bias. He switched to the *Washington Times,* a conservative newspaper with a much lower circulation and little impact, simply because he was tired of taking flack from Pretoria for the sins of his editors in New York. Peter is a South African with a stake in the country, and he would never do anything disloyal. He is also a respected journalist, probably the most knowledgeable correspondent ever to report on South African affairs in the American press. His byline did far more good for South Africa in *Newsweek* than it does in the *Washington Times.*

Like Peter, I am a child of Africa. I grew up in Cape Town, Port Elizabeth, Durban, Johannesburg and Pretoria. My father is buried there. I speak Afrikaans, a little Zulu, a little Xhosa. I feel more comfortable with farmers from Alldays (I have even hunted with them) than I do with Jesse Jackson. I understand the country and its problems. Yet it took a lot of persuading to get *Newsweek* to send me there. They wanted to send a black correspondent, thinking he would have more rapport with the people in Soweto. And when I finally arrived, I too spent most of my time in Rhodesia, with side trips to Beirut and the Falklands war.

In my four-year spell as *Newsweek's* southern Africa bureau chief, which ended two years before the state of emergency began, the magazine devoted only three cover stories to South Africa: one on Botha's apartheid reforms, one on South African military prowess, and one on the Group Areas Act and the Homelands policy. The first elicited an ecstatic response from the government. The second was greeted with some reservations and *put in my file,* as they say. The third got me in very hot water indeed. I was called on the carpet in Pretoria, harassed by the security police and vilified by the SABC. What made it laughable, however, was that the selfsame SABC had just done praising me for being the first correspondent to expose the Matabele massacres. A hero one week, a villain the next.

My *Newsweek* replacement in South Africa was also white. But his only qualification for the job was that he came from Detroit; the editors figured there were a lot of blacks in Detroit so he would feel right at home. That is the kind of thinking that Pretoria has to grapple with.

It may feel that the pressure is off for now. The state of emergency has curbed much of the civil unrest that occurred in 1985 and 1986. The townships have been placed under military control, and the ANC is back to doing what it did before: conducting a war of attrition with bombings, grenade attacks and other forms of urban terrorism. The security services have had considerable success in plugging infiltration routes, uncovering caches of weapons and neutralising terrorist cells with the help of informers. But *Spear of the Nation (Umkhonto we Sizwe),* the ANC's military wing, managed more than a bombing a day for two months preceding the municipal elections of October 1988.

The government now is trying to buy the loyalty of moderate blacks by improving housing and other social amenities. Millions of dollars have been earmarked for development of the townships over the next few years.

This is at best a stopgap solution. It appears to be predicated on perpetuation of the Group Areas Act while doing nothing to address the fundamental question of political rights for the disenfranchised black majority. Until there is movement on these fronts, the ANC will continue its guerrilla war, moderate black leaders like the Zulu Chief Gatsha Buthelezi will refuse to be coopted by limited power-sharing formulas and South Africa will continue to get a bad press.

Pretoria finds it particularly galling when men like Bishop Tutu and Allan Boesak travel abroad giving press conferences in which they advocate more sanctions and disinvestment. It is clearly against the national interest, if not treasonous. But instead of gnashing its teeth in helpless rage about the gullibility of the Western press, the South African government would be better served by using it ... just as Tutu and Boesak are using it to their advantage. Their remarks on advocating sanctions and disinvestment should be published in South African newspapers, not banned. Foreign correspondents should be allowed, nay encouraged, to go into the townships to gauge the reaction of black workers whose livelihood has been ruined by the pullout of American firms such as Kodak. Their stories would put a different slant on what Messrs Tutu and Boesak are saying.

Of course, apartheid remains the peg for most anti–South African reporting. To get a better press Botha must stop nibbling away at the edges of this policy and tear down its cornerstones. Admittedly, the emergence of a strong right wing within the National Party and the growing inroads made by the Conservative opposition have made that more difficult. The president cannot afford to move too quickly. This too he blames on the US press; for not crediting him with the reforms that he did manage to achieve, thus exposing him to ridicule by his own people with a subsequent loss of confidence and support.

But that is killing the messenger. No correspondent in his right mind can ignore the Race Classification Board which, with a perfectly straight face, issues an annual report listing the number of blacks who have become coloured and coloureds who have become white. It would take a very thick South African not to imagine how bizarre this sounds to American readers.

# SOUTH AFRICA AND THE SOVIET UNION
## by Christopher Coker

*Washington Times:* "Are you suggesting that the USSR now seems
to have a better grasp of real politik than the United States?"
*P.W. Botha:* "I think so."[1]

*John Fowles:* "Like all mystics ... he is baffled, a child before the
real now; far happier out of it, in a narrative past or a prophetic
future, locked inside that weird tense grammar does not allow: an
imaginary present."[2]

For forty years South Africa had comforted itself with the assumption that its
links with the West were indissoluable, that its own view of itself as a Western
state would see it through to the end of the century, and if necessary beyond.
The Simonstown base, the Cape sea route and its strategic minerals were assumed
to be interests that were not spurious but real. Although relations between Pretoria
and the West were often strained, it recognised that relations frequently appeared
to be more collusive than cooperative, subject to temporary set-backs whenever
a Democrat was elected to the White House or a Labour prime minister to
Downing Street, rarely, if ever, was the relationship itself questioned.

The Reagan administration, with its offer of a "strategic partnership"[3] between
the United States and South Africa, fostered a belief in a set of propositions
about the strategic importance of South Africa which were rarely questioned
because they had been taken for granted for so long. The destabilisation of Angola
seemed to match the destabilisation of Nicaragua, its support of Unita the more
questionable than American support of the Contras. Between 1981 and 1984
South Africa and the United States discovered a community of interest that
exaggerated the importance of Pretoria, and even its regional role.

It is never easy to challenge central beliefs. The imposition of sanctions by
the US Congress removed the keystone of the arch of the South African bridge
with the West without which the whole structure could not stand. The schedule
of repayment of South African debt required by the Western banks, together
with increasing "disinvestment" by American and European companies, who
proved fairweather partners, far less friends, inflicted more damage than the
desultory campaigns of violence of the ANC. South Africa belatedly woke up
to the fact that its relations with the West were essentially hollow, that it could
expect more, not less, pressure in the future, that it had already been dismissed
by the US Department of Commerce as a typical Third World state, economically
unviable, subject to prolonged periods of political unrest.

It was inevitable that sooner rather than later the South Africans would look
seriously at "the Soviet card", the option of moving closer to the Soviet Union
at the expense of the West. In this essay I shall not be so much concerned
with the tactical question of whether it is better to run the risk of courting the
Soviet Union, or to court the danger of not doing so. Both risks are severe.
The first, however, is the severer because it represents a challenge to forty years
of thinking about communism and the Russian threat. Those who would like
to find a basis of accommodation with Moscow are asking a great deal. They
are asking South Africa to abandon most of the shibboleths by which government

**Above:** Luanda during the Portuguese period was a beautiful town. Fort Jesus is now a military prison and museum displaying Portuguese and South African "atrocities".

**Right:** A sign familiar to most South Africans who spent holidays in Mozambique before Frelimo took over.

BENVINDO
WELCOME
WELKOM

PORTUGAL

MOÇAMBIQUE WELCOMES YOU

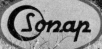

OFERECE-LHE O MELHOR SERVIÇO PARA O SEU CARRO
OFFERS YOU THE BEST SERVICE FOR YOUR CAR

**Above** Daniel Chipenda, of the Chipa Squadron, takes the salute near Nova Lisboã in central Angola. Al Venter served for a while with this unit to get his story.

**Left:** Chinese-trained parachute troops of the FNLA with their instructors at an airstrip in northern Angola, shortly before the failed attack on Luanda that gave the MPLA power in Angola. The FNLA was a protégé of both the Chinese and the Americans.

**Below left:** A dead boy in a Kampala cesspit. Such atrocities are sometimes seen in some African countries where life has deteriorated to a level of brigandry and mere survival.

**Above:** A long column of FNLA men marches towards Luanda. Most of them had set out from Zaïre. They were routed outside Luanda by a combined force of MPLA and Cubans.

**Below:** Children with wooden guns march under the orders of a young commissar (right) in the streets of Luanda. The revolution concentrated on young people to establish continuity of control.

**Above:** The Portuguese army in Guinea was one of the first to use airborne nurses, often dropped by parachute at isolated garrisons.

**Right:** A Portuguese army nurse attends a wounded soldier brought back by helicopter.

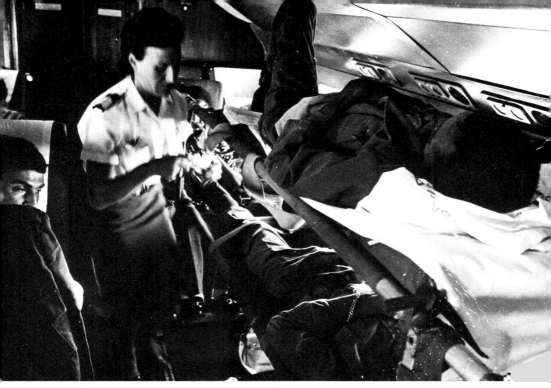

**Left:** Captain João Bacar (left) one of the most decorated officers in the African campaigns. He was brutally killed in an ambush soon after he had taken Al Venter on an operation near the Guinea border.

**Below:** A Portuguese soldier found wandering delirious in the bush after a skirmish in the interior. He was airlifted to safety.

**Above:** Many of the more serious casualties were flown to Lisbon for treatment. This group came out of Bissau.

**Above:** The Portuguese Air Force strip at Nambuangongo. Small aircraft were often the only means of communication between isolated garrisons.

**Right:** The road to Nambuangongo in northern Angola. Convoys had to be strongly protected.

**Above:** A Portuguese Air Force plane at Luanda airport shortly before independence. The belongings of tens of thousands of refugees lay scattered all over the main towns. Most of this stuff was pillaged by the rebels.

**Below:** A Unita sympathiser burnt to death outside the town of Nova Lisboã shortly before independence. All three movements, MPLA, FNLA and Unita committed horrible atrocities.

**Top right:** A Portuguese Alouette helicopter hovers over a convoy on the Tete road in central Mozambique.

**Top left:** Dissident civilians in the streets of Lourenço Marques soon after the army coup d'état in Lisbon. Emotions ran high as preparations were made for the Portuguese army to leave.

**Below left:** The first press conference at the governor's palace after Frelimo had been installed. All journalists were searched on entering the building.

**Below right:** Hundreds of refugees saved by the arrival of the French Foreign Legion gather at Kolwezi airport during the Katangese invasion of May 1978. Many of their compatriots were killed by these Angolan-backed rebels.

**Above:** Aerial view of Tete during the Portuguese era. It was a vital communication centre during the war. Most of the surrounding terrain was dominated by Frelimo.

**Above:** Conditions in Angola were often indescribably harsh for this European army. The Portuguese were hampered more than the rebels, who did not need roads or railways.

**Left:** To the glory of fallen heroes, members of an Angolan FAPLA unit on parade salute comrades killed in battles against the South Africans and Unita.

**Below left:** A Portuguese Air Force plane refuels at a remote base near N'Riquinha in eastern Angola.

**Above:** Much of Portuguese Guinea was swamp, a nightmare for troops trying to maintain order in the face of a resourceful enemy.

**Right:** General Antonio de Spinola with leather gloves and monocle, during an official reception in Portuguese Guinea.

**Above:** Luanda in the early Seventies was one of the most beautiful towns in West Africa. It has since deteriorated into a vast slum with few services or amenities.

**Right:** After the coup d'état in Lisbon, discipline in the colonies deteriorated. These Portuguese paratroopers had been ordered to guard a strategic depot, but they were slack in their duties.

**Above:**
Portuguese army
camp at Zemba
north of Luanda.
Rebel activity in
the area was so
intense that it was
supplied almost
entirely from the
air.

**Left:** A mine
casualty is
prepared to be
flown to a hospital
in Angola. This
man lost his hands
and his eyes.

**Below left:**
Portuguese army
patrol in the oil-
rich province of
Cabinda.
Aggressive,
concerted action
by the government
kept insurgency to
a minimum.

**Left:** Black Portuguese soldiers on patrol in Portuguese Guinea. These units, *Commandos Africanos*, were among the most efficient and ruthless colonial forces in the country.

**Above left:** An armed camp in Portuguese Guinea. Note the ragged trenchline and the heavy gun emplacements. Many of these camps came under heavy attack by the PAIGC from across the borders of Guinea and Senegal.

**Below right:** Portuguese marine patrol along an estuary in the interior.

**Above:** Surplus NATO vessels such as this barge were used effectively to carry men and supplies along the rivers. It was rather like Vietnam in places.

**Right:** Camouflaged with monkey skins, these black commando units were very effective in bush operations.

**Above:** FNLA soldiers with heavy machine-guns on parade in northern Angola.

**Right:** Cuban soldier on guard in the streets of Luanda.

policy has been determined since 1948; they are asking the state to abandon its crude rhetoric of anti-communism and recognise the Soviet Union as a "legitimate" actor in the region; they are asking the National Party to defy public opinion and admit that the forces opposed to it are essentially nationalist, not communist in inspiration. In short, they are asking for "the politically impossible", a commodity that could be supplied only by the Afrikaner establishment: a commodity the government has so far shown little interest in supplying.

## The View from Moscow

Nothing prepared the world for the advent of Gorbachev except one thing: growing concern in Russia, first enunciated under Andropov, that Brezhnev's "forward policy" in the Third World had been disastrous.

Ideologically, the Soviet Union could not have made its position clearer than in June 1983, when Andropov told the CPSU Plenum that the success of socialism outside the Soviet Union would turn largely on the economic fortunes of Russia itself. Its economic failings were clear long before Gorbachev came to power. The renewed theme of "socialism in one country" anticipated *perestroika* by several years.

Economically, the allies of Russia in southern Africa found themselves not wards, or welfare dependants, but despised poor relations, supplicants cooling their heels in the antechamber of history. "It is one thing to proclaim socialism," Andropov reminded Samora Machel. "It is another to build it."[4]. By 1984 Mozambique had been effectively written off as a "scientific socialist country"; even as a "natural ally" of the USSR. Demoted in the socialist lexicon to a "historic ally" instead, it was clear that there were many in Moscow who found its claim to be a Marxist-Leninist state absurdly "premature".

Much though they might complain about the Nkomati Accord or the Lusaka Agreement, it was clear that the Russian leadership had no intention of propping up shadow Marxist states against South African destabilisation, short of ensuring that their leaders remained in power. In the late 1970s the MPLA and Frelimo had been hailed as genuine "vanguard Marxist-Leninist parties", likely to be more reliable than the bourgeois nationalist leaders whom Khrushchev had embraced twenty years earlier. Nkrumah and Keita had relied on their own personalities to keep them in power in Ghana and Mali; Brezhnev hoped that scientific socialism would take root in southern Africa and institutionalise communist rule.

History, as usual, decided otherwise. Although the MPLA declared itself a vanguard party in 1977, it too has had to be propped up against enemies both internal and external. For the most part, it has been dismissed by Ulyanovsky, a senior member of the International Department of the CPSU, as a party "guided by the ideals of Marxist-Leninism" not a party that can lay claim to being Marxist-Leninist.

Ten years before the election of Gorbachev Karen Brutents's important work on national liberation movements warned the Third World that there were no short-cuts to socialism; that socialist states in the Third World could no longer look to the USSR to bail them out, as Mali had done in the mid-1960s; that the support they could expect "in a spirit of proletarian internationalism" was likely to be very limited indeed. In time the Soviet Union came to prefer "the non-capitalist road to development" precisely because it was an intermediate step on the road to socialism; as the Grenadan ambassador to Moscow recognised (in the event rather belatedly) "to adopt an overtly Marxist-Leninist path ... is to court alienation and take a deliberately long route to national liberation."[5]

Like Mozambique, Grenada may have derived a certain psychological security from its declaration of Marxist intent, but not the physical security on which Frelimo depends for its survival. Unlike Grenada, its leadership has survived because it has not been let down by its own revolutionary theory. "To believe that Grenada was not in anybody's (i.e. the American) backyard," Anthony Thorndyke wrote, "was an exhilarating experience, but it was an illusion."[6] The Nkomati Accord was recognition enough that Mozambique was firmly in the South African backyard, despite its treaty of friendship with the Soviet Union.

Ideological realism is not the only reason why Brutents and others are now urging the Soviet leadership to turn to a new generation of "bourgeois" African leaders who will not need unending military support, as much as the present weak and narrowly based clients of Russia; why there is in his voice and that of other academicians a new note of pessimism, from which prolonged study of the 1960s had allowed the Soviet Union to escape. If the Russian leadership is rather more sympathetic to the Ulyanovskys, even to Cassandras with disagreeable messages that turn out to be true, it is because military support for its southern African clients is proving increasingly costly.

If supplies of Russian arms to Africa since the early 1980s have risen exponentially both as a percentage of total arms sales to the Third World (34 per cent) and to Africa itself (54 per cent), the Russian share of supplies of arms to the Third World has considerably declined. The main explanation seems to be that the Soviet Union has become increasingly unwilling to sell arms without a substantial financial return in hard currency. Since 1975 hard–currency deals have never fallen below 80 per cent of total sales.[7]

Nevertheless there has been a striking contrast between sales and actual payment. If low prices and favourable credit terms have given way to high prices and stricter terms of repayment, many African states seem to have defaulted on their debts, with the notable exception of such oil-rich countries as Libya and Algeria (which together with Ethiopia are the three largest markets for Russia in Africa south of the Sahara).

Some authorities have argued that the value of sales of Russian arms is two or three times higher than most estimates suggest, and therefore that the repayment of debt represents a much higher burden for the recipient than had been previously acknowledged. If that is true, it must also be true that military help has become a correspondingly higher burden for the Russian economy to sustain. One authority has calculated that its actual receipts may only be 40 per cent of the CIA estimates; or to put it another way, that the net deficit in Russian trade has been running at US$2 billion or more for several years, partly because it has not been paid for the arms that it has sold.[8]

What are we to make of these figures? They explain – to begin with – why so many arms have been sold to the two countries that can actually afford them, plus the most strategically important of the allies of Russia: Ethiopia. In the early 1980s Ethiopia imported arms valued at 140 per cent of its total export earnings, at a time when its foreign exchange reserves fell by half. Clearly it was in no position to pay for them. A large proportion seems to have been written off as "aid", the rest sold on generous credit terms with payments that have been indefinitely deferred.

In southern Africa the Soviet Union seems to have made little out of the sale of arms, except from Angola (which managed to repay half its foreign debt to the Soviet Union just before the collapse in oil prices in the summer of 1987). Mozambique has not been so fortunate. It has no oil of its own; indeed it imports two–thirds from the Soviet Union. Despite the visit of a high–level military delegation to Maputo in June 1982, deliveries of arms did not increase. Indeed, in dollar value they were less in 1983 than they had been in 1978, when relations with South Africa were considerably more cordial and the threat from Renamo much less acute.

With the exception of a handful of MiG–21s and MI–24 helicopters, Soviet–bloc sales to Mozambique have been of ageing and increasingly poor equipment. Czech T–54/55 tanks, armoured personnel carriers and howitzers of similar age are far too old to engage South African forces. Romania has even dumped obsolete Alouette 3 and Puma helicopters which, although no longer built in France, are still built under special licence for the Third World market.

As a result Mozambique has been complaining about the delivery of obsolete and inappropriate arms since 1981. Its shortage of helicopters in particular has made it almost impossible to carry out proper counter–insurgency operations. In a word, the two Marxist–Leninist powers in the region have discovered that their allies expect an economic return, and that the region is not yet so vital that they qualify for "aid" like Ethiopia. Despite fifteen years of support for Frelimo when it was in the bush, its allies have behaved meanly and feebly; not like effective allies at all.

Thirdly, and perhaps even more important, the Soviet Union has found itself on the defensive in southern Africa as it has almost everywhere else. The great wave of revolutions that so weakened the world position of America in the 1970s – fourteen in all – has ended for the time being. The United States has managed to contain them (in El Salvador), or set them back in Angola (with the help of South Africa) or forced the USSR to pay an exorbitant price for its continued presence (80 per cent of all Russian aid is now channelled to the communist world). Contrary to the popular caricature of the Reagan presidency as lacking finesse, it seems to have stumbled upon the secret of containment on the cheap, a price tag of US$200 million in Nicaragua (in aid to the Contras since 1981), and a mere US$27 million a year for Savimbi's movement in Angola. Perhaps it was symptomatic of the innate pessimism with which the Soviet Union looks at the Third World that in a recent article by Lyudmila Alexandrovskaya there was not one mention of the USSR or its allies in the answer that the author gave to her own question: "Where do Africans place their hopes in this decade?"[9]

Unfortunately, the Soviet Union cannot afford to turn its back on southern Africa, to look on in the future in a mood of subdued passivity. George Orwell may have been right in predicting that the only "ism" that would eventually prove itself right this century would be "pessimism", but whether it would like to or not the USSR cannot remove itself to the margins of southern African history without forfeiting its status as a superpower.

Like the United States it has the interests of its own allies to look after, especially because ever since the early 1970s it has encouraged Eastern Europe to look to southern Africa as a market for raw materials to reduce its dependence on Russian supplies. There are now about 200 East European enterprises in the Third World, of which half are in Africa south of the Sahara, the great majority in southern Africa, and mostly in mining.

The East Europeans have good cause to look outside the Soviet bloc for cheap raw materials. During the last ten years the export prices of raw materials have been rising much faster than the prices of machinery and consumer products. They also have to live with the serious danger that the Soviet Union will not be able to supply raw materials indefinitely. Some CIA reports paint a picture of serious shortages in production over the next ten to twenty years, especially in lead and zinc. The Soviet Union has already been forced to double its imports from Africa of bauxite and alumina; indeed it now depends on foreign imports for half the alumina consumed every year.

Eastern Europe has had to live with the prospect not of short-term deficiencies of the kind that have always plagued the West as a result of such cyclical factors as unexpected crises or protracted strikes, but long-term shortages arising from a *structural* deficit in the socialist bloc at a time of over-production outside it. Eastern Europe has already suffered from such shortages in aluminium and coking coal at a time of over-supply in the world market.

Even if none of these factors were important, however, the allies of the Soviet Union would still face an apparently intractable problem in southern Africa. To their consternation they have discovered that the Soviet Union has no control over events in the interior; that like the West in the 1960s and 1970s they themselves are prey to the depredations of national liberation movements over which they have no control or influence. In 1977 attempts to pump out the Chipinga 7 mine (in Moatize) after severe flooding were hampered by persistent Rhodesian raids on the railway line, which in turn stopped the supply of diesel fuel for the pumps. Five years later the East Germans stood by helplessly as attacks by guerrillas opposed to Frelimo brought the renovation of the Condo-Derunde railway to an abrupt stop, causing a bottleneck to the Moatize fields, where more than a year's production of coal was stockpiled. In January 1986 Renamo began mortar-bombing the East German compounds in Moatize. The following year East German geologists were specifically targeted by the MNR to draw attention to the number of East German planners seconded to the National Commission for Planning.[10] The attacks have continued ever since.

Clearly, with these considerations in mind the Russian attitude to South Africa and its role in the region is likely to have changed considerably since 1975. Only South Africa can provide the security that its allies need; only Pretoria can restore conditions to where they were in the late 1970s, when instability in the region, although significant, was not economically damaging to Russian interests.

It is even more interesting that its attitude to change in South Africa itself seems to have changed, particularly since the end of the "unrest" in the townships that followed closely upon the declaration of the second state of emergency. Possibly in 1984 the Soviet Union expected more of the unrest than it should have. Recruitment by the ANC was far greater in that period than it had been after the last spontaneous outburst of black resentment in Soweto in 1976. It did not give the movement the capacity for serious military operations. Over 500 members of the ANC have lost their lives since, many in the ill-conceived attempt to disrupt the all-white election of 1987.

The election itself was a blow to those in the Kremlin who were committed to the Leninist proposition that a split in the ruling class was a necessary, if not a sufficient, pre-condition for a revolution; that a grassroots struggle from the bottom up could not prevail on its own. The consolidation of the right seems to have proved some of its assumptions in 1984 to have been hopelessly naïve and unrealistic.

In addition, the destruction by the police of the ANC network in the Western Cape in 1987 and the arrest of more than fifty of its members abruptly ended the attempt by the ANC to begin the mass-based "people's war" that it had declared in 1986. The setback may not have been as serious as the "post-Rivonia stalemate" in 1963, when almost the entire leadership of the ANC was captured in a raid by the police, but it forced Tambo and the leadership to accept the principle of a "negotiated settlement" with the government "under the right conditions" and the need for a dialogue with whites in the interim, of which the meetings with IDASA in Dakar (1987) and Frankfurt (1988) were a case in point.[11]

Several Western observers have also tended to treat seriously a number of Russian statements that confirm what some had begun to suspect as early as 1982, when Buthelezi met officials of the Russian embassy for an informal discussion in Washington; that Russian commitment to a revolutionary struggle may not be entirely unequivocal. Inevitably special attention has been paid to a number of unusually frank statements by members of the African Institute in Moscow, especially by its two deputy directors, Gleb Starushenko and Leonard Goncharov.

Starushenko's proposal for a two-chamber post-apartheid Parliament, in the second of which each race would exercise a veto, would be a far more radical concession to the white minority than the twenty guaranteed seats offered by the British in the post-independence Zimbabwean Parliament at Lancaster House. Although the Russians were quick to insist that Starushenko was speaking on his own behalf, not on behalf of the Institute, its Director, Anatoly Gromyko, tried to drive the same point home during a trip to the Congo a few months later.

It is also interesting that Leonard Goncharov dismissed the language of revolution in the townships in the ANC journal as an infantile disorder, a remark addressed to the Trotskyist young comrades, a comment that echoed Lenin's criticism of "the infantile left". When asked whether he expected a socialist South Africa in his lifetime, Goncharov replied rather obliquely: "In ten years, or a hundred – I'm an optimist."[12]

It should be noted that much of the debate about South Africa has been conducted by academics, and on a very narrow front. Many observers take a low view of the importance of academicians, especially Starushenko. Despite the failure of an ANC mission led by Paulo Jordan in March 1987 to persuade Moscow publicly to repudiate Starushenko's proposal, an article in *Africa Communist* in May and Goncharov's own remarks at a conference in Harare two months later suggested that his comments had embarrassed the Soviet government.

Throughout 1987, however, the evidence of a radical re-assessment of Russian support for the ANC grew stronger, not less. In Washington Victor Kremenyuk, No.3 in the Institute of the US and Canada, declared that a "revolution" in South Africa would not be in the interests either of the region or of the world. In October Boris Asoyan, a senior adviser to the Soviet Foreign Ministry, called for a fundamental reappraisal of Russian policy towards South Africa, and for an honest and open discussion of previous "miscalculations" about political developments. Asoyan's brief appointment to the Soviet embassy in Lesotho enabled him to set up a network of contacts in South Africa before he left. Even a senior Russian official, Y.Y. Vagris, refused to approve all the conditions that the ANC had set for a post-apartheid South Africa.[13] The support which Gorbachev gave to the *principle* of ethnicity at the Soviet Party Conference in the Summer of 1988 must have disturbed the ANC even more. As one member of the Soviet Central Committee said despairingly during a visit to the West: "We are fed-up with national liberation. We cannot carry the ANC into the Union Buildings, and we don't even wish to do so. We were very unfortunate to have blown up the ANC's self-conceit out of all proportion."[14]

Clearly the Soviet Union is a long way from repudiating the ANC or the SACP, whose association with the movement remains stronger than ever. Much though individual Russian officials may despair of an imminent transfer of power, or even deprecate a revolution, the ANC has about 35 per cent of the black vote, or more support than any other black organisation. Unlike Zimbabwe, the Soviet Union is not obliged to choose between two sides each of whom lays claim to be the "legitimate" representative of the dispossessed majority. The ANC will have to be supported if Moscow is to retain the influence that it already exercises.

If it were ever to alienate the movement, it might even push it into the embrace of the West. Despite becoming a counter-revolutionary power in the region propping up a political order that it established in the late 1970s, it would be doubly ironic if it encouraged the West for the first time in its history to back a quasi-Marxist movement before power had been transferred. Nevertheless there is no doubt that relations between the ANC and Moscow have changed in the direction of greater realism on both sides; so much so that the more radical members of the US Defence Intelligence Agency even proposed trying to "coopt" or arm the movement in the closing days of the Reagan administration.

Recent visitors to Moscow have found a disposition to persuade the ANC to talk to other black groups, from those that it despises, such as Inkatha, to Cosatu, whose claim to represent their own constituencies Moscow regards not only as legitimate, but not to be ignored. Insofar as this move has the support of the SACP, which has preached the need to win the liberation struggle first before any attempt is made to ensure the victory of socialism, the ANC is likely to shed its more radical image. To the extent that the SACP is prevailed upon to recognise that the African National Congress is not the sole representative of black opinion, it may even realise a democratic future by recognising the burden of its non-democratic past.

### The view from Pretoria

For South Africa to move closer towards the Soviet Union would mark a radical break with an alignment with the West that goes back forty years or longer, an alignment that has produced two results, one transient, the other more enduring.

The first was a reluctance to accept that as long as apartheid remained in force the West could or would not choose to accept South Africa as an ally. It is difficult to explain what Pretoria expected to get out of the association, out of membership of NATO, for which it strove until 1952, out of the Simonstown Agreement with Britain (1955), which was taken no further, or even the trilateral defence talks with Britain and the United States until the latter withdrew in 1959. It was so eager to be seen as a member of the Western community that its identity as an African state was denied altogether.

That was a transient mood, dictated by the exigencies of the moment, the pace of decolonisation, the fear of communism, the wish not only to defy the "winds of change" but also successfully to "ride the whirlwind" of black nationalism.[15] The other widespread attitude to the Soviet Union, which proved more resilient, was the illusion that the Soviet "threat" was greater than ever, that the appearance of the Russian navy in the Indian Ocean in 1968 and intrusion of Russian military power into southern Africa itself in 1975 offered South Africa another opportunity to play a part that Britain and the United States had denied it in the 1950s.

It was the single most dangerous illusion that South Africa entertained, an illusion begotten by ignorance of the history of the West, by its refusal to attach any importance to the rhetoric of Western politicians which even the always realistic Europeans did not dare to repudiate without putting their own probity in doubt. Writing in 1984, after looking at 25 years of alleged "collusion" by NATO with South Africa, I suggested that not only was the notion totally without foundation but that the recognition of South Africa as another Third World African nation (a discovery NATO made many years before the US Department of Commerce) might well make the eventual emergence of a non-aligned black South Africa much less damaging to the Western Alliance than many commentators had predicted, and also explain why, despite old African fears, NATO had never had much interest in forestalling majority rule.[16]

Ideologically, therefore, South Africa should have prepared itself to change horses some time ago. My main purpose is not to challenge the old view of partnership with the West, which has long since been discredited, but to test whether an alignment with Moscow is possible or desirable. It would not, of course, be the first time that the Soviet Union had changed horses; it did so in 1977, dropping its old ally Somalia for the old ally of America, Ethiopia. Nor would it be the first time that the Soviet Union had abandoned communist parties in "bourgeois societies" whenever it has been convenient: abandoning the Egyptian Communist Party to its fate in the late 1950s was the price that the Soviet Union was prepared to pay for a partnership between "the Sphinx and the Commissar".

More realistically, the Soviet Union would probably prefer a more neutral position on the part of South Africa that would be to the disadvantage of the West without committing the Russians to a collusive association. As it happened, the old isolationism of the National Party in the 1930s found a distinct echo in a speech given by the Foreign Minister in Zürich in March 1979, in which he threatened to give serious consideration to adopting a neutral position between the two blocs if the United States continued to penalise Pretoria.[17] In a private meeting outside Johannesburg in the Autumn of 1988 Pik Botha reassured the chief southern Africa correspondent of *Isvestia* that the Republic might even move in Moscow's direction if circumstances were to justify such a political *volte face.*

Perhaps neutrality is as far as South Africa could go, given its deep-rooted antipathy to communism and its more recent fears of a "total onslaught". The total onslaught may have had its day; it may (as its chief prophet General Malan has admitted) have become a currency devalued through overuse;[18] but it has helped to justify rising defence budgets, white conscription and the employment of conscripted troops beyond the borders of South Africa. Can South Africa afford to dispense with "the Soviet threat"?

At the moment the question remains open. In the past it was part of the intellectual baggage of apartheid, persuading the white population to treat black unrest as a manifestation of communism rather than of genuine black nationalism (as it is has been treated in the staff colleges since 1984).[19]

In asserting that the fear of communism in South Africa is irrational I am not arguing that its use by the government is not rational; on the contrary. It is no less real for being an *idée reçue,* even if it is an idea behind its time, not ahead of it. I am saying that even if South Africa wished to open a dialogue with the Soviet Union it would pay a price that might prove too high in social cohesion at home and political credibility abroad. Ideologically South Africa has less room for manoeuvre than Moscow, which has always been able to re-interpret history to fit the political realities of the moment: "In the nuclear age," *Pravda* commented on 14 November 1986 "in conditions where ... the whole world is enmeshed in military alliances and blocs, violence can easily change from being the midwife of history to its gravedigger." Working within narrower historical limits, South Africa has to be much more circumspect about changing tack, or sleeping partners (to use Chou en Lai's image of the superpowers during the early years of détente).

South Africa does appear, however, to be genuinely committed to looking at the Russian threat more realistically, assessing its options in the region, studying whether deals or informal agreements might be worked out. The Department for Foreign Affairs has created a Soviet desk under Pieter Bezuidenhout and on at least ten occasions in 1987 it established contact with Russian officials to explore the possibilities of a Russian–South African understanding.

Logically, given the depth of anti-American feeling and distrust of the West, the time is now ripe for an alignment of sorts. But politics is never logical. In reality, Heisenberg's "indeterminacy principle" which in physics has substituted cause-and-effect probabilities for cause-and-effect certainties has long held sway. In politics the probabilities of something not happening are greater than any certainties that they will. Nations may exercise choice, but they seldom make the right choices. Enemies rarely become allies overnight.

If South Africa is re-assessing its relations with the Soviet Union from the perspective of change at home, it is also being forced to re-assess its commitment to arming its own allies in Angola, with all that that may entail for its future security.

The South African Defence Force originally embarked on its military adventures in Angola to remove the need for continual frontier defence, to maximise its net disposable power, and to engage its enemies not on the frontier but beyond it, a strategy that the Israelis call "anticipatory counter-attacks".

Persuasive though it may be in theory, it has proved very costly in practice. In 1983/4 operations in Angola accounted for 73 per cent of the defence budget (minus pay and pensions). At times the "raids" (as they are still euphemistically called in the world press) have entailed an enormous application of power: 250 armoured cars and no fewer than 90 Centurion tanks during one operation alone in 1981. Over time the South Africans have been unable to keep up with two developments that may one day severely limit their operational capability: (1) the unexpected willingness by the Soviet Union to arm its allies at a faster rate than Armscor can resupply the SADF (R5 billion of arms to Angola between 1984 and 1985 alone); (2) the thoroughness with which the Russians have built a vast network of surface-to-air missiles in the south, which has effectively bottled up the SAAF in the extreme south-east of Angola. As the chief of the air staff admitted recently: if the "air umbrella" grows any stronger it will become more effective, and proportionately more difficult to neutralise; long-range operations will no longer be possible without heavy casualties on a scale that may deter South African politicians from engaging the Angolan army in the future.[20]

These realities have recently been brought home by the most disastrous of the campaigns that South Africa has waged since 1978: the indecisive siege of Cuito Cuanavale, which involved four battalions of the SADF, 8 000 men in all, as well as six months of preparations during which a thousand trucks a day carried arms and equipment from Rundu to Angola and the western Caprivi Strip. Despite lobbing 200 shells a day from positions five miles away, the town did not fall.[21]

Once the Angolan war became one of attrition and the struggle one of technological capability as each side tried to leap-frog the other in the race for military dominance, South Africa was bound to favour a negotiated settlement.

In these circumstances the temptation to do a deal with the Soviet Union has become more attractive, not less. The problem, of course, is that if a settlement should be negotiated it will be difficult for South Africa not to recognise the legitimate rights of the Soviet Union in the region, to complain as Henry Kissinger did in 1975 about Soviet "involvement" in Angola long before the arrival of the first battalions of Cubans led him to condemn "Soviet intervention" in the civil war. It would be all too easy for the Soviet Union to replace the United States as the most significant external actor, to acquire a quasi-legitimate status in the eyes of the outside world which would transform the politics of the region in a way that it would be difficult for South Africa to challenge once it had become a fait accompli.

There is a third community of interest between the two countries, however, that may lead them to swallow their ideological misgivings and circumvent the practical difficulties that any negotiations might give rise to. South Africa needs regional stability as much as the Soviet Union does, perhaps more, since its greatest fear is that of a superpower condominium that would leave it with precious little room for manoeuvre.

Five changes in attitude (which may prove to be more apparent than real) have contributed to a radical re-assessment of Russian policy in the region, all of which suggest a more realistic Russian approach to regional instability.

First, Gorbachev has challenged the idea that the blame for instability in the Third World should be laid entirely at the door of the West. Instead, the Soviet Union now admits that it often has deep roots in the past, and is conditioned by causes over which the West has little, if any, understanding – let alone control.

"Each regional conflict has its own particular causes," wrote Karen Brutents in February 1987. ... "Every regional conflict must be approached with an understanding of its own particular nature."

Secondly, national liberation wars are no longer described as "inevitable"; indeed Brutents and others have called them "ruinous" because they are not only costly, they are rarely "won". The Soviet Union has all too often found itself having to keep Marxist régimes in power when their opponents have taken to the bush.

Thirdly, instead of dismissing the connection between Russian intervention in the Third World and détente with the United States, the new leadership in the Kremlin has admitted that Brezhnev's "adventurism" in the late 1970s was largely to blame for ending détente.

Fourthly, at the 27th Party Congress Gorbachev singled out regional conflict as the most dangerous development in the world now, one that if left to fester could lead to war between the superpowers, a view in which he was supported by the Director of the Institute for World Economy, Yevgeni Primakov.[23] The Soviet Union seems to have accepted that far from being contained, regional wars usually spread and intensify, a point that the Russian leadership was at pains to drive home during a visit by Kenneth Kaunda to Moscow in 1987 during which Gorbachev took the opportunity to remind Kaunda that the primary duty of the Frontline States was to limit the struggle in southern Africa, not to invite in the superpowers to resolve it by means of their own choosing.

Finally, in a speech at Vladivostok in 1986, Gorbachev insisted that countries could no longer expect to buy total security for themselves at the expense of total insecurity for others; that in the modern era security could only be relative, a fact that was as true for regional powers as it was for the Soviet Union and the United States.

In Angola the South Africans came to the conclusion (rather belatedly) that any further instability of American devising might persuade Unita to move north out of the South African orbit. For months the Americans had been urging Savimbi to distance himself from Pretoria by leaving Jamba and moving beyond the Benguela railway, where he could be supplied from an American base in Kamina (Zaïre). The decision to take Cuito Cuanavale particularly angered Savimbi, since he was pushed into besieging a target of little strategic significance to Unita, which it could not have held in any case even if the town had fallen.

The South Africans were also clearly alarmed that the United States opened talks in January not only with the Angolan government but also the main Cuban negotiator, Jorge Rysquet; talks about which the South Africans were not informed, and which they first learned of from public radio.

In the past the South African attitude to the Soviet Union was to despise communism, and in the depth of its loathing consistently to fail to get to grips either with the country or with its ideology. If it has now come to terms with the ideological changes under Gorbachev, it cannot be entirely reassured on that count either. For the Soviet Union is still a power whose frontiers of policy-making are determined by calculations of what the United States is likely to tolerate. Its more "responsible" view of regional conflicts has been dictated by the need to establish better relations between Russia and America, not to buy a settlement of regional conflicts at America's expense.

The US factor is vital, for the Soviet Union will not accommodate South Africa if by doing so it were to jeopardise its still unstable relations with the United States. It is notable that when Goncharev suggested a joint Russian–American approach to southern Africa at a conference in Harare in 1987 he chose to cite neither a Russian document nor a speech by the ANC, but the report of the US Secretary of State's Advisory Committee on South Africa.[24] If there is a "window of opportunity" in Angola for Moscow and Pretoria to come to an arrangement, it is unlikely to remain open for long.

### A Russian-South African alignment?

One could argue that this is not the best period for South Africa, at least, to open a dialogue with the Soviet Union. South Africa seems to have reached a condition of stasis, a reaction to the disappointed hopes raised by the reform programme, a time of re-assessment that may see South Africa retreat even further into itself at home, suppressing dissent in the press and banning still more organisations. In such a climate of reaction, can we really imagine better relations with a traditional enemy, now that its traditional ally has departed the field? There are two areas, at least, that we should look at before answering that question.

### 1. Angolan Settlement

Inevitably any discussion of a Soviet deal on Angola will be influenced by the Russian withdrawal from Afghanistan, the circumstances in which it takes place, and the form that it takes. During one of his meetings with Kaunda in 1987 Gorbachev suggested that the proposals on the table for "national reconciliation" in Afghanistan could "also be applied fully in a resolution of the problems in southern Africa".[25]

Is the analogy, although plausible, entirely convincing? In Afghanistan the Soviet

Union has suffered a military defeat, however it may try to disguise the fact, a serious setback that may have cost the lives of 25 000 Soviet soldiers needlessly sacrificed for a government hardly worthy of Russian support. In Angola its main allies, the Cubans, have made it known that they would be willing to stay on almost indefinitely as long as their foreign exchange costs were met: not surprisingly perhaps, since until 1988 few Cuban troops actually saw any fighting.

In Kabul the Russians began "broadening the base of the social revolution" several years before pulling out, even inviting back the former Minister of Planning under the monarchy to improve the economic performance of Afghanistan. In Angola the MPLA has been prepared to coopt the FNLA as it did in 1987, repatriating 12 000 FNLA guerrillas into the bargain under a general amnesty, which the government could easily afford to grant. So far, however, the Angolans have shown no willingness to cooperate with Unita in a genuine coalition administration, even if they have not ruled out dividing the movement by offering a portfolio or two to the members of Unita in the north.

Whether the Afghan analogy holds good or not, there are two items on the agenda that South Africa and the Russians might discuss. The first, and possibly most realistic, is the demilitarisation of the south. In September 1987, just before the Angolan army made its most recent offensive, the MPLA came near to agreeing with South Africa on withdrawing all Cuban troops north of the Benguela railway.[26] When Philip Nel, the director of the Institute for Soviet Studies at Stellenbosch, visited Moscow about the same time, Anatoly Gromyko also raised the question of demilitarisation as an interim solution to the problem. Unfortunately, when the Soviet Union last suggested such a policy in the late 1970s, the MPLA objected that such a cynical manoeuvre would challenge the sovereignty of Angola, which according to the terms of its Treaty of Friendship and Cooperation the USSR was pledged to defend.

A less likely subject for discussion is a coalition government. In March 1988 General Malan stated that if the Soviet Union really was ready to see "a free, non-aligned and neutral government" in Kabul, Pretoria was ready to live with a non-aligned Angola. His insistence on a coalition government, while failing to mention Savimbi by name, suggested to some observers that South Africa was ready to exclude him from a settlement, if circumstances made it necessary or unavoidable. During Nel's visit the Russians had suggested that a coalition government could be negotiated if Savimbi were excluded; that the intermittent talks between Unita and the MPLA in Lisbon and Geneva over the past two years had shown that the only obstacle to such an agreement was Savimbi himself. This may become more crucial, not less, in any extended run up to free elections.

Plausible though both propositions may be, one must also acknowledge the difficulties that South Africa would have in "selling" such an outcome to its own constituents in the army and military intelligence (the least imaginative and most suspicious of the parties concerned). Clearly, there are many in Pretoria who genuinely believe that without the support that South Africa has given to Savimbi Pretoria would long ago have forfeited its role as an important factor in Angolan politics, whatever its claims to "regional superpower" status might be. Allowing the Soviet Union a free hand in Angola as a guarantor of a coalition government, even if South Africa were to guarantee the position of Unita (a Geneva-style 1955 conference which recognised the claims of two members of a government, rather than two countries) would call for a degree of diplomatic finesse, and a knowledge of the Soviet Union, that the South African Foreign

Service does not possess, and probably never will, as many South African diplomats are the first to concede.

If Angola is interested in coopting Unita, but not in power-sharing, how long would it be before Unita turned against South Africa, its former patron? In 1982 Savimbi insisted that he was not a capitalist, recalling the remarks that he had made to a group of Western journalists in an interview eight years earlier in which he had insisted that "socialism" was the only answer to the problems of Angola.[27] What the Soviet Union, on the other hand, could expect from the presence of Unita in the government is a decidedly more militant black representation at the expense of the mestico elements that still dominate the MPLA. South Africa has every reason to recall that the attempted Alves Coup in 1977 was a Russian-supported attempt to restore black influence in Luanda, a coup that the Cubans put down without referring the matter back to Moscow. Whatever his ideological shortcomings, the Russians are unlikely to find Savimbi's racial politics either unexceptionable or unacceptable.

There are other South Africans in the security world who would question whether the purpose of a regional deal with the Soviet Union should be an end in itself or a means to an end. If a means, then the exercise might neutralise South Africa while confirming the MPLA in power. It could be defended on one assumption alone: that Angola was the only question that divided the two powers. They would maintain, on the contrary, that South Africa has two alternatives that are both more attractive and realistic than the one we have just discussed – pressing until the Russians are either expelled from Angola or choose to leave of their own accord; or forcing Moscow – by holding out until 1989 or beyond – to make even more concessions until it had effectively become the junior partner in any future negotiations.

If such thinking were to prevail, South Africa would find refuge in a fanciful world even more remote from reality than a world of great-power brokering, of deals between two ideologically opposed powers. Jorge Luis Borges wrote that the greatest magician would be "he who cast such a spell upon himself as to believe the reality of his own creation". It is an achievement that is still not beyond either military intelligence or the government that it serves.

## 2. Russian-South African economic ties

An actual alignment with the East need not, of course, require formal diplomatic links or any public re-assessment of interests.

It could take the form of economic collusion (breaking the coal embargo by selling coal cheap to Bulgaria; or the United Nations embargo on the exploitation of Namibian resources by selling uranium through British mining houses to the Soviet Union – to cite two actual, not speculative examples).

Business has already been the main medium of ties between South Africa and the Soviet Union; although the medium has not yet become the message. So far De Beers and Anglo-American have been the main actors; gold and diamonds the main commodities.

De Beers has worked closely with the Soviet Union since 1926. In the mid-1970s its payments for marketing Soviet diamonds represented the third-largest Russian source of hard currency after the sale of gold and petroleum, even surpassing the sale of arms.[28] Any wish that the Russians may have had to set up their own cartel has been defeated by the other services that De Beers provides, including industrial diamonds, which are not found in the Siberian mines. Rumours persist that the South African Reserve Bank actually handles a Russian account.

With gold there is no formal marketing arrangement as with diamonds, but there is an informal agreement about gold pricing, what the South African Chamber of Mines has referred to coyly as a system of "collusive price leadership" between Anglo-American and the Wozchod Handellsbank in Zurich (a Western subsidiary of the Bank for Foreign Trade in Moscow). Any hope of coordinating the marketing of gold has so far proved an aspiration that is unlikely to be realised.

Both countries, of course, produce an even greater proportion of platinum than gold or diamonds. For years Rustenberg Mines has produced studies of the Russian platinum industry in the hope of finding some basis of agreement on marketing. In 1980 the Chairman of Rustenberg Platinum went to Moscow to try to get agreement on a market price.

South Africa and the Soviet Union have been cooperating on the marketing of platinum for years, although neither will admit it. For that matter neither country has felt the need for a formal arrangement, or cartel, when they are both prepared to exchange information. Suggestions that Lonhro is trying to form a cartel with Anglo-American through its ownership of Western Platinum in South Africa, and possible purchase of a 30 per cent shareholding in Consolidated Goldfields, are not very plausible. (Anglo sold its stock in Lonhro in the 1970s – a fact the company must now regret.)

Western Platinum is the smallest of South Africa's three largest reefs, producing only a quarter million ounces a year, or 10 per cent of total exports, compared with up to 1,2 million ounces for Rustenberg and 800 000 for Impala. In addition, marketing by the two countries would be made difficult by the very different structures of their respective platinum industries. Like Canada, the Soviet Union derives most of its platinum group metals from nickel, which determines total production figures in any year.

South Africa, in contrast, produces its nickel as a derivative of platinum. The Novobrisk complex is the only mine comparable to South Africa's reefs, but its production is notoriously unpredictable, possibly because of bad management. At times there can be 50 per cent differential in Russian production targets, a critical differential if the market is as finely balanced as it is.

Information on future production figures is really all that South Africa and the Soviet Union need exchange in order that both may know well in advance whether the market is going to be soft or firm; a prediction which will largely determine the price of platinum and ensure that neither country loses out at Canada's expense. Such information is usually passed to the Russians through the Moscow Narodny Bank in London.

Lonhro's involvement in these transactions is neither necessary, nor even desirable given Tiny Rowland's mercurial reputation.

Unfortunately, the Russian demand for platinum is increasing faster than supply, although whether that is due to falling production or even a calculated policy of stockpiling to capture the world platinum market in the 1990s (as the Soviet Union tried to do with palladium in the 1970s) is still uncertain. The palladium experience has not been forgotten. In 1988 the Soviet Union changed its marketing policy once again to increase revenue from its sales of palladium. As the "swing supplier" it can still shut down palladium capacity when prices are low; in 1988 it did so by cutting supplies to the West by 25 per cent.

On the other hand, there is no doubt that South Africa could provide knowledge and skill that the Soviet Union urgently needs in open-cast mining (it is far cheaper to exploit old mines in Siberia than to open new ones); in "detonics" (the science of detonation) in which South Africa still leads the field; even in the management of high capital, high risk ventures such as the ailing Russian joint-venture mining projects the investment costs of which under the present Five Year Plan (1985-90) are likely to be four times higher than was predicted in 1976. The South Africans could do a lot to smooth out some of the problems that have contributed to this situation, such as improved smelting and metal-rolling, to mention only two areas in which the Soviet Union still lags behind the West.

All these initiatives have come from South Africa. One that has its origins in the Soviet Union was tentatively put forward by Anatoly Gromyko at a meeting in Salzburg in 1986: whether South Africa would be prepared to sell technology to the USSR through European or American subsidiaries, technology now prohibited under the existing Cocom regulations. The matter of transfer of technology has become more sensitive, not less sensitive since the Toshiba scandal and the successful attempt by the Reagan administration to get 300 additional items added to the Cocom list.

As a country that has never been a party to the Cocom regulations South Africa finds itself in a unique position. That is especially true of the computer industry in which, although many US companies have pulled out, they still maintain franchise and marketing agreements that enable South Africa to buy the most up-to-date technology. By agreeing to a management buyout, IBM has been able to sell directly to ISM (and thus to organisations that it was prohibited from doing business with before it officially disinvested: companies such as Infoplan, a Johannesburg-based data-processing company that serves the SADF). At the main SADF research and development centre, CSIR, two up-graded IBM 370/158s provide half the computing power for the Centre for Computing Services (CCS), which simulates war-games. The Armscor subsidiary, Eloptro, has been using a hired Hewlett Packard 21 HX computer in the manufacture of electro-optical systems for military equipment.

Some computers as we already know, have reached the Soviet Union through illicit channels (notably a VAX 11-782 in 1982). The scope for such sales remains significant, especially of the Cyber 170/750, which was the subject of much controversy in 1981 because of the argument that it could break the American cryptographic codes, an argument that was resolved only through the personal intervention of the Secretary of State. The problem with computer sales, of course, is that they are not easy to disguise in trade figures; they are such high value that they can invariably be traced to source.

Not so the sale of deep-sea oil-drilling technology via European subsidiaries engaged in exploiting the Mossel Bay and Kudu natural gas fields. Some of these companies, such as John Brown Engineering (UK), through its subsidiary Crawford and Russell (itself a member of IMEMO, one of a number of joint ventures which intend exploiting the Mossel field) have access to highly sensitive technology – such as the zeolyte catalysts used for converting gas into methanol. As the manager of IMEMO said some years ago: "The whole purpose of the project ... was the transfer of technology (from the West) to South Africa."[29] Crawford and Russell are also said to be drilling in the Kudu fields off Namibia, potentially a far larger return than Mossel Bay. The conversion of gas into oil has become so refined in recent years that it is now cheaper than converting oil from coal, a technology in which South Africa leads the world.

Problems would abound even here, however, if South Africa chose to make some of the technology available to the Soviet Union. Any sale that blatantly defied Cocom regulations would incur a high "social cost" – the support of those

Western politicians who are still prepared to speak out on behalf of South Africa, unlike most of their conservative fellows who have lost their ancient pre-occupation with the strategic importance of South Africa. Looked at objectively, the transfer of technology must still be considered an improbable element of a probable political trend – a dialogue between the Soviet Union and South Africa.

## Conclusion

It is difficult to conclude, in fact, that there will not be a dialogue in the years to come; though what form it may take must remain an open question. It is likely that both powers will try to arrive at a respite in their conflict, what the Russians call a *peredyshka*, a breather, or what Churchill more brutally called a "loaded pause", a period of consolidation and avoidance of risk while forces assemble in the wings.

Will the pause represent "a window of opportunity", to use that much over-worked phrase? All we can say is that there are some moments in history that are more open than others; and that South Africa and the Soviet Union may be moving towards such an opening. There is no guarantee that when they do either power will seize the opportunity, or even recognise it for what it is.

Thirty years ago Henry Kissinger argued that statesmen with a vision of the future invariably fail to communicate it to their fellow men because they cannot validate its "truth". I suspect that that may be the fate of those in South Africa who would like to see closer relations with the Soviet Union, just as it may defeat those Russian officials who may be interested in closer relations with Pretoria. "Nations learn only by experience; they 'know' only when it is too late to act." Statesmen, said Kissinger, must act as if their intuition "were already experience, as if their aspirations were truth."[30] It is a fine principle on which to act, but it is not a very realistic one. As John Fowles said in the novel that I quoted at the beginning of this essay, it requires of politicians an ability to communicate to the public and to each other in "a weird tense grammar does not allow: an imaginary present".

## FOOTNOTES

1. *The Washington Times,* 14 March 1988
2. John Fowles: *A Maggot,* (London: Pan: 1986) p201
3. For the terms of the strategic partnership which had never been explicitly offered before, see Christopher Coker: *The United States and South Africa 1968-85: Constructive engagement and its critics,* (Duke University Press: 1986) p255
4. For some of the more recent ideological changes mentioned in this essay, see Francis Fukuyama: *Moscow's post-Brezhnev reassessment of the Third World,* RAND Paper R/3337 (February: 1986)
5. Cited: Anthony Payne: *The international crisis in the Caribbean,* (Baltimore: Johns Hopkins University Press: 1984) p82
6. Anthony Thorndyke: *Grenada: politics, economics, security,* (London: Frances Pinter: 1985) p101

7. Robin Luckham: "Soviet arms and African militarisation" in Robert Cassen (ed). *Soviet influence in the Third World,* (Sage: 1985) p101
8. Alan Smith: *Soviet trade relations with the Third World, ibid,* p152
9. Cited: Winrich Kühne "What does the case of Mozambique tell us about Soviet ambivalence towards Africa?" in Helen Kitchen (ed). *Angola, Mozambique and the West,* Washington Paper 130 (Praeger: 1987) p116
10. For Eastern Europe dependence on Southern Africa see Christopher Coker: *The Soviet Union, Eastern Europe and the New International Economic Order,* Washington Paper 111 (Praeger: 1984) p38
11. *South Africa Report,* (SA): 1 January 1988
12. For Goncharov's full interview see "Soviet policy in Southern Africa." Interview with Dr Leonard Goncharov, deputy director, Institute of African Studies (Moscow) *Work in Progress,* No.48 (July 1987)
13. *The Citizen,* 8 March 1988
14. *Front File Southern Africa Brief 2*: 5 April 1988
15. Harold Macmillan referred to the "winds of change" during a speech before the South African House of Assembly in 1960. During his New Year address to the nation in January 1977 John Vorster gave warning: "The storm has not yet struck. We are only experiencing the whirlwinds which go before."
16. Christopher Coker: *NATO, the Warsaw Pact and Africa,* (London: Macmillan: 1985) p143
17. Deon Geldenhuys: "The neutral option and sub-continental solidarity: a consideration of P. Botha's Zürich Statement." (Johannesburg: South Africa Institute of International Affairs: 1979)
18. See Christopher Coker: *South Africa's security dilemmas,* Washington Paper 126 (Praeger: 1987) p27
19. Kenneth Grundy: *The militarisation of Southern African politics,* (London: Tauris: 1986) p74
20. *South Africa's security dilemmas,* op cit. p87
21. *Intelligence Services in Pretoria maintain that it was never the intention to take Cuito Cuanavale in the first place, but rather to "cement the garrison into its bunkers" and force massive diversion of interests from other fronts. Had they taken the town, says a spokesman for Chief of Staff Intelligence, the situation would have been unacceptably reversed. Ed.*
22. *SWB (BBC) Su/8506/C/2:* 3 March 1987
23. *SWB SU/8199/C/21:* 5 March 1986
24. *Front File Southern Africa Brief 1*: 5 April 1987
25. *SWB SU/0014 A5/3:* 1 December 1987
26. *Africa Confidential 29:3* : 5 February 1988
27. John Marcum: "Unita: The politics of survival" in Kitchen *Angola, Mozambique and the West,* op cit. pp11–12
28. For the most extensive historical discussion of South African contacts with the Soviet Union see Kurt Campbell: *Soviet Policy towards South Africa,* (London: Macmillan: 1986) pp94–126
29. *The Financial Times:* 10 March 1987
30. Henry Kissinger: *A World Restored: the Politics of Conservatism in a Revolutionary Age,* (New York: Grosser and Dunlop: 1964) p157

# COUNTRIES IN THE CROSS-FIRE
## *by Gerald L'Ange*

Bands played and crowds cheered the soldiers marching to the troopships when South Africa went to war in 1914 and again in 1939. It was much the same, though with less fanfare, when South African airmen went off in 1951 to fight in Korea for freedom and democracy under the flag of the United Nations.

The next time South African soldiers went to war was in 1975; and then they did it in secret.

They slipped across the Namibian border into Angola to fight and die without their countrymen knowing it. Although their government considered they were still fighting for freedom and democracy it dared not tell about it, because by now South Africa was an embarrassing ally.

In the intervening period it had refined what it called racial differentiation, and what others called racial discrimination, and institutionalised it as apartheid. As a result it had become a pariah, forced out of the Commonwealth, barred from its seat in the General Assembly of the United Nations and banned from the Olympic Games.

In the invasion of Angola the pariah showed its teeth, and proved that it could bite as hard as ever.

That was the beginning of a series of strikes across the border that were the bloody punctuation of what is now seen as an era of destabilisation in the southern subcontinent of Africa.

It has been an era of violence and terror, of economic warfare and political brawling, of famine and flight, of espionage and sabotage, of suffering, sorrow, controversy, anger and destruction. It has shaken the subcontinent from the Atlantic to the Indian Ocean and is still doing so.

In that period, as international opposition to apartheid boiled up higher than its creators had ever imagined, the government in Pretoria was seen by most of the world as not only having oppressed the blacks within its own borders but as having embarked on a policy of keeping the other countries in the region unbalanced to serve its own selfish ends.

It was seen as having set out to undermine their economies, to influence their internal policies through economic blackmail and military threat, to foment insurrection and insurgency on their soil. It has been accused, in doing these things, of causing the deaths of tens of thousands of people, of spreading starvation, misery and destruction.

As always with warfare, political or military, the truth has sometimes been one of the casualties and the measure of South African guilt has at times been obscured by the mendacity and opportunism of some of its opponents.

What ultimately passes through the sieve of history may differ in some ways from the popular notions of the present. But what will never be disputed is the tragedy of it all; tragedy measured between what might have been and what is.

Southern Africa might by now have been a region of peace and prosperity, enjoying high international respect. By exercising ideological tolerance and promoting common interests, the nations of the region could have cooperated in developing their great mineral and agricultural resources and have formed an economic bloc perhaps as influential in the Southern hemisphere as the European Community is in the Northern.

But it has been nothing like that. Most of these countries are torn by war or political strife. Far from prosperously exploiting their resources, most of them are struggling for bare survival. For all its potential richness, the region includes some of the poorest countries in the world. Cooperation in economic development remains rudimentary.

In any international measurement of deprivation several of the southern African countries would be at or near the top. Their situation contrasts markedly with that in South Africa, or rather white South Africa, whose economic efficiency, productivity and prosperity emphasise the backwardness of black South Africa and of most of the rest of the continent.

By almost every yardstick — gross national product, electricity generated, railway and road networks, number of telephones, government budget, vehicles registered, average income, steel production – white South Africa far outstrips all its neighbours combined, and in some categories all Africa combined.

The gross national product of South Africa, excluding the independent homelands such as the Transkei, is four times greater than the combined gross national products of Angola, Mozambique, Zimbabwe, Zambia, Botswana, Lesotho and Swaziland.

Its budget is more than double theirs combined, its exports more than five times, and its imports more than double.

South Africa's relative prosperity has often been attributed by critics of apartheid not to white enterprise and skills but to the lucky existence of mineral wealth and to the exploitation of cheap black labour. Both claims are only partly true.

Without the gold, diamonds, platinum, chrome, coal and other underground resources South Africa clearly would not be as prosperous as it is. And neither the competitiveness of its exports nor the living standards of its whites would have been as high without the advantage of a vast labour reservoir of unskilled blacks, for long unorganised and unrepresented by trade unions.

Yet it cannot logically be contended that without the minerals and the cheap labour South Africa's physical and climatic endowments would not have attracted Europeans in the same way as did, say, New Zealand (this was in fact happening long before the discovery of diamonds and gold) and that it would be any less developed and prosperous than that country of limited mineral resources.

It can, however, be argued that New Zealand, unlike South Africa, has not suffered from the handicap of having its development retarded for nearly half a century by government policies shaped by racial fears rather than economic sense — a factor, incidentally, that has contributed substantially to the tragedy of the subcontinent.

As the dominant economic power in the region, South Africa is the natural nucleus of any subcontinental economic grouping, and indeed its government has long envisaged the Republic in that role — but on its own terms.

It is a matter of history that those terms — tolerance of apartheid — have been rejected by the neighbouring states. It made no difference that the terms were reduced to tolerance of an evolutionary approach to racial justice, for to a large extent those states had little faith in the will or the ability of Pretoria to bring about racial justice.

Political leaders in some neighbouring states might more readily have accepted South African leadership of a regional economic bloc if Pretoria had agreed unequivocally to abandon apartheid. Against that, the ideologues of Pretoria would argue that if South Africa had abandoned apartheid it would not have been able to maintain the development that made it the most powerful country in the subcontinent – and has hauled the neighbouring states upwards on the coat-tails of its economy.

Though not expressly intended as such, the derogation of blacks implicit in this attitude is at the core of the conflict between Pretoria and the neighbouring capitals.

If the architects of apartheid ever seriously expected the black states to tolerate it as an internal South African affair they were deluding themselves, however. For the neighbouring states, as for the rest of Africa and for black people all over the world, it would have amounted to self-betrayal.

Even President Banda of Malawi, the only African leader to have exchanged ambassadors with South Africa, never intended that to be seen as condonation of apartheid. It was an act of economic self-interest.

Still less did President Houphouet-Boigny of the Ivory Coast mean to imply acceptance of apartheid in his intermittent flirtations with Pretoria. Far from accepting apartheid, his intention was to persuade Pretoria to abandon it.

If apartheid had been seen by the neighbours only as an attempt to protect the culture and way of life of the whites from being swamped by the black majority, it might have found understanding, sympathy and tolerance. But few in the bordering states have ever seen it as simply as that. It was rather seen as exploitative, hegemonistic and essentially cruel.

Neighbouring blacks not only saw apartheid as intolerably insulting to their race: they also saw it as predatory and menacing. Apartheid could survive, they believed, only by destroying or weakening its antithesis, non-racism, the existence of which across the border exposed the immorality and ultimate impracticability of apartheid.

To sustain apartheid, in their view, Pretoria must not only subjugate the blacks in South Africa but also block the development and influence of those in the neighbouring states. Therefore, when Pretoria appeared several years ago to have embarked on a campaign to destabilise these states, they were quite ready to believe it.

Their mistrust of Pretoria was deep-rooted, going back even beyond attempts by the Union of South Africa to incorporate Bechuanaland, Basutoland and Swazi-land, back even to the attempts by the Boer republics to engulf the Basotho and the Swazis. To this day the Basotho have not abandoned their claim to the Conquered Territory stretching from the western border of Lesotho deep into the Orange Free State, which they say was taken from them by the Boers; nor have the Swazis abandoned their desire to regain the Kangwane area of the Transvaal.

It was not without some apprehension that the Batswana, the Basotho and the Swazis gave up British protection for independence in the Sixties, in the shadow as they were of the white giant to whom they were bound by economic necessity but whose intentions they mistrusted.

For all their suspicions of South Africa and their resentment of its racial policies, however, the bordering states were compelled to rely on it in varying degrees for commodities and manufactures that they could not get as cheaply elsewhere, for electricity, for transport routes to the sea, for medical and other services, for markets for their products and, almost without exception, for jobs for the relatively large proportions of their populations that their own economies could not employ.

First with the discovery of diamonds and gold and later with the development of its industries, South Africa was a magnet for one of the largest recurrent mass migrations in the history of Africa.

Over the past dozen decades millions of migrant workers from Lesotho, Mozambique, Zimbabwe, Zambia, Malawi and Botswana came to South Africa as the "Gastarbeiter" from Turkey came to West Germany; tolerated as temporary sojourners but barred from permanent settlement, grateful for the work and the pay but resentful of the impermanence and indignity.

Like the Mexican "wetbacks" who poured illegally into the United States, like the penurious Europeans who had poured in legally before them, black people from the neighbouring countries have for many years sought the South African Utopia. They have entered the country openly if possible but surreptitiously if necessary.

The futility of the hope did nothing to warm these visitors to white South Africa, nor did experience of apartheid at first hand. It rather exacerbated the need-hate relations between South Africa and its neighbours. The more the neighbouring states have become dependent on South Africa the more they have resented it. For many years practical considerations dictated that they must accept the situation with the best grace possible; but as political dissatisfaction grew among black people inside South Africa, and particularly when it became organised and militarised by the black freedom movements, notably the African National Congress, the neighbouring states were forced to adopt increasingly political attitudes themselves. In the United Nations they had to stand up and be counted along with the vocal and voting opponents of apartheid.

When the freedom movements resorted to armed struggle from the shelter of the neighbouring countries, they became directly caught up in the struggle whether they liked it or not.

Inevitable retaliation by South Africa across the borders put its neighbours into the front line of the conflict.

That term, 'front line', first acquired both a symbolic and a literal meaning in the conflict in Rhodesia, in which Zambia and Botswana, and later Mozambique, sided with the black nationalist movements. With Angola, they formed the group of Frontline States to consolidate opposition to white domination in Rhodesia. Tanzania, though not physically part of the southern subcontinent, was brought into the group through the zealotry of President Julius Nyerere and the partial dependence of both the group and the nationalist movements on Tanzanian routes to the sea.

The association had been born of the collapse of Portuguese colonialism in Africa, which shattered both the eastern and western flanks of the white redoubt across southern Africa and exposed Rhodesia to the full force of black nationalism. When Rhodesia gave way the group was strengthened by the addition of the new Zimbabwe.

Now the Frontline States could turn their full attention to supporting the South African black movements in what they saw as the final battle against white domination in Africa. With the Pan Africanist Congress of South Africa torn by internal conflict, it was left to the ANC to lead the attack, which now became increasingly violent.

Whether the black freedom movements were justified in resorting to violence, whether they truly had, as they say, exhausted all peaceful alternatives, is a question that has largely been ignored in the international community's eagerness to end apartheid.

Once the ANC had resorted to violence as a deliberate and sustained policy it was not an issue that could be canvassed without questioning the *bona fides* of what was seen as the leading anti-apartheid organisation. And any questioning of opposition to apartheid was something that grew closer to heresy the more firmly apartheid became entrenched in the international view as an evil beyond question.

ANC violence has been condemned as terrorism by the South African government and by right-wingers in the West but in virtually no political camp has serious attention been given to whether there is any validity in the ANC's claim that the point had been reached when violence was the only way to end apartheid — or, indeed, to the argument that the violence was justified by the violence of apartheid itself.

In neither political nor academic circles has much examination been made of whether apartheid's victims might have been closer today to ridding themselves of it if the ANC, which claims to act in their name, had chosen to adhere to its long-held policy of non-violence. It is interesting, even if now only academic, to speculate on what might have happened if, for instance, the ANC had chosen the infinitely more difficult and painful path of passive resistance so clearly signposted by Mahatma Gandhi yet never travelled to its end by any movement seeking political liberation.

Whether it was justified or not, the ANC's resort to violence has had one ironically perverse effect: it has made it more difficult for the government to abandon apartheid if it ever really wanted to do so — as it now claims it does.

ANC violence, far from forcing the capitulation of the government, has galvanised white, right wing extremists, compelling the government to make a sympathetic shift in the same direction to protect its own right flank. It has become increasingly impossible for the government to negotiate with an organisation dedicated to violently overthrowing it and increasing the level of that violence.

At the same time the ANC has used violence to discourage any other blacks claiming popular support to negotiate with the authorities, leaving the government searching almost desperately for ways to execute its professed desire for the dismantling of apartheid.

In this situation the ANC has been forced to step up the level of its violence against the white establishment, if not with much hope of overthrowing it then at least as an act of self-justification.

The room for manoeuvre has thus become progressively more restricted on either side. Negotiation and compromise have been blocked and the contest in South Africa has become not so much the fight for human rights that it is popularly seen as in the outside world but a struggle for political power, with heavy racial overtones.

With violence being met with counter-violence, the prospect of reconciliation has receded ever further, as was perhaps inevitable when the largest and most influential political organisation representing blacks in South Africa abandoned peaceful protest and took up the gun, the bomb and the landmine.

The government plainly could not allow the ANC's insurgency to succeed, for to bow to violence would have meant its own quick demise. And so a mortal conflict was begun.

The authorities might have been able to tolerate the occasional bombing of an electrical pylon but when the ANC spectacularly sabotaged the Sasol oil-producing plants in the Orange Free State and Transvaal in June 1980 the flames became a beacon of resistance to many blacks and a challenge was thrown down that the government could not ignore.

Nor could the government tolerate the rocket attack in August 1981 on the military base at Voortrekkerhoogte near Pretoria, ineffectual though it was in terms of damage, nor the bombing of part of the Koeberg Nuclear Power Station near Cape Town in December 1982, or any other ANC military action calculated to win respect within the country and abroad and demonstrate a capability to challenge the armed might of Pretoria.

No less intolerable to the government — and even to the government's white opponents — was terrorism against civilians, for which the ANC has been blamed with increasing frequency.

When it first adopted violence the ANC ostensibly followed a policy of avoiding soft civilian targets and attacking only police and military personnel and installations. Public utility facilities such as railway lines, power pylons and the Sasol and Koeberg plants do not fall within this definition but appear to have been seen by the ANC as legitimate targets because of their para-statal character.

Initially a fairly conscientious and consistent effort appears to have been made to avoid harming civilians although it was not long before the target legitimacy was expanded to embrace civilians directly assisting the police or military, such as farmers, who invariably cooperate with the security forces in anti-insurgent activities, especially in border areas.

The "hard-target-only" policy was founded on the ANC executive's acute awareness of the damage that could be done to its quest for international support and the support of moderate white South Africans if it were to be seen openly to make terrorist attacks on civilians.

But the policy came under severe strain for two reasons: firstly, selective violence demands more discipline in the field than the ANC leaders were able to maintain from their headquarters in Lusaka, Zambia; secondly, the policy did not receive unanimous support within the executive itself. As a result, it became progressively more blurred.

After it had added the farmers and others on the perimeters of the security forces to the target list the ANC went on to make it known that it had decided to step up its armed struggle and in the process innocent civilians would inevitably get hurt; caught in the cross-fire, as it were.

The ANC presumably placed in that category the casualties caused by its explosion of a large car bomb in 1983 outside an office block in Pretoria housing military as well as civilian offices. In this attack, coinciding with the afternoon traffic rush, 18 persons, most of them civilians, were killed and 217 injured.

In no way, however, could the cross-fire theory be applied to the detonation of a bomb in a shopping centre at Amanzimtoti on the Natal coast when it was crowded with Christmas shoppers. The shards of glass that swept like razor-edged grapeshot through the shoppers also cut deeply into white sympathy with the ANC.

While it had no difficulty in claiming responsibility for the Pretoria bombing because of the military element in the target, the ANC was put in a dilemma by the Amanzimtoti blast. The executive could not admit to this bombing without risking the alienation of the moderate whites whose support it needs if it is to be seen to be true to its rejection of racism of any kind.

To deny responsibility, however, risked alienating the radical blacks who are powerfully dictating the shape of liberation politics in South Africa, and whose support the ANC needs even more than that of the whites if it is to retain its position in the vanguard of the black struggle.

The dilemma appears to have been heightened by the organisation's practice of arming supporters after they have received only rudimentary training in secret inside the Republic, in contrast to the relatively extensive training given to ANC cadres in foreign bases. This practice seemed by the middle of 1988 to have left considerable numbers of limpet mines in the hands of people with only a tenuous grasp of or loyalty to the old rule of avoiding civilian casualties.

As bomb after bomb went off across the country around that time, with several clearly aimed deliberately at civilians, it appeared either that the executive had simply lost control of those into whose hands they had put the bombs or that the relative moderates in the hierarchy had been defeated on the soft target issue by the radicals.

Like the Pretoria bombing of 1983, some of the 1988 bombings had a tenuous link to official targets, such as the blast in a restaurant in a building in Pretoria that also contained some government offices and the blast in a street near Krugersdorp police station.

But others were clearly aimed solely at civilians, notably the explosion in a Roodepoort shopping centre that killed four persons and injured 14 and the car bomb set off, apparently by remote control, amid crowds streaming out of the Ellis Park stadium in Johannesburg after a major rugby match, killing two of the spectators and injuring 35.

The impression of a radical change in ANC policy was strengthened not only by these bomb attacks but also by statements made to Western journalists by leaders of the ANC's military wing in Lusaka in June 1988.

These leaders argued that the whites had been left largely untouched by the political upheaval and insurgency in South Africa and remained free to enjoy their privilege and prosperity. Only through violence aimed directly at them, could the whites be jolted out of their sweet life and made to accept the need to abandon apartheid.

The militants' statements were quickly followed by assurances from the ANC executive that there had been no change in the policy of not targeting civilians.

A strong impression remained, however, that the militants had exposed a fundamental rift within the ANC hierarchy that could have a severe impact on the organisation's bid to extend its traditional support in the communist bloc and Third World into the Western world.

While the ANC executive has equivocated on the issue of attacking civilians, for the government the matter was clear-cut from the beginning. Neither terrorism nor insurgency — and the government makes no distinction between the two — could be allowed. If civilians were to be attacked by the ANC it would only strengthen the need to stamp out the attacks at their source; and perhaps also increase the ruthlessness of the methods used.

For Pretoria the matter became even more clear-cut when the ANC began to use landmines, which, laid mainly on country roads near the borders of the countries through which they were transported, were even more of a danger to civilians on the farms than to the soldiers patrolling the roads.

Like the bombs, the mines do not distinguish colour of skins, and most of the casualties have been black farm-workers; more victims of the cross-fire.

Already angered by these deaths, the whites were yet more infuriated by the killing of their own kind by mines. Pictures on the evening television news of the shattered vehicle in which white children had been killed were enough to put most whites solidly behind whatever the government chose to do to stop it and take vengeance on those who laid the mines or abetted them.

Thus the neighbouring states were drawn even deeper into the conflict, and the front line became a real zone of battle rather than a merely rhetorical term.

The Frontline States turned a defiant face to what many of their people saw as the bully next door. Despite tribal and language differences, the struggle of the black people of South Africa for freedom and dignity was theirs too; for it was their own dignity that was being insulted when South African blacks were oppressed, and it was for the dignity of blacks everywhere that the ANC was fighting.

The part played by the neighbouring states in the struggle was crucial from the beginning. For the ANC to be able to conduct armed insurgency in South Africa it needed either bases in neighbouring countries or transit routes through them from bases in more distant countries.

The assertion by the ANC that it operates from bases inside South Africa is unsupported by any evidence. While it has the ability to train military and political operatives clandestinely inside the country, any military bases large enough to sustain operations of any importance would quickly be detected by the efficient intelligence services and destroyed by the formidable security forces.

The evidence points overwhelmingly to the ANC having launched its incursions into South Africa from bases in Zambia and Angola, using transit routes and facilities in Mozambique, Botswana and Zimbabwe.

These countries deny helping incursions, but Pretoria has rejected the denials. It remains a moot point whether some or all of the incursions have been carried out without the knowledge of the neighbouring governments or even despite their efforts to prevent it.

Whatever the origin of the insurgency, to destroy or at least limit it became fundamental to South African government policy and probably the most important element in its foreign policy.

No other consideration outweighed it in its relations with the neighbouring states nor, probably, in its relations with other countries, including its former friends in the West.

The first response by Pretoria to insurgency from across the border was two-fold: it launched military strikes directly at the ANC bases in neighbouring countries and it put political and economic pressure on their governments to stop the ANC making such use of their territory.

It assured the people and governments of those countries that the strikes were not aimed at them or their armed forces but only at the insurgents or terrorists. It also insisted that the strikes were made only after the governments of the countries affected had failed to respond to requests to take action to prevent the insurgents from using their soil.

But when the South African commandos struck, they struck hard and ruthlessly, coming in swiftly in the night, making straight for selected targets and leaving behind them blasted houses, riddled bodies, bloody mattresses, shattered furniture, wailing families, shaken and angry governments and local defence forces put to shame by their inability to stand up against the superior power of the invaders.

Seldom, if ever, have the South African Defence Force met any resistance from the local armies anywhere except in Angola. That was how it was when the commandos hit ANC houses in Maseru, the capital of Lesotho, on the night of December 9, 1982. It was not the first raid into a neighbouring territory or even into Lesotho; the commandos had attacked before on January 31, 1981. But it was the most devastating attack yet and its ferocity shocked the continent and beyond.

Forty-two bodies lay in the broken and blackened houses when the South Africans withdrew at daybreak across the Caledon river. Only twenty of the dead were South African expatriates, the rest mainly Basotho, innocent victims, perhaps, who had had the misfortune to get in the way of soldiers who dared not stop to ask who was an armed insurgent and who was not before they threw their grenades through the windows and shot into the beds and wardrobes; or perhaps who did not care.

The first raid in strength across the border had taken place the year before on January 30, when South African commandos attacked three ANC houses on the outskirts of Maputo, the capital of Mozambique, killing several members of the ANC and losing one of their own men in a short but sharp exchange of fire.

Botswana did not feel the heavy hand of the commandos until 1985, but when they did come it was their strongest raid yet. On June 14 ten targets widely scattered throughout the capital, Gaborone, were attacked in a carefully planned and coordinated operation. For nearly an hour the commandos shot up their targets, mostly houses, making as much noise as possible to frighten the town's residents and discourage them from renting out houses to South African expatriates in future.

Again the raiders left behind them smoking ruins and bullet-riddled bodies, 12 this time, mostly South African exiles.

Again there was no sign of the local armed forces. Officials in Botswana said later that the Botswana Defence Force vehicles had been immobilised by caltrops strewn by the South Africans outside their barracks to puncture their tyres.

The most ambitious operation across the border took place on May 19, 1986, when the SADF simultaneously made ground strikes on ANC targets in Gaborone and Harare, Zimbabwe, and an air attack on an ANC complex outside Lusaka, Zambia.

The death roll was low – two persons killed in Lusaka and one in Gaborone; but the political effects were severe. International feeling against South Africa hardened, and the faltering efforts of the Commonwealth Eminent Persons Group to find a peaceful solution in South Africa were killed stone dead (a result that many in the West and elsewhere thought was no doubt the prime purpose of the raid).

Not all these attacks in neighbouring territories have been straightforward military operations, however. There have been others of a different kind, not carried out by soldiers in uniform, blasting noisily at their targets, with a press statement afterwards, but small raids executed furtively by men in civilian clothes and travelling in civilian vehicles. Sometimes they were hooded by balaclavas, and usually they used silenced weapons.

Always the targets have appeared to be members of the ANC, but not always has the intention been to kill them; sometimes they have been kidnapped. Never has there been any acknowledgement of responsibility by anyone in South Africa or elsewhere. Officially South Africa denies any complicity, but their denial rebounded embarrassingly in one case when two innocent Swiss people were abducted from Swaziland, apparently in mistake for members of the ANC. They had to be returned by the shamefaced South African authorities through their mystified trade commissioner in Mbabane.

In the bloodiest of the surreptitious raids, a strike on December 20, 1985 on houses in Maseru occupied mostly by South African exiles, nine persons were killed. The formal denial by South Africa of complicity was rejected by the Basotho.

Most of these raids have taken place in Swaziland, and some have verged on the bizarre, such as when a group of men broke into the offices in Manzini of a Scandinavian organisation helping refugees and seized most of the files.

When chased by security guards they fled in cars, firing out of the window at their pursuers in fine Hollywood style as they made speed towards the border.

A raid in 1984 on the police station at Bhunya was no less bizarre, when armed men held up the constables on duty and freed four members of the ANC held on charges of illegal entry and possession of arms. The raid was presumed to be the work of the ANC, but they denied it and said that it had been carried out by South African agents posing as ANC who had taken the prisoners across the border into South Africa to be dealt with there.

There have been a number of hit-squad attacks on members of the ANC in Swaziland; the victims in several cases being shot in moving cars. A senior official of the ANC was killed in that way, together with two companions, in July 1987. As they drove from Matsapha airport after arriving on a flight from Maputo their vehicle was overtaken by another and sprayed with machine-gun fire.

Pretoria may have seen all the strikes across the border as legitimate acts of self-defence against imported terrorism, but to the neighbouring countries they were just another element in the South African policy of destabilisation. They considered that Pretoria was actuated by more than simple fear of insurgency in seeking to unbalance its neighbours economically and psychologically.

Pretoria was seen firstly as wishing to cripple the development of the neighbours to make it seem that black states cannot thrive and secondly as aiming to prevent South African blacks from getting ideas about emulating those next door.

Useful though it might be as a stick with which to beat apartheid, the second motive is less plausible than the first. To answer it Pretoria can point to the large sums of money poured into the independent homelands to make them viable, and to the aid that South Africa gives to its neighbours.

A third theory is that Pretoria sought to hamstring its neighbours' economies to ensure their continued dependence on its own economy. In accepting this theory the neighbouring states implicitly rejected the assertion by Pretoria that its own interests lie in having stable and prosperous neighbours.

Yet another motive was ascribed to Pretoria: discouraging the neighbours from supporting sanctions against South Africa by holding over them the threat of economic retaliation.

Any assessment of the motives that might lie behind destabilisation and of its effects is unrealistic without defining the term itself. But even that becomes a subjective activity, for the popular definition has progressively broadened until it now embraces almost any act by South Africa that might be construed as hostile to its neighbours. Preoccupation with destabilisation has in fact reached the point of paranoia.

Destabilisation, the bastard son of apartheid, has come into being only recently in southern African politics but already it threatens to outgrow its parent as the evil that the world most loves to hate.

For the anti-apartheid lobbies everywhere the notion may have appeared at a convenient time, just when the heinousness of apartheid was being diluted somewhat by reforms, small and reluctant though these were seen to be.

There is nevertheless much evidence to support accusations of deliberate destabilisation by Pretoria. The only area of serious dispute appears to be in the extent of the practice, the methods used, the effects and which branches of government may be responsible.

The raids on ANC targets by the SADF have been lumped together with all other alleged acts of destabilisation, despite the assertion by the SADF that the attacks had strictly military objectives and despite the evidence that the commandos took some care to avoid damaging public installations or clashing with the local security forces.

There is at the same time strong evidence that such installations have deliberately been the targets of sabotage raids not aimed directly at the ANC. Positive proof linking the saboteurs to Pretoria has been rare, but circumstantial evidence has often been strong enough to convince the most dubious of foreign governments.

There was more than enough evidence for most in the capture in May 1985 of Major Wynand du Toit of the SADF within shooting distance of the oil installations at Cabinda, the Angolan enclave in the Congo. The story by the South African government that he was looking for ANC bases, not oil tanks, was universally disbelieved, especially as he was reported to have confessed soon after his capture that he was on a sabotage mission, and there was no evidence that there were any ANC bases in Cabinda. His retraction of his confession after his release in an exchange of prisoners appears not to have cut much ice among the critics of South Africa.

If the ubiquitory belief is correct, du Toit and his men (most of whom escaped by sea after being surprised by Angolan troops) were there to damage the Angolan economy by crippling the oil production on which it is almost wholly dependent. The purpose would presumably have been to increase the pressure on the MPLA government in Luanda to stop aiding the ANC and perhaps also to send home the Cuban troops in Angola and negotiate a political settlement with the Unita rebels that would deprive the Swapo insurgents of Namibia of their bases in Angola.

Only once has South Africa confessed to acts branded as destabilisation but it argued that they were committed not to destabilise but on the contrary to stabilise.

The confession came after the headquarters of the Mozambique National Resistance (Renamo) rebels in the Gorongosa area of Mozambique had been overrun in August 1985 and diaries found that proved that South Africa had conducted secret dealings with the rebels in Mozambique after signing the Nkomati Accord prohibiting such contacts.

Faced with this evidence, the SADF admitted that it had maintained communications with Renamo after Nkomati, had taken supplies to the rebels and had even flown a deputy cabinet minister, Louis Nel of Foreign Affairs, into Mozambique for meetings with the rebels. But the SADF said that the purpose of all that was not to circumvent the Nkomati Accord or to help the rebels in their efforts to overthrow the Frelimo government. All they had done, acting for the South African government, was to try to persuade the rebels to agree to peace talks with Frelimo, they said.

It was a breach of the Accord, the South Africans admitted, but only a technical one. Frelimo did not accept the explanation. After failing for so long to get conclusive proof of South Africa's guilt they had no intention of being cheated of the bonanza provided by the Gorongosa documents. For Frelimo and most other enemies of apartheid the documents were absolute proof that Pretoria had secretly supported Renamo as part of a wider effort to destabilise the Marxist government in Maputo.

In any case, they pointed out, they had no intention of negotiating with the rebels and had never asked South Africa to arrange it.

An examination of the English translation of the document discloses no incontrovertible evidence, however, of continued South African supplies on a large scale to Renamo after Nkomati, although there certainly is evidence of an intention to do so.

There are references to arms drops that cannot easily be explained away but little that would stand up to the conventional courtroom test of being proved beyond reasonable doubt.

Taken with all the other evidence of secret supplies for Renamo, the Gorongosa documents might be enough to convince most people outside a courtroom of South African guilt. That certainly is how they have been taken by a world eager to believe the worst about South Africa, despite protests by the SADF that some of the documents as eventually produced by Maputo were forgeries.

Some of the other evidence of South African support for Renamo after Nkomati was more than circumstantial.

There was the case of the three South African soldiers shot dead by local troops in the south-eastern corner of Zimbabwe in August 1982. The explanation by Pretoria that they were former Rhodesians serving with the SADF who had gone into Zimbabwe on a private and unauthorised mission was universally rejected. For the rest of the world the only logical explanation was that the soldiers had been surprised while travelling through Zimbabwe on an officially authorised mission to link up with Renamo inside Mozambique.

Some attempts by Frelimo to prove South African complicity with Renamo have verged on the desperate, such as when they produced a white man's hand that had been found where saboteurs had blown themselves up in a botched attempt to cut the oil pipeline from Beira to Zimbabwe.

Suspicious though it was, there was nothing to prove either the nationality of the hand or any connection between its deceased owner and South African officialdom.

The discovery of large parachutes of the kind used for dropping military vehicles and other heavy loads was also suspicious but not conclusive. They had been fished out of the lake in which they had been hidden, said Frelimo, after the local people had heard aircraft flying overhead in the night.

When oil storage tanks at Beira port were blown up one night Frelimo and many others found it difficult to believe that Renamo had the ability and resources for such advanced sabotage.

There was no doubt in official minds that it had been done by South African commandos coming in by sea, even though the tanks had been attacked during the Rhodesian war by Rhodesian commandos who had apparently come across country.

If this were not proof enough of South African support for Renamo, Frelimo could point to the destruction of navigation buoys in the approaches to Beira harbour, a job that could not by any stretch of the imagination have been done by Renamo, whose naval resources could never have consisted of more than a few dugout canoes.

South Africa's alleged support for Renamo is probably regarded as the worst case of destabilisation, with even worse consequences than support for the Unita rebels in Angola. So severe and widespread is the havoc resulting from the fighting in Mozambique that it is almost beyond the comprehension of comfortable Westerners, whether measured in human suffering or in national economic destruction.

The horrors of massacre and mutilation, pillage and destruction, famine and disease, are some of the worst even in the appalling history of Africa.

Yet if blame is to be apportioned it can only be done subjectively. The Frelimo government says it would never have happened if Renamo had not been formed by the Rhodesians in retaliation for the Mozambican government allowing the Rhodesian nationalist guerrillas to operate from bases inside Mozambique. And Renamo would never have been able to continue to function as a rebel force after the Rhodesian war ended if it had not been taken over, armed and trained by South Africa.

The South African response is that, while it did take over the training and supply of Renamo from the Rhodesians, it stopped after the Nkomati agreement. Some in Pretoria also argue that Renamo might not have been able to exist if Frelimo, instead of turning itself from a liberation movement into a one-party dictatorship, had allowed the allocation of political power to be done by the people through a free election open to other parties besides Frelimo.

Not all the suffering in Mozambique can be blamed on the rebels. Much of the killing and looting is done by bandits – real bandits, as distinct from the use of the term by Frelimo to describe Renamo, because of its reluctance to admit the existence of political dissent in Mozambique.

Some of the attacks on civilians have been blamed, probably justifiably, on Frelimo soldiers who took to robbery because their rations and pay were tardy or non-existent.

Frelimo may to some extent have grasped at the notion of destabilisation as a distraction from its own economic, political and military failures. Even Frelimo has conceded the failure of its more extreme socialist policies by scrapping them and restoring some measure of free enterprise. These policies would have damaged the economy even if there had been no Renamo and no war.

It has been convenient rather than convincing to blame all the troubles of Mozambique on Renamo and South African destabilisation rather than on bad government policy. One effect of that may have been to magnify international conceptions of destabilisation far beyond the reality.

At times it has been difficult to decide whether in crying destabilisation Maputo has been covering something up or whether it really believes its own accusations. A case in point is the crash of a Russian Tupolev airliner on a hillside just inside South Africa on October 19, 1986, and the death in it of the first president of Mozambique, Samora Machel.

Almost from the time the news of the crash broke the government news media accused South Africa of deliberately engineering it to kill Machel. This assertion was maintained even after the South African commission of inquiry, consisting of a high court judge and two aviation experts from Britain and America, had found that the plane crashed through grave and fundamental errors by its Russian crew.

The Mozambican news media and even senior government officials propounded the theory that the plane had been lured off course by a false navigational beacon inside South Africa and stuck to it even after it had been refuted by the commission of inquiry.

In this the Mozambicans were encouraged by the Soviet Union, which could not afford the political damage that would have been caused by an admission that the President of Mozambique had been killed in full flower through the incompetence of a Russian aircrew in a Russian aircraft.

According to unconfirmed but credible reports, the false beacon theory was not accepted at the upper levels of the Mozambican government, and certainly not by Machel's successor, President Joaquim Chissano, who is said to have refused to fly in the Russian plane subsequently allocated for presidential use. He apparently insisted on flying in a Boeing from the regular Mozambican airline.

Nevertheless, accusations of South African responsibility for Machel's death continued to flow unabated out of Maputo.

From the wreckage of the aircraft there came something else: the first evidence that destabilisation was not entirely a South African practice. According to documents that the South Africans said they found in the wreckage, a few of the Frontline States have themselves engaged in a bit of destabilisation... and not directly against the arch enemy, South Africa. Minutes of a meeting purporting to have been found in the wreck suggest that President Machel had been plotting with the government of Zimbabwe to undermine President Banda unless he abandoned his alleged support for the Renamo guerrillas and loosened his dependence on South Africa.

There was talk at the meeting of setting up a fifth column in Malawi to overthrow Dr Banda's government if he refused to comply with the demand, and even of blowing up bridges in Malawi to cut its trade routes through South Africa by way of Zambia if he refused to reroute his imports and exports through Nacala port in Mozambique.

This arm-twisting seems to have worked so well that soon afterwards large numbers of Renamo insurgents appeared near the borders of Malawi, having apparently been expelled by Banda. Malawi subsequently sent troops to help to protect the railway line to Nacala against attacks by Renamo.

International cooperation in protecting the transport routes linking the landlocked neighbours of Mozambique with the sea was an inevitable consequence of the failure by Frelimo to crush the rebels; perhaps it is the only growth industry in Mozambique apart from the supply of arms.

For Zimbabwe and Malawi the roads and railways through Mozambique offer the shortest and cheapest links with the sea and a better alternative than the longer routes through South Africa. After the Tazara line linking Zambia to Dar es Salaam port in Tanzania they are the next best route for Zambian exports and imports.

The favoured method of protecting the railways is to establish defensive corridors along their length. It worked so well in the pioneer Beira Corridor, running from Beira to Mutare in Zimbabwe, that it is being applied to the lines from Malawi to Nacala and from Zimbabwe to Maputo.

The corridors are expensive to hold, however, and however valuable they may be to the hinterland states, they contribute little more than tariff revenues to the development of Mozambique.

Their very nature cuts these sterilised channels off from the districts that they pass through, and unless the districts can find some way to get their produce and their purchases to and from the railways through the Renamo siege their populations can do no more than watch the trains going by.

Once firmly established, the corridors might provide secure lines dividing Mozambique into areas that could progressively be cleared of Renamo, but even as a long-term prospect this offers little hope of providing the solution Mozambique needs.

Only an end to the fighting, either through the defeat of one side or the other or through a political settlement, can give the country the peace that its young men and women have never known and enable it to develop its riches.

A military victory by either side is improbable, however. The armed forces of Frelimo appear too feeble to win, even with the help of 12 000 Zimbabwean and the few thousand Tanzanian and Malawian troops deployed in the country, almost all of whom are engaged in protecting the railways and towns rather than seeking to crush Renamo in the bush.

Renamo for its part appears to have neither the military strength to defeat Frelimo nor the ability to form an effective government if it were to win power. It has yet to demonstrate the ability to seize and hold any extensive area.

Frelimo is no more capable of crushing Renamo than the Portuguese were capable of defeating Frelimo during the guerrilla war. The largely undeveloped, rugged and bush–covered terrain gives the guerrilla fighters a high degree of invulnerability.

If South Africa continued to supply and train the rebels it clearly did not do so to a degree that could ensure them victory. The rag–tag Renamo, who are seldom armed with more than the ubiquitous AK–47 rifle, rocket-propelled grenades and mortars, certainly do not look like an army supplied from the abundant resources of Pretoria.

Appearances tend rather to support the assertion by Renamo that it captures most of its weapons from the poorly organised and motivated soldiers of Frelimo, who are sometimes not much less rag–tag than the rebels.

Pretoria says it has no wish to see Renamo in power. The managers of South African foreign policy say Pretoria does not care who holds power in any neighbouring state as long as they provide stability and prosperity. Nor do they believe that Renamo would be capable of that if it were to take power.

The argument in Pretoria is that a military victory by Renamo would simply send Frelimo back to the bush to fight a guerrilla war as it did against the Portuguese, and Pretoria would be no better off.

This argument did not go down well in Maputo or, indeed, in any of the Frontline capitals. It was conceded there that the South African government might not want to see Renamo in power, but it was argued that neither did it want to see Frelimo in undisputed control, free to carry out its own economic and social policies, to choose its own allies and to support the ANC.

South African support for Renamo, it was believed, was maintained at a level carefully calculated to keep it too weak to overthrow Frelimo but strong enough to keep it and the whole country unstable and incapable of threatening South African interests.

In support of this argument it was said that while Pretoria might not have been supplying the rebels with effective weapons it was giving them what they needed most to keep the government off–balance: ammunition, the guerrilla fighter's staff of life.

Whatever views might have been held privately in Maputo, the Frelimo government publicly took the position that South Africa had consistently and deliberately violated the Nkomati Accord, and never signed it in good faith in the first place. Yet Frelimo did not at any time suggest that it might abrogate the agreement.The signing of the agreement was not without pain for Frelimo, for in doing so it was in a sense betraying the rest of Africa. It probably signed in the belief that South Africa, since it was the principal supporter of Renamo, could paralyse the rebels by withholding its support. It was probably thought in Maputo that Pretoria was not only able but willing to pull the plug on Renamo to ensure that Mozambique kept its side of the bargain by expelling the ANC and denying it further facilities for propagating insurgency in South Africa.

What went wrong with the Nkomati Accord? The reasons are hard to find. Frelimo appears to have kept its side of the bargain by sending the ANC packing and blocking its operations across the border. South Africa asserts that it also honoured its commitments, apart from the "technical violations" it said were intended to bring about a settlement.

It is widely believed, however, that the SADF pumped large quantities of supplies across the border to Renamo, enough to last for two years, just before the Accord was signed. Maputo says, though, that Renamo ran out of ammunition well within two years of the signing and was then given further supplies from South Africa.

For its part Pretoria maintains that Renamo broke the agreement by not expelling all the ANC from Mozambique and by allowing them to resume their activities after a while. The available evidence suggests, however, that this happened on a significant scale only from 1986 on.

However disappointed Frelimo may have been at the apparent violation of the agreement, it had at least one good reason for not repudiating it; to do so would have left Pretoria free to help Renamo openly and therefore more effectively than it could while pretending to honour the pact.

South Africa would also have had less reason to reduce its destabilising activities and would have no hesitation about striking openly and heavily at the ANC in Mozambique.

South Africa for its part made no move to abrogate the Accord, despite its accusations of Mozambican betrayal, because it still attached some value to the agreement. Its signing had been treated in Pretoria as a great diplomatic triumph, the showpiece, in fact, of South African diplomacy in Africa. Even the severest critics had to admit that the pact gave South Africa a measure of respectability that it could not have assumed before in a hostile continent.

For both sides there were considerable economic as well as political benefits to be gained from the pact. In addition to providing economic aid to Mozambique, South Africa was to clear the way for substantial private investment, notably in tourism.

Nkomati's bright hopes were short–lived, however. A year after the signing the Accord was effectively nullified when the Frelimo government, angered by the disclosures in the Gorongosa documents, withdrew from the Joint Security Commission that had been set up to monitor violations of the pact.

Why it chose this course rather than taking the matter to the JSC is not known.

The action was followed by a steady deterioration in relations between the two governments, although Maputo stopped short of expelling the South African trade mission or recalling its own official representatives from Johannesburg.

South Africa's persistent denials that it had continued to aid Renamo fell on deaf ears in a world unwilling to give credence of any kind to a régime as odious as the apartheid one. Pretoria's credibility had in any event been strained by too many denials of what was later admitted as fact, especially in the military field.

The three–year freeze in relations ended almost as abruptly as it had begun and again Maputo's reasons were obscure. However, its decision to heal the breach not only revived Nkomati's earlier hopes but inspired new ones in a South African government more eager than ever for acceptance in black Africa.

These hopes were further spurred by the coincidental revival of the Angola–Namibia peace talks, which in turn renewed the optimism that had been raised by the signing of the Lusaka Accord with Angola in the same year of heady diplomacy as Nkomati.

At that time the two agreements had appeared to herald a new era in which realism and pragmatism would overcome the revulsion felt in black Africa for apartheid and draw black states into a stable if unenthusiastic association with South Africa.

In the same way as the Nkomati Accord was viewed by Pretoria essentially as a means to suppress the ANC, so the Lusaka pact was seen primarily as a mechanism to block incursions by Swapo into Namibia from the safety of bases in Angola.

Common to the troubles experienced with both pacts was the accusation that South Africa was to blame because of its continued support for the rebels who sought to overthrow the governments that Pretoria had concluded the agreement with: Renamo in Mozambique and Unita in Angola.

While South African support for Unita is classed by its opponents as an act of destabilisation, like its support for Renamo, there is an important difference: Unita has much more respectable credentials than Renamo.

Some of the critics of Renamo say its only claim to be a liberation movement is that it is fighting against a government that was not elected but imposed on those whom it presumes to govern. Renamo, they say, was conceived in sin of an opportunistic liaison, a political one-night-stand, as it were, between white Rhodesia and a group of former soldiers and policemen of the colonial régime in Mozambique who, when the Portuguese decamped, fled across the border, not for ideological reasons but because they feared retribution for past crimes.

Far from serving the ideal of ridding Mozambique of its unelected and undemocratic government, it is said, the group served the Rhodesian government by attacking the Mozambican bases of the Rhodesian black nationalists.

Only later did the Renamo movement grow from this bastard birth, taking in genuine opponents of the Marxist rule of Frelimo and defining its objectives and policies.

Renamo rejects this version of its origins as Frelimo propaganda. It insists that Renamo was formed by a former Frelimo guerrilla commander who was gaoled after independence because he tried to promote private enterprise. He escaped and fled into the bush to form a new guerrilla movement, which asked the Rhodesians for arms and later turned to South Africa when Rhodesia collapsed.

Although Renamo policies are not widely known because of its extraordinary inability to promote its objectives and identity, they are fairly clear to those few who have been able to get within sight or hearing of them. Essentially they envisage a multi-party political system and a democratically-elected government, free enterprise and a free-market economy, and guarantees of fundamental freedoms.

The movement asserts that it seeks negotiations with the Frelimo government to establish a constitutional system acceptable to the majority of Mozambicans.

Far from projecting an image of democratic rectitude, as these policies would suggest, however, Renamo has acquired an international reputation for thuggery, brutality and political aimlessness.

How much of that is justified, how much is a creation of Frelimo propaganda and how much comes from the confusion of Renamo with real bandits it is impossible to determine in the mess that Mozambique is now.

In contrast to the obscure and dubious past of Renamo, Unita is a model of respectability, able to trace its freedom-fighting lineage back into the colonial past of Angola. Although not as old as the MPLA now ruling in Luanda, Unita was fighting a guerrilla war against the Portuguese long before independence in 1975. The only blot that its opponents have been able to find on its escutcheon is its alleged cooperation at one time with the Portuguese against the MPLA.

The association of Unita with South Africa began in earnest only after independence, when the MPLA had seized control of the capital, Luanda. This had followed the departure of the Portuguese and the collapse of the Alvor agreement providing for an interim government and ultimately elections to choose the first full government.

The prospect of the Marxist MPLA taking power in Angola and providing a haven for the Swapo insurgents from Namibia was too much for Pretoria. It moved quickly to help Unita in its fight to keep the MPLA from seizing control of the country, first sending small-scale military help, then a strong force of South African troops, with the approval of the United States and the promise of American support.

After nearly reaching Luanda in a swift and militarily brilliant thrust up the coastline, the South Africans were forced to withdraw when the Americans got cold feet and stopped their support. It was around this time that the South Africans first met the Cubans.

Whether the South Africans invaded Angola because Cuba had sent in troops first to ensure victory for the Marxist MPLA or whether the Cubans went in after the South Africans has become an historical chicken-or-egg argument. The weight of evidence strongly supports the view that the Cubans were first to go in, however.

The result of the South African withdrawal was that Unita retired to its strongholds in the south-eastern corner of Angola, and the third movement that had been fighting the Portuguese, the FNLA, began a decline into irrelevancy.

While the MPLA busied itself with consolidating its position in Luanda, Unita gathered its strength in the bush fastnesses of the south-east until it was ready to make powerful guerrilla strikes at the MPLA.

Whether the South Africans supplied Unita with arms and provisions right from the beginning is one of the secrets locked in the safes in Pretoria. For several years South Africa denied helping Unita, despite strong evidence to the contrary. It was only in 1987 that Pretoria openly confessed to helping the movement.

The South African withdrawal from Angola was quite different from its furtive entry; the troops rode out in review order with the minister of defence taking the salute from a dais erected just inside Angolan territory. After that South African backing for Unita came in two forms: initially in supplies, and possibly training, later in direct offensive action by South African troops. Both were seen by the outside world as acts of destabilisation directed against the Angolan government. Even in the United States, this view prevailed, despite the US having refused to recognise the communist MPLA government.

The precise extent of the activities of the South African armed forces in Angola is difficult to determine, for the SADF has publicly admitted only the basic facts, while the MPLA has almost certainly exaggerated them for propaganda purposes.

As far back as the early Eighties, however, accounts were coming out of Angola of bombing and strafing raids by South African aircraft on towns, convoys, roads, bridges and railways in the south. Ostensibly the attacks, if they were indeed carried out by the South Africans, would have been directed at Swapo camps, transit points and supply facilities. In one case at least the destruction of a bridge by commandos appeared to be intended to cut the Swapo line of supply, the railway from the port of Mocamedes. But the MPLA asserted, and the world believed, that the attacks were intended to destroy the transport communications of south-western Angola to discourage the MPLA from providing Swapo with the means to maintain its insurgency in Namibia.

Until 1985 most of the strikes by the SADF into Angola seemed clearly to have been directed at Swapo targets rather than in support of Unita. There may have been limited actions by special units in support of Unita, but the main strikes, such as the attack on the Swapo base at Cassinga, were directed at Swapo only. The South Africans were in fact at pains to avoid tangling with the MPLA or Cuban forces, although they sometimes did.

This changed in 1985 when Unita appeared to have serious difficulty for the first time in repelling an offensive on their south-eastern stronghold by a powerful MPLA force heavily armed by the Soviet Union and backed by the Cubans. The offensive was turned back, but according to Luanda only after South African aircraft had been sent in against the MPLA armour.

In the next dry-season offensive by the MPLA in 1986 South African help was apparently neither needed nor given, for the attackers were beaten off with the aid of Stinger anti-aircraft and Tow anti-tank missiles provided by the United States.

In 1987, however, South African ground and air forces went to the aid of Unita when the rebels found themselves hard pressed by a powerful attack by the Cuban and Soviet-backed Fapla army of the MPLA government in the Lomba river region. The South African ultra-long-range G-5 cannon, said to be the most effective in the world, is believed to have been used then for the first time in battle, with devastating effect.

Making the first open admission of sending South African troops to fight in support of Unita, the Defence Minister, Magnus Malan, said that had it not been done Unita would have been defeated and the way would have been opened for Soviet influence to spread throughout southern Africa.

He did not elaborate, but he probably had in mind the possibility that the defeat of Unita in the Lomba river offensive would have led to the fall of Mavinga to the south, which has a strategically important airstrip.

The capture of Mavinga would have made possible the eastward extension of the "umbrella" military line that the Russians had established for the MPLA across most of the southern part of Angola. Each umbrella consists of an airfield with MiG aircraft, usually piloted by Cubans, and ground-to-air missiles and radar to detect enemy aircraft and guide the missiles and the MiGs in repelling them.

With their diameters overlapping, the umbrella bases stretched from the coast half-way across Angola, forming a line that the South Africans would try to penetrate at their peril, for the MiGs could attack ground forces, and both the MiGs and the missiles could repel attacking South African aircraft.

This modern African equivalent of the French Maginot Line and the German Siegfried Line was clearly not intended primarily as a defence against the Unita guerrillas but against the South Africans, whether they were operating in support of Unita or against Swapo. Behind that line Swapo can set up safe bases from which to launch hit-and-run strikes into Namibia.

It was thus seen by the South Africans as an offensive rather than a defensive installation, threatening what it regarded as its own legitimate right to defend Namibia against Swapo and ultimately South Africa itself against ANC and other Soviet-backed insurgency.

The umbrellas covered the whole of southern Angola down to the Namibian border, except for the south-eastern corner, where Unita has its capital of Jamba.

Extension of the line would bring even Jamba within range, making it difficult if not impossible to defend, and could threaten South African bases in Namibia, including the important one at Mpacha near to where the Caprivi Strip, thrusting deep into the subcontinent, makes a strategic junction with Zambia, Zimbabwe and Botswana.

Together with the enormous flood of armaments that the Soviets poured into Angola, the development of the umbrella line doubtless convinced Pretoria of hostile and expansionist Soviet ambitions in southern Africa and strengthened conviction in Pretoria of the need to confront that expansion in Angola rather than wait for it to reach the borders of South Africa.

A primary purpose of the umbrella system was to challenge the aerial supremacy held by the SADF in southern Angola and in this it appears to have had considerable success. By early 1988 the Angolans and Cubans were in fact claiming total success.

Their claim was made with increased confidence after the Cubans had established new air bases at Cahama and Xangongo in a giant leap southwards that brought the Namibian border within striking range of Cuba's MiG-23 jets.

The Cahama and Xangongo bases were set up during the surprise southward advance by the Cuban forces into the area immediately north of Ovamboland in the first half of 1988. As the year drew to a close the South Africans were uncertain whether the advance was intended merely as a face-saving prelude to a withdrawal of the Cuban troops or to increase the pressure on Pretoria to advance Namibian independence, whether it would be turned into an eastward thrust towards Jamba or whether it was in preparation for a confrontation with the SADF by way of setting up a shield for Swapo incursions across the border.

Even the South Africans admitted, however, that the Cuban advance had changed the military balance in the region. Towards the end of 1988 it seemed clear that it would have an important effect on South Africa's future military strategy and possibly also on the Angolan-Namibian peace negotiations.

Which way the Cubans jumped might also throw light not only on their own intentions but also on those of the Soviet Union, which was thought to have the power to bring the Cubans to heel if it wished.

South Africa's view of the Soviet Union as an alien intruder bent on domination in Africa has clearly had a powerful influence on its decisions to wage war beyond its own borders. It helps to explain Pretoria's persistent accusations that it is the Soviet Union and not South Africa that is the destabiliser in the subcontinent and that it is the ANC (which Pretoria believes to be communist-dominated) that must primarily be blamed for the violence in and around South Africa.

It is in Angola that South Africa is on the firmest ground in its argument that its military actions across the border are essentially defensive and intended neither for territorial expansion nor political hegemony.

While its protestation that it has no colonial ambitions anywhere may be received with more than a little scepticism among its immediate neighbours, especially Lesotho, it carries more weight in distant Angola.

The Frontline States nevertheless deny the legitimacy of the right claimed by South Africa to strike across the border at Swapo, just as they deny its right to attack the ANC in neighbouring countries. The legitimacy, in their eyes, lies with the resort to violence by Swapo to end the "illegal" occupation of Namibia by South Africa and with the use of violence by the ANC to overthrow apartheid.

Questions of legitimacy have long dominated Namibian politics, both internally and externally. International efforts to get South Africa out of the territory have had to be based squarely on the premise that its presence there is illegal. Their main foundation is the finding of the International Court of Justice that the old South African mandate from the League of Nations was no longer valid nor, therefore, was its continued presence in Namibia.

Without the opinion of the World Court the opposition to "occupation" of Namibia by South Africa could claim no more than moral validity; the World Court has given it legality, though not undisputed legality.

It was the need for legal validation of their case that made the opponents of South Africa go to the World Court, even though its findings are not binding unless its jurisdiction is accepted by all parties to a dispute; and because South Africa refused to accept the jurisdiction of the Court in the Namibia dispute its decision remains only advisory and not binding.

But even those Western powers that at first refused to accept the recommendation of the Court have over the years swung round to accepting it tacitly because the sheer weight of international opposition has made it politically inexpedient for any government to do otherwise. Thus the presence of South Africa in the territory appears to have been made illegal not so much by the force of international law as by the weight of international opinion, and most countries, certainly those of the Third World that dominate the United Nations, take the view that international law is synonymous with international majority opinion.

The fact that Pretoria considers the UN attitude nearer to mob rule than the rule of law has made little difference to the prevailing world view. South Africa has, after all, had another conviction at the bar of global opinion: it was found guilty of apartheid, which has formally been declared by the UN General Assembly to be a crime against humanity.

Thus while most of the world condemned military incursions into Angola by South Africa as unlawful aggression and destabilisation, Pretoria continued to regard them as legitimate acts of self-defence against illegal attempts by Swapo to take power in Namibia by force of arms. The decision of the World Court and a cataract of resolutions from the General Assembly and the Security Council were taken by Swapo as total validation of its resort to violence. But Pretoria has dismissed that as opportunistic justification of what was essentially an attempt, supported if not inspired by Moscow, to impose one-party Marxist rule on the territory.

While shooting it out with Swapo, Pretoria continued to insist that it had no desire to swallow Namibia; it wanted only to exercise its mandated responsibility to bring the territory to independence according to the wishes of its inhabitants. But the assertion had a ring of bogus piety in the ears of the rest of the world as it watched the painfully laboured efforts by South Africa to find out what the wishes of the inhabitants in fact were.

With some justification, the South African government said that it was not easy to establish the wishes of so disparate and quarrelsome a collection of ethnic groups as the inhabitants of Namibia. But even among those who sympathised with Pretoria in this question there was a strong suspicion that it could long ago have come much nearer to granting independence if it were not afraid of seeing a Marxist (Swapo) government in power on yet another of its borders.

South Africa continued patiently to argue its case in the Security Council, the only major UN forum where it is still has a voice; but it also turned to other means to promote its case, hiring expensive legal and public relations firms to lobby for it in Washington and other Western capitals.

In the meantime it proceeded with attempts to nudge the squabbling internal political parties into a cohesion capable of refuting the claim by Swapo to be the sole legitimate representative of the inhabitants. The endorsement by the General Assembly of this claim was the second important pillar of legitimacy on which the opponents of South Africa based their case. But up to the time of writing it continued to be tested by the *ultima ratio regum:* the gun.

It was a David-and-Goliath contest in many ways, except that David in this case was not very good with the sling. Against the formidable South African military machine, the most efficient in Africa, the Swapo guerrilla fighters were singularly ineffective.

Ineffective, that is, in their failure to compel Pretoria to leave Namibia. They were incapable even of penetrating to the white heart of the territory, let alone of exercising control over any part.

Every year they came down from their bases in Angola in small lightly-armed groups, running the gauntlet of the constant patrols that the South Africans maintained in southern Angola to intercept them before they crossed the border.

Once over the border the danger was even greater as the insurgents began a deadly game that they could have little hope of winning. Waiting for them was a military machine so powerful and ubiquitous that it made their chances of returning alive to Angola virtually negligible. Against the Swapo insurgents with their Kalashnikovs, their light machine-guns, mortars and rocket-propelled grenades, the SADF and the South West Africa Territory Force could deploy skilled trackers, spotter aircraft, helicopter gunships, jet fighter-bombers and soldiers specially trained in anti-insurgent tactics and moving swiftly in helicopters and armoured vehicles, including the formidable Ratel armoured personnel carrier, or mounted on motor-cycles or horses.

Coming south in the wet season, when there is plenty of water in the bush and rains to obliterate their tracks, the insurgents usually "bombshelled," that is, scattered in smaller groups at first contact with the security forces.

With a cunning developed over years of furtive incursions, they have been known to travel for long distances by clinging to farm fences, walking sideways along the bottom strand of wire, to avoid leaving footprints. They fixed the hoofs of cattle to the soles of their boots. They walked backwards for miles. They laid false trails leading to ambushes.

Seldom were these tactics successful for long against their relentless hunters. Only two or three times did they ever penetrate through the Ovamboland tribal area (from where they got most of their recruits) and reach the white farming area to the south, where the aim was to attack farms and road traffic in an attempt to undermine morale and demonstrate that Swapo could successfully challenge the might of Pretoria.

Over the years a few farms were attacked and a few whites killed, but never was the resolution of the white civilians at the sharp end of the conflict seriously weakened. Seldom was the infrastructure damaged much more than the occasional cutting of a power-line.

Stigmatised as they have been by atrocities against civilians and the cowardly carnage of the mine, the tactics of the insurgents in southern Africa will always be the subject of hot controversy that tends to lose sight of the sheer courage needed to undertake many of their ventures.

A strong element of cynicism is apparent, however, in the wide acceptance that the means adopted in the struggle against Pretoria's rule in South Africa and Namibia are justified by the end.

In the case of Swapo, the cynicism appears to have reached the same extreme as was demonstrated by the generals who sent waves of troops in futile charges on to the barbed wire and the machine-guns in the first world war. The commanders of Swapo in Angola knew how few of their men ever returned from their missions across the border, and they knew how slender were the chances that they would succeed.

Yet they sent them on these suicidal expeditions year after year, apparently willing to sacrifice them to sustain the fiction that Swapo was waging an effectual guerrilla campaign.

From that the conclusion is inevitable that the commanders deliberately concealed from the men they sent south the overwhelming odds against their returning alive. If this is not the case, the insurgents were either astonishingly stupid or astonishingly heroic.

The men apparently used as cannon-fodder by the Swapo commanders might have believed the assertions that their organisation made about casualties inflicted on the SADF and SWATF, but it is inconceivable that the commanders did. Even allowing for cover-ups by the SADF, the boasts by Swapo were patently outrageous to any knowledgeable observer.

An accurate estimate of the number of SADF and SWATF personnel killed since the Namibian conflict began in 1966 is difficult to make since the SADF does not disclose an aggregate and few independent counts have been made. A rough guess would put the SADF figure in the high hundreds.

While some analysts have calculated that the South African losses are proportionately at least as great as American losses in Vietnam, the psychological impact has not been as severe. Despite a rather feeble campaign in South Africa against conscription, public opposition to the fighting on what is euphemistically called "the border" has not reached anything like the level reached by domestic American opposition to the fighting in Vietnam.

For sparsely populated Namibia (about 1 200 000) the loss of life has been high. It is estimated that as many as 20 000 lives have been sacrificed on both sides and among non-combatants caught in the cross-fire. More than half of these — 11 000 — are estimated to have been Swapo fighters.

The greatest losses to Swapo occurred not in Namibia but in Angola, where the SADF and SWATF not only tried to intercept their incursions into Ovamboland but also sought to hit them in their bases before they set out for the border.

Until recent operations in support of Unita most of the SADF strikes across the border were directed ostensibly at Swapo. In some cases the target was uncertain, such as an operation that appeared to have been intended mainly to knock out the radar installations at the Menongue "umbrella" base.

There was, however, no doubt about the target in what appears to have been the most destructive raid of all, the attack on the important Swapo base at Cassinga, deep inside Angola. Swapo maintained that it was not a military base but a refugee camp, and that nearly all of those killed were women and children and other civilians not directly concerned with military activities. Swapo not surprisingly extracted the maximum propaganda benefit out of the incident, and what it describes as the Cassinga massacre has become a day marked each year with mourning and appropriate political activity.

Although South Africa has admitted that some of those killed at Cassinga were women and children living in the camp, it insists that it was essentially an insurgent base and that most of the casualties were among Swapo fighters. This has been confirmed privately by SADF soldiers who took part in the operation.

The Cassinga attack has nevertheless become entrenched in the annals of Swapo as a South African atrocity, and the bitterness so created will be carried over into the independence of Namibia, whenever that may be and whoever wins.

Figures for the number of civilians killed in the Namibian conflict are even more difficult to obtain than those for combatants, for the civilians usually have died in a shadowy and brutal fringe war in which neither side wishes its part to be made public. That there have been atrocities is clear, but even the facts of the atrocities are hard to get, let alone who was responsible. One name that repeatedly crops up, however, is Koevoet, the sobriquet of the police anti-insurgency unit.

As in all guerrilla wars the Namibian civilians were the subject of a contest for their "hearts and minds". In late 1988 it was generally agreed that Swapo were winning that particular contest, at least, and had the political support of most black Namibians, especially among the Ovambo tribe, the largest in the territory.

Only a free and fair election could accurately reveal whether that was so, however; and even taking into account the difficulty of holding elections under the prevailing circumstances few outside government circles seriously challenged the impression prevalent in the world at large that Pretoria was not prepared to consider holding elections until it was pretty certain that they would not put Swapo into power.

For some sceptics this remained true even after South Africa's cooperation in the Angola-Namibia peace talks that began in 1988 with Cuba, Angola and the United States.

At the time of writing these talks appeared, however, to offer the greatest promise of success in all the long and frustrating efforts to bring independence to Namibia.

What distinguished the negotiations from previous settlement initiatives was that some of the major players were beginning to feel the cost of the Angolan war.

The Soviet Union appeared to have lost interest in continuing to pour costly weapons into a conflict the arms had failed to win for its protégé, the MPLA. As in Afghanistan, the Soviets appeared to have decided the Angolan war was an unacceptable financial and political burden on the effort to promote *glasnost* at home.

South Africa had for years accepted as politically worthwhile the financial cost of the war and of its subsidisation of the Namibian budget, in return for which, contrary to popular international belief, the Pretoria government received no material reward. To that cost, however, had now been added the possibility that its involvement in Angola could become more expensive in both men and material with the increased effectiveness of the Luanda allies, particularly in the air.

The MPLA for its part was feeling the economic and political cost of its continued failure to subdue Unita and exercise effective control of the country, despite the best efforts of the Soviets and Cubans.

The success or failure of the negotiations was, however, dependent on several factors that remained hidden: whether the Soviets were really serious about seeking a peaceful settlement and would indeed close their armaments cornucopia: whether the MPLA believed it might lose Moscow's backing if it did not settle and could in the event of a settlement survive against Unita; whether the South Africans really believed they ought to abandon Namibia and whether they thought they could do so without exposing their own country to a risk of insurgency from an independent Namibia and the Pretoria government to a white right wing backlash of unacceptable severity.

There is an irony in the situation that is typical of all liberation struggles in southern Africa. The main objection to Swapo by Pretoria is its leftist character and its close ties with the Soviet Union. Yet those sympathies might never have prevailed in Swapo and its links with Moscow might never have become so strong if Pretoria had long ago allowed the inhabitants of Namibia to determine their own future.

One lesson taught by the struggles in southern Africa is that the longer whites in power have denied legitimate rights to blacks the more radical and resolute have become the groups fighting for those rights and the stronger has grown the demand for revolution rather than reform. So it was in Rhodesia; and so it is in Namibia and South Africa.

The damage that can result has been demonstrated most painfully in Mozambique and Angola, from whence the Portuguese in their flight took most of the skill and capital, leaving both countries not only in a state of political conflict but also in a state of administrative chaos from which neither has recovered. A strong argument can be made out that if the Portuguese in their five centuries in Africa had been readier to share the wealth with the blacks and impart more of their skills they might not have had to leave at all.

In neither Namibia nor Zimbabwe has the damage of liberatory warfare been so great as in the former Portuguese territories. There has been damage nonetheless. In Namibia it has been economic rather than structural; outside investment has largely dried up and exports have to run the gauntlet of political opposition overseas.

But Namibia has not retrogressed because of the conflict; it has rather marked time. It has in consequence continued to rely heavily on South African contributions to balance its budget rather than developing its own productivity.

Any examination of liberatory warfare in Africa must consider whether the whites had reasonable grounds to fear the swamping of their cultural and individual rights by the black majority. That is something for blacks who support the liberation struggle in Namibia and South Africa to ponder. But the whites concerned should also remember that nowhere in Africa have blacks who took over from colonial administrations, or even those who won wars of liberation, ever sought revenge against the whites.

It is in Zimbabwe that this general rule is being put to its severest test as the black majority government ushered into power by the Lancaster House agreement consolidates its plans to turn the country into a one–party socialist state.

The policy of reconciliation introduced immediately after Robert Mugabe's ZANU party won the independence election in 1980 astonished many whites in Zimbabwe and South Africa. It has since been pursued with sufficient dedication to have persuaded a large number of the whites who were in Rhodesia before independence to stay. Their political influence has become negligible, but their share in the economy, in agriculture, commerce and industry, is still dominant, even though they no longer have the power to dictate economic policy.

There remains a deep and pervasive sense of unease, however, about the security of their future and their way of life. The government, having finally reached an agreement of sorts with the rival ZAPU party, has moved quickly towards institutionalising a one-party state, and this has been accepted by the whites as inevitable.

How far the government intends to go towards the extreme socialism that has wrecked the economies of many other African countries remains a worrying question not only for the whites in Zimbabwe but also those in South Africa who see Zimbabwe as a possible model of their own future. Both wait to see how the government will balance the long-term benefits of free enterprise against the short-term demands of the huge black proletariat that is the main constituency of the ruling party.

There are strong suspicions in Zimbabwe that certain people in Pretoria have been prepared to go to any lengths to ensure that the Zimbabwe scenario does not become an attractive one for white South Africa. This may help to explain the apparent obsession in Harare with seeing apartheid overthrown. Given the number of suspicious incidents in Zimbabwe since independence it is understandable that the government should appear to be close to paranoia about South African destabilisation.

There is, in fact, clearer evidence of South African destabilisation in Zimbabwe than anywhere else. Much of it is inconclusive, but altogether it builds up a startling picture of cross-border machinations.

The government has not been able to prove South African complicity in the more spectacular incidents such as the successful sabotage at the Thornhill air force base soon after independence, in which about a third of the aircraft of the Zimbabwe Air Force were blown up, or in the bombing of the ZANU (PF) headquarters in Harare. But it has produced convincing evidence of South African espionage on a large scale and of South African support for armed dissident groups, notably the so-called Super ZAPU in Matabeleland.

Remnants of the powerful Zipra army of ZAPU that was outwitted and disarmed by the Mugabe government soon after independence have been blamed for much of the violence that afflicted Matabeleland. That this violence includes the murder of more than 55 white farmers either argues against South African complicity or imputes the most astonishing callousness and cynicism to some persons in Pretoria.

The evil hand of destabilisation is seen by Harare in the border checks on road and rail traffic that slowed the flow of goods across the border, and in the alleged obstruction of fuel deliveries.

Apart from the attack on the ANC office in Harare in 1986 there have been no admitted raids by the SADF on ANC targets in Zimbabwe, whose government claims, like those of all the neighbours of South Africa, to have barred insurgency across the border from its soil.

But South Africa replies, with apparent justification, that many of the insurgents who have come in to lay mines in South Africa come from Zimbabwe.

The same applies to Botswana, despite the persistent denials by the government in Gaborone that it has ever allowed such activities. Botswana also argues, however, that if South Africa cannot stop ANC insurgents from crossing its borders from Botswana, then it can hardly expect Botswana, with its infinitely smaller resources, to do so.

Retaliation by Pretoria, according to Botswana, has included blocking petrol supplies to storage tanks built for the express purpose of making Botswana less susceptible to a South African blockade.

South Africa has also imposed what appear to be deliberate obstructions of road traffic crossing the border, including one in December 1987. The ostensible reason was that the police were looking for arms and explosives after a threat by the ANC to carry out some spectacular act of terrorism during the Christmas season.

This might well have been the real reason for the detailed searches of vehicles at the border points but the stoppages would also have served the additional purpose of warning Botswana that traffic across the border might be stopped altogether if Pretoria were not satisfied that the Gaborone government was doing all it could to prevent the ANC from using its soil for insurgency in South Africa.

The Batswana did not need to be reminded of what had happened to Lesotho in 1986 when a border blockade, also imposed to enforce total suppression of ANC activity, saw the country quickly running out of essential supplies. The fact that the blockade precipitated a military coup that overthrew the anti–Pretoria government of Leabua Jonathan was a bonus for South Africa.

Surrounded as it is by South Africa, Lesotho is completely exposed to blockade. The other neighbours of South Africa, having alternative routes to the sea, are less vulnerable but far from safe against the interdiction of their trade routes by Pretoria. Most still rely on the South African Railways and Harbours to move their imports and exports, not by choice but because the alternative routes are either inadequate or cut by hostilities. The reopening of the railway lines through Mozambique from Zimbabwe and Malawi through defended corridors offers only a partial escape from the stranglehold of Pretoria.

The Tazara railway from Zambia to Dar es Salaam port likewise offers only partial relief at best. The Benguela line from Zambia and Zaïre to the Angolan port of Lobito has been cut for years by Unita.

It appears, therefore, that Pretoria will be able to wield the lever of transport blackmail for some time to come; but it can only use it fully at the cost of losing the considerable revenue that it gets in tariffs from handling its neighbours' goods and at the cost of losing its own trade with countries as far north as Zaïre, all of which forms a substantial proportion of South African foreign trade. The need would have to be seen to outweigh the political and economic cost entailed.

The transport weapon has, according to its alleged victims, been used both to discourage them from imposing sanctions on Pretoria and to dissuade them from supporting the ANC. South Africa has yet another weapon that it could use for the same objective, but again only at the cost of damaging its own trade with the hinterland countries. If it thought that the need justified the price, however, it could do what the Rhodesians did ten years ago to dissuade Mozambique from sheltering the ZANU guerrilla fighters. It could send in aircraft or commandos to destroy bridges, roads and railways in the Frontline States.

Such extreme measures would, of course, be tantamount to outright acts of war, going far beyond the attacks on ANC targets to which South Africa has so far confined itself in the states across its borders. They would create the risk that other countries could come to the aid of the Frontline States and plunge the region into a disastrous conflict.

That South Africa would go as far as that seems to be doubted by those in the international community who see support for ANC violence and for sanctions only as warning messages to white South Africa rather than as real threats to its existence. But it is doubtful whether anybody living in southern Africa would wish to see the question put to the test.

As for the possibility of internationalising the South African problem, there is already some precedent. In Angola the MPLA has been supported by more than 50 000 Cuban troops and enormous supplies of Russian arms. Unita has been given modern weapons by the United States and logistical and other support by several African countries. In Mozambique the Frelimo government which was from the beginning supplied with weapons from Russia, has more recently been supported by troops from Zimbabwe, Tanzania and Malawi, while some of its own troops are being trained by the British. Several other nations are giving military aid, support that might not have materialised, certainly not in such strength, but for the conviction of destabilisation by South Africa.

It is ironic that while South Africa is being castigated from all sides for destabilisation, it not only proclaims its innocence and its desire to be a good friend and neighbour but to a considerable extent puts its professions into practice.

Thus Mozambique, while accusing South Africa of destabilisation, accepted its economic and technical help in developing and running Maputo harbour and the railway linking it with South Africa. Mozambique happily took all the South African imports and exports that it could get and asked for more. When the traffic was diverted through South African ports Mozambique saw that as an act of destabilisation.

Mozambique, like Zimbabwe, Swaziland and Lesotho allows Pretoria to maintain a trade commission in Maputo and exports its own in Johannesburg.

For all their condemnation of apartheid, not only the Frontline States, who have no option, but also many other African countries, who do have an option, have steadily increased their trade with South Africa almost in direct proportion to the rising opposition to its racial policies.

More than 45 of the 50 African states trade with South Africa, nearly all surreptitiously through the back door to avoid being seen to be doing business with the untouchable.

In a continent of flourishing black (i.e. illicit) markets surreptitious trade with the land of apartheid may be the biggest black market of them all. It clearly demonstrates how large and mutually beneficial it might be if it all became open and legal.

This point is demonstrated even more convincingly by the slow progress made by the Southern African Development Coordination Conference towards its objective of lessening dependence by the member states on South Africa and promoting trade and development among themselves.

The best available figures suggest that since the SADCC was formed in 1980 seven of its nine member-states have increased rather than decreased their trade with South Africa. Only Angola and Tanzania, which are not well placed to trade with South Africa anyway, have not done more business with it. Botswana, Lesotho, Malawi, Mozambique, Swaziland, Zambia and Zimbabwe have all increased their trade with South Africa. At the same time their trade among themselves has increased to a lesser degree.

If South Africa really is trying to destabilise its neighbours, it is doing quite the opposite in countries farther north. In several it is operating aid projects, such as the stud ranch in Equatorial Guinea at which South African experts were trying to develop a breed of cattle better suited to tropical conditions, until Nigeria forced Equatorial Guinea to expel the South Africans in 1988 on the ludicrous grounds that the South African veterinarians threatened Nigeria's security. To promote associations like these is an aspiration to which the South African Department of Foreign Affairs gives high priority. Its efforts are symptomatic of the outcast's hunger for acceptance, which South Africa desires particularly in Africa.

When South African politicians say "We are of Africa", and suggest that white South Africans should seek their future in their own continent rather than in the Western world from which their ancestors came, they are probably quite sincere.

The swing by South Africa towards black Africa and away from Europe and America has undoubtedly been impelled to a great extent by the growing animosity of its former friends among the white countries of the West. What influence it will have on government thinking is not yet known.

Certainly some sections of the government do not seem to share the enthusiasm of the Department of Foreign Affairs for bridge-building in Africa, at least not at the present time and in the present circumstances.

The belief that South African diplomats are constantly having the rug pulled from under them by hard-line politicians and military leaders is well established. So thoroughly entrenched is the belief that South Africa is run by the generals that it has probably become ineradicable in foreign minds even if it should be shown to be untrue, which has not so far been the case.

The military leaders certainly play an extraordinarily large part in government in close collaboration with like-minded politicians which is not entirely surprising in a country that is in a sense at war. What is uncertain is the extent of the influence of the military men.

Military leaders are prominent on the State Security Council and their influence, and that of the politicians on the council, is capable of permeating down through the complex National Security Management system.

How influential they are in formulating and executing government policy remains to the general public a matter of conjecture — conjecture that receives little guidance from the government and even less inquiring from a white public that is being pushed increasingly into a defensive posture by international pressures that seem to many to be calculated to destroy rather than reform them.

The military leaders have themselves professed a belief that the best interests of South Africa lie in promoting stability and prosperity in the neighbouring states. However, in stating that belief in parliament towards the end of 1987 the Minister of Defence, General Magnus Malan, linked it to Pretoria's conception of South Africa as a regional power; which it undoubtedly is, both economically and militarily. It is how Pretoria uses its power that will obviously dictate not only the direction of events in the region but also how other countries see them.

And it is their impressions that will continue to dictate reaction from abroad, for these will be decided not by whether South Africa is destabilising its neighbours, but by whether the world thinks it is.

It is difficult to escape the conclusion that it is Pretoria's actions rather than the prejudices of the world outside that have shaped these conceptions. Pretoria may have only itself mainly to blame for the fact that the world has largely ignored its insistence that the chief causes of destabilisation in the region were Soviet interference and the unrealistic policies of dictatorial Marxist governments.

The South African government obviously does not enjoy its notoriety as a destabiliser. Its motives are defensive rather than aggressive; that only makes the situation even more lamentable and the possibility of a solution even more remote.

As this was being written, however, events were unfolding that promised change for the better in the subcontinent.

The long search for independence for Namibia found new hope through the American–brokered negotiations between South Africa and Angola and Cuba. South Africa surprised sceptics by keeping a promise to withdraw its troops from Angola and by proposing a date for implementation of the Namibian peace plan in Security Council Resolution 435.

From this point the negotiations became locked, ratchet–like, into an irreversible progression that led through a series of talks in New York, London, Geneva, Cairo and Brazzaville, to the signing of the Brazzaville Accord in December 1988 and, ultimately, to the tripartite agreement in New York that cleared the way for a Cuban troop withdrawal from Angola and independence for SWA/Namibia.

These developments powerfully contradicted Pretoria's reputation for deliberate destabilisation and gave South Africa a new measure of respectability in black Africa and further afield.

Pretoria had already improved its image when South Africa and Mozambique restored the Nkomati Accord by reinstating the mechanism for monitoring violations of the pact. The momentum started by these events was increased when President Botha met President Chissano of Mozambique at Songo, near the Cahora Bassa dam.

This meeting put the seal on an agreement between the two states, together with Portugal, to resume the supply of electricity to South Africa along the power line from Cahora Bassa that had been put out of action by Renamo sabotage.

By implicitly accepting, through these actions, that South Africa was no longer supporting Renamo, the Frelimo government made the destabilisation accusations virtually untenable, at least as far as Mozambique officially was concerned.

The Songo meeting was followed in quick succession by meetings with Presidents Banda of Malawi, Mobutu of Zaïre and Houphouet–Boigny of Ivory Coast and King Moshoeshoe of Lesotho. South Africa's patient diplomatic drive in Africa was bearing fruit; several African states were showing a willingness to adopt a more pragmatic attitude towards South Africa. Even though they still condemned apartheid, they were giving South Africa the benefit of the doubt on its insistence that it was not practising destabilisation.

Pretoria's hope was that the new attitude, despite it being demonstrated only by states which already had some dealings with the Republic, would spread in Africa and that it would encourage more states to deal openly with South Africa in both diplomacy and trade.

Destabilisation could not be dismissed as easily as that, however. While Pretoria was wooing Africa, a series of trials were being held in Zimbabwe and Botswana that appeared to have at last brought destabilisation to account in a courtroom.

The accused, mainly whites, were charged with offences relating to the death of Zimbabwean and Botswanean citizens during alleged attempts by commandos and secret agents to strike at ANC personnel.

Some in Pretoria may have viewed the trials as vestiges of a discarded past, yet suspicions remained, especially in Mozambique, that elements in South Africa that disapproved of the diplomatic initiatives were continuing to support destabilisation. These suspicions were strengthened by a series of attacks on railway and power lines from South Africa that followed soon after the revitalisation of the Nkomati Accord.

In South African diplomatic circles, however, hopes remained high that acceptance in Africa could still be achieved, if not on terms of tolerance of apartheid then at least on terms of tolerance of a gradual rather than immediate dismantling of it.

It was doubtful, however, whether the aim could be achieved on either term without much stronger concessions to black demands than Pretoria had so far offered.

But if the government could be faulted on this, so perhaps could the African countries for making no effort to ease the fears of whites about what might happen to them if they relinquished even a degree of power to the black majority.

There can be no question of the whites voluntarily giving up power without such assurances and part of the southern African tragedy is that these have rarely been contemplated, let alone given. Blacks in South Africa and elsewhere in Africa, together with apartheid's opponents throughout the world, have offered to the increasingly beleaguered whites only a stark choice between destruction through economic sanctions or taking their chances under black domination. Not surprisingly, most whites have preferred to cling blindly to power.

Although apartheid is doomed, as even its creators have acknowledged, its enemies around the world have persisted in seeing the South African issue in the outdated terms of winning the rights of the majority rather than as what it should logically now become: a question of reassuring the minority so that the whites can make the enormous contribution they are capable of making to the prosperity of a South Africa without racial discrimination of any kind.

As a consequence of the intransigence on both sides, however, there has been a progressive decline of the opportunity available to both blacks and whites to get the maximum benefit from what they jointly could contribute to their common welfare ... and that of the subcontinent.

The chances of the white–dominated South African economic machine being harnessed for the good of blacks in South Africa and other countries in the region have dwindled as anti–apartheid attitudes have hardened and narrowed and the machine itself has been damaged by sanctions.

At the same time it has become less likely that the blacks would reject the extreme forms of socialism that have caused so much ruination in Africa and embrace instead the free enterprise ideals that have brought prosperity elsewhere in the world.

Neither the intransigence nor the violence has been confined to the South African government and its opponents. The calamity of southern Africa has been made worse rather than better by the imposition of economic sanctions, which may yet be regarded by objective historians of the future as the cruellest form of violence to be inflicted on the region.

Those in the foreign anti–apartheid lobbies, the United States Congress and elsewhere who have promoted sanctions may never have seen them as a form of violence but only as a means to end apartheid and destabilisation. Some have been actuated by sanctimonious fervour that could not have stood close examination of motives or effects, others by cold personal ambition that was equally indifferent to the results.

Yet if violence is defined according to the suffering that it causes, then sanctions, if pushed to their limit, must become the worst scourge that South Africa has suffered in modern times, causing greater human misery than apartheid or insurgency.

No advocate of sanctions has yet been able to demonstrate that black liberation and black dignity are to be found in the enduring and hopeless poverty that sanctions would bring.

Considerable hope remained, however, that the achievements of 1988 would help to reverse the process and allow whites and blacks to move at last towards a pragmatic accommodation, with the blacks giving the whites something other than punitive incentives to abandon apartheid and the whites offering the blacks a genuine prospect of apartheid being abandoned.

Whether one of these should come before the other or whether they could come about simultaneously were questions that had hardly been addressed, let alone answered, as the year drew to a close.

There is no doubt, however, that a persuasive rather than coercive approach offers the best chance of South Africans finding peace and prosperity.

Therein may lie also the best hope for the subcontinent.

# THE RHODESIAN ISSUE IN HISTORICAL PERSPECTIVE
## The Demise of Rhodesia
*by Richard Wood*

On 31 December 1987, at its new stadium built by the Communist Chinese, while Shenyang F-7 supersonic jet fighters (the Chinese version of the MiG-21) screamed overhead in triumphant salute, Zimbabwe took the last steps to enable Robert Gabriel Mugabe to achieve his life-long ambition to become its first executive president.

A few days earlier Mugabe had finally healed the twenty-four-year-old schism in the African nationalist movement by reuniting his Zimbabwe African National Union (ZANU) and Joshua Nkomo's Zimbabwe African People's Union (ZAPU). In the offing is the declaration of a one-party state, part of the second nation-building phase of Mugabe's Leninist revolution.

There was no surprise in all this. A one-party state of the Marxist-Leninist model had been the aim of Mugabe and his party from the early Sixties. Some commentators, particularly from the Western media, have tried to pretend otherwise, but never Mugabe. The most uncomfortable of the opponents of the Rhodesian government throughout the nationalists' long struggle, Mugabe could never be accused of being a compromiser or a deceiver.

His aims were always plain. He openly embraced the Marxist-Leninist formula and, despite the constraints of the Lancaster House Agreement, adopted its four-step programme for securing power and consolidating it. Mugabe based the structure of his party on the Russian model and made its praesidium a more powerful instrument than his cabinet. The Marxist Red Star, over which the Zimbabwe Bird is superimposed, was included in the design of the national flag not merely as a trendy concession to fashion in post-colonial Africa: it symbolises Mugabe's intentions.

"Inevitable" is a word that historians use with caution; but, given the racial imbalance, a black-dominated state, not necessarily of Marxist-Leninist persuasion, was probable, and was generally accepted as such. Indeed, its inevitability was acknowledged in 1965 by the Rhodesian Front cabinet, hours before declaring independence unilaterally. Only the most myopic white supremacist could have believed that the whites, never more than five per cent of the population, could have dominated Rhodesia much beyond the 1980s. Black participation in politics had been retarded by qualified franchises rather than total exclusion. The whites had tried racial partnership (but without reforming the crucial division of land) and then at times had shied away from the idea of even sharing power. Yet it was accepted, despite "the never-in-my-lifetime" or the "thousand-years" quips and black indifference to registering as voters that, in the end, the blacks would dominate.

As with all programmes of reform, the pace of change was inevitably always too fast for the "haves" (the whites) and too slow for the "have-nots" (the blacks). The white objective was to inculcate Western democratic values slowly and thoroughly, and in particular the Westminster parliamentary system. Hindsight tells us how vain that was, because that system, in its pure form, nowhere survives in Africa in 1988, having been supplanted by executive presidencies, one-party states and military régimes. Only in Botswana does the two-party system survive in a practical form. All the Rhodesian blacks were not entirely at odds with the aim of the whites, but they were impatient to progress. After the second world war the black nationalists, like all other nationalists, wanted exclusive power. White resistance to such aspirations led the nationalists to choose the violent route to power from the early 1960s, with willing help from Russia, China and the like. These countries supplied the training and weapons that would bring about the military stalemate in the bush that drove the politicians to settle. The reality of that stalemate was confirmed at Lancaster House in 1979 by the commander of the military wing of ZANU, Josiah Tongogara.

As early as December 1949, the formidable, if tactless, Sir Godfrey Huggins, then Prime Minister of Southern Rhodesia, had spelt out the realities. In a speech intended to promote the idea of federation with Northern Rhodesia (now Zambia) and Nyasaland (now Malawi), Huggins acknowledged that hitherto he had always favoured amalgamating the Rhodesias to create a powerful economic entity capable of surviving the stresses of the post-war world. Huggins said, instead:

"amalgamation was turned down by the British government, not on economic grounds, but because they were determined to carry out the policy of trusteeship of the native peoples which, of course, entails the retirement of the trustee when the ward grows up."

There was little surprise in this, because the British government had said as much in a white paper in the previous year, 1948.

Huggins explained that he preferred the evolutionary policy of a racial partnership which would ensure the permanent survival of the influence of the white. Chiding the British Labour government for adjusting its views to please ill-informed opinion within its party, Huggins said:

"It took many hundreds of years for the British people to evolve their present system of government, but these people see nothing absurd in the suggestion that a primitive people, only recently knowing no form of government except that of a military despot and his attendant train of wizards and witch-doctors, and even now ridden with superstition, should quite suddenly be transmuted into a people who understand the Westminster system of government and who are capable of bowing to the will of the majority without having a revolt every now and then."

Huggins said that he preferred to begin the African's political education in local government. Taking the risk of being called a heretic, Huggins conceded that,

"it is possible that our system of government might not suit the African."

Huggins urged the adoption of federation for a number of reasons and declared that, otherwise, Southern Rhodesia could be surrounded by black-dominated states. He did not, he said,

"... relish the prospect of an independent native state as a neighbour. Native states tend to revert to type, and in place of an autocratic chief they would have a dictator and his friends. The rule of existence among the natives when we came here was communistic and a mixture of the Russian system with hereditary dictators."[1]

It would be a mistake to over-emphasise white appreciation of inevitabilities, at least before 1945, because until then the blacks were not seen as representing any political or other threat in the foreseeable future. In 1945, however, a congress of Huggins's governing United Party debated the removal of the franchise from the few hundred blacks who had registered as voters. Even T.H.W.(later Sir Hugh)

Beadle, the future Chief Justice and then a parliamentary secretary, while opposing the proposal, thought that no more black voters should be enrolled. Huggins dismissed all such suggestions.

The problem of the decolonisation of Rhodesia was unique in British Africa. The possession of power by the local whites was rooted in the way in which the country was founded with the impulse coming from acquisitiveness and imperial vision to be found in the Cape of Good Hope rather than in London. The visionary was the 37-year-old Cecil Rhodes, whose British South Africa Company despatched the column of 150 pioneers, 500 police and 117 ox-wagons north from Kimberley on 6 May 1890 to exploit the Royal Charter granted in 1889 after Rhodes's agent, Charles Rudd, had secured a concession from the Matabele king, Lobengula.

Britain never directly governed the territory. The Company set the pace and Britain followed. On 13 September 1890 the pioneers raised the British flag on a dusty patch of veld that would become Cecil Square in the heart of Salisbury, now Harare. In 1891 the British government proclaimed a protectorate over the two main tribal areas, Matabeleland and Mashonaland. In 1893 whites from Mashonaland conquered Matabeleland, and in 1895 Britain allowed the name "Rhodesia" to be adopted. British confidence in the Company was shaken but not destroyed by the abortive Jameson Raid of 1896 and by the Company's handling of the blacks' armed rejection of the enveloping white rule in 1896/7.

The whites gained a political role when – to restrain the Company – a Legislative Council was created in 1899, comprising the administrator of the Company, five Company nominees, and four members elected on a non-racial franchise based on literacy and property qualifications. If blacks could qualify, they could vote. Rail links were established to the sea through the Cape and Mozambique. Roman-Dutch Law, rather than English Law, was adopted, and the civil service was drawn from the Cape. In short, Southern Rhodesia was a product of the sub-imperialism of the Cape.

The Company had been given control of the territory for 25 years and soon irritated the settlers. In 1914 its rule was extended for a further ten years because Britain was reluctant to add to her direct responsibilities. The whites became increasingly restless, and after the first world war in a referendum they opted for self-government rather than union with South Africa. Winston Churchill, then the Colonial Secretary, concurred, and self-government, with certain reservations, was granted in 1923. Under the reservations the British Parliament could veto any law that affected black rights or amended the powers of the legislature and its establishment. The Legislative Assembly comprised thirty members. To qualify for the non-racial common roll, the electors had to be literate, adult British subjects, owning property worth £150 sterling or receiving an income of £100 per annum. In addition, a convention was established that the British Parliament would not legislate on matters that were within the competence of the Southern Rhodesian Legislative Assembly unless asked to do so by that Assembly.

The Company received a financial settlement and, after an election in 1924 which returned Sir Charles Coghlan as the first Premier, the whites were left in charge of Southern Rhodesia, believing that after a suitable apprenticeship she would become a dominion. This belief was reinforced in the next year when the British created the Dominions Office and placed Southern Rhodesian affairs in its care. The impression was strengthened further when, after the Statute of Westminster had defined dominion status in December 1931, the prime minister of Southern Rhodesia was invited to all conferences of Dominion and later Commonwealth prime ministers because his colony was self-governing and, although not a dominion, was responsible for its own defence. Gestures such as being the first member of the British Empire to send men to war in September 1939 demonstrated not only loyalty but independence. In the event, Southern Rhodesia committed, in proportion to the size of her population, more men to war service than any other country in the Commonwealth.

The virtual independence of Southern Rhodesia was demonstrated by Britain never invoking her reserved powers, even though the Southern Rhodesian government enacted legislation that confirmed the segregation of the land and enforced job reservation. One reason was that the Southern Rhodesian government was careful to clear such legislation informally with the British. In one case everyone, including the British, were careless enough to accept the Land Apportionment Bill of 1931 before they realised that it was *ultra vires* of the Constitution. On discovery, necessary amendments were made and the Bill passed into law. The established "native reserves" were unaffected, because they were protected by the Constitution. What was at stake was the fate of 75 million acres outside the native reserves. Under the Act, 49 million acres, including the urban areas, were allocated for purchase by the white population of 50 000. By contrast only 7,4 million acres could be bought by the 1 000 000 blacks. 17,8 million acres were unassigned and the remainder was left as forest and game land. This was done even though the whites by then had not yet occupied half of the 31 million acres that had been alienated to them by 1925. There was no white land-hunger. Indeed, by 1965, they had bought only 32 million acres. In 1931 the blacks had adequate land, but a burgeoning birthrate would soon change that. The whites might have been over-provided for, but they would come to see the Land Apportionment Act as their *Magna Carta;* as the guarantee of the survival of their influence.

The question of land was a fundamental black grievance. The rapidly-expanding population soon found that it had insufficient land. When the pioneers had arrived there were something like 200 000 blacks. This population had grown to 870 000 by 1921, to 1 080 000 by 1931, to 1 430 000 by 1941 and to 2 000 000 by 1950. In 1988 Zimbabwe had a black population of 9 million, 45 times the population of 1888 (if the population of Britain had grown at the same rate it would have multiplied from 33 million then to 1 485 million now!) Relying heavily on immigration (though a selective immigration policy was adopted to avoid the "poor white" problem which beset South Africa), the growth of the white population failed to match that of the African. By 1921 there were 33 800 whites; by 1931, 50 100; by 1941, 69 300; by 1950, 138 000; and twenty years later the population had grown to 275 000. Independent Zimbabwe has a white population of about 100 000.

The growing black population was confined mainly to the reserves, and tilling them by traditional methods soon exhausted the soil. Attempts by the government to change those methods, including destocking, only gave rise to resentment. Yet, despite the overcrowding, most indigenous blacks chose to remain in the tribal areas. That forced the white farmers, miners and industrialists to recruit foreign labour, mainly from Nyasaland (now Malawi). This practice persisted until the 1960s. The great hydro-electric dam at Kariba, for example, was built with such foreign labour in the late Fifties.

The question of employment was another black grievance. Unskilled employment was virtually all that was offered to blacks until the Federal era, when the economy expanded and laws enforcing segregation were progressively repealed. The regulation of labour began early. The Masters and Servants Act of 1901 excluded Africans from trade unions. The African Labour Regulations of 1911 prevented employers from poaching one another's black workers by offering better pay and conditions. This did not apply to white employees. In 1931 the Public Services Act confined skilled black employment in the civil service to teaching and nursing. Then in 1934 the white trade unions induced the passing of the Industrial Conciliation Act to prevent any competition for jobs from the blacks being trained in the government trade schools. The Act excluded blacks from the definition of "employee" and thus reserved skilled employment for whites. As African workers were still under the 1901 Act, the growth of their unions was inhibited.

African schooling, a further serious cause of grievance, had been given to the Christian missionaries by the Native Education Ordinance of 1907, but until then white children had also been dependent on the churches for their education. The racial separation continued, which is not surprising, given the realities of the day. There was no integration in other British territories. White education was placed under the Department of Education, while the Native Affairs Department supervised the teaching of blacks. The separation meant that, given the times and the politics, the white children were inevitably favoured, and much more per head was spent on them than on the blacks. In addition the government preferred technical education for the blacks, which excluded them from clerical and other jobs already being performed by blacks in the neighbouring British protectorates. And, as we have seen, technical training provoked the white workers to secure the exclusive Industrial Conciliation Act of 1934. Until the 1940s the government simply provided two trade schools and left the missionaries in charge of the rest. Blacks like Robert Mugabe who wished to get a secondary education had to do so through correspondence courses. In 1942 the government took over responsibility for urban black schooling and in 1946 opened the first secondary school for blacks at Goromonzi, outside Salisbury, and two more in Bulawayo in 1949. After that the educational opportunities expanded with a multiracial university offering courses from 1956. But the gap between the levels of funding remained as wide as ever, with £8 sterling per annum spent on a black child by the Southern Rhodesian government and £108 on a white by the Federal government, which was responsible for non-African education after 1953.

Ignorant, perhaps, of any black grievances, the whites, immediately after the second world war, having governed Southern Rhodesia successfully for 25 years, believed that they had earned dominion status. Southern Rhodesia was attracting white immigrants. African nationalism was as yet unnoticed, because that crucial generation of black leaders, the first products of the African secondary schools, were at university at Fort Hare in South Africa and elsewhere. By 1947/8 the choices for Southern Rhodesia were either to join South Africa; or to seek dominion status, which a select committee of the Southern Rhodesian Legislative Assembly recommended; or to unite with Northern Rhodesia and Nyasaland in the expectation that the great new state would become a dominion. Union with South Africa had been rejected in 1922, and few still advocated it. In any case the British government was unlikely to allow it. Amalgamation or federation with the northern territories had been suggested at various times since the 1890s. Schemes had been proposed and a number of commissions had sat, but the Southern Rhodesians had hitherto never been particularly attracted to the idea and the blacks of all three territories had regarded it with wary suspicion.

After the war, the British Labour government began the process of decolonisation that its party had suggested in 1943. Accordingly, in March 1946 Britain (and France) withdrew from the Lebanon, Britain recognised the independence of Transjordan and carried out a constitutional change in the Gold Coast, allowing an African majority in the legislature for the first time. In January 1947 Britain gave Nigeria a form of self-government, and in April it referred the problem of Palestine to the United Nations. In August the British government conceded independence to India, casting away her "Jewel in the Crown". In February 1948 Ceylon was given dominion status, and in May the British mandate in Palestine was terminated.

This programme continued with decisions announced at almost monthly intervals for the next twenty years. Thus it is surprising that Clement Attlee's government should have responded to demands from the young white leader of the unofficial members in the Northern Rhodesian Legislative Council, Roy Welensky. In the closing stages of the war, believing in the concept of the dominion of greater Rhodesia and convinced that rule by the Colonial Office was stifling Northern Rhodesia, Welensky had begun to press for amalgamation with Southern Rhodesia. Southern Rhodesia had hitherto hesitated, but burdened with war debts and the problems of providing for the influx of white immigrants, unification with Northern Rhodesia, where copper was booming, became most attractive to the Prime Minister of Southern Rhodesia, Sir Godfrey Huggins. Amalgamation was unpalatable to the British, however, because it would mean the adoption of the Southern Rhodesia Constitution for the whole area. Northern Rhodesia was a protectorate, and it was the British intention that ultimately it would revert to its protected persons, the blacks. In the context of post-war attitudes to empires, racialism and so on, no British government, and particularly no Labour government, was going to leave the fate of the blacks entirely in local white hands. As a sop to the whites, therefore, the British responded by creating in 1946 the inter-governmental Central Africa Council to coordinate the administration of migrant labour, civil aviation and hydro-electric power. That would hardly satisfy the amalgamationists, and the Labour government would have to go further.

Not only was Britain beginning to divest herself of her Empire, but she knew that African opinion was opposed to any form of union between the Rhodesias. In particular, the northern blacks, many of whom had worked in Southern Rhodesia, disliked its legalised segregational policies, even though at home they faced colour bars of equal obnoxiousness, albeit not enshrined in law. Indeed, the blacks in Southern Rhodesia could qualify for the vote if they could meet the qualifications. In Northern Rhodesia the vote was denied to blacks, as British Protected Persons, unless they took the step of becoming British subjects. In Nyasaland there was no electoral system. What the Africans feared was perpetual white hegemony, which could block the path to power of the ambitious. In the Fifties, as before the second world war, the northern Africans would lead in applying political pressure. Pressure from the African nationalist movement led by Dr Hastings Banda of Nyasaland on a responsive Britain would be the rock on which the Federation of Rhodesia and Nyasaland would founder.

In October 1948 the British government indicated informally to Huggins and Welensky that, while it would not contemplate amalgamating the Rhodesias, it would consider federating them with Nyasaland. The distinguished British historian, Lord Blake, has described the product of this decision as "an aberration of history – a curious deviation from the inevitable course of events, a backward eddy in the river of time".[2]

Why did Attlee's government do that and then in late 1951, after examination by three conferences, proceed to make a formal commitment to federation? The answer lay in its shocked reaction to the unexpected result of the South African election on 28 May 1948. Although the British Labour government opposed the amalgamation, it wanted a liberal counterpoise to the Afrikaner state, which a greater Rhodesia might supply. Misreading their political mood, it also feared that the Southern Rhodesian whites might seek to join South Africa. Its alarm was not great enough to make possible the unitary amalgamated state that the whites would have preferred, but there were additional reasons for federation. One was that, after the British spy, Klaus Fuchs, had soured Anglo–American relations in the nuclear field, Britain needed Southern Rhodesian chrome and other minerals for the production of her own atomic bomb. A federation would exploit the economic strengths of the region, and in so doing relieve Britain of the financial burden of Nyasaland.

Mindful, however, of its responsibilities as protector, Britain would not allow any Federal government intrusion in the daily life of the African. It wished to shield the northern Africans at least from the influence of the local whites who would be elected to the Federal Assembly. If federations are to be successful, it is essential that matters common to all member states should be dealt with by the central government. Thus the Federal edifice was erected with a fatal flaw. In Southern Rhodesia African affairs remained the responsibility of the government of the colony, in Northern Rhodesia and Nyasaland these matters were to be dealt with ultimately by Whitehall. Dissension in this crucial area of government was guaranteed.

The upshot was that, far from abandoning its set political course in the case of these protectorates simply because the Federation existed, the British Colonial Office continued to prepare them individually for independence in step with the general advancement of all dependencies throughout the Empire.[3] Democratic self-government within the Commonwealth, based on the Westminster template and universal adult suffrage, was the ultimate intention. The African nationalists were not slow to exploit the opportunity and soon demanded immediate change. The British government began to respond after the Suez débacle of 1956, and even more after Harold Macmillan had been returned to power in the "never had it so good" election of 1959.

Turning towards Europe and away from the Empire, and reluctant to have to fight wars of liberation with impatient nationalists, Macmillan appointed Iain Macleod Colonial Secretary to liquidate the Empire as quickly as possible. For example, Macleod gave Tanganyika independence in 1961 instead of in 1970 as his predecessor, Alan Lennox-Boyd (later Lord Boyd), had intended. Kenya received independence in 1963 instead of in 1975. Macleod thought that it was more dangerous to go too slow than too fast. He earned the gratitude of the African nationalists and the venomous hatred and suspicion of the local whites, whose reaction blighted his political career. Macmillan replaced him in 1962 with Reginald Maudling, and then with Duncan Sandys, both of whom nonetheless continued his policies. Territories that had hitherto been considered unready were rushed to independence after brief experience of self-government. In the process, in 1962, and because of the demands and threats of Dr Banda, Nyasaland, the least developed territory of the Federation, was given the right to secede from it. The precedent was set. A like demand could not be resisted from Kenneth Kaunda in Northern Rhodesia, and the short life of the Federation was terminated on 31 December 1963. It had been an economic success but it had never been allowed time to consolidate before the British concessions were made to the demands for territorial change. With self-determination an unquestioned creed in the post-war world, the Rhodesias and Nyasaland had, because of secession and consequent disintegration, simply swung out of Lord Blake's "backward eddy" into the mainstream of history.

The African nationalists in Southern Rhodesia came a poor third to Banda and Kaunda in the effort to break the Federation, but then their affairs were not administered by Britain. It was more difficult for them to influence her and, short of suspending the 1923 Constitution, there was little that she could do for them in response. In any case, even within Southern Rhodesia, the northern Africans had been the vanguard of African nationalism almost from the outset, with the Nyasas, Clements Kadalie and Robert Sambo, attempting to sponsor black trade unionism there in the 1920s. Later the Southern Rhodesian branches of the African National Congresses of Nyasaland and Northern Rhodesia would raise money for their parent bodies as well as raise the levels of local political awareness and agitation.

This is not to suggest that the Southern Rhodesian blacks left everything to foreigners. After the bloody uprisings of 1896/7 and a brief armed rebellion by the Shona chief Mapondera in 1900, the blacks in Southern Rhodesia eschewed violence, misleading the whites to believe that they were entirely content with or apathetic to their rule. Although the blacks who qualified generally did not register as voters, there were attempts to raise a number of black associations. As early as 1914 the Matabeleland National Home Movement sought to remedy the grievance over land when the tribal reserves were threatened and their quality was poor. Abraham Twala, a Zulu teacher, formed the Rhodesian Bantu Voters' Association in 1923. Other associations appeared at that time, but without conspicuous success. In 1934 Aaron Jacha created the African National Congress; but again support was limited. The Reformed Industrial and Commercial Workers' Union, which was in close liaison with the South African Communist Party, was more effectual.

The Southern Rhodesian Africans were not immune to the effects of the global events of 1939-1945, nor would they fail to notice the general promotion of self-determination afterwards. There were small successes. Through a strike in 1945, black railway workers secured an increase in pay and recognition of their union. The African National Congress was resuscitated by the Reverend Thomson Samkange, but it remained rather ineffective. There was a half-hearted general strike in 1948. In 1951 the execution of soil conservation measures in the form of the rigorously applied Land Husbandry Act angered the tribesmen and provoked non-compliance. The significance of this reaction was that it offered the African nationalists a chance to gain some influence in the tribal reserves, where most of the population lived, and where hitherto the tribal hierarchy and the Native Department held sway. It was, however, the discontent in Nyasaland and Northern Rhodesia that caught attention as the black nationalists protested, through strikes, boycotts, visits to London and other actions, at the prospects of federation blighting any chance of African self-determination. In August 1953 violent unrest in southern Nyasaland was such that police reinforcements from the Rhodesias had to be called in. The African nationalist protests were ignored, and the Federation was brought into being in September.

If the ten years of the Federation, 1953-1963, saw the Southern Rhodesian African nationalists taking a less vigorous part in opposition to white aspirations than those of the north, they did show a new militancy, establish fresh contacts (the police believed that Joshua Nkomo formed links with the Russians as early as 1956) and begin the struggle that would end at Lancaster House in 1979. Building on support gathered through African anger at the Land Husbandry Act, the young nationalists, notably James Chikerema, George Nyandoro, Edson Sithole and the Nyasa, Dunduza Chisiza, created the City Youth League, which would become the African National Youth League. Their first success was a bus boycott in Salisbury in September 1956, which led to a night of violence that gave Southern Rhodesia her first taste of civil commotion for almost sixty years. There had been a strike at the Wankie Colliery in 1954, compelling the then Prime Minister, Garfield Todd, to declare an emergency and to deploy troops, but there had been no violence. True to form, in 1956, Todd declared a state of emergency when the railway workers came out on strike within a week of the bus boycott. This strike was soon over.

Growing in stature, the Youth League in September 1957 merged with the African National Congress in Bulawayo, creating a national movement with Nkomo as its President. The re-invigorated ANC threatened the internal peace of Southern Rhodesia by encouraging the flouting of the law, intimidation, boycotts, the extortion of money and challenging the authority of the government and its officials. All this induced the new Southern Rhodesian Prime Minister, Sir Edgar Whitehead, to ban the ANC in early 1959 after declaring a state of emergency as part of a coordinated effort to stem unrest in all three territories. Inspired by Banda and his African Congress, the disorder in Nyasaland had reached the proportions of an insurgency, and reinforcement by the Federal Army was urgently needed. Thus the Southern Rhodesian emergency was declared first, on 25 February 1959 the ANC was banned and hundreds of its members were detained. That done, the troops departed for Nyasaland to help to restore order there.

Whitehead had been a compromise choice for the premiership after the ousting of Garfield Todd, a missionary and rancher, by a cabinet revolt in early 1958. Todd had been enthusiastically elected in 1954, but increasingly his liberalism had dismayed the whites. The governing parties in the Federation had adopted the multiracial policy of partnership, but Todd's approach to reform had been cautious. Even so, when he sought to remove legislation like the Immorality Act, he aroused suspicion among his electorate if not among his colleagues. Todd belonged to the circle of white liberals who were supporting the ANC. Indeed, once ousted from power, he would soon throw in his lot with Nkomo and support his faction, ZAPU, right through the oncoming struggle. This association, his domineering style of leadership and other factors led Todd's Cabinet to revolt. This crisis, however, was not simply the result of dissatisfaction with his intentions or with his policies. Something else happened that influenced his colleagues which they vowed never to disclose, perhaps even to him. However unavoidable their action might have seemed to them, their removal of Todd was a fatal blow to the chances of Africans continuing to believe in white liberalism.

Todd's achievements included a reform, in October 1957, of the Southern Rhodesian franchise, which kept a complex version of the common roll. It was the product of a review by Sir Robert Tredgold, the Federal Chief Justice,[4] and was designed to increase the number of blacks who could qualify and to bring blacks into the legislature for the first time. Although Todd forced the reform through with threats of resignation, few blacks responded and no black members were forthcoming. The African nationalists, watching the changes being made in the Empire, wanted universal suffrage.

Awkward, deaf, half-blind and unmarried, Whitehead was never a popular leader. But he was highly intelligent and perceptive. Sensing that the Federation might be short-lived, he hoped to see Southern Rhodesia gain virtual self-government, ready for independence. He realised that he had to accommodate black aspirations to achieve the multiracial democracy that was his goal. Thus he continued Todd's programme of reform until voted from power in 1962, and did so despite the uncertainty created by the undermining of the Federation by the British and by the violent unrest among his black population that he had to confront. If his policy looked like the carrot and the stick it was unintentional.

Despite his emergency counter-measures, which began in February 1959 with his banning of the ANC, Whitehead and his ministers steadily introduced changes in the liquor laws (which had been designed to save the African from the fate of the North American Indian), in land tenure in the urban areas - allowing Africans to purchase land in the designated townships - and in racially restrictive employment practices in the public and private sectors. The state lottery was opened to blacks. Multiracial clubs were allowed in European areas. Private schools were permitted to become multiracial. Swimming-baths and cinemas were opened to all races — not without controversy. The pass system was scrapped and the tribal chiefs were given a council to reinforce their standing in their community and so counteract the influence that the nationalists were beginning to gain in the rural areas. In the end Whitehead promised, if re-elected in 1962, to secure a black majority in his parliament within fifteen years, to outlaw racial discrimination and to scrap the Land Apportionment Act. He was moving too far ahead of his electorate, and he would pay the price. His voters lacked his confidence in the multiracial society as they saw the imperial experiments in Africa around them degenerate and some, as in the Belgian Congo, collapsing into bloody chaos. They found no reason to be confident about black rule. Violence was near at hand too, in the black townships where the nationalists strove to gain support by fair means and foul. Whitehead's reforms could never satisfy the demand for self-determination. In any case he had no opportunity to complete his programme of reform.

When confronted, governments must either act or abdicate. In 1959 the internal unrest in the townships could not be ignored, and new security laws were needed to replace the emergency regulations. After much controversy in parliamentary, legal, public and church circles, Whitehead's government gave themselves the powers of preventive detention and of banning organisations and preventing disturbances. These powers proved insufficient to damp down the unrest, and each fresh outburst brought a new tightening of the law.

The uncompromising response of the African nationalists was to replace, on 29 December 1959, the banned ANC with the National Democratic Party (NDP) led by Michael Mawema, a railway trade unionist, in the place of Joshua Nkomo, who had escaped detention in early 1959 by going abroad. The new party demanded the total emancipation of the people, majority rule and Africa-wide cooperation to abolish colonialism, racialism, tribalism, and all forms of racial or national oppression. A further cause of militancy was that Whitehead's efforts towards virtual independence for Southern Rhodesia challenged the African nationalists' demands for a one-party state. The nationalists feared that if Whitehead secured popular support for a multiracial democracy his state might be invulnerable.

In late 1959 Whitehead began his campaign to persuade the British to remove the reservations in the 1923 Constitution before the Federal constitutional review in 1960. In 1953 the architects of the Federation had hoped that in seven years it would have proved itself worthy, perhaps, of dominion status. By 1959, however, the British government doubted the chances of survival of the Federation. Gone was the optimism of 1953 and in its stead were ideas of secession, which were soon to be confirmed by the controversial Monckton Commission that Macmillan appointed after assuring Welensky categorically in July 1959 that it would not consider secession but simply examine how the Federation could be improved.

The British by then, in fact, were intent on extricating themselves from Africa in the most advantageous manner possible. The northern African nationalists were bent on secession, while the Southern Rhodesian nationalists concentrated on securing their position at home. Welensky's white opposition, the Dominion Party, led by Winston Field, a tobacco farmer in Southern Rhodesia, proposed the replacement of the Federation by a "Central African Alliance", a customs union comprising an independent Dominion of Rhodesia, the Protectorates of Nyasaland and Barotseland and a special "Northern Territory" in the north-east of Northern Rhodesia which would be treated as part of the Rhodesian dominion. No one outside the Dominion Party considered the Alliance seriously, but its adoption split the party. In June 1960 its Southern Rhodesian division adopted a policy of "Southern Rhodesia first" and broke away.

Whitehead hoped to get the virtual independence of Southern Rhodesia signed and sealed before any disaster struck the Federation. But part of his reason was that the British had begun to take a hand in the framing of Southern Rhodesian legislation. Hitherto the Southern Rhodesians had only shown the British the final product or particular clauses of which they thought the British might disapprove.

The British, however, intended to stall Whitehead and Welensky until their general election in Britain in October 1959, and after that they would await the findings of the Monckton Commission. In any case, given the mood of the moment, they were reluctant to strengthen the powers of the Southern Rhodesian government until it was more representative. When Whitehead argued that, but for the Federation, Southern Rhodesia would have been a dominion, the British began pedantic negotiations over new safeguards to replace the constitutional reservations and would not be hurried by his warnings of the disastrous effects of the continuing political uncertainty, which included a growing tide of white emigration.

Whitehead's demands brought insistence from the British Labour Party that African opinion should be consulted on any changes. This implied universal suffrage. Leading members of the NDP went to London to oppose his influence. Emboldened perhaps by the reception given to them by the Commonwealth Secretary, Lord Home, the NDP from July 1960 demanded power and thereby raised the political temperature in Southern Rhodesia. Almost immediately Whitehead was faced with violent urban unrest and his inevitable response only increased the difficulties of Southern Rhodesia. The arresting and charging, under the Unlawful Organisations Act, of Michael Mawema and his close colleagues, Sketchley Samkange and Leopold Takawira on 19 July 1960, provoked short but violent protests in Salisbury and then in Bulawayo. The trouble brought the first of many subsequent demands for the British to invoke their powers, which they would deny they had, to suspend the Southern Rhodesian Constitution and for armed intervention to set up a popular democratic government. This appeal came from Garfield Todd and Joshua Nkomo, then the international director of the NDP in London.

Whitehead's response was to continue his programme of reform but at the same time to enlarge his police force (always of a modest size by British standards) by recruitment and by establishing a large multi-racial volunteer police reserve. The violence was not stemmed. In September there was unrest in the steel and cotton industries, and Whitehead himself had to escape through a window after trying to address a hostile crowd in a hall in the Highfield African township. Becoming more aggressive, the NDP replaced Michael Mawema, who was ill, with Leopold Takawira; and then, a month later, it elected Joshua Nkomo as its President, despite his self-exile abroad. It also decided to boycott any elections until there was "one man-one vote". The NDP demanded the suspension of the Constitution and pressed for a round-table conference to draw up a new one.

Further violence in October was serious enough for the police to lose their enviable record of not having killed anyone in the course of their duties that century. Seven blacks were killed in prolonged unrest. Whitehead strengthened his powers to combat the violence but, in doing so, he provoked the British government to suspend the constitutional negotiations. The British recoiled further when Whitehead's Minister of Justice, Reginald Knight, introduced the Law and Order (Maintenance) Bill, which greatly increased police powers and laid down heavy penalties for arson, stoning and intimidation. Such was the indignation among church leaders, the press and the legal fraternity that the government withdrew the bill for reconsideration. Even so, the Chief Justice of the Federation, Sir Robert Tredgold, was alarmed enough at the state of the nation to resign in an attempt to take over from Whitehead and lead a national government.

After a stern exchange with Whitehead and Welensky, the new Secretary of State for Commonwealth Relations, Duncan Sandys, agreed that the Federal review should be held in early December concurrently with other territorial conferences, including the conference on the Southern Rhodesian Constitution. This conference was necessary because the British insisted that the African nationalists should play a part in any settlement. The Law and Order (Maintenance) Bill, somewhat modified but still giving the government draconian powers while limiting access to the courts, passed into law in November. This display of inflexible reaction lost Whitehead the sympathy of the British public, despite his reforms. The Monckton Commission had sanctioned secession from the Federation and the Federal review conference, which opened on 5 December 1960, was a farce. Not even bothering to produce an agenda, the British government had clearly decided that the Federation was redundant and that they would rapidly introduce black majority rule in the two northern territories.

The Federal conference resulted in walk-outs by the African nationalists, Banda, Kaunda and Nkomo. In defiance, Whitehead excluded the NDP from the constitutional conference and began without them. This forced Nkomo to apologise because he was eager to attend. The surprise of the conference was a hint from Sandys that the removal of the reservations was conditional upon an adjustment to the franchise. The power to make the adjustment was already held by the Southern Rhodesian Legislative Assembly and therefore it was not on the agenda. After the conference reconvened in Salisbury in mid-January 1960, a constitutional formula was quickly agreed to by everyone except the Dominion Party. The reservations were replaced by a constitutional council empowered to review legislation, by a declaration of rights and by provision for certain amendments to the Constitution to require not only acceptance by a two-thirds majority in the House but submission to the British government for approval or to referenda of the four race groups of the territory voting separately. The common roll franchise was abandoned for a two-roll system with broadened franchise qualifications to elect fifty "A" roll and fifteen "B" roll members. There was a cross-voting system to give each roll an influence in the election of the members of the other. The idea was to give Southern Rhodesia her first African members and to provide a means for the Africans to capture seats on the "A" roll.

Whitehead proclaimed the agreement a victory for moderation and promised his electorate a referendum to sanction it. His party, the Southern Rhodesian Division of the United Federal Party, welcomed it at a congress where only a single voice, that of Ian Douglas Smith, dissented. Smith, the Federal MP for Gwanda, objected to the dropping of the common roll. Nkomo faced worse dissent, which forced him to recant. A month later the NDP threatened that, unless acceptable changes were made, it would continue the struggle outside the Constitution. The course of history could have been very different if the African nationalists had exploited that Constitution to achieve their aims instead of pursuing the goal of total power through the barrel of a gun. But to be fair, they did it when the British government was responding to such threats elsewhere in Africa and in the Empire at large.

Whitehead and Sandys ignored the NDP. The Constitution was drafted and Whitehead succeeded in having the convention, on the understanding that the British Parliament would not legislate for Southern Rhodesia without prior consent, written into it. In June the British and Southern Rhodesian parliaments ratified the agreement. The NDP condemned it and held a somewhat farcical referendum, on the basis of adult suffrage, on 21 July, which rejected it. Despite a spasm of violence two days before, Whitehead's referendum was conducted on 26 July in peace with the blacks ignoring calls to strike. The happy result for Whitehead was a 2:1 victory, and he proclaimed the birth of a Rhodesian nation in which Africans would play a full part in its political life.

Rhodesians could be forgiven if they thought that there was nothing more to be done; but the British drafters were to make further difficulties about the precise wording, and they slipped in a standard clause, 111, which seemed to undo everything else and leave the British with power to amend what they liked. It was in fact a purely technical matter – the British Parliament, having no constitution, cannot be bound by any law in theory – but it raised fears about the perfidy of the British. The Constitution was enacted by Order in Council in December.

Buoyed up by the good sense of his electorate, Whitehead continued his programme of reform while the NDP concentrated on dissuading any blacks from registering as voters. A rising tide of disorder provoked the government to ban the NDP on 9 December. Nkomo, who was in Dar es Salaam attending the Tanganyikan independence celebrations, again demanded that Britain suspend the Constitution. He returned to Salisbury and on 17 December announced his interim presidency of a new African nationalist party – the Zimbabwe African People's Union (ZAPU) which aimed to secure majority rule.

In 1962, when the fate of the Federation dominated the political scene and the British government conceded the right of secession to Nyasaland, this demand to suspend the Southern Rhodesian Constitution was taken up in the United Nations. The British responded by declaring that they lacked the constitutional right to intervene, and eventually they summoned Whitehead to New York to support their arguments.

In Southern Rhodesia an election was due and the parties prepared themseves for the campaign. Confident of the support of its electorate, Whitehead's party proposed a total repeal of the Land Apportionment Act. In response, Ian Smith resigned from it to form his own Rhodesia Reform Party. Then in March this party united with the Dominion Party as the Rhodesian Front. Their leader was Winston Field, who had abandoned Federal politics. The Rhodesian Front pledged itself to retain the Land Apportionment Act; to reject enforced integration and African domination; to foster equality of opportunity and justice for all; to promote economic development; to improve the position of the tribal authorities and to obtain independence for Southern Rhodesia within the Commonwealth if the Federation broke up.

Whitehead meanwhile continued his programme of reform. He was forced, however, to tighten his security legislation further when violence and strikes greeted a visit in May by R.A. Butler, by then the British Secretary of State at the newly created Central Africa Office. The legislation was enacted in early September just before threats were issued by one "General" Chedu of the Zimbabwe Liberation Army who proclaimed the "Zimbabwe Revolution" and demanded that the blacks join his army.

If this smacked of fiction, it was followed by an outbreak of sabotage and arson. Nkomo's response to it was that he could not stop the disorders until the Constitution had been changed. The succession of petrol bombings and other attacks on life and property provoked the inevitable bannings, detentions and police raids. During one raid considerable quantities of explosives and fuses were found in a house belonging to Robert Mugabe. Elsewhere quantities of home-made weapons were discovered and in December two cars were stopped and found to be carrying sub-machine-guns, pistols and explosives. 1 094 persons were arrested, and the most serious case of arson was the burning down of part of the BSA Company's forests near Melsetter. The war of liberation, or "Chimurenga", may be said to have dated from that moment.

True to form, Nkomo was in Lusaka when the ban on ZAPU was announced and, before he returned to join his members in restriction, he went first to Dar es Salaam to establish an external ZAPU committee led by the Reverend Ndabaningi Sithole. Nkomo then demanded British armed intervention, the removal of Whitehead's government, the reinstatement of ZAPU and a conference on independence. Continuing violence, though at a low level, led Whitehead to declare that ZAPU would not be allowed to reappear in another guise.

Uncertainty, with the evident collapse of the Federation and chaos elsewhere, was affecting morale as well as the economy, and Whitehead's statements on land and Africanisation had a profound effect. When summoned to the United Nations by Britain to explain the banning of ZAPU, he defended his record and stated that he envisaged the advent of black government within fifteen years. Later, on the eve of polling, he said that he expected to have blacks in his cabinet shortly. His tactlessness and personal unpopularity contributed to his defeat, but the Rhodesian Front also fought a clever campaign, playing on fears. By offering the civil service a pension fund and firm government, the Front swung vital seats. The non-registration of Africans, because of intimidation or genuine belief, ensured that the cross-voting effect of the "B" roll was minimal.

Whitehead was heavily defeated on 15 December. The Rhodesian Front secured a five-seat majority through gaining 35 "A" roll seats. The United Federal Party was left with 15 "A" and 14 "B" seats, and an independent, Dr Ahrn Palley, one "B" roll seat. Denying that the policy of his party was apartheid, Field wasted no time in naming his cabinet, which included Ian Smith as Minister of the Treasury.

The Rhodesian Front inherited a legacy of unrest. Indeed, it faced an undeclared war, but one that it would have to take seriously only in the late Sixties. Furthermore, the Front began to govern in the atmosphere of the final collapse of the Federation in 1963, with all that that entailed for public morale, the economy, the redundancy of civil servants and much more. The northern territories were moving rapidly to independence, and it seemed logical that Southern Rhodesia, being the most experienced in self–government, should do likewise. The Front took up the question at once with Butler, arguing that the 1961 Constitution with minor adjustments would serve as a basis for independence because it did not bar eventual African domination.

The securing of independence became the main objective of the Rhodesian Front, but the British government could not contemplate giving a territory independence on any other basis than adult suffrage. Yet they kept holding out the hope that something slightly less than majority rule would suffice, though they would never give Field precise conditions for independence. The truth was that they regarded white rule, whatever its value, as an anachronism in the brave new days of independent Africa and they would not risk offending the Afro-Asian members of the Commonwealth and the United Nations by sustaining it.

Field's demands for independence were evaded, and his image abroad was tarnished by his severe reaction to the unrest at home. Mandatory death sentences for petrol-bombing were introduced and security was improved. It was further improved in August 1963, when the African nationalists split, Sithole becoming the leader of a radical faction called the Zimbabwe African National Union (ZANU), leaving Nkomo with the rump, which he called the People's Caretaker Council until it too was banned and ZAPU was resuscitated outside the country. The split was important for the future of the country because it resulted in the dispatch of young men for guerrilla training in China, with Mugabe's future security minister, Emmerson Mnangagwa, leading the first lot.

The trouble in the townships would simmer on, but the new government sought to secure the rural areas by building on Whitehead's policy of improving the image of the tribal leaders and giving more responsibility to local rural councils. Care was also taken to develop the rural infrastrucure.

After the fate of the Federation was sealed by the decision in March to allow Northern Rhodesia to secede, Field and Welensky threatened to stay away from the dissolution conference unless Southern Rhodesia was given independence on the basis of the 1961 Constitution immediately. Butler stalled Field, and his seeming intransigence convinced Field that Southern Rhodesia could lose her fair share of Federal assets by his action. In fact Butler knew that the conference could not be held without Southern Rhodesia. Field accepted a vague assurance from Butler that something would be done for Southern Rhodesia and went to the conference. A chance was lost that might have forced the British hand.

After that no progress was made on the matter of independence. A British general election was due in 1964 and Macmillan's replacement as Prime Minister, Sir Alec Douglas-Home, was reluctant to take a decision that might break the Commonwealth. The Rhodesians were frustrated, and the prospect of the return of a Labour government did nothing to encourage them. Indeed, Harold Wilson, the new leader of the Labour Party, had assured Nkomo in March 1963 that when the Labour Party came to power it would ignore the convention and force a new constitution on Southern Rhodesia. Threats of unilateral action on independence began to be muttered. Indeed, Welensky, on his last visit to London as Prime Minister, warned Sandys that the Front would declare independence unilaterally.

In fact, despite the few alternatives open to it in 1963/4, the Rhodesian Front government regarded such a declaration as a last and least desirable action. Indeed, Field was to resign because he could not contemplate it. It was not, however, a new idea. In 1956 Huggins had threatened it when the British refused the Federation dominion status. The Dominion Party proposed it regularly, while the British Labour Party and its press speculated about it at intervals, half expecting it if they were returned to power. In October 1958, after a comment by the Dominion Party, Welensky had dismissed it as impracticable because it would be resisted by force of arms by the Colonial Police in Northern Rhodesia and Nyasaland. Yet, because he had wind of future British intentions, he had the feasibility of a Federal UDI examined seriously. He was advised that it was not worth doing because of the ramifications of its illegality in international and domestic law, its effect on the economy, on markets, on Commonwealth preference and much more, including providing the blacks with a justification for a rising. Six months later, in early 1959, when the Nyasaland emergency was at its height, both Welensky and Field threatened a UDI, and would do so again in 1960, when the Colonial Secretary, Iain Macleod, risked the stability of the Federation by concessions to Banda. In February 1961 Macleod so feared a Federal UDI, in reaction to his plans for majority rule in Northern Rhodesia, that he induced the British defence chiefs to begin to move troops. A terse word within the British Cabinet from Julian Amery avoided a confrontation, but not before the Royal Rhodesian Air Force had flown a photographic reconnaissance of Nairobi that confirmed British intentions. In May 1961 a senior Federal civil servant suggested a coup d'état to thwart the British plans for Northern Rhodesia; and, when the violence was at its height in Katanga and Northern Rhodesia was in crisis, Welensky hinted at a break with Britain. He repeated it in private, quite seriously, when Duncan Sandys indicated that secession would be granted to Banda. In January 1963 Butler arrived in Salisbury, asking Field if Welensky would take unconstitutional action. Welensky would not, but some of his ministers suggested it soon afterwards. Welensky, of course, had been handicapped by the disparate nature of the Federation, its huge area, rampant African nationalism, the paucity of his forces and the prospect that the British colonial civil servants in the north would resist and, in any case, would have to be replaced. The Rhodesian Front government had few of those problems and had won the allegiance of their civil servants and their servicemen.

The lack of progress on independence, despite a visit by Field to London, brought Ian Smith to power in April 1964. His opponents presumed that unilateral action was now intended. His advent was greeted with riots in the African townships over the almost immediate detention of Nkomo and others. The security position was worrying, with the first of the terror killings, the murder in the Eastern Districts of P.J.A. Oberholzer, who had the misfortune to be ambushed in July.

The political uncertainty made a settlement imperative. Smith continued the negotiations with the Conservative government, but they insisted on the need to satisfy the Commonwealth. Indeed, they refused what was by now presumed to be the right of Southern Rhodesia to attend the Commonwealth Conference that year. Locally and internationally this was seen as a slap in the face and made UDI more likely. Smith's acid response drew a stiff British warning about the consequences of a UDI. Whitehead concluded that it was the moment for a political come-back. Belief that UDI would be taken also brought Welensky out of retirement to fight a bitter by-election against it in October. At the Commonwealth Conference President Kenyatta insisted that the essential condition for Rhodesian independence must be majority rule. He demanded the release of the detainees and a constitutional conference. Douglas-Home, who had begun by declaring that Britain could not intervene, capitulated and agreed. The members of the Commonwealth also vowed never to recognise a Rhodesian UDI. In July, in fact, Smith denied that UDI was his intention, and he repeated that when he met Douglas-Home in September. Again there was no progress, except that Douglas-Home said he would accept the 1961 Constitution as a formula for independence if Smith could prove that the majority of the inhabitants of Rhodesia were in favour of it.

Smith returned home, announced a referendum and in haste convened an *indaba* of tribal chiefs and headmen. The Rhodesian government argued that, since eight out of ten Africans lived in the tribal areas and since the membership of the African nationalist parties was concentrated in the towns, the chiefs represented tribal opinion. On 14 October, the eve of the British poll, Smith invited the British government to send observers. The Conservatives disliked the idea of the *indaba* and refused. It was a very reactionary idea in days when African nationalists in the Commonwealth could demand what they liked. On 15 October Harold Wilson was returned and his Colonial Secretary, Arthur Bottomley, concurred with the Conservative decision.

Smith held the *indaba* and his referendum, both of which confirmed his proposals on independence. They mattered not. Wilson and Bottomley would not, and perhaps (given their narrow majority in the Commons) could not, allow the perpetuation of white rule. In any case, Wilson took fright immediately and issued a stiff warning on the consequences of unilateral action, thereby arousing the hostility of the Rhodesian government. Deadlock ensued until early 1965, when negotiations were re-opened half-heartedly. The British were startled when Smith held an election that gave him what he asked for, a two-thirds majority. In fact he captured all fifty of the "A" roll seats. Wilson did not, and indeed could not if he wished the Commonwealth to survive, invite Smith to the Prime Ministers' meeting that year. The subject of Rhodesia dominated the meeting, which pressed for unimpeded progress to majority rule. Afterwards Bottomley laid down the five principles[5] upon which all negotiations would thenceforward be based. Everything depended on the interpretation of the principles. The fifth, for example, ordained that any settlement had to be acceptable to the population as a whole, but Wilson would not countenance another *indaba*, while Smith would not allow a referendum because that would concede "one man–one vote". The parties were farther apart than they had been when Field had begun negotiating in 1963.

In October 1965 Smith visited London, but at once realised that Wilson would concede nothing. At a loss to know what to do, Wilson thought only of referring the matter to a commission of Commonwealth leaders and then to a Royal Commission, but the Rhodesians remembered the perfidy of the Monckton Commission and rejected it. Preparations had been laid for UDI in the sense that reliable personnel had been placed in key positions, the loyalty of the forces had been assessed and a state of emergency declared. The decision itself was taken reluctantly and late in the day. On 11 November 1965 Smith proclaimed the independence of Rhodesia.

Britain reacted with anger to this first rebellion by a British territory since the American revolution. But the use of force, despite vociferous demands from the Africans, was not contemplated. Wilson dared not risk it with his small majority and the possibility that his forces would not fight. Smith knew that force would not be used because his High Commissioner in London, Brigadier Andrew Skeen, as a former British soldier, had sounded out old colleagues in the British army. Wilson chose to apply the sanctions that he had long threatened if UDI were declared, and he backed them by deploying two carrier task forces to cut off the Rhodesian supply of oil. Wilson lengthened the odds by taking the problem to the United Nations to secure world cooperation through selective mandatory sanctions in 1966 and by making them total in 1968. On the surface the world cooperated, but underneath its trade continued through false bills of lading, barter and other means. The economy was tightly managed by the Reserve Bank of Rhodesia and the relevant government departments. Tobacco-growing continued, often subsidised, but the farmers diversified and fed the growing population. Where goods were expensive to import, or unobtainable, local substitutes were made or grown, the wine industry being a good example. Rhodesia had abundant coal but no oil. Petrol supplies were eked out by mixing in ethanol derived from sugar. Rifle and other ammunition was not manufactured, but aircraft bombs soon were. Small arms began to be made, though most weapons had to be bought from abroad or captured. Fuel, arms and ammunition constituted the Rhodesian Achilles' heel and would be exploited when the Prime Minister of South Africa, John Vorster, wanted his way.

Rhodesia suffered periodic oil shortages but survived. Otherwise sanctions were largely evaded, and with determined effort she even managed to keep air force jet aircraft flying, a crucial asset when the war intensified. The effect of sanctions was naturally cushioned by the cooperation of Rhodesia's neighbours, Portuguese-ruled Mozambique and South Africa. Neither recognised Rhodesia but both kept her routes open to the sea, and, in the case of South Africa, supplied many of her wants and later provided her with help to keep her armies in the field. The Rhodesian economy even grew, partly because of the need for self-sufficiency. In the Seventies, however, crippling drought, world depression, high oil prices, the cost of war and then the loss of Mozambique as an ally in 1975, imposed severe strains, never severe enough, nonetheless, to force a surrender.

Just as Field in 1963 faced the two problems of settling the independence question and counteracting the violence of the African nationalists, so did Smith in 1965/6. The declaration of independence, while it may have satisfied his followers, and it certainly welded the white community together, was not acceptable in international law until Britain sanctioned it. Britain did not wish to and would not risk the Commonwealth for Rhodesia or her standing with the United Nations, for that matter. In the end the Rhodesians had to secure a British blessing for a formula for independence. The war was fought with that clear knowledge. Even if African nationalism could have been beaten into submission, the question of recognition would have remained. The political solution was always paramount.

The Rhodesians might have thumbed their noses at the rest of the world, but contacts with London were resumed almost immediately to resolve the independence problem. They culminated in talks on board the cruiser HMS *Tiger* in early December 1966. A development of the 1961 Constitution with a senate added and designed to bring more Africans into the house was discussed. The British insisted that a quarter of the membership must consist of elected Africans to block effectively any undesirable amendments. The test of acceptability of the plan was to be by an assessment by a Royal Commission, and appeals could be made ultimately to the British Privy Council. A broad-based cabinet was to be chosen by the Governor in which the Front would maintain a majority. The Governor was to have full legislative powers while Rhodesia returned to legality. He would be the commander-in-chief and could, if necessary, call upon British military assistance. The Rhodesian Cabinet, in the event, were not prepared to risk giving the Governor such a free hand and thought that the right of appeal to the Privy Council seemed to deny full independence. The settlement was rejected. There is a point that most commentators forget, which is that it would not have satisfied black aspirations and the war would still have been fought. Legitimacy would have made it easier to fight but, as with all wars, there would have had to be a surrender or a settlement ultimately.

Relations with Britain deteriorated. Wilson opted for tougher sanctions and the Rhodesians fought small incursions of insurgents from Zambia. The legality of decisions of the courts brought confrontation with the estranged Governor, Sir Humphrey Gibbs, but contacts on the settlement question were maintained and, indeed, the effort to settle was sustained until the end in 1979. Formal talks were held on board HMS _Fearless_ in 1968, but they were fruitless, with referral to the Privy Council seeming to be a sticking point. The Rhodesians by then were considering a new constitution after the report of the Whaley Commission recommending racial parity as the goal rather than racial domination. In 1969 Smith brought in a new constitution and had it overwhelmingly confirmed in a referendum along with the idea of becoming a republic. The new constitution allowed all races other than African to elect fifty members of a House of Assembly while the Africans could elect eight members directly and another eight through their chiefs and councillors. There was a Senate consisting of ten chiefs, ten Europeans elected by the House of Assembly and three members nominated by the Head of State. The number of African seats could increase to fifty, but never more, when the African contribution to income tax equalled that of the other races.

A republic was proclaimed in 1970, and the return of the Conservatives in Britain under Edward Heath brought back Sir Alec Douglas-Home to the Rhodesian problem. Negotiations were renewed, secretly at first, leading to the signing of an agreement with Smith in November 1971. There would be no broad-based interim government, no appeal to the Privy Council. The Constitution was adjusted so that the Africans could eventually dominate. The number of seats remained the same, but a mechanism was introduced to allow the number of African-elected seats to increase as the number of registered voters grew. The Senate was unaltered, but the power to amend was inhibited. With the settlement came guarantees of lifting the emergency in force since 1965, the release of detainees, land reform and offers of British aid and training. The settlement was welcomed. Smith was mobbed by excited blacks. Garfield Todd expressed approval. The acceptability of the settlement was to be tested by a Royal Commission under Lord Pearce, and if it had begun its work immediately and completed it speedily, there would have been some hope of success. Rhodesia would have been legitimate but still facing the African nationalists. Instead, while the volume of protest grew both abroad and locally, the British allowed Pearce and his commissioners Christmas at home. They chose men with experience of Africa to do the work on the ground, but many were from the Colonial Service that had been so hostile to Southern Rhodesia during the days of the Federation. Before the Commission finally began work in January 1972, the African National Council had been formed, with a strong core of nationalists led by Bishop Abel Muzorewa. With the aid of university students and school pupils on their long summer vacation, the ANC waged a commendably effective campaign to ensure that those whom the Commission consulted rejected the settlement. Having heard the opinions of less than six per cent, the Commission concluded that African opinion rejected the settlement while the Europeans accepted it.

After this rejection came an intensification of the war as the forces of ZANU in particular sought to secure a foothold among the tribesmen in the north-east at least. Since the incursions in the late 1960s the Rhodesian forces had been reinforced by the equivalent of a battalion of South African police used as infantry. The counter-insurgency effort was, in theory at least, led by the Rhodesian police – the British South Africa Police – who deployed small anti-terrorist units (PATU); the Para-military Support Unit, which was to increase to battalion strength; and the police reserve, which began by reinforcing policemen at work and ended doing all manner of military tasks. The army itself had a regular white battalion, the Rhodesian Light Infantry (RLI) (at full strength through the inclusion of young men doing their national service); a black battalion, the Rhodesian African Rifles (RAR) which had a fifth company; white national service independent infantry companies amounting to a battalion; a small specialist reconnaissance unit, the Special Air Services (SAS) and eight battalions of territorials and reservists of the Rhodesia Regiment with varying commitments according to age. Asians and coloureds were drafted into a transport unit and later into a defence regiment with whites. There were units of engineers, signals, armour, artillery and the like. The latter would expand out of necessity as the demand for their services grew and they would draw their manpower from the territorial and reserve battalions as well as recruiting young blacks. A successful mounted infantry regiment, the Grey Scouts, would also be formed. An intelligence corps, a psychological warfare unit and the formidable special warfare unit, the Selous Scouts, all drew on the pool of white manpower. The Selous Scouts were nonetheless mostly black regulars. When the example of Malaya was followed and the tribesmen were moved into protected villages, a separate defence unit, the Guard Force, required whites as well as blacks. The police force had been a totally regular force, but in the Seventies it too began to employ national service officers and, of course, so did the Rhodesian Air Force. The white part-time soldiers were deployed by the company rather than the battalion, but this did not mitigate the disruption of their lives. This, plus boredom, discomfort, some danger and above all the lack of a certain political future, swelled the ranks of the young whites who emigrated. By 1979 the dispersion of their manpower meant that some reserve infantry companies could muster fewer than thirty whites. Their performance in the field was still in general effective, and never having been defeated in the field, their morale remained high. The Rhodesian forces believed themselves to be an élite force, and perhaps they were. But it is worth remembering that 80 per cent of their manpower was black.

Although 20 000 or 30 000 people would die in the bush-war, life in Rhodesia for the whites was never made totally unbearable. There was no war in the towns, where good police intelligence hampered the African nationalists. The war had by no means run its full course when the political settlement was achieved in 1979. The rural whites faced danger, and many were killed; but at the end of the war there were still 6 000 white farmers on the land. It would have been easy enough to drive them off it. They were vulnerable every time they left the homestead. Their enemies, however, usually ran at the sound of gunfire. But that is what the guerrilla was expected to do. To stand and fight lost the advantage and cost lives unnecessarily.

The military wing of ZANU, the Zimbabwe African National Liberation Army (Zanla), concentrated on indoctrinating the population and on recruiting. For a long time they had to rely on abduction. Later, the increasing tempo of the war alienated young people, and the insurgents gained more willing recruits who would go for training or serve locally as *mujibas* – look-outs and runners. Zanla and the ZAPU's Zimbabwe People's Revolutionary Army (ZPRA) built up their system of contact men and attempted to build their political base among the masses, which they did without notable success and to persuade or intimidate them to provide safe havens, services, food and other supplies. Their lack of success was illustrated when the tribesmen ignored their direct orders to the contrary and turned out in hundreds of thousands to vote for Bishop Muzorewa in April 1979. A sure sign of the insurgents' sense of insecurity was an increase in murders of tribesmen. It was also done to put into effect the first phase of Mugabe's revolution. A cynic was to say in 1980, when Mugabe emerged the victor at the election, that Mugabe had not won the war, he had just intimidated his voters for the past ten years.

The military response to the insurgency was profoundly affected by the coup in Portugal in April 1974, because it gave Zanla the whole of Mozambique as a safe haven. The Rhodesian government made the mistake in the first phase of the war, 1966-1972, of putting the forces on a care-and-maintenance basis, and in the process it failed to provide additional black infantry battalions. By 1979 there were only three, and the last one had barely been formed. There were always more black recruits than places in the ranks, and the additional battalions could have mitigated the effect of the call-up on white morale. These battalions would have needed white officers, and there was much unused leadership potential in the white units.

The government also failed to relate their political objectives to the operational and strategical needs of the military. There never was enough effort put into the gathering and correct interpretation of intelligence, which is of prime importance in counter-insurgency warfare, and insufficient attention was paid to its results. The government did not intrude into the military sphere, as Churchill did, and promote on talent. The Joint Operations Command (JOC) system was successfully instituted at district level early in the war on the ground. Later Combined Operations Headquarters was set up under General Walls, but the policy remained one of reaction, and not much coherent military strategy was devised. Perhaps that was impossible as long as the political objective remained so elusive.

Rhodesians had fought in Malaya, but the conflict facing them was very different, so that solutions such as the protected village programme, designed to cut the insurgents off from their supplies of food and comfort, was never as great a success as it had been in Malaya, where a minority had tried to influence a majority of a different race. Expensive mistakes were made, such as attempts to mine the borders to cut down freedom of access. The minefields simply did not work and were not worth the effort to lay and maintain. The proliferation of units was not prevented, with consequent dispersal of scarce resources and trained skills. When the political effort produced the internal settlement of March 1978, units of auxiliaries were formed, ostensibly from converted Zanla and ZPRA fighters, and deployed. They could have denied the bush to the insurgents by living among the tribesmen and using the same tactics. However, few had ever fought, and most were drawn from an urban riff-raff. Poor discipline and lack of imagination in their deployment robbed them of effectiveness.

The Rhodesian security forces nonetheless gained a formidable reputation. They quickly mastered tactics appropriate to their terrain and their opponents. The threat of the anti-vehicle landmine was neutralised by inventive adaptation of vehicles to reduce the severity of the blast. A unique mine-sweeping vehicle was produced which further reduced the threat. The use of pseudo-gangs, a network of observation posts and, above all, the development of the concept of "fire force" reaped an impressive, if grim harvest. The operational demands on the forces were excessive. Paratroopers found themselves making three operational jumps a day – something that no other such troops had ever done. One- and two-man missions deep into neighbouring countries were not infrequent. When external camps were attacked, the shortage of suitable aircraft, pilots and trained personnel often meant that the attacking force, in the early stage at least, would have equalled a reinforced platoon in another army. Internally the fire force units – three were usually the most deployed – comprised a locally-adapted Alouette III helicopter with a 20mm cannon and carrying a ground commander, three Alouettes carrying "sticks" of four infantrymen each, and, later, a Dakota with up to 18 parachutists. Often the fire force was reinforced with ground-attack aircraft, usually the Lynx (the Cessna 337G) and sometimes the Hawker Hunter or the English Electric Canberra. When summoned to a sighting of an insurgent group, the gun-armed helicopter, or "K-Car", would orbit and put down fire while its ground commander ordered the other helicopters to place their sticks in "stop" positions. The paratroopers would then jump and sweep the area. Despite the small number of troops involved, these tactics allowed the fire force units to achieve kill rates of over 80:1.

As the war intensified after 1975, the Rhodesian forces and their opponents soon reached a point where neither was likely to win. The regular forces were stretched to the limit to contain the situation and the territorial and reserve forces were needed simultaneously as soldiers to fight the war and as civilians to maintain the economy. Their enemies, Zanla and ZPRA, gained a hold over large tribal areas, but they would have been crushingly defeated if they had attempted conventional warfare, since they lacked air cover. Nkomo's ZPRA posed the greatest threat in a conventional sense, but their base was in Zambia across the Zambezi river. They lacked a bridgehead across the river and had long vulnerable lines of communication. Zanla had severe logistical problems and lacked the morale, discipline and training for positional warfare. Neither force had adequate reserves or air support.

Thus the war would be fought to a stalemate, and a political solution was always needed. In 1974/5 the South African government forced a ceasefire. They were influenced by the Pearce Report, the changes in Portugal, the evident imminent loss of Mozambique, the misreading of daily reports in Pretoria, where it was concluded that the Rhodesians were being defeated when, in fact, they had never done so well, having reduced the numbers of insurgents in the country to less than 100. John Vorster believed that he had to woo Africa, which he did secretly and with some success. Kaunda wanted to end the war, and with his cooperation an abortive meeting was held in August 1975 at the Victoria Falls – in a coach on the bridge over the Zambezi river. The meeting ended in deadlock when the African nationalists reneged on an agreement signed on their behalf by the Zambian government.

Undeterred, Vorster kept up the pressure on Smith. He withdrew his police, and then in protest against Rhodesian incursions into Mozambique he recalled vitally-needed helicopter crews, though not their aircraft. By then the American government, at the behest of the British, had decided to take a hand because they wished to stop the growth of the Russian and Cuban presence in southern Africa but they had been forced by the US Congress to end their clandestine intercession in Angola. Henry Kissinger, President Ford's Secretary of State, met Smith in Pretoria in September 1976. A pressing reason for Smith's cooperation was that Vorster had cut off his fuel and ammunition. The official reason was congestion on the railways as a consequence of Machel's closing of the borders, but the congestion miraculously cleared when Smith made his *volte face* of 24 September and publicly announced that he would accept black majority rule, after two years of interim government. A conference at Geneva followed to settle the interim arrangements, but Mugabe, who had been released from detention during the ceasefire and had recently ousted the Reverend Sithole from the leadership of ZANU, would not accept the plan agreed with Kissinger, to which Smith rigidly adhered. Mugabe wanted power and he believed he could get it through sustained violence.

The Anglo-American initiative was taken up by the new secretaries of state, Cyrus Vance of the Carter Administration and David Owen of the British Labour government. Their plans came to nought despite a sustained campaign and many hours flown. Smith turned his back on them and arrived at a settlement on 3 March 1978 with Bishop Abel Muzorewa, and Reverend Ndabaningi Sithole, and with a tribal leader, Chief Chirau. Muzorewa had enjoyed checkered fortunes since the Pearce Commission, but he had managed to remain head of the ANC (renamed the United African National Council or UANC). Sithole now led the rump of ZANU. An interim government was formed with an executive council and a chairmanship that rotated among Smith and the others. Joint ministers were appointed to give the blacks not only a share of power but also some experience of it. A constitution was negotiated that proposed a House of Assembly of 100 with 28 seats reserved for whites for ten years to allow them to block amendments to entrenched provisions. There would be universal suffrage, using a party list system, but the white MPs would be elected by standing for twenty constituencies with the remaining eight being elected by the white section of the outgoing parliament. After ten years, or the second general election, a commission would sit to consider what was to be done with the white seats. A Senate would hold ten blacks elected by the black MPs, ten whites elected by the white MPs and ten chiefs. There was to be a justiciable bill of rights, and a compromise name was given to the country of "Zimbabwe-Rhodesia". The Rhodesian electorate, in a referendum on 30 January 1979, overwhelmingly accepted the new constitution, and in February the Rhodesian Parliament passed it into law. At the same time all racial discrimination was abolished except for the reservation of the tribal areas.

A ceasefire was agreed – but largely ignored – and detentions were lifted, likewise bans on parties, ZANU and ZAPU included. Smith had some communication with Nkomo, but the shooting down of a Viscount airliner in September by ZPRA put an end to that, and soon ZAPU and ZANU were proscribed again. They were free to take part in the forthcoming election if they accepted the ceasefire and abandoned violence. True to form, they would not compromise. After the Viscount, Nkomo could not. He was beyond the pale. The British attitude, however, was that ZANU and ZAPU had to be part of any settlement. The Rhodesian view was that given the support of the electorate and international recognition, a moderate black government could not only survive but defeat the extremists. The British Conservative Party was inclined to support the internal settlement, and indeed promised to do so, but their new leader, Margaret Thatcher, decided that it would be better to include ZANU and ZAPU. The view of the British Foreign Office was that it was absolutely essential that this should happen, and in the end it was the view that prevailed.

When the new constitution was unveiled in January 1979, James Çallaghan, the British Prime Minister, dismissed it as unlikely to produce the peace that everyone sought. Callaghan wanted a wider settlement and elections supervised by the UN. The UN Security Council, in March, went further and declared the elections null and void before they had even been held. The world was conditioning itself against the return of Muzorewa. When the Conservatives called on 15 March 1979 for observers to be sent to the Rhodesian election, Callaghan argued earnestly that such a move would be "totally misunderstood" in the rest of Africa. A parallel attempt to send observers was made in the United States Congress, but it was blocked in the House of Assembly. The Anglo–American governments urged instead that Zimbabwe-Rhodesia should accept their solution. In the end the British Conservative Party sent a team of observers led by Lord Boyd, the former Colonial Secretary, and it was joined by a variety of private observers from America, West Germany and elsewhere.

With the exception of Lord Chitnis, who changed his mind once he left Rhodesia and perhaps sensed what would happen, Boyd's observers found the election, held over 17-20 April, to be as free and fair as was possible in the circumstances. Ignoring the threats of the insurgents, 63,9 per cent of the estimated electorate of 2 900 000 adults returned Muzorewa's UANC. It won fifty-one seats, Sithole's ZANU gained twelve and a third party, the United National Freedom Party, nine. In the white election the Rhodesian Front swept the board. Muzorewa combined with it to form the Government of National Unity. Electoral disputes between Sithole and a dissident group led by James Chikerema, however, marred the image of national unity.

The guerrillas were stunned by the degree to which the tribesmen had defied them. The Rhodesian security forces mobilised every man they could muster to protect the election and to eradicate the threat to it. Two hundred and thirty insurgents were killed in the three days of the election and 650 in the month of April. The insurgents either went to ground or surrendered. The Zanla commanders left the country for orders, and for six weeks their men did nothing. The war virtually stopped.

If, after being elected in May, Margaret Thatcher had stuck to her party's promise in its election manifesto and recognised Muzorewa's election as having fulfilled the six principles and then supported him, as she supported Mugabe in 1980, history might have been very different. With popular support at home and legitimacy in international law, a government led by Muzorewa might have defeated Mugabe and Nkomo. But Thatcher changed her mind, the murders in the tribal areas increased as the insurgents sought to reassert their influence, and the morale of the security forces and the public sank. Across the borders Mugabe and Nkomo tried to unite their bitterly divided forces and parties into what they would call the Patriotic Front (PF). The first sign that Thatcher would hesitate was in her rejection of Francis Pym as Foreign Secretary and the appointment of Lord Carrington, whose approach to Rhodesia was one of expediency not principle. Carrington was later to earn dismissal for such a policy over the Falklands, and there has been speculation that Thatcher's reaction then was a result of her experience of allowing her Foreign Office to call the tune over Zimbabwe.

While the Zimbabwe-Rhodesians waited, the pressures on Thatcher increased. The Foreign Office did not want Britain to have to prop up Muzorewa, whom the world saw, wrongly, as a puppet of Smith, and be drawn into an interminable war. The United Nations, as might be expected, had repeated their rejection of the election and much of the Commonwealth, the secretariat and members did likewise, with Malcolm Fraser of Australia enjoying brief prominence in the van of protest. Thatcher was new to the premiership, but it must be said that she was, as she has demonstrated, quite capable of making up her own mind. Nigeria exploited the disarray to nationalise British Petroleum and General Obasanjo, the head of state, would combine with Malcolm Fraser to attempt to force Thatcher's hand at the Commonwealth Conference to be held in August.

On 22 May 1979, Margaret Thatcher reminded the Commons that the final responsibility for returning Zimbabwe-Rhodesia to legality still rested with the British Parliament. She said that if the fifth of the six principles (that the Constitution had been approved by the people of Rhodesia as a whole) had been honoured it would be "our duty to bring Rhodesia back to legality". Zimbabwe-Rhodesian hopes were raised. But Lord Carrington sent Lord Harlech on a tour of Africa, and he reported the totality of the opposition, while Nyerere gave public warning that recognition by Britain would be tantamount to a declaration of war on the nationalists and their host countries. President Carter then decided, in June, not to recognise Zimbabwe-Rhodesia, and he resisted pressure to lift sanctions. The Frontline States also gave a warning of the damage that Britain would do to her relations with them. Thatcher knew, and said as much on a visit to Australia, that her party would not renew sanctions when they came up for review in November. It looked as if she would do what the Rhodesians wanted. Then she showed her hand through Lord Carrington, who said in a debate in the Lords on 10 July that the British government would soon reveal proposals to bring Rhodesia to legal independence on a basis acceptable to its people and to everybody else. Muzorewa's opportunity was lost. His people wanted peace, and without world recognition he could not secure it. When they voted again, they rejected him.

When the Commonwealth met in Lusaka in August, Thatcher faced the curious threat of seeing Britain expelled from the organisation and turned her back finally on the promise to recognise Muzorewa. She had dealt a fatal blow to the moderate cause in Zimbabwe-Rhodesia. The Commonwealth then blessed the British plan for a constitutional conference. Smith, perhaps, would have defied the British and rejected their invitation to the conference at Lancaster House in September. The timing of the conference ill suited the offensive planned by his forces, but Muzorewa, confident of his popularity, agreed to go.

By that time Mugabe and Nkomo had entered a marriage of convenience for the purposes of the conference and to overthrow Muzorewa. Their unity had long been pressed on them by the OAU and the suppliers of aid. Yet their armies, Zanla and ZPRA, would not train together and when they met in the field, they fought bitterly. Their strategies also differed markedly.

Nkomo's ZAPU and ZPRA contained Shonas in their leadership, but the fighters were either Ndebele or from associated tribes living in Matabeleland. The movement therefore had an ethnic element linked to the Ndebele warrior tradition. Overestimating the popular appeal of Nkomo, the Soviet Union chose to back ZPRA with arms and instruction. Ideological training was given, but it imparted no more than a veneer of Marxism. This was recognised by the Rhodesian government which, until the Viscount was shot down in 1978, several times came near to settling with Nkomo. The strategy of ZPRA was to leave Zanla to fight the war and to intervene at a decisive moment with a well-trained conventional army. This plan was recognised by the Rhodesians and by Zanla. ZPRA deployed 3 000 men in Rhodesia as a vanguard preparing the way for the conventional army. Zanla responded with an offensive into Matabeleland, which ZPRA countered by penetrating the tribal areas in north–west Mashonaland. ZPRA was confident that it would be able to recover any ground lost in Matabeleland when the time was ripe. Nkomo, despite the split of 1963, also hoped to dominate the partnership with Mugabe. However, the Rhodesian security forces, using their air power and paratroopers to advantage in raids across the Zambezi in 1979, destroyed the ZPRA munitions and stores and by blowing bridges limited its ability to move and deploy.

Nkomo's ZAPU kept its military wing firmly under control, in contrast with Mugabe's ZANU. Yet although Mugabe's political and military wings had little contact, they both adhered to a common strategy, which had the firm objective of securing political control of the Shona tribes. Taking terrible punishment from fire force, Zanla persisted in this effort. As the war intensified so the civil administration suffered and Zanla profited, even attempting to replace it with its own administration. As it did this, the political wing, ZANU, bent its entire effort to securing external support. It did not receive support from the Soviet Union, even though Samora Machel, who played host to ZANU, did. Zanla's arms supply came in through indirect routes from the Eastern bloc countries and from Pakistan. Gradually, the Zanla supply network was bound in with that of the FPLM in Mozambique, which complicated the Rhodesians' task when attacking it. Mozambique supplied transit camps that harboured insurgents briefly before they were sent into Rhodesia. The recruits from Rhodesia were sent to Tanzania, Libya and Ethiopia for training. The strength of Zanla inside Rhodesia in 1979 was about 10 000 trained men.

In answer to these strategies, the Rhodesians in 1978 adopted the concept of protecting what was called "vital asset ground", which contained economic assets such as mines, fuel dumps, factories, key farming areas, bridges, railways and the like. The second principle was to prevent Zanla from using the "ground of tactical importance " (in other words the tribal lands) as a base from which to carry out attacks on crucial assets. It was into these areas that auxiliaries were intended to be deployed in large numbers to help to re-establish the civil administration and to destroy the links between the insurgents and their political supporters. They would deny the ground to Zanla. At the same time the Rhodesian security forces would use their crucial strategic mobility in fire force and high-density troop operations against the troublesome areas infested by Zanla. In addition, the security forces would prevent many incursions by means of border control wherever it could be effected, for example on Lake Kariba. Finally, the forces would raid neighbouring countries, particularly Mozambique and Zambia, to disrupt the Zanla and ZPRA command and control, to destroy base facilities, ammunition and food supplies, to harass the reinforcements, and to hamper movement by aerial bombardment, mining and ambushing of routes.

To complement this effort, the politicians were expected to present a united front to the world, for it was crucial to gain international recognition; but that the politicians failed to achieve, along with the raising of sanctions. The Rhodesian strategy lacked flexibility. The security forces strove to contain the situation in the expectation of a political solution. The military strategy was not closely related to the political effort. In 1979 the politicians were divided, and that was exploited by the Patriotic Front, who pretended and appeared to be united by contrast. Everything had been wagered on international recognition and the ending of sanctions. Everything had been staked on the British Conservative Party keeping its promise on recognition. And, let me repeat, such recognition would have been a hammer blow to Zanla when its morale was shattered by the tribesmen ignoring its boast that the election would not take place. Once the British had committed themselves to a conference, Muzorewa's government had few political options left and it was necessary to improve its position by military means. It could have used the strategic mobility of the security forces to exploit the situation in the neighbouring countries. Perhaps because of British persuasion, that did not happen.

In Zambia President Kaunda acted as host to some 25 000 fighting men from ZPRA, Swapo and the South African ANC. His army was outnumbered, and these foreign armies threatened the political stability of Zambia. The conventionally-trained ZPRA army was growing in size but could not be moved out of Zambia because the Rhodesian forces had sunk the ferry across the Zambezi at Kazangula and destroyed boats along the river and in Lake Kariba. They held, of course, the two bridges at the Victoria Falls and at Chirundu. Then later in 1979 they made a coordinated attack on the secondary bridges in southern Zambia. They ignored the bridges over the Zambezi but cut the Zambian railway line to Tanganyika. That put Kaunda at Muzorewa's mercy, because his only lines of communication ran through Rhodesia. To succeed in an invasion of Rhodesia, ZPRA had to establish the bridgehead across the Zambezi. They also needed air support to allow their armour and infantry to survive and to keep their supply line open. Nkomo was having pilots trained, but Kaunda knew that their appearance would lead to the destruction of his airfields. Zambia was truly a front-line state, right in the firing line.

In Mozambique by mid-1979 Frelimo was totally committed to supporting Zanla. Zanla used FPLM supply lines, while FPLM sent 300 men into Rhodesia to support Zanla. The storing of Zanla arms caused the Rhodesians to stop attacking the transit camps, as they had done since 1976 with deadly effect, and switch to air attacks on Frelimo armouries. The success of this effort forced Frelimo to move their bulk stocks back to the coast out of reach, knowing that even the Rhodesians would hesitate to bomb Maputo. Mozambique, fearful of South African intervention, had to put up with a constant Rhodesian presence in its provinces. The Rhodesians mined the roads in Mozambique to slow up the resupply of the Zanla forces and thereby caused numerous civilian casualties. By that means they forced Zanla to curtail their operations inside Rhodesia because of the difficulties of bringing in reinforcements and obtaining ammunition, weapons and supplies. The Rhodesian effort, however, failed to deter FPLM from supporting and reinforcing Zanla.

In September 1979, however, when the conference at Lancaster House was sitting, the Rhodesian forces enjoyed a change of fortune in the course of a reaction to a threat to the Rhodesian lifeline to South Africa, the railway from Rutenga to Beit Bridge. The Rhodesians feared that a large concentration of FPLM forces at Mapai just south of the southern border of Rhodesia would be used to help Zanla to seize ground that would be declared a "liberated zone ". The Rhodesian raiders cut five major bridges deep in Mozambique, including the rail bridge across the Limpopo river at Barragem. The main FPLM bases were also attacked from the air. The success of the raid, at the cost of some casualties, was that it shook FPLM on to the defensive, severely damaged their communications and supplies, and prevented Zanla from consolidating their hold on the tribal areas on the border. The object was not to damage the Mozambican economy, but that was how the raid was depicted by Frelimo and Western commentators, who alleged that it not only delayed the movement of war material forward, but also cut the main food-growing area off from its markets. The second factor that weakened Mozambican confidence was the growing security problem within the country as the *Resistencia National de Mozambique* (RNM or Renamo) began to operate effectively in the Manica, Sofala and Tete Provinces. The RNM was, of course, greatly helped by the Rhodesians, and scored a number of successes, attacking the Revue dam, the Beira fuel farm and cutting road and rail links. The RNM also had a good deal of success in recruiting from among the ranks of FPLM.

These two pressures on Machel made him desperately keen to see a settlement in Rhodesia. Accordingly he persuaded a somewhat reluctant Mugabe to attend the Lancaster House conference. Thus the combination of political and military pressures did force his hand, but Muzorewa's government failed to put that strategy into effect in other fields. In November, *Operation Manacle* was cancelled when the troops were on the start line. If it had been carried out, it would have destroyed every important bridge in the Tete, Sofala and Manica Provinces. It would have cut the Zanla supply lines as well as further upsetting Machel. There is no doubt that it would have gravely weakened Zanla, but the political strategy was out of step and it was aborted.

The British worked hard and skilfully to divide the Zimbabwe-Rhodesian delegation and they succeeded. They isolated Ian Smith from even his white associates. General Walls found himself cast in a political role. The Zimbabwe-Rhodesian delegation had arrived at the conference in a seemingly strong position. Muzorewa, however, was anxious not to appear a puppet. He immediately revived an argument of the previous year about the number of white seats, demanding 20 instead of 28. The British encouraged this show of independence while David Smith, a veteran Rhodesian Front minister, split the Rhodesian Front and sided with Muzorewa. Generally, the Zimbabwe-Rhodesians chose to offer concessions to appear reasonable and to get the conference over quickly in order to have an early election before ZANU and ZAPU could establish their support among the electorate.

The Patriotic Front realised that they had to prolong the conference to enable their internal parties to emerge legitimately and to build up their support. Delay also was used to prevent the Rhodesian forces from gaining the strategic ascendancy. As they dallied, sure enough the programme of external raids was curtailed and eventually cancelled. Delay also allowed Zanla and ZPRA to recoup their losses. Russia intruded and began to supply ZPRA with war supplies in bulk. The strategy of delay perfectly suited the conditions and fatally weakened the position of the Zimbabwe-Rhodesian government. The Patriotic Front used the threat of withdrawal to gain concessions, but when Zambia and Mozambique insisted that they must settle, these threats sounded hollow. The Patriotic Front's gain was that it retained its freedom of action, which the Zimbabwe-Rhodesian government did not.

The British, under the forceful chairmanship of Carrington, drove through their solution. The party list system was retained. There were to be a hundred seats in the Legislative Assembly of which the whites would retain twenty for the first two elections. There was a bill of rights, a partly-elected and nominated senate, guarantees on pensions and other safeguards. Most difficult to arrange was a ceasefire, but in the end a plan for the gathering of the insurgents at assembly points and supervision of them by a British–commanded Commonwealth force was accepted. Until a government had been elected a governor, Lord Soames, was to exercise executive and legislative power. Smith predicted that the outcome would be a transference of power to Mugabe. The British and everyone else hoped he was wrong. They pinned their hopes on a divided House and a coalition that would include Muzorewa, Nkomo and Smith.

The odd thing is that the Zimbabwe–Rhodesian government accepted the ceasefire arrangement without any adequate mechanism to prevent the inevitable violations. Furthermore, the assembly-point arrangements favoured the Patriotic Front. ZPRA used the ceasefire to establish a series of heavily defended strongpoints to constitute the bridgehead for the force with which they hoped to recover the initiative from Mugabe. Zanla ignored the restraints imposed by the ceasefire. They kept a significantly large proportion of their forces outside the assembly points while sending in *mujibas* to make up the numbers expected. Zanla infiltrated 8 000 guerrillas into the eastern border area alone. They brought in large quantities of arms and ammunition and cached them near the assembly points. Inside the assembly points the *mujibas* were given intensive training. Zanla managed to re-stock with arms and ammunition and to treble the strength of its forces inside the country. The guerrillas outside the assembly points went to work on the population to ensure victory at the polls.

The plan worked. The Commonwealth forces were too weak to intervene and there was nothing that Muzorewa's government could do but protest to Soames, who arrived in early December, demanding the disqualification of Mugabe's ZANU (PF) or the declaration of the result as null and void. General Walls asked Mrs Thatcher to make such a declaration. The signs of what was going to happen were clear, even if few of Mugabe's opponents wanted to believe them. An example was the fact that neither Muzorewa's UANC nor Nkomo's PF (ZAPU) could hold meetings in the Victoria Province or in Mashonaland East. The British, however, had come so far that they were not prepared to turn back. They would pretend, for evermore perhaps, that what had happened was for the best. Mugabe's trump card was to threaten to continue the war.

When the election was held Mugabe, to his evident surprise and the dismay of his opponents, was the outright winner with 57 seats. Muzorewa was eclipsed, reduced to three seats; Sithole was eliminated, gaining none; and Nkomo only secured twenty in his traditional areas of support.

The whites were taken aback, because they had been led to believe that Muzorewa stood as good a chance as any. Furthermore, the white men, called up to protect the election, had been assured by General Walls and his senior officers that Mugabe would not be allowed to take power even if he won the election. He would be eliminated, it was hinted, in a coup. As has since been revealed, the demise of the Zanla–ZPRA command was plotted with precision and assaults on the assembly points planned and, in one case, rehearsed.

On the day when the result of the election was announced, 4 March 1980, key points were seized but the order to act never came. Whether "good sense" prevailed or doubters hesitated is not known. Officers trained in the British tradition, and of British stock, are virtually programmed against illegal action, at least by themselves. It is something that they never contemplate. The consequences, of course, are incalculable. Even if Mugabe had been eliminated, could a substitute black leader have been found? In any case, the world was hardly likely to accept him.

Instead, Soames could embrace Mugabe as the winner and the Commonwealth monitoring force could extricate itself rapidly from its exposed and dangerous position in the middle. The whites were left to vote with their feet, leaving the blacks to undergo Mugabe's application of "scientific socialism" and all that it entails.

Could the Zimbabwe-Rhodesia government have chosen some other path? Support and recognition by the West were always in doubt, but the government might have entered the last stages in a stronger bargaining position if they had adopted a total strategy[6]. The Zimbabwe-Rhodesian economy was stronger than all those of the Frontline States and Muzorewa could have exerted economic pressure on them while using his military options, such as threatening conventional war. This might have provoked outside intervention, but it might have been a risk worth taking. While the results of this pressure were awaited the auxiliaries could have been used to neutralise the insurgent forces already in the tribal areas. The external strategy could have been to contain the Zambian threat while steadily raising the odds in Mozambique so as to force Machel and Frelimo to abandon their support for ZANU and Zanla. In fact the raids into Zambia in late 1979 had cut her communications and had made her reliant on the railway from South Africa through Rhodesia. The Zambian side of the plan was therefore mostly accomplished. The situation in Mozambique lent itself to the device of direct support for the RNM to secure the central provinces while the Rhodesian forces systematically destroyed the economic assets of the other regions. Frelimo would have had to face the dilemma that military retaliation from them would have provoked a crushing response that could have triggered a successful counter-revolution or a coup at least against Machel from within the leadership. Mozambique was unlikely to get much real support from outside, and certainly not enough to save her economy. The Russians might have offered support, but Machel had seen what had happened to Angola in like circumstances and would have hesitated.

Muzorewa's Government of National Unity, regaining flexibility, would have re-opened a number of options. A separate deal with Nkomo would have been possible. The peace talks could have been stalled until the pressure on the Frontline States began to tell. Limited Western recognition might have been forthcoming to prevent a regional war. The Government of National Unity could have dictated the peace terms. Its apparent strength would have appealed to its electorate and it could have stolen the threat of the resumption of the war itself from Mugabe.

Of course, there would have been risks. The Cubans could have intervened, but that was unlikely, as they were already over-extended, and South Africa would immediately have been drawn in. Defeat of the Cubans would have provoked Soviet intervention, the success of which was far from guaranteed. The small town of Umtali (now Mutare) was exposed to retaliation, but then Beira was equally so. There were political dangers but Rhodesia had demonstrated that she could withstand international pressure. She could have continued to sponsor the RNM to keep Mozambique in line.

All this would have turned on the question of whether the white Rhodesians would have been prepared to pay a high price for their political survival and whether South Africa would have underwritten it. That is a question that historians cannot answer.

While there is little point in speculating on what might have happened, there are lessons to be learned for South Africa from the Rhodesian experience even though there are important differences in the circumstances of the two countries. Rhodesia, for example, was landlocked and therefore entirely dependent on the goodwill of Portugal and South Africa. When Portuguese help was lost through the coup of 1974 and South Africa decided that it did not need a buffer state, majority rule was forced upon Rhodesia with all that followed.

The whites in South Africa, like the Rhodesians before them, strive to retain power in the face of overwhelming black population growth. The blacks, as they did in Rhodesia, aspire to govern themselves, and frustrated by no or only slow progress have already resorted to violence. There seems little place for the moderate. Yet, in Rhodesia in 1979, it was possible that black moderation could have endured, given support from the West. That was withheld; and, as the world is still obsessed with self–determination, moderation in South Africa is equally unlikely to be encouraged from without. A unitary solution under African nationalist control would be seen widely as a just solution as it was for Rhodesia.

To thwart the aspirations of their African nationalist opponents, white South Africans have a number of assets which Rhodesia did not possess. South Africa has a powerful economy. She has a long coastline and good ports. Short of mandatory sanctions and a naval blockade, economic measures are unlikely to force a white surrender of power. And power is the prize, it must be reiterated. Sanctions spurred Rhodesia towards self–sufficiency, but she never made her own ammunition and had to import fuel, both of which made her vulnerable. South Africa is self–sufficient in almost everything and has lived with fuel and arms sanctions for years.

The possession of one's own ports is, obviously, not the entire answer to sanctions. A cooperative neighbour's port is necessary to disguise embargoed trade. As the main regional power, South Africa is in a position to ensure access to that. There are other significant differences. Rhodesia had a majority tribe (the Shona), South Africa has not; therefore a policy of divide and rule is feasible. South Africa is a sovereign independent country, which Rhodesia was not; and that is a most important difference when defying the world because, in the end, if international recognition were ever to be granted, Britain had to sanction any settlement in Rhodesia. South Africa is not obliged to depend on a foreign power constantly looking over its shoulder to its domestic and Commonwealth constituencies, allowing outsiders like Julius Nyerere virtually to dictate policy.

It needs to be repeated that the Rhodesians found that African nationalists like Robert Mugabe do not compromise, do not accept anything short of a hand-over of power, because the aim is not simply justice but control. Marxism–Leninism is likely to be adopted by any victorious African nationalist, despite the failure of totalitarian socialism worldwide, because it remains the best method for revolutionaries to secure power and to retain it.

If the low–intensity warfare being experienced in South Africa should be stepped up then, perhaps, the Rhodesian experience offers lessons to be learnt. That is not to ignore South Africa's considerable and successful conduct of counter-insurgency warfare in South West Africa. The response to an insurgency is governed by many factors, such as terrain, cross–border sanctuaries, numbers and so on. The winning and retaining of the support of the mass of the population is vital if an insurgency is to be quelled. Timely reform and coordinated military and political strategies are obviously crucial. Not only must the guerrilla fighter be eliminated but the discontent upon which he feeds must be neutralised. In Rhodesia reform came slowly and strategic coordination was wanting. Yet Muzorewa was returned in 1979 and the war in the bush was fought to a stalemate.

Rhodesia has taught us that the fundamental grievances – land, education and employment – must be addressed, and an acceptable method of at least sharing power is necessary if South Africa is not to be lost to extremism. The guerrilla fighter in Rhodesia was not always accepted by the people he lived among or else there would have been no need for a sustained campaign of terror. ZPRA, for example, managed to survive in northern Mashonaland. A key lesson of the Rhodesian experience was the need to win over the rural African or at least not to alienate him. The pace of reform is always a matter of controversy; but without reform the insurgent cannot be denied the support of the mass of people who will hide and feed him.

The lack of political initiative and the frustration of their ambitions are not the only factors in the alienation of a people. If a guerilla war has to be fought, the use of area weapons can instantly lose support by killing bystanders. Civilian casualties, mass punishments, crude interrogation or the enforced removal of people, their belongings and livestock can also serve the insurgents' cause. The fundamental ability of the old Boer fighter, the ability to kill with the first shot, is of prime importance. Guerrillas cut and run and civilian casualties rise when firing is wild. Equally, ruthlessness gains extremely shortlived rewards, as it denies the counter-insurgency forces the one commodity they cannot function without – intelligence. Rhodesians could have improved both their shooting and their collecting of information.

Guerrilla fighters are rarely defeated by military means alone, and the Rhodesian experience was no exception. It is difficult for the guerrilla fighter to win if he has no conventional forces to hold ground. Therefore the possession of potent air power proved in Rhodesia to be crucial in bringing about at least a stalemate and making the seizing of power unlikely. It was air mobility that compelled her neighbours to drive the insurgents to the conference table. South Africa possesses both these assets and will neglect them at her peril.

Rhodesia lacked skilled military manpower but made good use of what she had. She gave to the art of counter-insurgency warfare the fire force concept. Gangs found by intelligence and observation were encircled and killed. The Rhodesian experience showed that enormous forces need not be deployed if, through intelligence, the whereabouts and strength of the guerrilla forces are accurately known. The use of small sections – four men each – means that more ground can be covered. Each section must be in radio contact and have a machine-gun of the potency of the MAG. The use of pseudo-gangs, a knowledge of languages, the ability to track and the like are all vital lessons from Rhodesia.

The maintenance of the morale of the forces cannot be ignored. In a prolonged guerrilla war, the Rhodesians found their regular units, both white and black, to be prime assets. Constant call-ups of civilian forces sap public morale as much as casualties. The protection of the rural civilian is important and necessitates the use of farm guards, mine-proof vehicles and radio networks.

Tactical measures will not, however, resolve the future. The aim should have been to reform in advance of demand; and the hour is late.

## FOOTNOTES

1. The Papers of Sir Roy Welensky, 14/3,f.125f. (These papers are a closed collection and are housed in the Bodleian Library, Oxford.)

**Above:** Men and women soldiers of the MPLA on parade during the formal annexation of a base camp in northern Angola shortly after independence.

**Below:** Mozambican civilians embrace senior Portuguese officers after the coup d'état which led to the collapse of authority in all three Portuguese provinces in Africa.

A Frelimo rally in Lourenço Marques (later Maputo) at first as well patronised by whites as by blacks. Attitudes soon hardened though.

**Above:** *Operation Protea* was probably the most successful of all the cross-border raids into Angola by the South African Defence Force.

**Far right:** Long rows of captured Russian artillery at army headquarters at Oshakati, Ovamboland, after *Operation Askari.*

**Below:** Improvised ferry for armoured cars across the Kunene river in southern Angola.

**Above:** A display of Eastern bloc mines and booby-traps. Russia has exported vast quantities of military equipment to Africa in the past twenty years, with few lasting results.

**Below right:** Al Venter examining explosives at a PLO base in Kampala. Together with the Libyans, the PLO has launched many destructive missions against pro-Western countries in the region.

**Below left:** During *Operation Super* two hundred Swapo insurgents were killed by a small "special forces" squad in the arid south-western regions of Angola adjacent to the Kaokoveld.

**Above:** A Rhodesian patrol searches a *kraal* suspected of harbouring insurgents near Chipinga.

**Below:** During the Rhodesian war, patrols were an everyday event. In the end it was South African pressure and economic collapse that put the socialist Robert Mugabe in power in Salisbury (now Harare).

**Above:** Few of the Portuguese who took part in this demonstration against South Africa and Rhodesia remained in Mozambique after independence. Ironically, many came to South Africa.

**Right:** The anguish of an uncertain future is visible in the face of this Mozambican woman, just after the abortive counter-coup in Mozambique.

**Above:** A Russian cargo-vessel is buzzed while rounding the Cape. Russia does not make much use of the Cape route.

**Below:** The first president of Angola was Agostinho Neto. He was a strong supporter of Russian influence in Africa and died of cancer in a Soviet hospital.

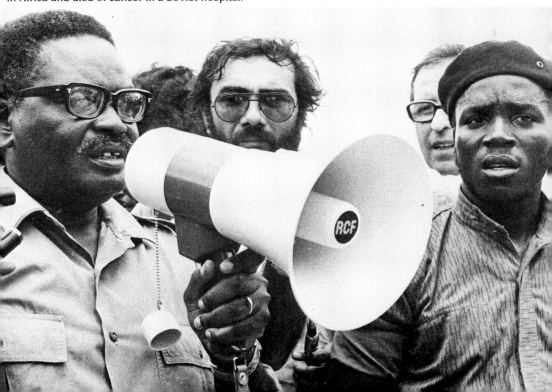

**Above:** Tete road to the north in central Mozambique. It was pitted with holes made by mines, and ambushes were frequent though mostly ineffective.

**Left:** A captured Frelimo rebel informs a Portuguese officer of the positions of his own side. The best intelligence came from members of Frelimo who were "turned" against their former comrades.

**Above:** A Portuguese officer offers a light to a Frelimo rebel during the ceasefire in Mozambique, 1974.

**Below:** Joachim Chissano, of Frelimo, with Admiral Vitor Crespo in Lourenço Marques just before independence. Crespo organised the socialist takeover of the government of Mozambique.

**Above:** British soldiers waiting to be airlifted home after rescuing President Julius Nyerere of Tanzania from an attempted coup d'état in Dar es Salaam in the early Sixties. The history of southern Africa might have been very different if the British had not intervened.

**Below:** Freedom-fighters of a different sort were trained in the eastern region of Nigeria to fight the Nigerian army, backed by the British and the Russians during the Biafran war. That was one of the saddest cases of colonial intervention in Africa after independence.

**Above:** Russian tanks captured by South African forces in *Operation Protea*. The Angolans lost US$1 000 million worth of equipment.

**Below:** A South African Army column en route for an Angolan destination in the early Eighties.

**Above left:** Search-and-destroy mission in Mozambique. To burn all the huts and kill all the livestock was regular policy of the Portuguese armed forces in Africa, notably in Mozambique.

**Left:** Rhodesian and Portuguese forces often cooperated along the Zambezi river, especially where their joint interests were affected. This was a Rhodesian operation.

**Above right:** Portuguese units move into position in central Lourenço Marques in an attempt to avert a counter-revolution in Mozambique after the coup d'état in Lisbon.

**Right:** The face of the Portuguese fighting man in Africa, often still in his teens and hardly inspired with zeal for a war to which he was ill-suited.

Landmine! A Rhodesian truck comes to rest against a tree after detonating a mine in north-eastern Rhodesia. The driver was only slightly hurt.

2. From Robert Blake's foreword in J.R.T. Wood, *The Welensky Papers: A History of the Federation of Rhodesia and Nyasaland*, Durban, Graham Publishing, 1983, p15.

3. In Africa in 1956 the Sudan was proclaimed an independent republic in September. Britain granted the Gold Coast independence and it became the Republic of Ghana in March 1957. The British rebuffed an attempt by Lord Malvern (formerly Sir Godfrey Huggins) to obtain dominion status for the Federation of Rhodesia and Nyasaland. In August 1957 Malaya became the Federation of Malaysia; in November Jamaica obtained full internal self-government, while Britain declared Bahrein independent. In 1959 Cyprus was made independent and Singapore and Jamaica were granted self-government. In 1960, faced with insurrection and under American pressure, the Belgians rapidly advanced the Congo to independence, the British did likewise with Somaliland, and France created the republics of Dahomey, Mauritania, Niger, Upper Volta, Ivory Coast, Chad, CAR and the French Congo. That October Nigeria became independent and a republic in the next month. 1961 saw Ruanda and South Africa become republics. Independence was achieved by Sierra Leone, while in May Tanganyika achieved full internal self-government with Julius Nyerere as its prime minister. The pace of change became furious. In January 1962 Western Samoa became independent. In March Uganda attained self-government. By April the West Indian Federation had to be dissolved. In July Belgium made Ruanda and Burundi independent. In August the British did likewise with Jamaica and Trinidad and Tobago, and in December allowed Tanganyika to become an independent republic within the Commonwealth.

4. Tredgold kept the common voters' roll and recommended that the more property or income the voter had, the less educational requirements were needed. These requirements were ignored if the voter had an income of £720 sterling per annum. The highly qualified needed less income and there were special voters who needed literacy and £180 per annum. The special votes would never count for more than half the general votes cast in a constituency. The principle of this devaluation of the common roll was not questioned but the mechanics of it were, resulting in the income qualification being set at £240 per annum and the influence in the constituencies being reduced to a third. With a threat of resignation, Todd successfully insisted that adults with ten years of schooling should qualify provided that they had been in continuous employment for two years and earned at least £120 per annum. In addition preferential voting was introduced to deal with the situation where there were more than two candidates contesting a seat.

5. These were that:
   5.1 The principle and intention of unimpeded progress to majority rule, already enshrined in the 1961 Constitution, would have to be maintained and guaranteed.
   5.2 There would also have to be guarantees against retrogressive amendment of the Constitution.
   5.3 There would have to be immediate improvement in the political status of the African population.
   5.4 There would have to be progress towards ending racial discrimination.
   5.5 The British government would need to be satisfied that any basis proposed for independence was acceptable to the people of Rhodesia as a whole.

    5.6  Wilson added in February 1966, as a sop to white fears:
        Regardless of race, no oppression of the majority by minority, or of the
        minority by the majority.

6. G.K. Burke, "Insurgency in Rhodesia – the Implications", *RUSI and Brassey's*
   *Defence Yearbook 1978-79,* London, l980, pp26–40.

# REVOLT IN THE TOWNSHIPS
*by Mike Hough*

## 1. The Concept of Political Violence

Political violence can be defined as "acts of disruption, destruction, injury whose purpose, choice of targets or victims, surrounding circumstances, implementation, or effects have political significance, i.e. tend to modify the behaviour of others in a bargaining situation that has consequences for the social system".[1] In addition to stressing the bargaining aspect, acts of political violence may, however, also be strict coercive measures or acts of terror on behalf of the protesters.

A riot has been described as an outbreak of temporary but violent mass disorder. It may be directed against a particular private individual as well as against public authorities, but it does not necessarily mean an intention to overthrow the government itself. In this respect, riot stops short of insurrection, rebellion or revolution, although it may be a preliminary to the latter. The American, French and Russian revolutions were preceded by persistent rioting.[2]

The most significant types of riots have been religious, political, economic and racial, and are (at least partially), indexes of social unrest. Underlying political and socio-economic conditions tend to create unrest potential, which is then triggered by a particular event or events.[3]

Theories of urban violence include conspiracy theories, the criminality theory, the teenage rebellion theory, the class struggle theory, the police brutality theory, the social-psychological theory, the historical-economic theory, and the structural-situational theory. Obviously too, politics and the political system are also often intimately linked to riots.[4]

In the South African situation, it is obvious that both political and socio-economic factors contribute to unrest and revolutionary potential. While government reform measures combined with the repression of violent dissidence have succeeded in limiting the manifestations of revolutionary and unrest activities, reform has also increased expectations among the black population especially, and repressive measures have met with international condemnation and sanctions. Revolutionary organisations such as the African National Congress (ANC), have also attempted to integrate unrest as part of the revolutionary process, and this has of course complicated actions directed at removing the root causes of unrest.

It has been stated that it would be futile to diagnose the present unrest in South Africa only as a well-coordinated attempt to create ungovernability and chaos in the townships, and that it is important to analyse township conditions within the wider structure of South African society.[5]

A matrix of conditions contributing to unrest potential in South Africa could include the following:[6]

* Youth and young adult unemployment.
* Bitterness about the failure to reach desired educational levels in a school system with unacceptably high failure rates.
* Economic recession and inflation, leading to severe shortage of spending money.
* Mobilisation by activists in political movements, more focused than but nominally under the umbrella of the UDF (United Democratic Front), and perhaps the National Forum.

* Feelings among Africans of being relatively even more deprived than before through the introduction of parliamentary rights for coloureds and Indians.
* Stress of overcrowding in townships.
* Opportunities that unrest offers for anti-social behaviour like looting, vandalism and displays of public aggression.
* Corruption or ineffectiveness in local leadership, creating popular resentment.
* Absence of a respected and legitimate local leadership in the townships to reinforce respect for authority.
* Counter-reaction by police units too thinly spread and sporadically present to deter rioters by strength of numbers.
* Absence of internal policing in the townships, capable of recognising individuals and distinguishing between leaders and followers, hence discouraging activism.
* Boredom–stress: stress occurs as a result of boredom. Juveniles observed to suffer social malaise or boredom often respond to the situation by acts of aggression "for kicks". This is particularly true in South African black townships which, having been established as "locations" or dormitories for working populations, have a low level of variety and social diversion.
* Encapsulation: populations or groups forced close together by residential circumstances have a higher propensity to collective dissidence and protest than groups intermingled with others in heterogeneous circumstances. The clearest illustration of this is among encapsulated workers (dockers, miners etc), but the principle also applies to segregated and ghetto populations.
* Urban reforms and promises of reforms by the authorities that have revived expectations without providing definite information on results. Universally, reform has tended to operate as an accelerator of unrest and violence in societies with a high degree of relative deprivation among large parts of the population.
* Urbanising populations are not necessarily inclined to unrest or violence, but the pressure of urbanisation can incline others in urban communities to violence.

As is generally the situation with rioting, longer-term as well as particular trigger factors seem also in South Africa to have combined in creating various riot cycles. Three main unrest cycles can be distinguished: the 1960 Sharpeville riots, the 1976/7 Soweto riots, and the present unrest cycle that began in September 1984. The emphasis in this chapter will fall on the 1984 unrest cycle and on insurgent activities in the period 1984 to the present. The period before 1960 is only briefly referred to, while a survey of the period 1960 to 1984 is given.

## 2. Urban unrest in South Africa: from Sharpeville to Soweto

Before 1960, when the Sharpeville riots brought South Africa its first serious unrest cycle, bus boycott campaigns, organised as a protest against fare increases, passive resistance campaigns and worker stay-away occurred. In 1952, the so-called "defiance campaign" was organised with the support of the African National Congress. In certain cases this was accompanied by violent incidents, although it was originally intended as a form of passive resistance against legislation such as the Group Areas Act and the Voters' Representation Act.[7]

The Sharpeville riots of March 1960 were preceded by rioting in the Transkei and some parts of the Transvaal, and by the African National Congress Conference held in December 1959. The most important resolutions adopted at the conference dealt with the economic boycott, which referred to both an international boycott of South African goods and to an internal boycott of listed "Nationalist products". It was also agreed to launch a vigorous campaign against the "pass laws" (influx control).

The Pan Africanist Congress (PAC), a rival movement to the ANC supporting the black consciousness ideology, also held a conference (its first) during December 1959.[8]

The PAC also decided to launch a campaign against the pass laws, as well as a "status campaign", to achieve courteous treatment for blacks in shops. The pass laws campaign would begin on March 21, 1960. Members were urged to leave their passes at home and to surrender themselves for arrest at the nearest police station. It was therefore a form of passive resistance. The ANC was dubious about the details of the PAC pass laws campaign, and decided not to support it in that form.[9] The PAC campaign began as planned, with large crowds joining in at some townships. It was at Sharpeville, a black township, that the main disturbances occurred. A crowd of a few thousand demonstrators clashed with the police; stones were thrown, and the police opened fire on the crowd. It was later officially announced that 67 blacks had been killed and 186 wounded.[10]

A similar situation occurred in Langa, a black township near Cape Town, on March 21, 1960, followed by disturbances in black townships near Johannesburg. In the latter case, people who ignored the call to stay away from work were assaulted by other blacks.[11]

On March 24, 1960, the South African government banned all public meetings in specified areas, and on March 30 a state of emergency in certain districts was proclaimed, followed by arrests and detention. A temporary relaxation of pass raids was announced, to protect blacks who were being intimidated by other blacks not to carry reference books.[12]

During April 1960, the *Unlawful Organisations Act* was promulgated, which led to the ANC and the PAC being declared unlawful organisations. As a result, both these organisations went underground.[13] In August 1960, the state of emergency declared after the Sharpeville riots was lifted.[14]

The next serious cycle of unrest in South Africa, after the 1960 Sharpeville riots, occurred in 1976/7 with the Soweto riots.

The riots, breaking out on June 16, were on a larger scale than had ever been experienced in South Africa. The trigger was the language issue: the use of Afrikaans as one of the media of instruction in black schools. Applications for exceptions from this ruling could be made, but few were granted.[15]

On June 16, a protest march by some black pupils against the use of Afrikaans as a medium of instruction was held in Soweto. Again, after attempts by police to break up the demonstration, stones were thrown and the police opened fire.[16] This was followed by rioting all over Soweto, which spread to other areas in South Africa. By the end of June, the official death toll was 140, with more than a thousand people injured, more than 900 arrested and many vehicles and buildings damaged. School boycotts and worker stay-away campaigns also occurred, and fighting between residents and hostel dwellers in Soweto. Rioting, mainly caused by resentment over black education, continued throughout 1977, accompanied by school boycotts.[17]

After the outbreak of the 1976/7 rioting, a Commission of Inquiry was appointed by the South African government.

The Commission found that on the Witwatersrand especially, young children took part in the riots, although they did not understand what it was all about. Schoolchildren again usually initiated unrest incidents, or took a prominent part in incidents that had already begun. Schoolboys from Soweto also went to other urban areas or to rural areas, to start unrest there. Youths acted along with other groups, but also separately, in unrest incidents and took part in arson, looting and stone-throwing. They intimidated pupils and workers. Adults usually took part in unrest incidents started by schoolchildren and seldom initiated them. Some unrest also occurred in coloured townships in the Cape Province, while some white students at English-speaking universities also took part in unrest incidents.[18]

The Commission discussed different types of unrest incidents, such as illegal marches and gatherings, public violence, assault, murder, rape, wilful damage to property, theft and looting, arson, illegal strikes, and acts of terrorism.[19]

Intimidation, the Commission found, played an important part during the unrest. Where there was unrest, there was intimidation, and people on all levels of black society were intimidated to take part. Not all those of course, did so as a result of intimidation. Pamphlets were sometimes distributed:

"This is the second and the last. Nobody back to school – 20 July 1976. Black Power. You enter this school at your own risk. By SASO members: No School."

"Students and teachers, you will be fired. Those who go to school will suffer."[20]

Physical intimidation such as assault also occurred.

As for police handling of the unrest, the Commission found that they were unprepared in manpower, equipment and information. No general finding of intimidation of blacks by the police could, however, be made.[21]

Finally, the Commission found that certain underlying factors such as housing shortages, influx control and low pay contributed indirectly to the outbreak, while the language issue was the immediate cause.[22]

As the unrest developed, certain organisations such as the *South African Students' Organisation* took part in planning and executing the unrest. The ANC and the PAC distributed pamphlets and recruited suitable rioters for training as insurgents.[23]

The ANC subsequently declared that the events of 16 June 1976 came as "a complete surprise for everybody" and that the ANC "was not prepared for these events".[24]

After the Soweto riots, incidents occurred sporadically, and during 1980 a minor unrest cycle affected the Eastern Cape, Durban and the Western Cape, where riots broke out in coloured and black townships. This included unrest at schools, stonings and arson.[25]

### 3. The 1984 Unrest Cycle
In this section a survey of the development and consequences of the 1984 unrest cycle will be given.

### 3.1 The origin and development of the unrest cycle
Between March and September 1984, fourteen black local councils on the Witwatersrand announced increases in rents and service charges. In the second half of the year, protests against the increases, linked to educational and political grievances, erupted in the Vaal Triangle and elsewhere.

During unrest in September 1984 in the Vaal Triangle, four councillors were killed, and houses and businesses of councillors became targets for petrol-bomb attacks. Several town councils, including those of Atteridgeville, Soweto and Lekoa, suspended service and rent increases. In November 1984 it was reported that only four of the 22 councils in the affected townships were still fully operational.[26]

An invitation by the Soweto council in October 1984 to student and political organisations to discuss the situation was rejected by the United Democratic Front, the Azanian People's Organisation and student organisations such as the Congress of South African Students. They called on the council to resign.[27]

By January 1985 the unrest had spread to the Eastern Cape, with black youths rioting in Grahamstown and Port Alfred. By mid-February it had spread to the Orange Free State, and by June 1985 to the Western Cape and later to Natal. The riots were characterised by looting, stone-throwing, the use of petrol-bombs and clashes with the police. It was confined mainly to black and in a few cases Indian and coloured townships, and included several urban as well as rural areas, including self-governing territories such as KwaNdebele. The original causes that had begun the cycle were exacerbated by restrictions on the holding of funerals, the presence of soldiers in the townships and incidents resulting from various boycott campaigns. These included school boycotts, consumer boycotts of white businesses and worker stay-aways.[28]

The response of the government was to combine the continuation of limited reforms and measures to suppress unrest, and the South African Police and the South African Defence Force carried out combined operations in the townships.[29]

On July 21, 1985 a partial state of emergency was declared in 36 magisterial districts and extended to another eight areas in October 1985. The emergency granted the government and officials wide powers of search and detention. Before declaring the state of emergency, restrictions on and the banning of certain meetings were imposed by the government.[30]

On declaring the emergency the State President, P.W. Botha, said:

"... Every responsible South African has, with growing concern, taken note of conditions of violence and lawlessness which, in recent times, have increased and have become more cruel and more severe in certain parts of the country, especially in black townships. These acts of violence and thuggery are mainly directed at the property and persons of law-abiding black people, and take the form of incitement, intimidation, arson, inhuman forms of assault, and even murder. This state of affairs can no longer be tolerated. Thus far, the government has shown the utmost patience. However, I cannot ignore the insistence of all responsible South Africans, especially of the majority of the black communities, who ask that conditions are normalised and that they are granted the full protection of the law to continue their normal way of life. It is the duty of the government to ensure that a normal community life is re-established and that community services are efficiently rendered. Children must be able to receive tuition. Breadwinners must be able to fulfill their daily task. The life and property of all people must be protected, and law and order must be maintained. In view of the prevailing conditions, it is essential that the situation be normalised in such a way that the climate for continued dialogue in the interest of all people in the constitutional, economic, and social fields is ensured. Against this background, the government has... decided to proclaim a state of emergency."[31]

Political violence continued in 1986. The partial state of emergency declared during July 1985 was lifted on 7 March 1986. Unrest continued however, and on 18 May 1986, the Crossroads squatter community erupted into a battle between vigilantes (known as *witdoeke* or "fathers") and "comrades" in the satellite communities of Nyanga Bush and the Portland Cement Company. It was alleged that the *witdoeke* had the support of the security forces. Within one day, 14 people had been killed and 20 000 people had become homeless. On 20 May, KwaMashu and other Durban townships erupted as battles were fought between the United Democratic Front and supporters of Inkatha.[32]

Previously, during April 1985, conflict between the United Democratic Front and the Azanian People's Organisation had also resulted in 21 people injured and 35 houses damaged.[33]

On June 12, 1986 a second, country-wide state of emergency was declared in South Africa. The State President made the following statement: "... sporadic cases of violence have begun to increase again and they have begun to assume such proportions that I am of the opinion that the ordinary laws of the country which are now on the statute book are insufficient to enable the government to ensure the safety of the public and to maintain public order. In fact, the government has information at its disposal concerning what is being planned for the coming days by radical and revolutionary elements. This constitutes a real danger to all population groups in this country."[34]

The emergency regulations included provisions for arrest without warrant, detention for an initial period not exceeding fourteen days, and restrictions on the movement of people and goods. Under the regulations, orders were issued by the police placing restrictions on funerals, curfews were imposed in certain areas, and restrictions on coverage of unrest incidents by the media were imposed.[35]

After the declaration of the general state of emergency, incidents of political violence continued to take place in various parts of South Africa. These included clashes between people in the townships and "comrades", attacks on members of the security forces, demonstrations leading to violence and "necklacings" (the burning of a victim with a tyre filled with kerosene). Demands already made by some black organisations during 1985 included the lifting of the state of emergency, the release from detention and prison of political leaders and activists, the withdrawal of the Defence Force from black townships, the removal of all racial discrimination, the scrapping of lodgers' fees, the improvement of amenities, and permission for residents who had been evicted for non-payment to return to their houses.[36]

On June 11, 1987 the general state of emergency was extended for another year. A new detention clause allows any member of the police force to have a person detained for a period of up to thirty days without a written order by the Minister of Law and Order, whereas previously the limit had been fourteen days.[37]

During September 1987 conflict between Inkatha and the United Democratic Front (UDF) flared up in Natal. Clashes between these organisations in the Pietermaritzburg area represented some of the worst unrest incidents in South Africa during 1987. By October 1987, 52 people had already lost their lives, and by November the number was 170. The UDF-Cosatu faction accused Inkatha of destabilising "progressive" organisations, while Inkatha maintains that the conflict results from attempts by the UDF and Cosatu to make South Africa "ungovernable", to the benefit of the ANC.[38] The conflict continued well into 1988, with recent reports indicating that some form of truce had been reached, after increased numbers of the security forces in the troubled areas.

On February 22, 1988 the State President signed further emergency regulations, under which the Congress of South African Trade Unions (Cosatu) is prohibited from engaging in a wide range of specified political activities such as campaigns designed to stir up public opinion against the system of local government in

South Africa, encouraging boycott campaigns, or campaigning for opposition to a negotiated settlement to which the South African government is a party. Seventeen political and community organisations were also restricted in the carrying out of their activities and may, for instance, only act to preserve their assets, perform certain administrative duties or take legal advice or judicial advice or judicial steps. The Minister of Law and Order is empowered to consent to these organisations carrying out other activities only if the safety of the public or the maintenance of public order is not threatened, or the termination of the state of emergency is not delayed by such activities. The organisations listed in the schedule are the following:[39] The Azanian People's Organisation, the Azanian Youth Organisation, the Cape Youth Congress, the Cradock Residents' Association, the Detainees' Parents Support Committee, the Detainees' Support Committee, the National Education Crisis Committee, the National Education Union of South Africa, the Port Elizabeth Black Civic Organisation, the Release Mandela Committee, the Soweto Civic Association, the Soweto Youth Congress, the South African National Students Congress, the South African Youth Congress, the United Democratic Front, the Vaal Civic Association, and the Western Cape Civic Association.

### 3.2 Unrest incidents during the 1984 cycle

Some of the incidents and campaigns occurring during the 1984 unrest cycle have already been referred to. Statistics indicate a sharp increase in the period September 1984 to May 1986. This trend includes both incidents of unrest (for instance stone-throwing) and injuries and deaths resulting from such incidents.

After the declaration of a national state of emergency on June 12, 1986, a definite downward trend regarding visible unrest could be perceived. The graphs illustrate this situation.[40]

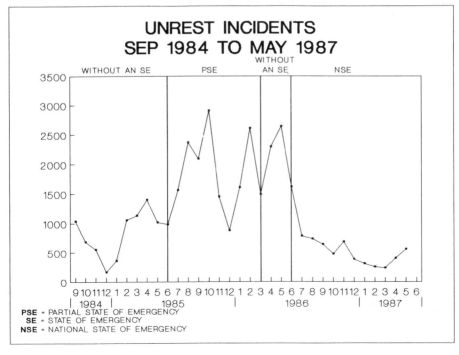

UNREST INCIDENTS
SEP 1984 TO MAY 1987

PSE = PARTIAL STATE OF EMERGENCY
SE = STATE OF EMERGENCY
NSE = NATIONAL STATE OF EMERGENCY

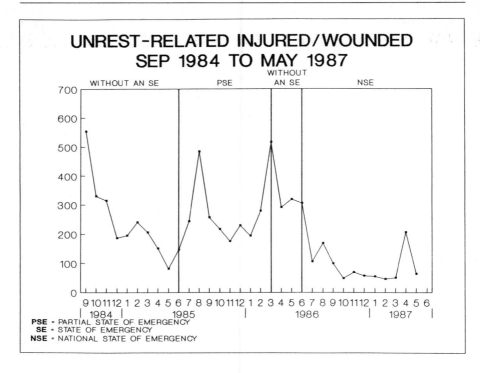

UNREST-RELATED INJURED/WOUNDED
SEP 1984 TO MAY 1987

PSE = PARTIAL STATE OF EMERGENCY
SE = STATE OF EMERGENCY
NSE = NATIONAL STATE OF EMERGENCY

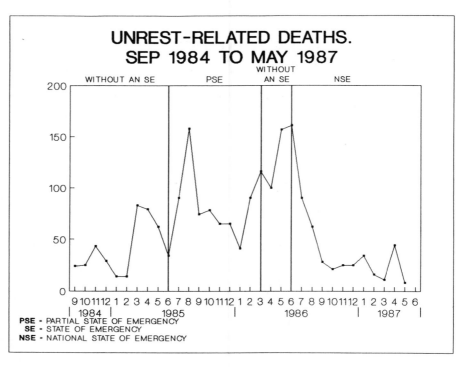

UNREST-RELATED DEATHS.
SEP 1984 TO MAY 1987

PSE = PARTIAL STATE OF EMERGENCY
SE = STATE OF EMERGENCY
NSE = NATIONAL STATE OF EMERGENCY

## INCIDENTS : AN OVERVIEW

| | 1984 | 1985 | 1986 | | 1987 |
|---|---|---|---|---|---|
| | SEP-DEC | JAN-DEC | JAN-JUN | JUL-DEC | |
| INCIDENTS | | | 12 255 | 3 701 | |
| average per day | 19,9 | 47,1 | 68 | 20 | Total number of Incidents ±30% of the total for 1986. |
| TOTAL | 2 433 | 17 188 | | 15 956 | |
| Decline | | | | -%70 | Includes stone-throwing, arson and petrol bomb attacks. |
| Stone throwing | | | 5 076 | 1 731 | |
| TOTAL | 1 555 | 9 936 | | 6 807 | |
| Arson | | | 1 964 | 547 | |
| TOTAL | 67 | 3 236 | | 2 511 | |
| Petrol bomb attacks | | | 1 949 | 618 | |
| TOTAL | 352 | 2 008 | | 2 567 | |

## DEATHS : AN OVERVIEW

| | 1984 | 1985 | 1986 | | 1987 |
|---|---|---|---|---|---|
| | SEP-DEC | JAN-DEC | JAN-JUN | JUL-DEC | JAN-DEC |
| DEATHS | | | 665 | 270 | |
| average per day | 1.0 | 2,2 | 3,7 | 1,5 | Total number of deaths ±48% of the total for 1986, |
| TOTAL | 121 | 819 | | 935 | |
| Decline | | | | -%59 | Vast majority of deaths due to black-on-black violence. |
| By Sec Forces | | | 211 | 66 | |
| TOTAL | 96 | 493 | | 277 | |
| By Black agitat. | | | 394 | 153 | |
| TOTAL | 20 | 293 | | 548 | |

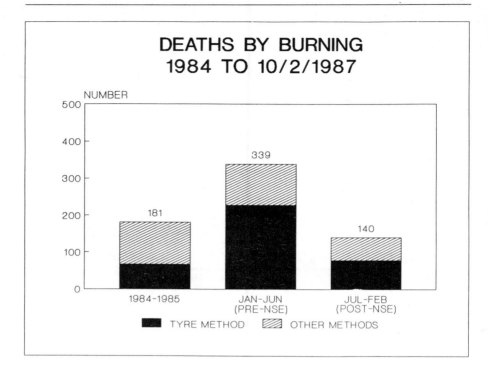

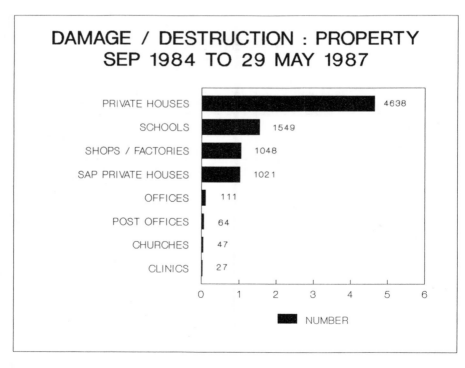

It has, however, repeatedly been stated by government spokesmen that unrest and revolutionary potential remains high, and as indicated on June 12, 1987 the national state of emergency was extended for a further year.

### 3.3 The general nature of rioting in the 1984 unrest period

The 1984 unrest cycle, which still continues, although in a much more limited degree, is the most wide-spread, the longest and at times the most intense and organised that South Africa has yet experienced. It also covers a broad range of factors, although the rent increase served as one of the "triggers". Furthermore, it involves a large number of national and local movements which are advertently or inadvertently concerned in some way or another, for example the ANC, the United Democratic Front, the Azanian People's Organisation, Inkatha, the Congress of South African Trade Unions, civic associations and student movements. In some areas, so-called "alternative structures", such as "people's courts" and "street committees" were also created, and were seen as a "step towards replacing official administrative structures".[41]

Major General Bert Wandrag, Head of the South African Police Riot Control, also stated that the police have frequently found that once a riot or some other form of unrest has begun ordinary criminal elements exploit the situation. Criminal acts include looting, arson, and murder, which may not have been the intention of the organisation or group responsible.[42]

Concerning the general character of the present unrest cycle in South Africa, General Wandrag commented as follows:[43]

"The type of riots perpetrated by the rioters in South Africa is unique in the sense that similar action is encountered nowhere else in the world. The riots are characterised by so-called hit and run techniques. Rioters and their leaders seldom act as one group. They would rather divide into twenty small groups to strike at targets, and instigate riots, by for instance setting fire to shops, beer-halls and community halls at various locations. They also murder people and overturn and set vehicles alight. As soon as they have committed their acts, they withdraw, only to congregate again elsewhere, a considerable distance away, to commit similar crimes.

"It is notable that the rioters are usually blacks. The SA Police are seldom confronted by white rioters. Considering the present explosive political climate, this situation also has a detrimental effect on black police who have to act against their own people.

"Another problem faced by the SA Police is the composition of the crowds. Usually the agitators appear among or behind the crowd to incite the people. In the ensuing tumult innocent bystanders get involved, and should the police eventually act, these innocents are the first to be hit, while the culprits get away.

"The present tendency is for women (many of them pregnant) and children to form the front line of rioters. Instigated by the agitators, they are the first to throw stones. Should these women and children become casualties during police action, the fact is exploited by both the domestic and foreign press to the advantage of the rioters.

"The effectiveness of the SA Police action forces the rioters to disperse quickly at the slightest possibility of a direct confrontation with the police. This of course seriously hampers arrest or linking arrested rioters to a particular riot situation.

"It should be borne in mind that the young black adults of today were youths during the 1976 riots. They are therefore 'experienced' in organising and executing riots. The older members of the black community are prepared to negotiate for peace, while the younger members form the militant wing of the rioters. They are not interested in negotiations, but only in instigating the so-called 'revolution'.

"Rioters are often accompanied by their own legal advisers as well as photographers to formulate complaints against the SA Police and obtain proof to substantiate their claims. Riots are no longer spontaneous and unplanned actions by a mutinous mob, but are skillfully planned in advance to be executed in a well-organised manner."

General Wandrag also said that in the areas afflicted by riots members of the police are often subjected to severe provocation. In view of the application of the principle of minimum force by the police, the fact that rioters at times made use of sharp ammunition and explosive devices caused serious problems. The lay-out of streets and townships, and narrow alleys in particular, also hampers the movement of riot control vehicles.[44]

In conclusion, General Wandrag commented as follows on black reaction to the unrest and the causes of unrest:[45]

"An encouraging backlash against the forces of anarchy and lawlessness can be detected in most areas where inhabitants have suffered because of unrest and lawlessness during recent times. Indeed, the combined military and police crime prevention exercise carried out at Sebokeng and elsewhere during 1984, while attracting the predictable international backlash at the United Nations and elsewhere, met with a different type of criticism by some of the residents who had suffered at the hands of criminal elements; they wanted to know why such an exercise had not been carried out sooner. It is a well-known fact that black members of the Force also play a vital role in quelling the political unrest.

"It is hoped that some good may yet arise from the present political unrest and turmoil, especially among the responsible township leaders in all spheres of community activity. Their influence and authority to discourage violence, crime and rioting are indispensable. Whatever political differences such communities may have with the government, they should at least realise that unrest and lawlessness are, at best, ineffective and, at worst, counter-productive in achieving the desired communal goals. Socio-economic frustration, especially in the present recession, is of course understandable. The plight of the unemployed also deserves sympathy".

## 3.4  The Van der Walt Report
A one-man Official Commission of Inquiry was appointed after the events of 3 September 1984. The subsequent report by Professor van der Walt, Rector of the University of Potchefstroom, highlighted the following events which contributed to the 1984 unrest cycle, originating in the Vaal Triangle, and then spreading all over the country.

### 3.4.1  Education
The report clearly states that although the real problem is not to be found in the education system, the schools were a convenient target and the pupils "remarkably cleverly handled and craftily involved". Van der Walt suggested three reasons why he found that the root of the problem was not to be found in the schools themselves, despite the prominence of pupils in the disturbances.

"...In the first place, it was time and again, in fact without exception, stated by all witnesses that the schools were not the real problem and that there was no doubt that education would return to normal as soon as some of the most pressing problems, especially the 'rent question', had been resolved. In the second place, my general impression that the black school system in the Vaal Triangle is, in many respects, ahead of that in other parts of the country was confirmed time and again. The mere fact that the Standard 10 pass rate for 1983/4 was 77,6 per cent, while it was below 50 per cent for the rest of the country, provides obvious confirmation of such a view. In the third place it is significant that, unlike previous cases of unrest, not a single school was burnt down in this area and damage, where it occurred, was done to the administrative block and not to classrooms. In the single incident where a principal's house was burnt down because he not only encouraged his own pupils to return to school but also attempted to inspire them to pass the message on to their fellow pupils, there is overwhelming evidence of the parents' sympathy towards him: from their own meagre resources they replaced some of his possessions, especially blankets.

"Add to this the fact that the majority of black pupils in South Africa live in the homelands (both independent and national states) and in practically all respects education in these states lags conspicuously behind that in the RSA; also the fact that 70 per cent of the schools and 30 per cent of the pupils under the jurisdiction of the Department of Education and Training are farm schools and that farm school pupils, in their turn, are generally behind pupils in towns and cities and the black education in the Vaal Triangle with all its shortcomings and limitations is still so much better than that in the homelands where, as yet, hardly any disruption of school activities has occurred.

"The root of the problem therefore obviously does not lie in the schools.

"This is not to deny that there is much room for improvement here as well. In my opinion, the top priority is to get the children to return to school, and the essence of my recommendations is that where schools have been misused for ulterior motives (or at least for non-education reasons), the school system should be utilised, not only in a vigorous attempt at convincing parents and children that they cannot afford to waste school time any longer; but also as a channel of information and as a means of communication at least to defuse some of the other grievances and to break through the ignorance.

"The chances of success appear to be reasonable. My overwhelming impression is that everyone, without exception, would like the pupils to return to school. In fact, some of them have already decided to do just that, irrespective of what may happen, while others claim, with greater or lesser vehemence, that this will happen automatically the moment the municipality has solved the service levy problem. Apart from these, there are organisations, such as COSAS, that make further demands. It is my impression, however, that their hold on the pupils is beginning to weaken, that they are becoming divided amongst themselves, and that the agenda behind the agenda is the political power struggle between COSAS/UDF/ANC on the one hand and Inkatha on the other."[46]

### 3.4.2 Local conditions.
The report states that this was probably the area where the real problem was to be found. As far as living conditions in general are concerned, van der Walt made the following comments:

"The effect of general socio-economic problems on the schools boycott and on the widespread unrest and violence in the Vaal Triangle should not be underrated. In the absence of these conditions there would probably still have been protest actions, but certainly not on such a scale, not with such intensity and not over so protracted a period of time.

"The whole country has been experiencing economic difficulties in recent years. The lower income groups are those that are the most affected. It is their purchasing power that has been hardest hit by price hikes and inflation. Add to this the fact that in an industrial area such as the Vaal Triangle there are thousands of workers whose income has been drastically reduced owing to the fact that at the very best, there are no longer opportunities for overtime work, that many of them are being restricted to a three-day week (and are being paid accordingly) and that obviously more workers have been laid off than the various firms will admit to.

"The situation would of course only be aggravated if thousands of black pupils, for whatever reason, terminated their school careers sooner than would otherwise have been the case. This means not only that there would suddenly be more job seekers on the labour market but also, what is more important, that they would be less adequately qualified; moreover, their chances of getting the better paid positions, and of experiencing the greater job satisfaction that goes with better pay, would be reduced correspondingly.

"Against this background black residents in the Vaal Triangle were all the more sensitive about the announcement of the tariff increase, which in point of fact was simply the last straw.

"Added to this is the fact that in recent years the physical living conditions of many black residents have taken a turn for the worse. The maintenance of many of the rented houses – so it was alleged – had deteriorated drastically; the improvement of roads, the laying out of parks and sports grounds, the provision of other community facilities, and so forth, had been either cut drastically or put off indefinitely in an attempt by the authorities to economise. True, some 25 000 trees had been planted on pavements or along the main routes, but most of them, according to officials, were not proof for long against the vandalism of some of the residents. Other complaints were about the lack of suitable storm water drainage at certain places, while there were areas, especially in the older townships, where the sanitary arrangements were still appalling. The effect of all this was that, although the average resident was paying more and more towards municipal service levies, he could not see any of it being ploughed back into the community."[47]

As to rent increases, which time and again were mentioned as the main cause of the unrest, the report stated that that was only the last straw:

"Time and again during the investigation one was told that the rent increases were the cause of the unrest. This is only partly true. In fact it had only been the final straw, the spark that caused the powderkeg to blow up. This becomes clear soon enough when a few elementary facts are examined.

"Last year's increase was much larger – on an average R9,00 as against this year's R5,50 or R5,90, depending on the ownership of the property. Furthermore, the increase was much smaller than that of most of the 27 local authorities which about this time also introduced rent increases. In any case, it does not match the rate of inflation. And, what is more, when the municipality decided not to implement any increases before 1 July 1985 this had no marked effect on the unrest. Indeed, the mere fact that the residents throughout speak of 'rent increases' while much more than rent (and especially certain service levies) is actually involved, already points to a basic short-circuit (to which I shall return at a later stage).

"On rational grounds the so-called rent increases can therefore not be regarded as the primary cause of the riots. However, what is at issue here are not purely rational factors, but a climate strongly charged with emotion. In a manner of speaking, the increases merely pulled the trigger.

"At the same time I cannot escape the impression that the whole matter of increases was handled over-hastily, unwisely, clumsily and insensitively. Since the Lekoa Municipality does not have enough competent officials, it is largely dependent on the assistance of the Orange Vaal Development Board. Apparently these officials were not able to submit a draft budget for the new financial year until a very late stage. I very much doubt whether the municipality actually realised the implications of the budget. Could it have been just another case of white officialdom deciding for the blacks what their standard of living should be and merely confronting them with the bill, instead of presenting them with various other possibilities (each with its cost implications) and leaving the choice up to them? In any case the way in which the announcement was made - by notice in certain newspapers (the *Rand Daily Mail* and *Beeld,* but not in, for example, *The Sowetan,*) instead of conveying the particulars by way of personal communication, does not testify to sound methods of communication. Immoderate haste is also revealed by the fact that the new tariffs could not come into operation on the proposed date because the prescribed procedure (approval by the Minister of Cooperation and Development and official publication in the *Government Gazette*) would not have been completed by then. It is therefore quite understandable for the rent increase to have been postponed by the municipality on 19 September 1984. One cannot help asking: Could they not have taken some thought at an earlier stage? Could they not at least have said: Sorry, we made a mistake? Instead, the Mayor is reported to have remarked laconically: 'For the time being, progress is out of the question and the municipality will be obliged to borrow money.'

"The Town Clerk's written communication with the residents was not without serious shortcomings either. It was resolved on 29 June to increase the tariffs, but an explanatory notice dated 2 August was distributed to all houses only from 6 August onwards. The decision to postpone the increase was also explained to residents by letter; unfortunately one such letter dated 23 October contained faulty information which had to be put right in a letter dated 31 October. In the already tense atmosphere this could not have done anything to boost people's confidence in the municipality."[48]

The report also stated that no resident spoken to had a good word for the Lekoa Black Municipality, but this did not indicate that the system of black local authorities had failed. "True, the impression is inevitable that the system was introduced over-hastily, that the preparatory work left much to be desired, that for the immediate future training is a very high priority and that there is urgent need for better and more personal communication with the black residents."[49]

Some of the matters mentioned are the ignorance of the public at large regarding local affairs; complaints about the quality of local representatives; allegations of corruption in black local affairs; and the problem of sufficient revenue for local councils. The reference in the report to the Orange Vaal Development Board, under whose jurisdiction four black local authorities fall, is also important. In addition to questioning certain aspects of the functioning of development boards, the report states: "The Orange Vaal Development Board clearly did not pay sufficient heed to signs that unrest was imminent. According to a report ... a trade union leader alleged that the Orange Vaal Development Board had been informed by letter six months before of the smouldering unrest about possible tariff increases.[50]

### 3.4.3 Political aspects.
The report referred to various political aspects that had played a part in the unrest. With reference to the tricameral parliament, from which blacks were excluded, it was stated that: "It is of course not without significance that the riots broke out specifically on 3 September, the beginning of the new dispensation."[51]

### 3.4.4 The role of agitators.
The report stated that both the police and the agitators were caught on the wrong foot on 3 September, and that agitators only began to take over later to steer the course of events more definitely. "Agitation and intimidation did undoubtedly play an important part. It would be short-sighted and unrealistic, however, to attach too much weight to this factor. On the other hand, what is shocking is the large extent to which people have played into the very hands of the agitators, thus making the agitators' work so much easier."[52]

### 4. Insurgency during the 1984 unrest cycle
It soon became clear that especially the ANC would use the opportunity to exploit the situation, both militarily and politically. The following table compares incidents of terror and sabotage in the periods before and after the unrest.

| Nature of incident | 24 Months before unrest | 24 Months of unrest (Sept 1984 – Sept 1986) |
|---|---|---|
| Attacks on police stations | 4 | 9 |
| Attacks on SADF buildings | 1 | 2 |
| Murder and attempted murder of police | 11 | 88 |
| Murder and attempted murder of civilians (including black councillors) | 3 | 118 |
| Murder and attempted murder of SADF | 1 | 9 |
| Armed robbery | 0 | 1 |
| Sabotage and attempted sabotage of: | | |
| Rail installations | 17 | 5 |
| Fuel and bus depots | 2 | 6 |
| Telecommunications installations | 0 | 1 |
| Business properties | 4 | 24 |
| Private properties | 4 | 5 |
| Water pipes | 0 | 6 |
| Government and public buildings | 23 | 21 |
| Power installations | 22 | 21 |
| TOTAL | 92 | 316 |

If a percentage analysis of terror incidents is made, a shift in targeting is obvious. In the 24 months before the unrest 79,34 per cent of all the acts of terror were aimed at key installations, while during the period of unrest only 30,06 per cent were aimed at key installations. Only 7,60 per cent of all acts of terror in the 24 months before the present unrest were aimed at civilians and private property while 38,92 per cent of all incidents of terror during the present unrest were aimed at civilians and private property. Attacks on members of the police in the 24 months before the present unrest totalled 11,95 per cent, while 27,84 per cent of all incidents during the present unrest situation were aimed at members of the police.

Sabotage has been the main tactic used in terrorist attacks and 57 per cent of all incidents since 1976 are sabotage-related. In the 24 months before the present unrest, 79 per cent of all incidents were sabotage-related, while only 39,31 per cent of all incidents during the current unrest are sabotage-related. Most such incidents have occurred in urban areas, although the ANC emphasises the importance of activating the rural areas in South Africa.

It is significant that only seven incidents of terror were committed with hand-grenades in the 24-month period before the present unrest situation, while 122 incidents of terror during the present unrest situation were committed with hand-grenades. There was also a marked increase in the use of attack weapons such as AK–47 rifles. Mines were also used for the first time during the present unrest situation, of which 87,5 per cent were used in the rural areas.

The unrest situation, an increased attempt by the ANC to intensify the activities of its military wing *Umkhonto we Sizwe,* an attempt at "local training", and an increase in infiltration through Botswana and Zimbabwe, resulted in a steady increase in the total annual number of incidents of sabotage and terrorism in South Africa, most of which can be linked to the ANC. The following table illustrates this trend.

| | | | | |
|------|---|-----|------|-----|
| 1976 – | 4 | | 1982 – | 39 |
| 1977 – | 20 | | 1983 – | 56 |
| 1978 – | 13 | | 1984 – | 44 |
| 1979 – | 12 | | 1985 – | 136 |
| 1980 – | 19 | | 1986 – | 230 |
| 1981 – | 55 | | 1987 – | 234 |

Counter-insurgency had, however, also been increased, and between 1976 and the end of 1986 more than 500 insurgents had either been killed or captured. Of these, 42,28 per cent were captured or killed during the present unrest situation. Between 1985 and 1986 more than 55 arms caches were discovered by the security forces.

As regards the ANC model for revolutionary warfare, the previous model, which would in the opinion of the ANC culminate in a conventional offensive against Pretoria in the classic Mao Tse-tung style, was also influenced by what the ANC saw as opportunities arising from the unrest situation. At the beginning of 1985, the ANC was indicating that the military activities carried out by the ANC had to be transferred into a "people's" war, actively involving the masses. It was also emphasised that South Africa should be made "ungovernable", and that an "alternative" power base had to be created. The participation of the masses would, in the ANC view, increase the likelihood of a "popular uprising" and the ANC had to associate itself with "popular grievances".[53]

By the end of 1986 the ANC was arguing that the South African government was no longer in control of certain black townships and that the ANC had facilitated the "question of organs of popular power - the street committees, area committees". Increasingly, reference was also made to the importance of winning over "significant sections" of the security forces to the ANC cause. Increasingly, too, the importance of trade unions was stressed by the ANC, especially the part played by the Congress of South African Trade Unions and the National Union of Mineworkers.[54]

Although the ANC has, despite its emphasis on "seizure of power", not rejected negotiations for a political settlement with the South African government in principle, the organisation has, in addition to refusing to abandon violence as a pre-condition for negotiations, stated that the ANC conditions for "considering" negotiations, would include the unconditional release of all political prisoners, detainees, captured "freedom fighters" and prisoners of war as well as the cessation of all political trials. The state of emergency would have to be lifted, the army and the police withdrawn from the townships and "confined to their barracks". Similarly, all repressive legislation and all laws empowering the régime to limit freedom of assembly, speech, the press and so on, would have to be repealed.[55]

Clearly, the ANC was arguing that it would attempt to use its violent activities to strengthen the ANC's negotiating position, if negotiations were to come about. Also, the ANC pre-conditions for a possible negotiated settlement were clearly intended to maximise ANC bargaining power in any negotiating system. The South African government, on the other hand, in view of white right wing pressure, could not be seen to give way under pressure to demands by the ANC.

At the beginning of 1988, the ANC began to admit setbacks in their attempts to transform unrest into insurrection, and blamed it on restrictions on organisations and the arrest of regional and national leadership.[56] At the Arusha Conference held by the ANC during December 1987, the emphasis seemed to fall on sanctions, trade union pressures and the division among whites as important instruments in achieving ANC objectives. Despite continued reference by the ANC to "seizure of power" and "people's" war, some commentators are now of the opinion that "the ANC is unlikely ever to be in a position, even within the context of wide-spread political unrest, to achieve a revolutionary seizure of power".[57]

## 5. Conclusion

In conclusion, a number of points regarding the general course of civil unrest in South Africa can be made.

First, civil unrest is not peculiar to South Africa. Even Western democracies such as the United States and Britain have experienced race rioting. More recently, Israel has experienced extensive rioting that in the opinion of many has become a civil war, and has been described as a "spasm of unrest that has transformed the occupied West Bank and Gaza strip into virtual war zones". It does, however, seem as if the riots in Israel differ in some significant respects from those which South Africa is experiencing. Rioting in South Africa has at times been accompanied by the use of sharp ammunition; it has largely been black-on-black violence (although the security forces, as in Israel, are also targets); it has tended to be more organised and precisely directed than in Israel, and the rioting in South Africa is also about black political rights in "white" South Africa, not about certain occupied territories that wish to rid themselves of foreign occupation as with the Palestinian rioters. The Arab population of Israel has also, however, taken part in some rioting, although unlike South African blacks, they have full political rights. But whereas South Africa has made it clear that a political solution, in addition to socio-economic reforms, should be sought, the Israelis have been less forthcoming. In the beginning of 1988, it was stated that "from the beginning of the riots, Israeli leaders had made it plain that they had no intention of even considering a political solution to the unrest". The Israeli Defence Minister, Yitzhak Rabin, stated: "We shall prove to the Palestinians ... that they will achieve nothing by violence."[58] Like South Africa with the ANC, the Israelis also face insurgency from the PLO in addition to unrest.

South Africa, however, has been exposed to far more condemnation for handling of the unrest than Israel. Even the relatively mild US rebuke of Israel was seen by the Israelis as exaggerated and hypocritical.

Secondly, the 1976 and the 1984 unrest cycles in South Africa particularly, have been characterised by the active engagement of children. Loss of parental control, educational discontents directly affecting school children, township conditions and the exploitation of young people by radicals have all contributed to this phenomenon. Conversely, detention of children, or the killing or wounding of children in unrest situations is of course always a sensitive and emotional matter.

Nor is the involvement of children in unrest situations peculiar to South Africa. In an interview General Yariv, head of the Jaffee Centre for Strategic Studies in Israel, stated: "Now we are fighting women and children ... we have to do our utmost not to open fire at all."[59]

Thirdly, it is clear that, to some extent at least, underlying and long-term causes of unrest in South Africa are identifiable, linked to political, economic and social conditions, especially as far as the blacks are concerned. Short-term or "trigger" factors such as rent increases have merely set in motion an existing potential for civil unrest. Often, too, clear danger signs existed before outbreaks of rioting that were not heeded sufficiently. In some cases, mistakes were obviously made in riot control, and to begin with the security forces were not sufficiently equipped, even in manpower, to handle the situation properly. South Africa is now one of the leaders in riot control and has become an exporter of riot control equipment.

Fourthly, although genuine grievances do play a significant part in civil unrest and in sustaining a given cycle of unrest, intimidation has certainly also been an important factor. The stone-thrower who attempts to intimidate others is in turn often intimidated. Revolutionary organisations such as the ANC, although not initiating unrest, certainly helped to create a climate conducive to unrest. The same can be said of many cases of foreign pressure and foreign propaganda directed at South Africa.

The ANC was also quick to exploit each of the unrest cycles, especially that beginning in 1984. This they argued, provided the opportunity to "mobilise" and "arm" the masses for a "popular uprising". In that way, unrest and revolution were to be combined into a strategy for the "seizure of power", directed by the ANC. Slogans such as "making South Africa ungovernable", and the attempts to support the creation of "alternative structures" such as "people's courts" and "street committees", underscored the ANC's revised strategic orientation of the ANC.

Fifthly, although reform in South Africa in conjunction with the maintenance of law and order, can in the long term create conditions that are less conducive to unrest, rioting and revolution, reforms also create rising expectations, which in themselves can lead to further manifestations of unrest. The ANC, while associating itself with popular grievances, rejects gradual change to the system and opposes any reform measures that may erode ANC support or unrest potential.

Sixthly, unrest cycles in South Africa have tended to become progressively more intense, more organised, more widespread and of longer duration. Also, the periods between cycles have tended to become shorter and since 1976 civil unrest seems to have become a permanent occurrence, ranging from small disturbances to large cycles, such as that beginning in September 1984. A backlash, however, has also developed in black communities, police presence on the ground has been increased (also through the introduction of black municipal police), and in addition to other reform measures, a programme to improve conditions in black townships has been launched. Alexandra, near Johannesburg, is one black township which is virtually being rebuilt.

Finally, South Africa is obviously paying a price for unrest. That is true of the whites as well as well as the blacks. The US "Anti-Apartheid Act of 1985", proposing a wide range of sanctions against South Africa, was at least partly inspired by the outbreak of renewed disturbances in South Africa during 1984 and the declaration of a partial state of emergency in 1985. Also, total direct damage, in the period September 1984 to April 1986 for example, amounted to R156 million. That excludes the indirect costs, such as human suffering, loss of production and increased social and political tensions and polarisation. Yet, however urgent the need for further and more effective reform may be, for the South African government merely to yield to ANC demands or those of some of the other more radical black organisations would only exchange the injustices of one system for still greater injustices and tyranny in the guise of "people's democracy". If middle ground is not found, no negotiated political solution is conceivable. Neither apartheid nor the extreme demands of the radicals offer such middle ground.

## FOOTNOTES

1. Zimmerman, E. *Political Violence, Crises, and Revolutions: Theories and Research,* Schenkman Publishing Co., Massachusetts, 1983, p8.
2. Seligman, E.R. and A. Johnson (eds) *Encyclopedia of the Social Sciences,* Vol.13, Macmillan, New York, MCMXIV, p386.
3. *Ibid.*
4. Lupsha, P.A. "On Theories of Urban Violence", in *Urban Affairs Quarterly,* Vol.4, No.3, March 1969, pp273–294.
5. Schlemmer, L. "South Africa's Urban Crises", in *Indicator SA,* Vol.3, No.1, Winter 1985, p3.
6. *Ibid,* pp3–5.
7. For an overview of this period, see Lodge, T. *Black Politics in South Africa since 1945,* Ravan Press, Johannesburg, 1983, chapters 1–8.
8. *Ibid,* p201.
9. *Rand Daily Mail,* 19 March 1960.
10. South Africa, *Debates of the House of Assembly,* Col. 4837, Hansard 12, April 5, 1960.
11. Lodge, T. *op cit,* pp216–224.
12. South Africa, *Proclamation No.90,* March 30, 1960.
13. South Africa, *Unlawful Organisations Act,* No.34 of 1960; and *Proclamation No.119,* April 8, 1960.
14. This was preceded by the lifting of the state of emergency in twenty mainly rural districts.
15. This issue is referred to again in the subsequent overview of the Commission of Inquiry into the Soweto riots.
16. *Rand Daily Mail,* 17 June 1976 and 18 June 1976.
17. *Star,* 21 June 1976; and *Rand Daily Mail,* 23 June 1976.

18. RSA, *Report of the Commission of Inquiry into the Unrest in Soweto and Elsewhere from June 16, 1976 to February 1977,* RP/106/1979, pp418–419. Page numbers supplied here refer to the Afrikaans edition of the Report.
19. *Ibid,* p420.
20. *Ibid,* pp435–441.
21. *Ibid,* p567.
22. *Ibid,* pp589–640.
23. *Ibid,* pp569–572.
24. *Sechaba,* January 1987, pp21–22.
25. Brewer, J.D. *After Soweto,* Clarenden Press, Oxford, 1986, pp86–87.
26. *The Star,* Johannesburg, 12 and 13 September 1984; *The Star,* 21 November 1984; and *Rand Daily Mail,* 15 September 1984.
27. *The Star,* Johannesburg, 16 October 1984.
28. South African Institute of Race Relations, *Race Relations Survey 1985,* SAIRR, Johannesburg, 1986, pp536–537; and *Indicator SA,* Vol.3, No.1, pp9–11.
29. *Indicator SA,* Vol.3, No.1, Winter 1985, p11.
30. RSA, *Government Gazette No 9876, Proclamation R120,* July 21, 1985.
31. *Sunday Times,* 21 July 1985.
32. See for instance: *Eastern Province Herald,* 19 May 1986 and 20 May 1986; *Cape Times,* 27 May 1986; and *Sunday Times,* 25 May 1986.
33. *Indicator SA,* Vol.3, No.1, Winter 1985, p9.
34. RSA, *Debates of the House of Assembly,* 18, cols 81108118, June 12, 1986.
35. RSA, *Government Gazette No 10279, Proclamation R108,* June 12, 1986, and *Government Gazette No.10280, Proclamation R109,* June 12, 1986.
36. See for instance: *City Press,* 13 July 1986; *Weekly Mail,* 20 August 1986; *Business Day,* 5 September 1986; and *The Sowetan,* 19 December 1986.
37. *Government Gazette No.10770, Proclamation No R95,* 1987, June 11, 1987.
38. *The Star,* Johannesburg, 27 October 1987 and 20 November 1987.
39. RSA, *Government Gazette No.11157, Government Notice No.334,* February 24, 1988; and *Government Gazette No.11156, Proclamation R23,* February 24, 1988.
40. The information contained in these graphs was supplied by the Directorate Research, Bureau of Information, Pretoria.
41. *The Weekly Mail,* 10 January 1986 and 17 January 1986.
42. Wandrag, A.J. "Political Unrest – A Police View", in *ISSUP Strategic Review,* October 1985, Institute for Strategic Studies, University of Pretoria, pp8–9.
43. *Ibid,* pp11–12.
44. *Ibid,* p12.
45. *Ibid,* p15.
46. RSA, *Report on the Investigation into Education for Blacks in the Vaal Triangle following upon the occurrences of 3 September 1984 and thereafter,* (Van der Walt Report), RP 88, 1985, pp9–10.
47. *Ibid,* pp27–28.
48. *Ibid,* pp28–29.
49. *Ibid,* p29.
50. *Ibid,* p36.
51. *Ibid,* p37.
52. *Ibid,* p58
53. See for instance: *Sechaba,* March 1985; *Sechaba,* April 1985; and *Documents of the Second National Consultative Conference of the African National Congress,* Zambia, June 1985, pp18–19.

54. See for instance: *Sechaba,* December 1986; *Sechaba,* February 1987; *Sechaba,* April 1987; and *Sechaba,* October 1987.
55. See for instance: *Sechaba,* December 1987.
56. See for instance: ANC, *Message to the People of South Africa from the National Executive Committee,* January 8, 1988.
57. *The Star,* Johannesburg, 21 November 1987.
58. *Newsweek,* 25 January 1988.
59. *The Star,* 1 March 1988.

# THROUGH THE LOOKING GLASS :
# The South African View
## by Douglas McClure

"When I use a word," Humpty Dumpty said, in a rather scornful tone, "it means just what I choose it to mean - neither more nor less."

"The question is," said Alice, "whether you can make words mean so many different things."

*Through the Looking Glass* by Lewis Carroll.

"One of the most dangerous weapons in the struggle against freedom is the weapon of the word. It forms part of a psychological propaganda war.

With a grim sense of irony, Marxist dictatorships are officially called 'people's democracies'. The struggle to enslave peoples becomes a 'freedom struggle' and political enslavement becomes 'freedom'.

South Africa now stands in the front line of this struggle."

South African State President, P.W.Botha (1986).

In 1957 Ghana under its "Redeemer" Kwame Nkrumah started the liberation avalanche in Africa. At that time Africa was regarded as the continent of the future, an investor's paradise and a potential example to the rest of the world of inter-racial cooperation, progress and development. Others, such as Julius Mwalimu ("the Teacher") Nyerere, Dr Hastings "Kamusu" Banda and Jomo Kamau Kenyatta ("Fancy Belt") of Kenya appeared in the forefront as politicians of stature at a time when African socialism was considered to be an effective alternative to the evils of capitalism and communism. The Western world, calling upon high-sounding moral principles, felt obliged to underwrite the new states both financially and morally, and poured millions into the coming millennium.

Less than a generation later, reports by the UN showed the life expectancy in 21 black African states in the 1980s to be markedly less than it had been forty years before. Income per head in Africa had become the lowest in the world, while its infant mortality rate was the highest. Almost 90 per cent of African people lived in countries where food production was declining to such a degree that in 31 black states it had entirely failed to keep pace with the increase in population and one in four black Africans was "severely malnourished". UNESCO estimated that more than 80 per cent of the black population were illiterate, and 45 per cent of the employable population were unemployed. According to the ILO 69 per cent of African people lived in conditions of "extreme poverty", a situation that has deteriorated since 1973, when the report appeared. Various UN reports showed that parts of black Africa were actually "undeveloping", 12 states having a lower GNP in 1975 than they had in 1970. So much for the millennium as forecast in the Fifties and Sixties.

Yet these facts seem to have entirely escaped the world at large, and even responsible Western leaders appear willing not only to pander to the demands of those who preside over the vast disaster that modern Africa has become, but they and certain organs of their governments give the impression of being determined to destroy the one country that might offer hope at the tip of the dark continent. South Africans may perhaps be forgiven for watching these antics with some scepticism.

Furthermore, the crisis of Africa is acknowledged by Africans themselves. The Ghanaian economist, George Ayittey, writes:

"Something has gone fundamentally wrong in black Africa, politically and economically...it is a disgrace that black Africa has not been able to produce a leader who places the interests of his people above his own egocentric thirst for power and self-aggrandisement." As the President of South Africa, P.W. Botha, has described it, Africa is a continent betrayed by those who were entrusted with its future:

"The former imperial nations are now far removed from the misery they have helped to cause on this continent and elsewhere in the Third World. They and the new imperialists in Africa, afford themselves the expediency to pay only lip service to the needs of the suffering millions of our continent who suffer in appalling poverty, famine and disease. They mask their guilt behind the campaign against South Africa."

No clearer illustration of this can be found than in the words of the late Lord Stockton, when as Prime Minister Macmillan he spoke of the winds of change blowing through Africa and said that the British government was planning the decolonisation of its African empire "in the belief that it is the only way to establish the future of the Commonwealth and of the free world on sound foundations". Macmillan no doubt sincerely believed what he was saying, but history has given his words a different interpretation. Far from identifying the real problems of Africa, the European powers were merely trying to escape from the rising tide of trouble that they were becoming caught up in. Dr Hendrik Verwoerd, the South African Prime Minister of the day, gave warning even then of the consequences of this precipitate withdrawal:

"When on an occasion such as this, on which we are perfectly frank, we look at (your policies) critically, then we see, unlike you, that there may be great dangers inherent in those policies." They were to prove prophetic words.

It was also during Macmillan's tour of Africa that a widely-read and highly-respected French author, René Dumont, wrote a book with the significant title of *False Start in Africa*. In 1986 he published another indictment of events in Africa. With total frankness he said that the situation in Africa was a disaster. The black continent was threatened with death... selfishness, incompetence and the waste of natural resources had effectively killed all hope. Neither independence nor aid nor progress nor years of prosperity had created the slightest chance that Africa could emerge from its misery and escape suicide. His book *Africa - I accuse* might have been written in South Africa, for all the impact it had on Europeans or policies cooked up in the corridors of power.

In South Africa itself the book was even quoted by the State President as evidence from an entirely independent source of precisely those African developments about which South Africa was most concerned. The speech, not surprisingly, went unremarked by the outside world.

The results of the colonial withdrawal from Africa were clear to South Africa. While the former imperial powers sat back in Europe, hordes of refugees, many of them owning nothing but the clothes on their backs, poured out of "independent" Africa in search of safety and sanctuary in the country described everywhere as a "threat to world peace". The flood continues to this day, creating the great irony of hundreds of thousands of black people, many of whom cannot speak English, prepared to risk life and limb crossing electrified fences and minefields (designed not to contain a captive population but to keep terrorists at bay) to find food, shelter, medical services and peace within the borders of South Africa.

These facts are repeatedly pointed out by the South African government, yet curiously, they are largely ignored by the international media, and President Botha's most cogent speeches lie unquoted.

Visiting southern Africa in l986, the British Foreign Secretary, Sir Geoffrey Howe, said that the winds of change had developed into a tempest. Like Macmillan he was partly right; but the survival of the African continent has little to do with the emotional catchphrase of "apartheid", a word that has come to represent the sum of all that is wrong with Africa and the abolition of which, it is supposed, will put the whole continent to rights.

That is not to suggest that the problems of Africa are either endemic or without the possibility of solution, but it is necessary to understand that many of the problems of Africa have been imported, particularly economic issues, resulting from centuries of greed and self-interest, culminating in the scramble between the European powers for African riches and territories; the arbitrary drawing of boundaries without regard to tribe or language; the exploitation of Africa for its valuable human, agricultural and mineral resources to the benefit of the nations of Europe; the transportation of great numbers of slaves across the Atlantic; the running of colonial economies purely in the interests of the colonial powers and the disastrous failure to prepare African leaders and populations to govern and administer their countries after independence. Those are also components of the winds that have been blowing over Africa and largely ignored by those in positions to know better.

As several South Africans have often stated, unless the world is prepared to look at the facts and to respond to them in kind, Africa will go down the drain. To suggest in l960 or in 1988 that South Africa is the root cause of the woes of Africa in general is the greatest injustice and insult to the African people.

Moreover, a development that many South Africans find extraordinary, is that when an event takes place like the meeting of the so-called non-Aligned Nations in Harare, the leaders of the Third World, often with the tacit support of the West, launch a volley of hatred against the one country that can really contribute to the development and security of southern Africa. The simple fact remains that nations such as Australia, Canada and New Zealand have neither the wish nor the ability to make the kind of constructive contribution that South Africa both could and would make in Africa.

Britain and France have shown their attitudes by voting with their feet and withdrawing. They care for little but their own special interests. The Australian motive for supporting sanctions against South Africa has less to do with their concern for the Africans (as the wretched condition of their Aborigines proves) than with their desire to sell their minerals and fruit in the markets buying from South Africa. The apparent altruism of the Canadians is belied by the appalling state of their own Indians, as was shown in l987 by Mr Glenn Babb, the incumbent South African ambassador to that country.

An increasing proportion of South Africans, both black and white, English and Afrikaans speaking, is coming to the conclusion that the animosity generated in some Western countries to weaken the position of responsible leaders such as Margaret Thatcher and Ronald Reagan, has very little to do with sincere concern for the welfare of Africa as a whole.

It seems rather a perverse determination to ensure that the one country that could do something positive and constructive has no chance to do so. In this looking–glass world right is wrong and wrong must therefore be right, Q.E.D.

Yet there is much to be said for a new wind of change across Africa, one that will discard the legacies of the past and blow into the future with hope.

South Africa is well qualified to act as such a force; for where else in Africa has a government shown a clearer objective, based on well-tried principles and realities, and all that with the purpose of creating a freer, fairer and better society?

The objective was declared by the Minister of Constitutional Development and Planning, Chris Heunis, in 1985:

"[we] seek to establish a democratic and just society in which everybody enjoys an effective say in all decision-making processes affecting their lives." The principles to be accepted for such a purpose include the preservation of Christian values and civilised norms; the sovereignty of the state; the independence of the judiciary and equality before the law; the preservation of law and order; safeguarding the spiritual and material welfare of all; ensuring human decency, livelihood and liberty; recognition of the group character of South African society, which requires that the self-determination of each group should be protected; private enterprise and free competition; and peaceful cooperation with other nations. In this catalogue of national principles and aspirations the notion that South Africans themselves, not vociferous dictatorial régimes elsewhere, will decide the country's future, is implicit. The realities of Africa and especially of South Africa centre on the fact that South Africa is a heterogeneous society with enormous differences in culture, values and levels of economic development. Such social diversity has naturally given rise to a great diversity of interests and aspirations, all the more conspicuous because the country comprises numerous minorities, so that no single group forms more than 20 per cent of the total population. What is seldom recognised, even by South Africans themselves, is that South Africa is itself also a "developing" country, and as such is undergoing an intense process of modernisation with all that that implies in rapid urbanisation, economic inequalities and unemployment. All these will demand the creation of new structures and rule out catchpenny slogans from outside.

To attain such an objective, some important conditions will be necessary. A certain amount of common agreement on basic objectives, values and norms must be reached. All participants in negotiations must show a willingness to reform and to cooperate in finding joint solutions.

There is a very close connection between reform and the economy. Change in one area has an effect on other areas, and it is often impossible to determine which is predominant under which circumstances. Experience has proved that political development, if it is not accompanied by an equal measure of economic and social development, can lead to serious discrepancies, frustrated expectations and national instability. Thus, political development and change are almost directly dependent on the strength and stability of the economy.

Reforms to broaden the democratic base put enormous strains on the financial resources of a country, the level of economic development and the strengthening of the economy, all of which are the pace-setters in constitutional reform. A further factor of considerable significance is that greater participation in decision-making implies the opening up of formal channels for communicating more ambitious economic demands. The economy then becomes a crucial determinant of the stability and effectiveness of the new democratic institutions and processes, for they have little hope of success if they do not offer or embody the prospect of still greater benefits for the majority of the population.

The economy also influences constitutional reform by determining what can be afforded and what cannot. To suppose, as many critics of South Africa do, that the country is engaged in a deliberate policy of destabilisation of southern Africa, at what must be assumed to be appalling cost, is an absurdity of the highest order when seen in that light. Such an assumption casts doubt on the sincerity of the South African government in its professed pursuit of genuine reform and on the repeated affirmations by the South African Defence Force that classic communist revolutionary warfare can only be contained by the military, who look to the politicians for a political solution.

A clear distinction must be drawn between the stated objective of democratic participation in government by all and the complexity of the structures through which the objective can be achieved.

As Heunis puts it: "Economic factors may and must influence the latter, but must never be allowed to detract from the objective." Political stability has a profound influence on foreign and local investment, for an unstable political environment means greater risk for the entrepreneur. There could be no stronger reason for South Africa to seek tranquillity and stability in Africa, to ensure a suitable environment for peaceful and progressive change. Nothing is more likely to discourage foreign investment, which is necessary for the realisation of such a programme, than the fear of internal and external disorder.

No one understands this better than those who would like to see the orderly and evolutionary development of South Africa fail. Indeed, it is such a view of South African politics that has largely caused the present economic difficulties of the country. The economic lever is all too frequently applied as a political tool to influence developments through sanctions or disinvestment campaigns. A recent study by the US *Journal of Defense and Diplomacy* has shown how futile, counter-productive and detrimental such conduct is, serving only to demonstrate the lack of understanding of the process of reform. Such gestures are effective only in impeding reform, and they seriously affect the African people, not only in South Africa but its neighbours too.

The Journal emphasises the fact that sanctions have slowed reform by further polarising the political forces in South Africa. No serious observer can doubt the sincerity of the President on reform when he is prepared to suffer the distress of a split in his ruling party. In 1988 three Nationalist seats in the Transvaal were lost to the Conservative Party, a fact that has in itself made further *rapprochement* between blacks and whites infinitely more difficult. Again, by raising black expectations that the white government can be overthrown, the talk of sanctions encouraged the intensification of violence and disruption which, despite all its efforts to the contrary, compelled the government to declare a national state of emergency. The result has been a society considerably less free than before, even if quieter.

By concentrating on labour-intensive industries, sanctions have thrown thousands of blacks out of work. The real effects are worse for their dependants, who number tens of thousands. Sanctions also reduce the resources available to create alternative jobs for blacks and make it difficult for the state to provide them with health, education, social-welfare and other services. If that has been the effect on the state, the impact on private enterprise has been even more serious. Many foreign corporations have pulled out of South Africa, abandoning their staff, both black and white; not for political reasons, but because the "hassle factor" back home was too great for the profits earned.

Other companies negotiated complicated sell-outs to local industries. According to one source, 160 new South African millionaires were created overnight. These local interests are not bound by Equal Opportunity Employment legislation; and although no study has been made to determine how black interests have been affected, it goes without saying that they could hardly be advanced by such developments. If it had not been for the rise (since reversed) in the gold price, the state would have been hard-pressed to compensate for these blows, or to finance the great increases in the 1987/8 budget for black education. No measure could have been more effectively calculated to create dissatisfaction and unhappiness among South African blacks than those measures which hurt social services and education. A more deliberate formula for destabilising South Africa could hardly have been invented.

Sanctions have also proved counter-productive in that the campaign has actually increased the concentration of wealth in the hands of white South Africans. Apart from the new millionaires, the number of unproductive government organs has also increased. The former Deputy Minister of Finance, Kent Durr, has repeatedly emphasised that the sanctions already put into effect have led to the freezing of thousands of millions of rands in the acquisition and storage of crude oil, capital that would have been far more profitably employed in the creation of jobs and investments, or on housing, health and education in the black townships.

Far from increasing the dependence of South Africa on the West, sanctions have actually broadened its trading base with the USSR and the Eastern bloc states.

Deposits formerly held in American banks to underwrite trade with the United States have now been transferred to the central banks of those nations that are prepared to trade with South Africa. Although it is not government policy to make public comment on trade relations, the *Journal of Defense and Diplomacy* states that the increasing numbers of Russian and communist bloc commercial agents and aircraft visiting South Africa confirm that there are growing trade links with these states, which means breaking the sanctions barrier and providing much-needed foreign currency for the Soviet Union and its satellites.

Nor are such links confined to the USSR. There are indications that the South African weapons industry has been invited to display its products in Peking before the 1990s. While trade in former Western markets has been badly affected, trade with countries in the Far East, particularly Japan, has greatly increased, to the point where certain business and financial interests in South Africa are concerned over the possibility of pressure by the US State Department on Tokyo to reduce its South African connections.

Paradoxically, sanctions have led to greater US imports of strategic minerals from the USSR and Eastern bloc countries. While the importation of strategic minerals is not forbidden by the US sanctions legislation of 1986, uncertainty about whether future sanctions will include such minerals has convinced importers that it would be wise to get their supplies from other countries, and the Soviet Union is in fact the only other source of certain minerals. Intelligent South Africans may be excused for wondering whether their country occupies such an important place on the international stage that the United States is prepared to put itself virtually at the mercy of its declared enemy merely to exert pressure on the knuckle-end of Africa. The minerals in question include:

*Chrome ore:* (stainless steel, super-alloys for aerospace and defence). Imports from the USSR increased to 6 440 tons a month (31 March 1987) compared with 479 tons a month in 1981-85, the base period.

*Antimony:* (bullets, computers, radar and sonar). Imports from the USSR have risen by 98 times in the base period.

*Industrial Diamonds:* (machining, precision–polishing). Imports from the USSR have risen by 100 times.

*Platinum bars and plates:* (catalysts, electronics, defence). Imports from the USSR have risen by five times.

*Ferrosilicon:* (armour, ships, tanks, submarines). Imports from the USSR averaged 1 407 tons compared with 346 tons in the base period.

Despite regular reports by the US Department of Commerce concerning the increasing dependence of the United States on the Soviet Union for crucially important strategic minerals, not least the Strategic Defence Initiative, Congress seems largely unperturbed. It was with incredulity that South Africans read reports towards the end of 1987 of proposals by Representatives Ronald V. Dellums, Senator Alan Cranston, Senator Ted Kennedy and Senator Carl Levin which, if put into effect, would prohibit imports of strategic minerals from South Africa unless the President attested that supplies were unobtainable from elsewhere. Yet nothing was said about purchases from the USSR.

An even more significant effect of sanctions on relations between the US and South Africa has been the weakening of American influence. The South African government, and many South Africans of all races, now believe that Washington has no sincere desire to act as a constructive contributor to a peaceful and lasting solution to the problems of southern Africa.

The whites are convinced that US politicians are eager to sacrifice South Africa on the altar of domestic political expediency. Margaret Thatcher and Helmut Kohl still command some credibility, Mrs Thatcher not least for her spirited defence of British determination to oppose sanctions at the Commonwealth meeting in 1987. The influence and respect commanded by Britain and Germany in South Africa puts the United States to shame, for unlike the American Congress and President Reagan, the European prime ministers are considered to occupy positions from which they can pursue their policies with determination, unimpeded by special–interest groups inspired by mischievous motives.

As American influence on the South African government and the whites has been permitted to weaken greatly, the American influence on black South Africans has likewise failed to strengthen. One factor has been the unemployment caused directly by sanctions, but even more, the pusillanimous flight of American companies has made it obvious that the United States does not really care, and seems more concerned with striking sanctimonious poses for the delectation of its own than with the hardships caused by US actions in South Africa. Moreover, South African blacks now realise that the programmes devised by the American corporations to promote black welfare in South Africa have failed to make any impression on apartheid.

An even more bitter irony, which would be comic if it were not so desperately serious for those affected, is the fact that South African blacks who personally recognised the value of such "social–responsibility" programmes and who had benefited by the presence of American companies, are now deeply resentful of disinvestment, now that times are hard and many of them have lost their jobs or are likely to do so.

To these men and women, the departure of the American corporations is not considered as opposition to apartheid or support for extending the black franchise; it simply displays a couldn't–care–less attitude.

On the other hand, those corporations and entrepreneurs who have courageously, often in the face of a subtle form of moral terrorism, resisted such pressures to withdraw from South Africa, deserve high praise. They also enjoy the respect and gratitude of their workers and a loyalty that trade unions will find difficult to destroy.

Their decision shows some faith in the South African economy and in the ability of South Africa to solve its own constitutional problems, and an understanding of the connection between politics and the economy. They are contributing to the stability and peaceful development of all southern Africa, for South Africa is as much in need of foreign capital, skilled manpower and technological resources, assistance and knowledge as any other Third World country. Therefore foreign investors should adopt much longer views of the prospects of investment and their continued presence in South Africa. The recent unrest, like the disinvestment campaigns, thus seriously impedes reform; but that of course is one of its main purposes.

Just as external restrictions on the South African economy retard the development of the entire region, so violence obstructs any positive and constructive reforms. It is precisely for that reason, not for repression or preserving the existing state of things, that the government has acted strongly against insurrection and violence, which, if it were permitted to run its course would kill the reform process stone dead. Certainly experience elsewhere has shown that some degree of uncertainty, instability and even violence is a normal side-effect of any process of constitutional, social, political and economic change.

Many people fear that they will lose benefits or privileges, and cannot believe that a new dispensation will work, at least in its early stages. It is quite possible (and it has been candidly admitted by members of the Cabinet) that a great part of the recent unrest can be attributed to such fears.

That is a consideration given serious weight in the highest government circles, as is proved by the President's address to Parliament after the elections in the House of Assembly in May 1987, when he said that the broadening of democracy could be sought in South Africa in more than one responsible manner. However, all who use the word "democracy" do not necessarily attach the same weight, values and meaning to it. To some it means a genuine broadening of democracy and a real expansion of freedom, but to others it is merely a convenient label for a radical clique attempting to seize power.

A careful reading of statements by the South African government, and this speech by P.W. Botha in particular, makes it clear that the leadership accepts that the question of constitutional change in any nation is a serious matter fraught with danger, not necessarily revolutionary or communist at all. Iran after the fall of the Shah is a case in point. In view of the demands and challenges of the realities, this is even more so in South Africa. But the most important criterion is that constitutional development and change must take place in a constitutional manner; and while the government readily accepts that there are people both inside and outside the houses of parliament who support government policy, it also recognises that there are others who do not share its views and reject them with vigour.

In itself the government sees nothing wrong with that, for it is a constitutional liberty accorded to all law-abiding citizens of any decent state. But what is most decidedly not acceptable is the fact that certain persons and groups should express their opposition and their attempts to promote alternative systems by methods that cannot be condoned by any decent state. These include activities that refuse to accept the lawful, constitutional mechanisms and institutions in South Africa;

approve of and use violence, intimidation and murder as instruments of political change; and are conducted in a manner that precludes the policies and leaders of those groups from being subordinate to the wishes of the electorate.

It is precisely such political activities, particularly when they are accompanied by contempt for the laws of the land, that the government feels bound to restrain if it is to fulfil its obligations responsibly and effectively. The fact that certain laws may not be acceptable to some people does not give them the right to contravene the law in general. The same is true of neighbouring states which, despite incontrovertible evidence of the sanctuary that they are giving to such people, not only do nothing to prevent them from entering South Africa in pursuit of their illegal and violent aims but positively help them within their own borders.

Furthermore, the government has observed with dismay the willingness of certain Western countries to be used as conduits or fronts for the transfer of funds from Russia and the Eastern bloc, as well as propaganda and other assistance to these overtly revolutionary groups. The rot has set in to such a degree in certain Western countries that it is no longer even necessary for the Russians to associate themselves with the organisations that they have fostered. Local communist and leftist organisations are easily capable of doing the work for them.

Subversive activities inside South Africa can no longer be allowed to be encouraged or financed from sources outside or their agents inside South Africa.

The world abounds with countries whose governments have been deposed and the system dismantled, under the pretext of freedom and democratic values. Such countries have invariably ended up in the Russian sphere of influence. What the South African government finds so ironic is that prominent persons and institutions in Western countries have given financial and moral support to the destruction of their own allies. Among recent examples we may cite Iran, Nicaragua and Rhodesia. The South African government is aware of the efforts and plans constantly being developed and rehashed to that end, and it devotes serious attention to those areas that are affected by the forces dedicated to illegal action.

Pride of place must be given to the African National Congress. It is not possible to assess the effectiveness of a revolutionary movement merely by counting its acts of sabotage, terrorism, intimidation (both intellectual and physical), propaganda and agitation. The ANC operates within broad limits. Although it was founded as a nationalist movement for the political liberation of South African blacks and the creation of a national consciousness, it has now become an outright Marxist-Leninist organisation. In a recent article in the US State Department Journal, *Problems of Communism,* titled "The ANC, Cadres and Credo," Michael Radu says it is a sterile exercise to argue the merits or demerits of the extent of the infiltration of the South African Communist Party and its penetration and control of the ANC. The communist role in the ANC is sixty years old, and that is also true of the so-called military wing, Umkhonto we Sizwe, since its creation. As Radu puts it:

"Until the mid-1970s, when the last non-Marxists were purged, one could make a reasonable case for the existence of internal tensions within the ANC between Marxists and non-Marxists. Today the only internal tensions are between the 'orthodox' (pro-Moscow) cadres of the SACP and the other 'unorthodox' Marxist-Leninists within the ANC's ruling National Executive Committee."

While sharing similar ideological tenets and carrying out similar practices, they may be said to differ over the question of race only in the credentials of leadership.

Although terrorism and sabotage are important components of ANC policy, they are by no means the only elements in the equation. Direct aggression can be effectively dealt with by the resources of the state, and although the impact is felt in coverage by the foreign media, now curtailed by the new measures adopted by the government, the possibilities of a takeover by the ANC through outright violence are so remote as to be hardly worth considering. The real danger lies in the propaganda assault on the national morale, the subtle psychological undermining of the security forces, the manipulation of the churches, schools, trade unions and universities for activities that can only be called subversion, and the effective isolation of South Africa in commercial, diplomatic and military relations. That demands a comprehensive policy capable of defeating the multifarious activities of the ANC, but also flexible enough to keep pace with changing circumstances under which the war is waged.

The military forces obviously have an important part to play, but theirs is not the be-all and end-all, for if the government is to win ultimately, it must discredit the ANC both in the neighbouring states and elsewhere.

Internally, what Mao Tse-tung called the revolution of rising expectations must be satisfied on the constitutional, social, political and economic level, proving that the government is more effective than the forces of violence, while the revolutionary ardour generated in the civilian population is contained, suppressed and neutralised. These are the classic principles of guerrilla warfare that have been applied in Malaya, Indo-China, Algeria, Rhodesia, Aden, Cyprus and Oman, and are now being adapted to the peculiar conditions in South West Africa/Namibia and South Africa. Ultimately such a strategy entails the identification of ANC activities at all levels and the adoption of the appropriate counteraction with the minimum delay and the maximum effect.

The recent state of unrest can be directly traced back to the late 1960s and early 1970s, when the ANC was trying to recover from the setbacks it had suffered in 1963. During the interim period the leaders were driven underground or arrested, or fled abroad, which created a gap on the revolutionary front, resulting in political apathy among the black population. During the latter part of that period the SACP-ANC axis developed a complex covert underground network with a secure foothold inside the country. This was conducted with the blessing of the exiled leaders in Lusaka and London.

To bring their underground movement into the open required the targeting, penetration and manipulation of a well-developed series of front groups and individuals. Some of these were specially invented for the clandestine work and purposes of the ANC, but many were perfectly legitimate, well-intentioned and of course always at the liberal end of the spectrum.

They were chosen because of their high repute among certain parts of the population. However, while such covert operations have their advantages, the use and abuse of front organisations also has serious disadvantages, as the ANC was to learn.

The essential problem is the question of ultimate control; for the larger front organisations become the more difficult they are to dominate and to direct along communist lines. Moreover, another curious fact about southern African revolutionary movements is that they have often been directed by European and Indian communists. It was, for example, no secret that the white-run Portuguese Communist Party dominated Frelimo in Mozambique, as well as from exile in Tanzania. Their influence persisted even after the departure of the colonial administration, for both Samora Machel and his successor Joaquim Chissano have been assisted by white Portuguese communists, who have shown signs of bitterness and disillusionment with the Utopia that they worked so hard to bring into existence.

The British Communist Party played an important part behind the scenes in Rhodesia, and the South African Communist Party has its share of European and Indian leaders.

From 1963 on the SACP found it expedient to base those stalwarts of the party who were not yet in gaol in South Africa or had been driven deep underground, well away from the country. Not only were they given sanctuary in the neighbouring states in Africa, but some surprising countries, ostensibly opposed to the export of terror in Europe, also made their territory available, despite the fact that the host governments must have fully understood the policies and plans of their guests.

Nonetheless they were prepared to provide means for the future destabilisation of one of their traditional allies. South African soldiers had fought alongside their own troops in two world wars. Furthermore, this did not prevent a remarkable network from developing inside the South African prison system itself, particularly on Robben Island and in the Pretoria Central Prison. This extraordinary clandestine system made possible consultation between the outside and exiled SACP leaders and their imprisoned comrades, such as Braam Fischer, Walter Sisulu, Govan Mbeki and Nelson Mandela. Bribed staff, cooperative non-political prisoners and visitors kept their comrades fully informed and consulted. Moreover, even in the mid-1970s, an attempt to penetrate Mandela's communication system on Robben Island failed when the agent on the spot, after spending six months with Mandela, told his handlers to go to hell. He had been turned and recruited by the man he had been sent to spy on.

In the early 1970s, the main objectives for infiltration were black youth organisations, black trade unions, some specially-invented ANC fronts and, of course, the liberal white English-speaking universities of Cape Town and Johannesburg.

By the mid-1970s, this policy had developed and changed. A large number of CP cells, mainly Indian and African, who acted as sleepers (agents who had been recruited but were still waiting to be actively employed) were now mobilised. It is likely that the order came direct from Moscow.

These cells and cadres were specially designed to coordinate the efforts of recently released comrades who had been gaoled since the failure of their endeavours in the 1960s. Many wavering activists found their previously doubtful communist loyalties actually reinforced by their confinement in gaol, so that incarceration became a badge of honour, proof of commitment and an opportunity for a sound ideological training!

An extensive campaign was launched at this time to sell the idea that detained communists were really only oppressed nationalists. How successful that operation proved to be may be judged from a poll conducted in Soweto during the mid-1970s, as cited by Gerard Ludi in his unpublished *History of the South African Communist Party*. It revealed that 90 per cent of all secondary-school pupils in Soweto considered Nelson Mandela to be the "true leader" of South Africa, and only two per cent had ever heard of the Rivonia treason trial. They were all convinced that Mandela had been fighting for the extension of rights to blacks, and, indeed, none of them knew of his membership of the SACP. However, it is even more remarkable that they attributed this astonishing ignorance to two black newspapers, *The World* and *The Post*.

While the attempts to penetrate the universities won only limited success in some faculties, the Black Consciousness Movement, or BCM, took off like a rocket. So fast did it grow and so large did it become that the SACP found, as it has discovered with the UDF now, that it was almost impossible to control. Membership ranged from genuine black nationalists who loathed the whites to those who merely despised the policies of the government. This was not promising material from which to make a full-scale communist revolution. As more and more senior posts were filled with genuine black nationalists, the SACP tried to form Marxist cells to steer the senior committees. To the dismay of the SACP, the black militants defeated the attempt and formed the South African Students' Organisation, SASO, led by Steve Biko, Abram Tiro and Harry Nengwekhulu.

Biko and Tiro did not hesitate to collaborate with the SACP. Harry Nengwekhulu refused such collaboration, maintaining that the BCM would be hijacked by the SACP and manipulated for their own purposes. For his trouble he was banished first to Venda, whence he fled to Botswana. He developed links with the International University Exchange Fund, with its headquarters in Switzerland, which liberally financed the anticommunist wing of the BCM. A highly-placed South African intelligence officer, Craig Williamson, who had been recruited into communist circles while posing as a student at the University of the Witwatersrand, was also in the IUEF. The Fund created a well-financed dissident element within the BCM that weakened control by the SACP over their own front organisation.

In 1976 the teaching of Afrikaans in black schools served as a pretext for massive civil disobedience by black schoolchildren and students against the entire white administrative system. Ironically they were mobilised by the very school system that they so vehemently rejected. The youth of Soweto erupted on to the streets. Even the ANC and the SACP themselves were caught off balance by the apparently spontaneous "mobilisation of the young masses", as it seemed to be at the time. Experienced political agitators found themselves swept along by the wave of juvenile hysteria.

It was said that between 200 and 600 deaths resulted, and certainly millions of rands worth of damage was caused. Zulu workers in the Transvaal saw their hostels ransacked and in some cases burnt down by hostile mobs. In retaliation they formed *impis* and hunted down the arsonists, murderers and rioters. Not surprisingly, the unrest died down.

Although the subsequent report of the Commission of Inquiry appointed by the government failed to find conclusive evidence to link the objectives of the SACP-ANC with the aims of the students, there was evidence to suggest that large numbers of pamphlets published and distributed by both organisations played a part in inciting the rioters after the first outbreaks of violence. The Commission noted that where there was agitation it exploited existing grievances such as discrimination, housing, pay, transport, trade, amenities, race relations and discipline.

Nevertheless, there can be no doubt that the KGB were aware as long ago as April 1976 that trouble was coming to South Africa in June that year. In his *History of Communism in South Africa*, Henry Pike describes an extraordinary meeting between Joe Slovo, a Colonel in the KGB and until 1987 leader of Umkhonto we Sizwe, and a former lover of his living in South Africa. Unknown to his wife, Ruth First, Slovo's twenty-year old affair with this woman had produced a son, who also attended the meeting in Trafalgar Square in London. At this rendezvous Slovo warned his former mistress to leave South Africa without delay, as there was great trouble in store for the country in the middle of the year.

The children's rising proved to the SACP that the potential for revolution was far greater than they had thought. As thousands of disaffected youngsters anticipated the inevitable crackdown by the security forces, they became ready recruits for Slovo's MK. Many of these children, much against their will, were taken to training centres run by the exiled CP movement in places as far afield as Angola, Mozambique, Algeria, Libya, the USSR, Cuba, East Germany and Nigeria. In 1978, according to Gerard Ludi, the ANC recruits in Nigeria were sent to Cuba. Some appalling stories have been told about these events.

In the latter part of the 1970s Ludi identified the following fronts which had been adopted or infiltrated by the SACP-ANC: AZASO, the Azanian Student's Organisation; the Soweto Committee of Ten; Azapo, the Azanian People's Organisation; COSAS, the Congress of South African Students; MWASA, the Media Worker's Association of South Africa; SATAC, the South African Teachers' Action Committee; BPS, the Black Priests Solidarity Movement; and many others.

An interesting point about these organisations was the extent to which they were funded from abroad, some by the World Council of Churches through the South African Council of Churches, and related bodies. Radio stations in the neighbouring states beamed incessant propaganda agitating for the overthrow of the "racist régime" in support of the SACP-ANC and its fronts. Such conduct was hardly in the interests of regional stability, although worse was to come.

By the early 1980s the ANC had begun to regain control of the BCM. The so-called "third force" of black radicals had either been assimilated or eliminated. The abducted teenagers of 1976 began returning in the 1980s as trained (though not very well trained) terrorists, infiltrating South Africa with the knowledge, if not the tacit approval, of the governments of Angola, Zambia, Botswana, Swaziland, Lesotho, Mozambique and newly independent Zimbabwe.

From 1987 onwards large caches of arms were secreted throughout the country, including the by now familiar AK-47 rifles (some of them with silencers for political assassination); landmines; anti-personnel mines, limpet-mines, hand-grenades, machine-pistols and large quantities of explosives, all of conspicuously Russian manufacture. Gone, at last, was the pretence that what was to come would not be a revolution inspired, financed, supplied and directed along classic Marxist-Leninist lines by the Soviet Union. Sporadic attacks on police stations, government buildings, public installations and commercial establishments preceded assaults on black policemen and other "collaborationist elements".

For the first time an extensive campaign of carefully organised political violence could be waged, as had been outlined by the SACP-ANC in 1961. Despite the repeated appeals by the government to neighbouring states to cease their support for a line of action that could only damage the entire sub-continent, only Swaziland responded with any degree of responsibility. It seemed as if Lusaka, Maputo, Maseru, Harare, Dar es Salaam, Gaberone and Luanda either refused to believe the warnings from Pretoria or to care about the consequences to their own people.

The South African government now found itself in a difficult position. If it ignored the support from abroad for internal subversion, the situation could only deteriorate. Diplomatic representations had been made many times, only to meet with rejection and sometimes, contempt. To declare war against the subversives, while not altogether impossible, would have been costly and could have led to a conflagration of Middle Eastern proportions or worse.

The problem was certainly not peculiar to South Africa - we see a similar situation developing today in Israel - and the government carefully examined the examples of other countries faced by the same dilemma.

Israel had invaded the Lebanon and created an Israeli *cordon sanitaire* in the early 1980s after repeated attacks by the PLO from that quarter. Britain had had the same problem in Aden, Malaysia, Borneo and Northern Ireland. In Aden the British Special Air Services had regularly carried out operations across the border. In a letter to *The Times* of London published on 19 June 1977, the former Director of Operations in Malaysian Borneo, General Walter Walker, stated that he had been "authorised by the then Labour government to conduct cross-border operations several miles deep into Indonesian Borneo" to establish a *cordon sanitaire,* so that eventually all contacts with the enemy had taken place on the Indonesian side of the border.

In Ireland, British SAS troops have been frequently apprehended on southern territory. That has always been ascribed to map-reading errors; so that when a small SAS team climbed in the Himalayas another letter to *The Times* from an irate Irishman asked sarcastically in view of their deplorable map-reading record in Ireland how they knew which peak they had conquered!

During the Vietnamese war the Americans had run covert operations in ostensibly neutral Laos and Cambodia. In his book on guerrilla warfare, *War in the Shadows,* a former officer of the US Marine Corps, Robert Asprey, emphasised the fact that "North Vietnamese units had knocked out a series of guerrilla outposts in southern Laos, in the important Bolovens Plateau area - outposts secretly organised by CIA personnel." Asprey says that the operations in Cambodia infuriated the US Congress, but they were defended by the US Secretary of Defense, Melvin Laird, as necessary to protect American troops. That cannot have been missed by the South African government.

The Rhodesians had faced a similar problem after the Portuguese withdrew from Mozambique. It was decided to use the Rhodesian SAS to train and deploy the anti-communist Mozambique National Resistance Movement. As Barbara Cole has described in her book *The Élite,* the Rhodesian SAS trained the infant MNR and accelerated their progress beyond measure. They transformed them from a rabble to an efficient organisation, to such a degree that it was rumoured that the MNR had played a part in compelling Machel to sign the Nkomati Accord.

Certainly, judging by experience elsewhere, the idea of underwriting proxy forces against those who support their own proxies in South Africa to overthrow the sovereign government by violence had strategic and tactical advantages. The ensuing level of conflict would be controllable, trading and diplomatic relations (of sorts) could continue, and there would be substantial political benefits; and the whole process could be stopped if the "frontline states" were prepared to stop destabilising South Africa.

Short of outright surrender, it was therefore the least damaging or costly option, and by 1988 it had brought both Mozambique and Angola to the negotiating table, which proved that it worked.

The drawbacks lay mainly in the field of propaganda where it was obvious that what Israel, Britain and the United States were capable of doing and getting away with, South Africa and Rhodesia were not to be allowed to in the diplomatic double-speak and treble standards of the world at large. It was to prove a bonanza to liberal academics, politicians and journalists. The cry went up that the racist régime was destabilising the sub-continent, while those responsible in reality for destabilising the region sat back elsewhere to watch the devastation caused by their handiwork. Yet the lesson from such bastions and paradigms of democracy as Britain and the USA was clear.

In fact it was only when Mozambique was one short step from total economic collapse, as much because of the inadequacies of her socialist system as the activities of the MNR, that Samora Machel consented to sign the Nkomati Accord with South Africa. But while the accord was a diplomatic triumph for both the United States (whose covert role in the negotiations has yet to be revealed) and South Africa, for Machel it did little to curtail the operations of the ANC, which were increasingly directed from Gaberone.

Networks throughout the country were coded and computerised. Great quantities of SACP-ANC propaganda, much of it printed in the Eastern bloc as well as in Western Europe, was distributed inside South Africa by church and educational institutions.

The KGB itself highlighted the Secunda SASOL project as a priority target. After the first attack failed to seriously disrupt the complex, ANC cadres began rehearsing on a full-scale model in Angola.

The "siege" of the Silverton Volkskas Bank, along the classic lines of the PLO, the Baader-Meinhof gang and the Red Brigade, signified an entirely new initiative. Although decisive action by the police effectively smashed the operation, the terrorists killed were given heroes' funerals in Pretoria and Soweto. This set the stage for an entirely new pattern: political funerals, for which ample cannon fodder was supplied by the ensuing violence. It was all rather ironic that this trend followed the IRA mould.

By 1985 embryonic "liberated zones" were being created in the townships. In Cradock, on the day of the first partial state of emergency, the Russian flag flew openly over the UDF meeting. Subsequently, in Alexandra, at a mass funeral attended by Western diplomats and some South African MPs, a large banner bearing the hammer and sickle dominated the proceedings.

To give general coordination in South Africa to the proliferating front groups, a vast umbrella organisation had been invented in August 1983: the United Democratic Front. As long ago as 1979 the SACP had said: "All revolutionary blacks and whites should strive to build in South Africa a broad democratic front, unifying all progressive forces under the revolutionary leadership of the ANC and on the basis of the Freedom Charter." Its more important affiliates included COSAS; the Release Mandela Campaign, the Natal Indian Congress and the South African Allied Workers' Union.

The leadership comprised many former officials of the ANC; the overt symbols of the UDF closely resembled those of other self-declared communist organisations and the political slogans differed little in their virulence or objectives. In 1985 Cosatu was formed, the Congress of South African Trade Unions, a huge black trade union umbrella, with a membership of almost half a million workers, under radical UDF leadership. The UDF adopted the 1955 Kliptown Freedom Charter as their constitution, a fuzzy-minded document proclaimed by the ANC as the basis of a new constitution.

It proposed a political system similar to the CPSU (Communist Party of the Soviet Union) idea of a dictatorship of the proletariat. Even Chief Mangosuthu Buthelezi denounced the UDF as a slimy stepping-stone to the ANC.

The watershed year was 1984. In contrast with the early Sixties, the violence did not surge up and then decline. In 1984 not a month went by without unrest in some part of the country. The remotest towns and villages were subjected to politicisation and mobilisation. In a curious way it was a tribute to the revolutionary fervour of the churches, trade unions, school teachers and university lecturers who preached the gospel of agitation. But that was not all. In the black townships of the Vaal Triangle, communications between the white administration and the black inhabitants had totally broken down.

Corruption, nepotism and chicanery aggravated an already unhappy and tense situation. The findings of the government Commission of Inquiry, led by Professor Tjaart van der Walt, described it as the explosion of immense individual frustration and irritation which, finding no formal outlet or channel for expression, detonated in the form (at first) of widespread unrest, arson and bloodshed.

In 1985 the patron of the UDF, Dr Allan Boesak, returned from a visit to Maputo and declared on the BBC World Service that the machinery was ready and waiting to propel Nelson Mandela to the forefront of the political struggle, just as soon as the government saw fit to release him. As the events of 1985 and 1986 took shape, it became apparent that the four-point strategy of the SACP-ANC was coming together: to isolate South Africa culturally, economically and diplomatically all over the world by mobilising a large number of communist fronts; to start a carefully planned terror campaign in the guise of a spontaneous uprising, with widespread intimidation, arson, sabotage, political murder and general anarchy to make the country ungovernable; to continue radicalising young people of all races, mainly Indians, blacks and coloureds, working through their schools, universities, technical colleges, trade unions and cultural groups; and to resuscitate in Cosatu the old South African Congress of Trade Unions.

About the same time an apparently spontaneous series of anti-South African demonstrations was started in the USA by radical black American organisations concerned with the civil-rights movement, led by a coalition under the aegis of Randall Robinson's Trans Africa movement. The demonstrations, which were designed to compel the imposition of congressional sanctions on South Africa were triggered off by two meetings in 1981 in collaboration with the US Communist Party, CPUSA.

On 8 June 1981 the first conference, "Building Forces for US Support Against South Africa", was held at Howard University, a black college in Washington DC. The speakers included Randall Robinson, Oliver Tambo and Canon Robert Powell of the American National Council of Churches. There were other delegates from the World Peace Council (a CIA-acknowledged Russian front), East Germany, Cuba, Algeria and other communist allies. Then from 9 to 11 October in the same year, another meeting was held under the aegis of the United Methodist Office for the UN at the New York Riverside Church: "A Conference on Solidarity with the Liberation Struggles of the Peoples of Southern Africa".

There is cause to believe that these meetings were arranged with the covert cooperation of the CPUSA at the behest of the KGB "rezident" in the American capital, Dmitry Yakushkin, who later that same year returned to Moscow.

In their book *The New KGB: Engine of Soviet Power*, William Corson and Robert Crowley say that on returning to Moscow Yakushkin assumed responsibility for all the foreign operations of the KGB, a job formerly done by Yuri Andropov. At this second meeting, the SACP received great honour, plus enormous financial, moral and physical support from the gathering. Similar operations were launched in Britain and several other countries in Western Europe.

Despite a first-class counter-intelligence operation in South Africa itself, a quarter century of subversive preparations began to pay dividends in the mid-1980s. All cells, terrorist cadres, specialist organisations, reconnaissance groups and couriers worked on the strictest "need-to-know" principle. Security service infiltrators found that they could smash only single cells. The SACP began to run itself on a family basis, making infiltration almost impossible. SACP staff who superseded the "need-to-know" principle were denied access to South Africa.

Thus the SACP command operated from Britain, Tanzania, Zambia, Algeria, Angola and so on.

The pattern of violence throughout the country really began with the full-scale riots in the Vaal Triangle in September 1984. From there the unrest spread systematically throughout the country operating through COSAS and youth organisations affiliated to the UDF. The highest incidence of violence first occurred in the Eastern Cape and the Pietersburg–Witwatersrand–Vereeniging area, but after the attempted protest march to Pollsmoor Prison, the Cape Peninsula became the focus.

At first sporadic and isolated, the incipient revolutionary situation became better organised throughout 1985. As chronic unrest spread, the government declared the partial state of emergency to restrict gatherings, stone-throwing, arson, and attacks on the property and persons of the police, lower government officials and other "collaborators". Grenades, petrol-bombs, acid-bombs and firearms were used in these attacks. The emergency gradually took effect and the ANC found it more difficult to run its crash courses on grenade-throwing, limpet and landmine operations and the use of explosive devices. In areas where the civil administration had begun to disintegrate with the failure of the electricity, refuse, postal and other services, law and order returned.

About three months into 1986, the State President lifted the partial emergency. He did so because the wide powers granted to the security forces had curtailed the violence. The ringleaders had been detained, a number of young activists had left the country and meetings inciting violence had tapered off. Immense pressure from abroad had been brought to bear on the country, particularly with the creation of the "Eminent Persons Group" by the Commonwealth Heads of State, who met at Nassau in the Bahamas late in 1985. Many countries attended the meeting, particularly African, whose track record in democracy owed much to the imagination.

The lull did not last long. Within weeks "necklace" murders became common, both inside and outside the townships. In one incident 33 people were "necklaced" in Lebowa. The government of Lebowa privately confessed that parts of the homeland had become virtually ungovernable. White farms in Sekhukhuniland were burnt to the ground. Farm labourers refused to go to work because of intimidation. In the Eastern Cape, herds and flocks were mutilated in Mau Mau style; sheep, cattle and goats were hamstrung and left to die.

White farmers were ordered to leave their farms or they would be "necklaced" as "enemies of the people". In the urban and rural areas, "people's courts" were established. These kangaroo courts were frequently used for personal vendettas on the pretext of politically or ideologically motivated "crimes against the masses". Light sentences involved a thrashing with a cane; more severe sentences resulted in the "necklace", by which the victim was trussed with barbed wire and burnt with a petrol-soaked rubber tyre round his or her neck.

People found buying from white shops were forced to eat their soap powders or drink their cooking oil. In the schools run by the Department of National Education, "people's education" was taught. The praises of Oliver Tambo and Nelson Mandela were sung, the Soviet Union was extolled as "the liberator of the oppressed masses" and the children played in "freedom parks" with toy AK-47s. Nevertheless the government still refrained from introducing another state of emergency.

By the beginning of June 1986, the intelligence services picked up alarming information about plans scheduled for June 16th, which indicated that a full-scale revolution might be about to break out. Student Representative Councils (SRCs) in the Vaal Triangle were to hand all their schoolbooks back to the Department of National Education and spend the day paying tribute to those who had died for the revolution.

In Port Elizabeth, Department of Education and Training centres were to be taken over and occupied. At English-speaking universities, the SRCs demanded public holidays and the cessation of all "élitist" examinations. The Atlantis Youth Congress in the Cape decided to replace the South African flag with the Russian and ANC flags where possible.

The UDF in turn announced a general stay-away, nationwide mass meetings, torch-runs and candle demonstrations in the windows of all UDF dwellings. The Western Cape division of the UDF planned a mass march on Pollsmoor Prison, and warned all persons that they should wear black T-shirts bearing the slogan "600 killed". Cosatu announced a general stay-away of all workers for June l6th and declared that in conjunction with the ANC, June l6th would be commemorated as National Youth Day. The South African Council of Churches not only approved the stay-away, but also called for a national day of prayer to destroy "this evil system in the RSA".

The ANC planned an extensive propaganda campaign with the theme "Strike a Blow for Freedom". COSAS was to be unbanned, and Nelson Mandela unconditionally released. June l6th would mark the turning-point in the freedom struggle.

Radio stations in the neighbouring states broadcast Oliver Tambo's call for the paralysis of every factory, farm and white household. The homeland governments and the tricameral parliament were to be destroyed, so putting a stop to the reform process, and "collaborators" would be forced to withdraw or be made to feel the "people's wrath".

Mass marches were planned for the Union Buildings in Pretoria and Parliament in Cape Town. The "people's militia" were to go on the offensive in the white suburbs, and all rents were to be withheld everywhere. All black municipal councils were to be replaced with "civic organisations".

In accordance with the "Mandela M-Plan" a cell was to be established in every street and every block to serve as the foundation of an alternative government. In the Eastern Cape the plan had reached street level in many areas, and black policemen abandoned the charred ruins of their houses to take shelter in protected sheds and barns. Movements in West Germany, Britain, the USA, Holland, Canada, France, Belgium, Norway and even Peru were to make coordinated calls for sanctions against South Africa.

It was for such reasons that the government found itself compelled to act, and in June l986 the State President declared a nationwide state of emergency. To many it seemed that the declaration had come at the last moment. It successfully disrupted the planning, led to a nation-wide decrease in unrest and ended or reduced the boycotts. In the national states and homelands, law and order began to return, while subsequent restrictions on the foreign media in l987 halted much of the publicity that the South African revolutionaries had achieved abroad.

The intended terror campaign never materialised, and the rand strengthened on the money markets, despite the imposition of sanctions.

Frustrated in their immediate aims, the ANC embarked on a widespread minelaying campaign, concentrated on the trade unions and reverted to a further round of internationally-mobilised propaganda attacks to put pressure on Western countries to intensify sanctions. The country had been saved from a communist revolution, aided and abetted by the "Frontline States", but in the words of the revolutionaries: the struggle continues.

In early 1988 seventeen organisations, prominent among them certain trade union groups such as Cosatu, were restricted by the Minister of Law and Order, Adriaan Vlok, thereby denying them the alternative course adopted by the SACP-ANC.

Certain clergymen immediately took up the cudgels and challenged the State President's conduct. Responding by letter to Archbishop Desmond Tutu, the President said: "What is clearly at issue here is your understanding of evil: is atheistic Marxism the evil, or does your view of evil include the struggle on behalf of Christianity, the Christian faith, and freedom of faith and worship, against the forces of godlessness and Marxism?" The President's letter pointed out the similarity of the Archbishop's approach to the jargon used by the SACP-ANC, and he asked whether the Archbishop was acting on behalf of the Kingdom of God or the kingdom promised by the ANC and the SACP.

Notwithstanding the alliance of forces deployed against South Africa, the government will clearly continue to strive for peace, order and stability. Secondly, the process of evolutionary reform on a constitutional, social and economic basis will continue in accordance with the multi-cultural nature of the country. Thirdly, South Africa will hold out the hand of friendship and cooperation to those who refrain from subversion, so that a common climate of peace, progress and prosperity can be constructively created, to the benefit of all.

The task of defeating the communist offensive in South Africa is difficult enough without the curious attitude of certain Western nations. While acknowledging the Russian influence, the Crocker group in the US State Department greet every new South African reform with demands for ever-more wide-ranging reforms, declaring that while the new measures give cause for hope, they are inadequate in themselves. On the other hand, measures adopted to prevent or anticipate communist-inspired insurrection are strongly condemned by foreign ministries in London, Washington, Paris, Bonn, Ottawa, Canberra and many other countries that ought to know better.

Developments in South Africa are therefore profoundly disturbing, compared with what happened to the allies of the West in Nicaragua, Iran, the Philippines, South Korea and Rhodesia. The South African government may be forgiven for wondering whether the Soviet Union is now regarded as the constitutional model for the new world order.

The accusations against South Africa are in striking contrast with the realities of her aspirations and ideals. The struggle, to use the jargon of the opposition, in southern Africa is not between black and white. It is an ideological struggle between the supporters of genuine freedom and stability and those who wish to force a socialist dictatorship on the states of southern Africa, which would deny freedom of worship, freedom of the individual, freedom of speech and economic progress.

The White Paper (1986) on Defence and Armaments Supply for the South African Department of Defence is enlightening about the Russian threat to southern Africa. Billions of dollars' worth of Russian arms, training and surrogate personnel have been poured into the region with a view to causing general havoc. These assessments are confirmed by the American Heritage Foundation in their report of February 1988, which says that "Africa has been the key testing ground in the struggle between the Reagan doctrine's support for resistance forces fighting

Soviet-backed communist régimes and the Brezhnev doctrine's insistence on the irreversibility of communist gains." Yet, strangely, while proclaiming the virtues of the Reagan Doctrine, organs of the Reagan administration have been actively working against it, as a high official of the administration now confirms: for more than five years the United States has been secretly providing military assistance (presumably along with that provided by the USSR) to the communist Frelimo régime in Mozambique. This despite the fact that since late 1986 the anticommunist MNR forces have been deployed throughout Mozambique to the point where Maputo is a city under virtual siege. Successive pledges by Frelimo to the US government to begin negotiations with the MNR have been repeatedly violated, while the propaganda war against South Africa and the MNR has intensified.

The most spectacular accusation centred on the alleged Homoine massacre, a small village on the Indian Ocean where 400 civilians, including children and pregnant women, were said to have been slaughtered in their hospital beds. Western journalists and diplomats were excluded from the area until the bodies had been buried. For the first week the only reports of the massacre came from the official Mozambican news agency. As subsequent information emerged, US officials lowered their estimates of the dead from 400 to 100, and even cast doubts on the report that the MNR had been responsible. Yet, predictably, South Africa and the MNR took a battering in the foreign press yet again.

At the end of 1987 the *Bulletin of the International Freedom Foundation* in Washington said: The economy of Mozambique is a shambles. 1987 was the seventh year of economic decline, while the interest on the US\$14 billion of foreign debt is 2,2 times the total revenue from exports. Eighty per cent of the labour force produce only 12 per cent of total food requirements. Famine is rife. So frequently is the drought blamed for this poor performance that it has become a joke to say that when the Portuguese pulled out they even took the rains with them.

Fifteen thousand Zimbabwean, 8 000 Tanzanian, 2 000 Cuban, 1 000 Russian, 800 Nigerian and 600 Malawian troops, supported by T-62 tanks and MiG-21/3 aircraft, have so signally failed to contain the relatively popular uprising led by the MNR that Maputo is making a "pragmatic" reorientation in its foreign relations with South Africa and the West, without relinquishing its associations with Russia or its role in the Russian propaganda war.

The record of the USA is little better in Angola, where Unita have won a substantial victory against the Russian general Konstantin Shagnovitch, commanding a mixed Cuban and FAPLA force of 18 000, supported by artillery, tanks, armoured personnel-carriers, armed helicopters and MiG-23s. Despite such enormous fire-power, Unita killed nearly 10 000 of the enemy, captured 80 tanks, about 400 trucks and armoured personnel-carriers, over a hundred field-guns, two complete radar defence networks and three surface-to-air SAM-8 Gecko units.

About US\$1,5 billion worth of Russian equipment found its way back to Unita. For its part the United States has supplied Unita with the crucially important Stinger anti-aircraft missile and TOW anti-tank missiles. But at the same time the State Department supports the commitment of the Gulf Oil Corporation to the Angolan enclave of Cabinda, which provides the Luanda régime with desperately needed foreign exchange.

In its first Bulletin for 1988, the International Freedom Foundation states that apart from Cabinda, where East German and Cuban troops protect US interests,

Angola is an economic wasteland. Food production since independence has fallen by 70 per cent and food shortages in the towns are chronic.

While food is grown in the zones under the control of Unita, the MPLA have ringed their farming communities with land- and anti-personnel mines, so further curtailing food production. Luanda carries a US$20 billion foreign debt, mostly owed to the USSR for arms, and it looks to the International Monetary Fund to bail it out.

Corruption at all levels of government is a serious problem. Aids is said to have spread 1 000 per cent over the last six years. Medical services are virtually non-existent in MPLA zones, which aggravates the spread of disease and malnutrition.

Yet again South Africa bears the brunt of foreign criticism for defending Western interests in a strategically crucial part of the world. As a result of South African support, both moral and material, the MPLA have indicated that they are ready to negotiate with Unita. The Longreach Short Term Forecast for March 1988 makes it clear that too high expectations from these negotiations should not be entertained; but the mere fact that Luanda is willing to consider talking must count as an important step in the right direction.

The first exploratory talks in London were alleged in certain well-informed circles to have originated from a Russian offer made through Canada to South Africa towards the end of 1987. It was the apparent result of four years of sporadic diplomatic contacts. Moscow is said to have suggested a deal whereby Russian and proxy forces would withdraw from southern Africa if Pretoria undertook to protect Russian interests there. Clearly, Swapo and the ANC would be abandoned in the process. In return, Moscow wanted South African diplomatic support for its policies in Central America, Afghanistan and, particularly, against Israel. It was suggested that the USSR also sought a boycott on minerals directed at the United States with respect to platinum group metals. Moscow also hinted, according to these sources, at its willingness to contravene Western-inspired sanctions and to guarantee a cheap oil supply from Iran.

There is no source or record of the South African response to this approach, although there was widespread discussion in diplomatic circles to the effect that a response of sorts was carried by Franz Josef Strauss, who died later in the year, when he returned to Europe after his visit to South Africa. Apart from the wide variety of political leaders that Strauss met on his visit to South Africa, his safari came soon after his visit to Moscow. Political commentators speculated that the response from Pretoria might have contained the following points: if the Kremlin sought withdrawal from southern Africa, as part of Gorbachev's policies of "glasnost" and "perestroika" then South Africa was willing to discuss constructive measures that might reduce the expenses of maintaining South West Africa, ensure regional peace and contribute to the general benefit and development of southern Africa.

While the South African government entertained no illusions about long-term Russian aims and ambitions in the region or anywhere else, it was perhaps possible that an accommodation could be reached that would give both sides a breathing space and permit new approaches and initiatives to be considered. On this basis, although South Africa had no intention of "protecting" Russian strategic interests in southern Africa, perhaps an agreement could be negotiated whereby Moscow could still withdraw in such a way that neither South Africa nor its local allies would any longer offer a threat to those parts of the continent in which Moscow perceived its strategic interests. If Moscow could persuade the Cubans to withdraw from Angola, the gesture would be an important contribution to stability and might ensure the realisation of Resolution 435 for the United Nations independence plan in SWA. If the Russians discarded the ANC and Swapo, the move would be appreciated by Pretoria. As for the problems in Central America and Afghanistan, Pretoria had no strategic interests outside Africa. Relations between Israel and South Africa were not a matter for discussion or negotiation. As for the proposed minerals boycott directed against the USA, Moscow might have been informed that South Africa did not believe in sanctions or counter-sanctions, except, perhaps, under the most exceptional circumstances. As for the possibility of sanctions-breaking and a guaranteed oil supply from Iran, these were serious matters that could perhaps be profitably explored in further talks.

Against this speculative background it is perhaps not surprising that exploratory talks took place in London between South Africa, Angola and others. A very wide variety of questions was raised, from the Cubans in Angola to the positions of Unita and Swapo in the event of the possible execution of UN Resolution 435. As a consequence of the London talks, the first fundamental negotiations began in Brazzaville, where the South Africans challenged the incipient Cuban concentration in south-western Angola on the northern frontier of South West Africa. Cuban sources at a senior level have disclosed that the Reagan administration official responsible for southern Africa, Dr Chester Crocker, was fully aware of the Cuban intention to hit the South Africans hard, "on their own turf", yet it was only when the South Africans themselves raised the matter with the Americans that State Department officials acknowledged the fact. During the Brazzaville talks, to the amazement of the South African delegation, the Angolans denied all knowledge of the build-up, saying that it was strictly a Cuban affair initiated by President Fidel Castro himself, without the consent or consultation of Luanda. Whether that statement was accepted by the South Africans at its face value or not, the South African team gave warning that unless the huge Cuban concentration ceased, all the options for a negotiated settlement could be seriously jeopardised. In retrospect, this clearly stipulated South African proviso seems to have been tacitly ignored by both sides.

By November 1988 the Cubans, East Germans, Russians and Swapo had established a series of well-equipped garrisons in the 5th Angolan District from the port of Namibe through Lubango to Ongiva with troops at Chibemba, Cahama, Humbe and Xangongo. The deployment exhibited all the classic characteristics of a Combined Arms Force designed for engagement with conventional regular army forces rather than guerrilla warfare against Unita. For strategists in Pretoria and elsewhere, it was logical to suppose that this force was intended for use against the South African Defence Force and not Unita. The force included Mi-24 Hind helicopters, artillery and 200 Cuban "spetsnaz" or SAS-type Cuban special forces, plus a pilot corps of 200 helicopter or fixed-wing pilots. Notwithstanding the South African threat, more Cubans continued to be deployed up to the time of writing.

The talks in Brazzaville were also instructive to the South Africans for other reasons. Local government officials pointed out to them that black Africa increasingly recognised that South Africa was the only African country in a position to help the continent with knowledge, talents, skills and other assets crucial to the survival of the continent. While the Frontline States were preoccupied with their propaganda assault against South Africa, they were reaping the benefits of its economic spin-offs. The African states beyond the "front line" were enjoying no such privileges. It was therefore in everyone's interests that the peace talks should succeed. The exchange of such confidences explained to the South Africans why four black countries had been prepared to act as host to the Brazzaville discussions.

By the time of the Cairo talks eleven black states were vying with one another to play host. Although at first very unproductive, the sudden appearance of the Russian official responsible for southern Africa, Mr Vladillen Vasev, just before the South Africans were preparing to leave Cairo, injected a new vigour and intensity into the Angolan and Cuban teams. Although there was some confusion about whether he actually met the Cuban and Angolan teams, his presence impressed the South Africans by its impact on the negotiators. Whether the incident had been staged for effect is impossible to determine at this point, but certainly that is a factor that cannot be ruled out. The South Africans were satisfied that the "man from Moscow" was interested in serious negotiating.

No sooner were these discussions over than a curious incident took place on the South West African/Angolan border when a Cuban–FAPLA force of 600 infantrymen and 35 tanks advanced in a three-pronged spearhead assault on the Ruacana–Caluquembe hydro-electric plant. The attack was spread across a three to five-kilometre front from Tchipa in the north and resulted in nearly 300 of the Cubans being killed, with the loss of nine tanks, for the loss of two Ratels and one South African soldier. Pulling their ground forces back from the mauling, the Cubans retaliated with an air strike by twelve MiG-21s flying below radar–detection level. They dropped between 12 and 18 bombs, one of which carried 548m beyond the retaining wall of the plant and killed 11 SADF men. Whatever the exact circumstances of the incident, neither side was prepared to be the first party to foreclose on the possibility of a negotiated settlement. The attack had, however, demonstrated just how thin the ice was on which the talks had been based.

A series of on-off negotiations led to the subsequent Geneva talks at which the South African Minister of Foreign Affairs, Pik Botha, surprised everybody with a masterly diplomatic stroke, by suggesting that Pretoria was prepared to move on Resolution 435 provided the Cubans were prepared to reach a satisfactory agreement on their timetable for withdrawal. He cited 1 November as the operative date for UN Resolution 435, but he also emphasised that certain pertinent questions still remained unresolved with regard to the source of funding for the execution of the UN Resolution. Soon afterwards the Secretary-General of the UN visited South Africa for talks with the State President, no doubt to clarify these and other matters. His brief visit followed hard on the heels of the much publicised SADF withdrawal from Angola. By contrast, disturbing reports in the press indicated that the Cuban–FAPLA forces were clearing a large area east of Cuito Cuanavale where yet another big offensive was being prepared, clearly aimed at Jonas Savimbi's Unita movement after the withdrawal of the SADF from the country. In October a fierce battle raged round Savimbi's birthplace, Munhango, on the Benguela railway line, a region of little strategic importance but of considerable psychological significance to Savimbi and his movement.

In September it had been generally revealed that an average of one ship a week was leaving Cuba for Angola with troops and equipment. An additional 10 000 Cubans had already been deployed in the country, together with forty MiG-23s. When challenged in the talks, the MPLA denied that these constituted fresh shipments and suggested that they were replacement forces in the monthly rotation of men. Not only was the story unsubstantiated, but the irony could not escape Western observers when it was pointed out by the South Africans that the MPLA and Havana must have uncharacteristically missed the propaganda coup of the decade in comparison with the highly publicised withdrawal of the SADF from Angola back to SWA. Indeed, the protocols agreed to at the Geneva talks implied withdrawal of the SADF from Angola between 20 August and 1 September. In return, Cuban and Swapo forces would withdraw north of the 17th Parallel 100km north of the Angolan-SWA border. It was also agreed that by 1 September agreement would be reached on a timetable for the Cuban withdrawal.

On 24 August the next round of talks in Brazzaville confirmed that Resolution 435 would be implemented on 1 November, but everything still hinged on the timetable for the Cuban withdrawal. Far from withdrawing, the Cubans were arriving in ever-increasing numbers. It was rumoured that USAF cargo transport aircraft were disgorging large numbers of Unita troops at the huge USAF base at Kamina in Zaïre. While Savimbi emphasised that he was certainly not abandoning Jamba, it was apparent to military analysts that he was busy opening a second front to take some of the pressure off Jamba. For General Mobutu these developments acquired a new meaning as the Cuban Air Force frequently violated his air space. Insult was added to injury when the Cuban representative at the peace talks quietly told Mobutu that if he did not adopt a more conciliatory attitude, Zaïre would be next on the hit list after South Africa had been sorted out. Not surprisingly, Mobutu almost immediately invited the South African State President to a public meeting at his magnificent vacation lodge, Gbadolite.

P.W. Botha's visit to Zaïre came soon after his visits to Mozambique and Malawi. Clearly, the President's predictions over the years that South Africa would prove to be the saviour of Africa seemed to be coming true with startling speed for Western European observers. The premature death of the leader of Bavaria, who had tried to help in initiating the talks, provided President Botha with the opportunity to visit Europe and inform certain Western governments at first hand on the latest enigmatic developments on the continent. Perhaps, appearing prominently in the discussions would have been the concern of the South Africans at the possibility of serious Cuban-FAPLA military action during the height of the confusion caused by the American presidential elections in November, or during the inauguration of the new president in January. Certainly, the obvious stalling by the Cubans at the talks on the question of their timetable for withdrawal, which delayed the date of the carrying out of Resolution 435 on 1 November 1988 by the South Africans, was an ominous reminder of the extreme delicacy of the proceedings. Other African leaders were also hopeful.

These difficulties notwithstanding a time-table was drawn up with US-Soviet collaboration by December 1988. The Protocols were signed before Christmas 1988 and SWA seemed set for independence by November 1989.

In Zimbabwe, Robert Mugabe has successfully created his one-party state, although so far he has failed to unite with Mozambique in a federation. Zimbabwe also suffers from a serious shortage of foreign exchange, an increase of 40 per cent in export earnings to service the foreign debt, an increase of the budget deficit to US$2,5 billion accompanied by a 16 per cent inflation rate and an increase in government spending to more than 55 per cent of the Gross Domestic Product. Although the activities of dissidents, termed "bandits", have formed a serious threat to internal security only matched externally by events in Mozambique, South Africa is still denounced as the main threat to Zimbabwe.

Zambia faces an appalling economic future, thanks to Dr Kenneth Kaunda's radical socialist policies and his refusal to accept the advice of the IMF reform programme, which called for reduced government expenditure, cuts in subsidies and imports and extensive rationalisation of the bureaucracy, which consumes 20 per cent of the GDP. Output per head was 35 per cent lower in 1984 than in 1974, which led the French socialist economist Professor René Dumont to say that "a rich man's pigs" enjoyed a better diet than most Zambians.

Not surprisingly, increases in the price of food in 1987 led to nationwide riots, with angry hordes of unemployed attacking symbols of the ruling UNIP party. Despite constant pleas from Pretoria, Zambia continues to give sanctuary to the ANC and is moving deeper into the Russian orbit, using scarce foreign exchange to buy large quantities of Russian armaments, including aircraft and tanks. It is significant that by mid-June 1988 Zambia's foreign exchange reserves had dried up completely.

Moreover, Western intelligence analysts are convinced that the Russian Embassy in Lusaka, headed by Oleg Miroshkin, is the most important Russian surveillance and intelligence-gathering centre in Africa south of the Sahara. With a staff of 130, its main task seems to be the organisation of the destabilisation of southern Africa. In that task it is helped by 200 East German and 450 Russian military "advisers" in Zambia.

Against this background it must surely be clear that South Africa has an irreplaceable part to play in all fields of life in the sub-continent, a constructive and responsible role, unlike that of the external powers. Therefore, provided it can be permitted to solve its own unique problems, in its own orderly and evolutionary way, in contrast to the "liberation" of violent revolutionaries assisted by interfering foreign powers, it may prove more than just a beacon of hope at the end of a dark continent.

With the help of South Africa, not only the South African region, but a large part of the entire continent may one day stand on its own feet, unfettered by external ideological and alien political and economic influences. The South African transport systems, industry, commerce, science and technology, agricultural as well as veterinary and medical services are not only the best on the continent but compare favourably with those of many "developed" countries. The announcement in 1988 that a feasibility study into a space programme would be completed by the end of the year says much. South Africa needs its own Communication and Surveillance Satellites.

Moreover, the State President has already made such an offer to the West and to Africa on questions as diverse as military security and stability in the sub-continent; economic development, aid and mutual cooperation; agricultural and industrial development and creation of employment; the conservation and utilisation of water resources; the development and utilisation of other natural resources and social development in health, nutrition and training. Sooner or later African leaders, in particular, will have to accept that South Africa holds the key to the potential wealth and resources of their continent, and that without South Africa there can be no prosperity.

It is therefore one of the greatest ironies of our curious looking–glass age that the very country which offers hope for the nations and peoples of the African continent should have become the object of destructive condemnation. As P.W. Botha put it in 1986:

"Still, the intensity of the phenomenon reveals a vague underlying realisation that what is now happening here is of vital importance, not only to our part of the world, but in some way also to humanity at large.

"In short, that something of universal significance must and shall be decided in this southern land of ours."

# AFRICAN MILITARY POTENTIAL - INTO THE NINETIES

*by Deon Fourie*

"War is not as easy as everybody thinks."
*Lt-Gen. Joseph Garba,*
*Chairman of Ghana's National Liberation Council, 1966.*

The object of this study is to assess the capacity of the sub-Saharan countries to conduct a prolonged military campaign against South Africa in what may be called "the short term". The depth has been limited by the breadth of the study. There are too many variables for one chapter to give the proper depth. War potential is a mass of continually varying factors: man, his political life, education, the economy, inventions, new techniques, topography and geography, material wealth and poverty. These factors in turn place a time limit on the conclusions. One cannot normally place that time limit too far away. If African countries were the only actors that needed consideration their parlous economies would allow more latitude than would be permissible for more advanced economies. It must be appreciated, however, that since the demonstration of Soviet intervention capabilities in Angola and in Ethiopia between 1975 and 1977, the capacities of the sub-Saharan countries themselves may play a far less important role than before. Whereas the capacity of military forces to fight remains relevant, it has become clear that the build-up of armaments may depend entirely on the willingness, particularly of the USSR, even in the period of *perestroika,* to provide arms to a belligerent. Of course, the possibility that foreign forces such as those of Cuba may be brought in to bear the brunt of fighting has also become very real. It is therefore difficult to determine what the period should be. Ordinarily, the "short term" is too short to allow for re-equipment, re-organisation, changes in standards of training and other factors influencing efficiency or fighting capability. In the "intermediate period" the changes may have begun but their effects are yet to be felt. In the uncertainties of sub-Saharan Africa, as was found in Angola and in Ethiopia, a combination of equipping and providing foreign expeditionary forces could result in immediate operations against opponents already in the field.

In view of these difficulties and the poverty of information on Africa, this analysis relies on four elements as guides:

1. The existence of forces large enough and equipped for prolonged operations far from home;
2. the existence of a balanced force of conventional arms to cope with an opponent's forces;
3. the ability to move and maintain forces long enough to complete operations;
4. unified political leadership effectively to establish strategy, and sound command and control by general staffs to execute the political and strategic decisions.

## Armies[1]

In 1987 the total armed forces of sub-Saharan Africa amounted to 1 295 400 of which armies number 839 550 excluding the South African army. Police and gendarmerie forces available would inflate the figures if they were capable of being added to military operations by their training and indeed if internal circumstances in the various countries permitted that. Of the total, a very substantial number can be mustered south of the Sahara. Figures however tend to mislead if they are not related to the order of battle of the African armies, i.e. the fighting arms and services and their organisation in brigades and divisions.

When conventional capability is to be assessed there must be an assumption that balanced forces containing the requisite proportions of "teeth" arms and services will be available to cope with the prospective enemy. Few of these countries have so organised their armies, let alone exercised them as formations. On the other hand, some have had the experience in the past twenty years of actually using formations in battle. Although Ethiopia had only an infantry mass of 35 000 with an armoured car squadron in 1966, twenty years later its regular army and People's Militia make up 313 000 men, organised into 22 infantry divisions and eight para–commando brigades with 750 tanks, 870 other armoured fighting vehicles (AFV), 700 field artillery pieces, air defence armaments and other medium and heavy weapons. The Nigerian force of 9 000 men in 1966 grew during the civil war to about 250 000 and has now been reduced to 80 000, organised as four divisions of 11 brigades. They are backed by 232 tanks, 565 miscellaneous AFVs and 522 field artillery pieces. Angola, which was a Portuguese colony until 1974, has 91 500 soldiers, 550 tanks and 500 artillery pieces. Zimbabwe has an army that, while large in manpower (46 000) as a result of the inflation caused by absorbing the former Zanla and Zipra forces, has only 43 tanks, 168 AFVs and 60 artillery pieces. Tanzania is similar, with 38 350 men, as against 1 700 in 1966, but only 96 tanks and 65 AFVs, although the artillery strength is 340 pieces. The Tanzanian increase can probably be ascribed to the war with Uganda, when its army deposed the dictator Idi Amin in 1979.

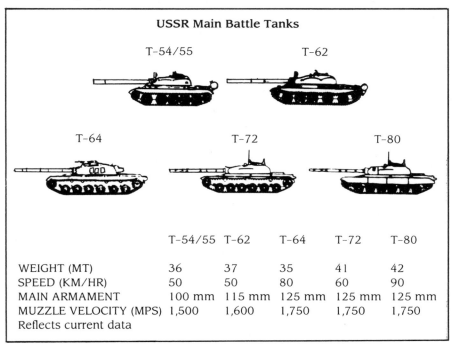

**USSR Main Battle Tanks**

|  | T-54/55 | T-62 | T-64 | T-72 | T-80 |
|---|---|---|---|---|---|
| WEIGHT (MT) | 36 | 37 | 35 | 41 | 42 |
| SPEED (KM/HR) | 50 | 50 | 80 | 60 | 90 |
| MAIN ARMAMENT | 100 mm | 115 mm | 125 mm | 125 mm | 125 mm |
| MUZZLE VELOCITY (MPS) | 1,500 | 1,600 | 1,750 | 1,750 | 1,750 |

Reflects current data

Challenge

Mozambique is the last army in the table of sub–Saharan countries with a really significant force on paper, consisting of about 35 000 men with 250 tanks, 264 AFVs and 250 artillery pieces. There are also several hundred Cuban, Russian and East German advisers, and 6 000 to 12 000 Zimbabwean and 3 000 Tanzanian troops helping in the campaign against the National Resistance Movement of Mozambique.

Of the remaining armies in sub–Saharan Africa, Zaïre and Uganda, have about 22 000 and 35 000 men respectively without significant quantities of armour or artillery. Chad, with 17 000, is involved in its own internecine struggle, using armed Toyota trucks instead of armoured vehicles. Of the rest two have armies exceeding 10 000, three have about 8 000, four about 6 000, five about 5 000 and two have about 3 000 men. The next step down is to fewer than 2 000 men. Most have no tanks or less than a hundred, as with their AFVs and artillery, except for Zambia, which has 153 pieces.

The total forces do not necessarily represent their capacities, however. When fighting formations such as brigades or even divisions are counted, only some countries have yet developed formations or at least their headquarters. These are Angola, Ethiopia, Ghana, Kenya, Mozambique, Nigeria, Tanzania, Zaïre and Zimbabwe.

Some others have loosely grouped "brigades", "regiments" or "brigade groups", such as Uganda, Togo and Madagascar. On paper the more significant forces could amount to the 22 divisions in the Ethiopian order of battle, together with another 84 "brigades" of varying structures and strengths. The number of men in the nine countries with formations amounts to 600 850. They may be backed by 1 950 tanks, 2 654 AFVs and 2 403 artillery pieces and multiple rocket-launchers. All this is a significant increase over the 12 armoured–car squadrons, two tank battalions and nine artillery batteries that the most important countries of twenty years ago could muster. Whereas in those post–independence days the total army strength for the newly–independent African countries of 157 200 would have been rudimentary infantry divisions inadequately protected against armour and artillery, they could present a very considerable force for South Africa to face in 1988. Moreover, with the exception of Ghana, the countries with the larger forces have all had recent experience in warfare of one kind or another.

What has this experience shown? In March 1988 an Ethiopian corps of three divisions was routed in Eritrea by a guerrilla force of the Eritrean Liberation Front.[2] Such a disaster was totally unexpected, considering the years of experience and the armaments that the forces and their commanders must have possessed. Reports from Eritrea were that from 18 000 to 25 000 casualties were suffered and that the Ethiopian government had wreaked severe punishment on their generals.

In Mozambique a force of about 20 000 rebels has kept the army at bay since the late President Samora Machel took command in June 1981 in an attempt to stop the depredations of the MNR.[3] Despite repeated campaigns, the overrunning of "bases", the help of British and Portuguese military training teams and the signing of the Nkomati Accord, the Mozambican army has been depleted by desertion, the selling or discarding of arms to the rebels and a general inability to defeat a rag–tag rebel force.

Zaïre had opportunities to demonstrate its military capacities in 1975/6 during the Angolan campaign and again during the two invasions of Shaba in 1976 and 1977. In the first campaign the armoured "brigade" trained by the North Koreans broke and fled in the face of the MPLA or the Cubans. This no doubt reflects on the North Koreans' inadequacy. For example, only one member of the training team sent to Zaïre knew any French. In 1976 the local regional commander in Shaba fled on foot before the advance of the so-called Katanga Gendarmes. No use was made of telephones or radios, and even military vehicles were abandoned. Only the use of radios by missionaries warned the government of the impending disaster. The general staff of the army was eventually replaced by a scratch staff of foreign advisers in Kinshasa. During the second invasion only intervention by foreign paratroopers saved the situation in Shaba.[4]

The Angolan forces (FAPLA) have had the only experience of fighting South African forces. However, South Africa has always been represented by rudimentary forces, probably of battalion size at most, often much less. Only during the 1987/8 offensive were 3 000 soldiers and Namibians engaged. FAPLA, the Angolan army of the MPLA, on the other hand, has been supported by formations of the Cuban army, numbering some 40 000 men to which an additional 10 000 of the 50th Cuban Division were added early in 1988.[5]

Since 1985 the FAPLA has been attempting to take the town and airfield of Mavinga to attack the forces of Unita. In each offensive, year after year, the FAPLA forces have been driven back to Cuito Cuanavale. In spite of considerable replenishment by the USSR, as well as staff and command help both by Russian and Cuban officers, four seasons of campaigning have made no difference to the position of FAPLA. In 1987/8, with about 25 000 soldiers deployed by the MPLA, including about a thousand Cubans, 4 768 were killed as against 31 South Africans up to 25 February. In addition 12 MiG aircraft, two SU–22s, 94 tanks, 372 logistics vehicles and 282 other vehicles were lost by FAPLA at a cost of three South African tanks and seven infantry combat vehicles, a light aircraft and a jet-fighter. In the process the 47th and 21st brigades of FAPLA were put to flight.[6]

The Nigerian army, now some 80 000 strong after having risen from 9 000 to about 200 000 during the Biafran war, fought its own campaign against the Biafran army between May 1967 and January 1970. Just as the war came to an end a report by the Defence Adviser to the British High Commissioner in Lagos, no doubt intended to predict the course of events for the British government, was leaked to the press.[7] It considered every aspect, from arms supplies to operational design, the relative strengths of the opponents and the effectiveness of command and staff work.

The report sharply criticised the inertia, dilatoriness, wastefulness, corruption and muddles of the Nigerian army and the inability of the staff to write intelligible English to those addressed. Before that is read as "typical" of African forces, however, it should be contrasted with the writer's tributes to the high morale, ingenuity, resourcefulness and comparative efficiency of the Biafran forces, especially their intelligence successes. Nevertheless, the military adviser made some cogent points about inability to abide by time schedules or to apply the principles of war and the influence of superstition on night fighting. What chiefly emerged from the report was that when the Nigerian forces were strong in elements of the pre-war regular army, as with the 1st Division, it never failed to take its objectives, however slowly. Poorly officered formations such as the 2nd Division, consisting of wartime-enlisted and hurriedly trained personnel had weak records in combat, staff and command. A report of this kind is rarely, if ever, published. Its significance is that it was a first-hand expert assessment which revealed that thoroughly well-trained, professional units could be produced in Africa as forces to be reckoned with and that it would certainly be a mistake to underrate the value of African soldiers. This assessment of the Biafrans also showed that educated people, as the Ibos tended to be, could be sound material when fighting for their own survival, which the Nigerian Federal Army was not.

Most of the forces described in these paragraphs tended to fall into the category of forces fighting for the purposes of governments, not for survival or for ideals. Perhaps, as with the Italian forces in Libya in the second world war and with the Argentine army in the Falkland campaign, this should be regarded as a critical factor when assessing their value.

The South African army has itself undergone great changes since it first began, in the early Sixties, to foresee the possibilities of clashes with other African forces.[8] Until the operations in Angola in 1975 and 1976, the tendency had been to develop a force largely concerned with counter-insurgency. Although a corps of two divisions had been established in 1974 to meet possible conventional threats, it had not been accorded great priority as the operations in South West Africa against Swapo attracted more attention and the South African Defence Force began to learn how to engage in counter-insurgency. The Angolan operations, however, indicated that while the art of conventional war had been maintained, this had not been at a sufficiently high level. With a better enemy the outcome of the operation conducted by fewer than 2 000 men could have been less fortunate. But in 1975 neither the MPLA nor the Cubans were a sufficient test. Nor was it intended that they should ever provide a better test. As will appear later in this chapter, the SADF engaged in a programme of achieving operational readiness. This included radical changes in training as well as modernising the stock of conventional armaments, as the Angolan campaign had shown arms such as artillery to be old-fashioned and in need of replacement. The modernisation was carried out very quickly and it was remarkable both in the lack of delay in providing new weapons and in bringing both full-time and Citizen Force soldiers to an operational level of readiness. Evidence of this was provided in May 1978, by the airborne attack on the Swapo base at Cassinga, 250km inside Angola, simultaneously with overland operations against several bases nearer the SWA border. Subsequently, a series of semi-conventional operations was carried out against Swapo bases in Angola, resulting ultimately in clashes with the FAPLA when the latter intervened in 1983 to prevent the withdrawal of South African forces. Later, the SADF again committed forces to the assistance of Unita, culminating in large-scale operations to prevent MPLA-Cuban moves to capture the town of Mavinga in south-eastern Angola in 1987. In these operations the combined Unita-SADF forces accounted for at least two Angolan brigades which were effectively destroyed.

The MPLA were driven back 250km to Cuito Cuanavale, from whence the attack had been launched. There they were held and prevented, despite several attempts, from renewing their advance southwards. Considering that the brunt of the fighting was borne by national servicemen and later Citizen Force soldiers temporarily called to relieve the former when they were discharged as their periods of service ended, the results of the operations are eloquent of the standards achieved by the army, both professional and non-professional. Perhaps the same might be said of the engagement at Calueque Dam on 27 June 1988 when heavy losses were reported to have been inflicted on the Cubans.

Strengths of the SADF are never divulged. The most recent estimates by the International Strategic Studies in *The Military Balance 1988/9* indicate that the Permanent Force numbers 19 900, including white, black and coloured troops, and 55 000 national servicemen with about 175 000 in the Citizen Force, 130 000 commandos and another 150 000 trained reserves. Bearing in mind that South Africa enlisted 406 000 volunteers in the second world war, it is not unlikely that a similar figure could be mobilised at present. Integration of different races has proceeded in the army, and with some four million men aged 18 to thirty, of all races, even the impact of industrialisation should not hamper the development of the army to adequate numbers, provided that they can be accommodated. In considering this, one has to avoid seeing an image of the second world war, when there was a long time in which to develop the Defence Force, which at the outbreak of war numbered only a few thousand and even after 1945 was reduced to 6 698 Permanent Force and 30 000 Citizen Force officers and men. In contrast to the assessment of the situation in those easy-going days, South Africa has to be in a position now to maintain what amounts to a standing Citizen Force, particularly the army, such as the Swiss. The SA army now has to be adequate to repulse a conventional force, to cope with the possibilities of a rural insurgency and to police the black townships. So far these forces have been adequate. A full-scale war would be more demanding, and more and more people other than whites would have to be involved. That in turn raises political questions, which, if solved, would probably eliminate the military problem. (See tables A and B on pages 442/443.)

**Air Forces**[9]
In the years since sub-Saharan states have gained their independence, air forces have changed considerably. Whereas twenty years ago the South African Air Force had a strength of 300 combat aircraft and 40 helicopters, there are now 324 combat aircraft and 188 helicopters; whereas Harvard (T-6G) training aircraft numbered 250 in 1966, today there are apparently only 130 in service, the rest being Mirage F-IZs, Mirage IIIs, Impala I/IIs, Canberras and Buccaneer S-50s.

In 1966 Ethiopia, Zaïre, the Sudan and Somalia had 63 combat aircraft. In 1988 fourteen countries have a total of 672 combat aircraft, with another 98 spread over 17 countries. Air forces numerically are: Ethiopia 150, Angola 133, Nigeria 96, Mozambique 70 and Zimbabwe and Zambia 53 each (see table). Of these most are MiG-23s (70) and MiG-21s (271), although their flying condition must be uncertain. Of a total of 97 transport aircraft in all sub-Saharan Africa in 1966 there are now 602, somewhat thinly spread. Angola has 91, Nigeria 61, Zimbabwe 37, others have twenty or less. South Africa has 109 transport aircraft; as against 202 helicopters of various types in South Africa, there are 451 elsewhere in Africa, of which a hundred are now armed. (See table on page 445.)

South Africa has about sixty light aircraft, to which several hundred privately owned aircraft could no doubt be added in an emergency for liaison, reconnaissance or even offensive purposes where anti-aircraft defences or enemy air activity was limited.

When, more than twenty years ago, the Carnegie Foundation financed a study of the needs for military action to deprive South Africa of Namibia, it was estimated that for "direct military intervention" 200 frontline aircraft with a reserve of 100, while 200 transport with a reserve of another 200 transport aircraft would be needed.

It was calculated that the operations would last four months, with 3 000 flying hours for a direct assault and 3 000 for a period of thirty days. (See diagrams on pages 446 and 447.)

Several factors influence the value of aircraft in Africa. In numbers the proposed

**TABLE A**

| COUNTRY | ARMY | TANKS | AFV, IFV APC | FIELD ARTY. MRL | AIR FORCE | COMBAT | ARMED HELI | TRANSPORT AC | TRANSPORT HELI | NAVY | VESSELS |
|---|---|---|---|---|---|---|---|---|---|---|---|
| South Africa | 75 000 CF 175 000 130 000 Cdo | 250 | 4 600 | 265 | 13 000 | 324 | 14 | 108 | 174 | 7 500 | 1 Frig 9 FAC 3 Sub 9 MCMV |
| Ethiopia | 313 000 | 750 | 870 | 700 | 4 000 | 150 | 22 | 13 | 52 | 1 800 | 2 Frig 8 FAC |
| Nigeria | 80 000 | 232 | 565 | 522 | 9 500 | 96 | – | 61 | 72 | 5 000 | 2 Frig 3 Corvettes 6 FAC 42 Patrol |
| Angola | 91 500 | 550 | 455 | 500 | 7 000 | 133 | 21 | 91 | 116 | 1 500 | 6 FAC |
| Zimbabwe | 46 000 | 43 | 168 | 60(?) | 1 000 | 53 | – | 37 | 26 | – | – |
| Tanzania | 38 350 | 96 | 65 | 340 | 1 000 | 22 | – | 20 | 6 | 700 | 18 Coastal Patrol |
| Mozambique | 35 000 | 250 | 264 | 230 | 1 000 | 70 | 12 | 12 | 14 | 700 | 23 Patrol |
| Zaire | 22 000 | 50 | 239 | 128 | 2 500 | 28 | – | 2 | 18 | 1 500 | 4 FAC |
| Uganda | 35 000 | 13 | 150 | 80 | ? | ? | – | 8 | 7 | – | – |
| Madagascar | 20 000 | 12 | 103 | 24 | 500 | 12 | – | 23 | – | 500 | 1 Patrol |
| Chad | 17 000 | – | 65 | 5 | 200 | 2 | – | 21 | 6 | – | – |
| Zambia | 15 000 | 60 | 78 | 153 | 1 200 | 53 | – | 30 | 31 | – | – |
| Kenya | 19 000 | 76 | 108 | 56 | 3 000 | 24 | 38 | 21 | 15 | 350 | 4 FAC |
| Ghana | 9 000 | – | 78 | – | 800 | 9 | – | 6 | 6 | 800 | 8 Patrol |
| Congo | 8 000 | 67 | 129 | 40 | 500 | 20 | – | 14 | 5 | 300 | 9 Patrol |
| (RSA excluded) | 748 850 | 2 199 | 3 337 | 2 838 | 32 200 | 672 | 93 | 379 | 374 | 13 150 | 4 Frig, 29 FAC, 101 Patrol, 3 Corvettes |

AFV, IFV, APC includes all types of armoured vehicles except battle tanks.

MRL multiple rocket launchers

FAC Fast attack craft, Frig = Frigates, MCMV =Mine control vessels.

Heli = Helicopters

(Source: The Military Balance 1988 – 1989, IISS, London, 1988.

**TABLE B**

| COUNTRY | ARMY | TANKS | AFV, IFV APC | FIELD ARTY. MRL | AIR FORCE | COMBAT | ARMED HELI | TRANSPORT AC | TRANSPORT HELI | NAVY | VESSELS |
|---|---|---|---|---|---|---|---|---|---|---|---|
| Guinea | 8 500 | 58 | 65 | 26 | 800 | 6 | — | 4 | 5 | 600 | 20 Patrol |
| Senegambia | 9 100 | — | 99 | 18 | 500 | 11 | — | 15 | 5 | 700 | 8 Coastal Patrol |
| Burkina Faso | 7 000 | — | 96 | 8 | 200 | ? | — | 21 | 4 | — | — |
| Cameroon | 6 600 | — | 69+ | 22 | 300 | 11 | 4 | 25 | — | 700 | 1 FAC, 3 River Patrol |
| Mali | 6 900 | 39 | 70 | 22 | 400 | 27 | 2 | 10 | 2 | 100 | 14 Patrol |
| Guiné-Bissau | 6 800 | 30 | 65 | 27 | 100 | — | — | 5 | 4 | 300 | 4 FAC, 6 Patrol |
| Ivory Coast | 5 500 | 5 | 52 | 4 | 900 | 6 | — | 15 | 9 | 700 | 3 River Patrol |
| Burundi | 5 500 | — | 54 | — | 150 | 3 | — | 4 | 5 | 50 | 5 Patrol |
| Liberia | 5 300 | — | 10 | 11+ | ? | 4 | — | 16 | — | 500 | 5 Patrol |
| Malawi | 5 000 | — | 34 | 12 | 150 | — | 2 | 8 | 15 | 100 | — |
| Rwanda | 5 000 | — | 28 | 6 | 200 | 2 | — | 7 | 13 | — | — |
| Central African Republic | 3 500 | 4 | 49 | — | 300 | — | — | 25 | 2 | — | — |
| Togo | 4 000 | 11 | 89 | 4 | 250 | 13 | — | 8 | 3 | 100 | 2 FAC |
| Benin | 3 800 | 20 | 23 | 4 | 350 | — | — | 12 | 4 | 200 | 7 Patrol |
| Niger | 3 200 | — | 64 | — | 100 | — | — | 12 | — | — | — |
| Botswana | 3 100 | — | 52 | 10 | 150 | 5 | — | 15 | 2 | — | — |
| Gabon | 1 900 | — | 82 | 12 | 600 | 10 | 5 | 21 | 14 | 500 | 1 FAC, 5 Patrol |
| | 90 700 | 167 | 1 001 | 186 | 5 450 | 98 | 13 | 223 | 77 | 4 550 | 8 FAC, 78 Patrol |
| TOTALS (A & B) | 839 550 | 2 366 | 4 338 | 3 024 | 37 650 | 770 | 106 | 602 | 451 | 17 700 | 4 Frig, 36 FAC, 179 Patrol, 3 Corvettes |

scale may be met. There is a wide variety of types available; however, of these only 431 combat aircraft are uniform, the various MiG types. To achieve decision through air operations there would have to be high levels of regular operational preparedness. The capacity to keep flying is the measure of its success, not simply numbers of aircraft available. That is determined, first, by the ability to keep maintenance at a high level. That means not only sufficient stocks of fuel, spare parts and munitions but also enough technicians and other ground staff. Rapid turn-round operational capacity may be more important than actual numbers of aircraft if they are not to be continually in the air. Inability to provide that kind of support seems to be characteristic of Third World air forces generally, despite the high quality of fliers. Good air crews are of course a *sine qua non* for an air force to be offensively decisive. A favourable air situation, never mind air superiority, needs pilots trained and experienced in combat flying techniques and tactics to defy anti-aircraft fire, to attack parked aircraft, fuel dumps and communications facilities, and to attack enemy aircraft in the air. That in itself demands standards of training seldom available to small air forces with limited budgets and facilities. Finally, numbers of aircraft and the capacity to replace losses are important. When numbers are small, losses cannot be easily borne. Most African countries have no production facilities for rapid replacement. Even South Africa with its production capability cannot quickly replace losses of modern jet aircraft. Countries that can be rapidly supplied by the Soviet Union or other Eastern bloc countries would have to supplement pilots and ground crews from the suppliers. An air force such as that of the MPLA (FALA), with 133 combat aircraft, if each were to fly three sorties a day and to suffer an attrition rate of only two per cent would have only 75 aircraft after ten days and perhaps 55 after 14 days. In the four weeks projected by the Carnegie assessment, if there were to be a two per cent attrition over two weeks with all planes flying three sorties a day, only fifty aircraft could remain operational. Those available to Angola, Ethiopia, Nigeria, Mozambique, Zambia and Zimbabwe could at the same rate of attrition still have 260 aircraft grouped together for operations. The point, however, is that all parties in Africa could barely tolerate even low rates of attrition, because of the impossibility of replacing aircraft from immediate local production.

These rates of attrition may seem artificial; and indeed this is difficult to judge accurately. While little is known of the other air forces, it is known that FALA (the MPLA air force) lost 53 aircraft in 1985 and about 26 in 1986. Despite claims made by Unita, most of these losses appear to have resulted from poor maintenance, failure to refuel, poor navigation, weak command and control and from attrition at the hands of their own forces, air defence and otherwise. While Angolan losses have often been caused by operational conditions, similar losses have been recorded in other African air forces such as those of Zaïre and Mozambique. The loss of the aircraft carrying President Samora Machel was apparently partly due to a number of characteristic failures in flying safety common to all Africa. This included failure to adhere to standard radio procedures in English, a language foreign to both pilots and ground control.

Air defence systems have also changed considerably since early independence. A variety of advanced air defence systems has replaced or supplemented the few superannuated anti-aircraft guns with which some countries began their independence. The new systems include not only a range of anti-aircraft artillery of high rates of fire but also missiles. The missile systems include the Franco-

## USSR Combat and Support Helicopters

**Mi-28/HAVOC**

| | |
|---|---|
| SPEED (KM/H) | 300 |
| RADIUS (KM) | 240 |
| TROOP LIFT | 0 |

**HOKUM**

| | |
|---|---|
| SPEED (KM/H) | 350 |
| RADIUS (KM) | 250 |
| TROOP LIFT | 0 |

**Mi-24/HIND**

| | |
|---|---|
| SPEED (KM/H) | 320 |
| RADIUS (KM) | 160 |
| TROOP LIFT | 13 |

**Mi-8/HIP**

| | |
|---|---|
| SPEED (KM/H) | 250 |
| RADIUS (KM) | 200 |
| TROOP LIFT | 26 |

**Mi-6/HOOK**

| | |
|---|---|
| SPEED (KM/H) | 300 |
| RADIUS (KM) | 300 |
| TROOP LIFT | 70 |

**Mi-26/HALO**

| | |
|---|---|
| SPEED (KM/H) | 300 |
| RADIUS (KM) | 370 |
| TROOP LIFT | 85 |

**Ka-27/HELIX**

| | |
|---|---|
| SPEED (KM/H) | 260 |
| RADIUS (KM) | 300 |
| NAVAL AIR VARIENTS | |

**Ka-25/HORMONE**

| | |
|---|---|
| SPEED (KM/H) | 220 |
| RADIUS (KM) | 250 |
| NAVAL AIR VARIANTS | |

| METERS | 0 | 10 | 20 | 30 | 40 |
|---|---|---|---|---|---|

## Comparable Tactical Aircraft
## USSR

| | Su-24 FENCER A/B/C/D | MiG-23 FLOGGER B/G/K | MiG-27 FLOGGER D/J | Su-17 FITTER D/H | MiG-25 FOXBAT B/D | MiG-21 FISHBED L | MiG-29 FULCRUM | Su-25 FROGFOOT |
|---|---|---|---|---|---|---|---|---|
| MAX SPEED (MACH) | 2.0 | 2.3 | 1.7 | 2.1 | 1.8 | 2.0 | 2.3 | 0.8 |
| RADIUS (KM) | 1,300 | 1,150 | 600 | 550 | 900 | 750 | 1,150 | 300 |
| ARMAMENT | 3,000 KG Bombs | 6 AAMs | 3,000 KG Bombs | 3,000 KG Bombs | — | 4 AAMs | 6 AAMs | 2,000 KG Bombs |
| WINGSPAN (M) | 10 (Swept) | 8 (Swept) | 8 (Swept) | 10 (Swept) | 14 | 7 | 12 | 15 |

METERS: 22, 11, 0

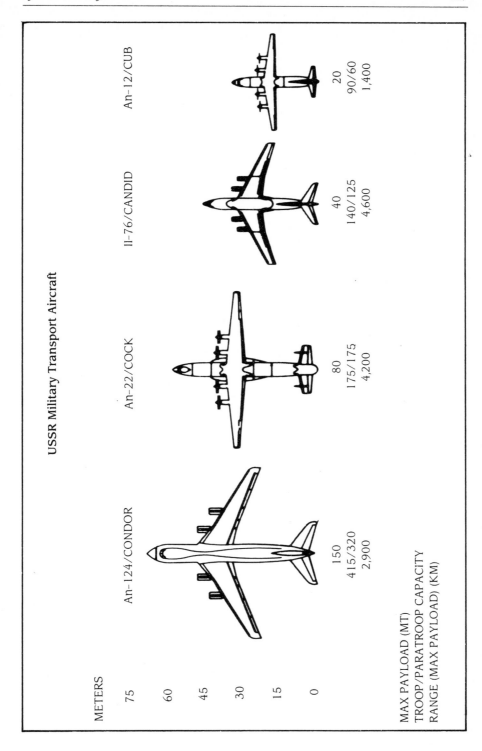

USSR Military Transport Aircraft

METERS

75

60

45

30

15

0

| | An-124/CONDOR | An-22/COCK | Il-76/CANDID | An-12/CUB |
|---|---|---|---|---|

MAX PAYLOAD (MT)
TROOP/PARATROOP CAPACITY
RANGE (MAX PAYLOAD) (KM)

An-124/CONDOR
150
415/320
2,900

An-22/COCK
80
175/175
4,200

Il-76/CANDID
40
140/125
4,600

An-12/CUB
20
90/60
1,400

South African all-weather Crotale (Cactus), the British Bloodhound, Blowpipe and Roland, the Russian SA-2 (Guideline), SA-3 (Goa), SA-6 (Gainful), SA-8 (Gecko), SA-9 (Gaskin) and the SA-13 (Gopher) and of course, the SA-7 (Grail or Strela) and the updated SA-14. The Russian missile systems, together with a variety of early-warning, surveillance and guidance radar systems are supplied to Angola, Ethiopia, Chad, Guinea, Mali, Mozambique and Tanzania. Fifteen countries, including most of those mentioned, also have stocks of SA-7 (Grail or Strela) hand-held missiles, of which Angola and Mozambique are each believed to have about 700. Nigeria and Malawi have stocks of Blowpipe, a British shoulder-aimed, hand-held missile. The most important of these missile systems from the point of view of field operations are probably the mobile SA-3, with a range of 29km, the SA-6, with a high-altitude range of 60km, and especially the air-portable quadruple-launcher SA-8, which like the SA-9 performs a battlefield defensive function, probably with only infra-red heatseeking guidance but possibly with the more dangerous semi-active radar homing (SARH). While electronic and other counter-measures have worked against missile systems of this kind, they have decided advantages, as the Israeli Air Force found in 1973, when the SA-6 inflicted serious losses on aircraft during the Yom Kippur war. The effect on all air forces of limited numbers in Africa is to fill them with a great sense of caution. Reports during the 1987 campaign in south-east Angola were that the mere hint of the presence of American Stingers in the hands of Unita was enough for FALA to operate at unrealistically high altitudes, even to the extent of "close-support" bombing from several thousand feet. An American source reported that the only time confirmation has been obtained of an aircraft's having been shot down by an Angolan SA-7 was that of an Angolan civilian Yak-40. The same source mentioned that a South African Impala returned to base in 1983 with an unexploded SA-9 lodged in its tail. (See diagram on page 449.)

What this signifies is difficult to assess with certainty. It is clear that in sheer numbers and perhaps characteristics of certain aircraft, South Africa no longer has absolute superiority. The armament bans on South Africa would also make it difficult to replace operational losses quickly, despite the existence of a fairly advanced aircraft industry. On the other hand, the Soviet Union demonstrated in Angola and in Ethiopia in 1975 and 1977 that it was capable, given the incentive, of lifting by sea and by air thousands of troops and more than US$1 000 million worth of arms. At that time about 200 aircraft were used, some even carrying crated MiG-21s.[10] Two questions have to be considered. One is whether, under the present political régime in the USSR, there is still a desire not only to prolong the operations in southern Africa but to raise the level. This may be the Cuban attitude, as the reinforcements in the Fifth Military Region in Angola have suggested. But at the time of writing it is not certain that after a series of military setbacks in Angola the Gorbachev government would wish to become more deeply involved. There have been reports of SAAF attacks having successfully taken place on the main base of Lubango in spite of the improved Angolan air defences. The other question concerns the quality of pilots and the desire to replace Angolan losses with Cubans or even Russians or pilots from other communist countries. The South African Air Force itself suffers from the attractions of employment elsewhere, but there are a fairly large number of pilots in the reserves who could be called back from civilian life. Another question is: to what extent could available aircraft be kept flying? Will quality in training, in flying and in maintenance make a crucial difference? That is important, for air power, even on the African scale, is necessary not only to break up and destroy enemy

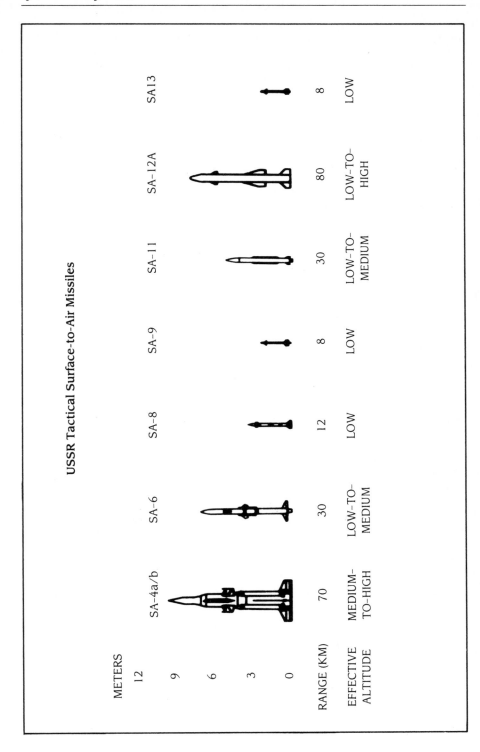

USSR Tactical Surface-to-Air Missiles

| METERS | SA-4a/b | SA-6 | SA-8 | SA-9 | SA-11 | SA-12A | SA13 |
|---|---|---|---|---|---|---|---|
| 12 | | | | | | | |
| 9 | | | | | | | |
| 6 | | | | | | | |
| 3 | | | | | | | |
| 0 | | | | | | | |
| RANGE (KM) | 70 | 30 | 12 | 8 | 30 | 80 | 8 |
| EFFECTIVE ALTITUDE | MEDIUM-TO-HIGH | LOW-TO-MEDIUM | LOW | LOW | LOW-TO-MEDIUM | LOW-TO-HIGH | LOW |

formations on the ground but also to disrupt lines of communication to prevent ground formations from maintaining themselves. Operations at various times in Angola have shown that the air arm may still play almost decisive parts. What will probably determine whether the air arm will be decisive for both sides in a conflict involving South Africa seems to be who the personnel of the opposing forces are going to be and to what extent external support will be given to the opponents of South Africa. It is certain that the economies of those countries will not allow large-scale domestic recruitment of pilots and technicians.

### Naval Forces[11]

The term "navy" can hardly be applied to naval forces in Africa south of the Sahara, with the exception of South Africa and a few Black African states such as Nigeria, Ethiopia, Angola and Kenya.

During the second world war South Africa developed a force that was numerically impressive (89 vessels); but the vessels were mainly whale-catchers and trawlers converted to corvettes and mine-sweepers. The Simonstown Agreements of 1955 began a programme of expansion to twenty vessels, which included two destroyers, six frigates, 12 minesweepers and three submarines.

The effect of an apparent belief in Britain becoming the source of vessels as well as the mandatory arms ban of 1977, which deprived South Africa of foreign replacements, radically altered the design of the SAN. The "blue-water" vessels have tended to disappear from the order of battle in favour of fast attack craft armed with guided missiles. The present strength is nine Minister class boats armed with Skerpioen surface-to-surface missiles. Although these boats have shorter ranges and can spend less time at sea than the previous escort vessels, the missiles give them a harder punch than the four-inch gun and an over-the-horizon reach, not available to the torpedo. While the replacement of the three Daphne class submarines by Agostas was stopped by the French government in 1977, it has been suggested that the present boats might be refitted, and the German press has carried reports in the past year that plans for Type-209 submarines have been sold to South Africa, and the Minister of Defence indicated in November 1987 that a project was under way to build submarines in South Africa. In the mean time two President class frigates with helicopter-carrying facilities have been retained with a view to reconditioning or conversion. Mine counter-measures vessels have also been kept on the strength. The vessels have apparently been given a longer reach by the commissioning in 1987 of a 12 500-ton replenishment ship, which has already accompanied FAC on a transatlantic voyage.

A naval force with a wide variety of craft giving it an extensive range of operations is that of Ethiopia, which is equipped with two Petya-II frigates, eight Osa-II missile-armed FACs and six torpedo-armed FACs, with seven inshore patrol-boats and eight landing-craft.

On the other side of Africa, the Nigerian navy has two MEKO-360H armed frigates, one of them armed with Otomat surface-to-surface missiles, six FACs armed with Otomat and Exocet SSMs and three Vosper-Thorneycroft corvettes. Two more corvettes were badly damaged by a corrosive fumigating agent that caused one vessel to sink at its moorings. Nigeria has 42 coastal patrol boats and two landing-craft.

Angola is the next in the sequence of large naval forces, with six Osa-II missile-armed FACs, five Shershen torpedo FACs and 13 patrol-boats and 14 landing craft.

Some of the vessels date back to Portuguese rule and may no longer be serviceable. The remaining naval forces have mainly coast guard characteristics, with 146 inshore patrol-boats, six large patrol-boats, 9 missile-armed FACs and 42 landing-craft, and two corvettes shared among Cameroun, Cape Verde, the Congo, Gabon, Ghana, Guinea, the Ivory Coast, Kenya, Mozambique, Tanzania and Zaïre, to mention only the more important.

The most lethal of these vessels are the Osa-II, La Combattante, Petya, Brooke Marine and Lürson, armed variously with SS-N-2, Exocet, Otomat or Gabriel surface-to-surface missiles. The SS-N-2 Styx was the naval missile that first drew attention to its power. That was after the Six-Day war when on 21 October 1967 a 70-ton Egyptian Komar FAC sank the Israeli destroyer *Eilat* with only three missiles. Since then its explosive power has been demonstrated as placing the FAC in a category comparable to that of heavier vessels. The casualties suffered by shipping during both the Falklands and the Iran-Iraq wars have since provided further evidence.

While the ship-borne SSM is more lethal and accurate than the four-inch gun commonly carried on African frigates and destroyers, it is certainly more versatile than the older form of torpedo. The fundamental change, however, is that the heavier punch can be carried on very small vessels. Small vessels mean smaller targets for an enemy to strike back at. The ranges of some missiles mean larger areas of sea and land that can be dominated than by the gun. There are also disadvantages. Smaller vessels have shorter operating ranges, fewer men to stand watches, shorter periods at sea and therefore on operations. Missiles can be affected by electronic counter-measures and by technological defects such as would never trouble the robust and simple gun. A higher quality of education is also demanded of a missile operator than of a gunlayer. Missiles make vessels more vulnerable than gunfire, however. While they make the "navies" of smaller countries more effective than ships armed with guns, they can easily deprive them of their navies and leave them unarmed at sea. Relative strengths accordingly become important. The possession by South Africa of only nine FACs is unimpressive compared with the numbers of SAAF aircraft. Few losses would become disproportionately significant.

What would tell in South Africa's favour would be the commitments that other countries' vessels would have in their own waters. Most naval forces in Africa are concerned with fisheries patrols, preventing smuggling, and internal security. Only Nigeria appears to have engaged in air-sea exercises in recent times. With numbers restricted, and with regard to the classes of vessels that predominate in African waters, it is probable that only Ethiopia with two frigates, 14 FACs and eight landing-craft (LC), Nigeria with one frigate, two serviceable corvettes and six FACs and two LCs and Angola with ll FACs and 14 LCs could conceivably carry out operations against a common opponent, and then only in combination. Even Angola, with evidence of vessels having been subjected to damage in home waters, might hesitate to permit her FACs to operate away from home.

Since only Nigeria has mine counter-measures vessels (two), besides South Africa, depleting coastal defences would invite the laying of mines in the path of merchant shipping and in harbour entrances, a task for which South Africa is equipped.

Finally, the navies in Africa suffer from the differences in languages, which would make command and control over a combined force difficult if not impossible.

One may conclude that it is doubtful whether direct attacks on South African ports could be made or whether South African naval vessels operating in formations or supported by air cover could be challenged. But what about South African merchant shipping sailing alone or without armed escort? Hit–and–run attacks carried out from the security of Nigerian or Angolan waters on passing shipping are conceivable. How would South Africa cope with that, or with any other naval threat to ships trading with her?

The best answer is perhaps to devise new doctrines for possible offensive as well as defensive operations. The Israeli conception of going out to meet the enemy wherever he may be, perhaps accompanied by aircraft, may prove to be the starting-point in gaining and retaining the initiative. In the minds of the Naval Staff in Pretoria there must always lurk the spectre of an enemy drawing assistance from elsewhere. Apart from the Russian navy, there is the Cuban navy, which has 18 FACs with missiles, three frigates and three submarines; or the German Democratic Republic, which has 19 frigates, five corvettes and 12 missile-carrying FACs. Or help might come from another Third World navy, such as that of Libya which, with a government with a reputation for recklessness, has three frigates, seven corvettes and 24 FACs, all armed with surface-to-surface missiles, and six submarines. In the absence of equivalent numbers the principal South African defence at sea might prove to be seamanship of high quality, in initiative and originality in leadership, and in operational strategy.

**Naval Forces**

| Country | FAC(G) | FAC(T) | Patrol Large | Coast | ALC | Frig | Corv |
|---|---|---|---|---|---|---|---|
| Angola | #6 | #5 | – | 13 | 3 | – | – |
| Cameroon | 1 | – | – | 5 | 7 | – | – |
| C.Verde | – | #2 | – | 3 | – | – | – |
| Congo | – | #*3 #1 | – | 5 | – | – | – |
| Ethiopia | *8 | 6 | 1 | 6 | 8 | 2 | – |
| Gabon | 1 | – | 1 | 4 | 4 | – | – |
| Ghana | – | – | 4 | 4 | – | – | – |
| Guinea | – | #*6 #3 | 1 | 10 | 2 | – | – |
| Ivory Coast | 4 | – | – | 6 | 1 | – | – |
| Kenya | 6 | – | – | 5 | – | – | – |
| Mozambique | – | – | – | 23 | 3 | – | – |
| Nigeria | 6 | – | – | 42 | 2 | 2 | 3 |
| Tanzania | – | #*6+4 | – | 8 | 4 | – | – |
| Zaïre | – | #*4 | – | – | – | – | – |
| South Africa | 9 | – | – | 9 | 6MCM | 1 | 3Sub |

Notes: *Osa (USSR) with SS–N–2
#Shershen (USSR) with torpedoes
#*Shanghai II (PRC)

## Mass Death — Chemical Weapons

This perhaps excessively dramatic sub-title refers to the weapons that may cause death and destruction on a mass scale, such as nuclear weapons and chemical weapons. The discussion of either in the African context may seem superfluous, but since the use of chemical weapons in Angola has been alleged, some mention of them seems to be called for.

Chemical weapons (CW) are easily acquired or manufactured and may be easily and covertly employed. Moreover, they have been used in Africa before. In the 1920s Mussolini authorised their use against rebels in Libya and in the invasion of Ethiopia in 1936 CW were employed against the army of Haile Selassie.

The Fascist government took particular care to conceal the use of poison gas. According to Spiers, rumours of the use of gas were denied, the press was censored and the Ethiopians themselves were accused of using gas. Later reasons were advanced for the use of CW with the argument that retaliation against Abyssinian atrocities justified extreme measures under the Geneva Protocol of 1928.[12]

There are now more cogent reasons why CW should be regarded as relevant to an assessment of armaments in Africa. Since the end of the second world war, in which CW were not used, there have been both allegations and substantial evidence of their use in several countries in the Third World. During the war in Yemen between 1963 and 1967, Egypt was accused of having used CW against the royal forces. In South East Asia the United States armed forces openly used riot control gases against the Viet Cong and herbicides to strip foliage from the Vietnamese jungle. Between 1975 and 1978 in Laos there were allegations of chemical warfare by the Vietnamese and the Lao People's Liberation Army against tribesmen. The reports from Laos were of aerial attacks in which coloured vapour was sprayed over villages, causing symptoms ranging from death to dizziness, intensely itching skin, blisters, bloody diarrhoea and vomiting. In 1978 Vietnam and the People's Republic of Kampuchea were also accused of using CW against the Khmer Rouge, using 60mm mortars, 120mm shells, 107mm rockets, grenade-launchers, mines and aircraft. In the year after the Russian invasion of Afghanistan in 1979, helicopters, aeroplanes, artillery and mines were used to deliver CW vapour against the Afghan mujaheddin.

President Carter raised the matter in the US Congress and in the United Nations after the publication of an American report in 1980. It resulted in a General Assembly Resolution (A/35/144C), approved by 78 votes to 17 with 36 abstentions, setting an investigation in train. From very sparse evidence a US plant pathologist found evidence of man-made mycotoxins in Cambodian vegetation where the so-called "yellow rain" vapour had been reported. Later, evidence was gathered from a wider range of sources, including people suffering from CW attacks, defectors, including a Laotian pilot who had delivered CW attacks, Vietnamese and Afghan army defectors and a captured military chemical specialist from the Russian army as well as from radio interception. In Afghanistan a Dutch journalist filmed an Mi-24 Hind helicopter spreading a yellow cloud over a village near Jalalabad in June 1980; he suffered from contamination while filming the injuries of Afghan villagers. The American conclusions at that time listed 261 CW attacks in Laos, causing 6 504 deaths from 1975 to 1981, 124 attacks in Cambodia, causing 981 deaths from 1978 to 1981, and 47 attacks at a cost of 3 042 deaths in Afghanistan from 1979 to 1981.[13]

In the course of the campaign in Iran, the same kinds of allegations were made by Iran against Iraq. For example, on 4 November 1984 Iran sent a letter to the Secretary General of the United Nations asking for an "examination of the medical and military evidence of chemical weapons employed by the Iraqi forces." Later that same month, there was a press conference in Teheran to present the opinions of foreign medical experts. *The Guardian* of 25 November and *The Times* of l December 1984, reported that British doctors had examined wounded Iranians and seen evidence of "nitrogen mustard gas blistering."

In March 1984 Iranian soldiers suffering from the effects of CW were flown for treatment to West Germany, Sweden, Britain and Austria. In Vienna on 10 March a statement was issued that laboratory testing had revealed that the men were affected by mustard gas and by the mycotoxins called "yellow rain". A United Nations report of 26 March concluded that there was evidence of the use of Tabun gas also.[14]

Except for Iraq, where it was suggested that some of the CW came from a pesticide factory in Iraq, all the CW mentioned are said to have come from the Soviet Union, suppliers of armaments to most of the countries south of the Sahara. That is not to say that they are the only manufacturers of CW. Nor can the supply of CW by Western suppliers be ruled out. But on the balance of probabilities, the evidence so far indicates that lethal CW have been sold by the USSR and used by their clients rather than by Western governments and their clients. Although Mikhail Gorbachev declared that the USSR no longer produced CW and denied that they had been exported, the document *Soviet Military Power,* 1988, issued by the United States Department of Defence argues that research and development of CW and training in their use continue in the Warsaw Pact countries. In October 1987 the USSR invited representatives of 45 countries to examine their chemical weapons and watch a demonstration of their destruction. They acknowledged that they had 50 000 tons of CW agents, including mustard gas, the nerve gases sarin, soman and VX. Small amounts of these gases inhaled or absorbed through the skin cause nervous malfunction and rapid breath. All can be delivered by the equipment already existing in Africa, such as 122mm and 130mm guns, aerial bombs and sprays. The BM-21 multiple rocket-launcher, which is an area saturation weapon, is perfectly suited to dispersing CW in minutes. The Russian ground forces have about 45 000 Chemical Troops (VKhV) with 30 000 CW reconnaissance and decontamination vehicles. All army units have a delivery and a decontamination capacity. Each soldier has protective clothing, a mask and decontamination kit. The purpose of CW with the ground forces is to deny ground or airfields to the enemy but not to destroy. In the three CW schools and the Timoshenko Military Academy for Chemical Defence, Russian commanders are taught to regard CW as a matter of course, and chemical phases are included in all military exercises and staff courses.[15]

So far the evidence of use of CW in Africa has been small and restricted to Angola. In the *International Defense Review* of January 1988 there was a brief report that FAPLA had used CW near Lucusse and near Cassamba, causing paralysis in dozens of survivors.[16] Some were demented and all were in great pain. The CW agent had apparently been dropped by Mi-25 helicopters. No official comment was forthcoming from South African or American sources, although it was believed that American "advisers" had seen the victims of attack. South African newspapers suggested at the time that doctors of the South African Medical Service had examined the injured, who were members of Unita. As in the past, when reports from Afghanistan that Russian forces had used CW were answered with counter-accusations that the US were breeding mosquitoes to carry viruses, the MPLA ambassador to Paris, Luis de Almeida, deplored the use of poison gas by the South Africans at Munhango and at Cuito Cuanavale.[17] He denounced the UPI for being used by Pretoria to gain the sympathy of the media to "promote disinformation against the People's Republic of Angola". Later a Swiss newspaper reported that a Belgian medical team led by Professor Aubin Heyndrickx, Head of the Laboratory for Toxicology and Criminalistics at the University of Ghent, had in 1988 examined CW casualties and submitted a report to the Secretary General of the United Nations. The conclusion read: "The toxicological and clinical examination of soldiers in the Mavinga field hospital brings one to the conclusion that there is high probability that they were subjected to nerve gas. This agrees with earlier examinations which where undertaken two years ago."[18]

He pointed out, however, that since the chemicals suspected had a short persistence, direct evidence of gas could not be found by the time the patients were examined. Nevertheless the injuries suffered were consistent with sarin and soman. The Swiss report said that a piece of indirect evidence of CW was that FAPLA soldiers were carrying the same protective equipment found on Russian prisoners in Afghanistan. As elsewhere, the difficulty of finding direct evidence of the use of CW after the lapse of time before an independent investigator is able to arrive on the scene, leaves the objective observer unsatisfied.

There seems to be little doubt that chemical weapons have arrived in Africa. The question that needs to be asked is whether they will play a significant part in future campaigns. Italian experience in the 1936 campaign indicated that they are affected by heat and soil in Africa. Perfect conditions to make them decisive may seldom occur; but that they can be used with some success was shown by the Italians, and in humid bushy country such as Angola they may be effective in certain seasons and localities.

## Command and Control
Dr Samuel Johnson once said that "the qualities which commonly make an army formidable are long habits of regularity, great exactness of discipline and great confidence in the commander". Experience in Africa would perhaps contradict the expectations expressed by Johnson. Apart from difficulties experienced in Nigeria and Ethiopia and other armies in recent campaigns against irregular forces, time and again mutual suspicion and mistrust have blocked advances to the objective of an all-African army or an African High Command, which would appear to be the first steps towards dealing with South Africa.

In the early years of independence the need for some central military control to help to overcome internal problems, such as the uprisings in the Congo (Zaïre) or the army mutinies in Tanzania, became apparent. In February 1964 two committees of African governments rejected the call for a joint military force. Soon after its creation the OAU Defence Commission met the Secretary General to "act as an organ of consultation, preparation and recommendation" aimed at combined action for external and internal defence and the liberation of colonial Africa. That attempt, and every succeeding attempt, led chiefly by Ghana, Nigeria and Ethiopia, was opposed, mainly by the French-speaking states. It appears that a general fear has worsened as more and more countries succumb to military rule or to extreme left governments. In some cases, such as that of Ethiopia, these have been mutually inclusive categories. Any controversial course that a Pan-African Command were to choose would inevitably be interpreted as the furtherance of the policies of the government providing the commander of the joint force. This has apparently continued to block the creation of a high command and a joint army. Perhaps the way in which the forces of Nigeria and Ethiopia have grown since 1963 has also served to frighten the OAU away from creating what might become a Frankenstein's monster. Moreover, stability is a prerequisite for an army designed to keep the peace between and within countries. It could not work if the forces and the commander were suspected of being partisan instruments of someone's political ambitions. The first requisite, therefore, is to find a commander who would be above suspicion.

The commander would have to be someone with experience in a stable, long-established armed force. The damage done to the older established armed forces by revolution and military coups makes that problematical. Out of 51 countries in Africa there have been 72 coups, of which only four were north of the Sahara.[19] Eleven still have military governments, including Nigeria, which has had five coups since 1965. Effectively, the government of Ethiopia, which has suffered three coups since 1974, is also military. These events speak of internal tension as well as of high involvement of officers in government. The net effect has been the weakening of armed forces, for the capable officers who would have been commanding troops are occupied with day-to-day administration. Because of the conspiratorial way in which they took office, they cannot think of leaving their posts to others to enable them to command forces in the field far from home. Leaders of coups may be replaced by younger officers, but the latter then need time to train and gain experience before they can think of taking the field.

Effective command and control also require standardised operating procedures and reliable and flexible communications. While training in Africa depends on the foreign military advisers and a variety of equipment, this may remain a difficulty. However, there has been a gradual move towards the use of Russian equipment which, if this were to become more general and uniform, could obviate the problem. However, the problem of different languages and poor French or English could be an impediment.

The problems of command and control seem to require that less attention should be paid to the concept of an all–African force than to the concept of a selected national force, specially cultivated and with money lavished on its equipment, or at most a force comprising closely–related countries, such as Mozambique and Angola. The latter, at least, has acquired some experience in engaging South African forces. Whether the experience would encourage the soldiers as much as it might their governments remains to be seen.

### Unity of Purpose
Numerous external tensions between members of the OAU have persisted since the various countries gained independence. Some have resulted only in harmless aggression, but some have led to full-scale wars. In most cases external conflicts have been associated with internal conflict caused by attempts by various groups or movements to secede from countries in which they had been incorporated, either by the former colonial governments or in the course of gaining independence. Probably the oldest post-independence secessionist civil war was that which began in the southern Sudan in 1955.

In Eritrea an insurgency against Ethiopia has smouldered since 1960, while Morocco has had to engage in operations against the Polisario Front on the borders of Mauritania since 1976. At various times movements have engaged in sporadic conflict with the régime in power. In Ghana, the Ewes opposed the government in 1956. In Zaïre, apart from the Katanga War of 1960 to 1963, there have been uprisings in South Kasai (1960), Kisangani from 1960 to 1964 and the Shaba "wars" of 1976 and 1977 , when Katanga Gendarmes invaded the mining area of Shaba, formerly Katanga. A civil war raged from 1967 to 1970 between the federal government of Nigeria and the self-proclaimed state of Biafra, which broke away from the federation in an attempt to set up an independent state for the Ibo people. In 1977 the Soviet Union and Cuba provided a considerable quantity of armaments and manpower to Ethiopia, when Somalia attempted to secure the Ogaden region from Ethiopia. This war was remarkable for the way in which Cuban soldiers were flown east to the island of Sal, across Africa and on to Ethiopia. There they were supplied with armaments flown south from the USSR to provide rapid support to the embattled Ethiopian government.

Wars or rebellions have continued intermittently during the past ten years between Libya and Chad, and in Uganda after the overthrow by Tanzania of the Amin régime. At first South Africa helped the rebel movement in Mozambique until the terms of the Nkomati Accord terminated it. Since the signing of the agreement there have been frequent accusations of continued South African aid to the MNR and, as frequently, South African denials of their having continued to foment rebellion. Considerable help has been given in Angola to Unita, which was one of the three political movements that rebelled against Portuguese rule in the early 1960s. At first both the FNLA and Unita were helped during the 1975/6 campaign, called *Operation Savannah* by the South Africans and *Operacion Carlotta* by the Cubans and Angolans. For a while after that no help was given to either. But at the end of the 1970s the South Africans once more provided help to Unita. The extent of it has never been made public except to describe it as "humanitarian" or to list commodities such as fuel, food and medical aid. In more recent years, since *Offesiva Segunda Congressa* in 1985, it has appeared that the help given has been more substantial and in positive military form. The first announcements about military help, however, were made only in December 1987 and April 1988, when the South African authorities gave details of operational assistance to Unita. The point, however, is that a civil war has raged in Angola for several years. Unita has been conducting a guerrilla campaign throughout Angola, occupying almost a third of the country in the south and dominating the countryside in many other provinces, capturing towns, even a small town on the Atlantic seaboard in 1984, and generally making a serious impact both on the economy and the security of the country. The civil war has required the supply by the Eastern bloc of enormous quantities of armaments and the help of the Cuban armed forces and contingents of military advisers from the German Democratic Republic (500), North Korea (100), the Soviet Union (950), including generals and staff officers alleged to have been engaged in operations, and Portugal, which provided a hundred pilots and technicians. About a thousand ANC (African National Congress) and 4 000 Swapo forces also apparently serve in combat against Unita.

The importance of the question of unity of purpose among the countries south of the Sahara remains related to the ambition, now over thirty years old, to form a pan-African army to defeat South Africa. Originally the brain-child of Kwame Nkrumah, the idea has recently been revived in Nigeria. Early in 1988, on Nigerian Army Day, the Chief of the Army Staff, Lt-Gen. Sani Abacha, announced the setting up in Lagos of a "special armed force... for the defence of other African countries". It will be called the Rapid Deployment Force and become operational late in 1988 or early in 1989.

Observers were of the opinion that the force was to be aimed at South African "intransigence and frequent military incursions into 'unfriendly' countries". The question remains whether African governments not wholly dependent for their existence on foreign forces, such as the MPLA in the face of Unita, would consider allowing foreign armies to operate within their frontiers, especially those proposing to lead the continent "from the front", as has been said of Nigeria. The divisions in Africa are related to language, sometimes tribalism, and religion. But the consequences of politics and political ambitions cannot be ignored. Not everyone wishes to see a tiger and her cubs roaming about their countries, as Kenneth Kaunda put it. Nevertheless, with countries such as Angola and Mozambique politically and economically *in extremis*, the possibility of their accepting Nigerian forces cannot be dismissed. That would mean greater numbers of troops that might have to be met by South African forces if they made cross–border raids against ANC bases or in support of Unita. Their quality might be indifferent, but these numbers can increase risks that cannot be left out of the reckoning. The presence of Nigerian troops alone or in combination with other African forces from Zimbabwe or Tanzania must therefore be added to the imponderables in any assessment of the future of armed forces and arms in Africa. Not only the South Africans but also the governments likely to be committed to playing host need to consider what kingmakers might mean to their own security. That was an experience not likely to be soon forgotten in Uganda.

### Logistic Support

The logistic support of an expeditionary force is a burden no less important than the strategic battle and the effects of its failure would be as decisive as defeat on the field of battle. The German field commander during the war in the Western desert in 1941/2, Field Marshal Erwin Rommel, defined a fundamental law of operations when he wrote that "... the first essential condition for an army to be able to stand the strain of battle is an adequate stock of weapons, petrol and ammunition... The bravest men can do nothing without guns, the guns nothing without plenty of ammunition, and neither guns nor ammunition are of much use in mobile warfare unless there are vehicles with enough petrol to haul them about. Maintenance must also approximate, both in quantity and quality, that available to the enemy".[20]

To win the game, the sub–Saharan armed force will have to play according to these rules. The penalty for infringement may be extreme.

The purpose of logistics is to provide armed forces with the essential means:

* to live, such as food, water, clothing, shelter and medical supplies;
* to move, including vehicles, transport animals, rolling stock, shipping, aircraft, fuel, lubricants, spare parts and forage;
* to fight, including weapons, defensive armaments and materials, armoured fighting vehicles and other combat equipment, ammunition and missiles.[21]

The critical requirements of resupply and the replacement of equipment lost in combat are fundamental, since so much is expended after being used only once. Without new stocks combat efficiency declines in direct proportion to the time spent in a theatre of war, particularly one far from home. As troops move farther forward their stocks must be moved to intermediate and advanced depots that need not only shelter but also defence.

Fuel and food are the most necessary supplies with the mechanisation of armies and the coming of the air arm. Men can exist for five weeks without food, but they cannot fight. They can exist without water for not more than four days. Not all troops consume food at the same level of abundance. In Burma Field Marshal Slim found that "... instead of 400 tons a day not considered excessive to keep a division fighting in more generous theatres, we could maintain our Indian divisions in action for long periods, without loss of battle efficiency or morale, on 120."[22]

To keep one division fighting for three months may need 3 000 tons of ammunition for artillery, including anti-aircraft artillery, and for small arms. Ammunition has become an important factor in resupply with the increased use of field artillery and automatic small arms. With mines and grenades and engineers' explosives added, 3 500 tons may easily be needed.

The supplies would be of little value without transport to provide the steady flow of supplies from the rear to the front. In the field this will be principally by motor lorry. American infantry divisions use 2 400 and a Russian motor rifle division needs 1 308 lorries and other soft-skinned vehicles. Even North Vietnam bought 15 000 trucks from its allies for a semi-guerrilla war in 1966. Indeed, each Viet Cong regiment needed two companies of porters for supply in the field. Motor vehicles themselves depend heavily on spare parts and fuel, without which operations cannot be conducted. Repair and maintenance facilities are also necessary. The absence in Africa of adequate railways means enormous difficulties and almost total dependence on road transport. But the absence of hard, well-maintained roads with all-weather capacities also adds to the logistic difficulties. A great deal of energy and material would have to be used on building and maintaining roads approaching South Africa.

The support of a modern army demands large resources and manpower and the entire nation may be involved in the case of underdeveloped countries. Skilled workers must join the armed forces to do the technical work needed by modern armaments and as officers. It is essential to have a sound, well-developed economy capable of continuing its normal routine along with the war. The real growth rates in Africa are not of that level. In general we must conclude that there is really no capacity to supply either present or future needs for war over a protracted period. Without developing manufacturing industries a belligerent is in no position to ensure the unhampered flow of essential material to the armed forces. It would also be hard put to find the foreign exchange with which to buy armaments and it would be obliged to ask for loans or gratuitous aid. There might be restrictions on the provision of aid, even if it were forthcoming from the USSR.

An armed force moving against South Africa would find its logistic capacities severely limited, therefore, by long distances, the lack of adequate road and rail links, underdeveloped economic and educational capacities and insufficient foreign exchange. An advancing army could, therefore, expect to suffer from serious deficiencies that would hamper its ability to reach South Africa in a condition fit for warlike operations until extensive and well-surfaced roads had been built from concentration areas in Angola, Mozambique, Botswana and Zimbabwe. The most economical form of approach would be by rail, so long as rolling-stock in working condition could be found. But since that would restrict routes, an invader would do better to wait until the number of roads approaching South Africa became adequate. Until then the advantage lies with the defender, who has less chance of being strategically surprised.

## Economic Factors[23]
In a study of the potential for military action of the sub-Saharan states only the short term can be examined with any accuracy. If military action is to be taken against South Africa it must rest upon a capacity to fight a prolonged war if it should be forced on the belligerents by South African capacities. The alternative would be that they would have to depend entirely for resupply on foreign suppliers. The duration of a war determines the extent to which the

natural resources must be used. A short war, like that between India and Pakistan in 1965 or the Falkland war of 1982, could be fought on the strength of existing stocks of ammunition, weapons, clothing and probably food, although the replacement of missiles and jet aircraft may impose a greater degree of urgency than in 1965. Almost all these stocks may be drawn from external purchases not necessarily directed to the needs of the war itself and acquired some time before. When a war becomes protracted and existing stocks dwindle, the capacity for war is no longer a function of inventory. In the absence of foreign suppliers a prolonged war will demand access to raw materials and the ability to manufacture. If raw materials are wanting, considerable resources in foreign exchange and credits will be needed to bear the additional burden of imported natural resources. Consumptions in war, moreover, are not merely changed to military commodities: they are additional to normal existence. Thus there are increased demands on resources.

A key to estimating industrial capacity for war is the availability of metals, non-metallic minerals, rubber, textile fibres and vegetable oil. Modern arms have raised the demands: during the second world war American supplies of copper, steel, aluminium and magnesium were increased by 70, 82, 429 and 3 358 per cent respectively. The output of metals as a whole increased by 68,5 per cent. No large arms producer can do without large supplies of iron, steel and energy, no matter how dependent they may be on imports for other raw materials. Metals are essential to tanks, armoured cars, guns, shells, lorries, cartridge cases, electronic instruments, batteries, paint and cans, while coal is needed to provide energy for manufactures. Gold and diamonds are necessary for payments.

Virtually every raw material needed is available in Africa. Apart from South Africa, Sierra Leone, Liberia and Mauritania, which are active exporters, there are considerable iron ore deposits in seven other countries, including Angola and Swaziland. Copper, manganese, tin and coal are available in Zambia, Zaïre, Ghana and Nigeria as well as in South Africa. Both Liberia and Nigeria are sources of natural rubber. But for the most part output in these countries has been sporadic and uneven. Only Zaïre seems equal to South African resources, although lack of organisation and poor communications tend to deprive the country of the full benefits.

Without the ability to manufacture, no amount of raw materials can be of much direct value for the maintenance in the field of a large army for an indefinite period. In the very short run, general economic strength is perhaps irrelevant; but from a few months to three to five years it becomes important. It is in that period that it should become possible to transfer a large proportion of resources to the production of munitions. Not all manufacturing industries are suitable for war production, which is specialised. The greatest contribution to the conduct of war comes from the steel and chemical industries, without which there can be no guns, vehicles or ammunition. By 1943, 80 per cent of durable goods produced in the USA were military, 66 per cent of all manufactures. Thus the significance of a country's war potential may be determined by the extent of its pre-war durable goods and chemical industries.

It may therefore be possible to evaluate the war potential of the sub-Saharan countries by an enumeration and comparison of actual production of capital goods such as ships, aircraft, motor vehicles, railway rolling stock, turbines, machine tools, optical instruments, electronic devices and radios and important chemicals. Such industries can be converted to war production and to expanded capacity.

Consumption of energy, although a crude indicator, may through large differences especially be used to compare war potentials of belligerents, mainly because of the growth of electro-chemical and electro-metallurgical industries. In 1984 six African countries produced 24 per cent of all African electricity, 44 produced 21 per cent and South Africa produced 55 per cent. In 1983 six African countries consumed 48 per cent of the crude steel, 22 per cent consumed 18 per cent and South Africa consumed 34 per cent. In 1984 South Africa was the only producer of electricity from nuclear sources. South Africa was the main producer of coal in Africa in 1984, producing five per cent of the world's hard coal. Twelve African countries exported only single commodities in the past five years, 23 exported a few primary commodities. Only Mauritius, Morocco, Tunisia, Zimbabwe and South Africa exported manufactured goods. Manufactures amounted to 26 per cent from Morocco, 28 per cent from Tunisia, 6 per cent from Zimbabwe and 22 per cent from South Africa. While manufacturing contributed to the gross domestic product significantly in Egypt (48 per cent), Mauritius (20 per cent), South Africa (23 per cent), Zimbabwe (29 per cent) and Zambia (22 per cent), other countries among a selection of twenty, including Ghana (11 per cent) and Nigeria (9 per cent) fell well below 20 per cent in 1985.

South Africa comes second in the list of countries assembling motor vehicles and Nigeria third, but the difference in absolute terms is that in 1979 South Africa assembled 208 000 passenger vehicles and 90 400 commercial vehicles while Nigeria assembled 68 900 commercial vehicles. Morocco was fifteenth in assembling commercial vehicles with 12 000, Tunisia seventeenth with 7 400, Algeria eighteenth with 5 900, and Egypt twentieth with 4 600 vehicles. With regard to passenger vehicles, the Ivory Coast was twenty-first with 7 000.

The only tyre manufacturers in sub-Saharan Africa in 1983 were South Africa with 5,6 million, Nigeria with 754 000 and Ivory Coast with 12 000.

In 1983 pig-iron and crude steel were manufactured in Zambia, Zimbabwe and South Africa (5,9m tons) and the principal African consumers were Angola, the Congo, Ethiopia, Gabon, Ghana, Guinea, the Ivory Coast and Kenya.

In 1983 radios were assembled in Cameroun, the Central African Republic, Gabon, Ghana, Mozambique, Nigeria, Rwanda, Tanzania, Zambia, Zimbabwe and South Africa – where 895 000 were assembled – with Tanzania and Nigeria next with about 100 000 each. Television sets were assembled only in Gabon (1 000), Ghana (2 000), Nigeria (208 000), South Africa (337 000) and Tanzania. (See Table C on next page.)

Perhaps the net effect of the industrial capacity developed by South Africa is best indicated by its armaments manufacturing capacity in addition to the normal industrial capacity. While the country has not become entirely self-sufficient, it is largely so and is not fundamentally dependent on foreign arms supplies. Through the development of a central armaments corporation employing 26 000 workers and through the use of contractors throughout its whole industry, 975 private companies employing about 70 000 people manufacture about 4 000 items, including 140 different types of ammunition. Not only has this freed the Defence Force from the ban on armaments imposed by the UN in 1963 and made mandatory in 1977, it has also enabled South Africa to export arms to 23 countries: artillery pieces, infantry fighting vehicles and troop-carriers, sold in Asia and in the Middle East.

The arms made in South Africa have gradually developed since the first arms industry was established during the second world war. But the arms now available have reached a much higher level of sophistication. They include not only arms

**TABLE C**

**Economic Factors**

| Country | Def Budget ($) | GDP '85/6 ($) | GDP Growth (%) | Inflation (%) | Debt ($) |
|---|---|---|---|---|---|
| Angola | 1,09 bn | 4,04bn | 0,0 | ? | 3,2 bn |
| Ethiopia | 446,86 m | 5,47 bn | 3,7 | -9,8 | 2,5 bn |
| Ivory Coast | 93,62 m | 6,81 bn | 3,2 | 5,5 | 8,0 bn |
| Kenya | 255,6 m | 5,77 bn | 5,3 | 4,0 | 3,5 bn |
| Madagascar | 59,9m | 2,72 bn | 0,3 | 14,5 | 2,4 bn |
| Mozambique | 146,53 m | 2,55 bn | -8,0 | 20,0 | 2,7 bn |
| Nigeria | 217,35 m | 68,01 bn | 1,0 | 5,5 | 22,0 bn |
| Tanzania | 223,42 m | 4,23 bn | 2,5 | 33,3 | 3,5 bn |
| Uganda | 10,92 m | 1,79 bn | -5,5 | 177,3 | 1,2 bn |
| Zaire | 45,28 m | 2,88 bn | 2,0 | 42,1 | 5,0 bn |
| Zambia | ? | 2,33 bn | 3,0 | 69,9 | 4,0 bn |
| Zimbabwe | 389,62 m | 5,60 bn | 1,0 | 14,3 | 3,0 bn |
| TOTAL | 2978,46 bn | | | | 61,0 bn |
| South Africa | 3,29 bn | 62,48 bn | 0,7 | 18,6 | 24,0 bn |

(Source: Military Balance, 1987 – 1988)

of foreign design adapted to local needs, such as the Eland armoured car, the Olifant tank and the Cactus (Crotale), but also missiles such as the V3C Darter air–to–air heat–seeking missile with a sighting device mounted on the pilot's helmet, frequency–hopping radios that alternate signals ten times a second to defeat interception and the G–6 46–ton 155mm gun–howitzer system with a range of 40 km, which is self–propelled and has an operational range of several hundred kilometres. There are also proximity fuses, fire–control systems, gun-sights, new types of bombs, mines, command and control communication equipment, computers, radar and electro–optical equipment and a 127mm multiple rocket launcher. In vehicles the corporation (Armscor) has developed the Ratel infantry fighting vehicle, which has been tested successfully in action, mounting a variety of guns, the Samil range of trucks, ambulances, field–kitchens, mobile operating–theatres, and gun–tractors and most recently, the Rooikat heavy armoured car. In addition the 450–ton FACs used by the South African Navy have been produced under contract by the local ship–building industry. Not only is the ageing Mirage III being converted to the improved Cheetah, with more modern radar and electronic devices, but an experimental attack helicopter, the XH–1 Alpha, has been built in prototype. In an interview in December 1985, the chairman of Armscor spoke of the development of missiles to increase the striking power of the Defence Force.[24] Many of these have been operationally tested in recent actions alongside Unita in south–eastern Angola and found to perform very well. Perhaps the low level of 31 deaths in the operations in 1987 may be accounted for in part by the quality of the equipment.

In *Arms Production in Developing Countries* Neuman mentioned that in 1979/ 80 sub–Saharan Africa had only two arms–producing countries. The only other besides South Africa is Nigeria. An Act setting up a Defence Industries Corporation to manufacture small arms and ammunition with German help was passed by

Parliament in 1964. Twenty years later Neuman says that Nigeria is still "in the early stages of domestic arms production" in spite of the size of her armed forces and of her GDP and population. Since other African countries are in various ways worse off than Nigeria, it is reasonable to assume that the arms production situation will remain unchanged for a long time. The assessment of economies in the *Military Balance 1987-1988* produced by the International Institute for Strategic Studies was that real economic growth for the African economies in 1986 had been disappointing; regional GDP rose by only 1,2 per cent compared with 2,8 per cent in 1985. Both figures were well below the growth in population, so that the GDP per head also fell. The oil exporters did worse than the importers, with income from exports falling by 44 per cent. The table shows that for a selected group of countries with pretensions to military power sub–Saharan debt reached US$61 billion. The *Military Balance 1988-1989* described a fall in regional GDP from $160 billion in 1986 to $127 billion in 1987, a per capita fall of $100 in one year. Excluding RSA, regional debt rose to $137,8 billion from $122,4 billion in the same year. At the same time these countries budgeted $2 978,46 million on defence. Since they did not produce arms, where do they come from?

**Foreign Aid**
The alternative to internal resources is foreign aid. Twenty years ago there were few signs of significant aid to Africa south of the Sahara, although the USSR and Czechoslovakia had begun to sell arms to Egypt in 1955. At that time, it also appeared to Western observers that the Russians were not prepared to give arms away free. Nor did it seem obvious then that there would be African countries that would, like Angola, rely on oil production to pay for armaments and the use of foreign forces. As many African countries were celebrating twenty years of independence, the Chief of the SADF, General Constand Viljoen said in 1982 that in the preceding five years Angola alone had received arms worth R10 000 million, while Mozambique had received arms worth R350 million and Tanzania, Zambia and Botswana had received arms costing R800 million, R200 million and R42 million respectively.[25]

Substantial deliveries of arms by the USSR to Africa really began with the decision to send the Cuban expeditionary force to Angola when *Operacion Carlotta* was started in 1975. This was the decision to help the MPLA in its attack on the two Angolan political parties which, under the Alvor Agreement of January 1975, were intended to rule Angola jointly. According to Andrew Pierre during this operation about $200 million worth of weapons were sent in support of 16 000 Cuban soldiers.

Later, the Russian reinforcement of and supply to the Cuban and Ethiopian forces during the 1977/8 war in Ogaden illustrated a newly exploited capacity to transport forces by air or sea. Pierre says that 200 aircraft were used to fly men and equipment to Ethiopia. Arms worth US$1 billion, 17 000 Cubans and 1 200 Russian advisers were sent to rescue Mengistu's government from the Somali army, which had itself been trained and armed by the Russians. This capacity appeared to do as much during the later years of the Brezhnev era to raise the prestige of the USSR in Africa at a time when it was declining.

As stated in the 1988 edition of *Soviet Military Power: An Assessment of the Threat* (p.30) the most important instrument for the spread of Russian influence in Africa south of the Sahara, has been the despatch of armaments and advisers. Clearly, the shake–up economy of the USSR has not been able to compete with Western economic aid as a form of influence. Even so, as Pierre has shown, the USSR remains second in exports of armaments in the world. Nevertheless, Africa has received about $15 billion worth of armaments from the USSR from 1980 to 1987. In several countries the support has been given indirectly through Cuba, to which enormous deliveries have been made. Not only has 60 per cent of armaments delivered to Cuba been received in the past ten years, according to the US Department of Defense, but 2 800 Russian military advisers serve with the Cuban forces. Annually, some $4,5 billion in economic aid goes to Cuba, but that is one of the few countries that the USSR considers it necessary to support economically. Andrew Pierre has called sales of arms "foreign policy writ large". It is apparent from the quantities of such aid to Cuba that the USSR has recognised the utility of cultivating Cuban political ambitions, not least in Africa where Cubans serve in several countries, from the 50 000 in Angola to several hundred in other countries. For the USSR the spread of military forces has been a means of eroding Western powers which compete with the USSR for markets and for influence; although until recently the Western countries appeared to stand helplessly in the wings. Indeed, not long ago a Russian attempt to sell arms even to Botswana resulted in a vigorous response from America.

**TABLE D**

**Major Soviet Equipment Delivered to the Third World 1981 — 1986***

|  | Near East and South Asia | Sub-Saharan Africa | Latin America | East Asia and Pacific | Total |
|---|---|---|---|---|---|
| Tanks/Self-propelled Guns | 3 720 | 585 | 500 | 660 | 5 465 |
| Light Armour | 6 975 | 1 050 | 200 | 660 | 8 885 |
| Artillery | 3 350 | 1 825 | 800 | 530 | 6 505 |
| Major Surface Combatants | 22 | 4 | 4 | 4 | 34 |
| Minor Surface Combatants | 28 | 18 | 39 | 37 | 122 |
| Submarines | 9 | 0 | 1 | 0 | 10 |
| Missile Attack Boats | 10 | 8 | 6 | 2 | 26 |
| Supersonic Aircraft | 1 060 | 325 | 110 | 210 | 1 705 |
| Subsonic Aircraft | 110 | 5 | 0 | 5 | 120 |
| Helicopters | 635 | 185 | 130 | 75 | 1 025 |
| Other Combat Aircraft | 235 | 70 | 50 | 90 | 445 |
| Surface-to-Air Missiles | 11 300 | 2 300 | 1 300 | 375 | 15 275 |

*Revised to reflect current information
(Source: Soviet Military Power, 1988)

Despite recent signs that the Soviet Union might wish to free itself from costly and unrewarding adventures in the Third World, it is unlikely that it would neglect opportunities in which much has been invested. Moreover, the political cost of abandoning clients when they are endangered would entail high risks. Foreign aid therefore appears to remain a significant factor for the future of African stability, from both the USSR and the USA and other Western powers competing with the USSR.

## Conclusions

This study of the future of arms in sub-Saharan Africa has indicated that in contrast to the parlous state of the armed forces in Africa soon after the achievement of statehood and independence in the early 1960s, several countries have acquired remarkably modern arms. Some have acquired what by previous standards could be regarded as vast armies. Some have been able to overtake the armaments of South Africa, partly as a consequence of the United Nations ban on the supply of arms to South Africa, partly as a result of the readiness of the USSR during the Brezhnev régime to provide arms free to the African countries. Whereas the South African government has been able to compensate adequately on the ground and to some extent even at sea through the local manufacture of arms, a problem that has not yet been easily solved is that caused by the lavish sale to the African governments, especially Angola and Mozambique, of MiG–23 aircraft and air–defence systems. Nevertheless, experience in Africa indicates that unless African forces are fighting in defence of their homes their performance in battle may be poor. Not only the losses suffered by the FAPLA forces in the failed campaigns to take Mavinga in 1987/8 and the previous two years serve as indicators of inadequacies. The severe defeats inflicted on the Ethiopian forces in 1988 by the Eritrean and Tigrean rebels testify to defects. Indeed, until the Cuban expeditionary force was flown in in great haste by the USSR in 1977, the performance of the Ethiopians against the Somali forces had been very poor and help was necessitated by impending defeat. These considerations also turn one's attention to the fact that of the stronger powers, regarded by the Africa Institute of SA as "military powers", internal or border conflicts remain incipient and this would tend to limit their ability to send forces elsewhere. There are, however, certain African countries that have sent forces elsewhere to help in the suppression of insurgencies or in the guarding of vital communications. These include Zimbabwe and Tanzania, with 6 000 to 12 000 and 650 troops respectively serving in Mozambique, apparently with some success. But the character of that campaign is different from a full–scale campaign against a balanced force with armour and artillery.

It is apparent that African armies do not possess highly mobile, balanced forces. The vast distances in South Africa and in the countries through which an army would approach, the poor communications and the topography of the continent, would therefore favour South Africa in a prolonged campaign not preceded by extensive re–equipment and preparation. Nor would the economies of Africa be able to sustain either the preparation needed nor even the conduct of a conventional war with present armaments. In other words, in the short term their capacity to operate successfully would be doubtful.

There remains the question of foreign aid. An important question is to what extent sub–Saharan armed forces could benefit from the injection of large quantities of advanced equipment. Unless education has developed enough to produce soldiers without robbing the economy of the services of people essential to its maintenance, the diversion of the educated to operating and maintaining technologically advanced arms could be damaging to already shaky economies. The implication is that as with the present tendency in Angola to use Cuban and perhaps Russian pilots to fly complex aircraft such as the MiG–23, the supply of such equipment generally would require greater numbers of foreign soldiers and airmen. That this is already the case is suggested by the fact that, apart from the tens of thousands of Cubans in Angola, there are 500 in the Congo, 500 in South Yemen, 500 in Ethiopia and in Nicaragua and 600 in Mozambique, apparently not part of Cuban military formations. East German, Russian and other military "advisers" in these numbers in Angola, Mozambique and Ethiopia, for example, also suggest that they play a part other than mere advisers. Some of the Russian personnel killed during *Operation Protea* in 1981 were apparently technicians maintaining equipment.

The conclusion seems to be that for any large-scale campaign to develop against South Africa or against South African forces deployed outside the country, foreign intervention would be necessary. Until *Operacion Carlotta* in 1975/6, no one in Africa expected that a Cuban expeditionary force of any significance would intervene on the continent of Africa. Even then, the intervention on a far larger scale on the side of Ethiopia in 1977 was probably even more unexpected, particularly the manner of its execution. The question that needs to be asked now is what the prospects may be for further intervention in Africa, especially against South Africa.

The Cuban reinforcements in Angola in June 1988 may serve as a case study. They followed on the recent atmosphere of détente after the Reagan–Gorbachev discussions in Moscow and also after the beginning of the Russian withdrawal from Afghanistan. Moreover, they took place in the weeks before the extraordinary conference of the Communist Party of the Soviet Union was due to begin in Moscow, a conference of critical importance to Gorbachev's future. According to what Fidel Castro told a meeting of foreign ambassadors in Havana, they were undertaken despite the détente and without the knowledge of the Angolan government. Expressing his displeasure at the cordiality in Moscow, Castro said he was prepared to go to war with South Africa. Any Cuban withdrawal such as the Soviet Union was carrying out in Afghanistan would mean 13 wasted years in Angola. Gorbachev's *perestroika* and *glasnost* programmes are censored out of the Cuban media. One has thus to ask whether reinforcement of the Cuban forces in future could proceed or whether pressure would be brought by the Soviet government to end further possibilities of force being used against South Africa. If it should be asked why the USSR should stop Cuba, the answer may lie in the new easing of relations with the USA and also in the attitudes toward foreign adventures, such as Afghanistan, which are costly and embarrassing. Angola, with the protracted war since 1976 and the inability in recent years to capture Mavinga, even with fresh equipment, Cuban participation and Russian advisers has been equally embarrassing. Cuban conduct would seem to be motivated by Castro's zeal as a revolutionary, made perhaps more urgent not only by signs that the USSR could apply pressure for Cuban withdrawal, but also by the cancer from which he is rumoured to be suffering. In the same way as Hitler, he may wish to conclude his "mission" before he dies. On the other hand, Castro may be operating in the same frame of reference as that described by Yehezkel Dror in his book *Crazy States*. According to Dror, it is sometimes rational for governments to behave as though they were "crazy". This may force other governments into desired positions far more effectively than if rational negotiation were tried.[26]

The USSR may now have abandoned the conduct that brought it into Africa with such apparent success in 1975 after some years of mediocre results. If that is so, the future may show the USSR struggling to find a way of backing out of Africa without too much damage to its relations with the Third World. If that interpretation is correct, the arms race in southern Africa and elsewhere in Africa may slow down, even if it does not end for the time being while the Russian economy is concentrated on more beneficial production. This would

**Above:** Rhodesians from all walks of life were required to do extended periods of service in the bush. It is remarkable that such a small nation was able to hold out as long as it did.

**Below:** A strange assortment of mine-protected vehicles appeared in Rhodesia during the war. This photograph was taken on the road to the Honde Valley, one of the most strongly contested regions in the war.

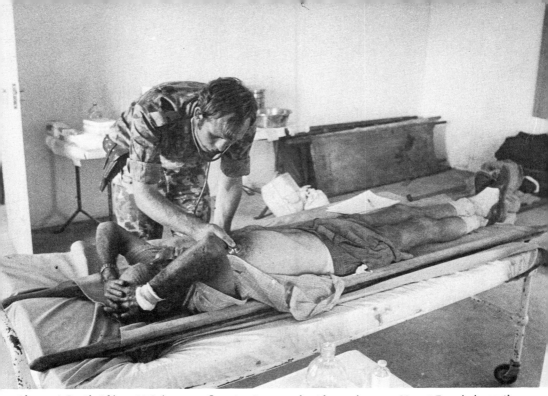

**Above:** A South African M.O. in camouflage treats a man hurt by a mine near Mount Darwin in north-eastern Rhodesia. South Africans from all arms served in Rhodesia.

**Below:** Looking at South Africa from the Rhodesian side of the Limpopo. Now South African soldiers are deployed on the south bank and their attention is focused on Zimbabwe.

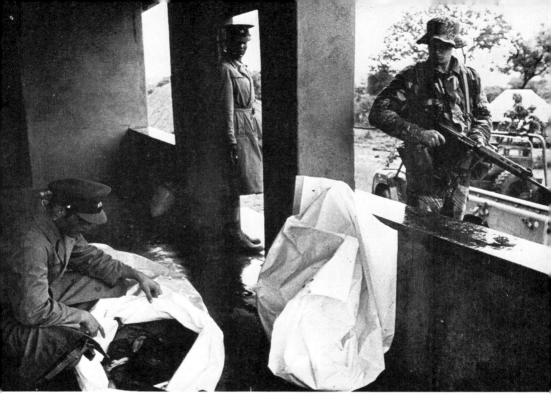

**Above:** Two ZANU insurgents killed in a fight with the Rhodesian security forces are identified by the BSAP.

**Below:** This ZANU unit, in training, was encountered near Nyamapanda on the Mozambique border with Rhodesia. They were photographed by Al Venter at the end of the Portuguese war while he was on his way back to Salisbury from Cahora Bassa.

**Above:** President Daniel arap Moi plays a crucial part in keeping East Africa stable. He is seen here at a meeting of the Organisation of African Unity in Mauritius during the late Seventies.

**Right:** Mercenaries have taken part in some African disputes, but they are a diminishing influence since Europe has shown increasing interest in maintaining stability throughout much of Africa. This group was in Angola after the Lisbon coup.

**Far left:** Chad soldiers man a Russian anti-aircraft gun captured from the Libyans. In spite of peace moves throughout much of Africa, the continent will see many more conflagrations of this kind.

**Left:** Literally "armed to the teeth", this Chad soldier awaits airlift to the north to meet the Libyan invasion.

**Above:** Helicopter pilot's view of some of the vehicles captured in a raid into southern Angola.

*Légionnaires* interrogate a Katangese rebel after he had been captured near Kolwezi in southern Zaïre. This rebel force was launched from Angola in an attempt to overthrow the government of Zaïre.

Zaïrean security forces totally failed to stop the Katangese invasion from Angola and depended on French and Belgian troops to drive out the attackers.

South African armoured strike force at rest in south Angola. The Ratel armoured car has been prominent in such adventures.

**Below:** Many South African soldiers will remember being airlifted to the border in SAAF C-130 or C-160 transports. That era is about to end.

South West Africans of all races are giving much attention to security now that independence is imminent. This is one of the units that have seen much active service on the Angolan border.

**Top:** The new line of defence is likely to be the Limpopo. A patrol of the South African Citizen Force on the banks next to the Zimbabwe border.

**Above:** The "Golden Highway" in South West Africa. This road along the Angolan border has been the supply line for a generation of South African soldiers fighting against Swapo.

**FROM TOP LEFT CLOCKWISE:**
Experimental helicopter test platform built as a prototype for a new gun-ship to be made by Armscor for the Air Force; 250kg bombs come off the assembly line; cluster bombs used to great effect in several wars, including those in Africa; 20mm GA-1 automatic cannon, born of experience in the

**A SELECTION OF WEAPONS PR**
**SOUTH AFRICAN ARMAMENTS**

Angolan bush war; SAAF *Cheetah,* which
strongly resembles the Israeli *Kfir.* The SADF
G5, a 155mm cannon which was used to
excellent effect at Cuito Cuanavale; and the
*Rooikat* armoured car, an 8 x 8 infantry
fighting-vehicle whose design enables it to
operate in the worst conditions of Africa.

BY THE
RATION (ARMSCOR).

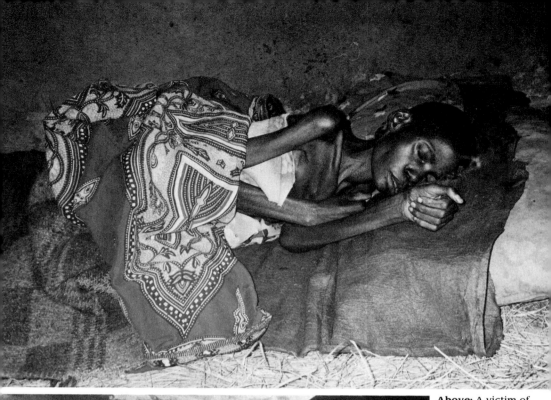

**Above:** A victim of Aids in Uganda. This horror will become increasingly common as it spreads throughout the continent in the Nineties.

**Left:** The huge lake behind the Cahora Bassa dam, which holds much promise for the future for all southern Africa.

**Below left:** A large crowd in Maseru is symptomatic of one of the greatest problems facing southern Africa in the future: overpopulation.

mean that the Cuban potential for armed conflict would also have to be brought under control without damaging relations. It is assumed that the USSR will not change its character so much that it would not return to the export of revolution one day when it has a sounder economy. Whatever might ultimately be the unintended results of Gorbachev's policies, one must assume that at present the Russian government does not intend to abandon its communist character. Thus the conclusion as to arms in Africa in the future seems to depend on the type of government that develops and the policies that it might pursue in Africa. At present it would depend on their reading of how to deal with the Third World, in particular with Africa and Cuba. If Afghanistan becomes a precedent, the situation may change radically, with Western powers no longer wanting to distribute arms as a counter to Russian successes in effecting sales and influencing government through supplies of arms. If the withdrawal from Afghanistan is seen as a failure that results not only in the overthrow of the communist government there but also in the overthrow of Gorbachev, or at least his reform programme. In the latter case, a hard-line communist return in the USSR might not necessarily mean a return to African adventures unless the Russian armed forces, in particular, believe that a return must be made. Reports of Russian racism, however, might indicate that, as with Egypt in 1972, military contacts might be diminished. The fact remains that in the immediate future Cuba has sufficient munitions of war to continue with a campaign of about a year's duration without Russian help against South Africa. If the South African forces, however, were to have some degree of success, the impact politically in Cuba may create an entirely new factor. In the mean time, South Africa should probably be more concerned about achieving the political changes that would not only deprive foreign powers of any legitimacy in intervention but also deprive the insurgent political movements of recruits by taking away any cause for young people to join them. While the SADF has shown that it is able to restore a degree of calm in the black townships, the politicians have yet to make the progress that will make the calm permanent.

**FOOTNOTES**

1. All data relating to the sub–Saharan armed forces numbers, equipment and organisation are taken from *The Military Balance, 1988,* pp120 to 145. Tables are derived from the same data.
2. *Indian Ocean Newsletter No.325,* March 26, 1988; *BBC Summary of World Broadcasts Middle East,* 0102 B/4 17 March, 1988 reporting Sudan National Unity Radio, also 0106, B/5 of 22 March 1988 and 0108, B/14 of 24 March 1988.
3. *The Economist,* 12 March 1988, p24.
4. *Strategic Survey,* 1978, IISS, London, 1979, pp100–101 and writer's interview with the Belgian officer who acted as Chief of Staff for the ad hoc staff of foreign advisers who took charge of the operations against the Gendarmes when the Zaïrean staff collapsed.
5. According to Roland Darroll, spokesman for the Department of Foreign Affairs, *Beeld,* 2 May 1988, pp1 and 2 and *Natal Mercury,* 7 December 1987, which reported the 50th Division's move to Angola.

6. Gen. J. Geldenhuys, Chief of the SADF, *The Star,* 19 April 1988, p1; *Pretoria News,* 19 April 1988, pp1 and 7; *Uniform,* 28 April 1988, p3.

7. "Scott report says 'Gowon can win by April -- if... '," *Sunday Telegraph,* 11 January 1970, pp8 and 9.

8. *Strategic Survey, 1978,* IISS, 1979, pp100–101; Gen. Geldenhuys, op. cit.; *Military Balance 1987-88,* IISS, London, 1987, p137; *Official Year Book of the Union of South Africa, No. 23,* Chapter XXIX, pp20–24, 1946; Government Printer, Pretoria, 1947; Deon Fourie, *War Potentials of the African States South of the Sahara,* SAIIA, Johannesburg, 1968, p22.

9. See the *Military Balance, 1987,* and also D.J. Earp, "The Role of Air Power in Southern Africa" in Hough, M. and van der Merwe, M. *Contemporary Air Strategy,* ISSUP, Pretoria, 1986; Cohen E.A., "Distant Battles–Modern War in the Third World", in *International Security* 10:4 Spring 1986, pp 152–4; Blake, B. (ed) *Jane's Weapon Systems, 1987/8,* Jane's, London, 1987, pp252–261, 752 and 755.

10. Payton, G.D. "The Soviet Ethiopian Liaison: Airlift and Beyond", *Air University Review,* Vol.3, Nov-Dec 1979, p69; *Strategic Survey, 1977,* pp14 and 21–2; *Strategic Survey, 1978,* pp94–95. Marquez, Gabriel Garcia, "Operacion Carlotta", *New Left Review,* 101–102, London, April 1977, pp130–2.

11. Goosen, J.C., *Our Navy,* W.J. Flesch, Cape Town, 1973. pp202–9; *German Tribune,* No.1264, 1 March 1987, p5, taken from the *Frankfurter Algemeine Zeitung;* Hill, J.R., *Maritime Strategy for Medium Powers,* Croom Helm, London, 1986, pp128 and 179; Moore, J. (ed) *Jane's Fighting Ships 1987/8,* Jane's, London, 1987, pp105 and 598; Blake, B. (ed) *Jane's Weapon Systems, 1987/8,* Jane's, London, 1987, pp481 and 483.

12. Spiers, E.M., *Chemical Warfare,* Macmillan, London, 1986, pp89–97.

13. op cit. pp104–108

14. *Keesing's Contemporary Archives,* Vol.xxx, pp32689 and 33058; see also Vol.xxxi, p34515.

15. Spiers, E.M., op cit. Chapter 6, "Soviet Chemical Warfare Posture", passim and *Soviet Military Power: An Assessment of the Threat,* 1988, US Government Printing Office, Washington, 1988, pp77–78.

16. *International Defense Review,* 1/1988, p11.

17. *ANGOP News Bulletin,* No.90, London, 10 February 1988, pp4–5.

18. "Setzt die MPLA sowjetisches Nervengas ein?" *Schweizerzeit,* 1 Juli 1988, p6.

19. *Africa Insight,* Africa Institute of SA, 17:4, 1987, pp53–60.

20. Fourie, op cit. p37; *Military Balance,* passim.

21. Fourie, op cit. p39.

22. op cit. p39

23. *The World in Figures,* The Economist, London, 1981, *United Nations Statistical Yearbook 1983/4,* UN Publications Division, New York, 1986, tables 125, 126, 135, 152, 172.

24. Fourie, op cit. p75; *This is Armscor,* n.d., n.p.; Neuman, S.G. "The Global Arms Transfer System" in Katz, J.E. *Arms Production in Developing Countries,* "The Armsmaker an Embargo Built", *Time,* May 9 1988; *Beeld,* 4 December 1985.

25. Steenkamp, W., "The SA Defence Force", *Leadership SA,* 2:4, Summer 1983, p56.

26. *Africa Insight,* op cit., pp65, 83, 96; *The Independent,* quoted in *The Star,* 16 June 1988, p9; for the concept of "crazy states" see Dror, Yehezkel *Crazy States.*

## SELECT BIBLIOGRAPHY

*Africa Insight,* Africa Institute of SA: 17:4,1987.

*African Economic Handbook,* Euromonitor, London, 1986.

Cohen, Eliot, A: "Distant Battles–Modern War in the Third World", *International Security,* 10:4, Spring 1986.

Fourie, Deon: *War Potentials of the African States South of the Sahara,* SAIIA, Johannesburg, 1968.

Hill, J.R: *Maritime Strategy for Medium Powers,* Croom Helm, London, 1986.

International Institute for Strategic Studies: *Military Balance 1988-89,* IISS, London, 1988.

Katz, James E: *Arms Production in Developing Countries,* Lexington Books, Lexington, 1984.

Matthews, Ron: *The Development of the South African Military-Industrial Complex,* Defense Analysis, 4:1, March 1985.

Meason, James E: "African Navies South of the Sahara", *US Naval Institute Proceedings,* 114:3, March, 1988.

Pierre, Andrew, J: *The Global Politics of Arms Sales,* Princeton University Press, Princeton, 1982.

Western Massachusetts Association of Concerned African Scholars: *US Military Involvement in Southern Africa,* South End Press, Boston, 1978.

# ARMSCOR TODAY - SELLING ARMS TO THE ENEMY

*by Willem Steenkamp*

South Africans are so used to the fact that their national economy rests on its wealth of rare and valuable minerals that it was a shock to them when they were told in 1987 that in foreign earnings the export of military arms and equipment ranked just behind gold and coal.

The South African arms industry now produces a wide range of arms: mine-protected vehicles, rifles, small-arms ammunition, field-cookers, a helmet-guided 20mm machine-cannon, towed and self-propelled 155mm gun-howitzers, advanced electronic gear, radio equipment, light and heavy infantry fighting vehicles, armoured cars, ground-to-ground unguided artillery rockets and air-to-air missiles.

At the same time it constantly modernises existing weapons, sometimes to the point where any resemblance to the original hardly remains, and carries out continual research and development, which has brought it near to producing an all-South African combat helicopter.

Some of its projects are so secret that they will not be known for a long time yet, and in fact may never be revealed if they remain part of the development process rather than resulting in a new product.

Thanks to its combination of imported technology, locally acquired experience, inspired corner-cutting and intensive research and development, the South African arms industry has taken less than forty years to develop to such an extent that the country is now an exporter of weapons and equipment... the tenth largest in the world, supplying no fewer than 23 different countries, many of which would not be seen dead speaking to it in any public forum such as the United Nations... and is the largest single exporter of manufactured goods.

Whether one approves of the causes of the development of the South African arms industry or not, it is a remarkable achievement.

The South African arms industry is now a huge complex of state-owned and private firms.

The backbone of the whole intricate network is a parastatal body called the Armaments Corporation of South Africa or Armscor. It consists of ten privately-owned subsidiaries, some with subsidiaries of their own, employing 23 000 workers of all races, and with assets of about R2,8 billion and an annual turnover of perhaps R2 billion in 1988/9: the equivalent of the entire gross domestic product of a nation like Zambia or Malawi.

Its influence on the South African economy is out of proportion to its size. While Armscor carries out large-scale manufacturing and development of its own, it also hands out work to a myriad of private firms.

At present it has more than 900 sub-contractors, employing something like 70 000 people, while another 1 200 firms supply it from their normal production runs. So great is the extent of the private sector that such firms manufacture between 70 and 75 per cent of the Armscor weapons. In May 1988 the general manager of Armscor, Johan van Vuuren, was quoted by *Jane's Defence Weekly* as saying that every job opportunity created within the corporation created six more in the private sector.

The scale of cooperation is gigantic for a country the size of South Africa and at its stage of industrial development. In a television interview in 1987 the chairman of Armscor, P.G. Marais, spoke of one export project (the nature of which he did not divulge) that employed more than 10 000 Armscor and other workers.

Yet another ripple effect of its operations is that it has had to introduce and develop new precision technology which in the ordinary course of events would not have been necessary in South Africa at this stage of its development. The result has been a spin-off that benefits the civilian population, much as the space race introduced new materials and methods to the world at large.

If a feasibility study announced in April 1988 proves satisfactory, South Africa intends to launch its own surveillance and communications satellite by late 1989 ... for which it will obviously use some of the intensive missile research work that Armscor has been carrying out for the past four years.

The corporation is a standing testimony to an unpalatable truth that no amount of political sleight-of-mouth can talk away: it is almost impossible to boycott a country that has plentiful natural resources, a well-developed infrastructure of industry and technical ability, much ingenuity, hard cash to buy what it cannot make and, above all, the will to paddle its own canoe.

In February 1988 the *Cape Times,* a harsh critic of most of the actions of the South African government wrote in an editorial while calling for an impartial study of the probable impact of widespread economic sanctions:

"One issue that the surveys will have to give a careful miss, however, is the performance of South Africa's weapons industry, which was virtually non-existent till arms deals with this country became subject to the most stringent compulsory sanctions internationally some ten years ago.

"Today the industry consists of a hundred private companies. Armscor alone is now the biggest exporter of manufactured goods in the country and is ranked third overall as a foreign revenue earner, beaten only by gold and coal.

"Such facts, clearly, would not fit readily into any argument about the efficacy of sanctions as a means of bringing Pretoria to its knees or destroying its morale."

What helped to scupper the international arms boycott of South Africa was the time factor. If it could have been applied swiftly and totally it might have hurt badly. But it took too many years to begin to bite. As a result South Africa had since the 1960s to prepare for the day when the taps would finally be turned off.

Then again, it was not dependent on hand-outs or arms aid like almost all other Third World countries, and there were too many other outcast states like Israel and Taiwan that made common cause with South Africa, while other nations were willing to deal with anyone as long as it suited their own interests.

That is not to say that the mandatory UN arms embargo imposed in 1977 has failed altogether.

It has forced South Africa to pay highway-robbery prices for some spare parts and secretly acquired technology, and it has certainly managed to prevent the South Africans from acquiring such equipment as long-range reconnaissance aircraft, larger warships and (so far) submarines; but it is a hollow victory, because Armscor and its private-sector partners not only can and do manufacture all the things needed to maintain internal stability, which was the main motive for the embargo in the first place, but are steadily expanding their range to include much larger and ever-more sophisticated products.

It is not going too far to say that the present state of South African self-sufficiency in weapons is, ironic as it may sound, the direct result of the actions of the anti–apartheid lobby actions.

In May 1988, a senior source in the Defence Force was quoted by Reuters as saying: "The arms embargo is the best thing that happened for technology in South Africa."

So Armscor flourishes and without apology. As its former general manager, Fred Bell, told journalists four years ago: "Our size was thrust upon us by our enemies, and we had to grow to the size determined by them ... We have a real war. The (South African) Defence Force is not playing a war game here, it's for real ... We started late and had to move fast."

Move fast it did. In 1964 the South African arms industry was so small that it was barely capable of copying a few thousand rifles under licence. Ten years later it could supply 30 per cent of the weapons needed by the SADF. Now, the local arms industry can supply about 95 per cent of all its needs, and the percentages are improving all the time as the worldwide clamp–down on weapons for South Africa continues to take effect.

In the interview in *Jane's Defence Weekly*, the general manager, Johan van Vuuren, spoke of the possibility that at some time in the near future Armscor might be required to deal simultaneously with thirty or forty systems:

"The simple reason is that the threat against us from the outside is so severe that the world will not wait for us. We will have to keep up with the Joneses, so to speak ... Whereas the arms embargo was originally intended to stop South Africa from buying arms elsewhere, now the embargo attempts to stop other countries from buying South African arms."

The main subsidiaries of Armscor are all over the country. Apart from the usual technical reasons for such decentralisation, there is also a conscious effort to locate plants, where possible, in such a way as to relieve local unemployment. In one case a factory was so sited that it would provide employment for a particular non–white residential area in the densely-populated Johannesburg-Pretoria region.

That might surprise foreign observers, who tend to believe that there is total racial polarisation in South Africa. In fact, Armscor is not a whites–only outfit, despite the "sensitive" nature of its work. It employs people of all races, and both its own subsidiaries and its multitude of contractors have a largely non–white labour force.

Armscor has few labour problems, and is not known to suffer from a sabotage problem, even though people from "oppressed" groups carry out most of the work on munitions. One reason for that, no doubt, is that there are many shades of political opinion among the non–whites of South Africa; another is that the corporation is an equal–opportunities employer and pays competitive salaries, provides a full range of benefits and runs extensive in–service training schemes to enable its workers to improve their position. It says that an average of 65 per cent of its employees undergo some form of further training every year; which of course improves their earning ability.

To attract the best intellectual potential it offers bursaries with no strings in engineering and related subjects at polytechnic and university level, then offers to recruit the best of them; about 75 per cent join.

The priorities of Armscor are well defined. In 1987 it announced that it would build a new factory at Houwhoek in the Cape primarily as a "think–tank" rather than test or manufacturing plant. In a television interview a few months later, the chairman, P.G. Marais, said of the Houwhoek plant that the prospects of the corporation looked very good for the next ten years; "but I think the potential is the people we have built up."

The main subsidiaries of Armscor are as follows:

ATLAS AIRCRAFT CORPORATION (Kempton Park): which builds, maintains and services various aircraft.

Subsidiary: TELECAST (Kempton Park): manufactures high-tech castings with special alloys, such as helicopter parts.

ELOPTRO (Kempton Park): manufactures optical and electro-optical equipment.

INFOPLAN (Pretoria): provides computer services.

KENTRON (Pretoria): designs and manufactures guided-weapons systems.

LYTTLETON ENGINEERING WORKS (Verwoerdburg): manufactures small arms, mortars and artillery.

MUSGRAVE MANUFACTURERS AND DISTRIBUTORS (Bloemfontein): manufactures and sells sporting rifles, shotguns and pistols.

NASCHEM (Lenz and Potchefstroom): fills mortar and aircraft bombs, heavy-calibre ammunition and mines.

PRETORIA METAL PRESSINGS (Pretoria): manufactures small arms and quick-firer ammunition.

SOMCHEM (Somerset West and Wellington): manufactures explosives, propellants, rocket-propellant systems, rockets.

SWARTKLIP (Cape Town): manufactures pyrotechnical products and commercial small-arms ammunition.

The corporation also has several test sites, such as the Overberg missile range on the Cape coast near Bredasdorp, the St Lucia range in Natal (now being phased out), the Eugene Marais vehicle-testing range west of Pretoria, and an artillery range near Copperton in the Northern Cape.

## THE HISTORY OF ARMSCOR

In a sense the South African home-grown arms industry began in 1803, when a young gunsmith called J.S.F. Botha set up a shop in Cape Town where he manufactured "sannas", as the frontier Boer farmers called their long smoothbore muzzle-loaders.

Botha was the first private gunsmith in South Africa. Up to 1795 all gunsmith's work had been the province of armourers belonging to the Dutch East India Company.

At first Botha imported complete weapons from Holland and sold them to the locals, but after the British permanently re-occupied the Cape in 1806 he began to import locks, barrels and walnut stock-blanks from Birmingham. He assembled the weapons and fitted them to the stocks carved from the imported blanks by local Muslim craftsmen. Later Botha's craftsmen also carved stocks out of native stinkwood and yellow-wood.

There is only a tenuous link between Botha's little factory and the huge present South African arms industry; and yet there are certain similarities. In both cases imports were reduced in favour of local production, the difference being not only in the scale of complexity but also the fact that most Armscor products are totally South African-made, which Botha's never were.

Modern observers tend to ignore such rather romantic historical connections and assume that the South African arms industry came into being as a result of the international weapons boycott, which began to take effect in the 1960s. In fact its seeds were sown long before that.

The first signs of a domestic arms industry can probably be found in the 1920s when the South African Air Force received what became known as the "Imperial Gift"... a large number of war-surplus aircraft, together with vast supplies of stores and spares, presented to the country by Great Britain from stocks left over from the first world war.

At first SAAF technicians did no more than assemble the crated aircraft and get them into airworthy condition; but later significant modifications were made to some types to adapt them to local conditions.

The first serious step towards 100 per cent local production of arms, however, began during the second world war, when it found its arms cupboards almost bare and its usual source of supply, Great Britain, so hard-pressed to meet their own minimum requirements that they had very little to spare.

The South African response was to begin local production. Already the most highly industrialised country on the African continent, it had no great difficulty in turning ploughshares into swords. The first radar sets to be built outside Britain itself were operating by 1940, while factories turned out 3.7-inch howitzers, simple but efficient armoured cars, small-calibre cartridges, artillery shells, aerial bombs, mortar bombs, steel helmets, army boots and innumerable other pieces of war equipment.

But it was a constant struggle to obtain imported parts and raw materials, and when the war ended in 1945 it was obvious that the question of a future local arms industry would have to be considered. In 1948 investigations into the establishment of such an industry got under way, and in 1951 the Defence Ordinance Workshop was set up at Lyttleton, near Pretoria.

The DOW was instructed to begin production of local arms and to acquire technical knowledge concerning the rapid conversion of local industry to war production if the need arose. It expanded in a modest way in the next few years, and by the early 1960s it was able to undertake licensed manufacture of the new service rifle, the Belgian FAL (locally known as the R1).

It was an almost laughably simple product compared with later Armscor weapons, but at the time it was all that could be manufactured with the limited trained personnel and manufacturing resources available.

The arms industry was soon to receive a considerable boost. The adoption of the R1 coincided with the first calls to UN members to boycott exports of military equipment to South Africa, and South Africa began to feel the effects of the call almost immediately. By the beginning of 1946 Belgium had rejected the possibility of future arms deals, the United States had stopped all assistance in the manufacture of arms for South Africa and Britain under a Labour government had cancelled 93 arms-manufacturing licences.

The response of the South African government was the Armaments Act, which removed arms procurement from the province of the civil service and established the Armaments Production Board, in which private industry was well represented.

The first task of the Armaments Production Board was to assess the already existing capability and know-how and to coordinate it for the purpose of manufacturing arms. The first step was to take over the DOW (which was renamed the Lyttleton Engineering Works) and the ammunition-manufacturing section of the South African Mint, which became Pretoria Metal Pressings. That was the beginning of an extensive programme of rationalisation and planning to harness local resources.

In March 1968 the Armaments Production Board was renamed the Armaments Board and given the task of controlling the manufacture, procurement and provision of armaments for the SADF. Manufacturing was to be the responsibility of a new body, the Armaments Development and Production Corporation of South Africa. LEW and PMP were then converted into privately-owned subsidiaries of the corporation. It was a pattern that has been followed ever since.

The following year the Armaments Development and Production Corporation took over the four-year-old Atlas Aircraft Company, which had been established to service the aircraft of the South African Air Force. This was followed in rapid succession by an existing fireworks firm, Ronden's, the Musgrave sporting weapons factory in Bloemfontein and two explosives factories belonging to African Explosives and Chemical Industries at Somerset West, near Cape Town, and Lenz, outside Johannesburg.

The process continued in the next few years, with the products becoming ever more ambitious and sophisticated: ammunition of all kinds, aircraft, armoured vehicles, communications, optical equipment and so on. By 1975, at the beginning of the first long incursion by South Africa into Angola, the corporation employed 16 000 workers and had assets of over R750 million.

At that point it was decided to merge the board and the corporation. The amalgamation took place *de facto* immediately, but its formal ratification by Parliament did not take place till 1977, months before a compulsory arms boycott was begun by the UN. Commandant P.G. Marais was appointed chairman of the new body, the Armaments Corporation of South Africa Limited, soon to be known simply as Armscor.

At the time the appointment of Marais, a farmer and part-time soldier from the arid Karoo, was widely regarded as a pork-barrel appointment, resulting from his friendship with the then Minister of Defence, P.W. Botha. But Marais turned out to be a dark horse. Under his chairmanship, which ended in November 1988, when he retired and was replaced by the general manager, Johan van Vuuren, the Armscor board of directors, (a minimum of seven and a maximum of twelve members appointed by the State President, with the Chief of the SADF as an *ex officio* member), has succeeded in forging a remarkable organisation that has achieved astonishing results with a fairly modest expenditure of money.

## HOW ARMSCOR WORKS
Armscor is the South African government's only organisation for the procurement of weapons (which does not mean that it is the sole supplier to Pretoria, witness the very successful Casspir armoured personnel vehicle produced by a private firm called TFM Limited to satisfy specifications determined by the police, and which is not in limited use by the military). "Procurement" covers a multitude of meanings. Buying is one part (and buying abroad does take place, although under a veil of secrecy), but even more important is the renewal of existing assets and the designing of new weapons and equipment for the future.

At the moment the procurement policy of Armscor is based on three legs:

### 1. Updating, upgrading, improving and adapting designs already in service
Armscor follows that policy as much as possible. because it obviously yields quick results and is cheaper.

An example is the Olifant battle tank. For years the South African armoured strength was dangerously low, as a result of an astonishingly ill-advised decision in the 1950s to sell most of its Centurion MBTs because no use was then seen for them. That led to a pressing need which in turn led to an ingenious solution: a detailed modernising programme on the shrunken Centurion inventory, plus a large number of Centurion hulls and turrets acquired under-the-counter from India and, it is said, Jordan.

The arrival of the Olifant on the scene was greeted with some scepticism. South Africans have always distrusted official pronouncements, and in any case the Olifant looked little different from the familiar old Centurion that the SADF had been using for so many years.

According to Armscor, however, almost all that remains of the original Centurion is the turret shell and hull. It has been ungunned, re-engined and converted from petrol to diesel and equipped with better gunlaying equipment and better transmission, drive and suspension.

The result is a vehicle that retains the Centurion's well-known capacity for absorbing punishment, but is faster, has a greater range, breaks down less readily and can fire larger shells more accurately.

The Olifant saw its baptism of fire against Russian T-54/55 and T-62 battle tanks during the fierce fighting in Angola in 1987 and 1988, the first time that South African tanks had seen action since the second world war. The Olifants apparently performed more than satisfactorily: in a severe armoured battle in November 1987, 62 out of 72 Angolan battle tanks were either "brewed-up" or captured, while the Olifants suffered two casualties: one tank lost a track as a result of a mine and another was hit in the engine compartment. The SADF has admitted losing another Olifant since then.

To be fair, the Olifant cannot be given all the credit for all that. South African armoured crews, particularly the officers, are far better trained than the Angolans, and their technical support is also much better. What it has proved, however, is that the Olifant is capable of engaging Russian tanks on at least equal terms.

Tanks are not the only armoured tracked vehicles made by Armscor. Others, such as recovery vehicles, repair-and-maintenance vehicles and bridge-laying vehicles are also made. Not much is known about them, but they are probably based on Centurion-Olifant chassis and hulls, and possibly older ones.

Another important updating programme is that being carried out on the ageing SAAF Mirage III jet fighters. The result is a new aircraft called the Cheetah, which has been fitted with canard wings and modern electronic equipment, designed as an interceptor and ground-attack fighter. As this is written the first squadron to be equipped with Cheetahs has just gone into service, and conversion work is proceeding on the remaining Mirage IIIs of the SAAF.

An interesting news item appeared in South African newspapers in October 1988 which claimed that Chile had just bought a squadron of Kfir fighter-bombers, reputed to have been jointly manuactured by Israel and South Africa. The announcement was greeted by the proverbial deafening silence from both Jerusalem and Pretoria.

## 2. Designing and development of new equipment for local requirements and according to the manufacturing capabilities of Armscor

Examples of these are the 6 x 6 Ratel-20 infantry fighting vehicle and the Buffel 4 x 4 mine-protected counter-insurgency vehicle.

The basic Ratel design has been expanded into a series, which now includes a tank-destroyer and fire-support vehicle that carries a 90mm gun instead of the infantry 20mm; a command vehicle; a logistics vehicle; and an 81mm mortar-carrier.

The Ratel has been thoroughly tested in battle and, according to Armscor, "the Army says (it) is extremely reliable. (Ratels) are basically the only combat-roved IFVs that exist in this (wheeled) configuration in the world."

As this is written it is not known whether the Ratel is nearing the end of the line as an operational vehicle, although a new design of IFV has reached the production stage.

Given the determination of the South African government to keep defence spending within reasonable limits (the 1988/9 defence estimates amounted to an acceptable 4,5 per cent or so of the gross domestic product) and the present preoccupation with aircraft and missile research, the answer would appear to be no, since the Ratel is more than adequate for foreseeable future conditions, has been thoroughly "de-bugged" and has been expanded into a family of vehicles.

The Buffel MPV, based on the Unimog is now definitely obsolescent after more than ten years of operational service, but it is not known whether it will be replaced soon.

As with the Ratel, however, replacement might be delayed by lack of money and the efficiency of the Buffel, in spite of various faults, such as top-heaviness and the lack of overhead cover. It is likely that it will soldier on for some time yet, possibly in improved form (a very similar vehicle called the Bulldog, based on the local Samil-20 rather than the Unimog and with a slightly different lay-out and overhead cover, has been designed and built, but is not known to be in production).

South Africans have always had a certain affection for artillery (the South African Artillery, for example, has supplied a disproportionate number of generals), and it is in that line that Armscor has scored its most notable triumph in the G–5 155mm gun-howitzer.

Designed at least partly abroad and brought to completion in South Africa, the G–5 has a maximum planning range of about 40km. It is believed to be superior to similar artillery pieces used by the NATO nations. It is rumoured to "shoot like a rifle", and it has been given the most credit for stopping a large-scale armoured advance in Angola in 1987 and 1988 on the territory held by the allies of South Africa, the Unita insurgents of Dr Jonas Savimbi.

The G–5 has now been developed into the G–6, the only wheeled 155mm self-propelled gun-howitzer in the world. The G–6 is a big but agile armoured vehicle, designed for the mobile warfare that the South Africans have been talking about and practising for years. The fighting in Angola in 1987 and 1988 was the début for the handful of G–6s in service, and they seem to have acquitted themselves well, although suffering some failures of components in the heat and stress of the protracted fighting. Yet these failures were a blessing in disguise, since they enabled the South Africans to embark on a comprehensive de-bugging programme.

The 127mm Valkiri multiple rocket-launcher is another local development designed to destroy the Russian BM–21 MRLs, which were first encountered by the South Africans during the fighting in Angola in 1975. The Valkiri is mounted on the back of a Unimog lorry and has a maximum planning range of 22km, slightly more than the BM–21. It uses extremely lethal shrapnel-filled rockets with a low minimum impact angle (20 degrees) and it can be fitted with either a contact fuze or a proximity fuze for airburst, which is said to be virtually impervious to jamming since it is fitted with a frequency-hopping device.

At the *Feria Internacional del Aire* (FIDA) air and arms show in Santiago de Chile in March 1988 Armscor unveiled a smaller version of the Valkiri, known as the Valkiri 5, which can be towed behind almost any vehicle.

Another success by Armscor is the V3B Kukri air-to-air missile, which is linked to a helmet sight worn by the pilot; all he has to do is look at the enemy aircraft and designate the target after it has been acquired. After that he can shift his attention to more pressing matters.

In 1988 the Kukri was overtaken by an even more advanced model, the V3C Darter, which is now in service and, like almost all Armscor products, is for sale as well.

The hint that Armscor might have developed a species of "smart" or guided bomb (about which it has said nothing to date) filtered through in October 1988. The SAAF Chief of Staff: Operations, Brigadier Jan Steyn, revealed that during the 1987/8 Angolan fighting, South African aircraft had carried out successful air-to-ground operations by adopting "a low attack profile and tossing bombs seven to ten kilometres with an accuracy of about 200 metres".

In October 1988 another weapon with overseas sales potential was announced: the Rooikat (Afrikaans for "lynx"). This is a very large (27 ton), yet low-profile eight-wheeled armoured car designed to replace the SADF's renowned but outdated Eland-90, local version of the Panhard AML-90.

According to Armscor officials, the Rooikat can travel 1 000km/h on a single tank of fuel, has a top road speed of 120km/h (60km/h across country) and can keep going even when two wheels are missing. It mounts a 76mm gun with passive night-sight equipment in a stabilised turret which has a computerised gun-laying system for greater accuracy and speed in firing, even on the move. It fires armour-piercing discarding sabot rounds at ranges in excess of 2 000 metres and can engage soft targets with high explosive up to 12km away.

Johan van Vuuren states that the Rooikat is "the most comprehensive system developed by Armscor to date and is superior to anything of its kind in the world". True or false? Time will tell. At a special show for technical journalists the Rooikat certainly lived up to expectation.

The Armscor network has also produced advanced frequency-hopping radio systems that are almost impossible to monitor, which enables battlefield commanders (or police and private security services) to achieve the ancient dream of speaking *en clair* without fear of their messages being picked up by the enemy.

Armscor has a finger in several other pies. It is able, for example, to produce armourplate and armoured glass of European and American standards. This is a matter of cardinal importance in a time when small hand-held weapons, much in use among the Third World enemies of South Africa, are improving in effectiveness almost by the day. The infantryman, still the basis of any ground fighting, is no longer as helpless against armoured vehicles as he was during the second world war.

### 3. Rationalisation, standardisation, simplification and consolidation
This part of the procurement process can best be illustrated by the Samil series of load- and passenger-carrying lorries. Formerly the SADF had over 200 types of such vehicles. This large variety was almost impossible to supply and maintain, many of the vehicles were old or obsolete, and most of them were inherently incapable of surviving the destructive combination of heat, dust, mud, bad roads and cross-country "bush bashing" of southern Africa.

The thorough revisions that began after the first calls for arms boycotts in the early 1960s led to a new generation of South African military lorries.

The result is the Samil range of diesel-engined military trucks. They are in three load-classes: two-ton, five-ton and ten-ton, and more than seventy different configurations, some armoured and others not, providing mine-protected troop-carriers, workshop vehicles, recovery vehicles, tankers, mine–protected ambulances and tippers.

Armscor has also developed a series of container bodies that can rapidly turn a standard Samil–20 two-tonner into a command post, an office vehicle, a communications centre or an artillery command post.

As with most Armscor products the Samils have been thoroughly battle-tested in Angola and Namibia and accordingly de–bugged. They have earned high praise for toughness and reliability.

How much of this three–part procurement programme is original and how much is simply cheque-book progress?

The answer is that there is an element of each. Critics of the arms industry have said that it is nowhere near as inventive or ingenious as is believed, and that many of the things that it produces and claims as its own work are close copies of weapons or equipment produced in other countries.

In some cases that is true; and Armscor often blandly claims total originality when it is obviously not so. The R4 assault rifle, for example, is so close a copy of the Israeli Galil that it even has the bottle–opening device that the designers of the Galil incorporated to prevent troops from damaging its magazine wells. The Cheetah and Centurion conversions are similar to Israeli models, while the G–5 gun and its ammunition incorporate the results of foreign developments in Canada and elsewhere.

It is possible that this trumpet–blowing merely disguises a reluctance to lose good sources by giving credit where it is due.

There appears to be a curious convention that governs arms sales (and presumably transfers of technology) to and by "sensitive" countries like South Africa: as long as neither the seller nor the buyer admits to the deal, all is well, even if details are given in authoritative publications.

That is why for years South African newspapermen were not allowed to photograph the P.122 light maritime–reconnaissance aircraft (local name Albatross) that South Africa had bought from Piaggio, even though the transaction was made public by such sources as *Jane's* "All the World's Aircraft" and the annual review of the International Institute of Strategic Studies, *The Military Balance*.

By ordinary standards it was a farcical situation. The general public had been told over and over again that the SAAF was flying Albatrosses, and the distinctive gull–winged aircraft had been on open view on numerous occasions at air shows. Probably a dozen reputable technical publications had noted that the SAAF had the Piaggios. But as long as no photographs of the aircraft appeared in South African newspapers it did not officially exist, and the wrath of the sanctioneers was not turned on the Piaggio firm.

The same sort of thing happened in the case of the Mirage F–1. For at least two years the F–1 was not officially acknowledged to be in service with the SAAF, although the SAAF could not resist a quick fly–past at an air show. (One alert photographer took a picture of it, and his newspaper then sat on it for about eighteen months before being allowed to publish it.)

That sort of thing occurs less often now that the South African arms industry has grown to its present state of self–sufficiency, but it still does happen. In 1987 there was a great public outcry when the South African Navy disposed of some of its British Ton–class minesweepers; some people accused the SADF of corruption and others damned it as shortsighted. What neither the Navy nor the press could divulge was that a new class of mine–hunters had been taken into service, but that there were conditions attached.

Exactly what these conditions were remains unclear at the time of writing: one story is that the hulls had been designed abroad, and that they were so clearly recognisable that a certain period of time had to pass before they could be officially revealed. It sounds rather odd, but it is no odder than other things that have happened in the South African arms–producing game.

Certain grey areas also exist about the F–1, which according to Armscor was at first locally assembled and then manufactured. To this day, long after the F–1 production line has closed, sceptics still say that little of it was locally manufactured, and that a myth was created to protect its makers, the French firm of Dassault, from repercussions. Only the people at Armscor's Atlas Aircraft Corporation know the truth, and probably not too many of them.

On the other hand, there can be no doubt that many of the products of Armscor are in fact locally designed and manufactured, in whole or in large part. It has built a series of strike craft closely resembling, although larger than the Israeli Reshef class, and last year it took into service a 14 000 ton fleet replenishment ship, the SAS *Drakensberg,* which was built from scratch in the yard of its subsidiary in Durban.

Its series of mine–protected vehicles, said to be the best in the world, are certainly of local design, as is the very efficient Ratel infantry fighting vehicle and a series of small arms including a light machine–gun and a semi–automatic shotgun; and its contractors produce a large variety of arms and equipment including very efficient radios and a hand–held multiple 40mm grenade–launcher called the MGL, which has given good service in the fighting in Angola and northern Namibia.

### ARMSCOR EXPORTS

In 1982, British troops who had overrun Argentinian positions in the Falklands War were intrigued to find their enemies' radios equipped with frequency–hopping devices superior to their own... and made in South Africa, of all places; although when asked about the truth of that, Armscor officials answer with nods and winks rather than outright confirmation.

Various reasons can be found for this reticence in an organisation that usually delights in flourishing its successes in public. One, no doubt, is an unwillingness to offend British sensibilities; it is generally accepted that it was only a coincidence that the Argentinians got the equipment in time to use it in the fighting. But there was much speculation in the press at the time, probably clandestinely started by British diplomats, that South Africa was supplying weapons to Argentina while the war was in progress.

The second reason illustrates a peculiar problem faced by no other arms exporter: revelations about arms sales would embarrass most or all of the 23 countries, both on and off the African continent, who buy weapons or military equipment from the great pariah at the same time as they piously raise their voices in favour of arms boycotts and other signs of disfavour against Pretoria in the United Nations and other international bodies. In other words, politics is politics, but business is business.

And it is a vastly profitable business for Armscor. Its products are in such keen demand that at the time of writing it had a backlog of orders worth R9 000 million, an impressive figure, considering that it was done in the face of the most extensive international arms boycott in history.

Why? Partly because the products of Armscor, most of them sturdy, cheap, fairly simple and needing little maintenance, are tailor–made for both the backward and advanced parts of the Third World.

As the chairman of Armscor says: "Sanctions, as far as Armscor is concerned, have never worked. At the end of the day, if your product is good enough, there will always be a buyer." Backing that policy is the powerful sales force Armscor has built up in the past six years, a team of marketing and weapons experts, some of whom spend six or more months of every year abroad peddling their wares.

Then again, Armscor is willing to sell almost anything from complete weapons systems (complete with back-up service and pre-delivery training) to propellants, spares, updating kits and even raw materials, to almost anybody without fussing about such things as end-user permits, since the pariah status of South Africa has freed it from the limitations of treaty commitments and even ethics.

It has restored something of the original meaning of the word "outlaw": a person who is literally outside the law and therefore is not bound by any of the constraints of organised society.

South Africa reached its final development stage as an arms producer in 1981, the year in which Somchem, a subsidiary of Armscor, commissioned one of the most advanced nitro-cellulose manufacturing plants in the world at Krantzkop, near Wellington in the Cape Province.

It was a time for stock-taking at Armscor. For years it had been fighting the clock to supply the SADF with the weapons and equipment needed to counteract the effect of the UN boycott and a hotting-up of the border war. Now that the worst immediate effects of the boycott had been warded off, it could stand back and plan for the future.

Ironically, the most immediate threat to the well-being of Armscor came not from outside enemies but from the SADF, whose orders for equipment of high quality were falling. Combined with a worldwide recession, it meant large cuts in production, the retrenchment of workers and the seeping away of essential but now under-used talents and knowledge.

The simple economics of arms manufacture also played a part. The only way to recover the investment in arms development and to reduce the unit manufacturing costs is to start mass production, and a country like South Africa can only afford to absorb so much of any particular military product, especially when the range is as wide as that of Armscor. Therefore any national arms industry begins to look outward at a certain stage of its development; not only to save itself money but also, with luck, to turn a profit from sales abroad.

As a result, says Armscor, it was necessary to start an export drive, not only to reduce unit costs but, with luck, to earn foreign money for research, development and manufacture, for which the government simply could not raise the huge sums needed.

The increased needs of Armscor were a direct result of the much greater sophistication of its operations.

In the early 1960s production consisted mainly in assembling imported components. The first French Panhard AML-90 and AML-60 armoured cars, known as the Eland in the SADF, were produced in that way (the Elands have been entirely locally manufactured since 1978, and largely South Africanised by at least seven important improvements and modifications).

The next phase consisted in the manufacture and assembly of low-technology parts, and by 1977 the Bedford lorries and Landrovers used by the SADF were two-thirds local content.

Since then some views have changed. For example, an important goal of the early days, assembly of a 100 per cent locally designed and manufactured parts, has long since been abandoned, since Armscor planners have come to understand that complete self-sufficiency of that kind was less important than efficient use of resources.

Self-sufficiency, as defined as long ago as 1983 by the then general manager, Fred Bell, consists in the ability both to design and to build a thing, not necessarily by manufacturing every last part used in the process; manpower can be more efficiently utilised by importing cheap and simple nuts-and-bolts components rather than wasting abilities and funds that could be better employed elsewhere by laboriously making them at higher cost just for the sake of making them.

Armscor came of age as an arms exporter in 1982, when its salesmen offered a range of sophisticated weapons and equipment at the Defendory '82 arms exhibition in Athens. Anti-apartheid pressure forced the display to close early, but not before buyers had satisfied themselves that it was no mere show-case exercise but genuine goods that were on offer.

The exhibition gave convincing proof that for immediate practical purposes the UN arms embargo of 1977 had not worked.

The Defendory '82 exhibition was followed up by the FIDA '84 exhibition in Chile, where the Armscor show-case stayed open to the end and made a great impression on visitors, and then the FIDA '86 and '88 shows, also in Chile.

The million-rand question is, of course: who are the 23 foreign customers of Armscor? For the most part this information is veiled in secrecy, made still deeper by the fact that to break into the international arms market is not easy, even for a nation that is not an outcast. As a result, observers of the South African arms industry have to reach their conclusions by stitching together or analysing a variety of hints, reports, rumours, official and unofficial disclosures, and the occasional confirmation or denial.

The international arms trade is governed by the ordinary rules of commerce, plus a few additional considerations. An important part of the success formula is to have a good product to sell. The other part is to find the right customers; and that is where selling arms can be more complicated than selling, say, refrigerators.

One problem is that many purchases of arms by small nations are tied to military aid programmes. It is not unusual for a small country to be given credit or cash to buy arms as long as it buys the products of the country that lends it the money.

Armscor salesmen have also to bear a burden peculiar to their situation: the fact that South Africa has been expelled by most world organisations, so that no country is willing to sign a military treaty with it, even if there are good reasons for doing so, or to be seen to buy weapons or military equipment from it.

This state of affairs has a strong bearing on the question of what Armscor sells, and to whom; and what might be called the "invisibility factor" is obviously of great importance: nations that are sensitive to anti-apartheid pressure but have money to spend will probably be interested in "invisible" or inconspicuous goods.

That sort of purchase can be of any size. For years now South African observers have been wondering about the truth of a reported deal in which a certain African country renowned for its anti-South African oratory is said to have bought large quantities of steel helmets made in Pretoria by an Armscor contractor and exported through Botswana. South Africa is so important a source of supply in an underdeveloped continent, however, that even firms outside the Armscor complex benefit; it is a fact, for example, that two prominent African opponents of the "apartheid régime" have some or all of their military uniforms tailored by private clothing companies in Cape Town and Johannesburg.

The invisibility theory determines that recognisably South African goods are harder to dispose of than those that look like goods obtained from more respectable countries, but that proved to be far less of a deterrent than it had seemed at the beginning of the export stage, as can be seen from the sales of such products as the G-5 gun-howitzer, the Ratel infantry fighting vehicle and the Buffel mine-protected vehicle.

There is no doubt that the products of the South African arms industry have seen service in places as far apart as Latin America and the Far East, although some of the stories remain only partly told, such as the one about the South African frequency-hopper radios used by the Argentinian forces in the Falklands war. The story goes that a large number of these radios were shipped to the Argentine "on approval" some time before the war broke out, but thanks to the defeat of the Galtieri régime South Africa was never paid for them and there were no follow-up orders.

No doubt the world will also have to wait a considerable time before it hears the full story of how it came about that Eland-90 armoured cars made in Pretoria ended up serving in the Moroccan army against the Polisario Front in the early 1980s.

One explanation that was heard at the time (although never confirmed or denied by Armscor or anyone else) was that the Moroccan government requested some Panhard AMLs from the French government, which could not supply them as its production-lines had closed. The French then made a deal with the South Africans to supply Morocco with Elands, the South African variants of the AML series, which though extensively modified were still familiar to the French-trained armed forces of Morocco.

The South Africans played ball and in due course the Elands arrived in Morocco, having been carefully laundered of all instructions and other markings that might disclose their origin. But the launderers missed the instructions on the oil-filters, which were in both the South African official languages, English and Afrikaans. When some of the Elands were captured, the cat was out of the bag.

But not disastrously so, it would seem, since the International Institute of Strategic Studies later reported that the Moroccans were also deploying Ratel infantry fighting vehicles entirely designed and built in South Africa. No doubt the Moroccans liked the price and the workmanship of the South African products; the finish and quality of the Eland hulls was said to have impressed the buyers.

The purchase by Sri Lanka in 1986 of Buffel mine-protected vehicles (a hundred of them according to some sources) to fight its exceedingly nasty racial civil war is less obscure. This deal took place in complete secrecy, only to become public knowledge when *Time* magazine published a photograph of Sri Lankan soldiers sitting on one of these unmistakably South African vehicles, which were developed in the mid-1970s, specially to overcome the landmine danger in the Namibian border war.

The unofficial word is that the Sri Lankans are very happy with their purchase of the ungainly and obsolescent but efficient MPVs; According to P.G. Marais, the Sri Lankans came under great pressure from India to stop the acquisition of the Buffels, "but they stuck to their decision".

Morocco is also said to be interested in acquiring South African mine-protected troop-carriers, although whether they want Buffels is not known.

A growing mass of circumstantial evidence indicates that Iraq and Iran have been the most important markets for both high- and low-technology South African weapons, in spite of heavy political influences. Iran is a foremost enemy of Israel, with which South Africa has had close ties since it became a nation in 1948; on the other hand, a considerable proportion of the small but prosperous and vocal Muslim minority in South Africa supports the Ayatollah Khomeini.

However, warfare is a great leveller in more ways than one, and three years ago the reputable publication *Africa Confidential* reported that Iraq had bought a large number of South African G–5 gun-howitzers, then a recent newcomer to the arms scene. Since then more evidence has come to light. In December 1987, for example, *Africa Confidential* published detailed information on South African shipments of arms to Iraq.

The publication said that between 1984 and 1985 at least five loads of armaments, which included detonators and shells, went from South Africa to Iraq with the "discreet blessing" of the United States government, the chief enemy of the Ayatollah Khomeini.

Judging by the report, persons of various nations had fingers in the pie, obviously a very profitable confection. According to *Africa Confidential,* one of the cargoes was valued at nearly US$30 million. The newsletter named as intermediaries a Swedish arms dealer called Karl Erik Schmidt of the Scandinavian Commodities Companies, the Elviemiek company of Greece and Tirrena Industriale of Italy.

Both *Africa Confidential* and the equally reputable International Institute of Strategic Studies have reported that South Africa has been supplying spare parts, ammunition and other materials of war to Iran as well as to Iraq. *Africa Confidential* has said that South Africa chartered ships to deliver arms to Iran, the cargoes carrying forged end-user certificates purporting to have been signed by Kenyan and Nigerian military officials. The Yugoslav government acted as intermediary in return for a rake-off of the profits.

Transactions like these illustrate the difficulty of enforcing arms boycotts when the target is not only able to fight back, like South Africa, but can guarantee profits large enough to tempt the saintliest humanitarian or socialist into doing the "apartheid régime's" dirty work for it.

The belligerents are said to be very satisfied with the G–5, and one source states: "Details of exactly what material is being supplied are sketchy, although it is known that (the G–5) has been supplied with ammunition, in vast quantities, to both forces... The sales are so extensive and in such demand that in spite of major (South African) operations in south Angola... much of the material now being delivered to the Middle East comes straight off production lines instead of being taken from stocks.

"The South Africans are under pressure to deliver in the Middle East before restocking their own strategic reserves, even though these must have been fairly severely depleted by the recent military venture into Angola."

This last statement is not necessarily correct. Losses of South African heavy equipment in the Angolan fighting at the time of writing had been so small that on May 16 the Chief of Staff: Finance, of the SADF, Vice-Admiral M.A. Bekker, openly told reporters that they would not be replaced because "were not going to set up a production run to replace three tanks."

However, re-equipping the SADF might well be delayed by large sales abroad. For example, the mechanised infantry forces of the SADF are crying out for the self-propelled version of the G–5, the G–6, of which only a few have been made so far. However, phasing G–6s into the mechanised infantry might be delayed if, as a usually reliable source indicates (although without offering proof) that both Iran and Iraq urgently requested delivery of the huge wheeled-gun system after it had been instrumental in defeating numerically superior Angolan forces in the fighting of 1987 and 1988. If true, this could depend on whether the Iran–Iraq war starts again.

It is also said that either Iran or Iraq or both have bought other South African-made equipment such as heavy mortars, automatic weapons and frequency-hopping radio systems. One rumour has it that some naval weapons have also been supplied, but no details are known; the only weapon used by the small and under-funded South African Navy that might be of interest is the Scorpion, a copy of the Israeli Gabriel naval surface-to-surface missile, carried by the missile gunboats of the SAN which, although locally built, are directly descended from the Israeli's Reshef-class vessels.

The same source quoted above also says that Iran and Iraq expressed keen interest in acquiring another star of the Angolan battles, the Valkiri 127mm artillery-rocket system; but in May 1988 the South African Minister of Defence, General Magnus Malan, categorically denied as a "damned lie" the accusation that the country was or had been selling arms to Iran. The MP in question did not produce evidence to contradict Malan, even though he could have done so under the protection of Parliamentary privilege, and the matter was dropped.

The Moroccans are said to be interested in acquiring South African artillery systems, although it is not known whether they want the G–5/G–6 weapons or the Valkiri.

The G–6 was introduced to Latin America at the FIDA arms show in Chile in 1988; the South Africans shipped one over and installed it in the Armscor pavilion, where it attracted a great deal of attention, and not just because of its impressive bulk. One very interested party was none other than Chilean President Augusto Pinochet Ugarte, who paid a personal visit to the South African pavilion, lingered a while before the G–6 and afterwards remarked to the general manager of Armscor that he could see a Chilean application for both the big SP gun and also for a small towed version of the Valkiri.

Armscor products with great market potential are the V3B Kukri and V3C Darter air-to-air guided missiles, which are designed for use on Mirage jet fighters, various marks and models of which are used by many Third World countries, although clients would be more difficult to identify because in this case the "invisibility factor" prevails.

The V3 missiles are a prime example of "invisible" weapons, since they have the same external dimensions and general appearance as their ancestors, the Matra Magic missiles. That is said to worry French arms salesmen, since it means that the V3 missiles can be used out of the box on aircraft fitted for the Matra, and in conjunction with the world-class helmet sight made by Armscor.

At the FIDA '88 arms show observers noted that the V3C on display (its trump-card parts carefully masked) was the subject of long and close scrutiny not only by the French but also by the Red Chinese, whose Norinco marketing organisation is also making considerable inroads into the Third World markets.

For poorer nations, committed to buying heavy equipment elsewhere under military aid agreements, many Armscor products would be attractive for their invisibility, cheapness and simplicity.

Prominent among these would be the frequency-hopping radio systems, as well as the variety of internal-security equipment offered by Armscor and its contractors. At the FIDA '88 show, the Grinel stand attracted considerable attention from military and private observers interested in a data terminal with a built-in encryption facility which works over a hopping link, so that the user gets two-way security. Exhibitors at the stand reported great interest in another product, an ultra-high-frequency single side-bank 100-watt radio for point-to-point networking and control communications, which Grinel claims is unique.

As I noted above, there appears to be no shortage of customers for the secure communications equipment, and because of the invisibility factor the potential market is large. Among others Morocco is said to be interested, and equipment which allows commanders to communicate *en clair* obviously has an added attraction for backward countries whose ill-educated radio operators would have difficulty in physically encoding and decoding messages.

Internal-security equipment, too, is a potentially profitable field for the Armscor network. Generally speaking, the world's arms manufacturers have not yet paid a great deal of attention to mine-protecting relatively small vehicles, while South Africa has done a large amount of research in this field as a result of its long, low-intensity counter-insurgency campaign in the northern areas of South West Africa/Namibia.

This has reached the point where Pretoria's Afrit concern, an exhibitor at FIDA '88, is offering a commercial light truck which gives the occupants a high probability of surviving the explosion of an anti-tank mine. At the FIDA '88 show the Afrit exhibit had two of these vehicles: one "out of the box" and another battered one which had detonated an anti-tank mine (which was also shown on a video film). This elicited great interest from representatives of the 26 or so nations attending or exhibiting, and particularly the *Carabineros*, the Chilean national police.

Gerrit van de Wetering of Afrit later remarked: "They simply could not believe that one can survive a mine explosion, till we showed them." His remarks were substantiated by another exhibitor, who recalled that visitors thought that one of the vehicles, an armoured light personnel carrier, was amphibious because of its characteristic V-shaped lower hull, designed to deflect mine-blasts.

Other internal-security exhibits that attracted much attention were the "Slingshot", which enables rubber bullets or "baton rounds" to be fired in machine-gun fashion, and a quick-deployable road barrier capable of instantly stopping any rubber-tyred vehicle.

South African automatic weapons are now being shipped to more than twelve countries that expect to have internal-security problems, one source claims.

Armscor rifles, mortars and other small arms are very saleable. It produces the 5,56mm-calibre R4 assault rifle, very similar to the "invisible" Israeli Galil, the 7,62mm Nato-calibre R1 self-loading rifle derived from the ubiquitous Belgian FAL, the handy SS-77 light machine-gun, 81mm mortars of the type used by most nations supplied from outside the communist bloc, and other standard or near-standard weapons.

Armscor also offers the MGL, a small hand-held launcher able to fire six 40mm grenades in rapid succession. It was developed as a direct result of South African experience in the Namibian border conflict and later used in action in that theatre. It is designed to fill the gap between maximum hand-grenade range and minimum mortar-bomb range, and it is an excellent weapon for bush wars.

Customers in this category are also conspicuous by their secrecy; there is a rumour that several Central and South American countries are using South African weapons. El Salvador is said to have acquired South African weapons and equipment through covert CIA routes.

Armscor also produces a wide range of small-arms ammunition, hand-grenades, flares, mortar-bombs and similar munitions, as well as larger articles such as 155mm artillery shells, 68mm unguided rockets and cluster bombs, all of standard calibre and fittings. The latest addition to the line are the CB-470 cluster bomb, which releases forty 6kg bomblets, and a 120kg pre-fragmented aerial bomb that sprays out hundreds of steel balls and can be set to explode before, on or after impact.

Armscor also offers a variety of heavy machine-guns and aircraft cannon. The helmet-sighted GA-1 cannon, which is available in either 7,62mm or 20mm calibres, can be installed on anything from aircraft to small vehicles because it is light (49kg) and recoil is so mild that if necessary it can be controlled by hand.

There is also the GI-2 20mm automatic cannon, for use against ground and aerial targets by infantry fighting vehicles, helicopters, ships and light vehicles. It can fire a variety of ammunition, from armour-piercing and incendiary to high-explosive and "multiple effect". It has a double-feed system that allows the gunner to switch from one type of ammunition to the other by moving a selector switch. The feed system will work regardless of its position, and recoil is mild enough for it to be fired manually.

South African-made spare parts range from simple goods to such high-tech products as gearboxes and rotor blades from the Puma helicopter, which is widely used internationally but is no longer produced by the country of origin, France, although some may still be in production by Romania.

Armscor can export kits for updating existing weapons, such as Mirages and Aermacchi MB326 (locally manufactured as the Impala) jet combat aircraft, and Centurion tanks. Intensive research and recent updating and battle-testing have given Armscor great experience in rejuvenating and improving existing equipment, a case in point being the Cheetah version of the Mirage III.

Armscor and its contractors also manufacture many civilian products such as expendable wooden air-supply platforms, each capable of being loaded with up to 12 000kg of freight and dropped from 1 000 metres on hilly, rough or bushy terrain where the landing site cannot be determined and prepared in advance.

For level ground there is a platform that can be fitted with aluminium skids and pulled out of an aircraft flying between two and five metres above the ground. It is guaranteed to slide to a halt within fifty metres.

There is also the Samil range of load-carriers and field-cooker units, which is said to have found a ready market.

A complete list of products offered by Armscor and its contractors would be too long to list here. Suffice it to say that at the FIDA '88 show there were no fewer than 150 items on display, and that did not include the entire range available.

## ARMSCOR: WHAT IS (OR MAY BE) IN THE PIPELINE

The chairman and his executives normally keep silent about what they have in the pipeline till the time is judged ripe for an announcement by the Ministry of Defence, which often unblushingly misuses security legislation to delay news of new developments so that it can obtain the maximum political benefit.

However, the corporation has long maintained an extensive research and development programme that absorbs many millions in any given financial year, and the result is that it has a wide variety of projects at various stages of completion.

According to one official "about 75 per cent of our brainpower is used in developing new-generation weapons for the future". Armscor officials say they get a disproportionate amount of mileage out of every rand by exhaustive preparation.

"The Americans can afford to build a missile and then fire off about 200 for evaluation," an official says. "We can't afford that way of working. So by the time we actually launch a missile it has already undergone hundreds of simulated computer firings in the laboratory."

A list of things that Armscor is working on at the time of writing could include the following:

**Missiles**
Armscor is engaged in extensive research on missiles. That is hardly surprising, since a technologically advanced country like South Africa can use missiles to make up for deficiencies where the arms boycott has really hurt: in aerial offence and defence.

The most crucial medium-term problem is a high-technology fighter to replace its ageing Mirage F-1s, since its chances of obtaining anything in the F-16 class are remote. Again, it is unlikely to be able to replace its handful of British Buccaneer strike fighters or its now-retired Avro Shackleton long-range maritime reconnaissance-bomber aircraft.

There has been much speculation that Armscor has recruited (by offering huge salaries) Israeli engineers who formerly worked on the now-defunct Lavi fighter project. As long ago as 1984 James Adams, defence correspondent for the London *Sunday Times,* stated in his book *The Unnatural Alliance* that South Africa had agreed to contribute finances for the development work, and in return would produce some components. The allegation was promptly denied by the Israeli ambassador to South Africa, Eliahu Lankin, as "a fantasy that I have no doubt is not objective."

Armscor has repeatedly denied that it is resurrecting the Lavi in a South African guise. Some local observers accept that, pointing out that in 1983, when the project had not yet run into the financial difficulties that led to its scrapping, a very senior SAAF officer rejected any such intention because, he said, the Lavi was not far enough up the spectrum to justify the enormous cost of starting a very limited production-run.

Since that was very much off-the-record at the time, it had a ring of authenticity; and if the Lavi was too low on the spectrum in 1983 it is even lower now.

Four years later, the credibility of Adam's information is somewhat dented by the fact that three other deals that he documented have not come to pass: in addition to the Lavi deal, he said, South Africa had ordered 36 Israeli Kfir Mirage updates and a number of Merkava battle tanks, and the two countries had agreed to cooperate in producing a submarine and an 800-ton surface warship. Or is it perhaps that the contracts of 1984 have been cancelled or delayed? Anything is possible, given the cloud that hangs over South African arms deals.

Nevertheless, the ghost of the Lavi still haunts the corridors of Armscor, and it appears that some Lavi engineers actually have been hired by South Africa. In March 1988 Johan van Vuuren told reporters: "One advantage is that there is a migrating work force in the aircraft world. They go where there is work, and aircraft developments don't come by the bunch."

Van Vuuren also made an interesting remark that provides a clue about the direction of some future Armscor development: "It doesn't take a genius to see that our biggest problem is going to be engines. Unless the political situation changes this is going to be a priority, in spite of the cost of development."

According to one report the SAAF has managed to upgrade its Mirage F-1s to the same standard as the Kfir; but that is no solution to the problem of finding a new-generation fighter, merely a postponement of the inevitable day of reckoning.

Given the South African government's apparently iron determination to keep defence spending under 5 per cent of the GDP, as it has done for the past ten years, the obvious answer is to concentrate on guided projectiles, and that is exactly what is happening.

In September 1986 P.G. Marais said, in an unusually explicit interview for so discreet a man, that his corporation was engaged in developing what he described as an all-embracing and comprehensive missile system.

Marais refused to say when the project would be completed, but he added: "Systems being developed include air-to-ground missiles, anti-tank missiles, long-range missiles, new guided missiles and a project to increase the range of sea-to-sea missiles."

He made it clear that heavy emphasis was being laid on long-range anti-aircraft missile defences as a fairly cheap way of matching the ever-more advanced aircraft being deployed by Angola and, in times to come, possibly other neighbouring countries.

Armscor was working all-out on new missiles to meet conventional attacks from neighbouring countries, and "missiles could totally replace fighter aircraft."

In what might have been a hint that Armscor is working on a ballistic weapon, he said that "long-range missiles are very much within our capability."

Since then he has said nothing more about that; but some South African military observers are pretty sure that Armscor is working on a small cruise missile.

One reason for this belief is that there is an urgent need for such a weapon. The Luanda government has constructed an extensive missile and radar network that covers most of south-western Angola, the area where most South African incursions take place because it is just north of the Ovambo tribal homeland, seat of the insurgency carried out by the South West Africa People's Organisation. The network also covers so much of Namibian airspace that a Mirage fighter from the Ondangwa air base can be picked up and tracked from the moment it leaves the runway.

The network has blunted the clear edge that the stringently selected and trained SAAF pilots have hitherto had over their opponents, and attempts to knock it out by aerial attack would result in the loss of irreplaceable machines and pilots who cost more than R2 million each to train.

Part of the then still incomplete Angolan network was knocked out by a low-level SAAF raid during an "external operation", *Operation Protea,* in 1981; but in a subsequent incursion, *Operation Askari* (December 1983 - January 1984) it was clear how things were going when an Impala II ground-attack fighter was hit by a Russian SA-9 missile, a type deployed since the earlier raid. It managed to return to base, but only because the warhead failed to explode.

What that means is that if, in any future incursion, the southern Angolan network could be disrupted or put out of action, the SAAF pilots would regain some of the edge and have a better chance of maintaining their superiority against Angolan aircraft without suffering unacceptable losses.

A strong indication that Armscor is already working on a project of that kind came as long ago as the FIDA exposition in Chile in 1984, when the corporation unveiled a small, light gas–turbine engine. Only 32cm in diameter, a metre long and 63kg in weight, the turbine was described as cheap, simple, reliable and requiring little maintenance, with a maximum operating life of only twenty hours.

The chairman of Armscor later noted that the little turbine had significant defence potential and could be used to drive long–range missiles, a "tremendous technological breakthrough."

Observers agree that while the dimensions suggest that it could be used for a remote–controlled vehicle or drone, the short life of the engine indicates a strictly one–way ticket, whereas RPVs are re–usable machines.

There can be little doubt that all that Armscor needs is to develop a suitable guidance system for a cruise missile to be a feasible proposition.

There is a possibility that cruise missile guidance systems are already being tested, although concrete evidence is small. Local military observers have been intrigued for months with an allegation of Angolan–origin that a tactically important bridge at the Angolan base of Cuito Cuanavale was knocked out late in 1987 by what P.G. Marais cryptically described as a "clever weapon".

Some reports indicate that the machine was not a missile but an RPV carrying an explosive charge, and it is no secret that Armscor has carried out considerable research and development work on drones. Till recently the SAAF was known to deploy a version of an Israeli RPV, but at FIDA '88 Armscor unveiled a new, locally–designed and built surveillance RPV called the Seeker. Whether the Seeker has or is being given another role is not known, nor whether it has a bigger but still secret brother.

On the other hand, it might not have been an RPV at all but the 10km bomb mentioned by Brigadier Steyn of the SAAF in October 1988. At this stage the matter remains obscure.

One question that hangs over the entire subject of missiles is whether South Africa would use them for nuclear strikes. At the time of writing there is no clear answer, because it depends on whether Pretoria has a nuclear device that works. That has never been confirmed in spite of intense speculation after an alleged nuclear explosion in the southern Indian Ocean in 1979, which according to the CIA was a joint test by Israel and South Africa.

However, observers point out that actually designing and building a serviceable nuclear device is not difficult for a country of the South African level of development; at least half of the problem is finding a suitable delivery vehicle. The fact that such a vehicle, in the form of a medium–range missile, now appears to be within sight can only aggravate the debate.

## A surveillance satellite

In April 1988 it was announced that the quasi–government Council for Scientific and Industrial Research had embarked on a feasibility study of building and launching a South African surveillance and communications satellite in 1989.

The news caused little excitement in South Africa, possibly because official spokesmen made it clear that there was no intention of building spacecraft or putting men into orbit. The Minister of Economic Affairs and Technology, Danie Steyn, said the satellite programme was designed mainly to supplement present space research programmes, which included satellites, data–transfer, communications and meteorological and geophysical monitoring systems.

Now, while all these are perfectly legitimate and respectable, two things were immediately clear to local observers: first, that missile research by Armscor would play a vital part in the design and building of such a rocket; after all, the first American rocket shots utilised virtually unaltered V–2s looted from Germany in 1945; and secondly, that such a satellite could be of great military value if the isolation of South Africa from the rest of the world were to increase. Communications and navigation in the virtual seas of bushveld in northern Namibia and southern Angola would no longer be in the hands of others, and if the satellite were placed in the right orbit South Africa would be secure in the knowledge that it was not being given only part of what was being picked up.

In a wider context, a South African satellite would be of such great commercial and strategic value that observers do not expect that the government will have any difficulty in finding the billions needed.

## A small attack helicopter

The groundwork for such a machine was completed with the unveiling in 1986 of the two-man Alpha XH–1 experimental attack helicopter, the main armament of which was a 20mm servo-controlled cannon in a chin mount. The local press immediately went overboard about the helicopter, calling it the equivalent of the high-tech helicopter in the popular "Airwolf" TV thriller series being screened at the time. In fact the XH–1 was nothing of the kind. It was essentially a rebuilt Alouette III, and it was exactly what Armscor wanted: a cheap flying testbed.

Its main but not only *raison d'être* was to evaluate the weapons system. That consisted mainly of the cannon, controlled by the gunner's helmet sight and capable of being elevated 10 degrees, depressed 60 degrees and traversed 110 degrees to either side. The XH–1 was also said to be used for evaluating rocket pods, and Armscor engineers built up a valuable fund of helicopter technology to get the project off the ground.

Having served its purpose, the Alpha project has now been mothballed for the foreseeable future because, as P.G. Marais said in 1987, no need for such a helicopter had been formulated by the SAAF; although if the SAAF were to find such a need the Alpha project would be resurrected and carried further.

## An attack-and-transport helicopter

At the time Marais's statement that there had been no demand by the SAAF for a small attack helicopter rang oddly in the ear, since South African airmen on the border have been crying out for just such a machine to replace the Alouettes and Pumas which they repeatedly take into whites-of-the-eyes situations.

In retrospect, however, it probably meant that Armscor considered it was practicable to develop only one new helicopter, and that a larger attack-and-transport machine was thought to have greater utility.

Nevertheless, in 1987, only a few months after the existence of the Alpha was made known, Armscor unveiled the XPT–1. Once again the popular press went into ignorant raptures; but the XPT–1 was not an operational prototype, merely a slightly modified Puma transport helicopter on which the knowledge gained from the Alpha project had been put to good use.

The XPT–1 carried the same 20mm helmet-weighted gun as the XH–1 and four outboard pods firing the standard 68mm air-to-ground unguided rocket. The obvious intention is to develop an answer to the formidable Russian Mi–24 now in service in Angola and Afghanistan.

After the unveiling Marais made it clear that South Africa had become capable of building Puma-sized helicopters.

Once the XPT–1 development programme had been completed, he said, an upgraded up-engined Puma would be built, and after that a helicopter so different from the original "that you could hardly call it a Puma... If the time comes when we must supply the air force with a combat helicopter, it will be a full-blooded combat helicopter and not just a souped-up version of something else".

The indications are that Armscor is pushing ahead with all speed on this project. The XPT-1 was unveiled just before a general election, in which the government was facing challenges from both liberals and conservatives, as these terms are understood in South Africa, and critics of the government were quick to label it a mere vote-catching stunt. Marais strenuously denied that. The XPT-1 had been unveiled as soon as it was ready for such exposure, he said. The engineers were already a week behind schedule, and the very tight programme did not permit a further delay of ten days or so till the election was over. (In the event the government won easily, although the liberals lost ground and the conservatives gained.)

The significant aspect of the unveiling of the XPT-1 was the revelation that Armscor had acquired the ability to make such high-tech components as gearboxes and rotor blades. This fact astonished observers abroad, so much so that a few weeks later, on May 23, *Jane's Defence Weekly* stated:

"It... showed photographic evidence of a greatly-developed industrial base for helicopter component manufacture... Even allowing for South Africa's long-established technical expertise, European observers were astounded by the advanced autoclave for manufacturing composite rotor blades. Previous assessments suggested that rotor blades were imported."

## An anti-submarine helicopter

There can be little doubt that the combat helicopter resulting from the XPT-1 project can be turned into a replacement for the ageing Westland Wasp ASW helicopters of the SAAF by fitting it with the necessary systems, including a torpedo-launching and rocket-firing capability.

Since a Puma-sized helicopter is considerably larger than a Wasp, this would probably necessitate some rebuilding of the hangar and landing facilities on the bigger ships of the SAN: two British Type 12 anti-submarine frigates and two fleet replenishment ships.

## A new tank

At some stage the Olifant-Centurion will need to be replaced. It is known that as long ago as the early 1980s the Armscor research and development boffins were engaged on that, having concluded, like boffins elsewhere, that the heavy battle tank was not yet obsolete in spite of premature obituaries after heavy losses by the Israelis in the Yom Kippur war in 1973.

It was generally acknowledged that the Israeli losses resulted not so much from the obsolescence of the battle tank as from incorrect handling in battle, including the tendency to go off without adequate infantry protection, and the use of improved small armour-piercing weapons such as the RPG-7.

For years a strong, up-to-date tank force had low priority, since the Eland armoured car series had proved adequate for the border war and the incursions into Angola. These circumstances have changed as the incursions have run into ever stiffer resistance; in *Operation Askari* in 1984 several Ratel IFVs were knocked out by Angolan T-55s, and on one occasion a Ratel column came close to becoming engaged in a direct confrontation with tanks. In 1987 Centurion-Olifants were deployed in Angola, the first time that South African tanks had been in action since the second world war.

The Armscor policy with regard to tanks is clear. In 1983 an official of the corporation told me:

"We can have equivalent firepower on a wheeled vehicle and lower maintenance and running costs, but if we're attacked by armour we need protection and the ability to withstand modern ammunition... The trend in the world is towards bigger tanks with heavier guns.

"We believe we can live with the upgraded Centurion till the 1990s, but then we'll have to put our own tanks on the ground."

### Other additions to the Ratel family

The basic Ratel-20, a large (14-ton) IFV carrying a 20mm gun, already has several variants. There is the mortar-armed Ratel-81 (revealed in 1987), a recovery Ratel, a command Ratel and a logistics Ratel. However, observers have identified three other possible variants.

The more urgent of the three is a Ratel carrying dual or quadruple anti-aircraft guns, because at present the South African ground forces are badly served in that respect, and there is no indication that the air situation, already rather poor, is going to improve soon, now that countries like Angola are beginning to develop effective aerial forces.

The only truly mobile AA-guns in service at present are hand-laid 10mm singles, mounted on an armoured, mine-protected Samil-20 lorry known as the Ystervark, or Hedgehog (although one Ystervark actually managed to shoot down an Angolan MiG-23 late in 1987); the only radar-aimed guns used by the ground forces, dual 30mms, are meant for the defence of static positions such as bridges and camps, and are mobile only in the sense that they can be packed up and moved from one place to another; they certainly cannot keep up with a highly mobile mechanised force travelling across country, a frequent situation in the trackless bushveld of northern Namibia and southern Angola.

Alternatively or in addition to AA gun Ratels the ground forces would benefit by having some fitted with air-defence guided missiles. The SAAF deploys some old but efficient Cactus-Crotale missile systems for airfield defence, but once again these vehicles would not be able to keep up with, or even stand up to, rapid cross-country movement.

A third variant of the Ratel that would be of some use would be one with twin launchers for anti-tank guided weapons.

Are any of these variants in development? It is difficult to say. But the requirements have been clearly identified, as was the need for a mortar-armed Ratel, which duly appeared.

### Active armour

One of the latest innovations in military technology is "active armour": blocks or plates of explosive attached to vehicles that detonate on being struck by the sort of shaped-charge projectile fired by portable launchers such as the RPG-7. This pre-emptive explosion totally or partly destroys the effect of the shaped charge.

It is not known whether Armscor is developing such armour, but it is deeply interested in anti-armour-piercing technology, and it has been working for a long time on a de-bugged alternative, ceramic armour, which one spokesman said was better than the British Chobham armour; after which nothing more was ever said on the subject. Like that famous apocryphal newspaper headline, "No News of the Pope", the silence can mean anything or nothing.

## More missile strike craft

The South African Navy now has nine Reshef-type strike craft, most of them built locally, and it appears likely that at some point more will be acquired. The question here is money. Because of the nature of the war that South Africa is fighting in Namibia and southern Angola, as opposed to any war that it might be fighting in the future, the SAN has long been kept on a tight financial rein, and it seems unlikely that more strike craft will be built in the foreseeable future.

One thing is sure: any new strike craft would probably look different from the existing ones, since the stormy seas around the Cape coasts have taught Armscor many lessons about the Israeli-derived boats, which were designed for the calmer waters of the Mediterranean.

Funds are always the difficulty. The SAN recently acquired five new mine-hunters, but apparently at the cost of a long-cherished dream of acquiring locally-built corvettes (the 800-ton part-Israeli vessels described by James Adams?); and its plans for its two Type 12 anti-submarine frigates remain obscure.

Till fairly recently the pride of the SAN was its squadron of three frigates. But a few years ago one sank after a collision and another has been stripped to the bones. The SAN at the time of writing has no intention of disposing of the stripped-down vessel, an indication that it and its still functioning sister ship might yet be rebuilt, always provided that the SAN can afford to man and run them on its very tight budget.

## A new submarine

That is another subject veiled in the greatest secrecy, but it seems that Armscor is or was working on a submersible to complement and eventually supplant the Navy's three Daphne-class vessels.

That is a long-standing requirement. In the 1970s South Africa ordered two French Agosta-class submarines and was about to take delivery in 1977 when France decided to observe the UN arms embargo and slammed the door on Pretoria's fingers.

The first hint of local production came in 1982, when Con Botha, a nationalist MP, said in Parliament that South Africa would soon have to consider building its own submarines.

In the same speech he mentioned that a new supply ship would soon be built; and sure enough, SAS *Drakensberg* was launched in 1987.

Subsequently the speculation was renewed when Captain Evert Groenewald, commanding officer of the submarine flotilla, pointed out that the life expectancy of a submarine was 20 to 25 years... and the Daphnes had been bought from France in the early 1970s. That means that they have now reached the mid-point, and it is possible that they will be upgraded as an interim measure while construction of a local submarine proceeds.

Technically both projects appear entirely feasible, since the Navy and Armscor have acquired a great deal of technical knowledge from the periodical stem-to-stern refitting of the Daphnes.

Armscor also probably has the necessary blueprints. In 1986 it became known that the West German government was investigating a well-known builder of submarines, Howaldtswerke-Deutsche Werft AG of Kiel, for selling a set of blueprints to South Africa for DM46 million (about US$26 million). A Luebeck engineering firm called IKL was also implicated.

HDW, which has built many submarines for the West German Navy and is

75 per cent owned by the Bonn government, withheld comment at first. So, naturally, did Armscor. Eventually HDW broke the silence to say that although it had dealt with Pretoria for years, the business had not included submarines.

A loud political row ensued, in the course of which it turned out that the right-wing West German politician Franz Josef Strauss had pressed unsuccessfully to allow HDW to build no fewer than eight submarines for the SAN. The West German opposition parties began to press for a parliamentary inquiry into the alleged sale, with speakers of the Social Democrats and Greens accusing Chancellor Helmut Kohl of favouring the deal. According to the Greens, Kohl was "deeply entangled in the arms trade with South Africa".

Kohl stonewalled at first, admitting only that Strauss had approached him on the subject of submarines for South Africa, but in December 1986 he admitted that the South African head of state, P.W. Botha, had directly asked him to approve the sale of plans when he visited Germany in June 1984.

The parliamentary inquiry duly began behind closed doors in January 1987, and when Kohl testified a month later he conceded that he had told Botha he would see that his request for West German submarines received careful consideration.

However, he added: "I rejected the deal after I had had it examined, as my office requires," and it was not till months afterwards that he had become aware that HDW and IKL had sold microfilmed blueprints, which had been taken to Pretoria in a diplomatic bag.

Asked why he had not summarily rejected the request at the time when it was made, Kohl explained somewhat lamely: "When a head of state asks me politely for something… then I think it's only correct that I should agree to consider it."

Later in the inquiry it turned out that one reason why Kohl had been willing to consider Botha's request was that the sale of completed submarines would have eased an unemployment crisis in the North German shipyards, till it became clear Pretoria was interested only in acquiring plans. It also came out that deliveries of the microfilm continued for five months after HDW and IKL had been told to stop the transaction, the last shipment actually taking place a day after the West German Minister of Economics, Martin Bangemann, positively forbade the transfer.

At that point HDW, which had refused to testify at the hearings, tried to give the money back, presumably in exchange for the plans that had been spirited to Pretoria. South Africa refused to take the money.

Later attempts to prosecute HDW and IKL failed, and the dispute spluttered on. In July 1987 the Greens MP, Ursula Eid, tried to visit South Africa to look into the alleged sale of plans, but she was not allowed into the country and was sent back on the first aircraft out.

The mystery deepened in November that year, when P.W. Botha, while launching the fleet replenishment ship the SAS *Drakensberg* in Durban, said he hoped to live long enough to see the first South African-built submarine. "This ship (the *Drakensberg*) is proof that we can do it."

Was that a pious expression of hope or a concrete hint of things to come? As with so many other aspects of the South African arms industry, it was anybody's guess.

The great submarine controversy went on. On January 12, 1988, the Kiel port authorities announced that they had dropped their investigations into the sale of the microfilm because the plans were not detailed enough to be used for the construction of submersibles. That being so, there was no evidence that either HDW or IKL had broken the UN arms embargo.

Later that month the submarines were back in the headlines when the Finance Minister of Schleswig-Holstein, Roger Asmussen, said that the money paid by South Africa, which had been frozen, would probably be returned, but he declined to say when it would take place. A Greens spokesman denounced Asmussen and the federal government, accusing them of a cover-up that had been agreed on under a clause in a contract signed in 1984. As a result he said, "we are certain that with the help of the Federal government, and Israeli complicity since as far back as 1980, South Africa and Israel will have the operational submarines by mid-1992".

Right or wrong? Again let us recall James Adams's assertion in 1984 that Israel and South Africa were cooperating on a submersible.

In the meantime the Greens have not given up on the submarine scandal, and as recently as March 1988 they renewed their attacks on HDW and IKL.

At the time of writing the case of the submarines remains open to speculation. Certainly there appears to be no technical reason why submarines should not be built at the Sandock Austral yard in Durban. The yard has the necessary capacity, having built all the locally produced strike craft as well as the 14 000-ton SAS *Drakensberg*, the largest ship ever built in South Africa.

Armscor makes no secret of the fact that the yard could build a medium-sized submarine, but it will not be drawn on whether such a project is actually on the cards. In 1987, when asked about the possibility of such a project, an Armscor spokesman, Johan Adler, would only make the guarded but interesting comment that "we're not so far down the line yet".

Whether submarines will actually be built depends on several factors, the most important of which is finance. In the end it might depend on how necessary new and larger submarines are judged to be, at a time when seaward defence continues to occupy third place on the list of priorities of the SADF.

## ARMSCOR: FINANCING
The financing of Armscor is a vexed subject. At various times opponents of the South African government have expressed doubts that the corporation could get so much mileage out of the comparatively modest sums available to it from a total defence expenditure of about 4,5 per cent of the GDP.

It sounds even more improbable when one considers that all this is happening at a time when South Africa is not only conducting a low-intensity internal-security effort at home but is also engaged in a counter-insurgency campaign in northern Namibia, which at times breaks out into full-blown conventional battles in Angola.

Since Armscor is part of the Ministry of Defence and is financed by it, the question that should be asked first is how the South African defence machine manages to accomplish everything it does on a military budget that is not only less than the British as a percentage of the GDP, but also has remained at virtually the same level for the past ten years.

Opponents of the South African government nurture dark suspicions that defence spending contributes to the uncomfortable rate of inflation, but the figures make it clear that the real culprits are over-spending on political structures, sloppy accounting, lack of control and top-heavy manning of the civil service.

It is significant that during 1987/8 State expenditure went up by 37,6 per cent in money actually spent, but defence expenditure by only 7,6 per cent. In fact, if it is correlated with the national growth rate, the military actually used less of the national resources than before.

Is this accomplished by cooking the books? Such accusations are vehemently denied by the able Chief of Staff: Finance, Vice-Admiral M.A. Bekker, who holds the purse-strings of Armscor as well as those of the armed forces themselves.

Bekker swears that there is no cooking of the books and no flow of unrecorded or disguised secret funds to keep the official defence budget at its present modest level. The SADF (and by extension therefore also Armscor) "can only receive money voted by Parliament," he told journalists recently. "All amounts can be traced through the estimate of expenditures, additional expenditures, Finance Act allocations and audited appropriation statements."

People who thought the military could spend money not voted by Parliament, he said, "don't understand the system … they're saying that people like Mr Harry Schwarz [a hawk-eyed opposition MP who is perhaps the finest financial brain among South African politicians] has cotton-wool between his ears, and I can assure you he has not".

Asked to comment on a statement by a liberal newspaper that the so-called "Special Defence Account", an important element of defence funding, functioned outside the jurisdiction of the State Audit, Bekker said that that had been so till 1978. In that year the dispensation had been withdrawn as one of the consequences of a national scandal about misuse of funds by officials of another ministry.

However, he admitted, in consultation with the Auditor-General the Minister of Finance could decide that some parts of defence expenditure might be excluded from the ordinary audit. Nevertheless, "this must be seen in the context of the general defence budget. In the (Auditor-General's) report of 1985/6, for example, a test audit of the Special Defence Account was carried out on sections exempted from the previous year, the sensitivity of which had diminished. Since 1978 there has been no expenditure against the Defence Act which has not been audited."

Bekker maintained that the Ministry of Defence was able to accomplish what it did on "a virtually flat budget" because of detailed planning to allow flexibility of response to various contingencies, holding down personnel expenses in the armed forces by maintaining a small regular component and large conscript and reservist assets, in spite of the inherent disadvantages of such a system, and by reducing operating expenses.

Military operating expenses began to rise sharply from 1977 as the Namibian border war, having puttered along since 1966, really got going, because for the first time the Swapo insurgents had a safe border from which to operate, since Angola had come under the Moscow-oriented MPLA government. Operating expenses reached a peak in 1982, at 69,4 per cent of the total military budget, but since then they had fallen every year to the 1988 level of only 56,8 per cent; although he predicted a possible rise to about 60 per cent from 1989 onwards.

Yet another "very important" contribution towards keeping down the defence budget was the money that Armscor earned from exports. As Bekker said:

"Take ammunition: you have to stockpile, because when you have reached your requirement you can't simply shut down the ammunition industry; you must retain it to produce ammunition in the future and carry out research and development. Thus the export of ammunition helps to cushion this industry.

"Basically I pay a subsidy to the ammunition industry. So I give them a certain minimum loading to keep them ticking over. If they export ammunition it lowers the subsidy, [and] export earnings go back into Armscor, not into the SADF."

In the highly competitive international arms business, he said, the standard procedure was "selling at marginal costs. All the countries work on the basis of covering direct costs, and any contribution to overheads is a bonus. Armscor also operates like that, so export profit is a subsidy.

"Remember, overheads are there whether one exports or not... exports cut overheads, so resulting in lower unit costs... Research and development is also an overhead."

How much Armscor spends and earns are secrets known only to a few. Now and again a few hints emerge. In the 1987/8 defence estimates, air defence was allocated R926,6 million more of the defence pie than the previous year; presenting the budget for that year, the Minister of Finance, Barend du Plessis, made some guarded remarks in which he indicated that a large slice of the increase would be spent on upgrading the old Mirage IIIs into Cheetahs. He also spoke vaguely of "certain programmes" that could not be deferred, which military observers took to mean the missile development projects hinted at by P.G. Marais the previous year.

It is likely that Armscor has had some difficulty in getting clients to cough up, and in fact there have been some hints to that effect from high government sources. No doubt it is a real problem, since client countries must finance such purchases without benefit of military-aid pacts or open borrowings.

Of course, payment need not be in money. Since Armscor operates in close cooperation with other government departments, it might be willing to take payment in kind rather than in cash: a tankerful of oil, say, in exchange for a shipload of arms or equipment. Such barter deals are not unknown elsewhere, and certainly not in Africa. The Soviet Union is particularly fond of such deals. In the days of Nasser, Egypt mortgaged its future cotton crop to pay for Russian weapons, and in war-torn Mozambique, the famous prawns are no longer an ordinary man's food; they are shipped to Russia in part-payment for the masses of obsolete weapons, far in excess of requirement, that have been palmed off on the Mozambicans.

There is an unconfirmed report that South African and Namibian troops using the Russian RPG-7 rocket-launcher in the border area (it is a weapon favoured by all sides) have found themselves issued with missiles stencilled in Arabic characters only. Products, perhaps, of some barter deal with a client state of Russia? It is something worth remembering next time the "non-aligned" world rises in unanimous indignation against the "racist oppressors" at the tip of Africa.

**ARMSCOR: THE FUTURE**

What of the future? The future of Armscor is, or course, closely tied up with political events in South Africa. It appears positively healthy if one agrees with those (including many opponents of the government) who believe that South Africa will evolve stealthily and almost involuntarily, in contra-distinction to the "Big Bang" theory which has become rather discredited by the fact that it appears no nearer to being realised than it was twenty years ago, when it first gained currency. It is a fact, for example, that in spite of the much-attacked state of emergency in force at the time of writing the South African government has not had to call up a significant number of its reservists, above and beyond its normal yearly training and operational mobilisations; in one command area larger than Britain fewer than 800 troops are engaged in internal-security duties, and so many non-whites apply to join the armed forces that in 1987 a new battalion had to be formed to take the recruits.

The stealth theory holds that such influences as market pressures and the ever-increasing need for skilled workers will break down apartheid at the person-to-person level, and in fact that has happened at a great rate in the past few years. "Petty apartheid" (ordinary ground-level segregation) has disappeared to a very large extent, although there is still much room for change.

Things are more problematical when it comes to dispensing with "grand apartheid" and introducing a more equitable national political dispensation. Some steps have been taken towards admitting people of colour to the direct processes of government; inadequate though they undoubtedly are, there is no going back to the pure-white days, and it appears likely that change will continue to take place, although probably in jumps and hiccups rather than by a smooth evolutionary process.

As one political observer once told me: "The difference between South Africa and Rhodesia is that the Rhodesian whites could never quite believe that there was anything basically wrong with their system, whereas the South Africans understand it quite well but aren't quite sure what to do about it."

Be that as it may, if the stealth theory prevails Armscor is likely to continue operating in its present fashion for the foreseeable future. That certainly appears to be its own assumption: in a television interview in 1987 the then chairman, P.G. Marais, stated that "the next ten years look very good." As a confidant of the State President, P.W. Botha, he obviously knows more than the ordinary outside observer; but if one takes his words at face value he is saying that for the next ten years it will be business as usual, only more of it; and his words, later in the same broadcast, might be worth remembering: the work of Armscor on various missile programmes, he said "will continue for many, many years."

Comments made in 1988 by the general manager, that the corporation was trying to identify defence needs fifteen to twenty years in the future, are also significant.

There has been much talk of a sort of alliance of "pariah nations", comprising such countries as South Africa, Israel and Taiwan. In the arms trade that would appear to be a fallacy, for several reasons.

For one thing, neither Israel nor Taiwan are pariah nations in the same sense as South Africa. Israel has the support of and easy access to a great part of the world, including the USA, as has Taiwan, whereas the doors have been slammed on South Africa all over the globe, partly as a result of unremitting propaganda by nations with a far worse civil record than Pretoria's, and partly by the South African government's unfortunate predilection for tactless and ill-timed actions.

But there is an even more cogent reason: both Israel and Taiwan are direct competitors in the Third World arms market, particularly Israel. While it might suit them to cooperate to some extent in transfers of technology and even components, that is where it is likely to end, unless a strong marketing imperative should arise.

That being so, one might well ask whether an association of "pariah nations" would serve any purpose in the sale of arms. He who operates alone takes greater chances, but he also enjoys greater profits if his ventures succeed.

Let us look at the curious affair of what might be called the "Red China flap".

On March 30, 1988, *Jane's Defence Weekly* caused a great to-do when it reported that an Armscor official had confirmed that the corporation had been invited to exhibit its products in Peking.

*JDW* quoted an unnamed official as saying that both Israel and South Africa had been invited, and "we accepted, but were later told that both South Africa and Israel could only exhibit after the show ended ... and then only to the People's Republic Army, not to foreign delegations."

Needless to say, there was an immediate reaction to this, but spokesmen for Armscor said simply that they had no further comment to make. Unofficially the word went out that the report was untrue; which, as it happened was correct, but only partly so.

Many weeks later a source in the arms industry told me that it was all an unfortunate misunderstanding. There had been such an invitation, but several years earlier, and it had been turned down for the reasons stated. *JDW* had got the facts right, but there had been a misunderstanding about the dates, he said.

But the whole episode raises an intriguing thought. Red China has developed a large arms-export industry, Norinco, which concentrates on marketing updated and reconditioned items of existing Russian or Chinese equipment used by so many Third World nations. It is a very convenient way of off-setting the overheads of the Chinese arms industry, but it is a dead-end, because Red China cannot afford to spend large sums on research and development; the truth of that is evident from the fact that Peking is spending millions on buying missiles and other equipment from the Israelis, equipment that the Chinese would not have bought if they had been able to make it themselves.

Therefore the question arises: Is this where South Africa and Red China might find one another? The Red Chinese may be friendly with the Americans these days, but what they need is robust, cheap, "soldier-proof" weapons and equipment, and lots of it. In other words, the sort of gear they might conceivably obtain, in suitably disguised form, from South Africa, either as direct imports or manufactured under licence. Bearing in mind the recent acquisitions by Peking from Israel, it might well be that South African research and development on missiles would prove interesting to Chairman Mao's successors.

That kind of fruitful exchange might also help South Africa with its abiding long-term problem, the lack of replacement for the Mirage F-1; for in spite of P.G. Marais's brave words, airspace-protection missiles are not a substitute for fighters; they are essentially defensive and very expensive one-shot devices. At the same time, high-tech fighters are becoming more and more costly, with most of the rise in cost due not to inflation but to the ever-more sophisticated equipment and materials required. All these factors mean that the possibility that South Africa might be able to afford to turn out short production runs of locally designed fighters is fading by the month.

The international arms market also presents infinite possibilities. For example, in 1983 a senior defence source told me that one arms dealer offered South Africa a large number of brand-new attack helicopters which were on the way to Iran, but were "diverted" when the Shah was deposed. The South Africans turned down the offer, he said, because the dealer could not provide the sort of back-up such a deal requires.

In retrospect, this might have been a bad decision; although another reason might have been a shortage of cash since the border war was at its height then and Armscor was in the final stages of various development programmes.

This demonstrates what can be obtained from the right seller at the right price. Given Armscor's aggressive overseas marketing drive, some bargain high-tech fighters may yet roll out at Atlas Aircraft amid bland assurances that they are not look-alikes but home-grown products.

# BIOGRAPHIES

## SIMON BARBER

Simon Barber is Washington correspondent for Times Media Limited's daily publications, including *Business Day* and the *Cape Times*. He also writes a weekly column for the *Sunday Times*. He began his journalism career with the *Sunday Times* in Johannesburg which he joined in 1977 after graduating from King's College, Cambridge, in classics. He has been based in Washington since 1978, where he was correspondent for Sir James Goldsmith's *Now!* magazine during its brief existence. He rejoined TML, or South African Associated Newspapers (SAAN) as it then was, in 1983. He lives in Sharpsburg, Maryland, close enough to the capital to commute but far enough away to avoid the contagion of its conventional wisdom.

Simon Barber is at present working on an expanded version of his chapter to be published later in 1989 by Ashanti Publishing.

## WILLIE BREYTENBACH

Dr Willie Breytenbach is Professor of Africa Studies at the University of Stellenbosch. Previously he was Director of Constitutional Planning in the Department of Constitutional Development and Planning in Pretoria. He held the same position in the office of the Prime Minister. Before that he was a lecturer in Anthropology and Applied Anthropology at the University of Pretoria, Chief Researcher at the Africa Institute and Head of Publications and Research with the South Africa Foundation.

He has a BA degree in African Studies, a BA (Hons) in Applied Anthropology, an MA in Anthropology from the University of Pretoria and a doctorate in Development Administration and African Politics from the University of South Africa in 1974.

In 1977 he was a Lester Martin Fellow at the Harry S. Truman Institute, Hebrew University of Jerusalem.

He has attended many international conferences in the United States, Israel, Greece, Britain, South America and West Germany.

Professor Breytenbach has published extensively on aspects of African government and politics, and on labour matters. He has for some years been lecturing to the Air, Army and Naval Staffs and the South African Defence Staff Colleges on aspects of strategic and political interest.

He was a member of the main committee of the Human Science Research Council on the Investigation into Intergroup Relations, the Interstate Working Group created by the meeting of Heads of State in 1982 to promote multilateral cooperation in southern Africa, and he was also the Coordinating Secretary of the Special Cabinet Committee on Black Constitutional Development that investigated the constitutional future of South Africa.

## FRED BRIDGLAND

Fred Bridgland has been a journalist for twenty years since graduating from St. Andrews University. As a correspondent for Reuters, he reported from India, the Middle East, London and Central Africa. He resigned from Reuters to write a book on the Angolan civil war, *Jonas Savimbi - A Key to Africa*, which has sold well all over the world and has recently been published in Portuguese.

Bridgland joined *The Scotsman*, as foreign leader writer (based in Edinburgh),

Europe correspondent (Brussels), and diplomatic correspondent (London). While at *The Scotsman* Bridgland won five journalism awards.

Bridgland was born in Corbridge, Northumberland. He has three daughters, all born in different capital cities – Annwen in London, Samantha in New Delhi, and Rebecca in Edinburgh.

## CHRISTOPHER COKER

Dr Christopher Coker was a Junior Research Fellow at Wolfson College Oxford, 1981/2, later becoming lecturer in International Relations at the London School of Economics in 1982. His most recent publications include *The United States, Western Europe and Military Intervention in the Third World* (Ed.) (Macmillan: 1988); *Constructive Engagement and its Critics: the United States in South Africa, 1961-85* (Duke University Press: 1986); *NATO, the Warsaw Pact and Africa* (Macmillan: 1985) and *South Africa's Security Dilemmas,* Washington Paper 126 (1987). He has written for journals such as *International Affairs, Strategic Review, Soviet Studies, Politique Etrangère, The Washington Quarterly, South Africa International,* etc. He was a Council Member of the Royal United Services Institute (1985-8); a Committee Member of the Institute for Foreign Policy Analysis; the Committee on Atlantic Studies; the Standing Committee on Atlantic Organisations; and the Project for the Anglo–American Successor Generation (Chatham House/ School of Advanced International Studies, Washington, DC). He was a Board Member of Brassey's Defence Publishers (1985-8) and Series Editor for International Security, John Spiers Ltd since 1987.

## DEON FOURIE

Deon Fourie is a Professor of Strategic Studies at the University of South Africa.

He has had an interest in military matters since he was a school cadet after the second world war. While teaching Public Administration he began lecturing on strategy to the Supreme Command of the SADF in 1968. In 1975 he introduced Strategic Studies as an independent subject at Honours level at the University. This has been followed by other universities in South Africa, at both undergraduate and graduate level. He has lectured and presented papers at teaching institutions and conferences and has published in France, Germany, Sweden, Britain, Switzerland and the United States as well as in South Africa. He has also broadcast on radio and television and acts as a consultant to the press, local establishments and foreign embassies.

## MIKE HOUGH

Professor Michael Hough was born in Johannesburg in 1944, and educated at the Afrikaans High School for Boys, Cradock. He took a BA degree at the University of Pretoria in 1965, with Political Science and Roman Dutch Law as his main subjects. In 1966 he took a BA (Hons) degree and in 1968, an MA in Political Science. In 1977 he received a PhD (Political Science) from the University of Pretoria and in 1980 a BA (Hons) in Strategic Studies from UNISA.

From 1968 to 1981 he lectured at the University of Pretoria, and since 1982 has been Professor of Political Science and International Politics at the University of Pretoria. Since July 1979 he has also been Director of the Institute for Strategic Studies at the University of Pretoria.

Professor Hough is a member of various associations, including the Joint Staff Course Association, the SA Defence College, the International Institute for Strategic Studies in London, the Advisory Council of the Interaction Systems Incorporated and Strategic Resources Information Centres, Virginia, USA, and a member of the Publications Appeal Board.

His special interests include Political Dynamics, Constitutionalism and Strategic Studies. His publications include subjects such as revolutionary warfare and national security. Professor Hough has in addition read papers on Strategic Studies and International Politics at conferences, and is regularly quoted on strategic matters.

## DAVID ISBY

David Isby, who wrote the chapter on *The Strategic Overview of Southern Africa towards the Nineties,* is the author of a number of books on defence subjects, including *Weapons and Tactics of the Soviet Army, Armies of NATO's Central Front* and *Russia's War in Afghanistan.* He is an expert on Soviet military affairs, low-intensity conflict, the NATO-Warsaw Pact theatre balance, conventional arms control and international transfers of arms. Isby has made fact-finding trips to Afghan resistance centres every year since 1984. He has lectured widely at staff colleges and academic conferences on both sides of the Atlantic and is a member of the International Institute of Strategic Studies.

He has experience as a national security consultant and an analyst, a legislative assistant in the United States Congress, an attorney (immigration and litigation works), and as an editor and simulation designer with *Strategy and Tactics* magazine. More recently David Isby has appeared in all forms of media as a commentator.

## HOLGER JENSEN

Holger Jensen a veteran foreign correspondent and editor before he left journalism to become a risk forecaster for multi-nationals, has lived and worked in Africa, the United States, the Soviet Union, Asia, the Middle East and Latin America. His 24-year-career with daily newspapers, the Associated Press, *Newsweek* magazine and *The Washington Times* spanned nineteen wars, revolutions and lesser guerrilla conflicts in such diverse trouble spots as Mindanao, Eritrea, Namibia and the Falklands. He was wounded in action in Vietnam, detained by Palestinian guerrillas in Beirut and won an Overseas Press Club award for his coverage of the Turkish invasion of Cyprus.

Born in Shanghai, of Danish and Russian parents, he was educated in South Africa, where he went to the Argus Journalism School in Cape Town and worked for *The Pretoria News.* He emigrated to the United States in 1963 and worked on a number of Californian newspapers before joining the Associated Press, first as an editor on the foreign desk in New York, then as a correspondent abroad.

He speaks Russian fluently, and was assigned to Moscow in 1969 but was expelled a year later for "activities hostile to socialist construction". Authorities objected to a series of articles that he had written about the dissident Vladimir Bukovsky, who was himself thrown out years later to found the Resistance International, a worldwide alliance of anticommunist groups.

Joining *Newsweek* in 1976, first as a correspondent and later as Chief of the Hong Kong bureau, he spent three years covering China, South East Asia, the Philippines, Taiwan and India. He was among the first American correspondents to visit China after normalisation of relations between Peking and Washington. He returned to his old hunting grounds in Vietnam and Cambodia to cover the bloody aftermath of the communist takeovers there and spent a considerable amount of time covering the communist insurgency in the Philippines and Muslim rebels of the Moro National Liberation Front on Mindanao.

In 1979 Mr Jensen was transferred to Johannesburg as chief of the southern Africa bureau for *Newsweek,* with responsibility for coverage of South Africa, Namibia, Botswana, Angola, Mozambique and Rhodesia.

### PAUL JOHNSON

Dr Paul Johnson was born in Lancashire in 1928. He was educated at the Jesuit Public School, Stonyhurst, and at Magdalen College, Oxford, where he studied history. He served in the British army from 1949 to 1951, with the rank of captain. From 1952 to 1955 he lived in Paris, working as Assistant Editor of the French monthly magazine *Réalités.* From 1955 to 1970 he was on the staff of the British weekly *The New Statesman,* as Assistant Editor, Deputy Editor and Editor. Since 1970 he has been a freelance author. His books include *A History of the English People, Elizabeth I: a Study in Power and Intellect, A History of Christianity, A History of the Modern World* and *A History of the Jews.* His latest book is *Intellectuals,* a case-study of the moral and judgmental credentials of intellectuals to give advice to humanity on how to conduct its affairs. Paul Johnson has also made many television documentaries and contributes to newspapers throughout the world, including *The Times* of London, the *New York Times,* the *Wall Street Journal,* the *Washington Post* and the *Los Angeles Times.* He writes regularly in the London *Daily Mail* and contributes a weekly column on the media to the *Spectator.* He travels all over the world and is particularly familiar with the problems of the mining industry, having written *Goldfields: a Centenary Portrait,* to mark the first hundred years of Consolidated Gold Fields. He is married to Marigold Johnson, executive director of a public affairs institute, and has four children. He lives in London and in Somerset. His hobbies are painting and hill walking. Paul Johnson is at present working on a historical study, a survey of world society in the formative years 1815-1830, to be called *The Birth of the Modern.*

### GERALD L'ANGE

Gerald L'Ange is a South African whose forebears have lived there since 1820. He has worked as a journalist for forty years in Africa, Britain, Canada and the United States.

During most of this time his work has been directly connected with Africa: as a reporter on the Johannesburg *Star* and other South African newspapers. He spent several years in Kenya during the Mau Mau uprising and for seven years was a correspondent at the United Nations in New York, specialising in Namibian, Rhodesian and South African questions.

He has also examined the African scene from Washington, where he was chief of the Argus Group bureau for two years.

He has served for over ten years with the Argus Africa News Service of the group, for most of the time as Editor. In that capacity he has travelled all over southern Africa and closely followed developments in the Frontline and other states.

### DOUGLAS McCLURE

Douglas McClure is a fourth-generation South African, born in Cape Town. Educated at Bishops in the Cape, he studied politics, philosophy, economics and British imperial history at the University of Michigan in the United States, before doing postgraduate studies in the sociology and politics of sub-Saharan Africa at the University of Edinburgh. In 1978 he lectured in the Department of International Relations at the University of the Witwatersrand, specialising in Russian naval penetration of the Indian Ocean. During the same period he worked as a Research Assistant at the South African Institute for International Affairs. In 1979 he joined the Political Science Department at the University of Cape Town, where he lectured in political economy, comparative politics and strategic studies. In 1979 he published a short book titled *The Soviet Threat to Europe and Africa,* which predicted the Russian invasion of Afghanistan. In 1983 he joined the South African Broadcasting Corporation.

### TOM McGHEE
Tom McGhee was born in Scotland and was educated at Daniel Stewart's College in Edinburgh. The Hitler war broke out just after he left school, and he finished up in the 2nd Parachute Battalion under its Colonel John Frost. He was wounded and captured in Tunisia and spent two years in prison camps in Italy and Eastern Germany until he escaped to Czechoslovakia, where he continued to shoot Germans with a band of partisans.

After the war he resumed his interrupted education at the universities of Aberdeen and Edinburgh, in science and modern languages. He then became an education officer in Nigeria, where he witnessed the transition from the old Empire to the new independent state. At the time he foresaw the later conflict between the Ibos, or "Biafrans", and the rest of the Federation.

Having acquired a lasting taste for Africa he came to South Africa after a period as a publisher's editor in Edinburgh. He was appointed Language Adviser to the SABC, from which he retired in 1965. He is now a full-time translator and editor for a government department.

As a broadcaster he was allowed wide scope as a theatre and cinema critic, and for many years he had a regular slot in which he had much to say, mostly caustic, about modern trends in the world in general and Africa (including South Africa) in particular. He is not impressed by the irresistible march of Progress and Technology.

### RON REID-DALY
Rhodesian-born, Major-General Ron Reid-Daly first became a soldier in 1951 when he volunteered to fight with C (Rhodesia) Squadron of the British Special Air Services, newly re-formed to combat communist insurgency in Malaya. Afterwards, he worked his way up through the ranks in the Rhodesian Army from trooper to become the Regimental Sergeant Major of the Rhodesian Light Infantry, at which time he was commissioned. In 1973, while still a Captain, he resigned his commission to retire on pension, but was persuaded by General Walls, the then Commander of the Rhodesian Army and later the Commander, Combined Operations, to stay on and form the Selous Scouts, a Special Force unit which distinguished itself in the Rhodesian war. The unit became one of the most effective counter-insurgent regiments anywhere in the world.

Major-General Reid-Daly finally retired from the Rhodesian Army in November 1979, just prior to the end of the war.

For a period after Rhodesian transition to black rule he commanded the Defence Force of the Transkei. Since leaving Rhodesia he has written a number of non-fiction books which have enjoyed wide success in South Africa and abroad.

## WILLEM STEENKAMP

Born in Cape Town in 1940, Willem Steenkamp comes from old South African stock, the first of his ancestors shipping out to the Cape of Good Hope as a soldier of the Dutch East India Company in 1699. His interest in military affairs comes naturally, since he is descended from a long line of citizen–soldiers who have fought in almost every significant war in which South Africans have been involved for at least 200 years, including a rebellion in which both his grandfathers came close to being executed for rising against the government of the day. He himself has seen service as a mechanised infantryman of the South African Citizen Force in Angola and South West Africa/Namibia and served a term on the ill-fated Joint Monitoring Commission of 1984.

He has also been involved in the fighting there as a front–line newspaper correspondent... he has been a journalist since 1961 and started covering the border war in 1973, when he was appointed defence correspondent of the *Cape Times* in Cape Town.

He has written a total of 14 books (fiction and non–fiction), several of them on military topics, and contributes to various overseas and local publications. He has won four writing prizes, two for fiction, one for enterprising journalism and in late 1988, the Barcom Prize for essays on military subjects, for an article on the future development of the South African Marines.

## AL J. VENTER

Al J. Venter, African traveller extraordinary, has spent thirty years covering the African beat. He has produced a dozen books on the continent and related subjects and more than 40 television documentary films on African countries.

His films on the Ugandan and Afghanistan wars and Aids in Africa have been seen in more than thirty countries, including the United States over the nationwide Public Broadcasting System. His documentary *AIDS – The African Connection* was nominated for the Grand Magnolia Prize at the 1988 Shanghai International Television Festival. He has also made films and reported on the wars in El Salvador, Angola, Rhodesia and Beirut.

Venter originally qualified as a Fellow of the Institute of Chartered Shipbrokers in London before turning to journalism. While in Cape Town during the late Sixties and early Seventies he was a correspondent for NBC (News) New York; the BBC; the *Daily Express* and the *Sunday Express* in London; United Press International and *International Defense Review* in Geneva.

He wrote the first book to appear on guerrilla warfare in southern Africa, published in 1969 by Purnells. It dealt with the guerrilla war in Angola, then developing. At the time he predicted that conflict would move southwards and eventually envelop all Rhodesia, and, ultimately, South Africa.

Al Venter has visited every African state except Lesotho. He has lived in Lagos, Nigeria and for a while in Nairobi. He spent almost a year in Angola during and after the Portuguese epoch. Since independence he has been into Angola many times, first with the FNLA as a combatant, then with Unita and later with South African forces on military operations. He was twice wounded on operations. He has worked closely with the Israeli Defence Force and has visited Lebanon about a dozen times in recent years.

## CRAIG WILLIAMSON

Craig Willaimson, now a director of companies and a politician in South Africa (he is a member of the President's Council for the National Party) is probably the best known South African intelligence agent.

For ten years, until 1980, when his true role was exposed by a defector, Williamson was a secret agent of the South African security police, and worked closely with the opponents of the South African government. He was vice-president of the National Union of South African Students, the deputy director of the Geneva-based International University Exchange Fund, vice-chairman of the International Non-Governmental Organisations Sub-Committee on Racism, Racial Discrimination, Apartheid and Decolonialisation. He addressed United Nations committees in New York on anti-apartheid action and worked for the ANC, the SA Communist Party and for *Umkhonto we Sizwe*. He travelled the world from his base in Geneva, meeting and working with revolutionaries from all over the globe, especially from South America and Africa. He attended conferences and planning sessions in Western capitals and behind the Iron Curtain.

In 1980, after being exposed as a South African government agent, Williamson returned to Pretoria, where he became the section head of Intelligence at Security Head Office. He retired in 1985 to go into business and politics.

Craig Williamson was awarded one of the highest South African decorations in 1983, when he received the South African Police Star for Outstanding Service, the S.O.E. He was also awarded the South African Police Star for the Combating of Terrorism and the South African Police Medal for Faithful Service. He has a degree in political science.

### RICHARD WOOD

Dr J.R.T. Wood, BA (Hons)(Rhodes), PhD (Edin.), was born in Bulawayo and brought up in Salisbury (now Harare) and educated there at St George's College. He spent some years in accountancy, and during that time he did his national service in the Federal Army and was then posted, as a territorial, to the First Battalion of the Royal Rhodesia Regiment. In 1959 the Federal Army reinforced the Nyasaland Police to combat unrest inspired by the African Congress led by Dr Hastings Banda. Dr Wood was present as a rifleman at the worst of the riots, at Nkata Bay.

In 1960 he went to Rhodes University, where he acquired two first-class degrees in history. In 1965 he won three scholarships and through one of them, a Commonwealth scholarship, went to the University of Edinburgh to take his doctorate with a thesis on Franco-British diplomatic history under the eminent diplomatic historian, David Horn.

In 1970 he was appointed the Ernest Oppenheimer Research Fellow at the University of Rhodesia (later of Zimbabwe) and, using the extensive collection of documents of Sir Roy Welensky, wrote the definitive history of the Federation of Rhodesia, which was published in 1983 under the title of *The Welensky Papers: A History of the Federation of Rhodesia and Nyasaland*.

Like most other Rhodesians, Richard Wood served in the Rhodesian forces from 1970 to 1980, as a rifleman in the Eighth Battalion, the Rhodesia Regiment, and later was commissioned into the Rhodesian Intelligence Corps, in which he was second-in-command of a small research unit.

Now a lecturer in history at the University of Durban-Westville, he is engaged in the research and writing of a history of Rhodesia from 1948–1980, concentrating on the constitutional, political and military aspects.

# INDEX

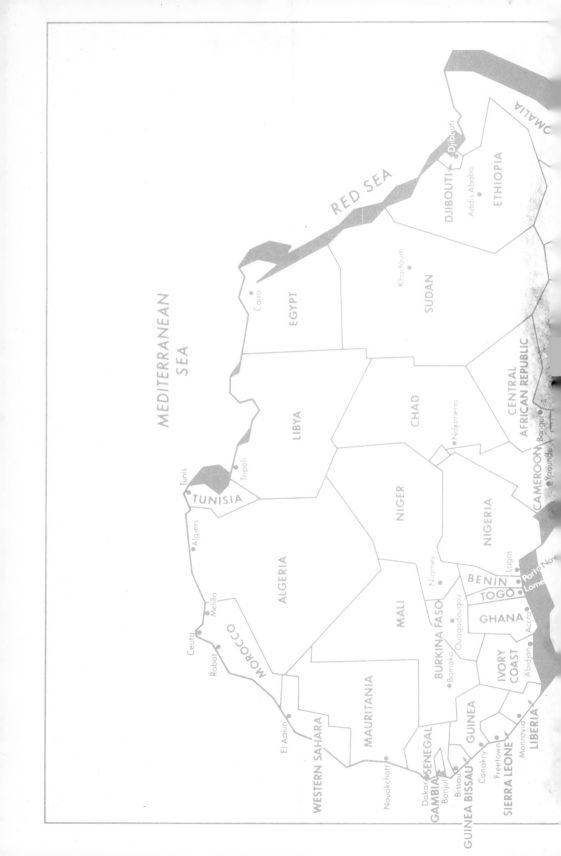